witches

THE COMPLETE COLLECTION

story and art by
Daisuke Igarashi

In the
olden
days...

there were
witches.

witches

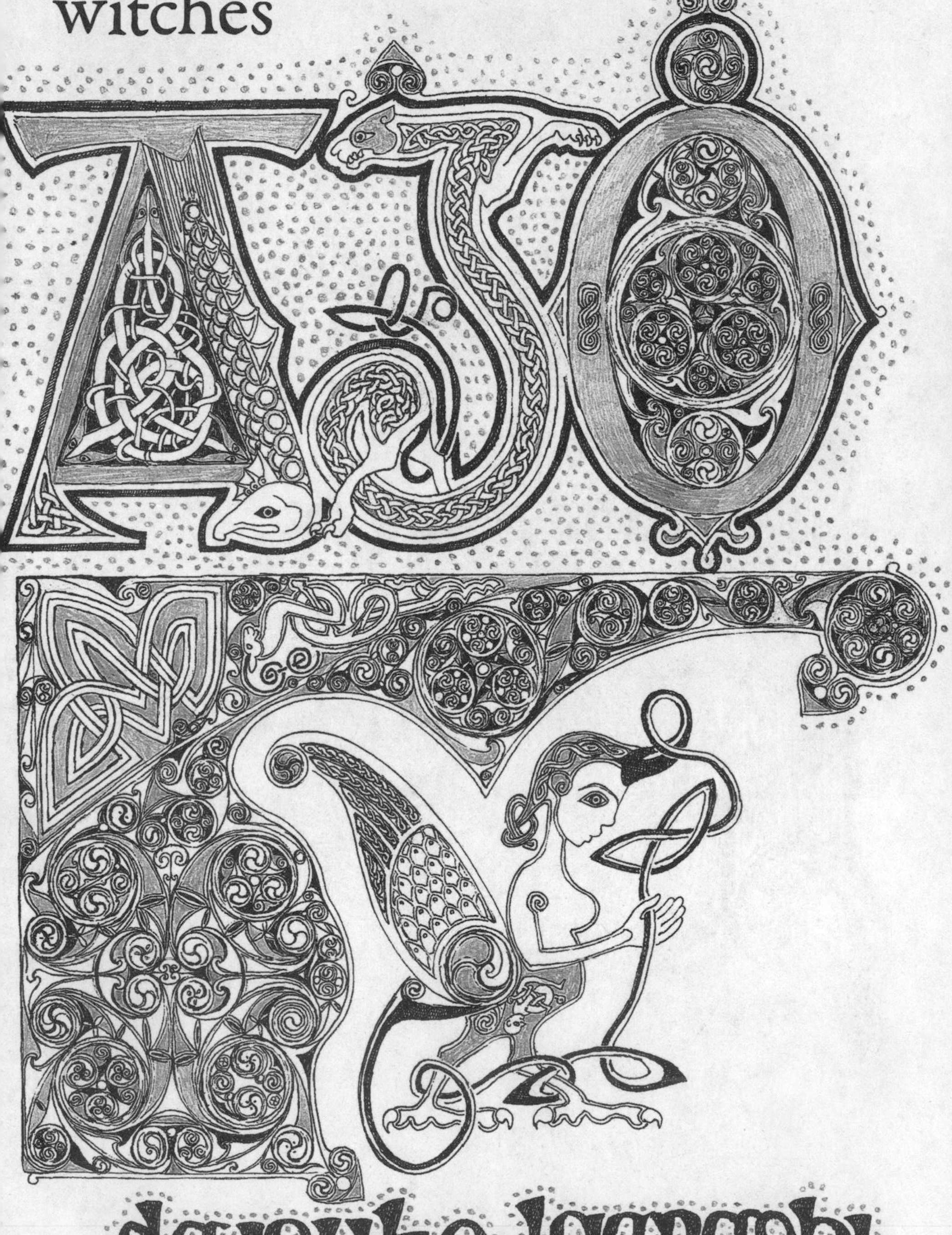

daisuke igarashi

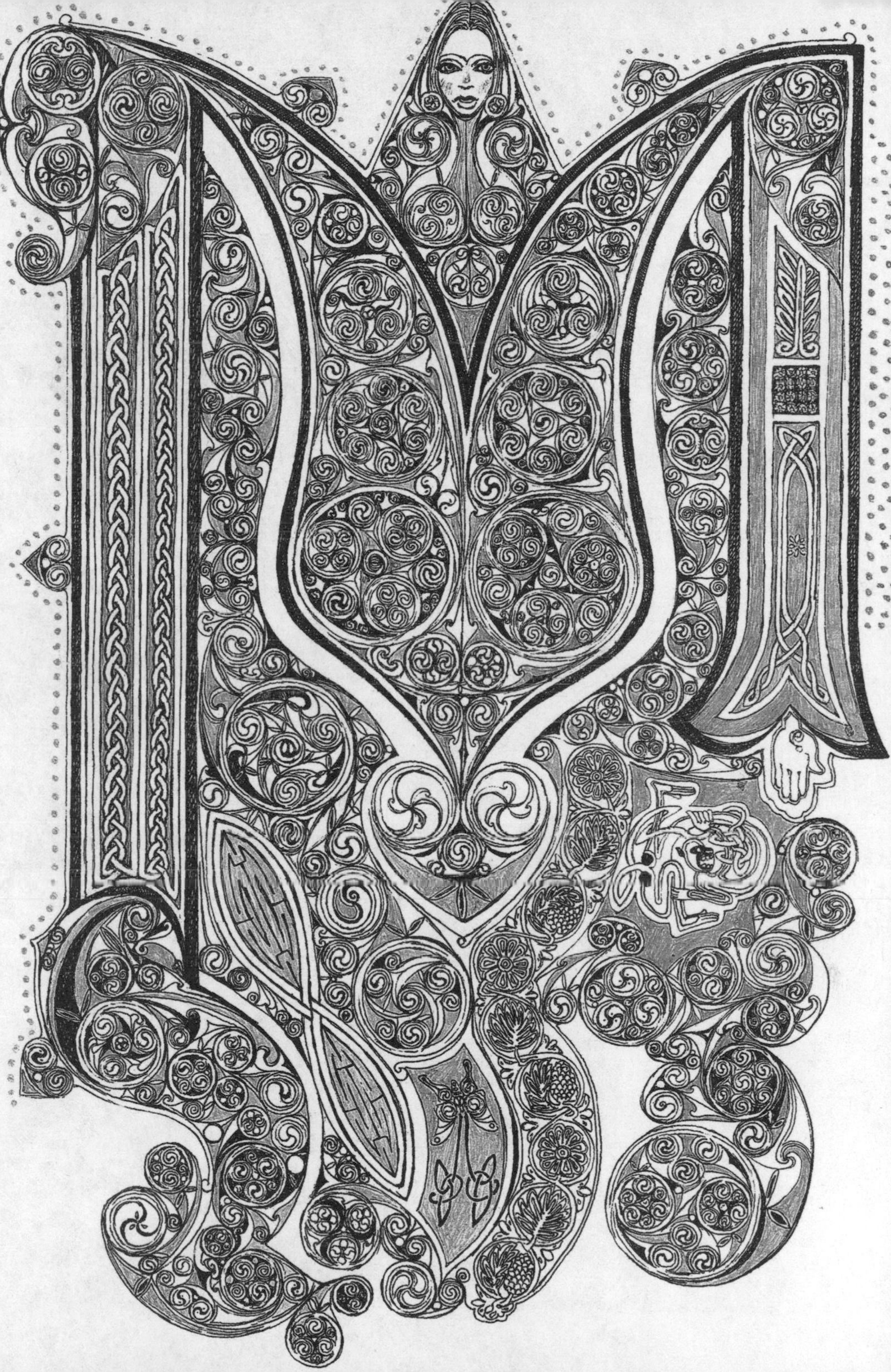

CONTENTS

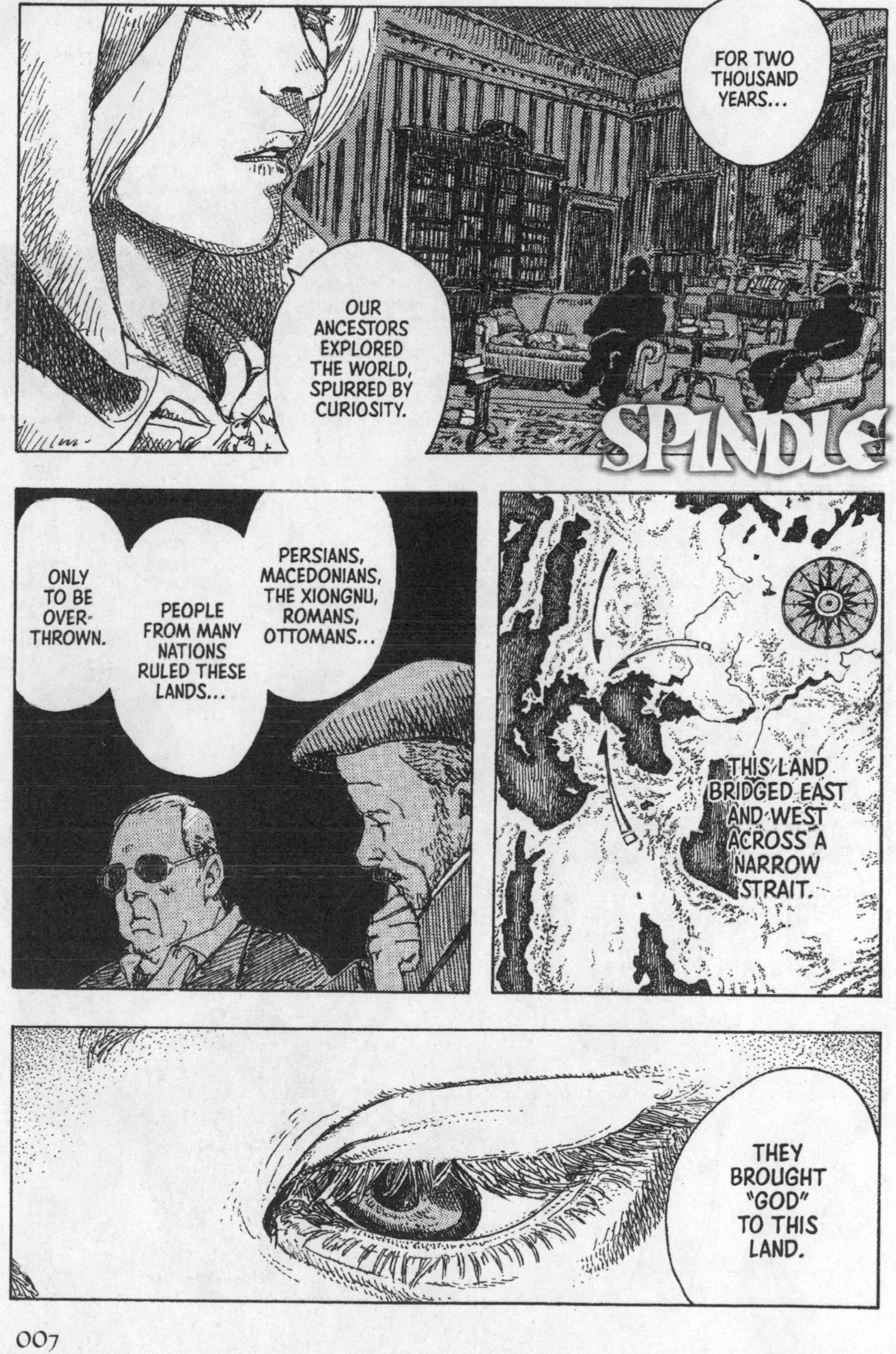
FOR TWO THOUSAND YEARS...
OUR ANCESTORS EXPLORED THE WORLD, SPURRED BY CURIOSITY.
SPINDLE
THIS LAND BRIDGED EAST AND WEST ACROSS A NARROW STRAIT.
PERSIANS, MACEDONIANS, THE XIONGNU, ROMANS, OTTOMANS...
PEOPLE FROM MANY NATIONS RULED THESE LANDS...
ONLY TO BE OVER-THROWN.
THEY BROUGHT "GOD" TO THIS LAND.

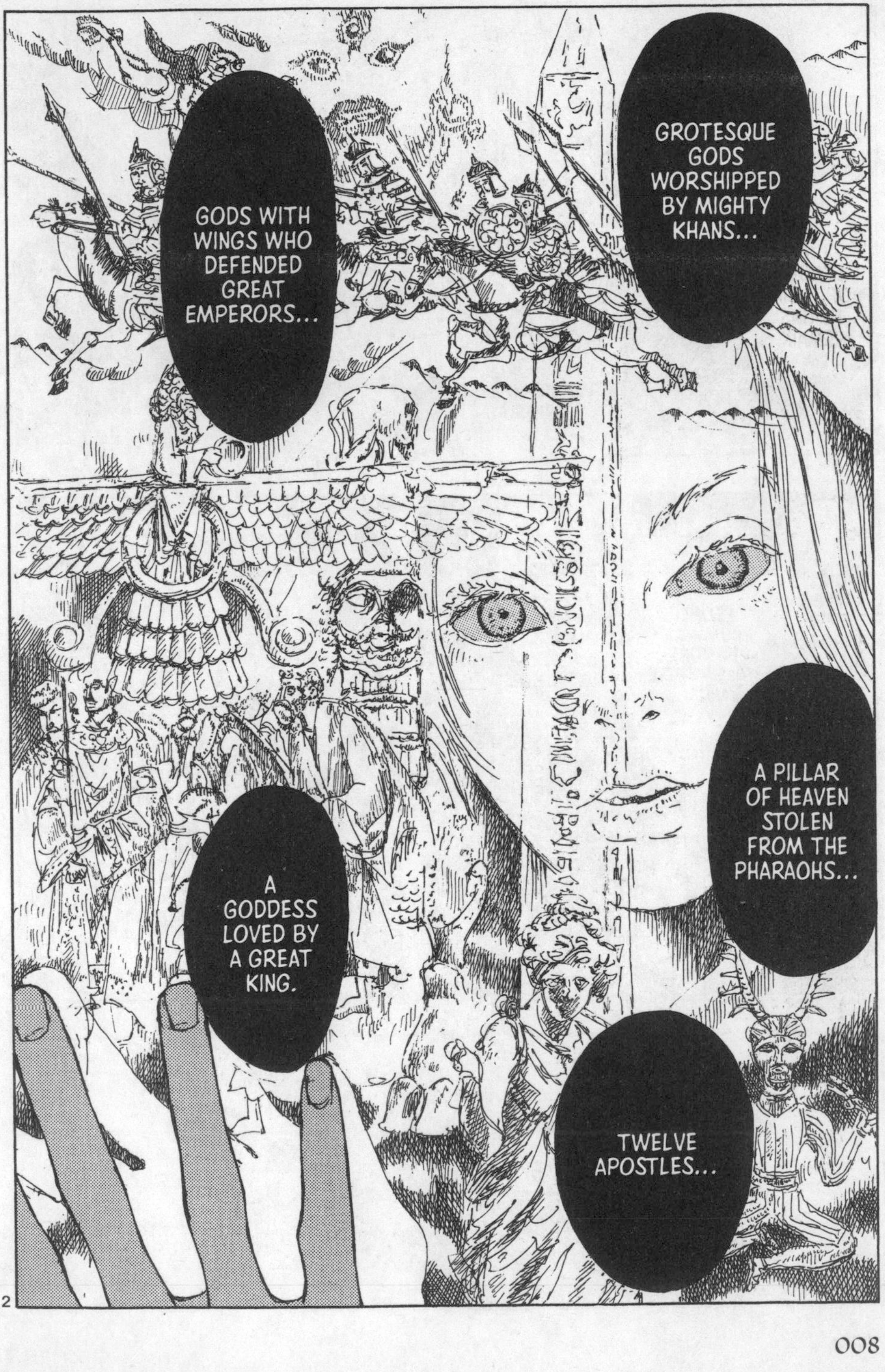
GROTESQUE GODS WORSHIPPED BY MIGHTY KHANS...
GODS WITH WINGS WHO DEFENDED GREAT EMPERORS...
A PILLAR OF HEAVEN STOLEN FROM THE PHARAOHS...
TWELVE APOSTLES...
A GODDESS LOVED BY A GREAT KING.

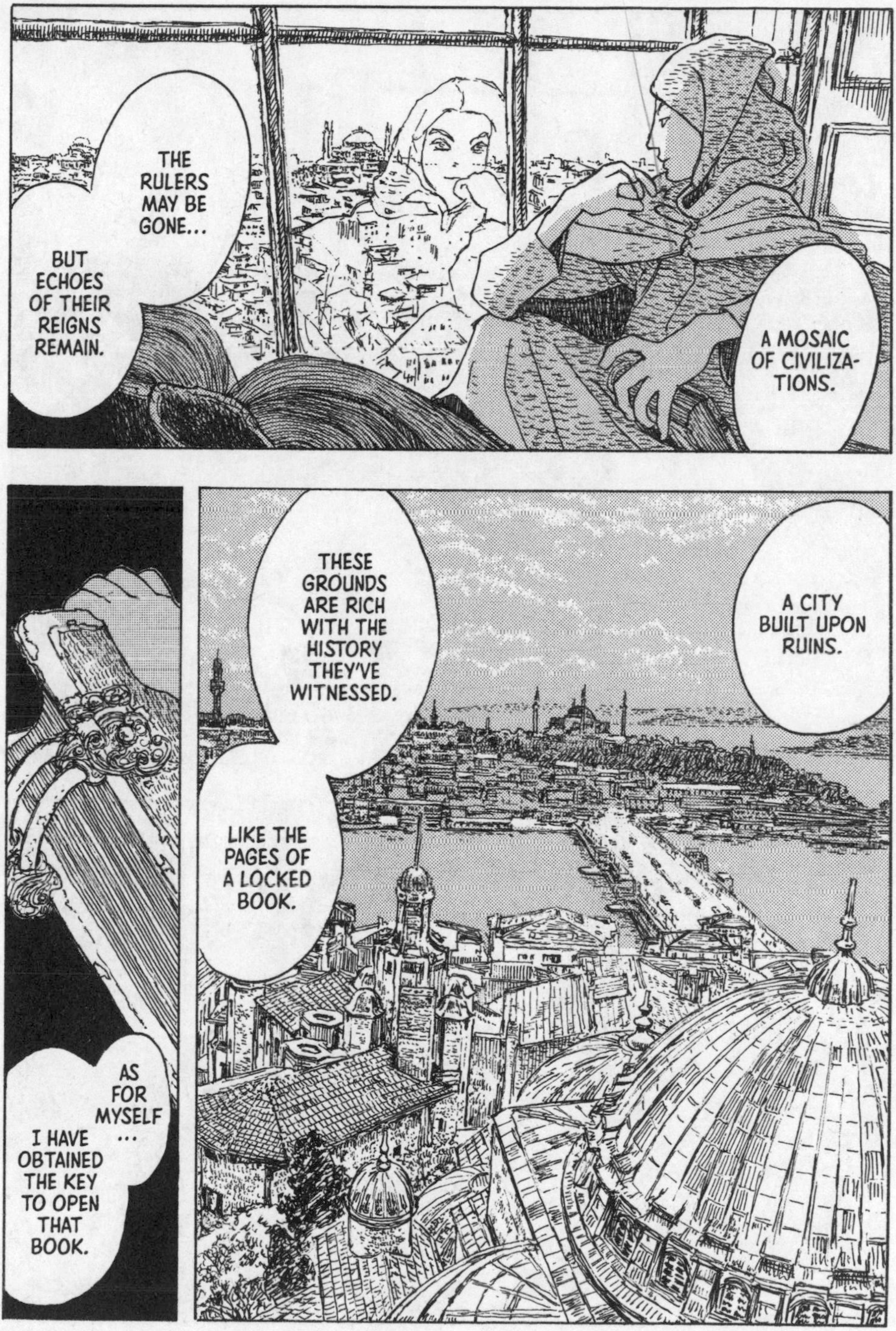
A MOSAIC OF CIVILIZATIONS.
THE RULERS MAY BE GONE...
BUT ECHOES OF THEIR REIGNS REMAIN.
A CITY BUILT UPON RUINS.
THESE GROUNDS ARE RICH WITH THE HISTORY THEY'VE WITNESSED.
LIKE THE PAGES OF A LOCKED BOOK.
AS FOR MYSELF...
I HAVE OBTAINED THE KEY TO OPEN THAT BOOK.

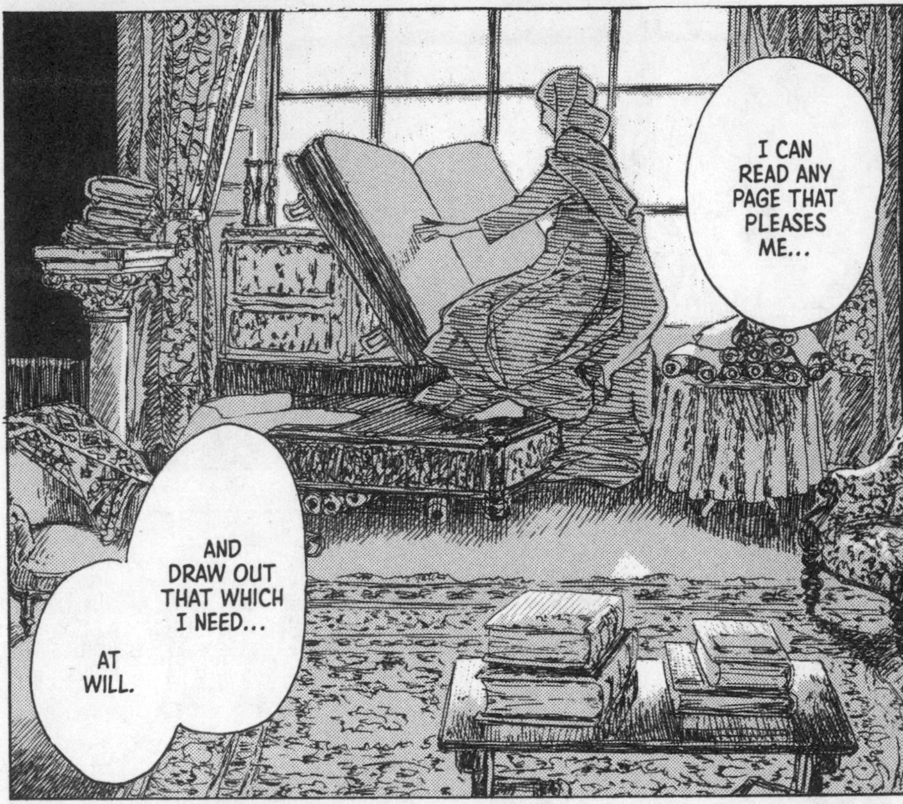
I CAN READ ANY PAGE THAT PLEASES ME...
AND DRAW OUT THAT WHICH I NEED...
AT WILL.
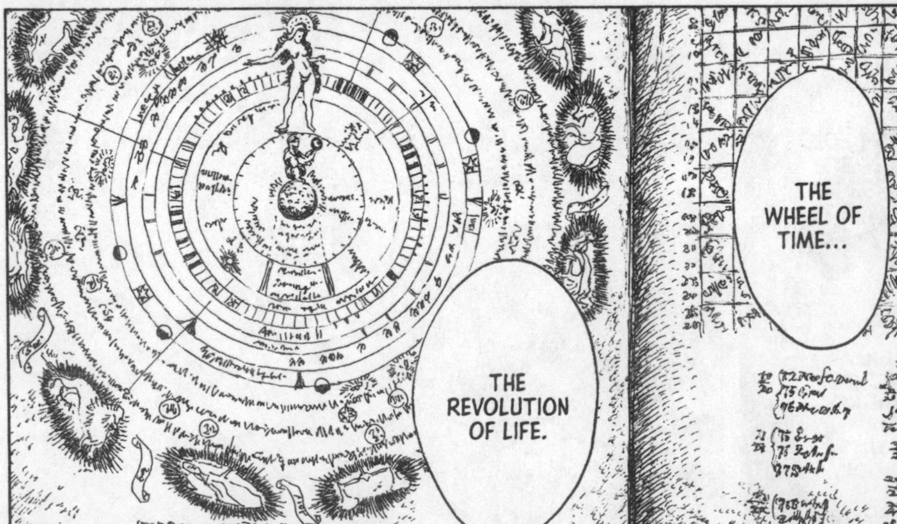
THE WHEEL OF TIME...
THE REVOLUTION OF LIFE.

IN THE VERY PALM OF MY HAND...
I HOLD THE SECRET OF THE WORLD.

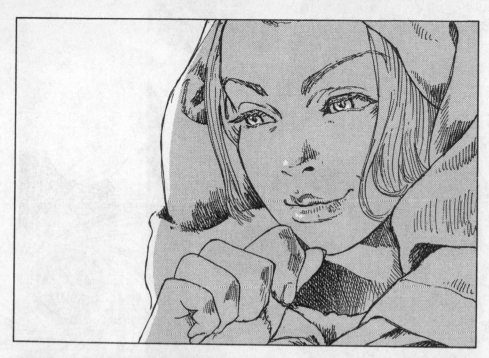

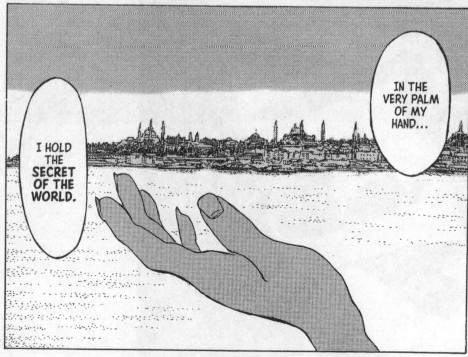

Spindle
- Part I -

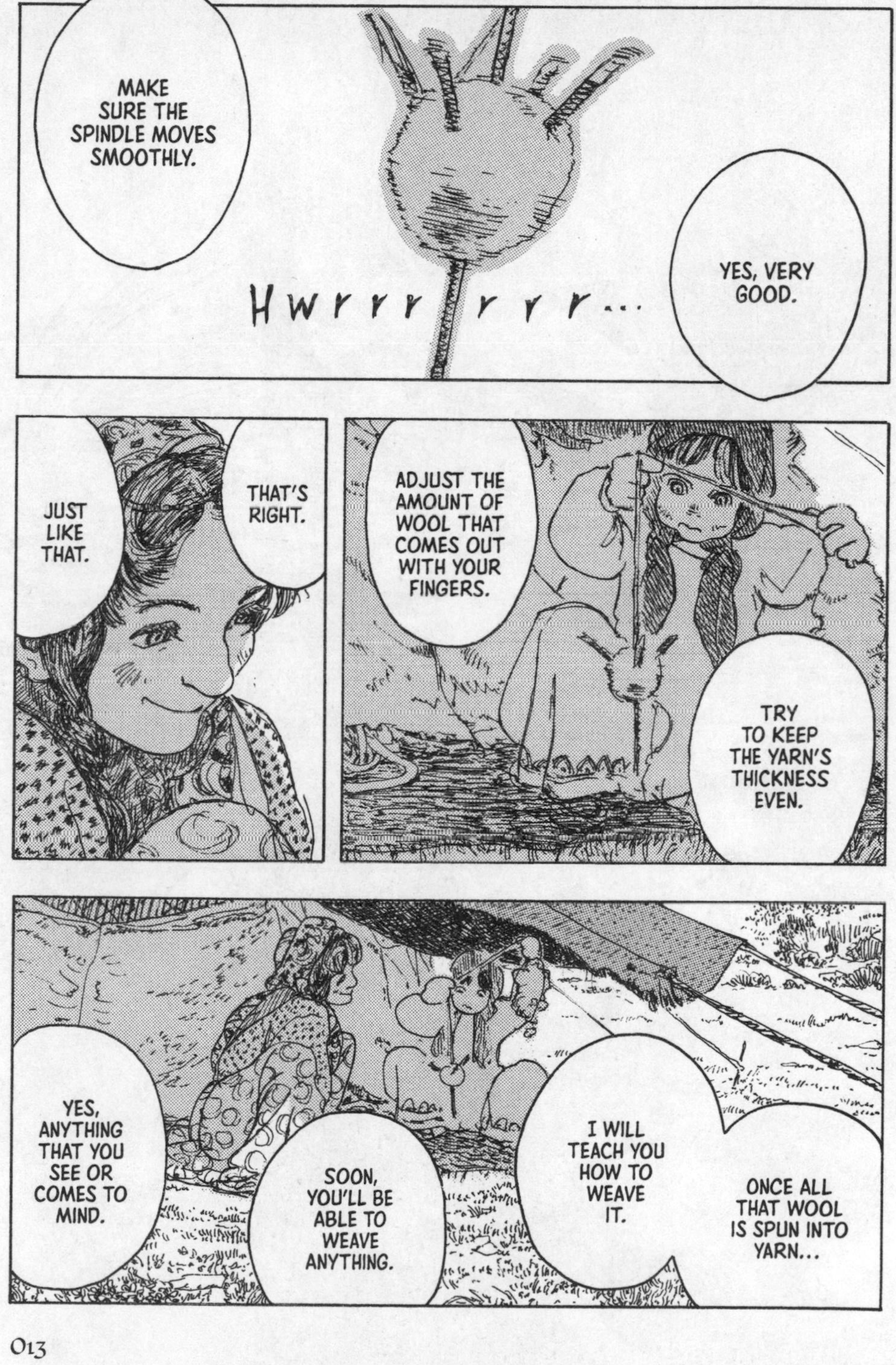
MAKE SURE THE SPINDLE MOVES SMOOTHLY.
Hwrrr rrr...
YES, VERY GOOD.
ADJUST THE AMOUNT OF WOOL THAT COMES OUT WITH YOUR FINGERS.
TRY TO KEEP THE YARN'S THICKNESS EVEN.
THAT'S RIGHT.
JUST LIKE THAT.
ONCE ALL THAT WOOL IS SPUN INTO YARN...
I WILL TEACH YOU HOW TO WEAVE IT.
SOON, YOU'LL BE ABLE TO WEAVE ANYTHING.
YES, ANYTHING THAT YOU SEE OR COMES TO MIND.

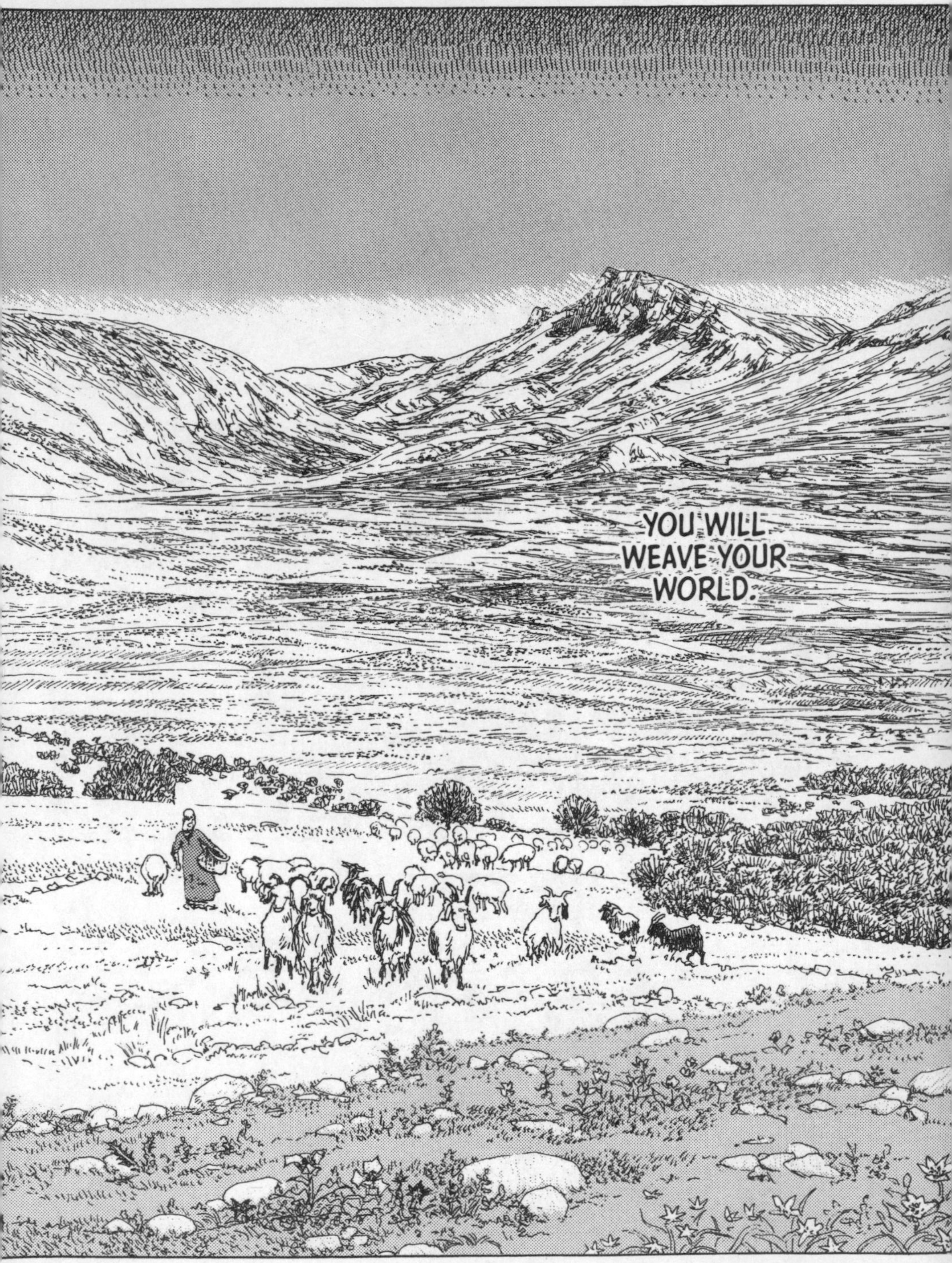
YOU WILL WEAVE YOUR WORLD.

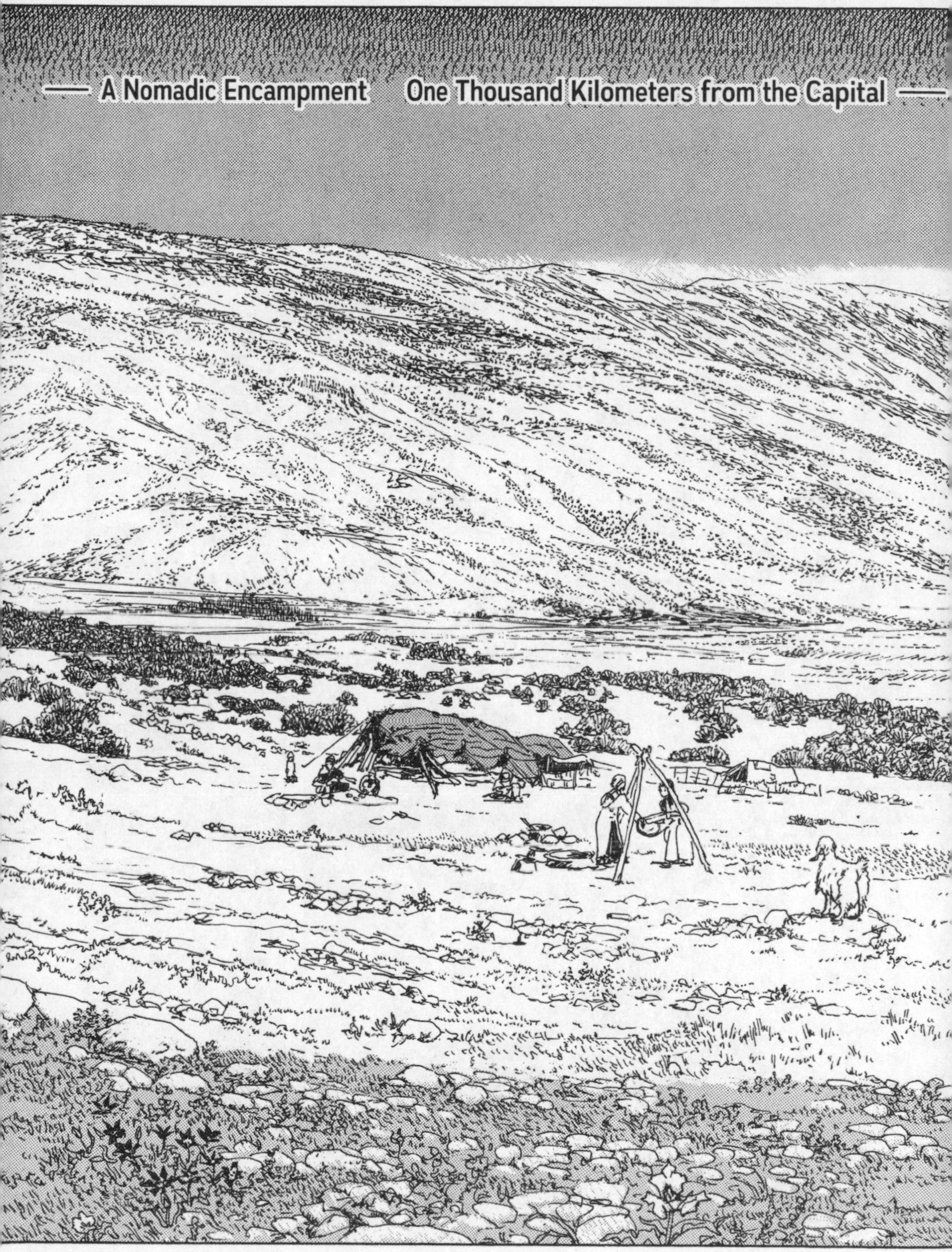
A Nomadic Encampment One Thousand Kilometers from the Capital

IT ISN'T THE SAME AS WHEN GODS CREATED THE WORLD...

BUT IF YOU TAKE GREAT CARE...

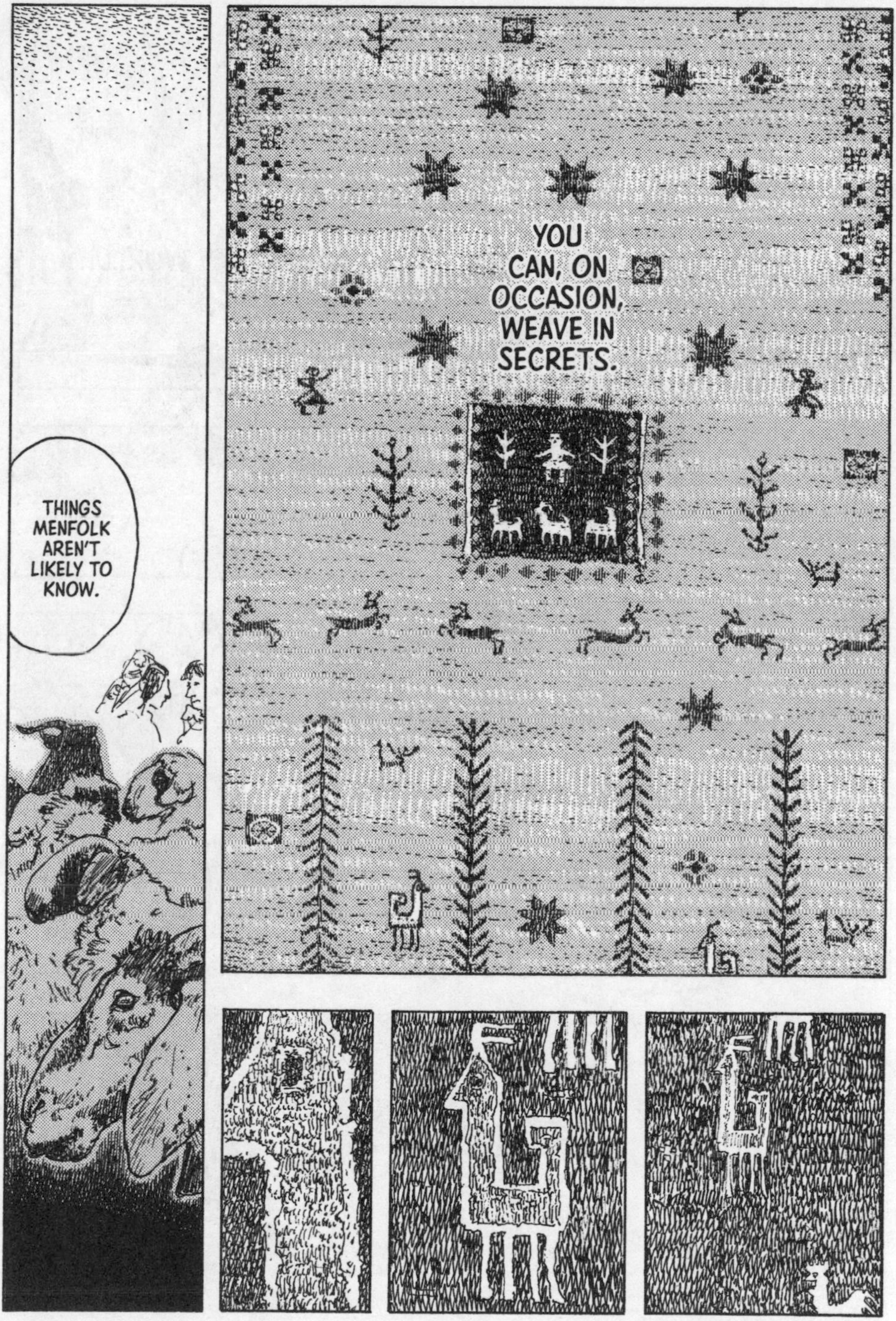
YOU CAN, ON OCCASION, WEAVE IN SECRETS.
THINGS MENFOLK AREN'T LIKELY TO KNOW.

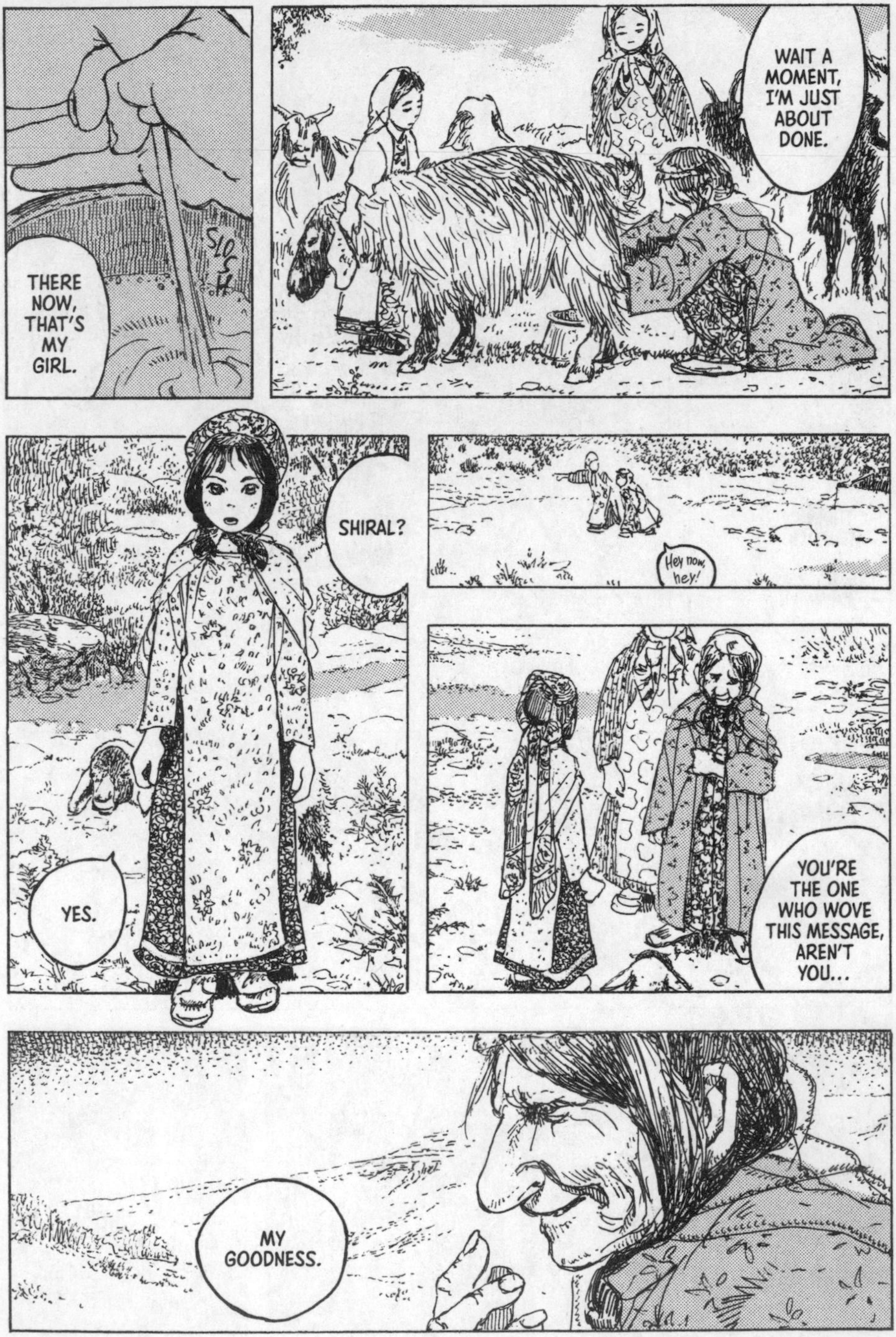
WAIT A MOMENT, I'M JUST ABOUT DONE.
SLOSH
THERE NOW, THAT'S MY GIRL.
Hey now, hey!
YOU'RE THE ONE WHO WOVE THIS MESSAGE, AREN'T YOU...
SHIRAL?
YES.
MY GOODNESS.

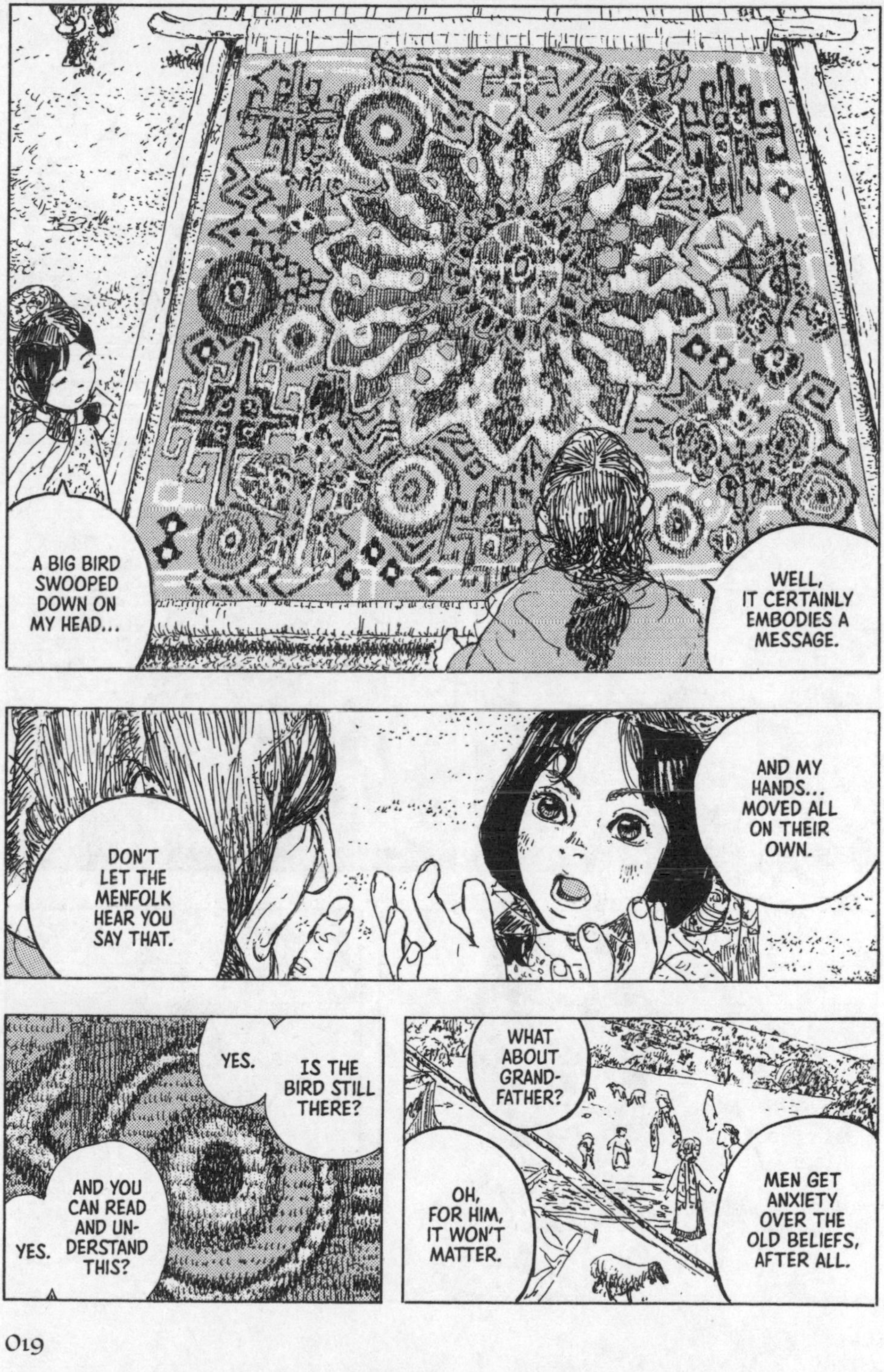
WELL, IT CERTAINLY EMBODIES A MESSAGE.
A BIG BIRD SWOOPED DOWN ON MY HEAD...
AND MY HANDS... MOVED ALL ON THEIR OWN.
DON'T LET THE MENFOLK HEAR YOU SAY THAT.
MEN GET ANXIETY OVER THE OLD BELIEFS, AFTER ALL.
WHAT ABOUT GRAND-FATHER?
OH, FOR HIM, IT WON'T MATTER.
IS THE BIRD STILL THERE?
YES.
AND YOU CAN READ AND UN-DERSTAND THIS?
YES.

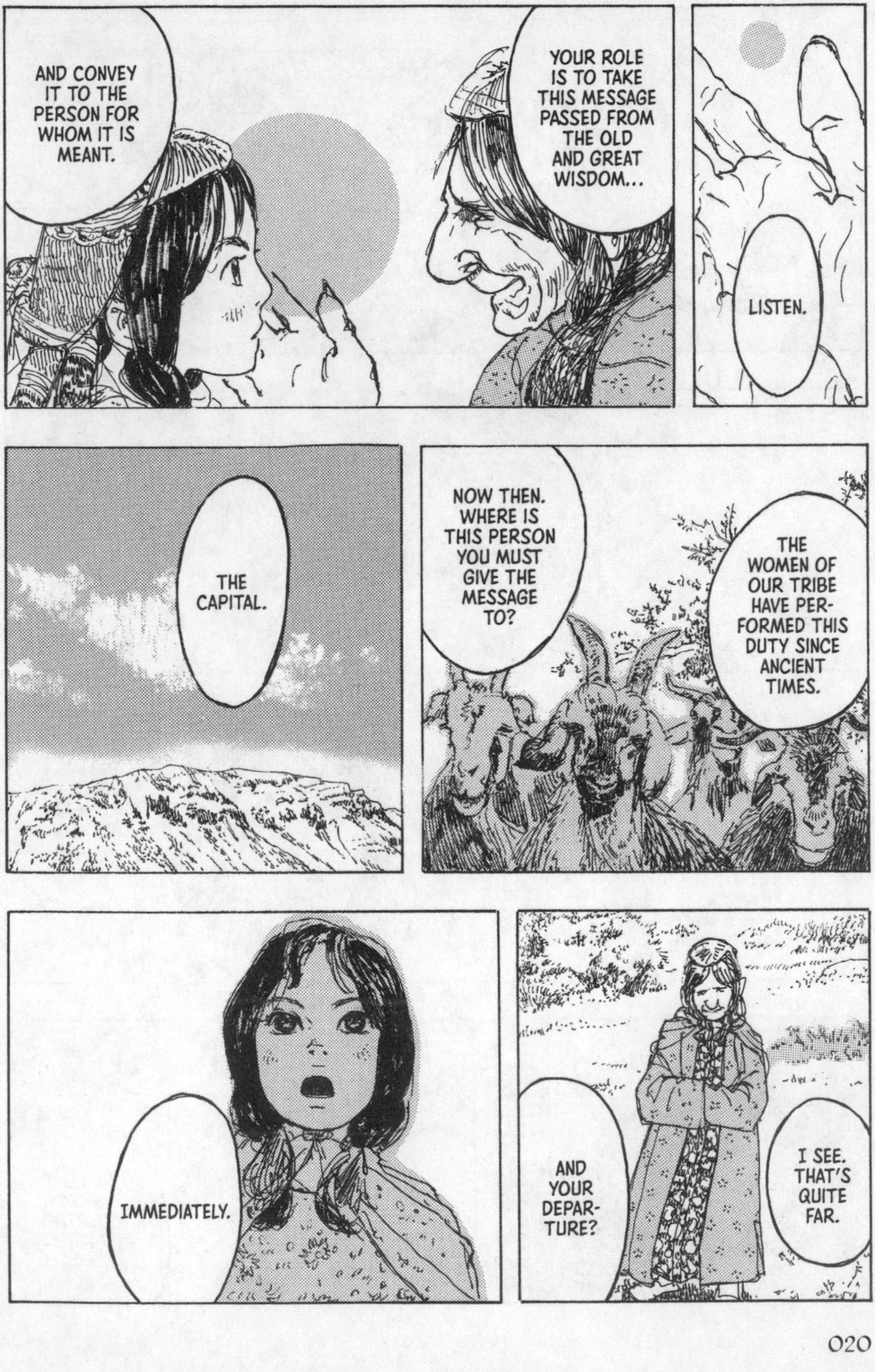
LISTEN.
YOUR ROLE IS TO TAKE THIS MESSAGE PASSED FROM THE OLD AND GREAT WISDOM...
AND CONVEY IT TO THE PERSON FOR WHOM IT IS MEANT.
THE WOMEN OF OUR TRIBE HAVE PER-FORMED THIS DUTY SINCE ANCIENT TIMES.
NOW THEN. WHERE IS THIS PERSON YOU MUST GIVE THE MESSAGE TO?
THE CAPITAL.
I SEE. THAT'S QUITE FAR.
AND YOUR DEPAR-TURE?
IMMEDIATELY.

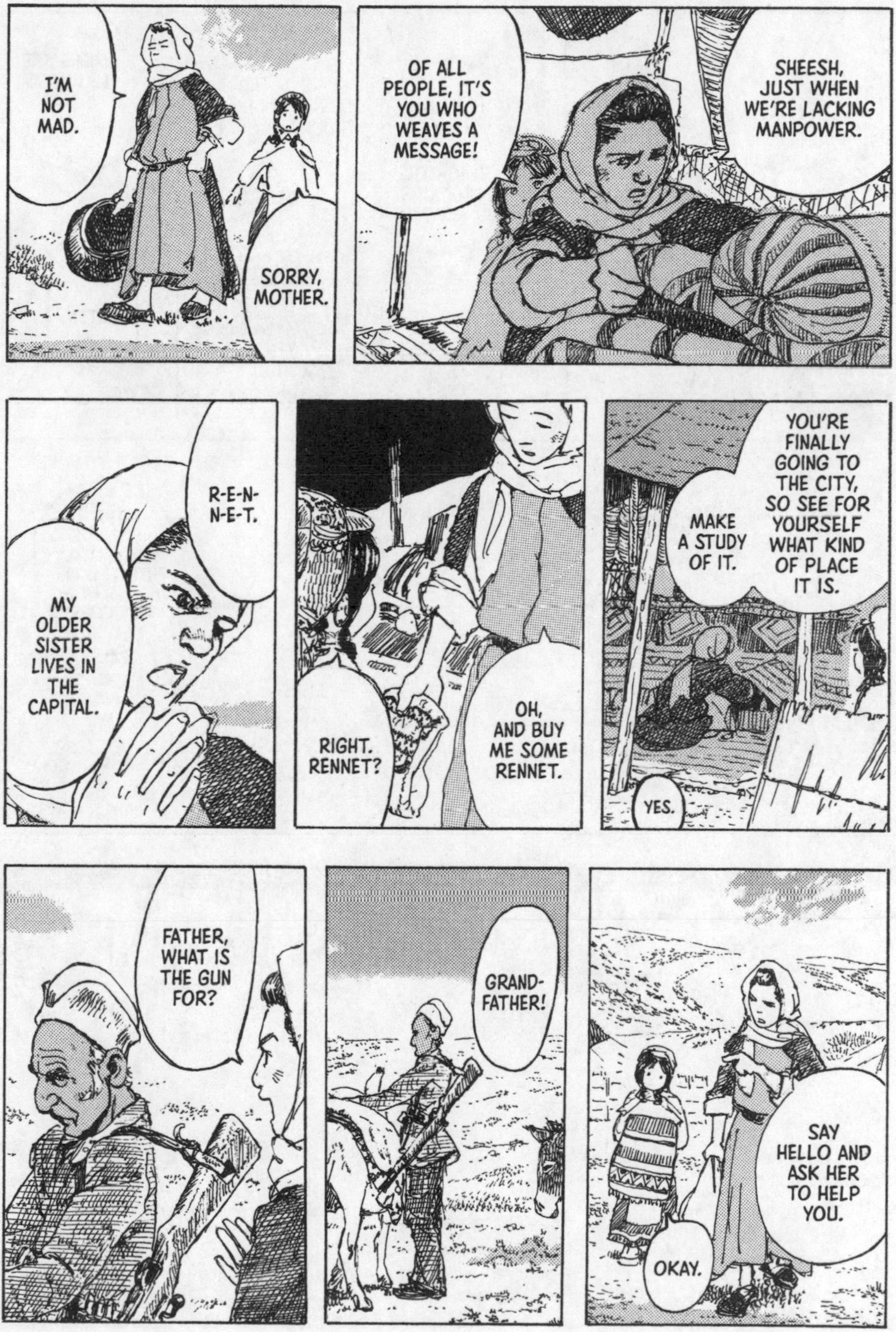
SHEESH, JUST WHEN WE'RE LACKING MANPOWER.
OF ALL PEOPLE, IT'S YOU WHO WEAVES A MESSAGE!
SORRY, MOTHER.
I'M NOT MAD.
YOU'RE FINALLY GOING TO THE CITY, SO SEE FOR YOURSELF WHAT KIND OF PLACE IT IS.
MAKE A STUDY OF IT.
YES.
OH, AND BUY ME SOME RENNET.
RIGHT. RENNET?
R-E-N-N-E-T.
MY OLDER SISTER LIVES IN THE CAPITAL.
SAY HELLO AND ASK HER TO HELP YOU.
OKAY.
GRAND-FATHER!
FATHER, WHAT IS THE GUN FOR?

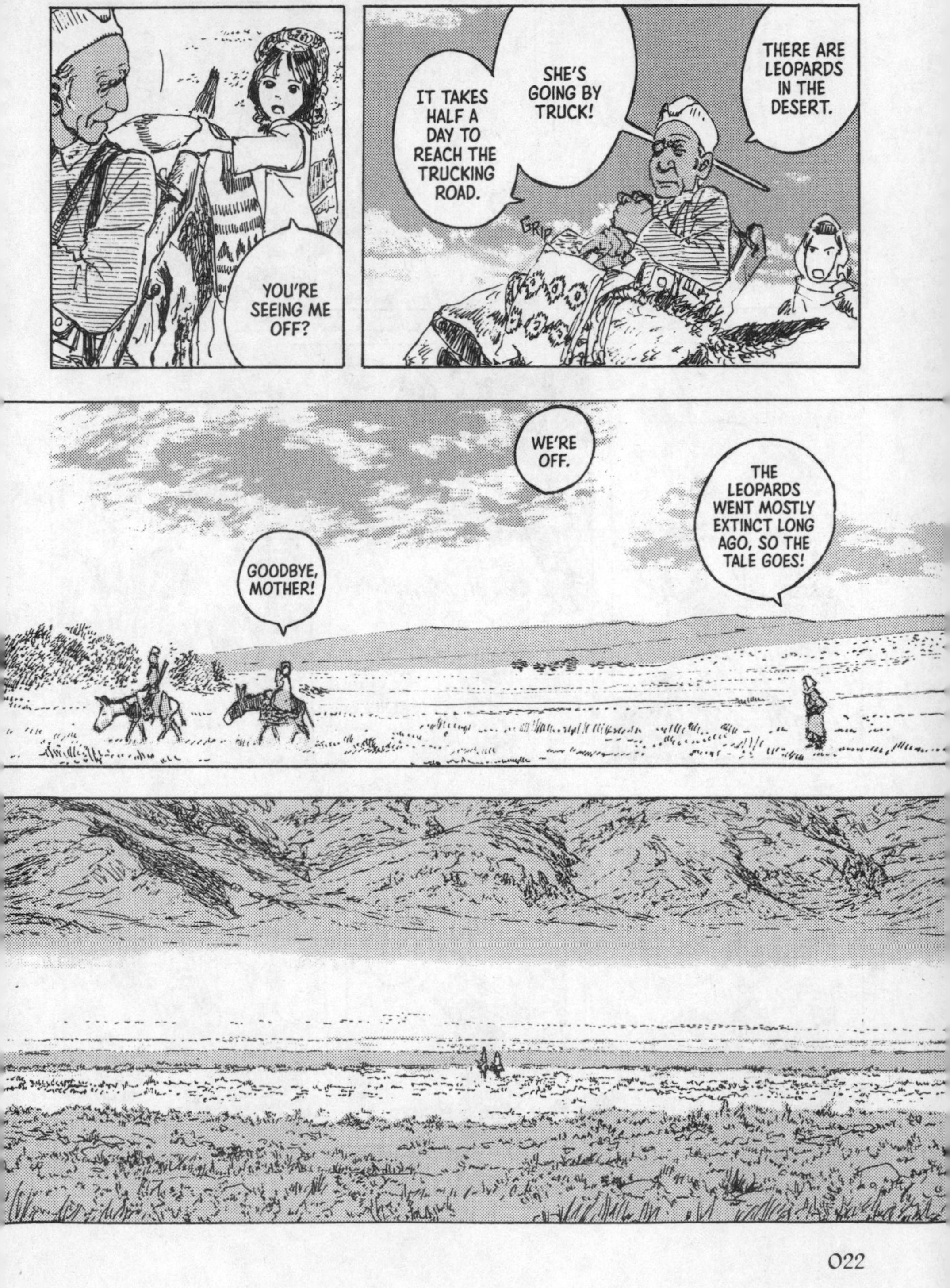
THERE ARE LEOPARDS IN THE DESERT.
SHE'S GOING BY TRUCK!
IT TAKES HALF A DAY TO REACH THE TRUCKING ROAD.
GRIP
YOU'RE SEEING ME OFF?
WE'RE OFF.
THE LEOPARDS WENT MOSTLY EXTINCT LONG AGO, SO THE TALE GOES!
GOODBYE, MOTHER!

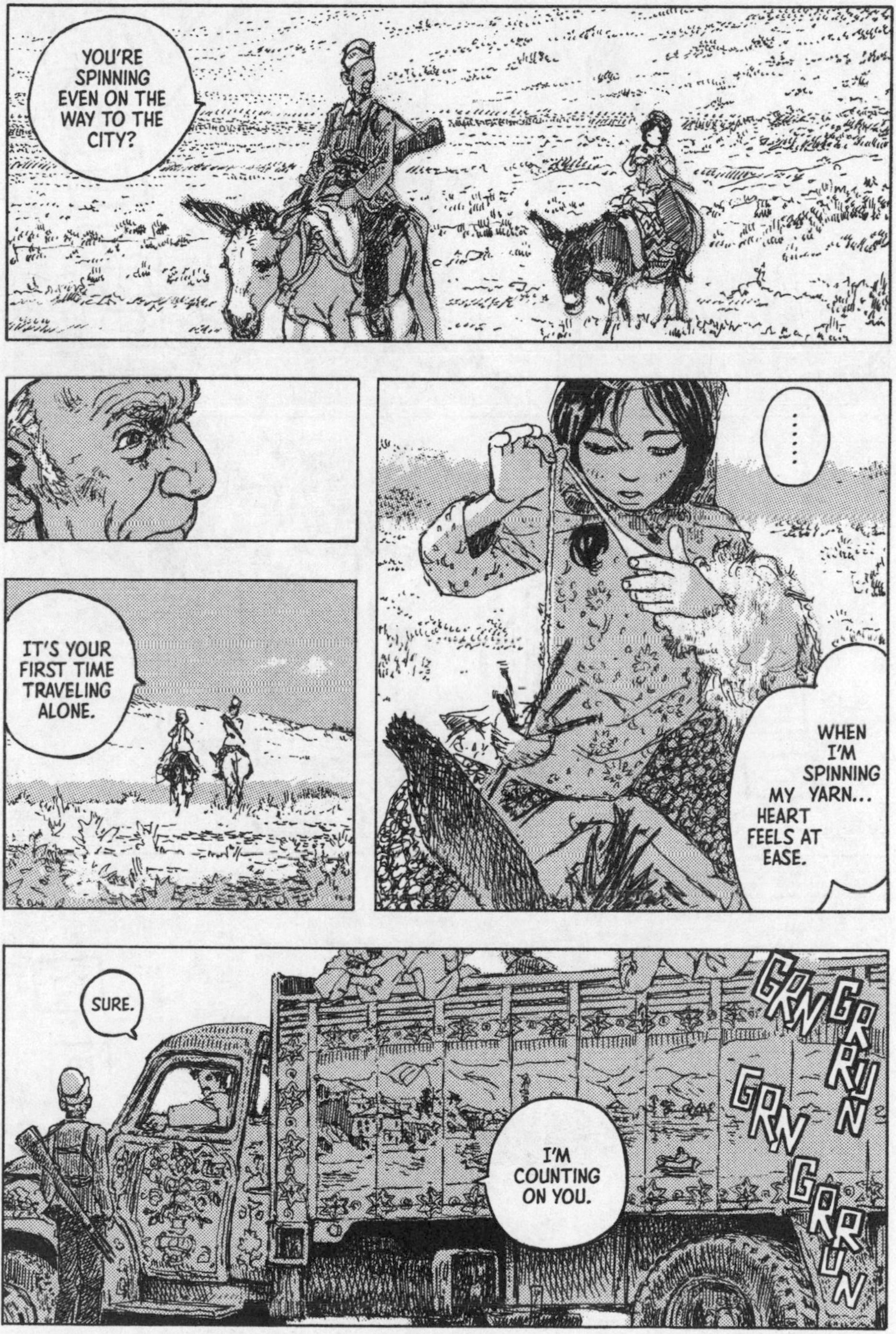
YOU'RE SPINNING EVEN ON THE WAY TO THE CITY?
......
WHEN I'M SPINNING MY YARN... HEART FEELS AT EASE.
IT'S YOUR FIRST TIME TRAVELING ALONE.
GRN GRRUN
GRN GRRUN
I'M COUNTING ON YOU.
SURE.

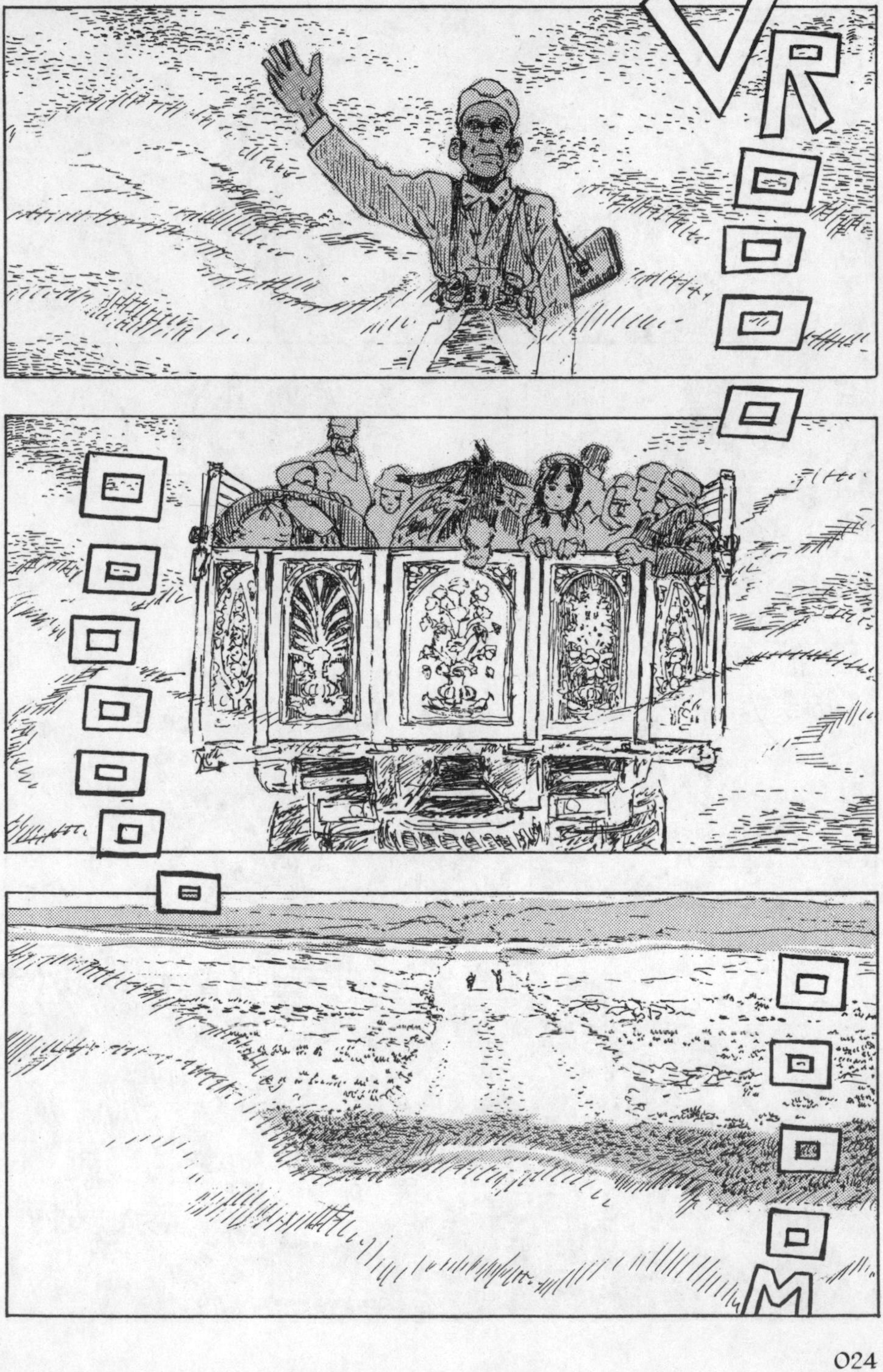
VROOOOOOOOOOOOOOOM

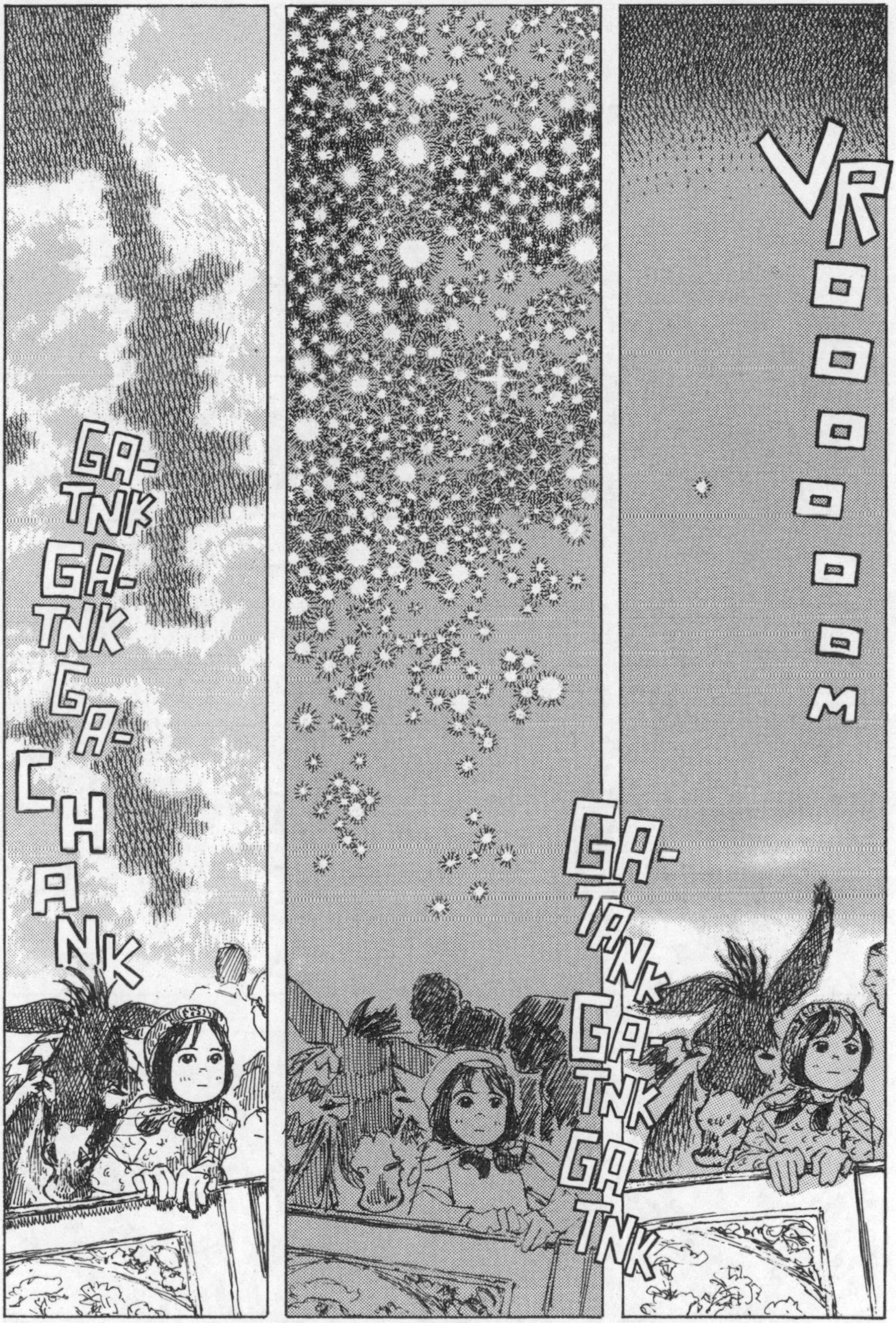
VROOOOOOM
GA-TANK GA-TNK GA TNK
GA-TNK GA-TNK GA-CHANK

— The Capital   Thirty Years Earlier —

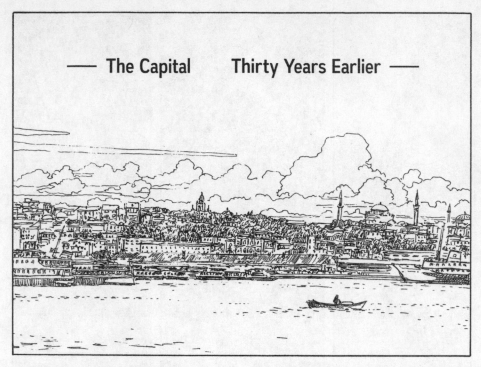

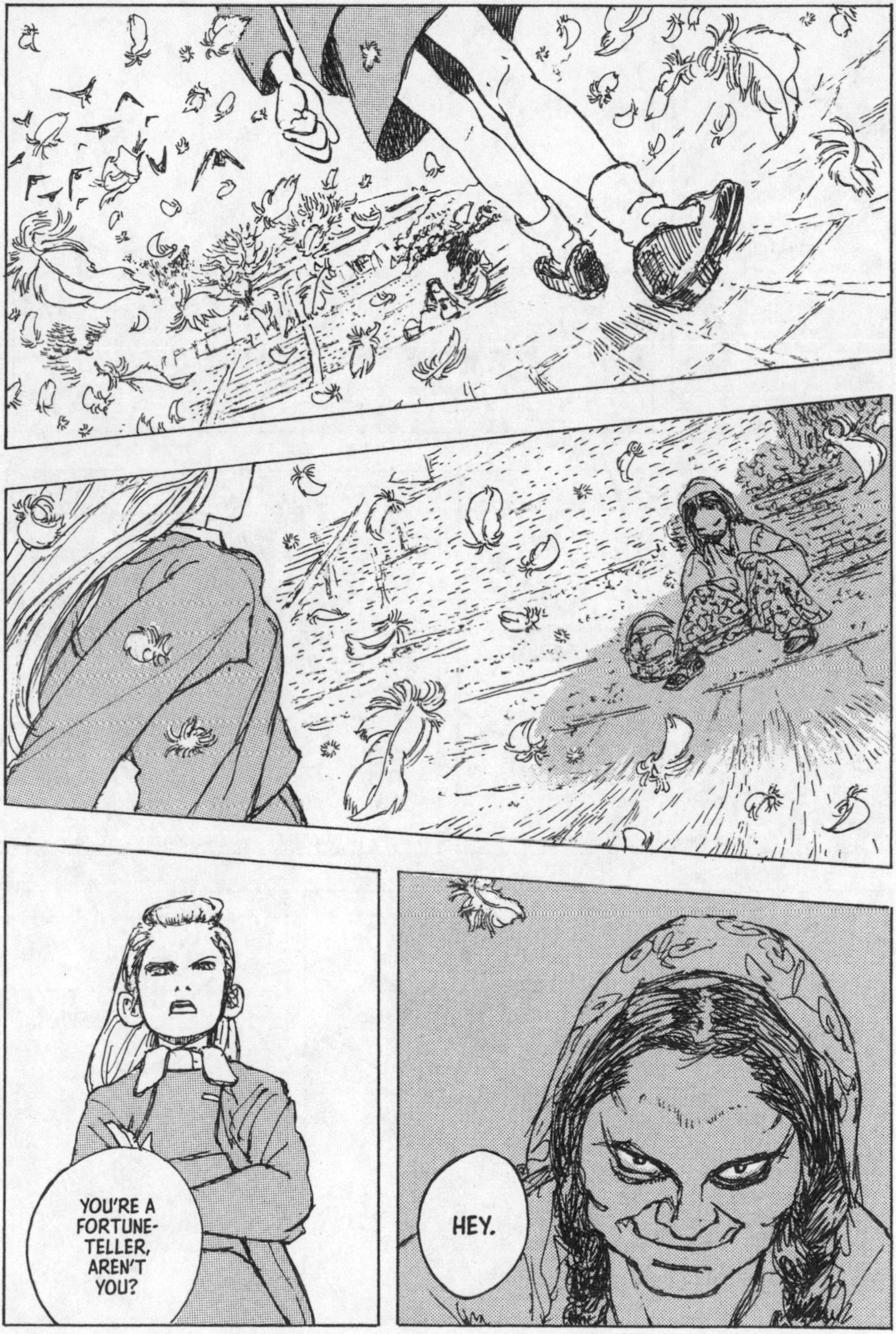
HEY.
YOU'RE A FORTUNE-TELLER, AREN'T YOU?

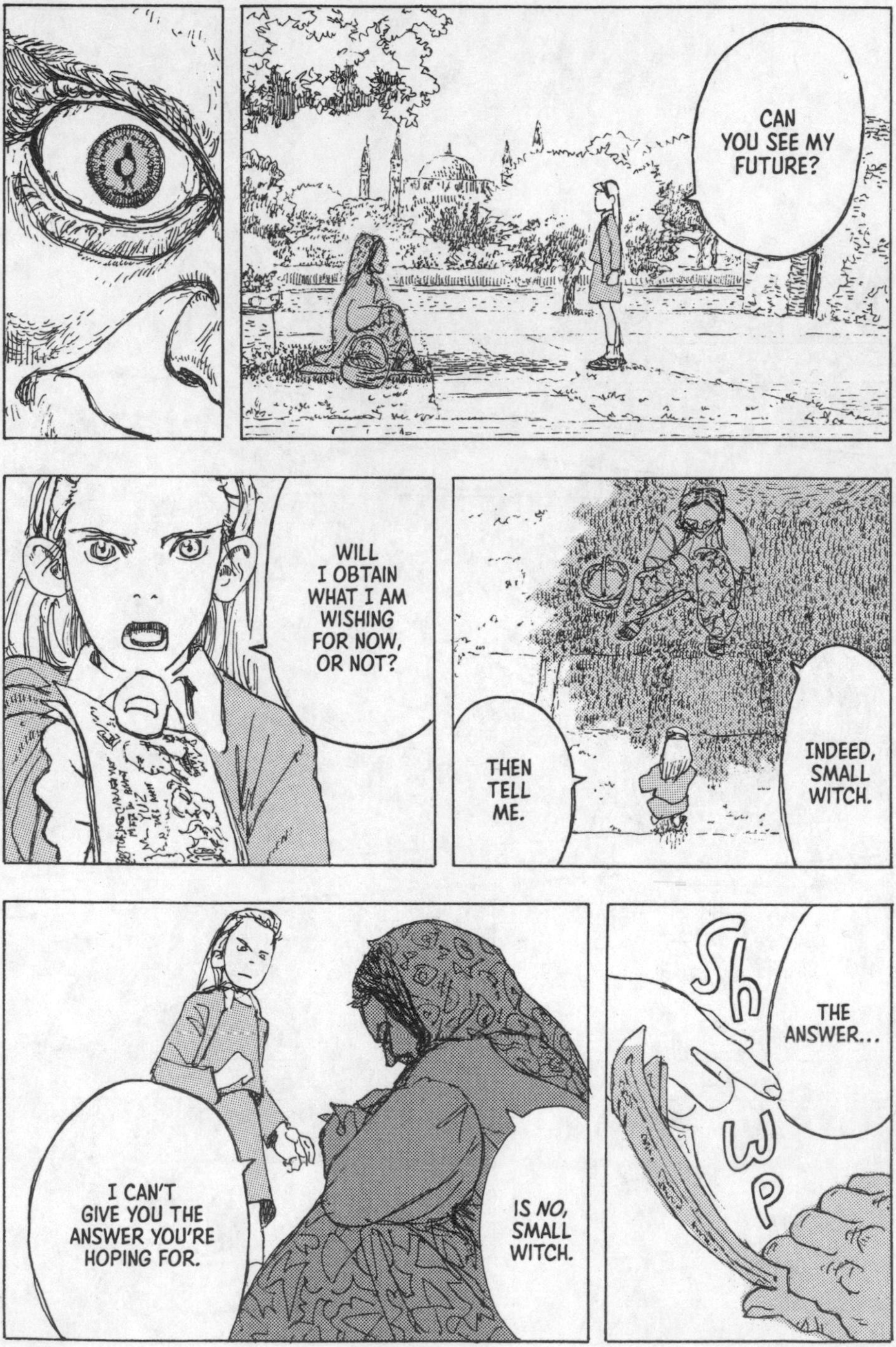
CAN YOU SEE MY FUTURE?
INDEED, SMALL WITCH.
THEN TELL ME.
WILL I OBTAIN WHAT I AM WISHING FOR NOW, OR NOT?
Shwup
THE ANSWER...
IS *NO*, SMALL WITCH.
I CAN'T GIVE YOU THE ANSWER YOU'RE HOPING FOR.

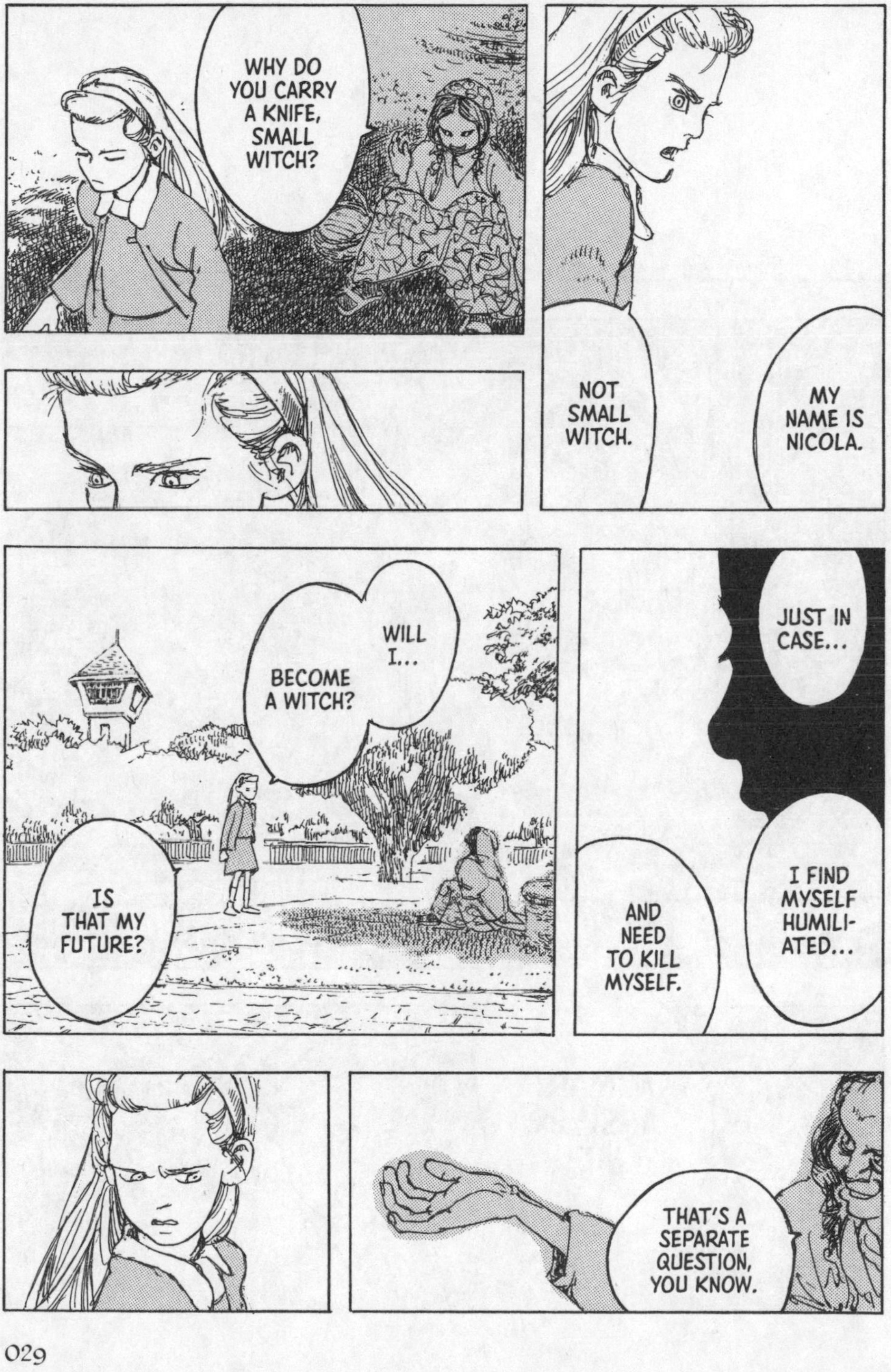
MY NAME IS NICOLA.
NOT SMALL WITCH.
WHY DO YOU CARRY A KNIFE, SMALL WITCH?
JUST IN CASE...
I FIND MYSELF HUMILI-ATED...
AND NEED TO KILL MYSELF.
WILL I...
BECOME A WITCH?
IS THAT MY FUTURE?
THAT'S A SEPARATE QUESTION, YOU KNOW.

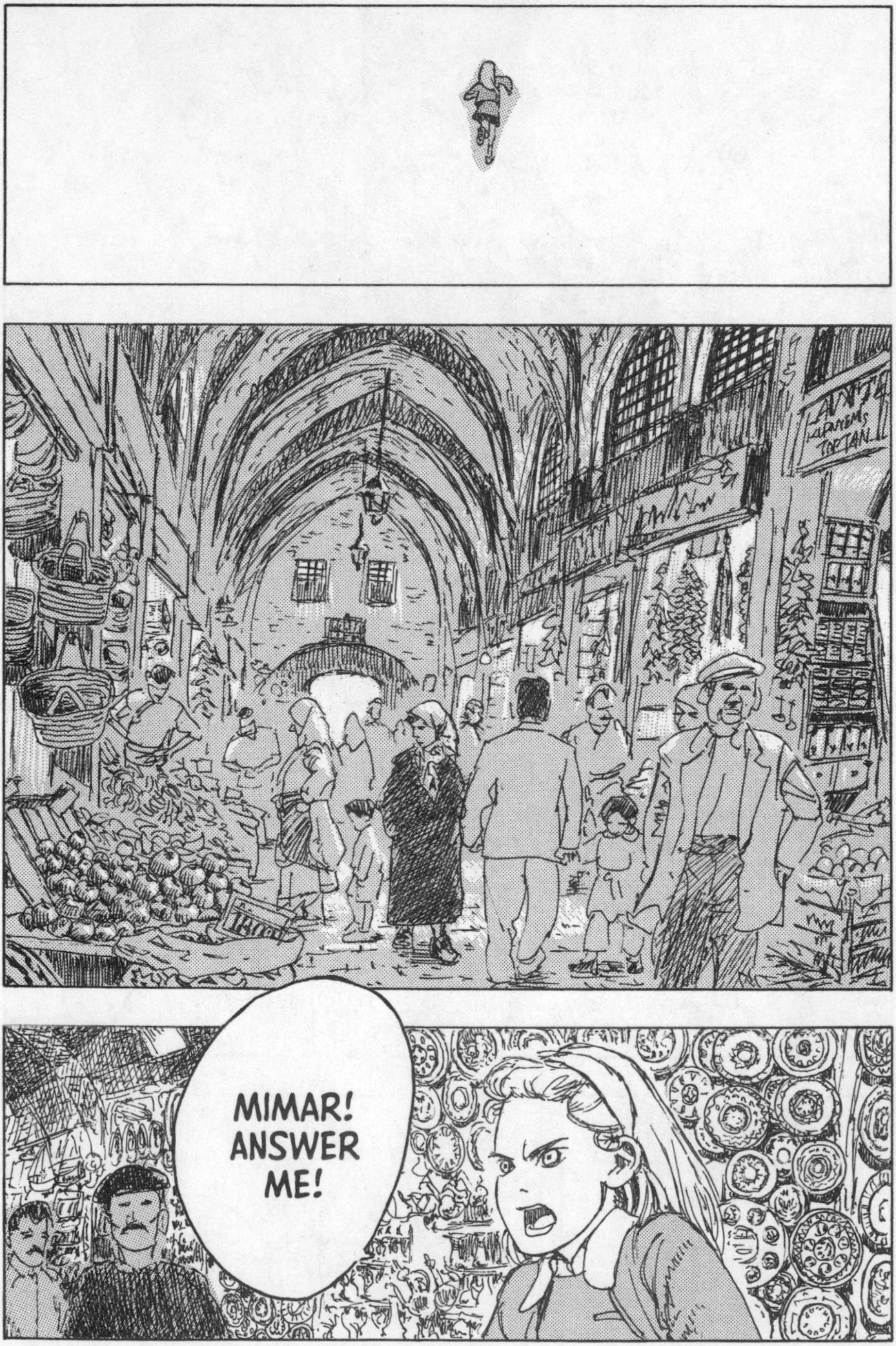
TOPTAN
MIMAR! ANSWER ME!

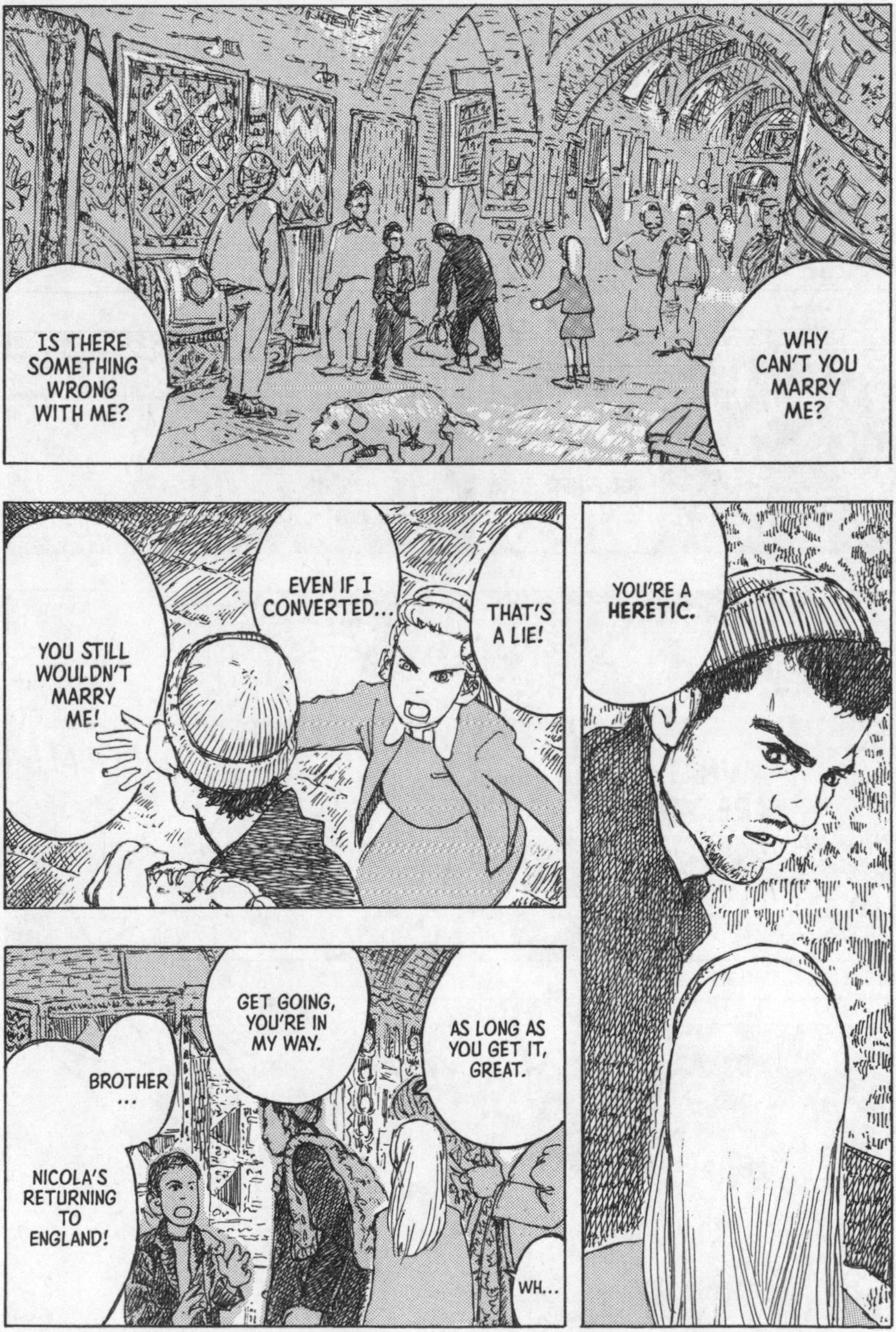
WHY CAN'T YOU MARRY ME?
IS THERE SOMETHING WRONG WITH ME?
YOU'RE A **HERETIC.**
THAT'S A LIE!
EVEN IF I CONVERTED...
YOU STILL WOULDN'T MARRY ME!
AS LONG AS YOU GET IT, GREAT.
GET GOING, YOU'RE IN MY WAY.
BROTHER ...
NICOLA'S RETURNING TO ENGLAND!
WH...

BROTHER...

MIFRIM.

IGNORE HER AND GET TO WORK...

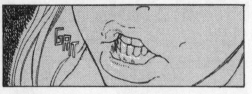

GRIT

WHAT ARE YOU DOING?!

NICOLA!!

26

STOP!

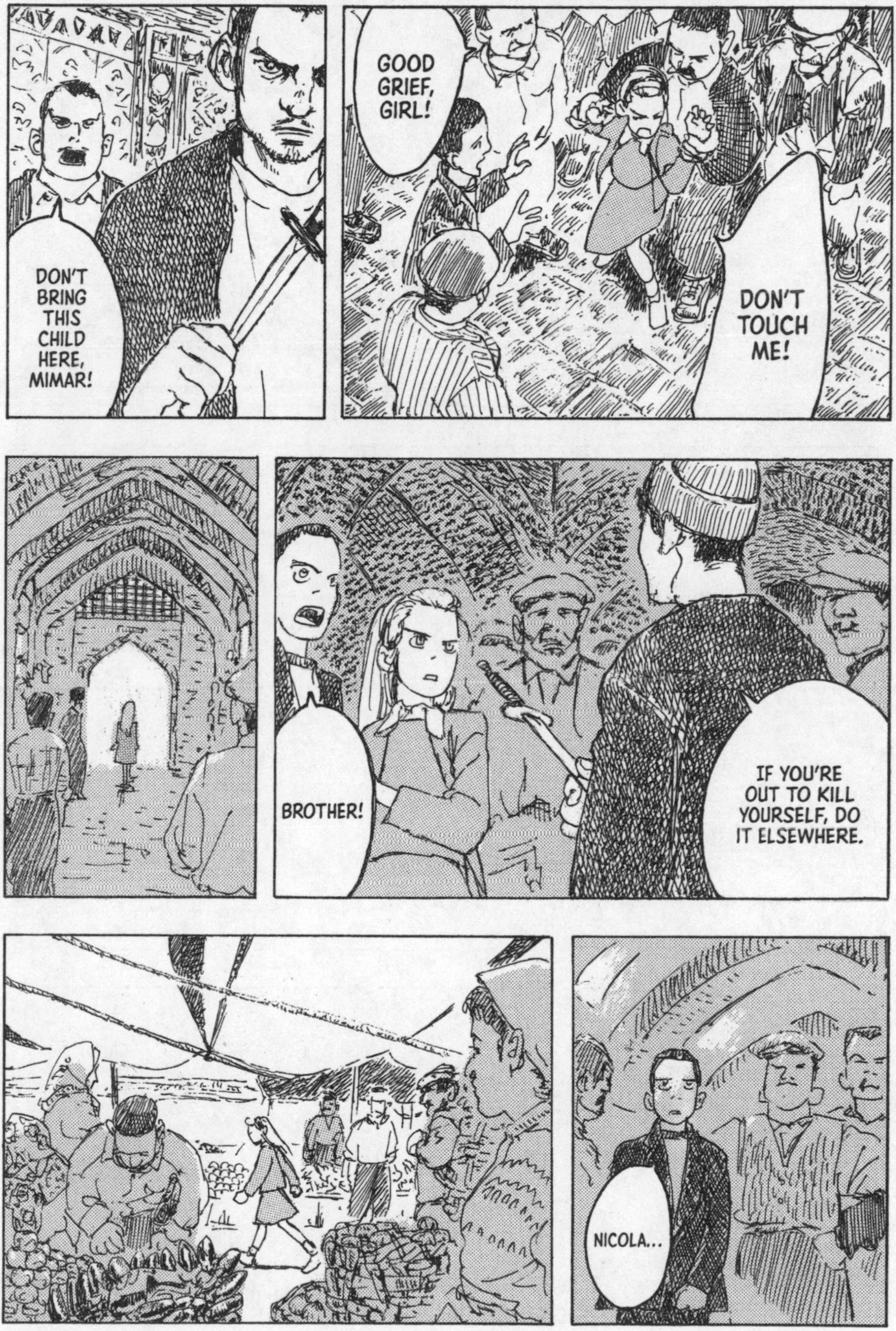
GOOD GRIEF, GIRL!
DON'T TOUCH ME!
DON'T BRING THIS CHILD HERE, MIMAR!
IF YOU'RE OUT TO KILL YOURSELF, DO IT ELSEWHERE.
BROTHER!
NICOLA...

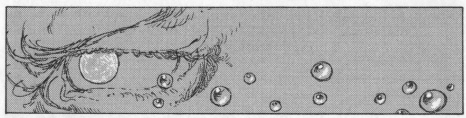

— **The Present** —

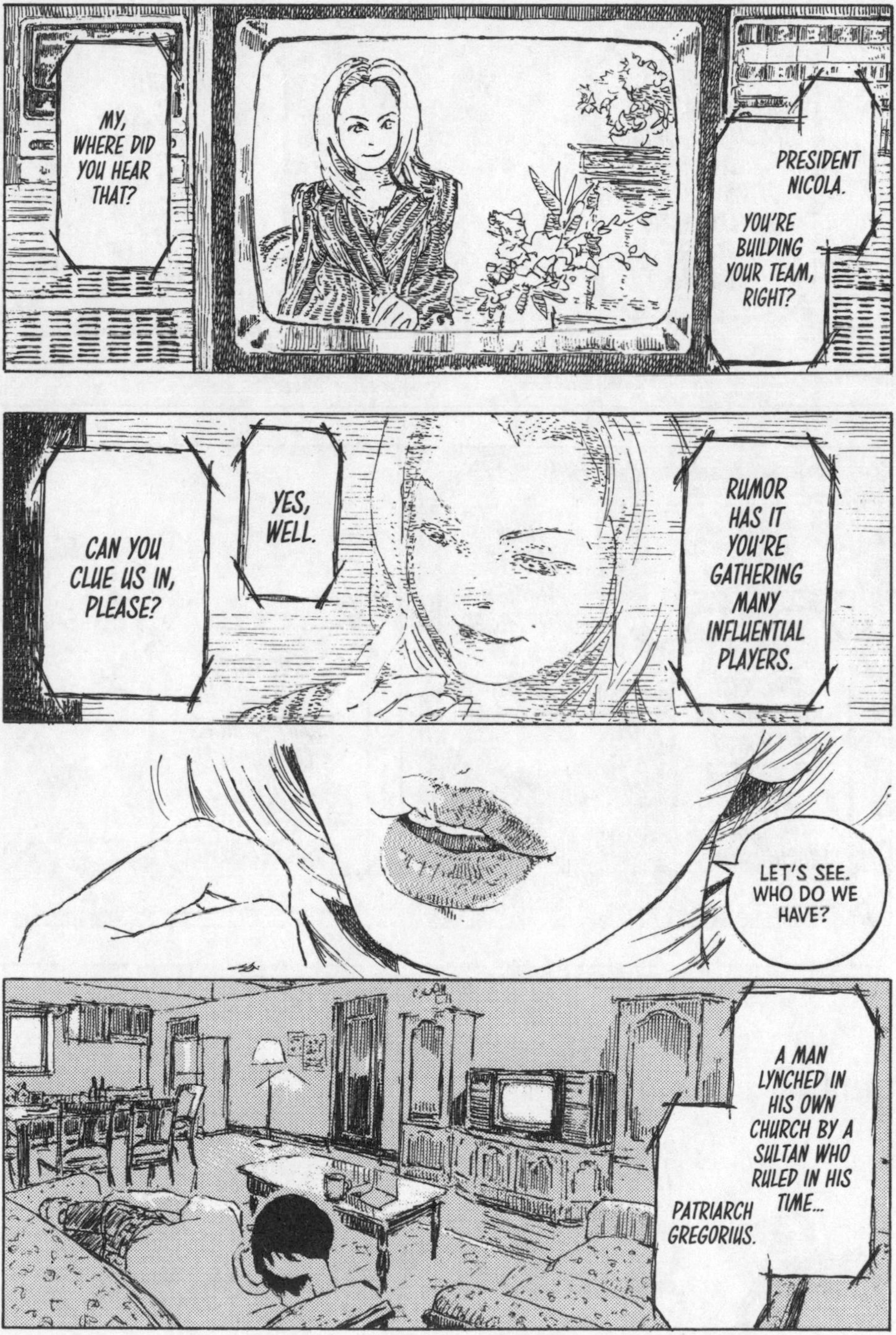
PRESIDENT NICOLA.
YOU'RE BUILDING YOUR TEAM, RIGHT?
MY, WHERE DID YOU HEAR THAT?
RUMOR HAS IT YOU'RE GATHERING MANY INFLUENTIAL PLAYERS.
YES, WELL.
CAN YOU CLUE US IN, PLEASE?
LET'S SEE. WHO DO WE HAVE?
A MAN LYNCHED IN HIS OWN CHURCH BY A SULTAN WHO RULED IN HIS TIME...
PATRIARCH GREGORIUS.

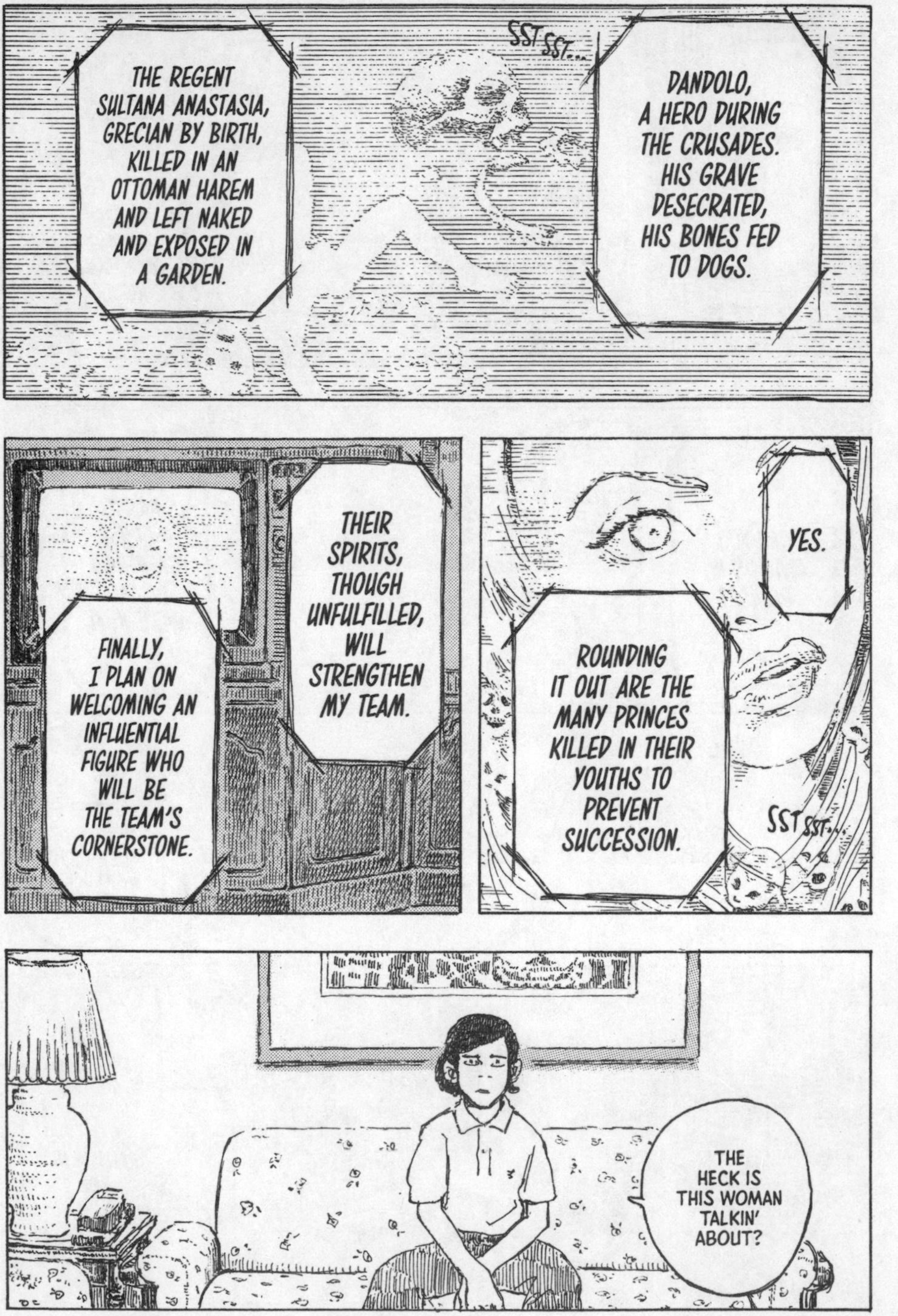

DANDOLO, A HERO DURING THE CRUSADES. HIS GRAVE DESECRATED, HIS BONES FED TO DOGS.
SST SST...
THE REGENT SULTANA ANASTASIA, GRECIAN BY BIRTH, KILLED IN AN OTTOMAN HAREM AND LEFT NAKED AND EXPOSED IN A GARDEN.
YES.
ROUNDING IT OUT ARE THE MANY PRINCES KILLED IN THEIR YOUTHS TO PREVENT SUCCESSION.
SST SST...
THEIR SPIRITS, THOUGH UNFULFILLED, WILL STRENGTHEN MY TEAM.
FINALLY, I PLAN ON WELCOMING AN INFLUENTIAL FIGURE WHO WILL BE THE TEAM'S CORNERSTONE.
THE HECK IS THIS WOMAN TALKIN' ABOUT?

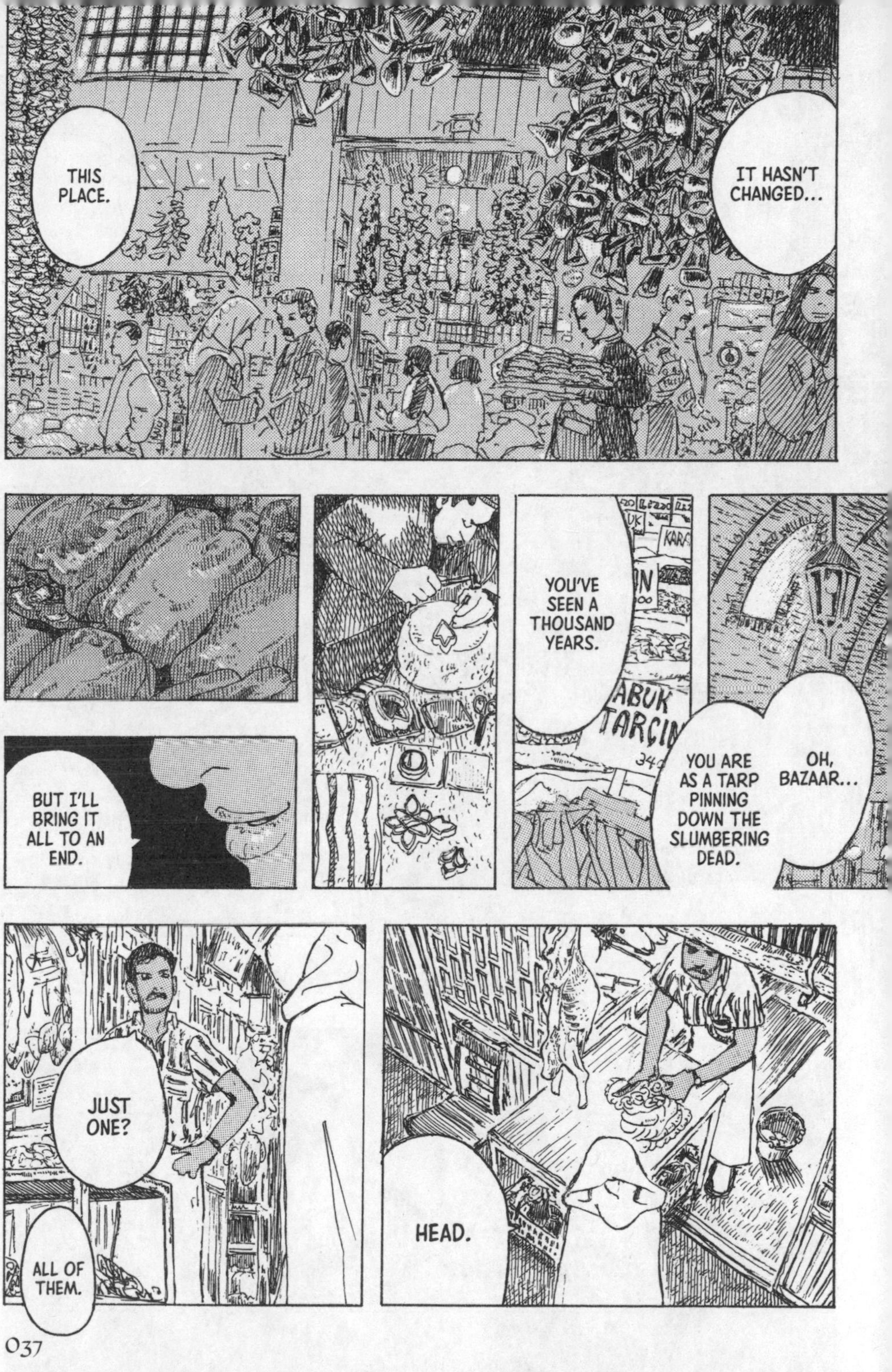
IT HASN'T CHANGED...
THIS PLACE.
OH, BAZAAR...
YOU ARE AS A TARP PINNING DOWN THE SLUMBERING DEAD.
YOU'VE SEEN A THOUSAND YEARS.
BUT I'LL BRING IT ALL TO AN END.
HEAD.
JUST ONE?
ALL OF THEM.

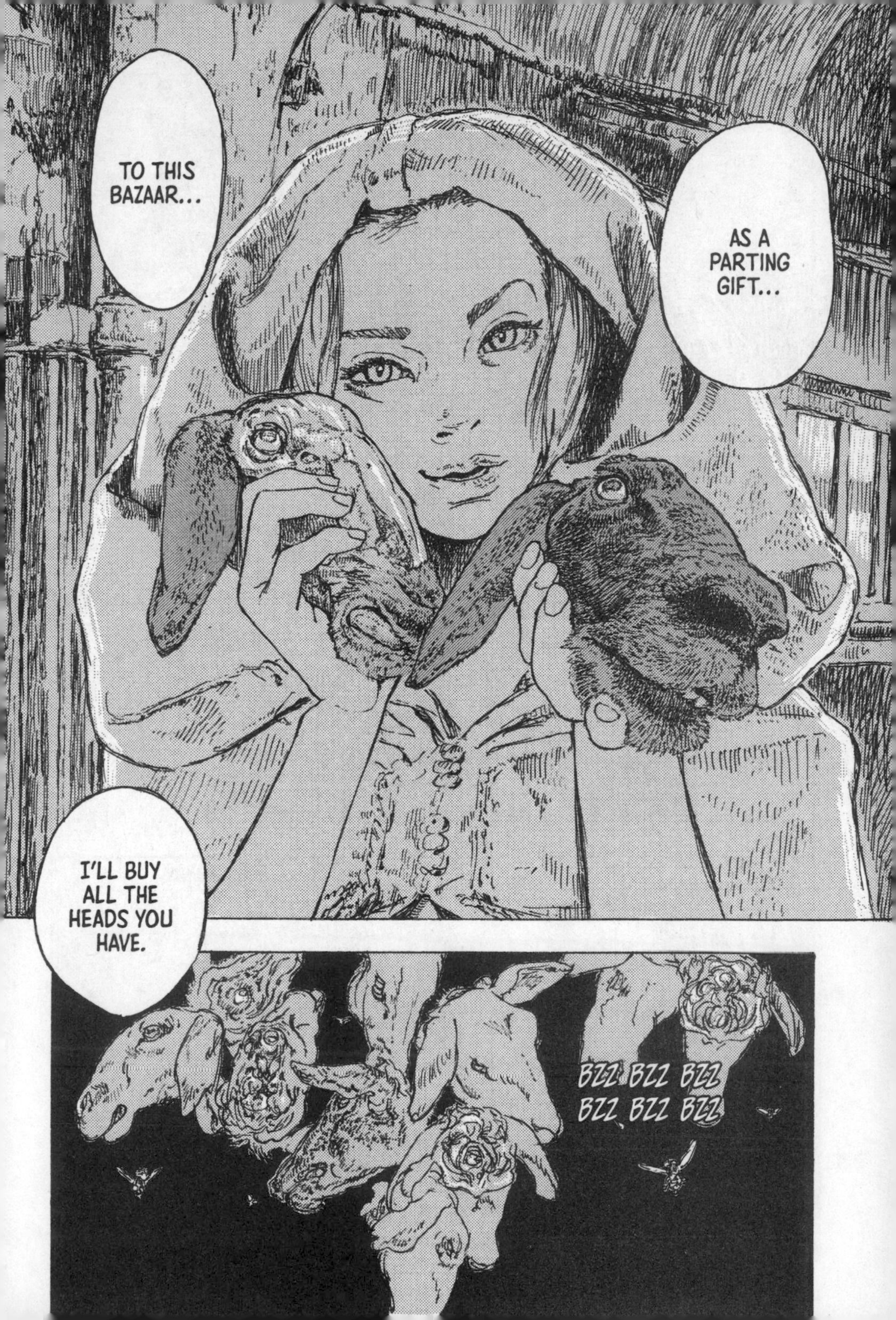
AS A PARTING GIFT...
TO THIS BAZAAR...
I'LL BUY ALL THE HEADS YOU HAVE.
BZZ BZZ BZZ BZZ BZZ BZZ

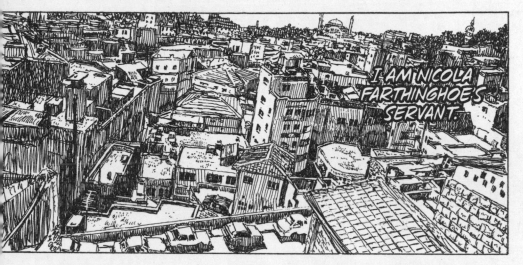

I AM NICOLA FARTHINGHOE'S SERVANT.
THAT WOMAN, SHE CLAIMED OUR BAZAAR WAS FILTHY.
SHE SAID SHE'LL CREATE A CLEAN MARKET FOR THE CHILDREN'S SAKE...
BY CRUSHING THE BAZAAR!
MY WORDS ARE THE WORDS OF FARTHINGHOE.

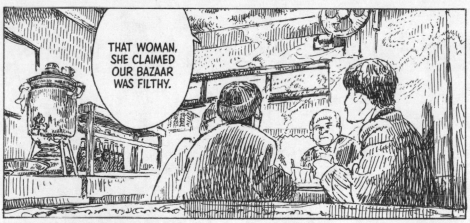

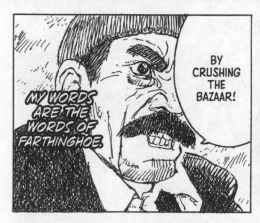

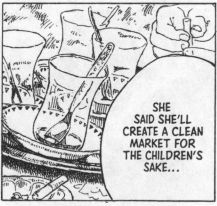

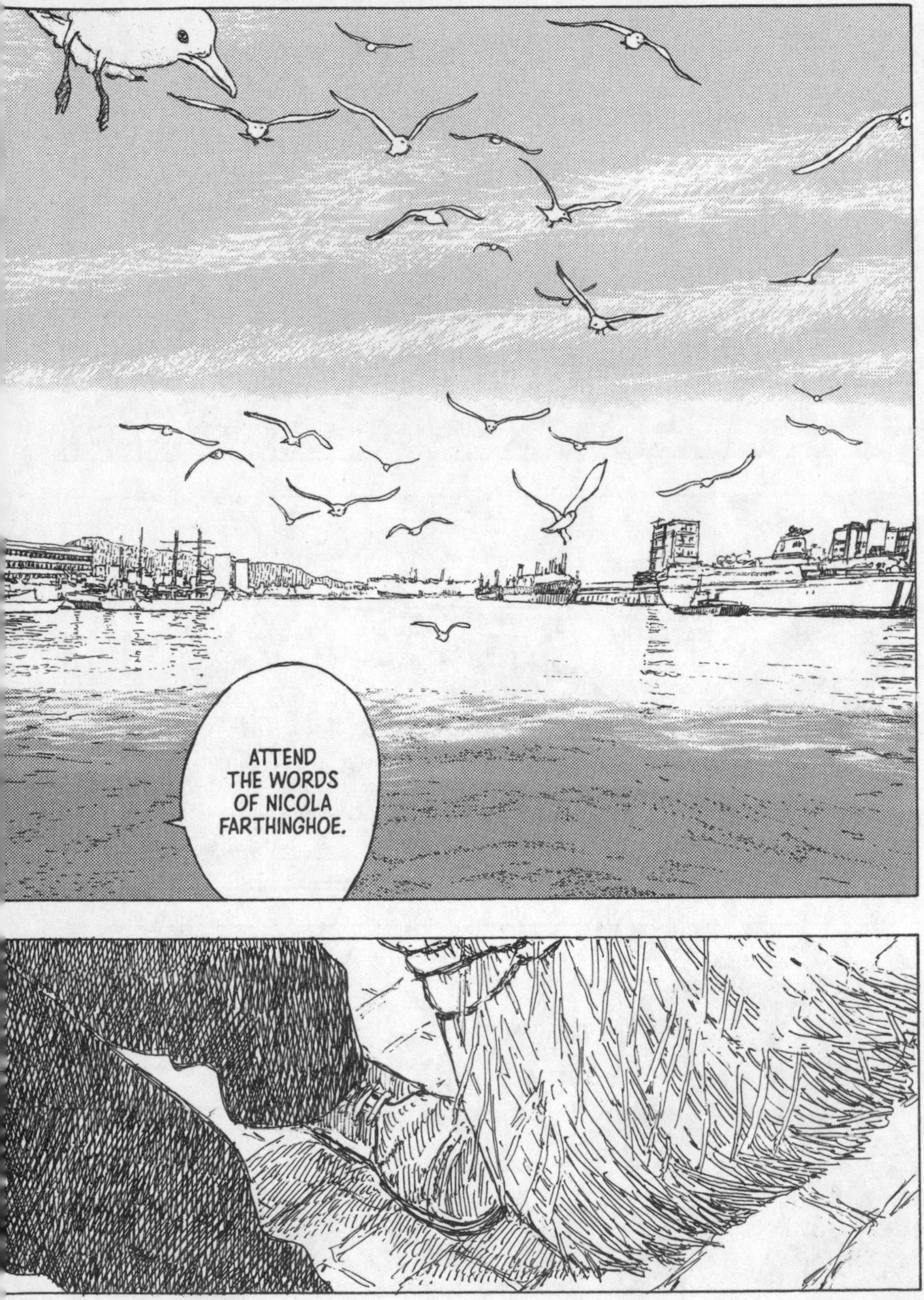
ATTEND THE WORDS OF NICOLA FARTHINGHOE.

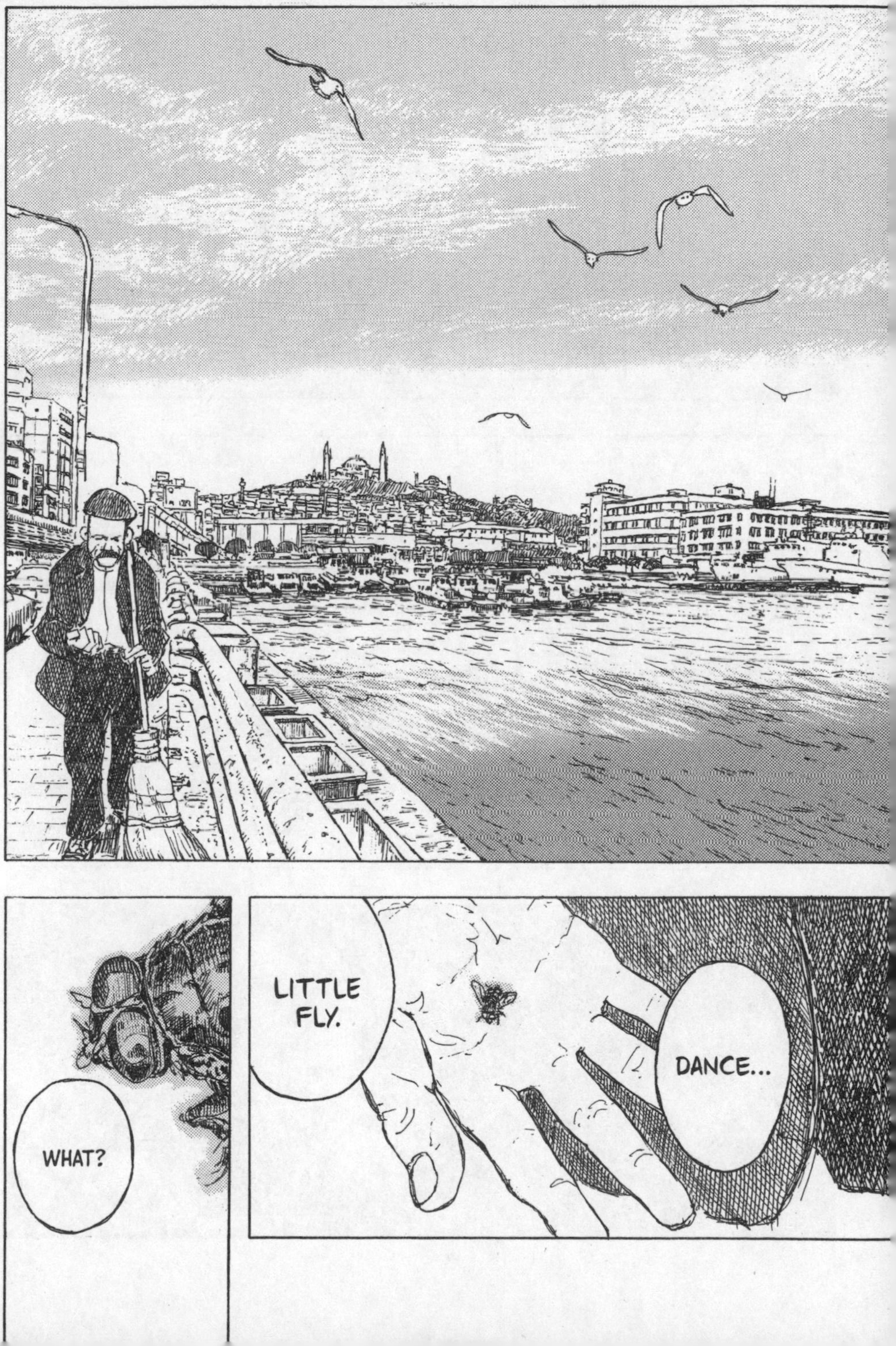
LITTLE FLY.
DANCE...
WHAT?

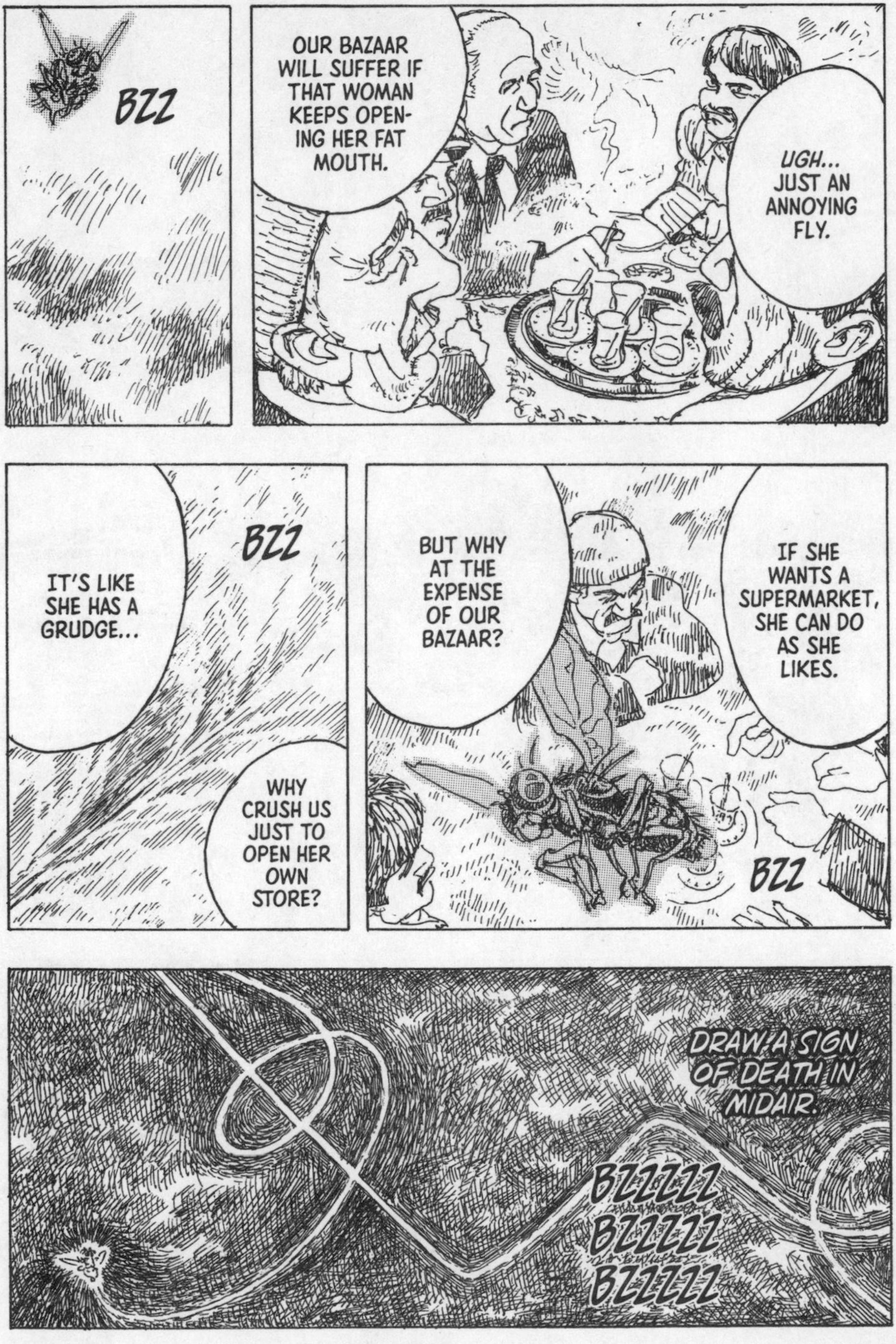
UGH... JUST AN ANNOYING FLY.
OUR BAZAAR WILL SUFFER IF THAT WOMAN KEEPS OPEN-ING HER FAT MOUTH.
BZZ
IF SHE WANTS A SUPERMARKET, SHE CAN DO AS SHE LIKES.
BUT WHY AT THE EXPENSE OF OUR BAZAAR?
BZZ
BZZ
IT'S LIKE SHE HAS A GRUDGE...
WHY CRUSH US JUST TO OPEN HER OWN STORE?
DRAW A SIGN OF DEATH IN MIDAIR.
BZZZZZ
BZZZZZ
BZZZZZ

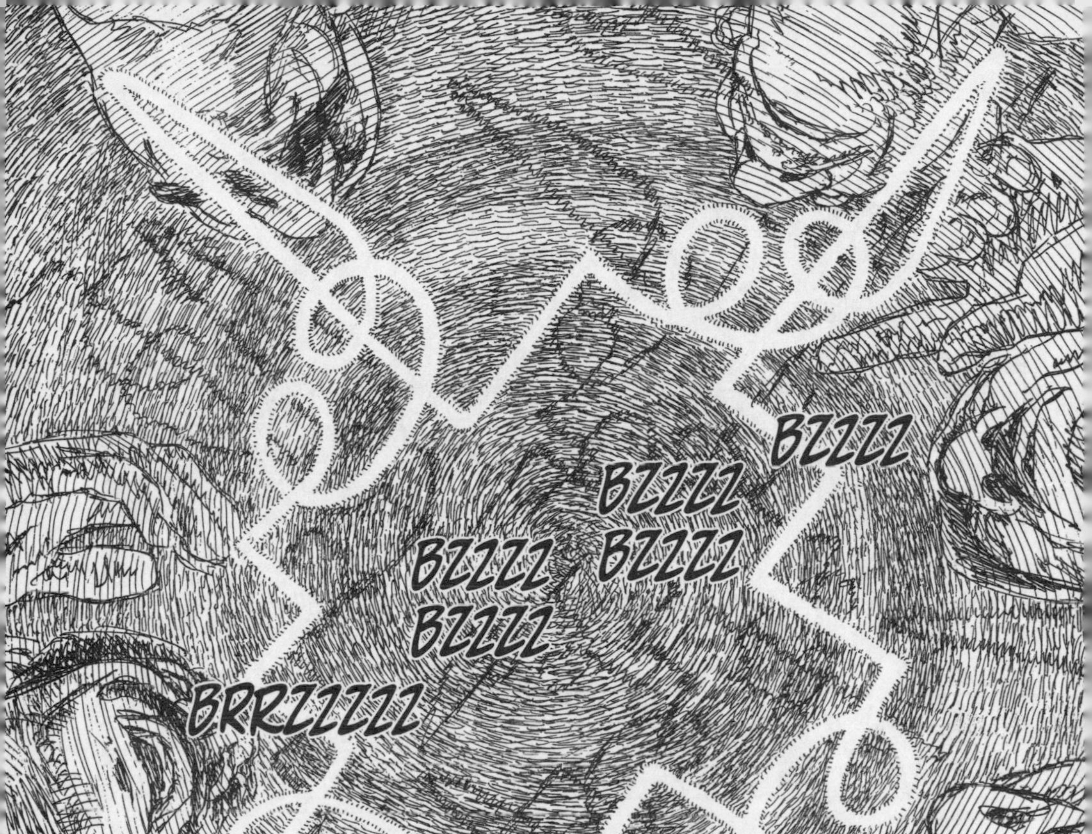
BZZZZ
BZZZZ
BZZZZ
BZZZZ
BZZZZ
BRRZZZZZZ

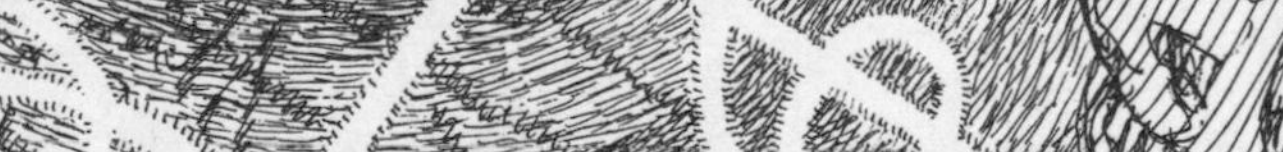
GENTLE-
MEN?

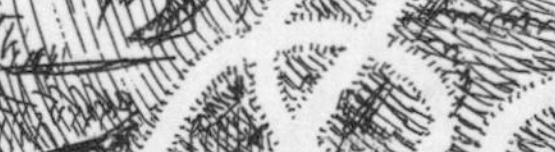
GENTLE...

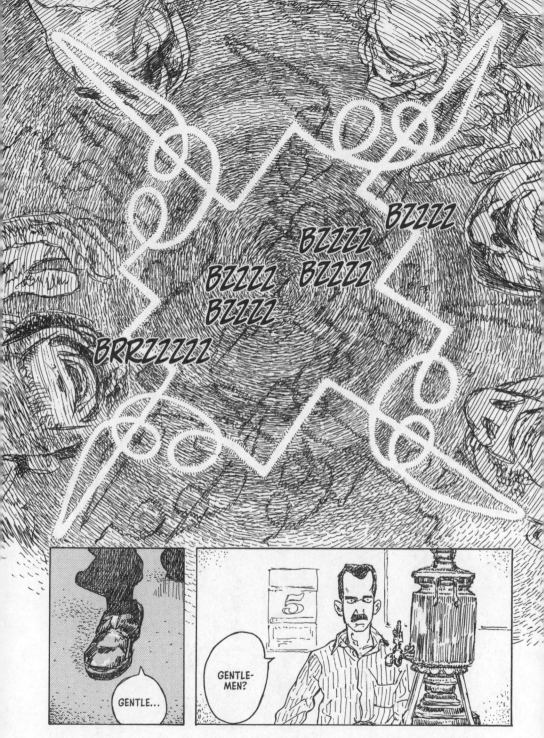

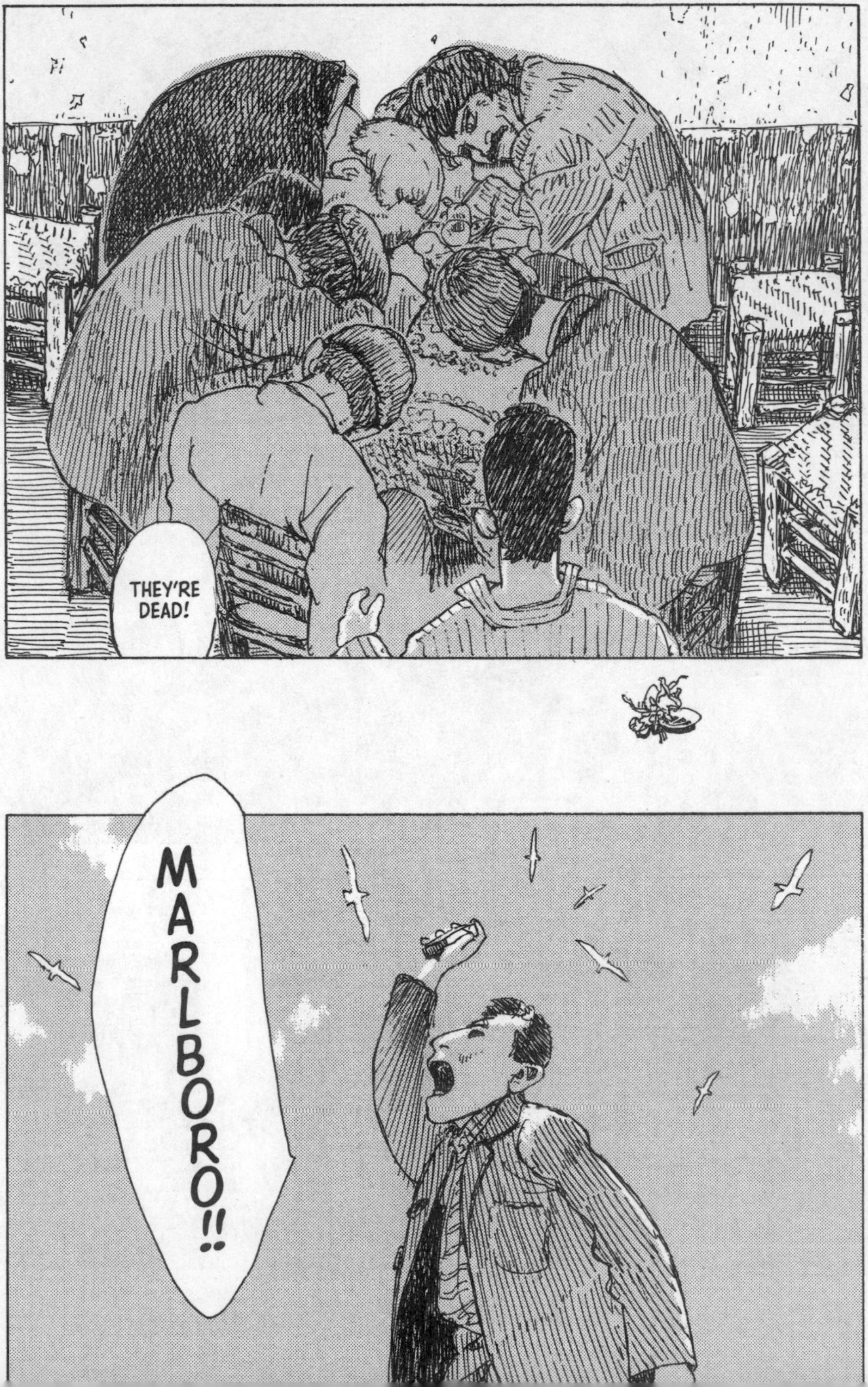
THEY'RE DEAD!
MARLBORO!!

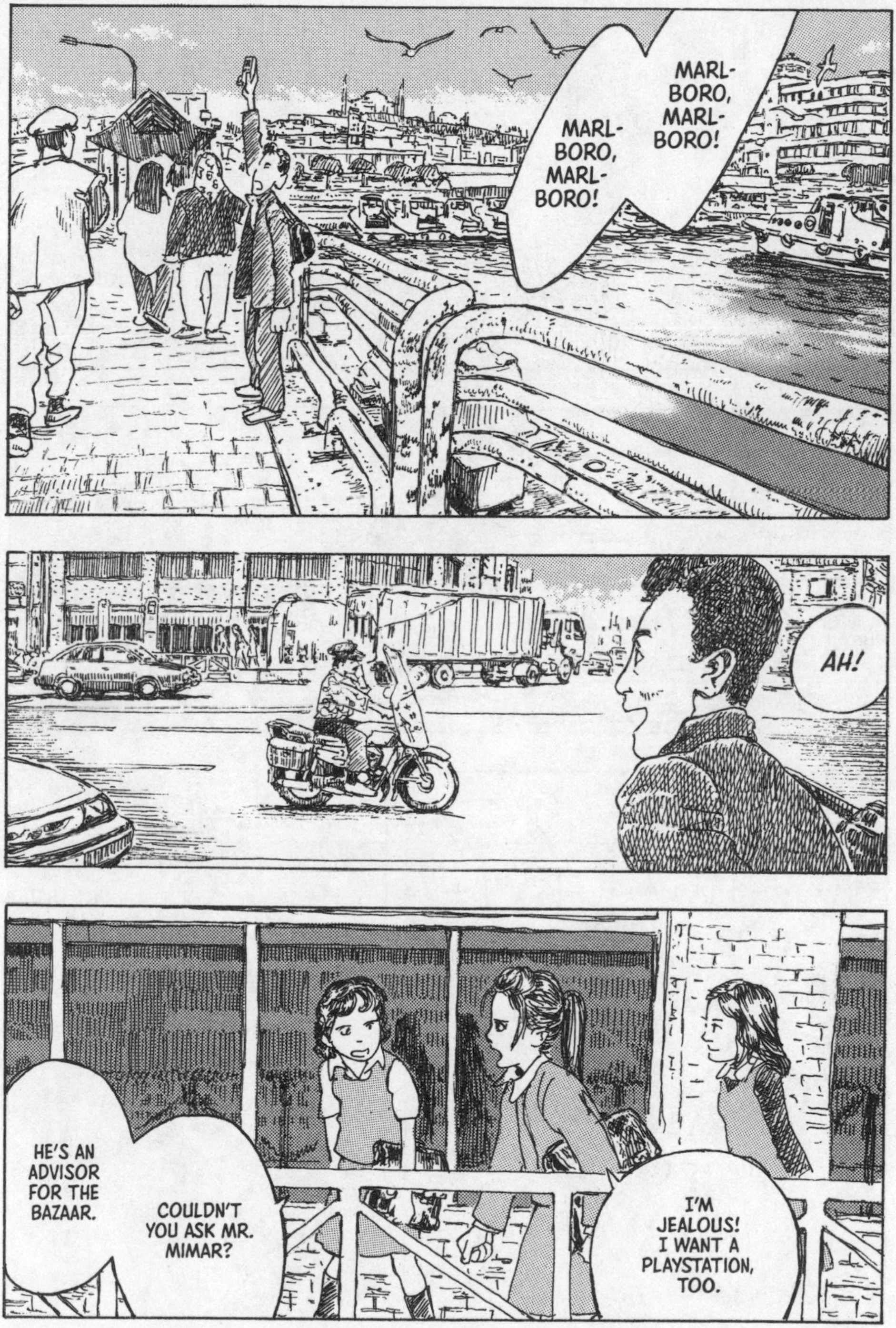
MARL-BORO, MARL-BORO!
MARL-BORO, MARL-BORO!
AH!
I'M JEALOUS! I WANT A PLAYSTATION, TOO.
COULDN'T YOU ASK MR. MIMAR?
HE'S AN ADVISOR FOR THE BAZAAR.

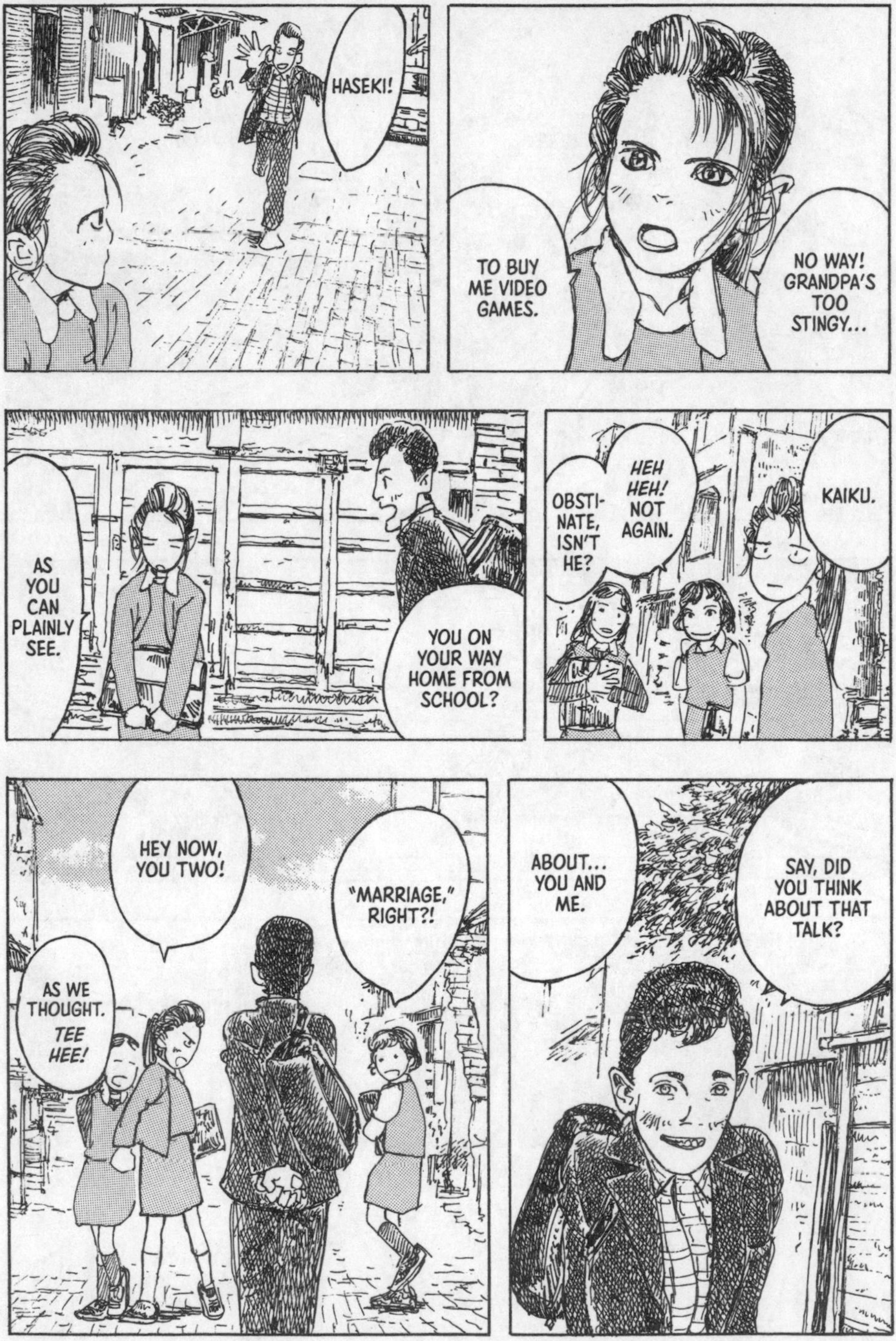
NO WAY! GRANDPA'S TOO STINGY...
TO BUY ME VIDEO GAMES.
HASEKI!
KAIKU.
HEH HEH! NOT AGAIN.
OBSTI-NATE, ISN'T HE?
YOU ON YOUR WAY HOME FROM SCHOOL?
AS YOU CAN PLAINLY SEE.
SAY, DID YOU THINK ABOUT THAT TALK?
ABOUT... YOU AND ME.
"MARRIAGE," RIGHT?!
HEY NOW, YOU TWO!
AS WE THOUGHT. *TEE HEE!*

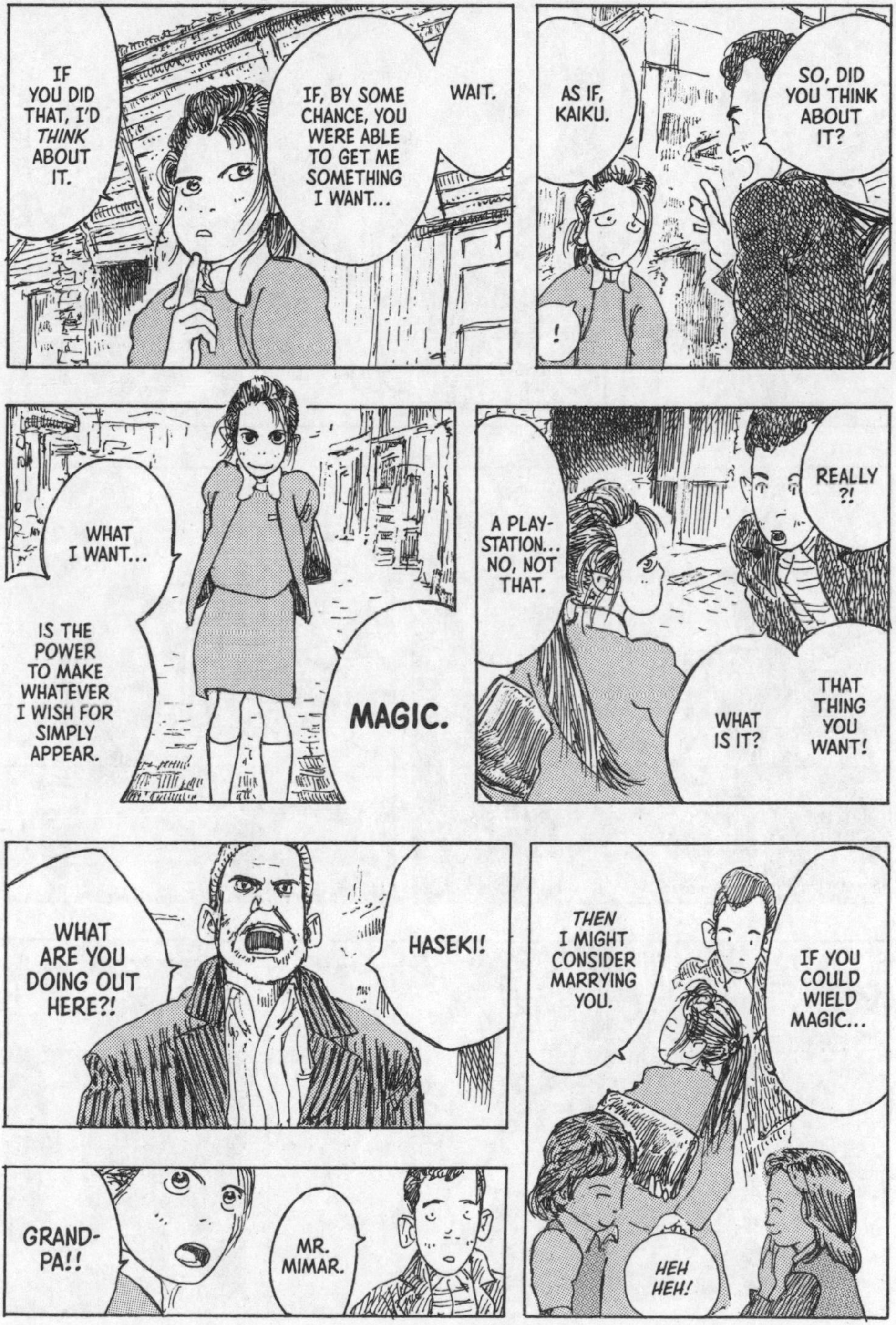
SO, DID YOU THINK ABOUT IT?
AS IF, KAIKU.
!
WAIT.
IF, BY SOME CHANCE, YOU WERE ABLE TO GET ME SOMETHING I WANT...
IF YOU DID THAT, I'D *THINK* ABOUT IT.
REALLY?!
A PLAY-STATION... NO, NOT THAT.
THAT THING YOU WANT!
WHAT IS IT?
WHAT I WANT...
IS THE POWER TO MAKE WHATEVER I WISH FOR SIMPLY APPEAR.
MAGIC.
IF YOU COULD WIELD MAGIC...
THEN I MIGHT CONSIDER MARRYING YOU.
HEH HEH!
HASEKI!
WHAT ARE YOU DOING OUT HERE?!
MR. MIMAR.
GRAND-PA!!

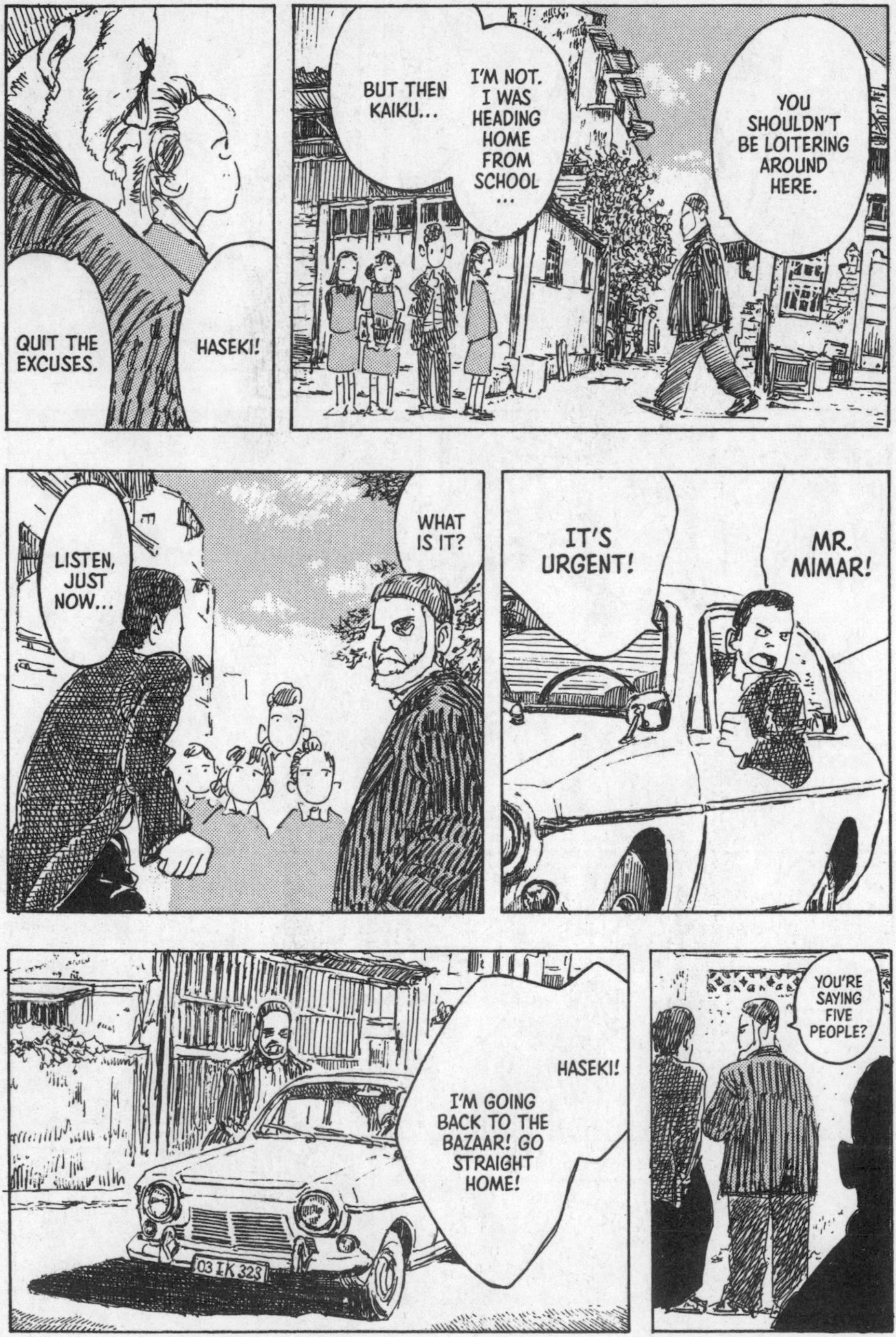
YOU SHOULDN'T BE LOITERING AROUND HERE.
I'M NOT. I WAS HEADING HOME FROM SCHOOL...
BUT THEN KAIKU...
HASEKI!
QUIT THE EXCUSES.
MR. MIMAR!
IT'S URGENT!
WHAT IS IT?
LISTEN, JUST NOW...
YOU'RE SAYING FIVE PEOPLE?
HASEKI!
I'M GOING BACK TO THE BAZAAR! GO STRAIGHT HOME!

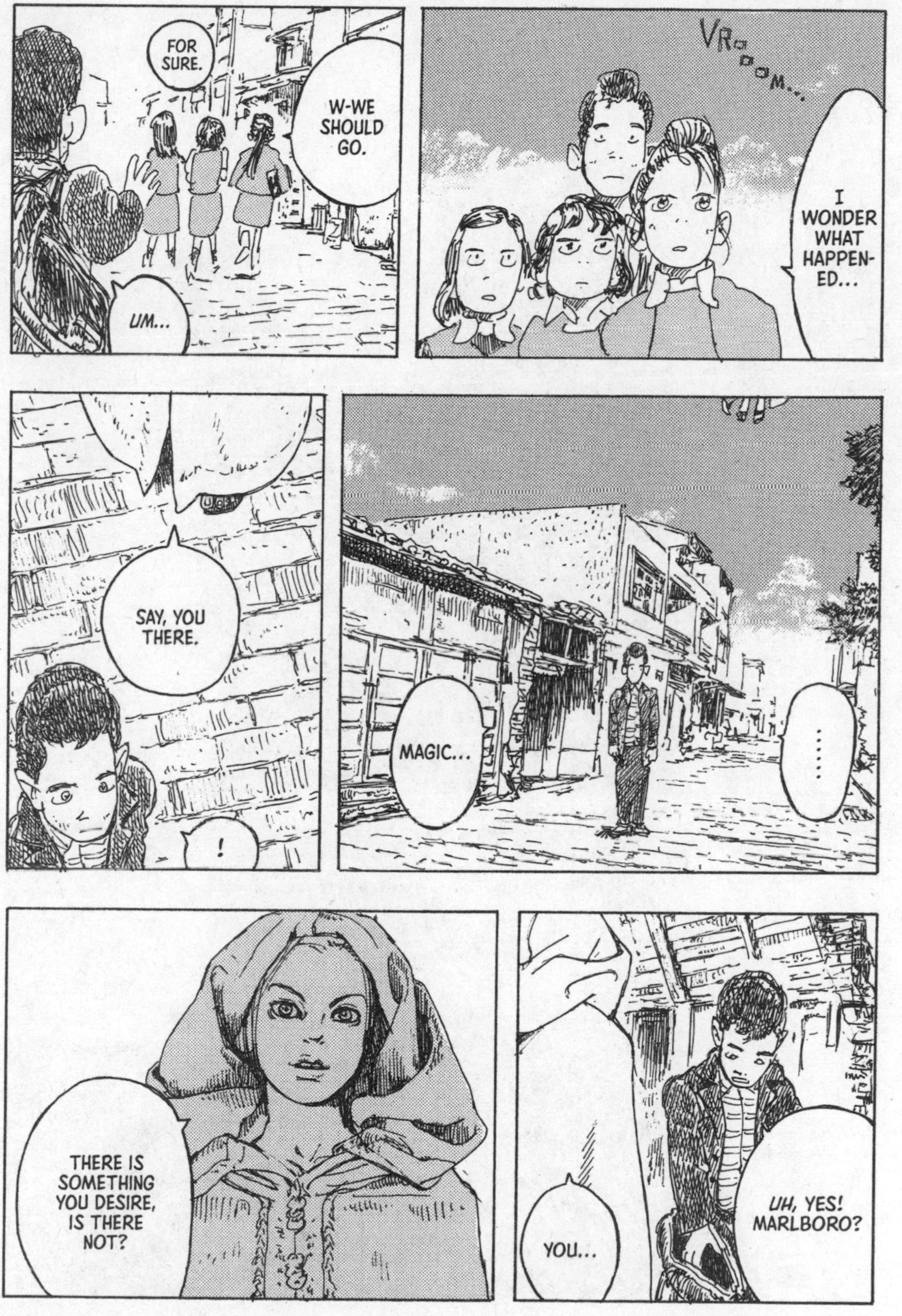
VROOOM...
I WONDER WHAT HAPPENED...
W-WE SHOULD GO.
FOR SURE.
UM...
......
MAGIC...
SAY, YOU THERE.
!
UH, YES! MARLBORO?
YOU...
THERE IS SOMETHING YOU DESIRE, IS THERE NOT?

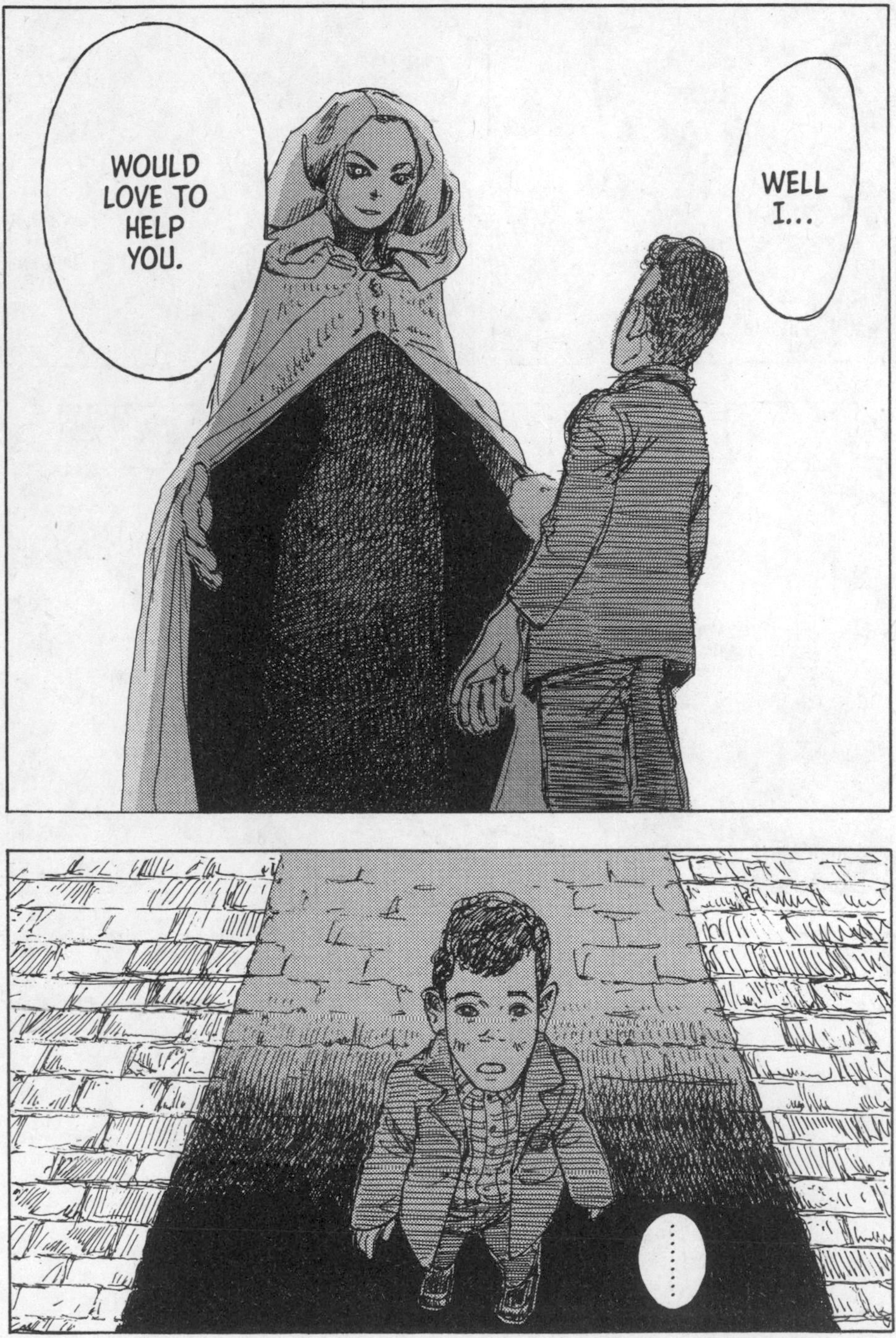
WELL I...
WOULD LOVE TO HELP YOU.
....

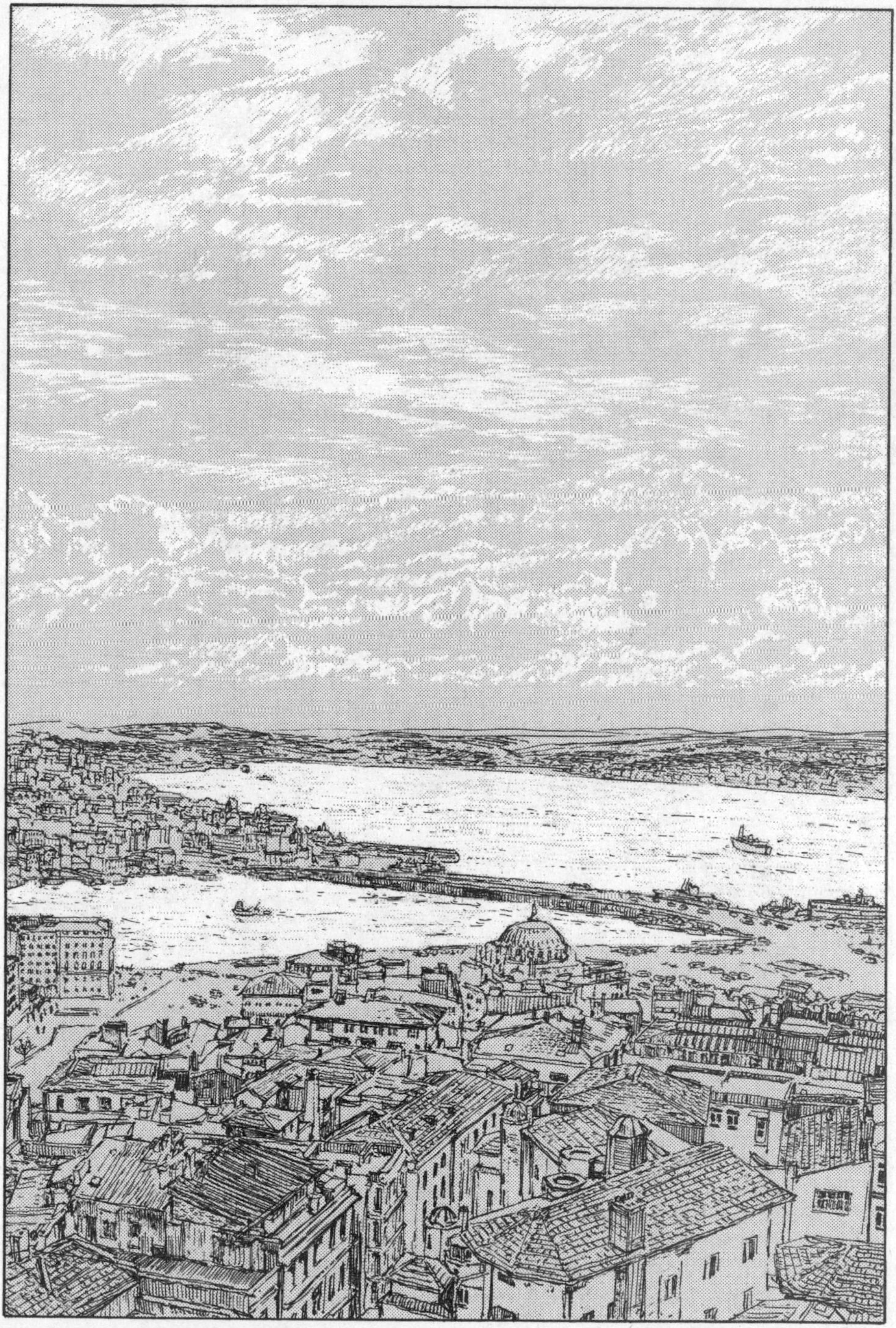

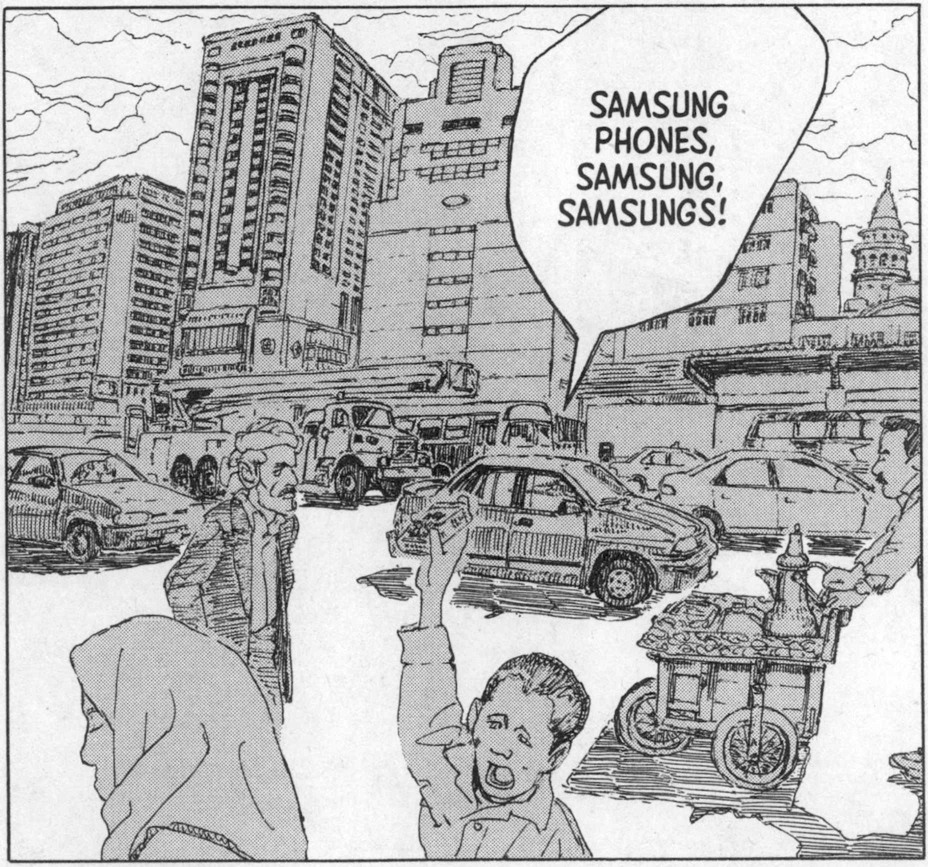
SAMSUNG PHONES, SAMSUNG, SAMSUNGS!

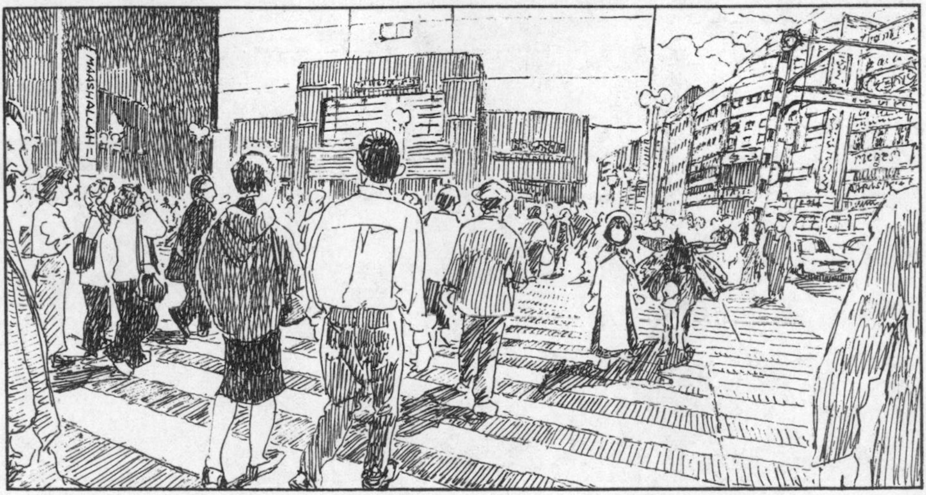
MAASHALLAH

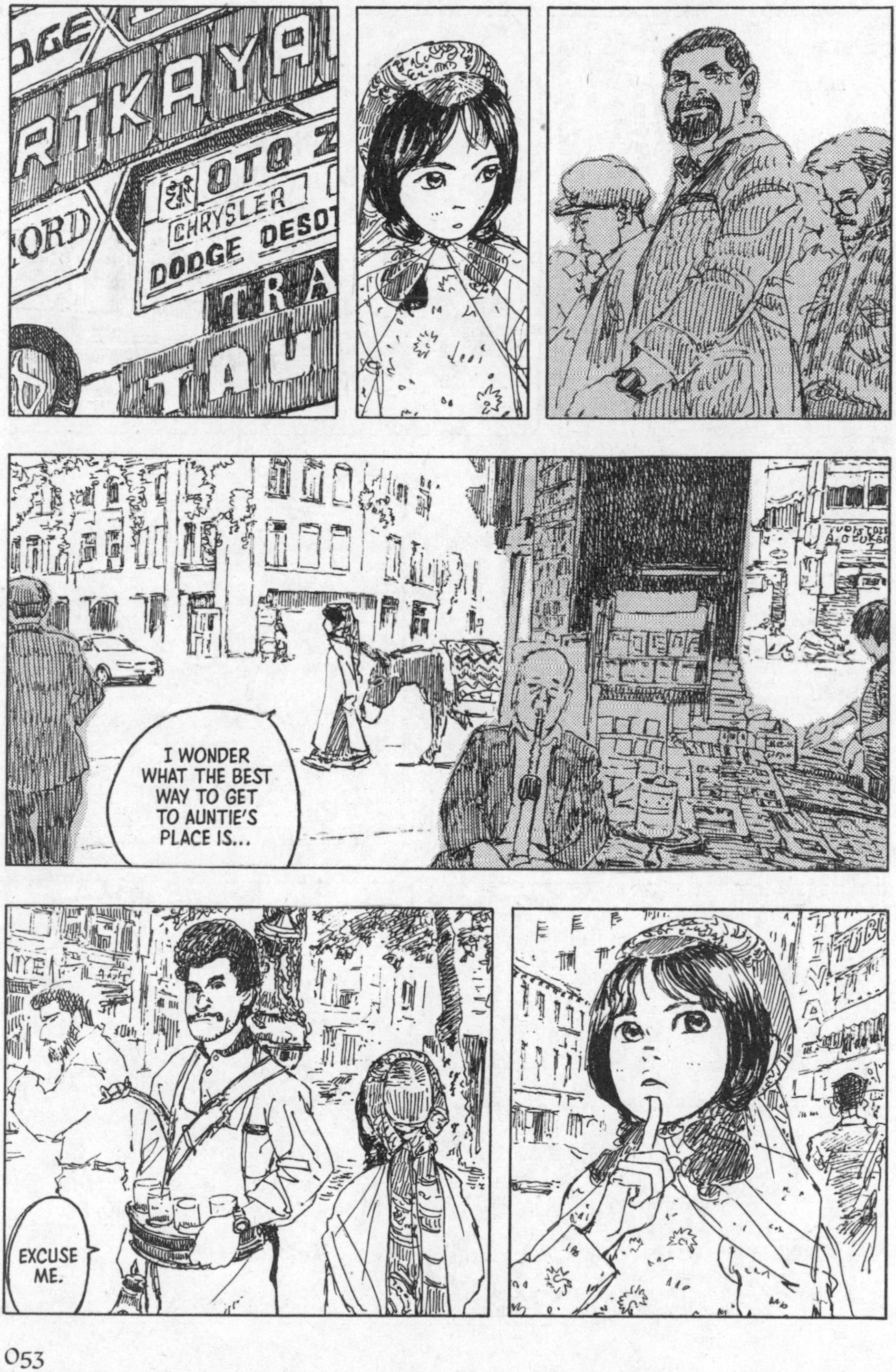
OGE
RTKAYA
OTO
CHRYSLER
DODGE DESOT
ORD
TRA
TAU
I WONDER WHAT THE BEST WAY TO GET TO AUNTIE'S PLACE IS...
EXCUSE ME.

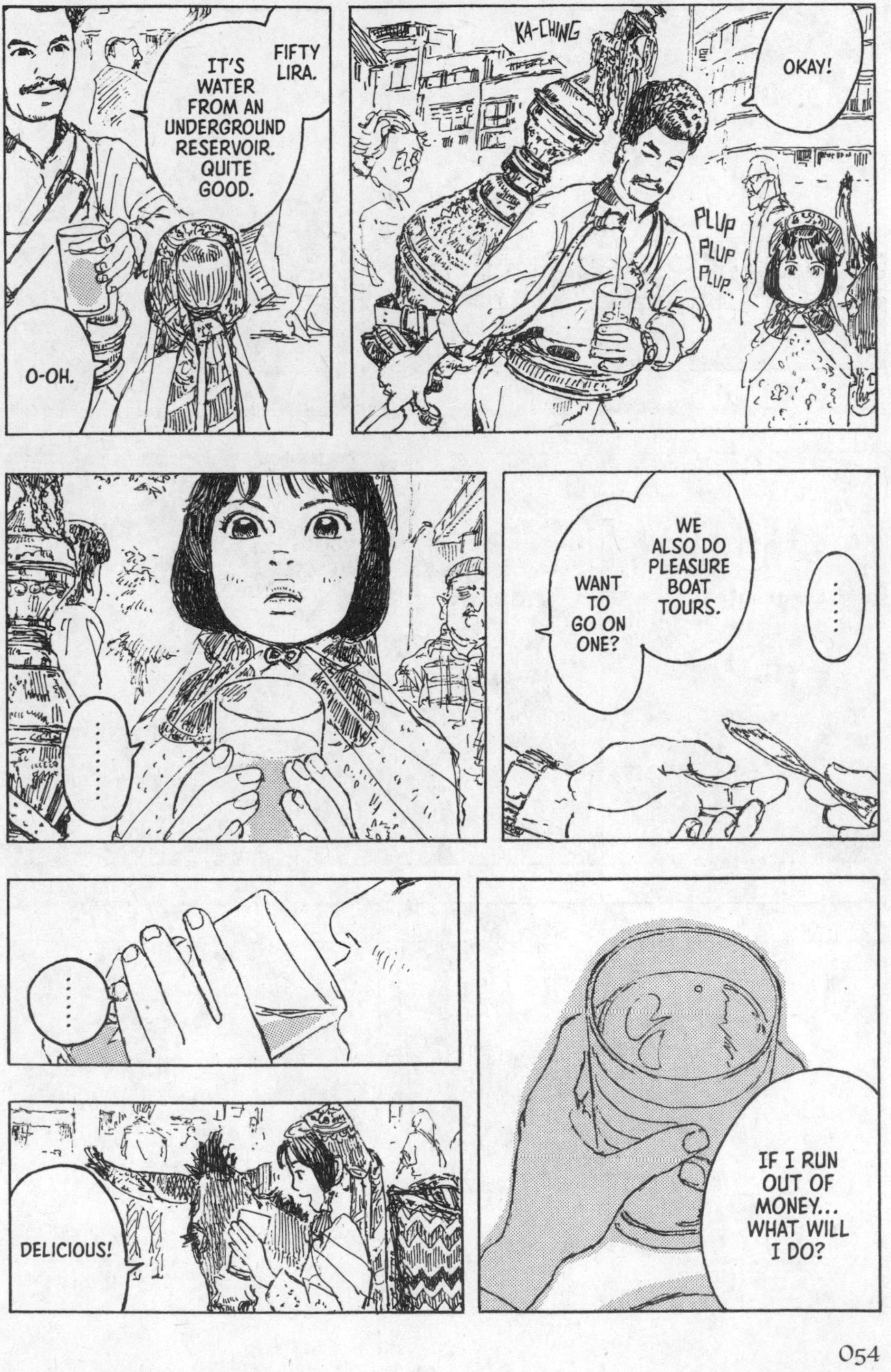
OKAY!
KA-CHING
PLUP PLUP PLUP...
FIFTY LIRA.
IT'S WATER FROM AN UNDERGROUND RESERVOIR. QUITE GOOD.
O-OH.
......
WE ALSO DO PLEASURE BOAT TOURS. WANT TO GO ON ONE?
......
IF I RUN OUT OF MONEY... WHAT WILL I DO?
......
DELICIOUS!

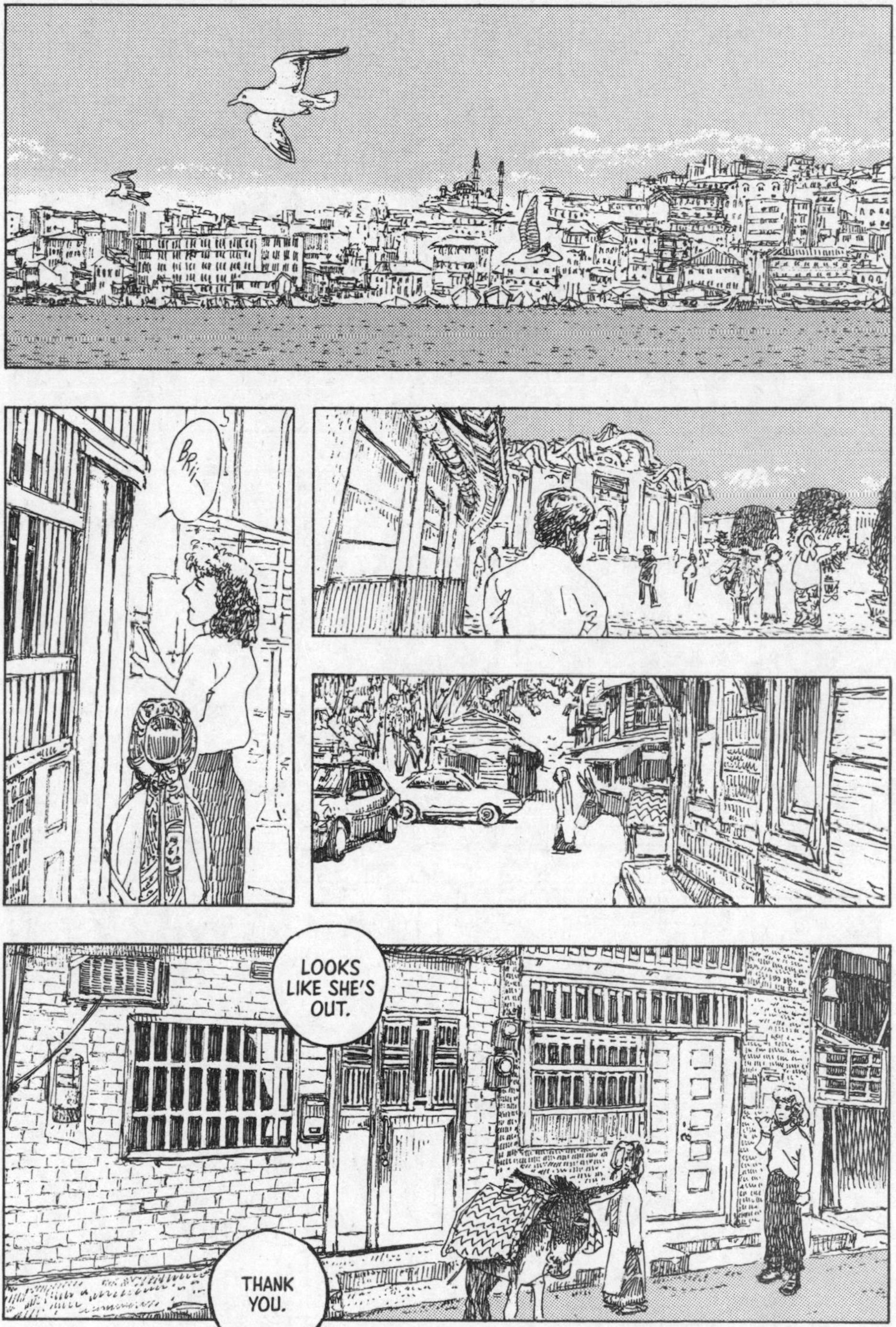
BRii
LOOKS LIKE SHE'S OUT.
THANK YOU.

Hwr———r

FLAP

GRR!

GRR!

FLINCH

NNRR!

056

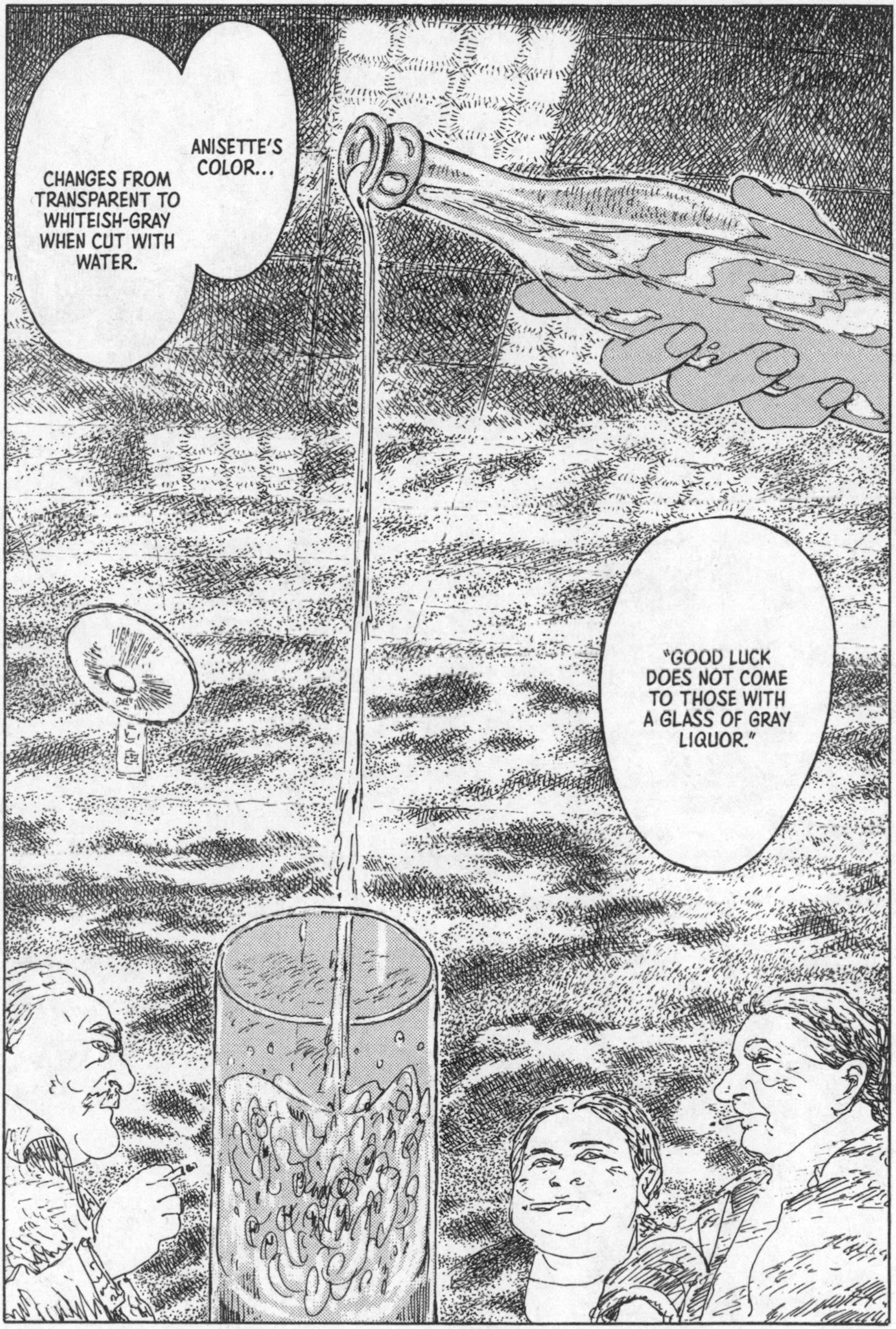
ANISETTE'S COLOR...
CHANGES FROM TRANSPARENT TO WHITEISH-GRAY WHEN CUT WITH WATER.
"GOOD LUCK DOES NOT COME TO THOSE WITH A GLASS OF GRAY LIQUOR."

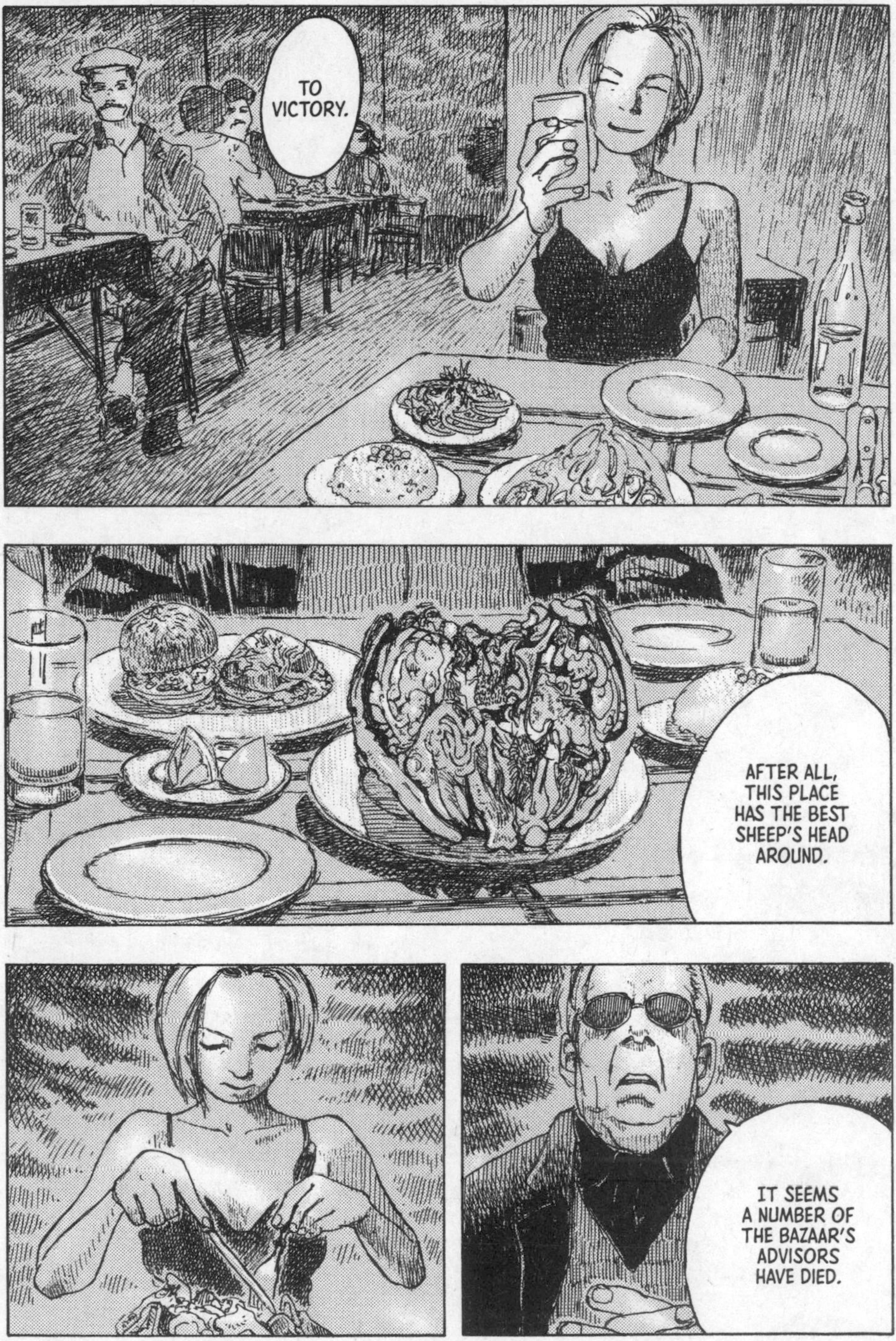
TO VICTORY.
AFTER ALL, THIS PLACE HAS THE BEST SHEEP'S HEAD AROUND.
IT SEEMS A NUMBER OF THE BAZAAR'S ADVISORS HAVE DIED.

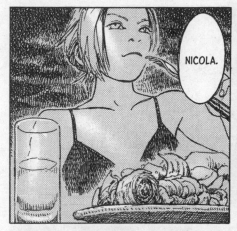

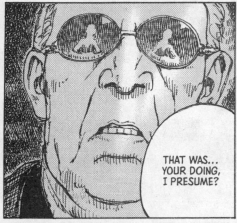

THAT WAS... YOUR DOING, I PRESUME?
NICOLA.
THOSE PEOPLE WERE ALWAYS GETTING IN MY WAY.
THEY NEEDED TO BE SHOWN THEIR PLACE.
THEY HAD TO BE MADE COGNIZANT...
OF JUST HOW INSIGNIFICANT THEY ARE.

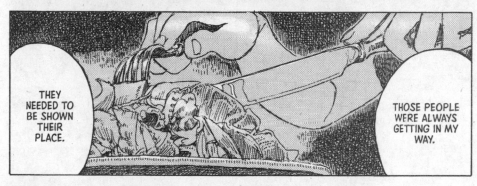

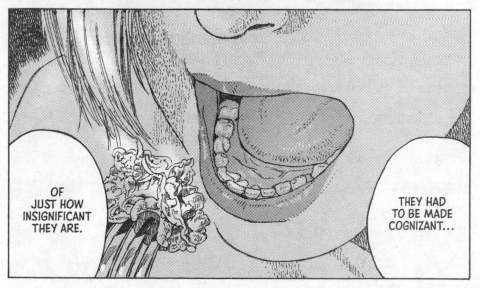

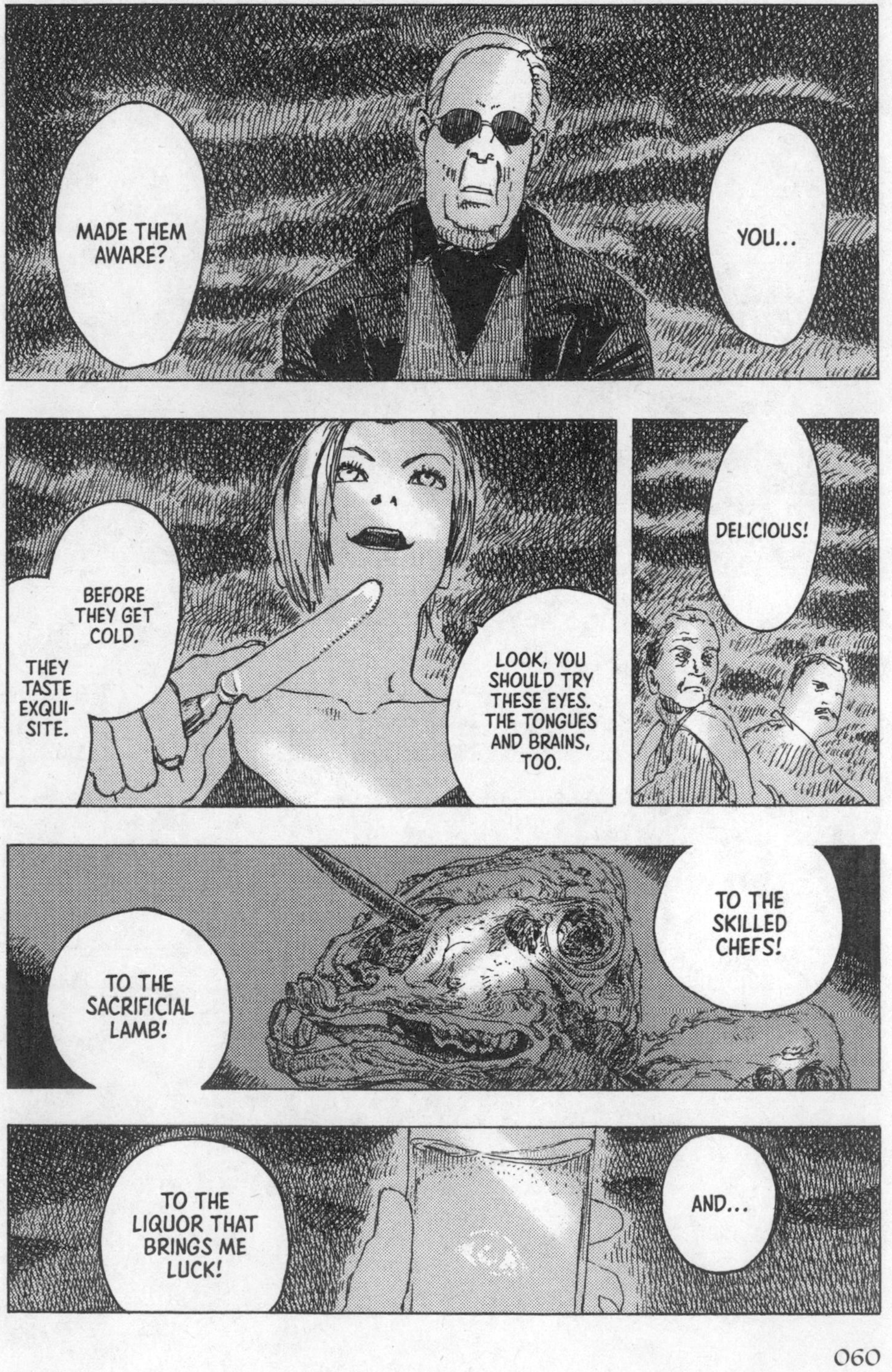
YOU...
MADE THEM AWARE?
DELICIOUS!
LOOK, YOU SHOULD TRY THESE EYES. THE TONGUES AND BRAINS, TOO.
BEFORE THEY GET COLD.
THEY TASTE EXQUISITE.
TO THE SKILLED CHEFS!
TO THE SACRIFICIAL LAMB!
AND...
TO THE LIQUOR THAT BRINGS ME LUCK!

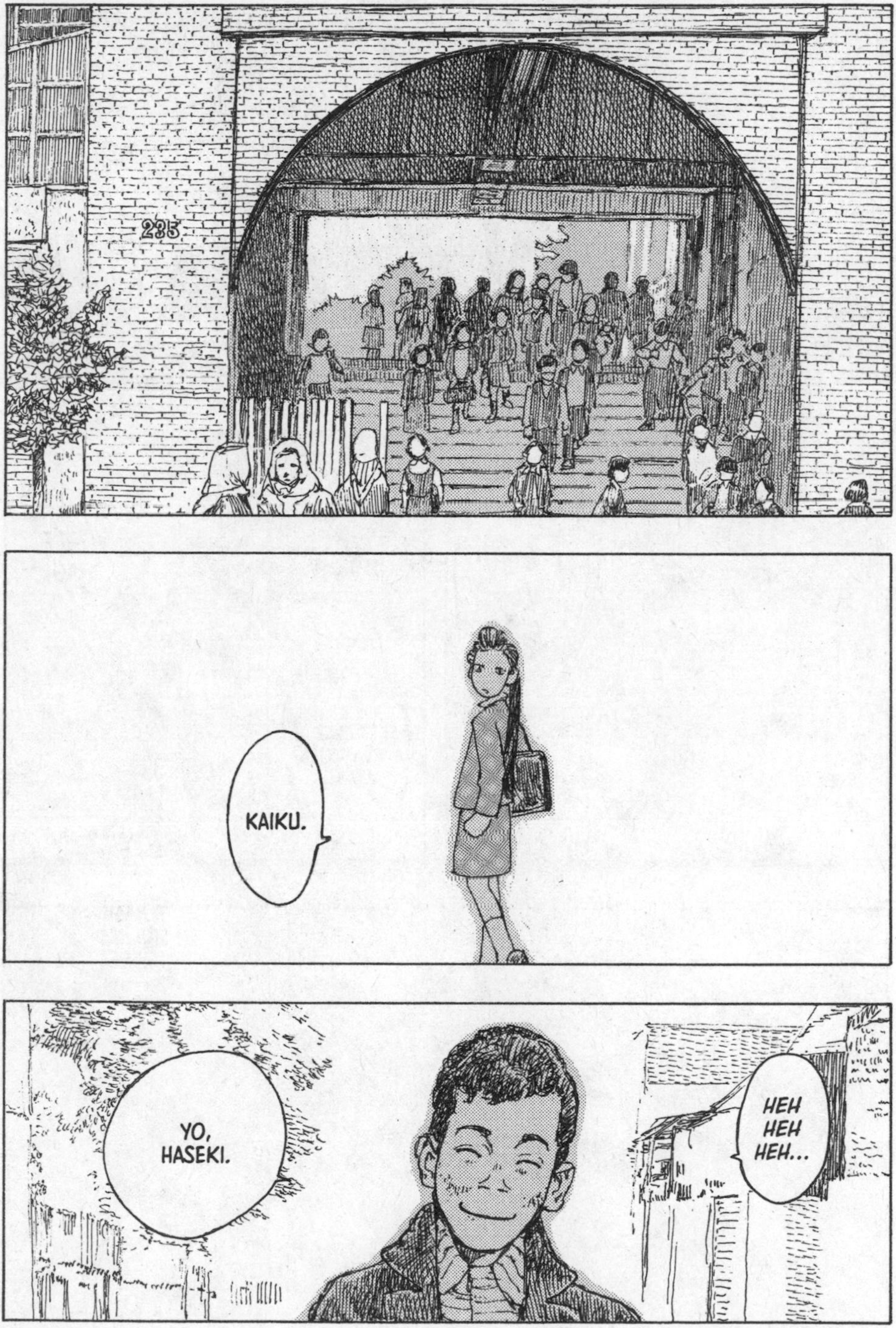
235
KAIKU.
HEH HEH HEH...
YO, HASEKI.

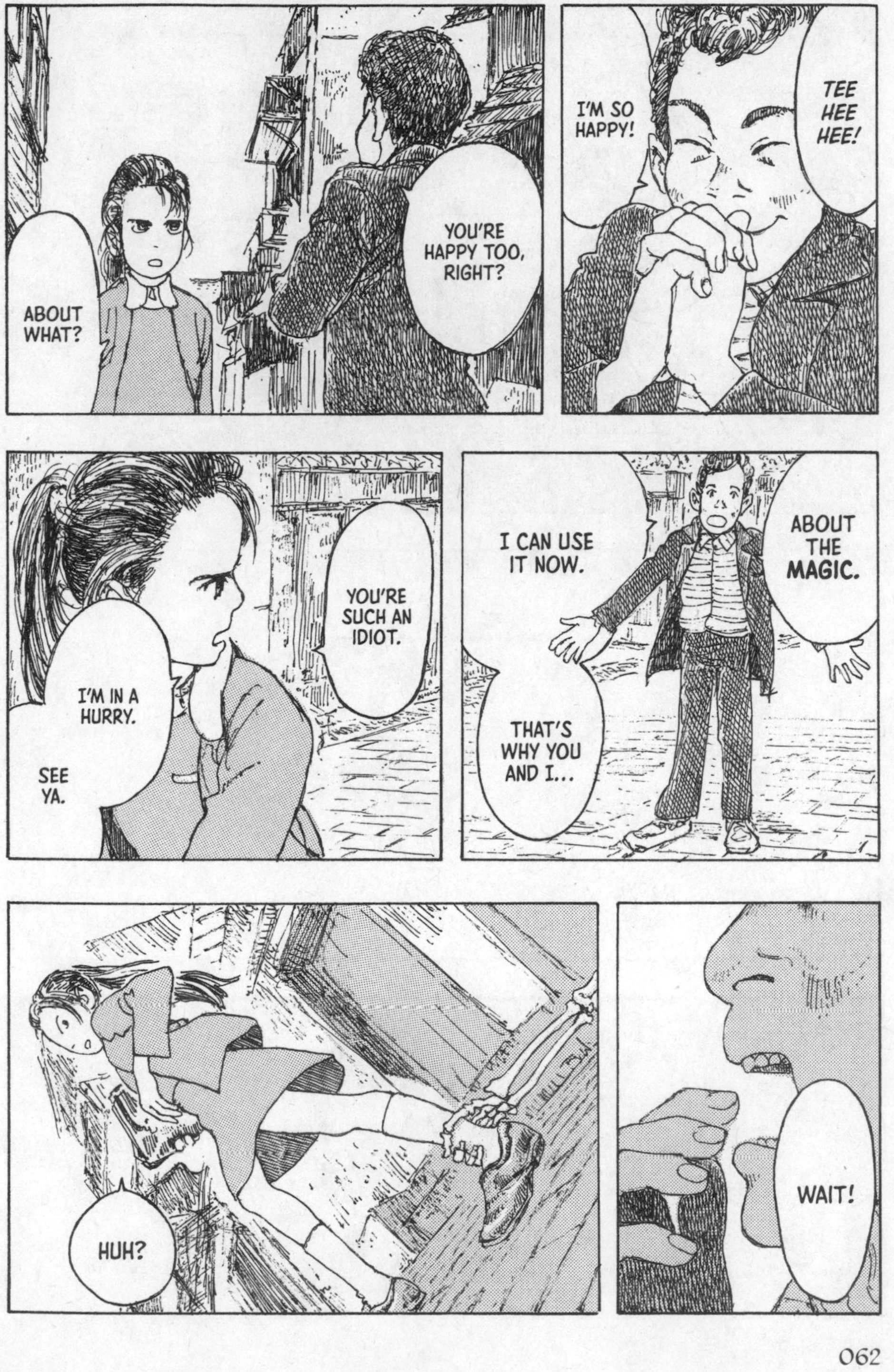
TEE HEE HEE!
I'M SO HAPPY!
YOU'RE HAPPY TOO, RIGHT?
ABOUT WHAT?
ABOUT THE **MAGIC.**
I CAN USE IT NOW.
THAT'S WHY YOU AND I...
YOU'RE SUCH AN IDIOT.
I'M IN A HURRY.
SEE YA.
WAIT!
HUH?

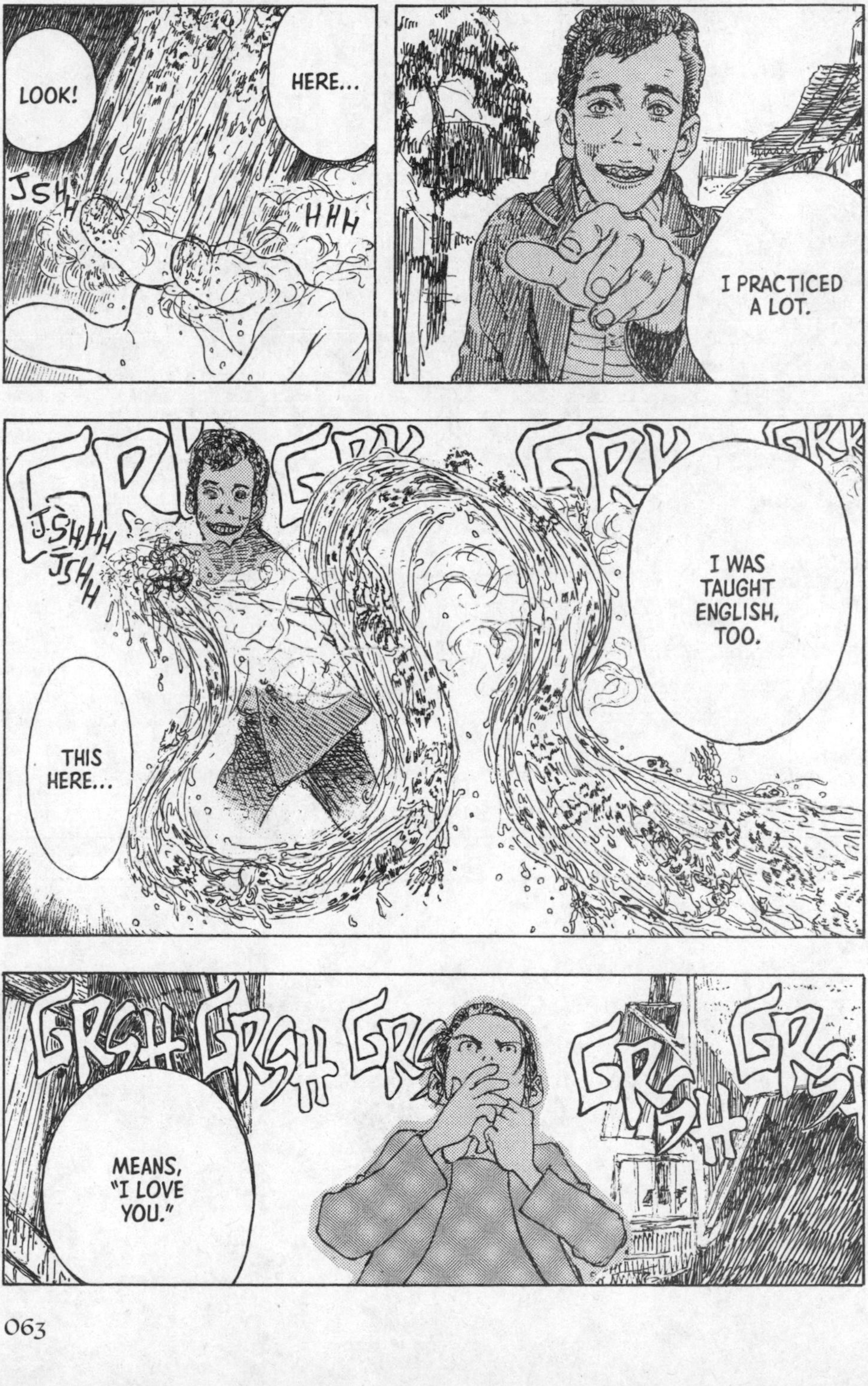
I PRACTICED A LOT.
HERE...
LOOK!
JSHHH
HHH
GRK GRK GRK GRK
I WAS TAUGHT ENGLISH, TOO.
JSHHH
JSHH
THIS HERE...
GRSH GRSH GRSH GRSH GRSH
MEANS, "I LOVE YOU."

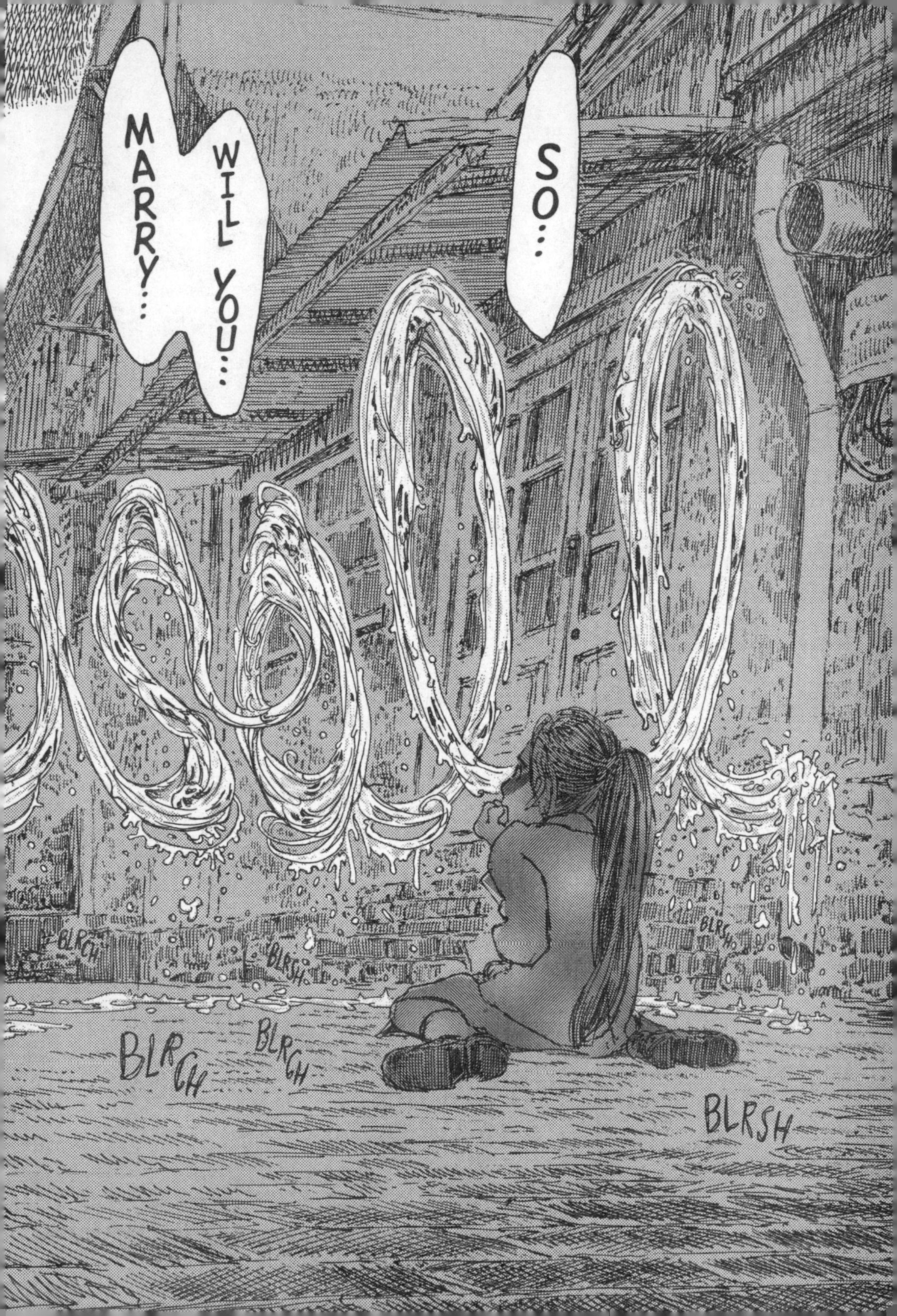
SO…
WILL YOU…
MARRY…
BLRSH
BLRSH
BLRCH
BLRSH
BLRCH
BLRCH

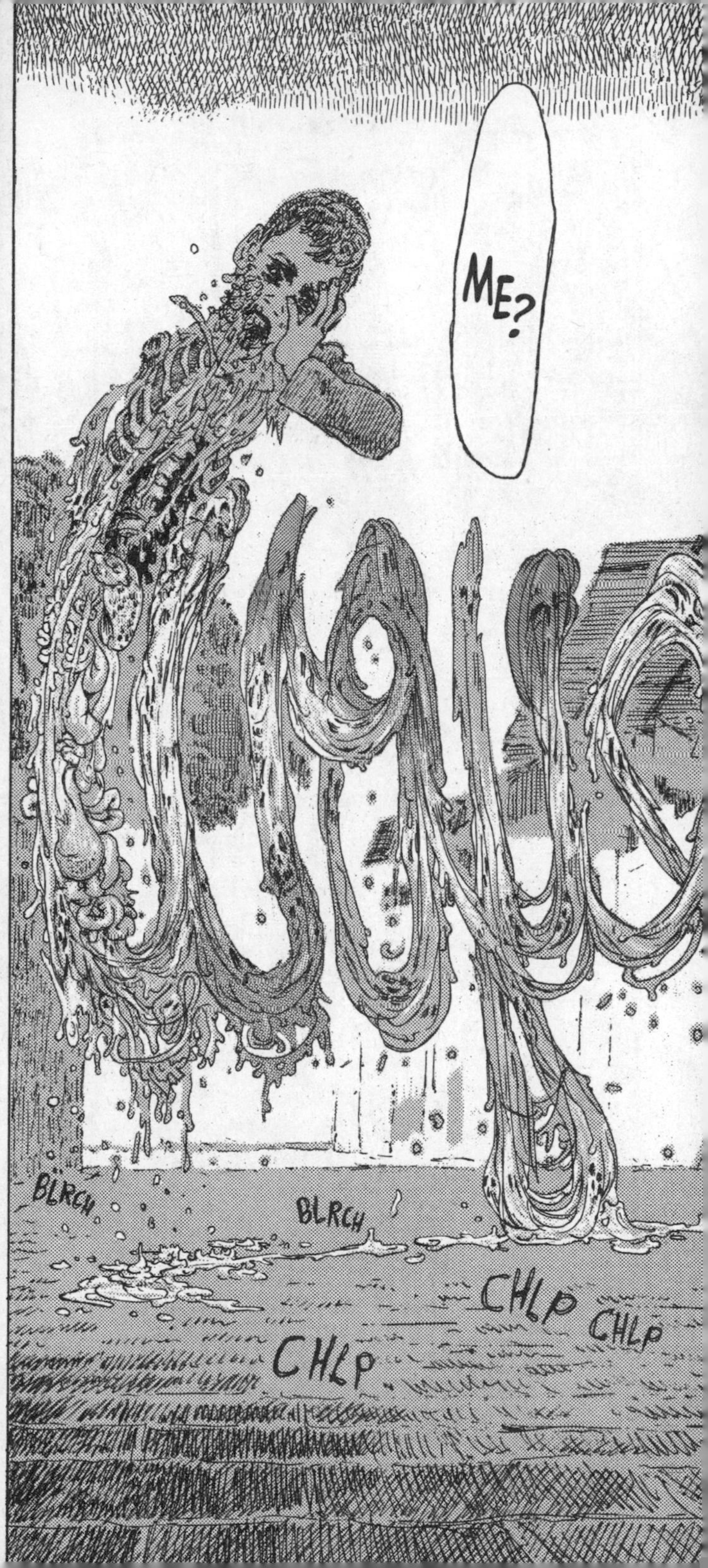
ME?
BLRCH
BLRCH
CHLP
CHLP
CHLP

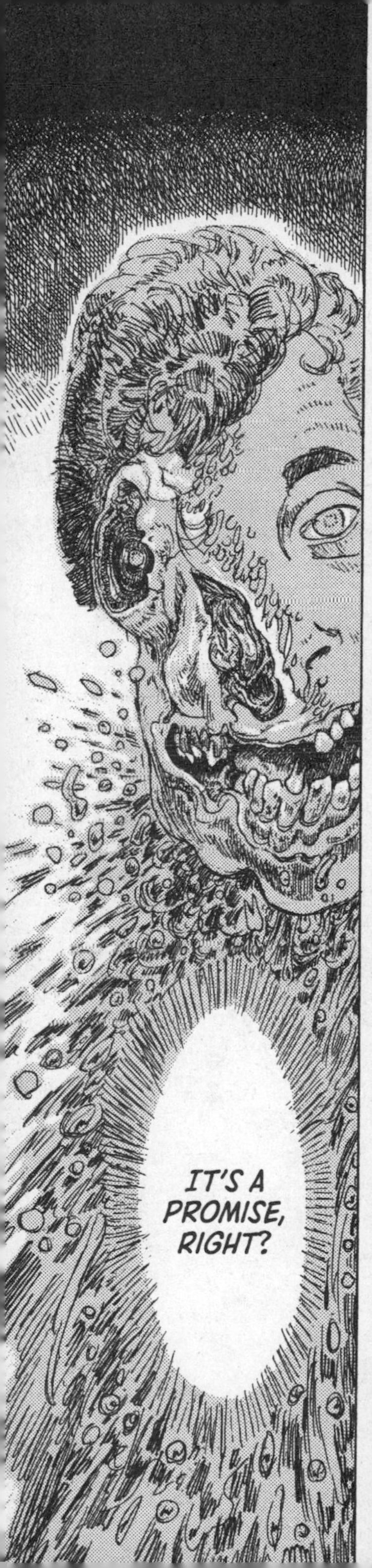
IT'S A PROMISE, RIGHT?

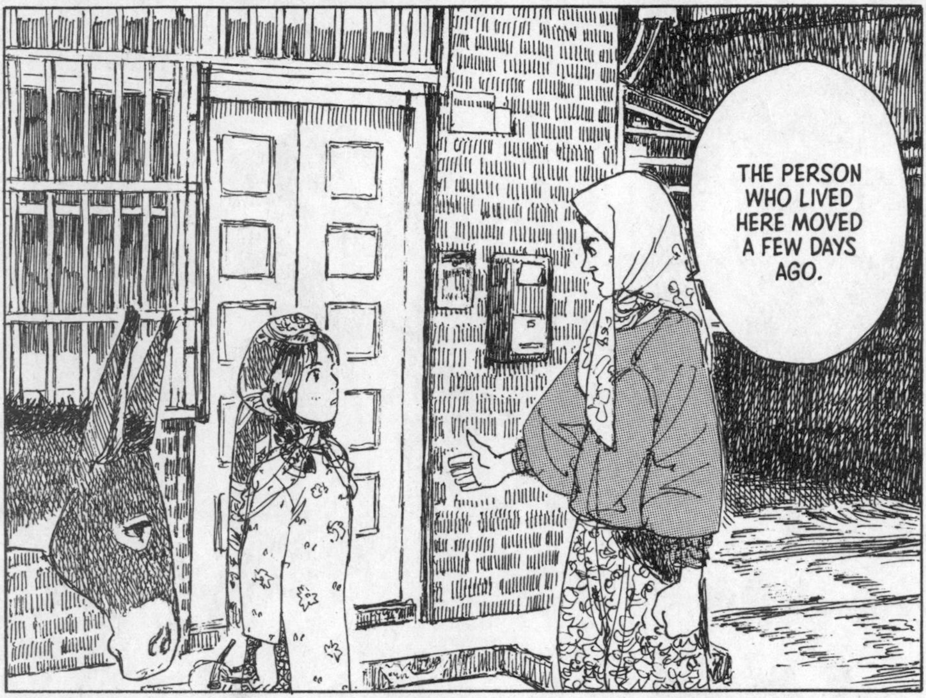
THE PERSON WHO LIVED HERE MOVED A FEW DAYS AGO.
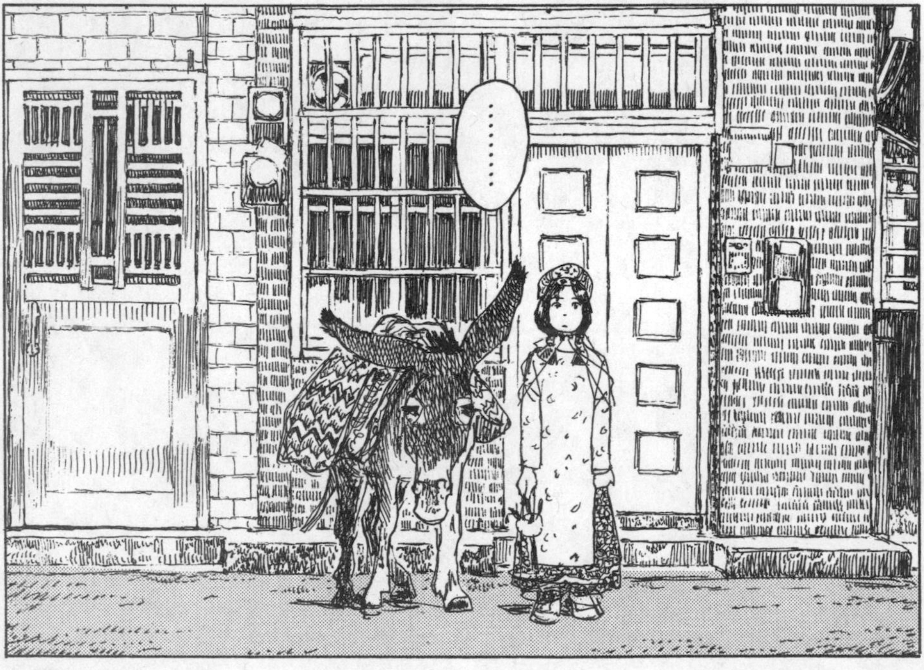
......

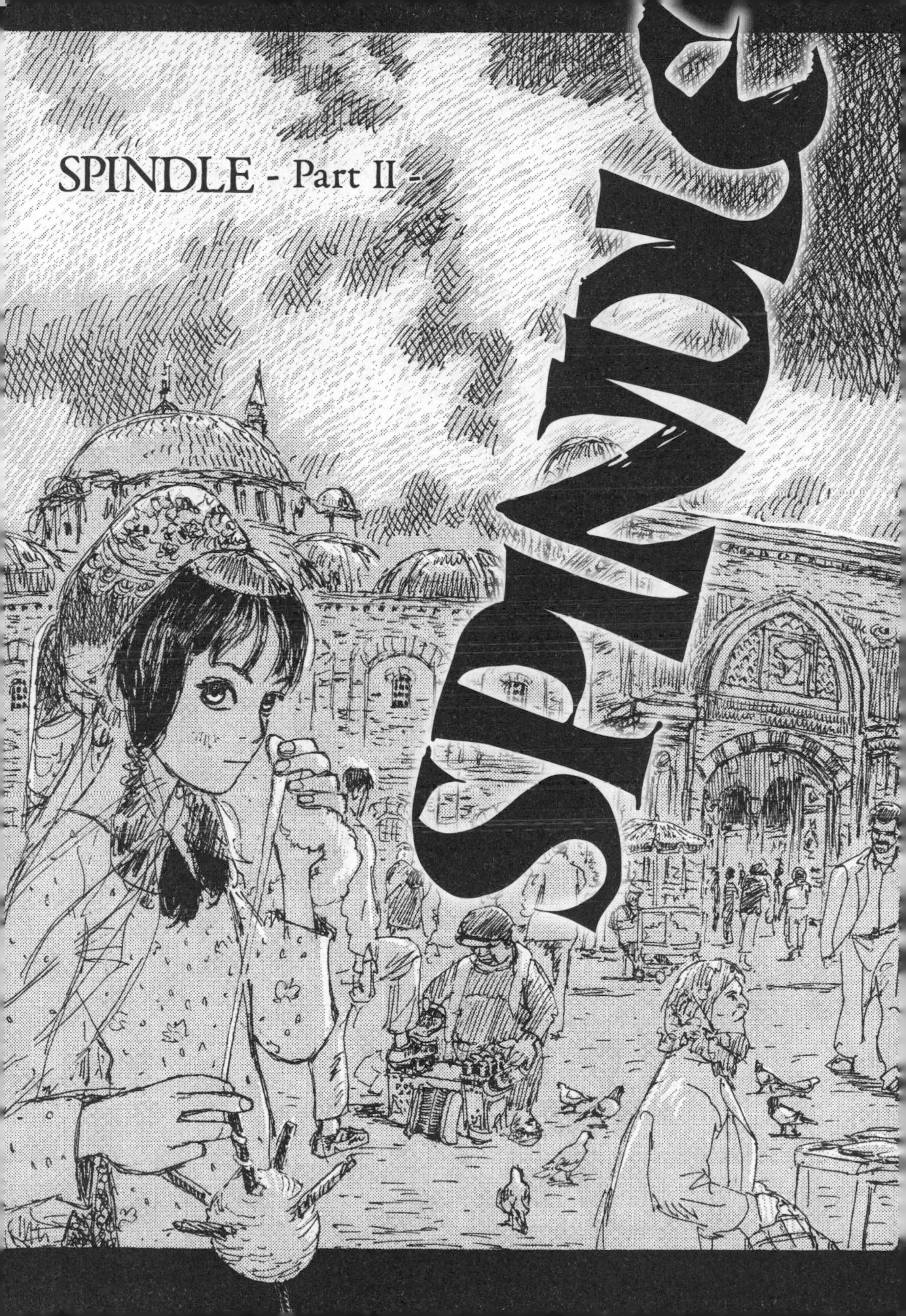
SPINDLE - Part II -
SPINDLE

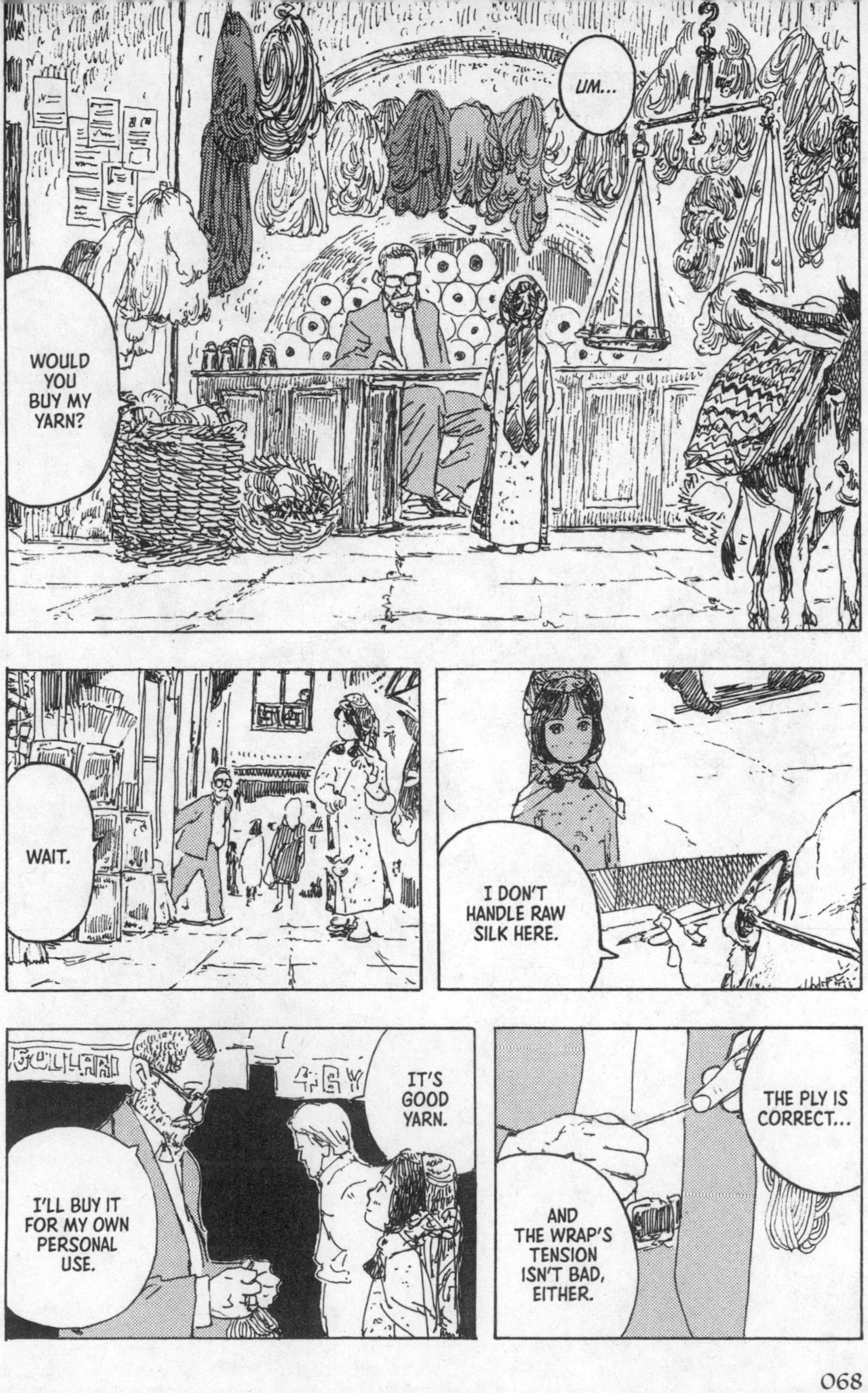
UM...
WOULD YOU BUY MY YARN?
I DON'T HANDLE RAW SILK HERE.
WAIT.
THE PLY IS CORRECT...
AND THE WRAP'S TENSION ISN'T BAD, EITHER.
IT'S GOOD YARN.
I'LL BUY IT FOR MY OWN PERSONAL USE.

WITH THIS, I CAN BUY WATER, FOOD...
AND RENNET, TOO.
OH, YOU'VE COME BACK, HAVE YOU?

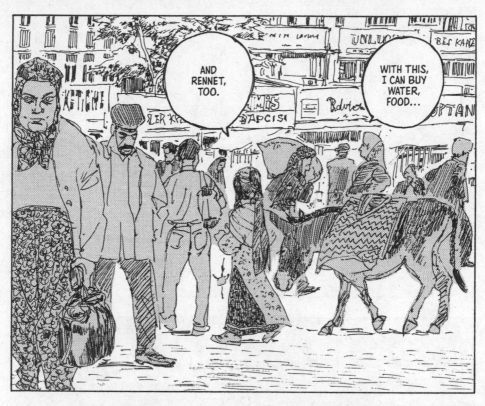

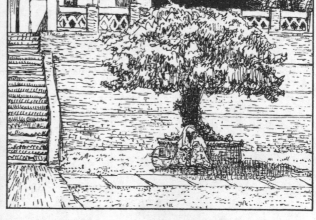

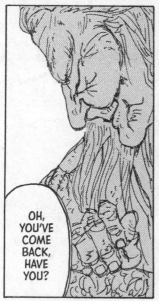

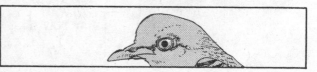

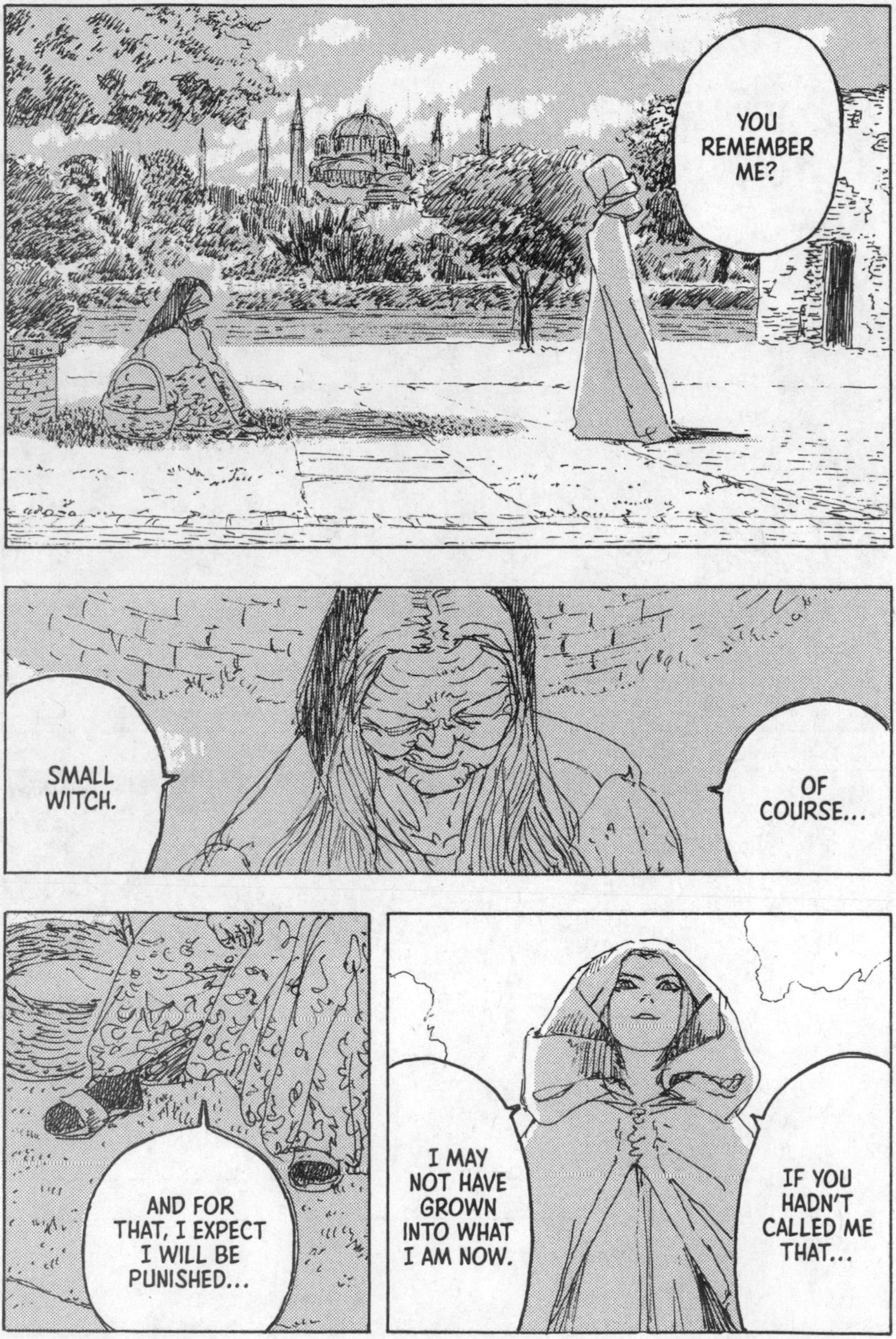
YOU REMEMBER ME?
OF COURSE...
SMALL WITCH.
IF YOU HADN'T CALLED ME THAT...
I MAY NOT HAVE GROWN INTO WHAT I AM NOW.
AND FOR THAT, I EXPECT I WILL BE PUNISHED...

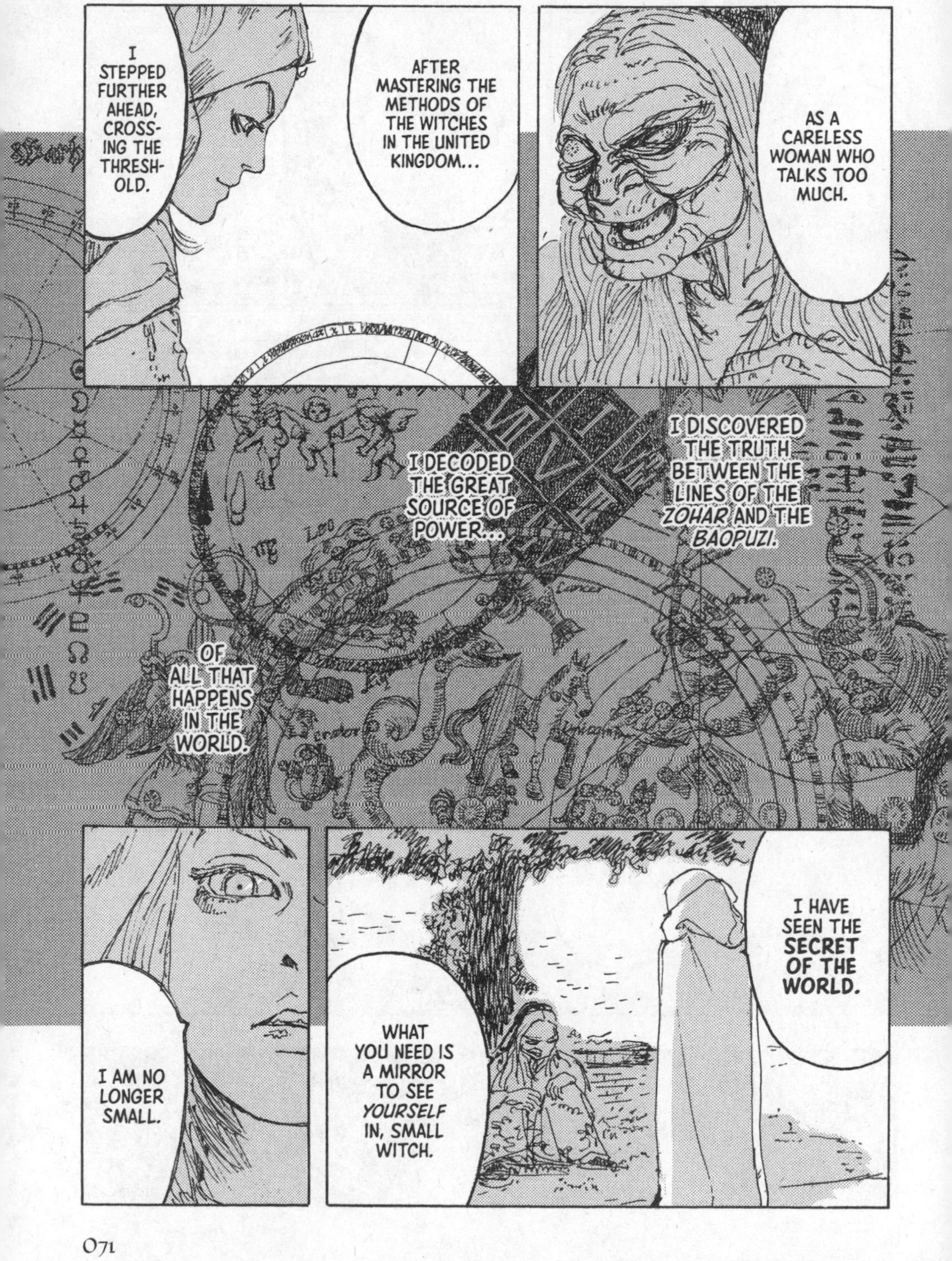
AS A CARELESS WOMAN WHO TALKS TOO MUCH.
AFTER MASTERING THE METHODS OF THE WITCHES IN THE UNITED KINGDOM...
I STEPPED FURTHER AHEAD, CROSSING THE THRESHOLD.
I DISCOVERED THE TRUTH BETWEEN THE LINES OF THE *ZOHAR* AND THE *BAOPUZI*.
I DECODED THE GREAT SOURCE OF POWER...
OF ALL THAT HAPPENS IN THE WORLD.
I HAVE SEEN THE **SECRET OF THE WORLD.**
WHAT YOU NEED IS A MIRROR TO SEE *YOURSELF* IN, SMALL WITCH.
I AM NO LONGER SMALL.

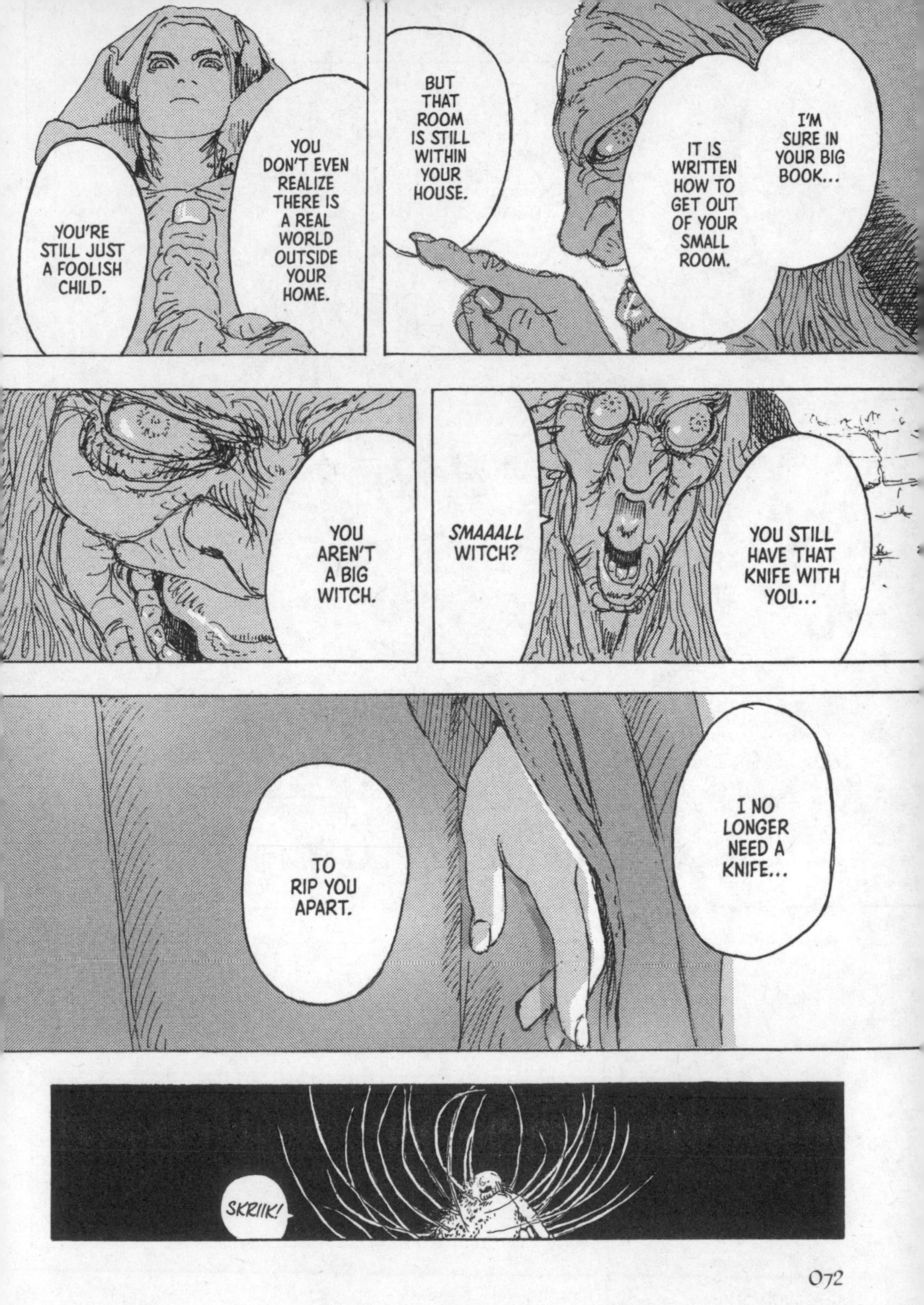
I'M SURE IN YOUR BIG BOOK...
IT IS WRITTEN HOW TO GET OUT OF YOUR SMALL ROOM.
BUT THAT ROOM IS STILL WITHIN YOUR HOUSE.
YOU DON'T EVEN REALIZE THERE IS A REAL WORLD OUTSIDE YOUR HOME.
YOU'RE STILL JUST A FOOLISH CHILD.
YOU STILL HAVE THAT KNIFE WITH YOU...
SMAAALL WITCH?
YOU AREN'T A BIG WITCH.
I NO LONGER NEED A KNIFE...
TO RIP YOU APART.
SKRIIK!

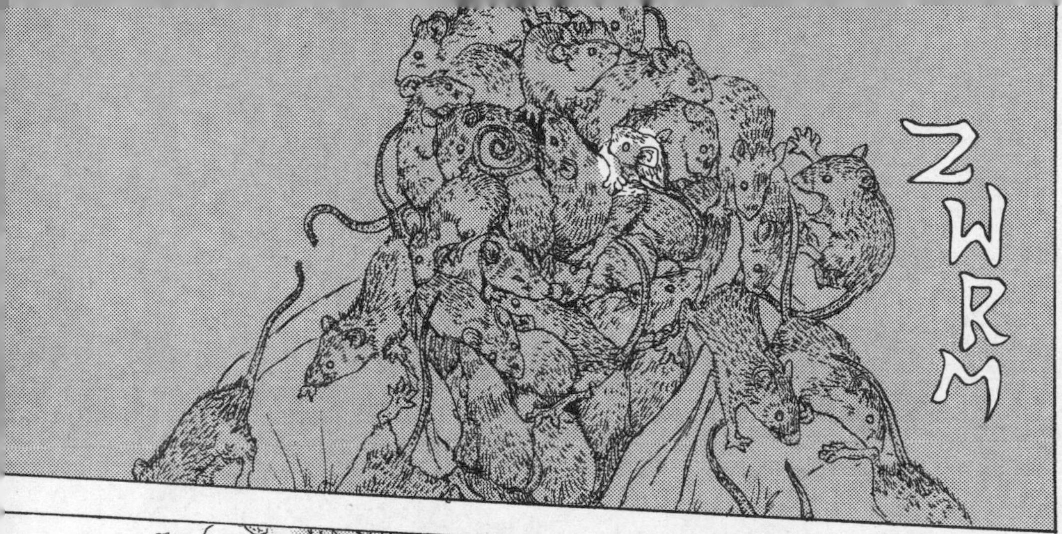
ZWRM

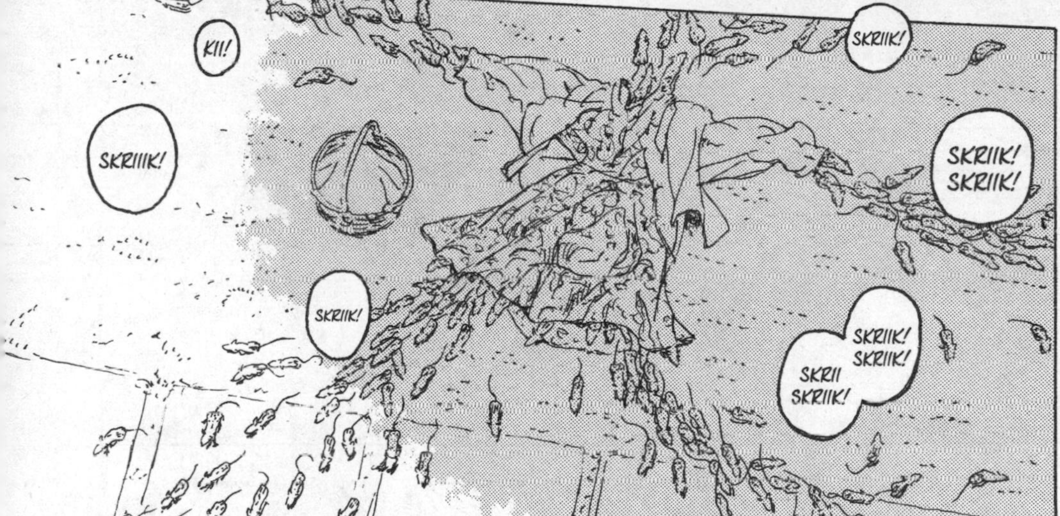
SKRIIK!
SKRIIK! SKRIIK!
KII!
SKRIIIK!
SKRIIK! SKRIIK!
SKRII SKRIIK!
SKRIIK!

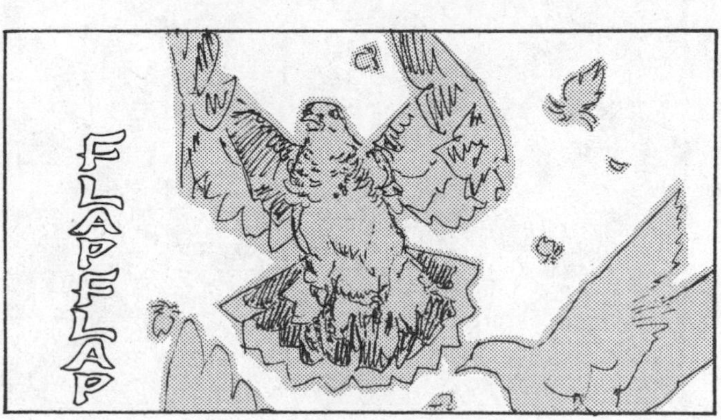
FLAPFLAP

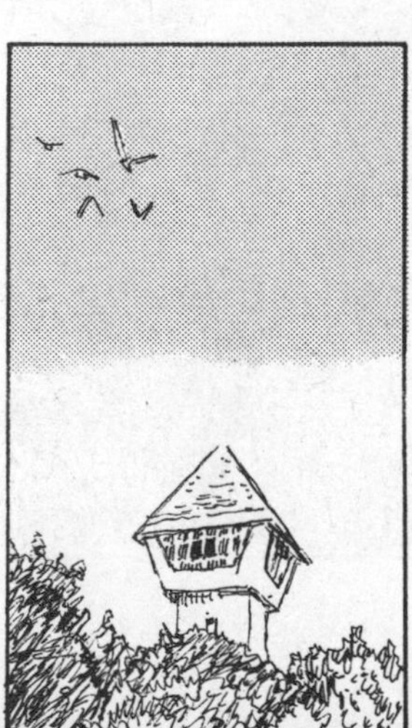

OY.
TWO OF THOSE.
SUGAR?
YOU'LL GET TWO CUBES.
THANK YOU, SIR.
THREE, OVER HERE!
MEETING AGAIN AFTER TWENTY YEARS, HUH?

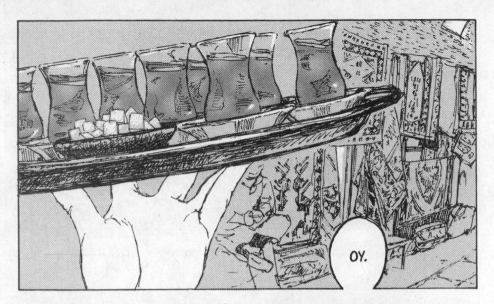

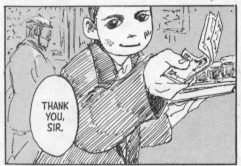

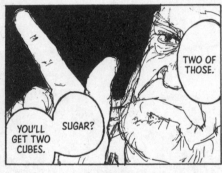

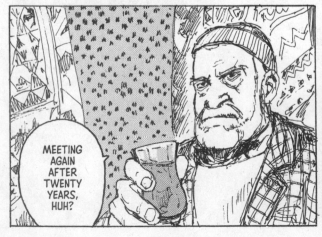

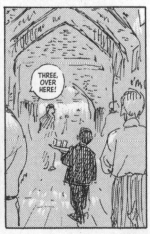

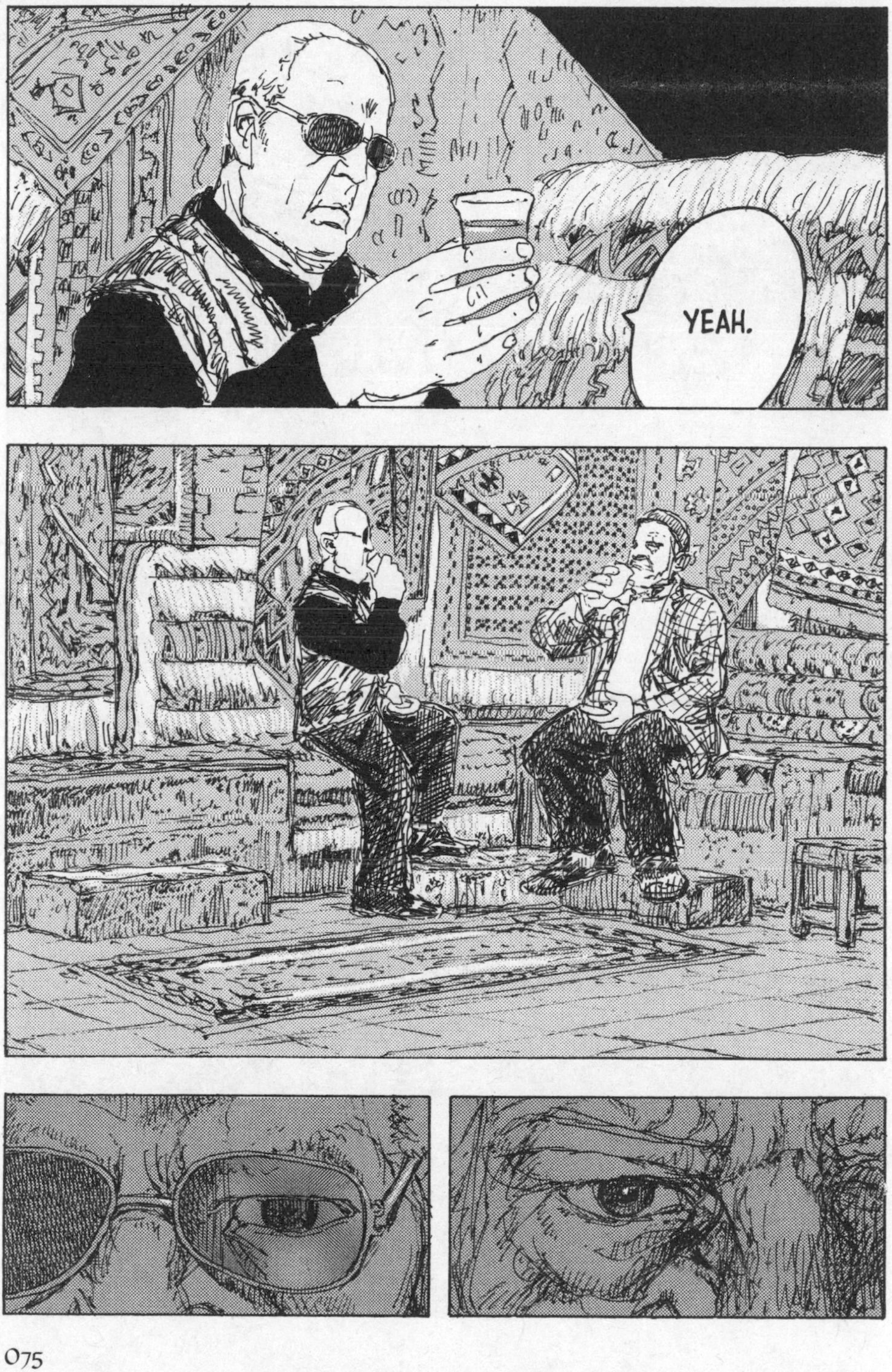
YEAH.

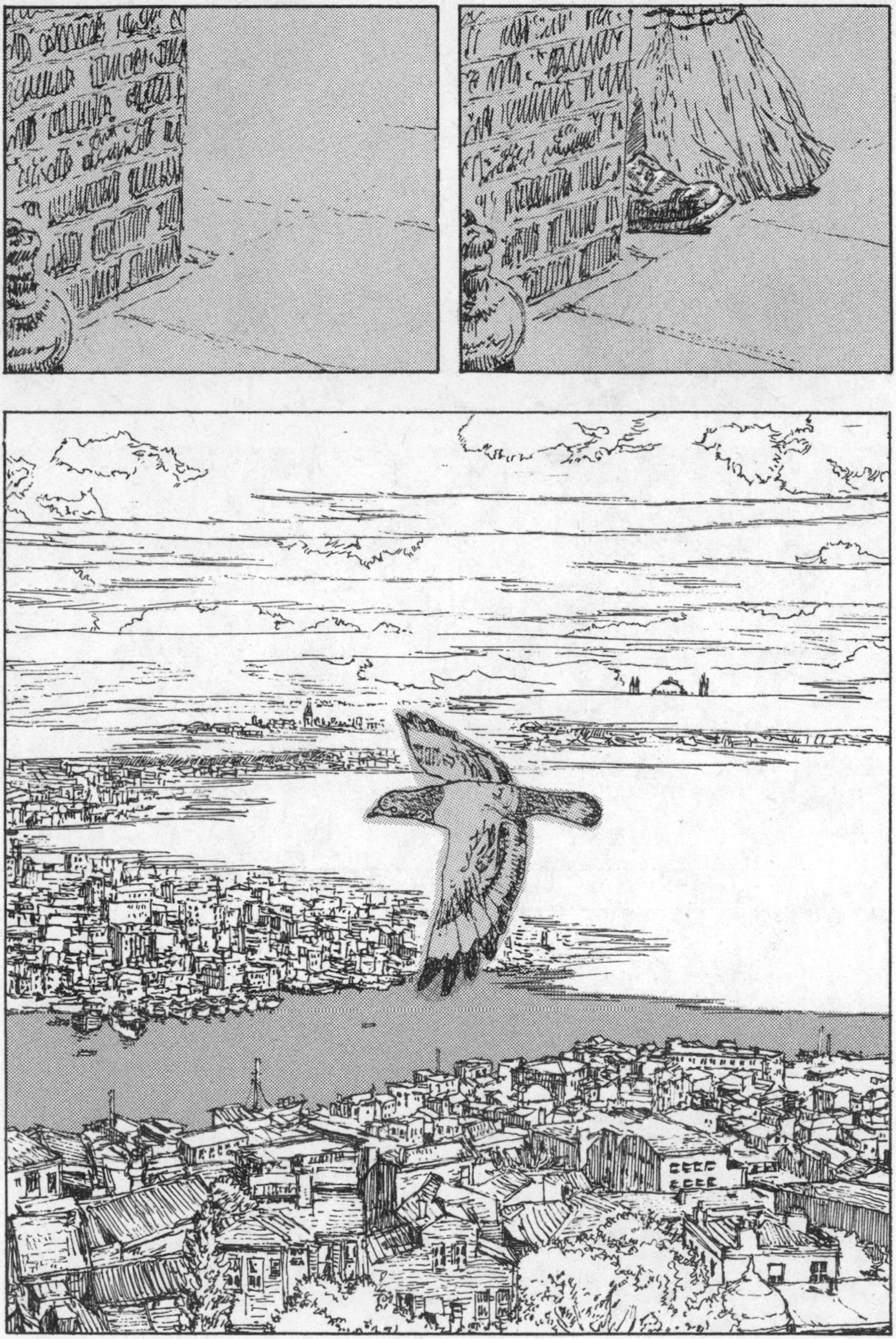

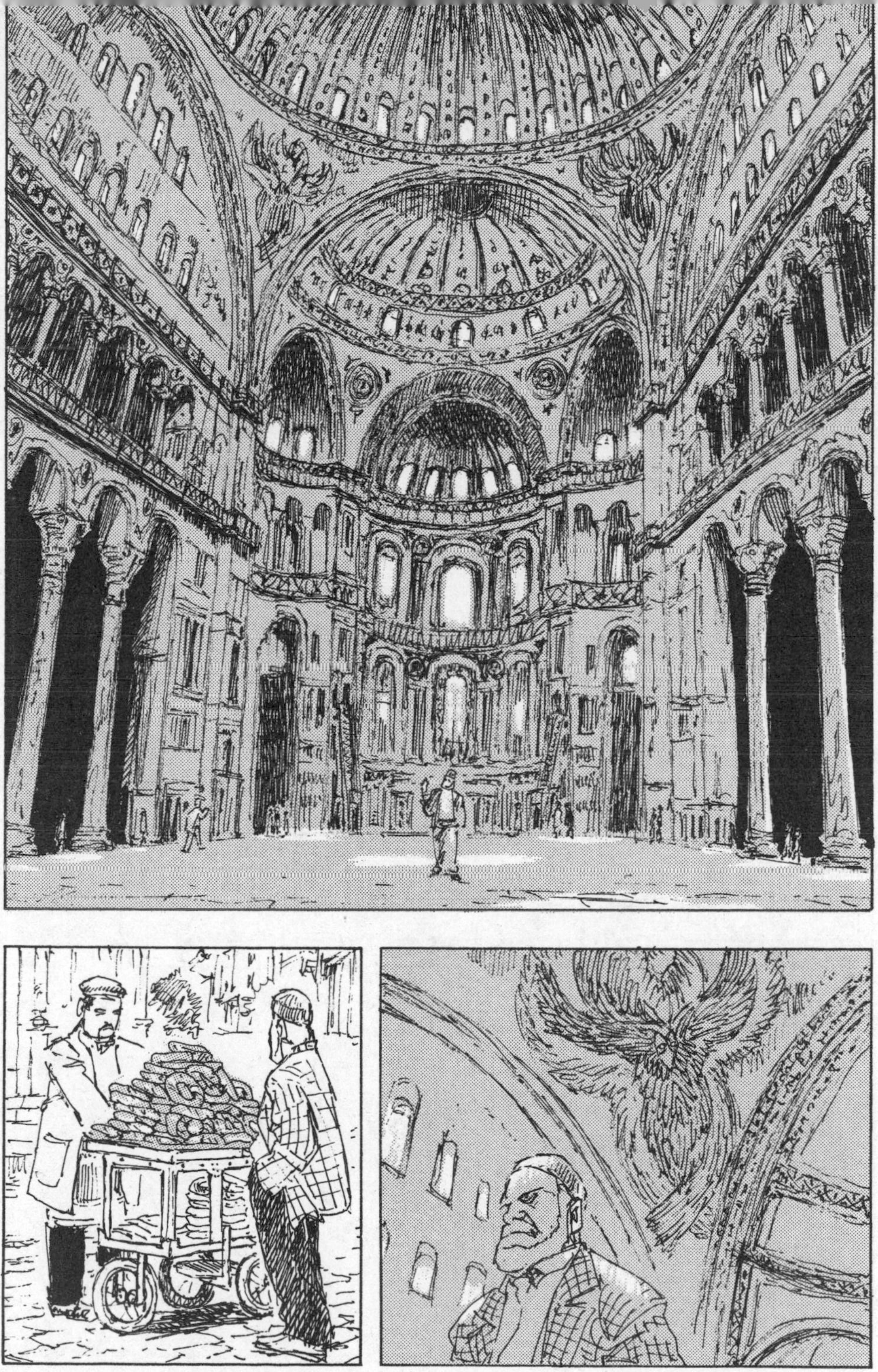

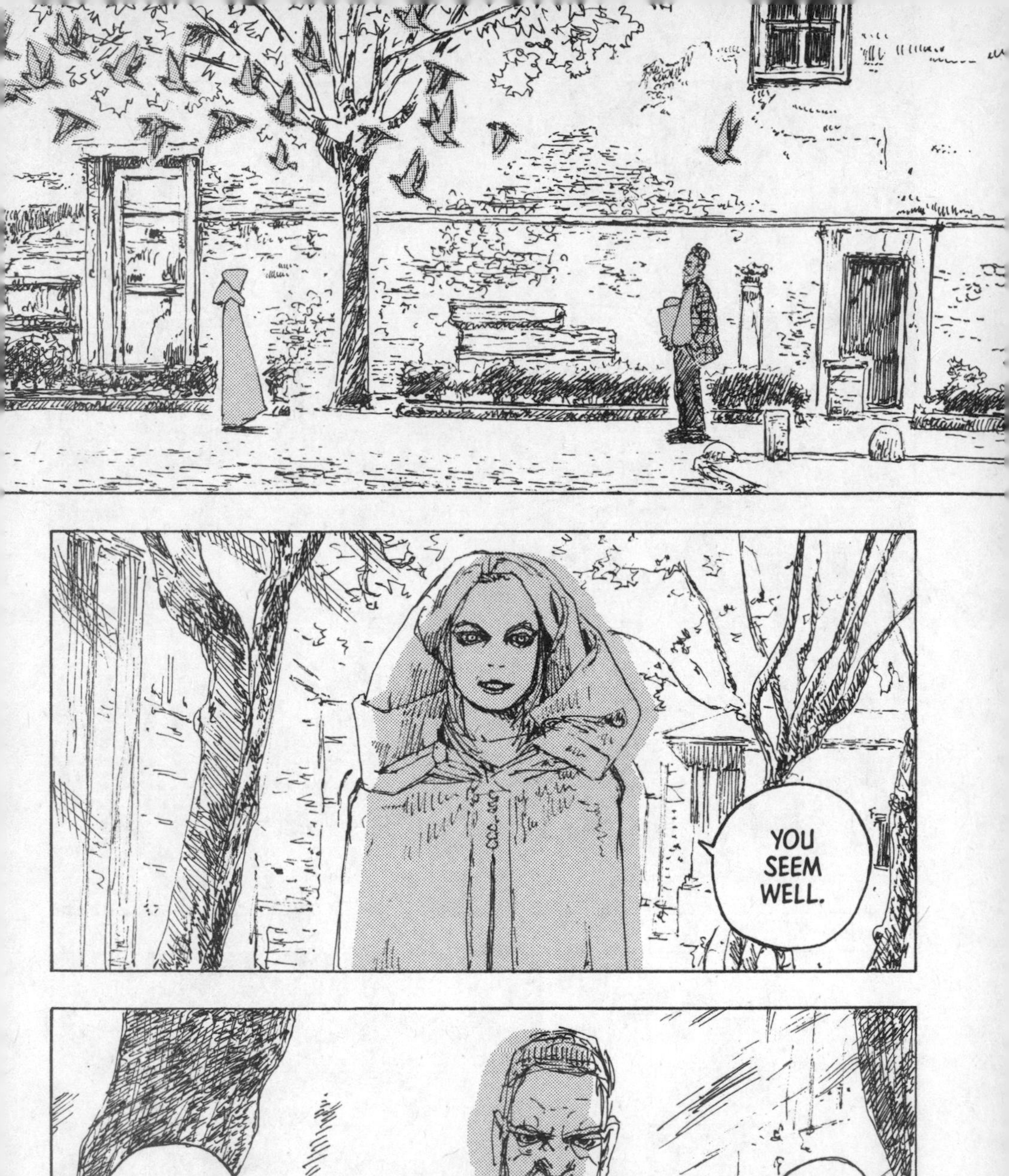
YOU SEEM WELL.
COMING BACK TO THIS CITY...
WHAT ARE YOU EVEN DOING HERE?

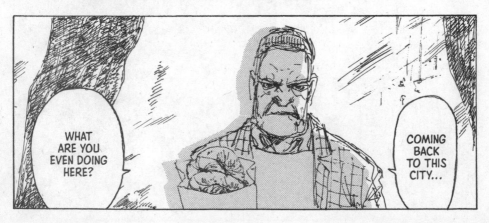

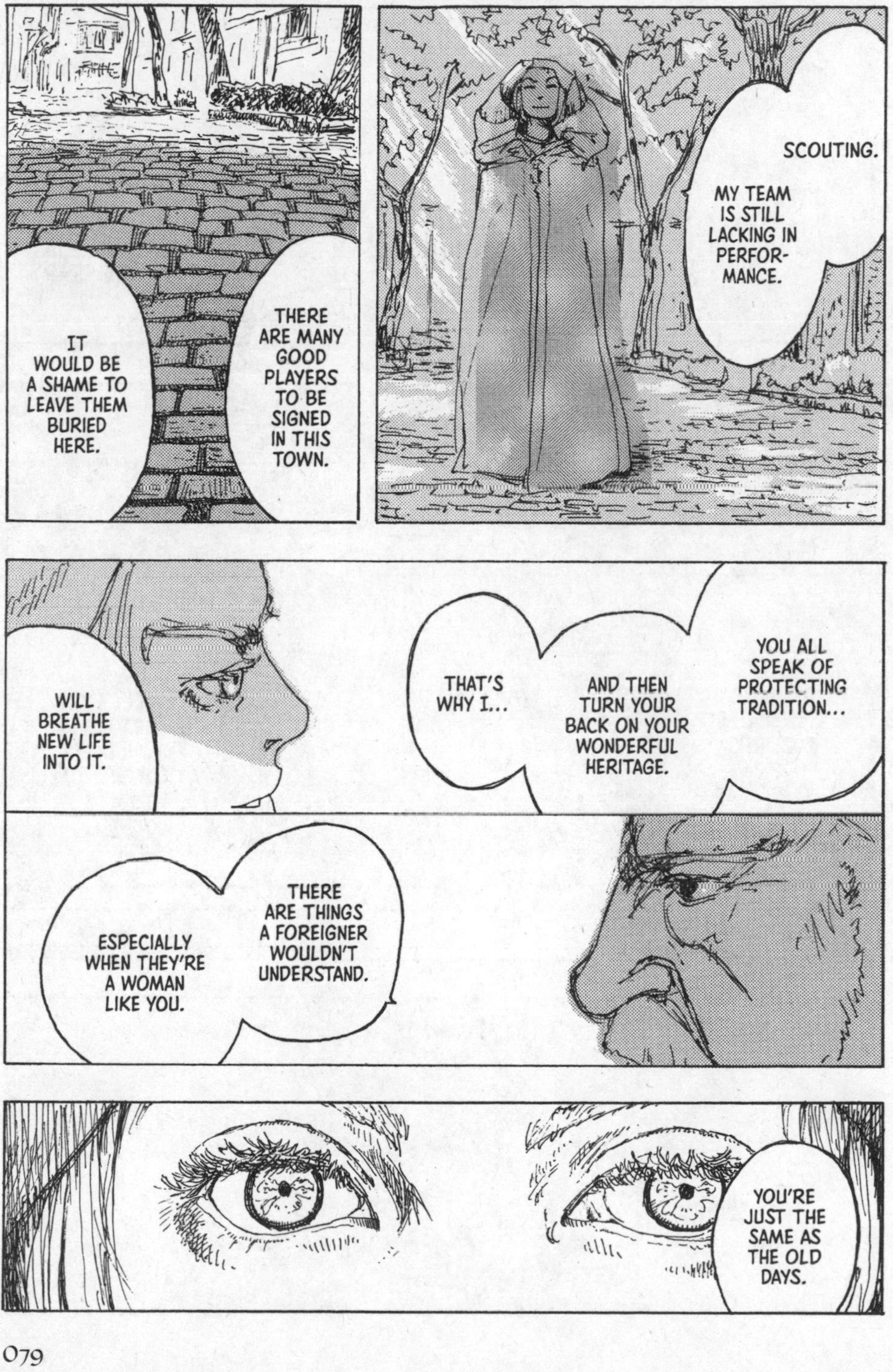
SCOUTING.
MY TEAM IS STILL LACKING IN PERFORMANCE.
THERE ARE MANY GOOD PLAYERS TO BE SIGNED IN THIS TOWN.
IT WOULD BE A SHAME TO LEAVE THEM BURIED HERE.
YOU ALL SPEAK OF PROTECTING TRADITION...
AND THEN TURN YOUR BACK ON YOUR WONDERFUL HERITAGE.
THAT'S WHY I...
WILL BREATHE NEW LIFE INTO IT.
THERE ARE THINGS A FOREIGNER WOULDN'T UNDERSTAND.
ESPECIALLY WHEN THEY'RE A WOMAN LIKE YOU.
YOU'RE JUST THE SAME AS THE OLD DAYS.

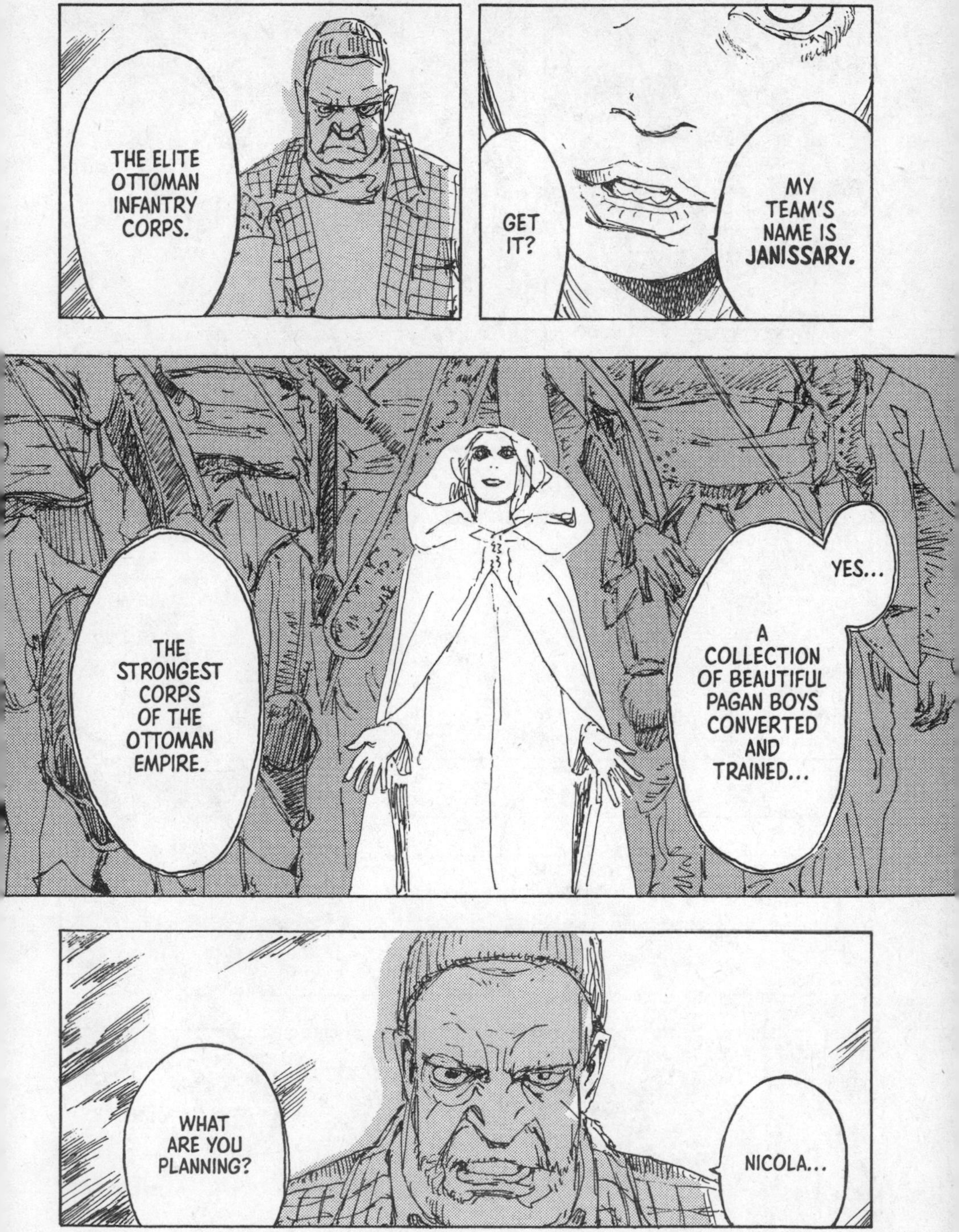
MY TEAM'S NAME IS JANISSARY.
GET IT?
THE ELITE OTTOMAN INFANTRY CORPS.
YES...
A COLLECTION OF BEAUTIFUL PAGAN BOYS CONVERTED AND TRAINED...
THE STRONGEST CORPS OF THE OTTOMAN EMPIRE.
NICOLA...
WHAT ARE YOU PLANNING?

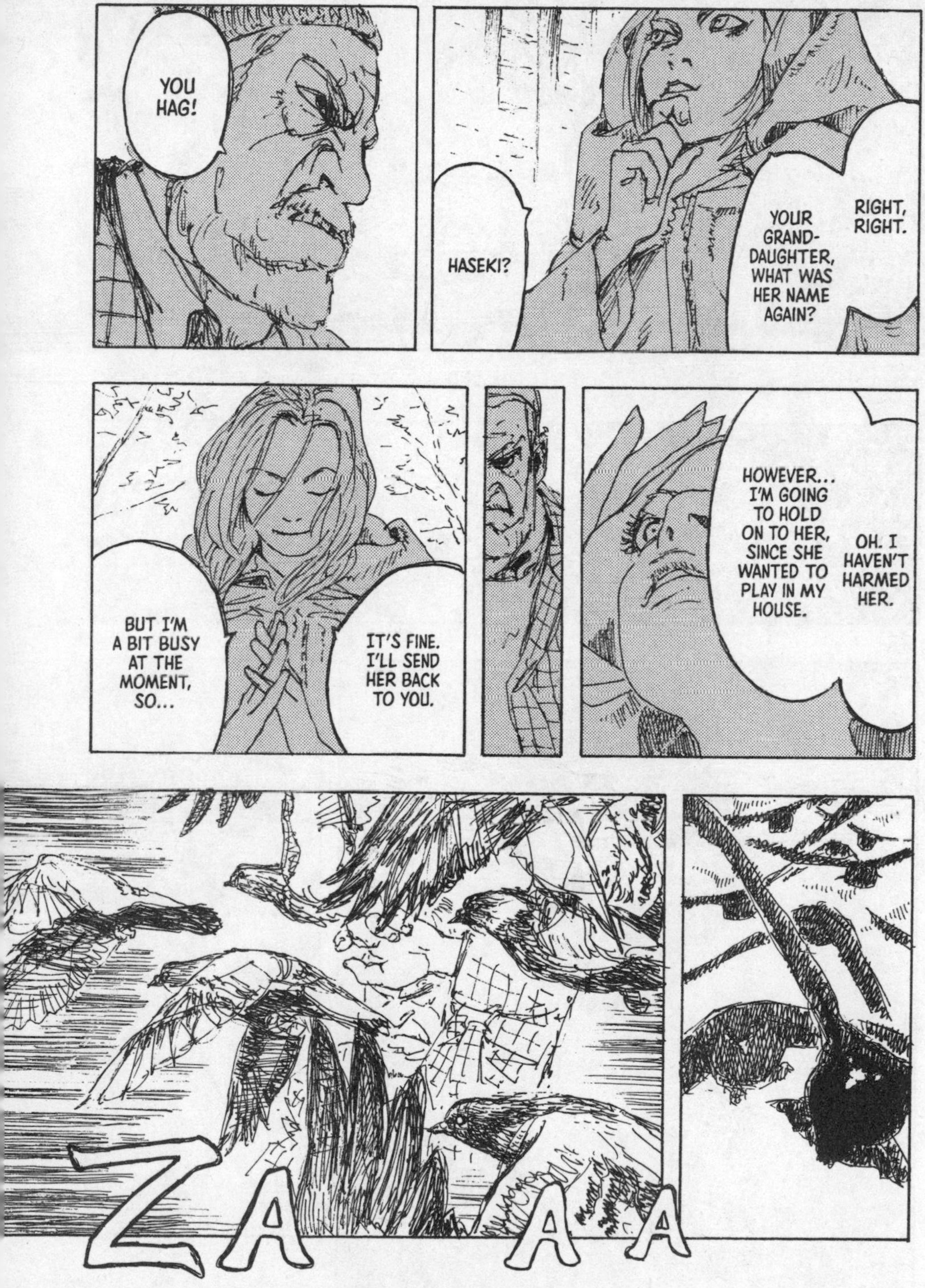
RIGHT, RIGHT.
YOUR GRAND-DAUGHTER, WHAT WAS HER NAME AGAIN?
HASEKI?
YOU HAG!
OH. I HAVEN'T HARMED HER.
HOWEVER... I'M GOING TO HOLD ON TO HER, SINCE SHE WANTED TO PLAY IN MY HOUSE.
IT'S FINE. I'LL SEND HER BACK TO YOU.
BUT I'M A BIT BUSY AT THE MOMENT, SO...
ZAAA

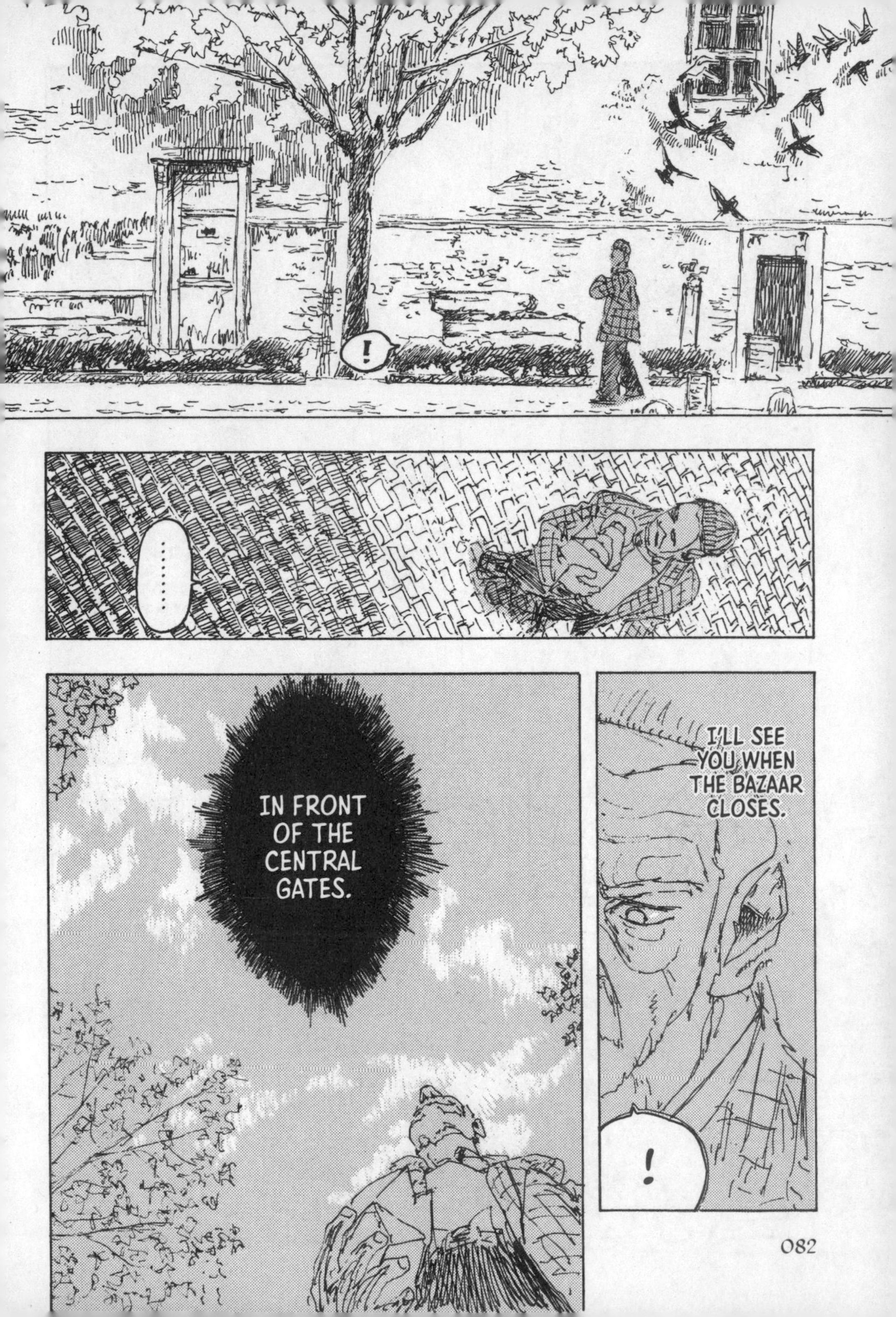
!
......
I'LL SEE YOU WHEN THE BAZAAR CLOSES.
!
IN FRONT OF THE CENTRAL GATES.

HEY!

WHERE CAN I BUY RENNET?

THANKS.

FINISHED.

UM...

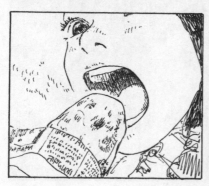

NO CLUE.

RENNET?

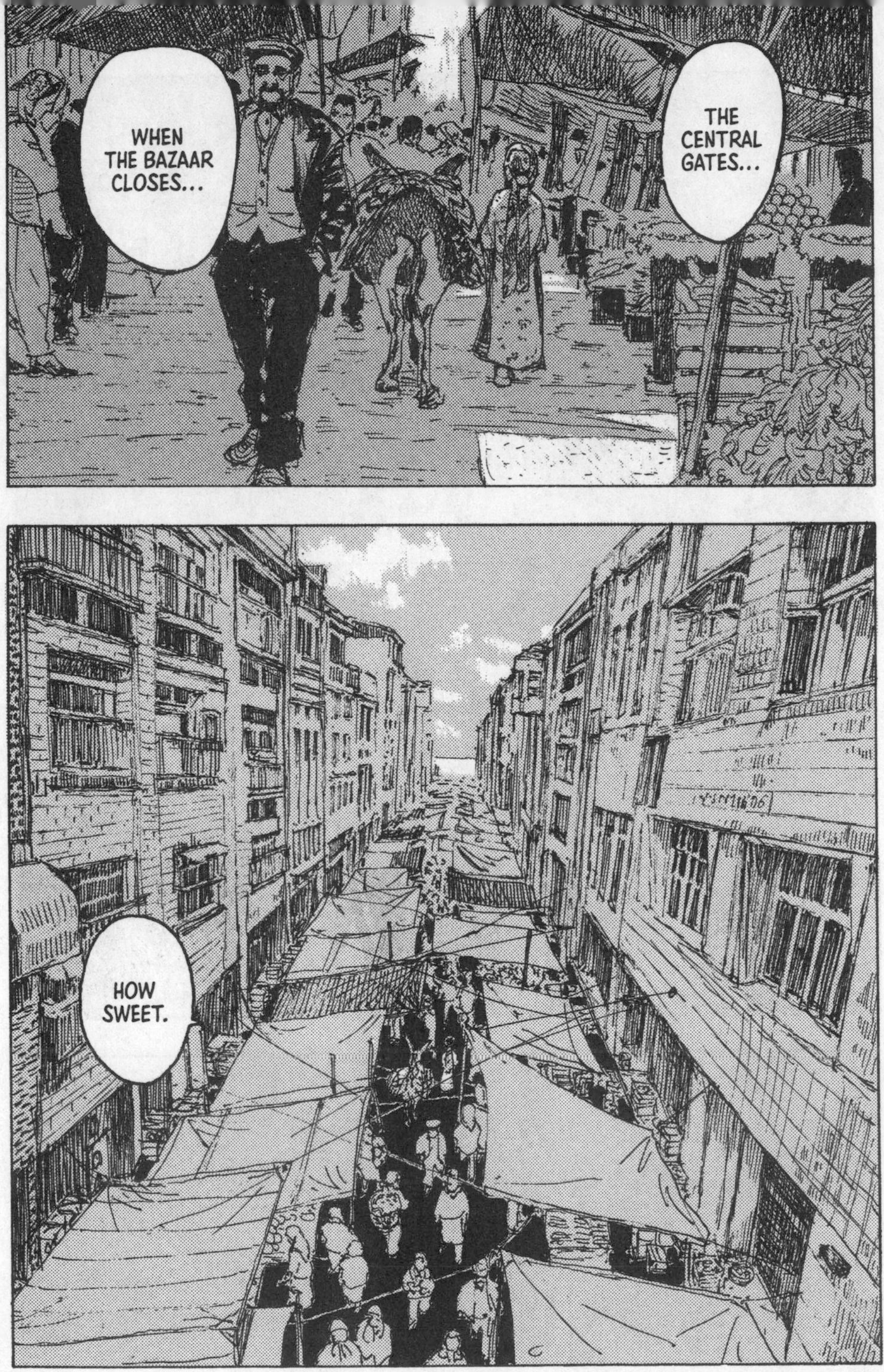
THE CENTRAL GATES...
WHEN THE BAZAAR CLOSES...
HOW SWEET.

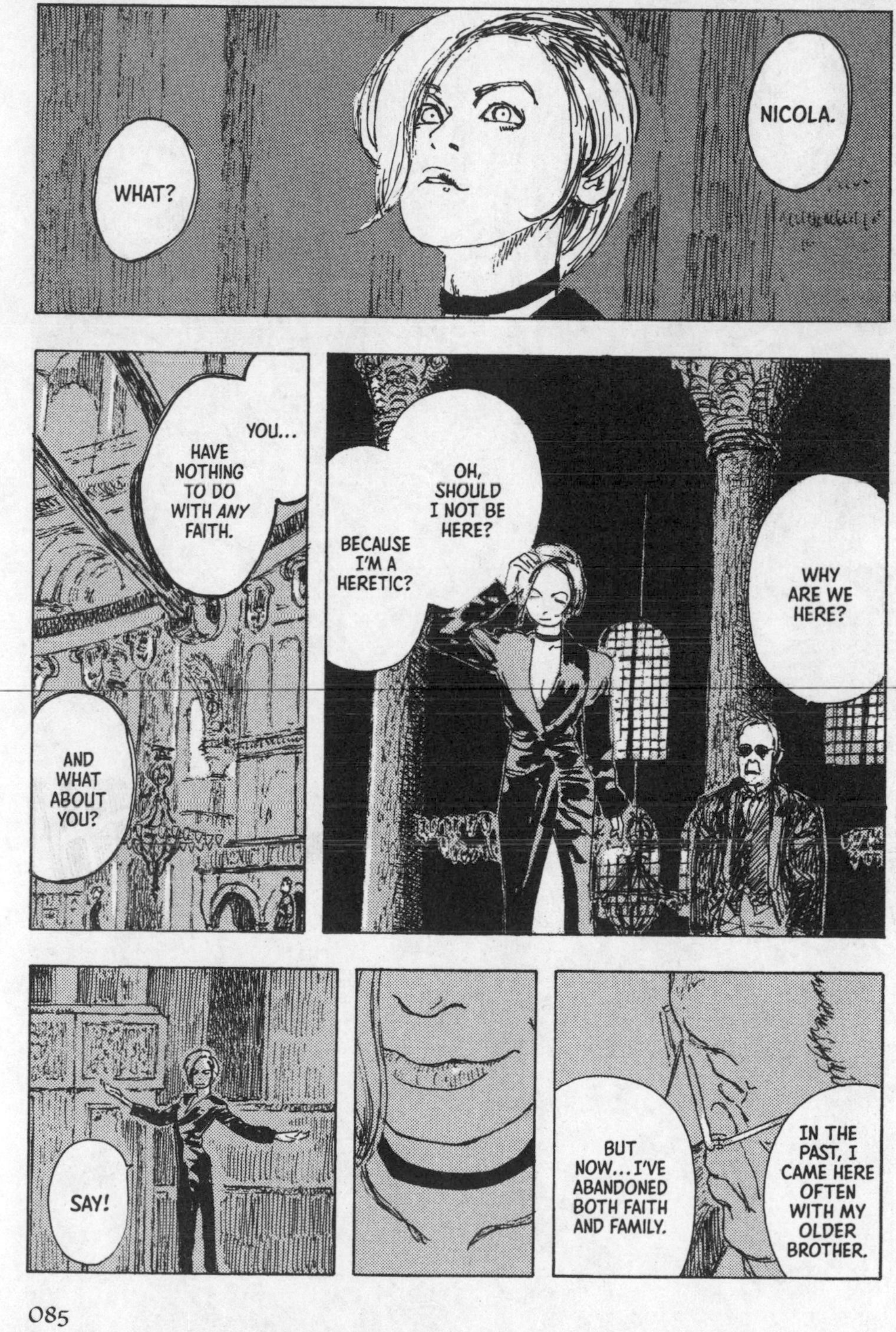
NICOLA.
WHAT?
WHY ARE WE HERE?
OH, SHOULD I NOT BE HERE?
BECAUSE I'M A HERETIC?
YOU... HAVE NOTHING TO DO WITH *ANY* FAITH.
AND WHAT ABOUT YOU?
IN THE PAST, I CAME HERE OFTEN WITH MY OLDER BROTHER.
BUT NOW...I'VE ABANDONED BOTH FAITH AND FAMILY.
SAY!

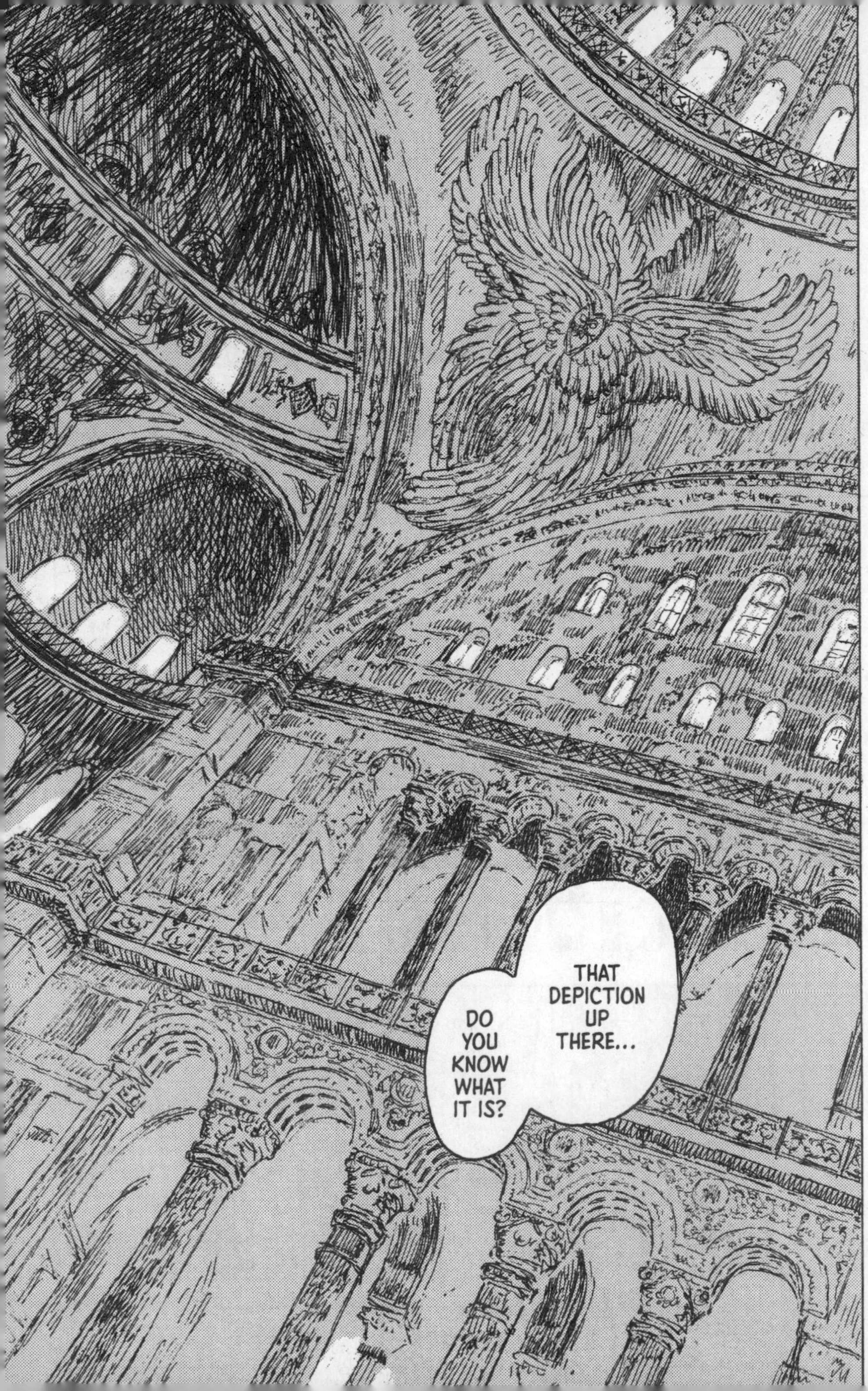
THAT DEPICTION UP THERE...
DO YOU KNOW WHAT IT IS?

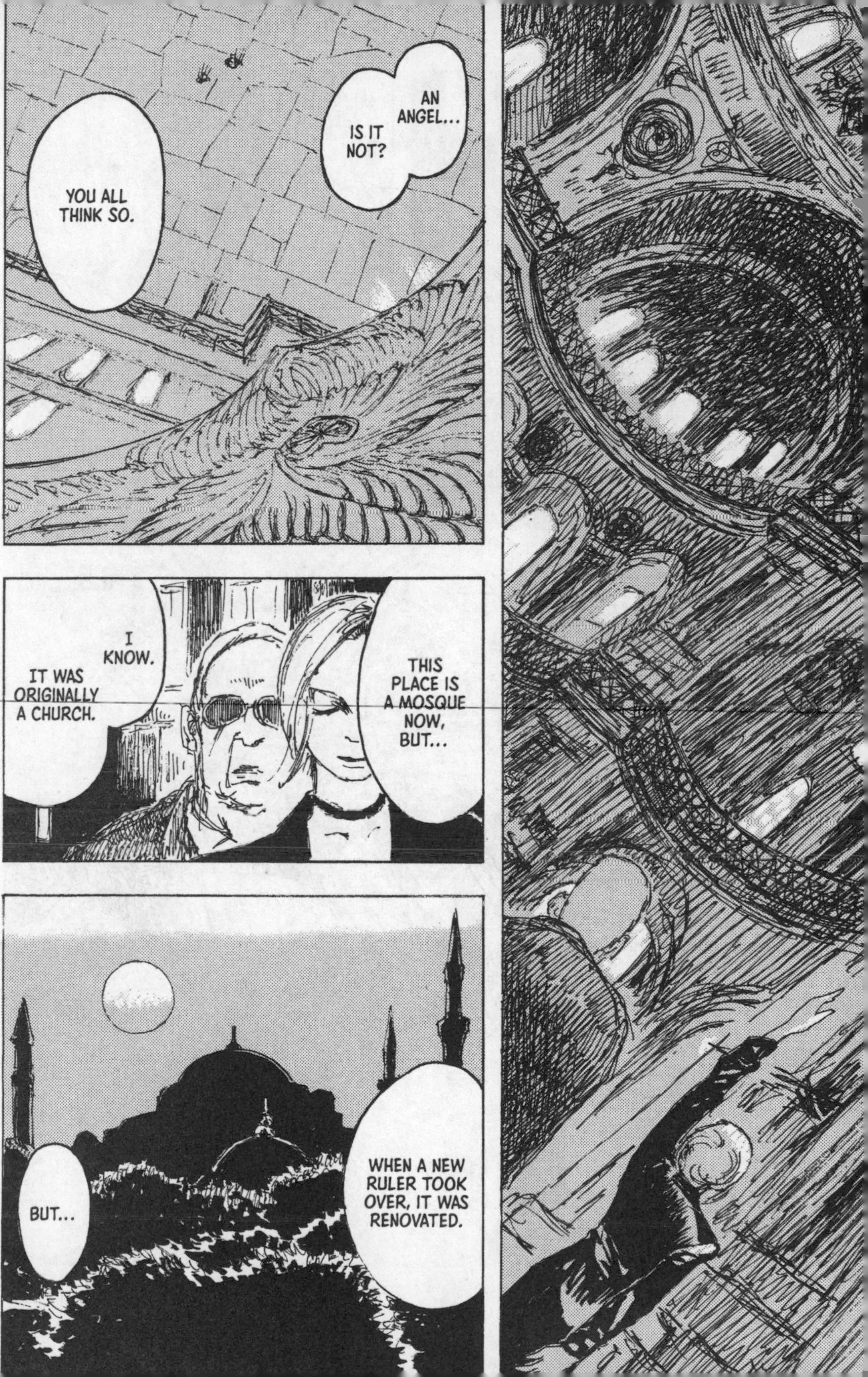
AN ANGEL... IS IT NOT?
YOU ALL THINK SO.
THIS PLACE IS A MOSQUE NOW, BUT...
I KNOW. IT WAS ORIGINALLY A CHURCH.
WHEN A NEW RULER TOOK OVER, IT WAS RENOVATED.
BUT...

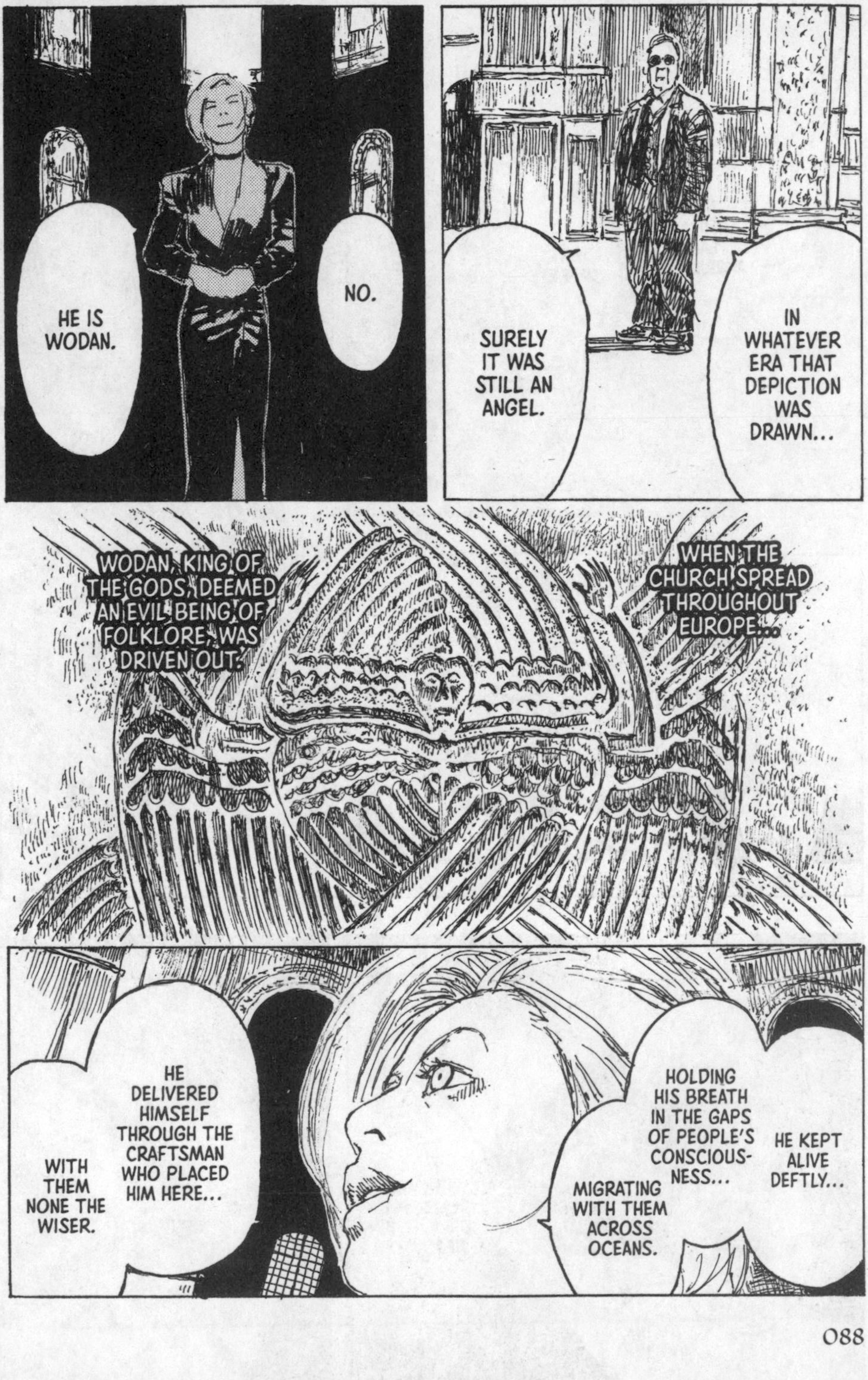
IN WHATEVER ERA THAT DEPICTION WAS DRAWN...
SURELY IT WAS STILL AN ANGEL.
NO.
HE IS WODAN.
WHEN THE CHURCH SPREAD THROUGHOUT EUROPE...
WODAN, KING OF THE GODS, DEEMED AN EVIL BEING OF FOLKLORE, WAS DRIVEN OUT.
HE KEPT ALIVE DEFTLY...
HOLDING HIS BREATH IN THE GAPS OF PEOPLE'S CONSCIOUS-NESS...
MIGRATING WITH THEM ACROSS OCEANS.
HE DELIVERED HIMSELF THROUGH THE CRAFTSMAN WHO PLACED HIM HERE...
WITH THEM NONE THE WISER.

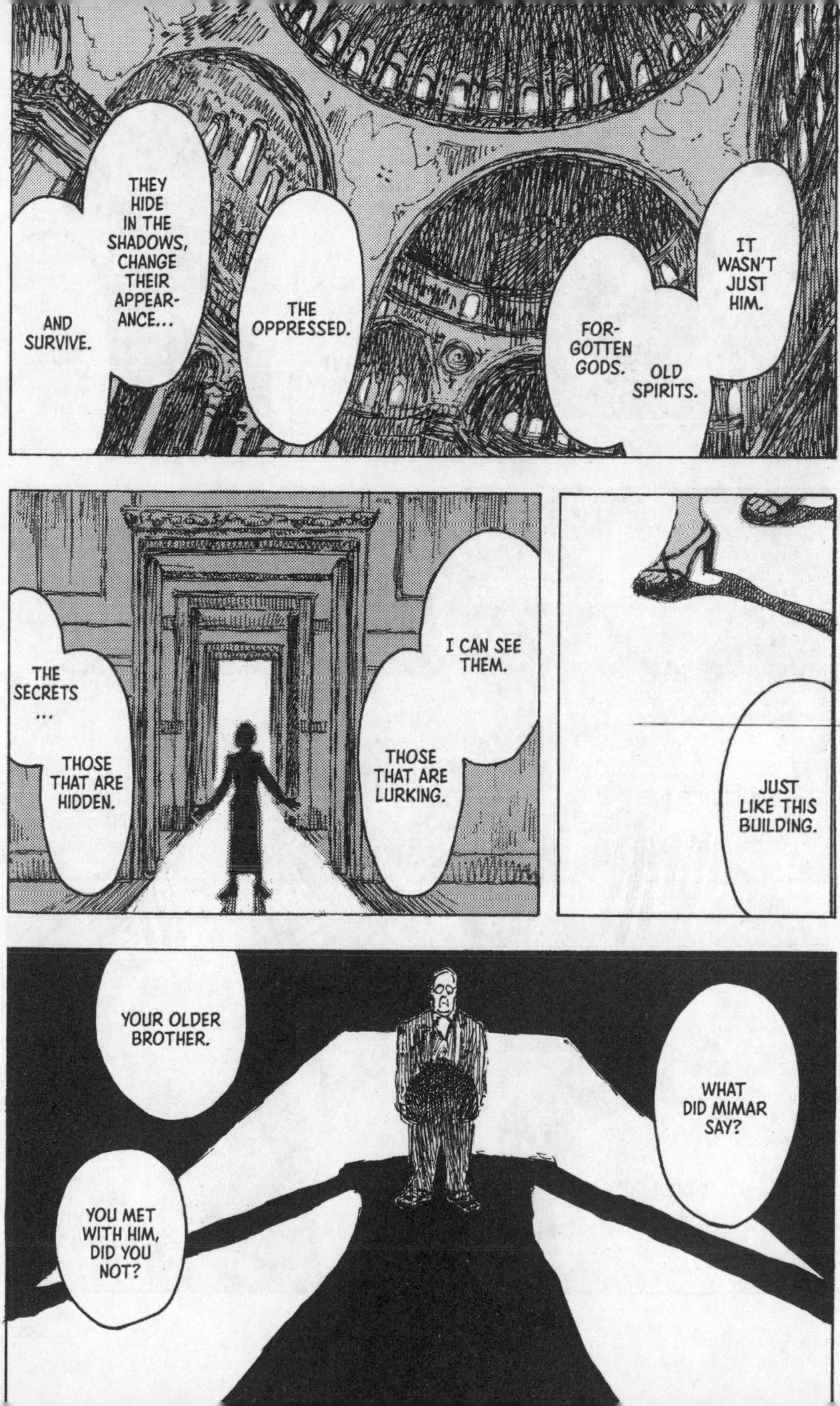
IT WASN'T JUST HIM.
OLD SPIRITS.
FOR-GOTTEN GODS.
THE OPPRESSED.
THEY HIDE IN THE SHADOWS, CHANGE THEIR APPEAR-ANCE...
AND SURVIVE.
JUST LIKE THIS BUILDING.
I CAN SEE THEM.
THOSE THAT ARE LURKING.
THE SECRETS ...
THOSE THAT ARE HIDDEN.
YOUR OLDER BROTHER.
YOU MET WITH HIM, DID YOU NOT?
WHAT DID MIMAR SAY?

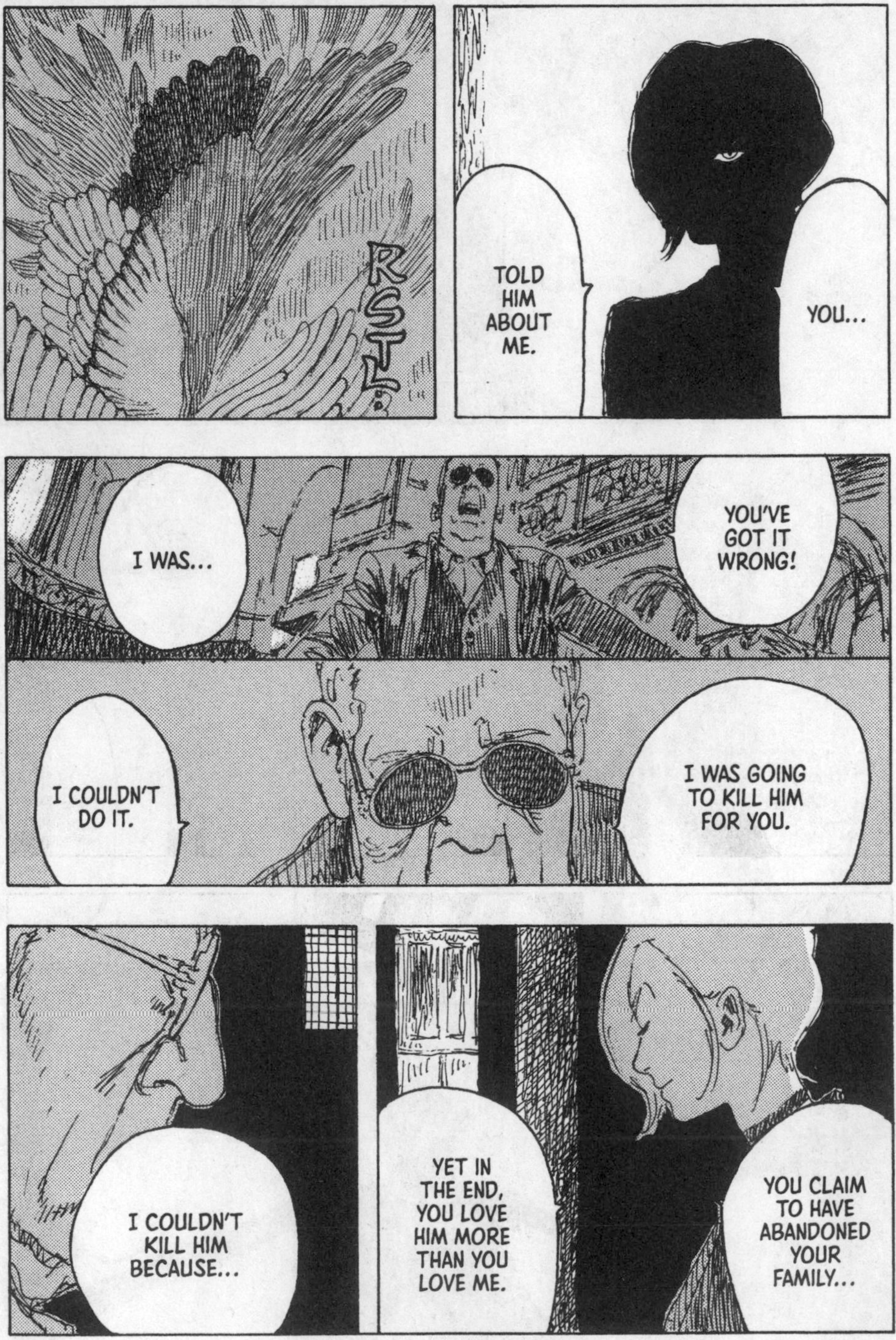
YOU...
TOLD HIM ABOUT ME.
RSTL
YOU'VE GOT IT WRONG!
I WAS...
I WAS GOING TO KILL HIM FOR YOU.
I COULDN'T DO IT.
YOU CLAIM TO HAVE ABANDONED YOUR FAMILY...
YET IN THE END, YOU LOVE HIM MORE THAN YOU LOVE ME.
I COULDN'T KILL HIM BECAUSE...

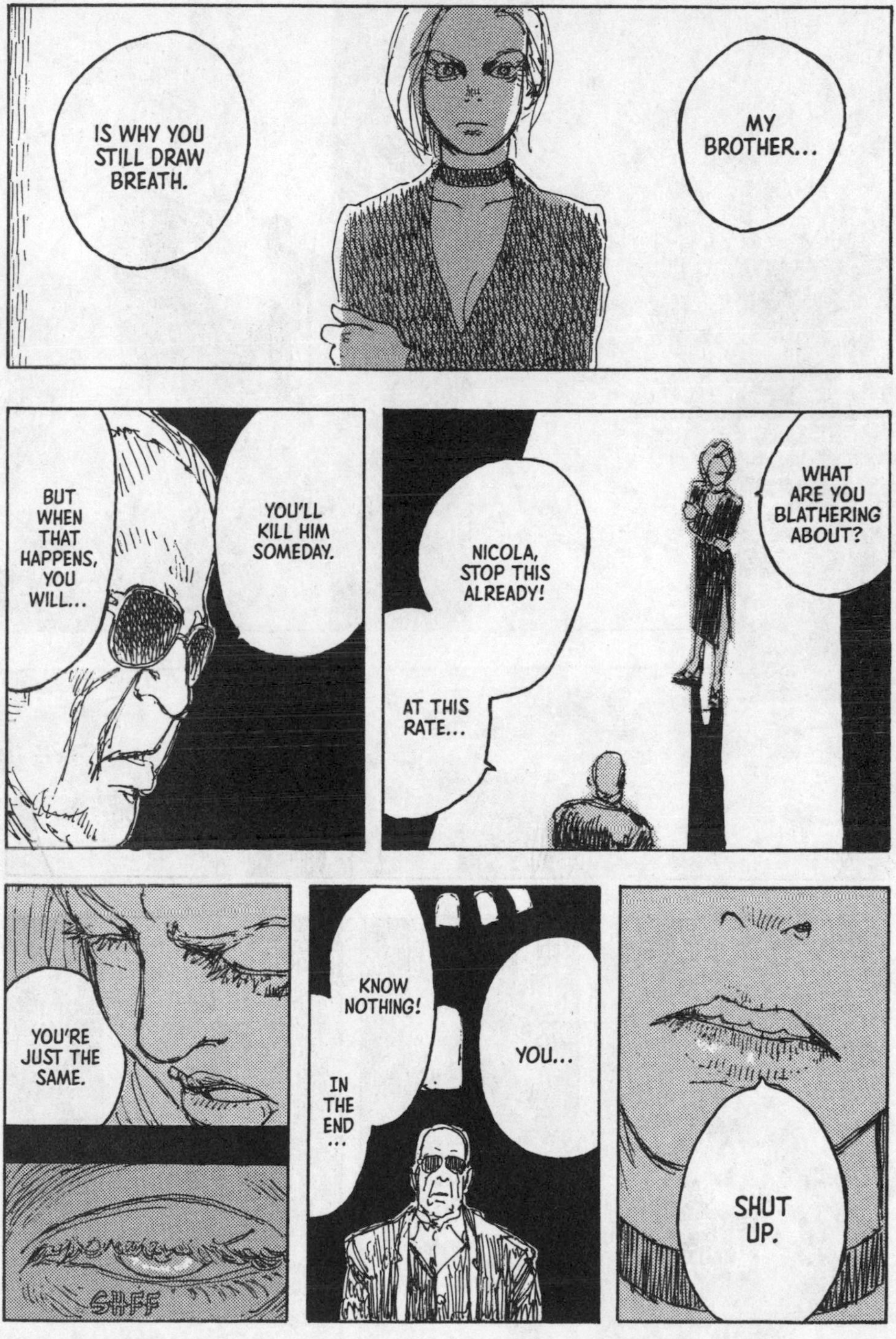
MY BROTHER...
IS WHY YOU STILL DRAW BREATH.
WHAT ARE YOU BLATHERING ABOUT?
NICOLA, STOP THIS ALREADY!
AT THIS RATE...
YOU'LL KILL HIM SOMEDAY.
BUT WHEN THAT HAPPENS, YOU WILL...
SHUT UP.
YOU...
IN THE END...
KNOW NOTHING!
YOU'RE JUST THE SAME.
SHFF

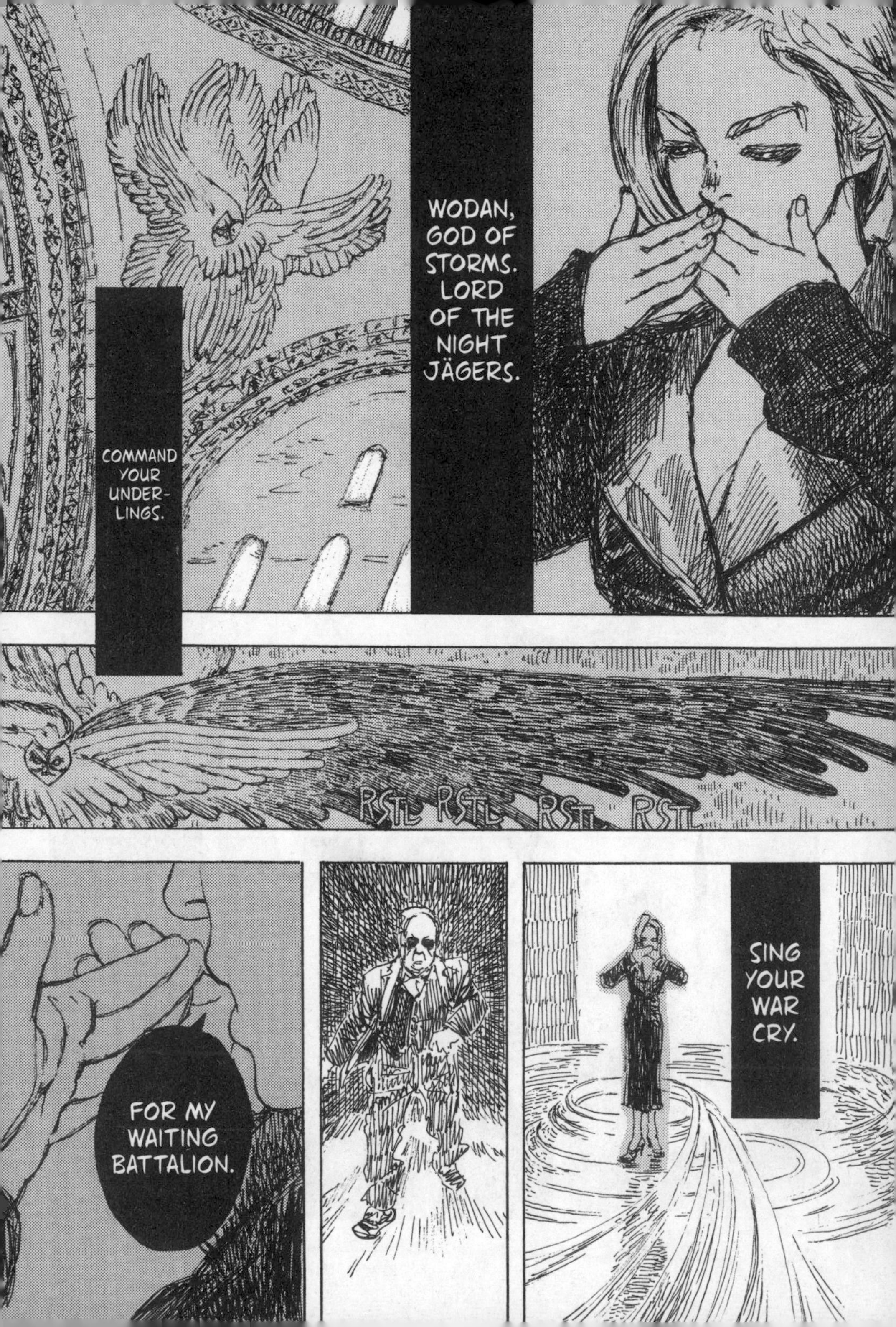
WODAN, GOD OF STORMS. LORD OF THE NIGHT JÄGERS.
COMMAND YOUR UNDER-LINGS.
RSTL RSTL RSTL RSTL
SING YOUR WAR CRY.
FOR MY WAITING BATTALION.

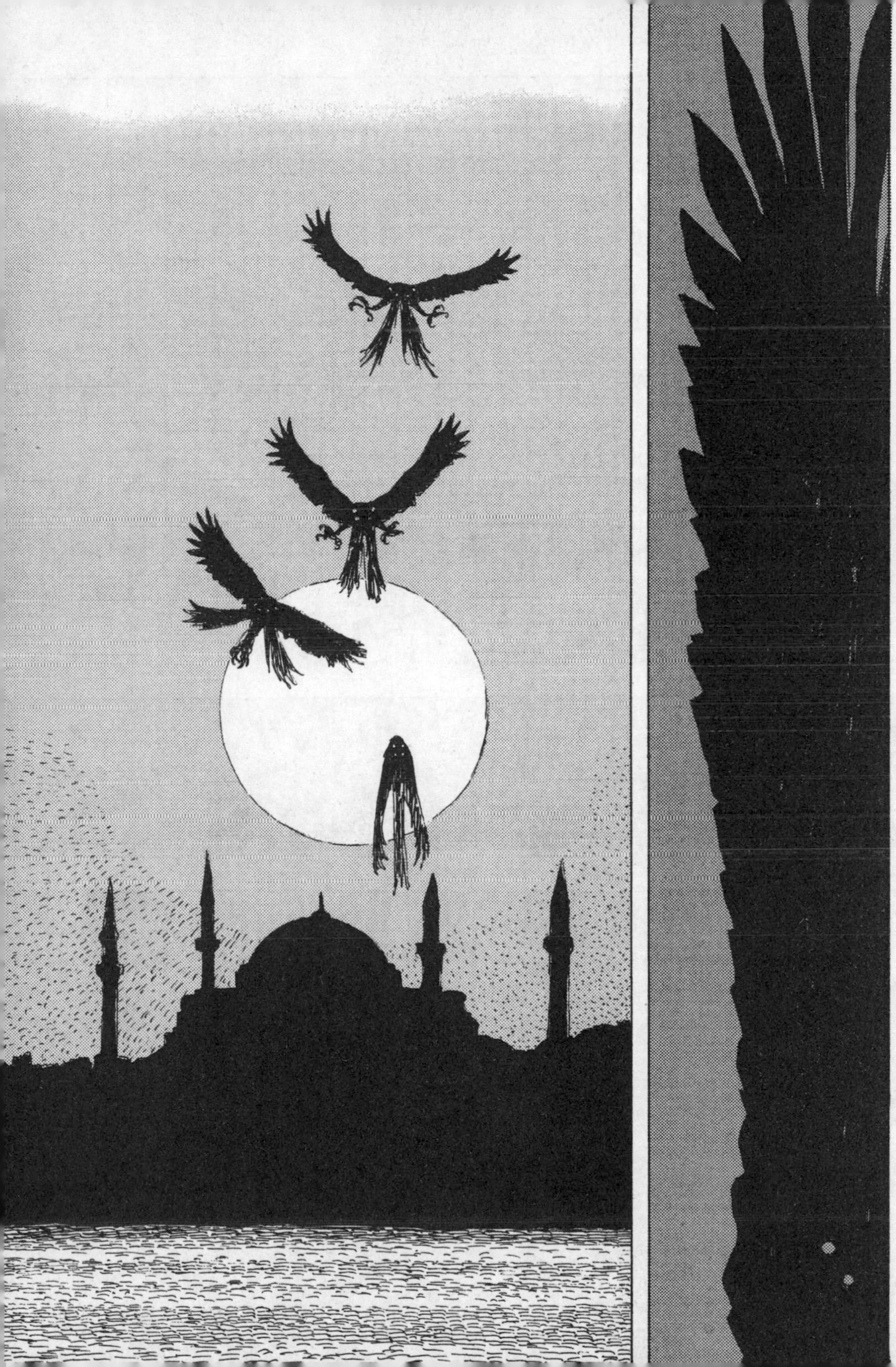

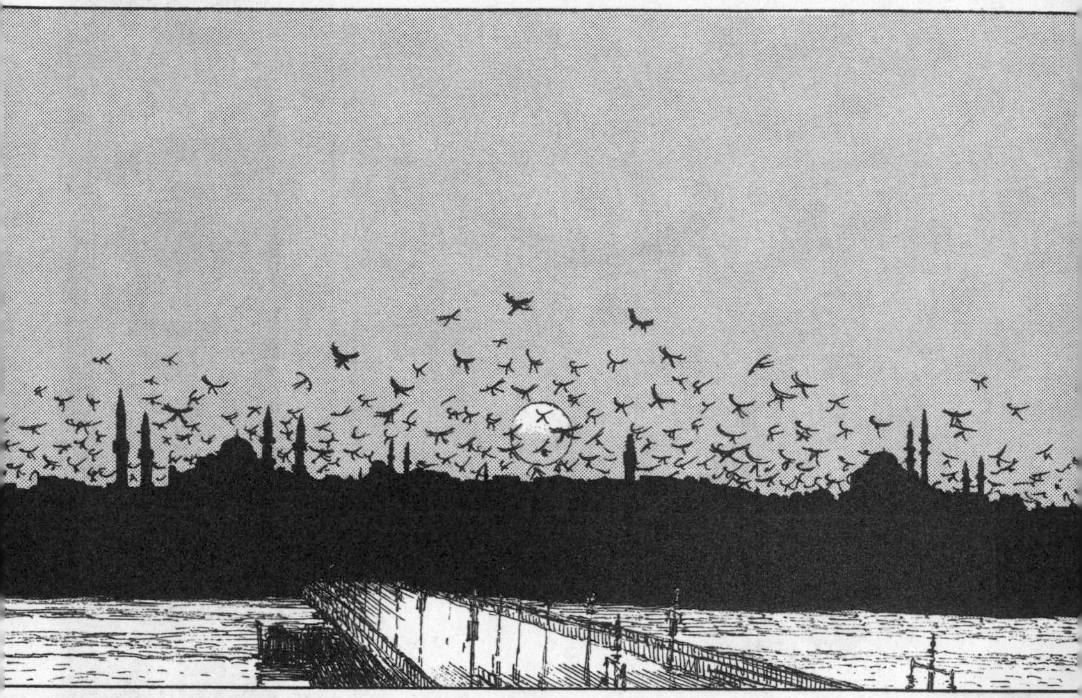
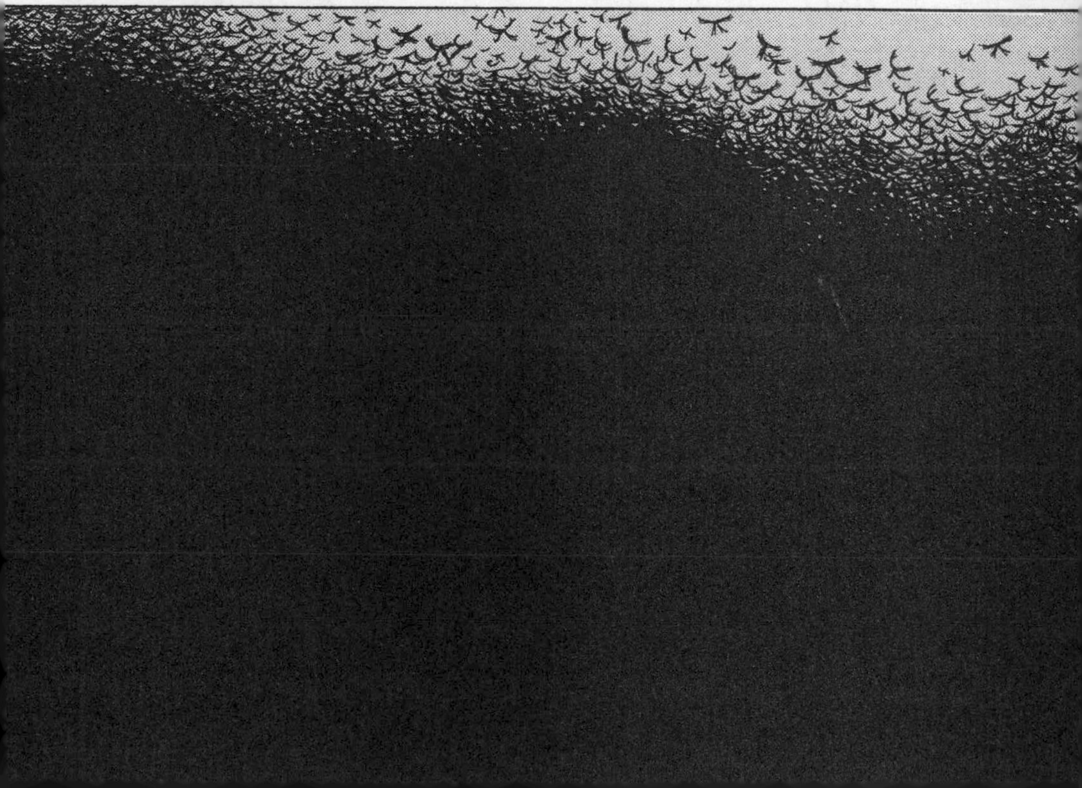

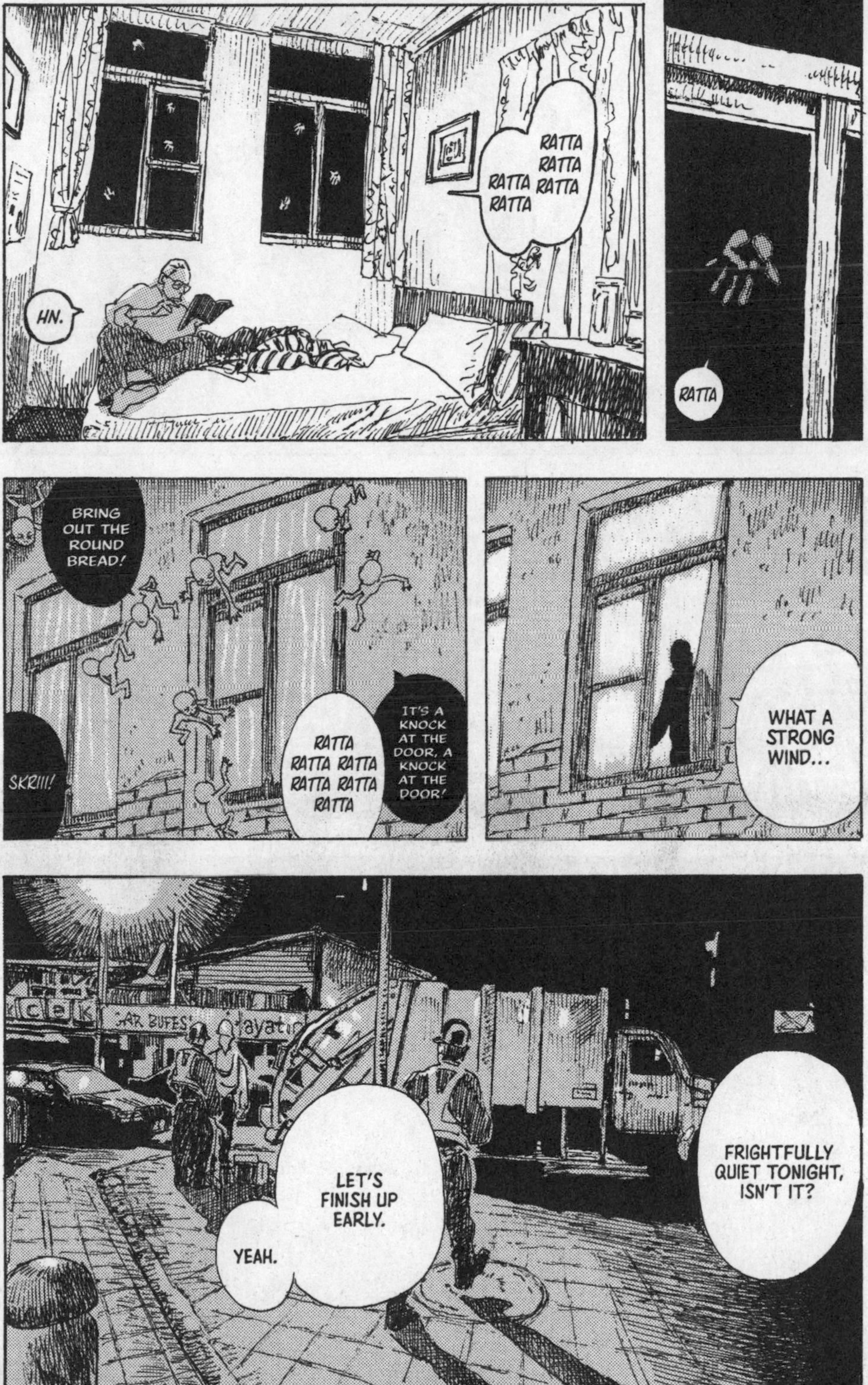
RATTA
RATTA RATTA RATTA RATTA RATTA
HN.
WHAT A STRONG WIND...
BRING OUT THE ROUND BREAD!
IT'S A KNOCK AT THE DOOR, A KNOCK AT THE DOOR!
RATTA RATTA RATTA RATTA RATTA RATTA
SKRIII!
FRIGHTFULLY QUIET TONIGHT, ISN'T IT?
LET'S FINISH UP EARLY.
YEAH.

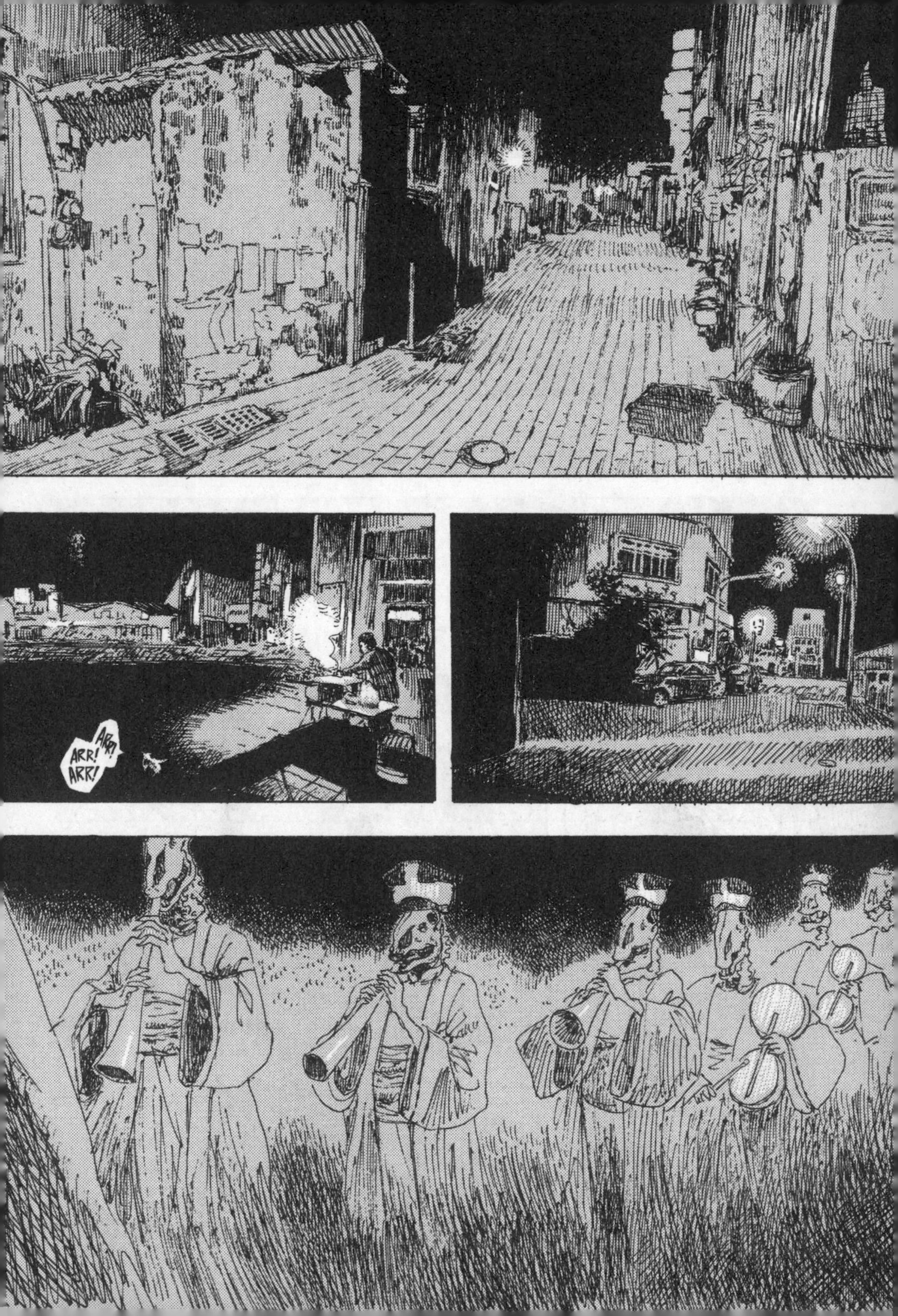
ARR!
ARR!
ARR!

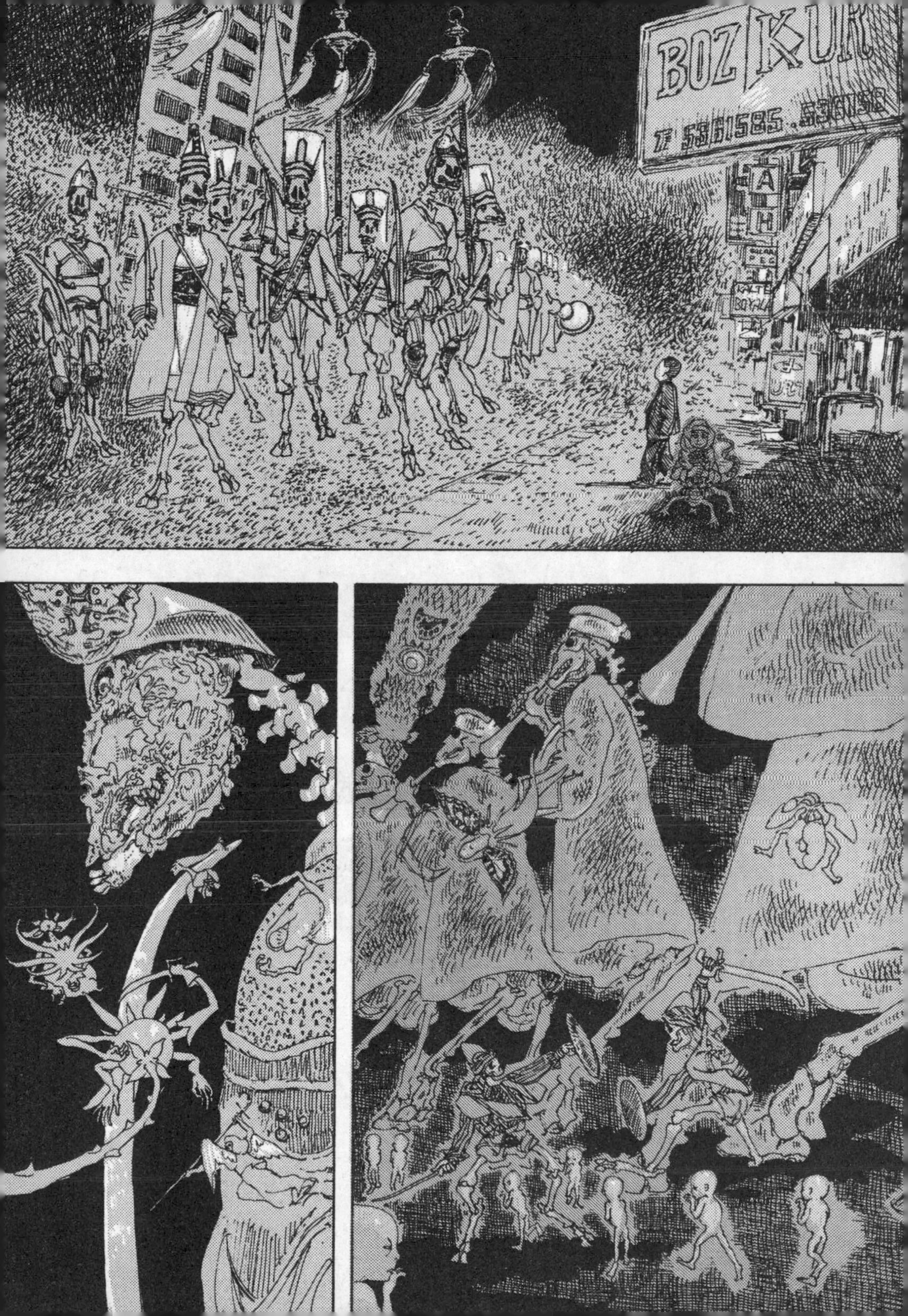
BOZ KUR
5361585
A
H

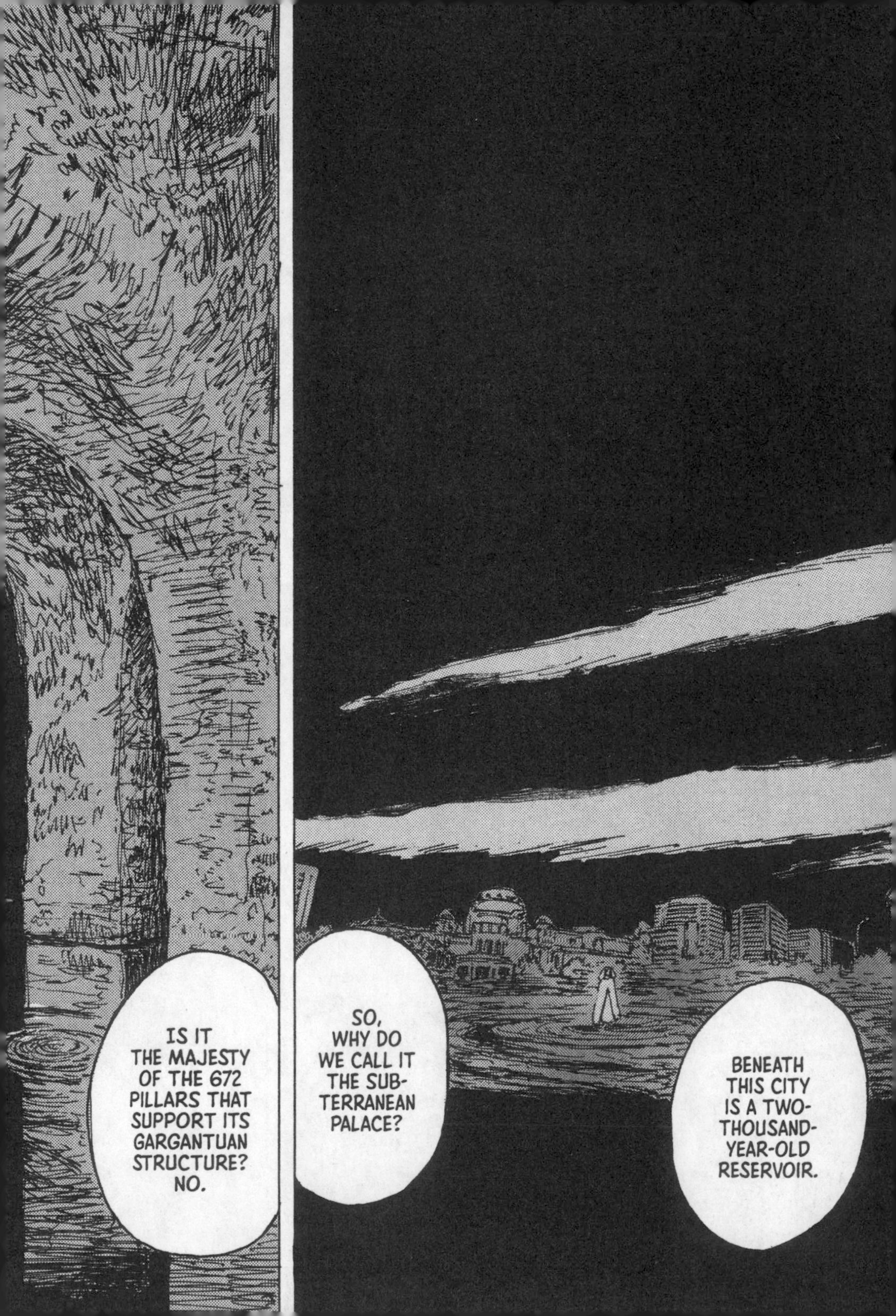
BENEATH THIS CITY IS A TWO-THOUSAND-YEAR-OLD RESERVOIR.
SO, WHY DO WE CALL IT THE SUBTERRANEAN PALACE?
IS IT THE MAJESTY OF THE 672 PILLARS THAT SUPPORT ITS GARGANTUAN STRUCTURE? NO.

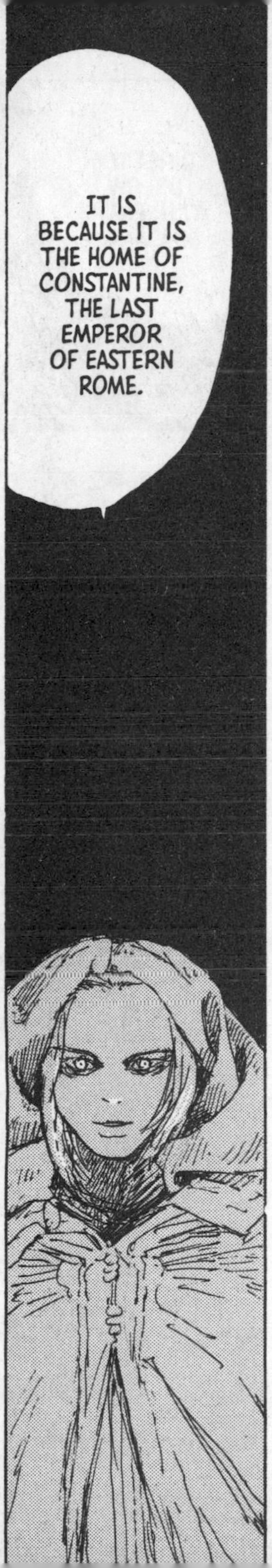
IT IS BECAUSE IT IS THE HOME OF CONSTANTINE, THE LAST EMPEROR OF EASTERN ROME.

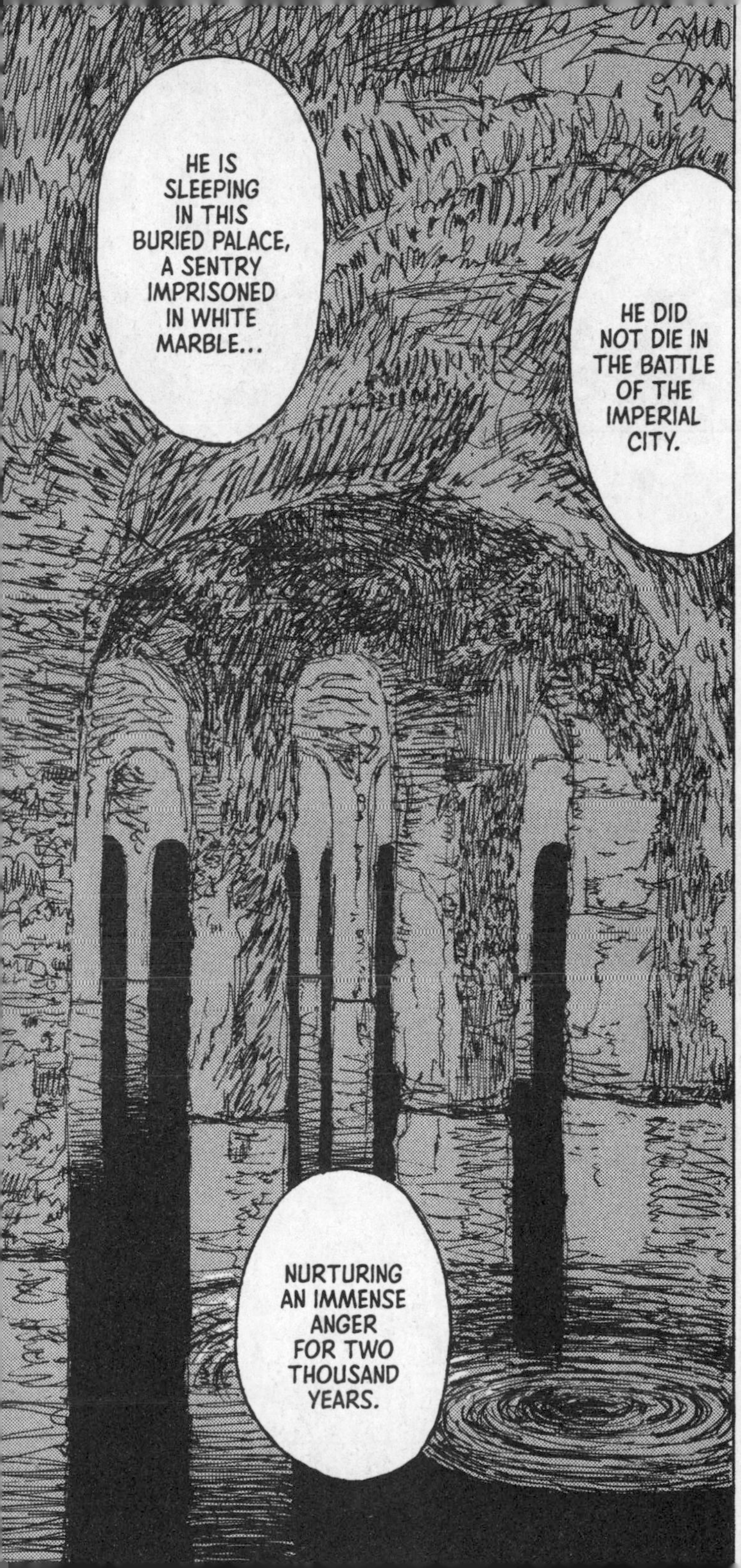
HE DID NOT DIE IN THE BATTLE OF THE IMPERIAL CITY.
HE IS SLEEPING IN THIS BURIED PALACE, A SENTRY IMPRISONED IN WHITE MARBLE...
NURTURING AN IMMENSE ANGER FOR TWO THOUSAND YEARS.

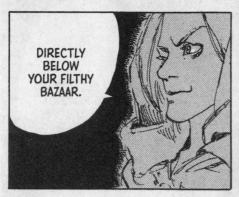

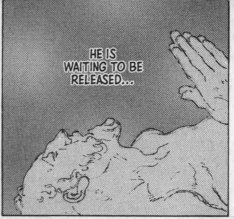

HE IS WAITING TO BE RELEASED...
DIRECTLY BELOW YOUR FILTHY BAZAAR.
DID YOU KNOW THAT THIS BUILDING...
IS A SEAL ENTRAPPING THE EMPEROR AND HIS GRUDGE?
MIMAR!

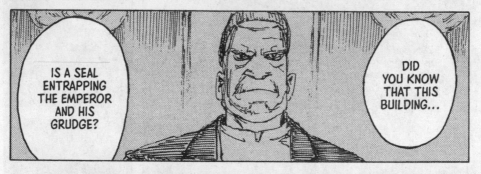

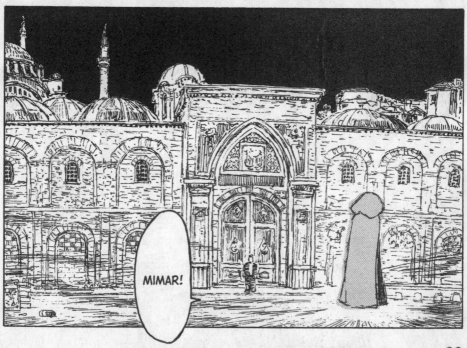

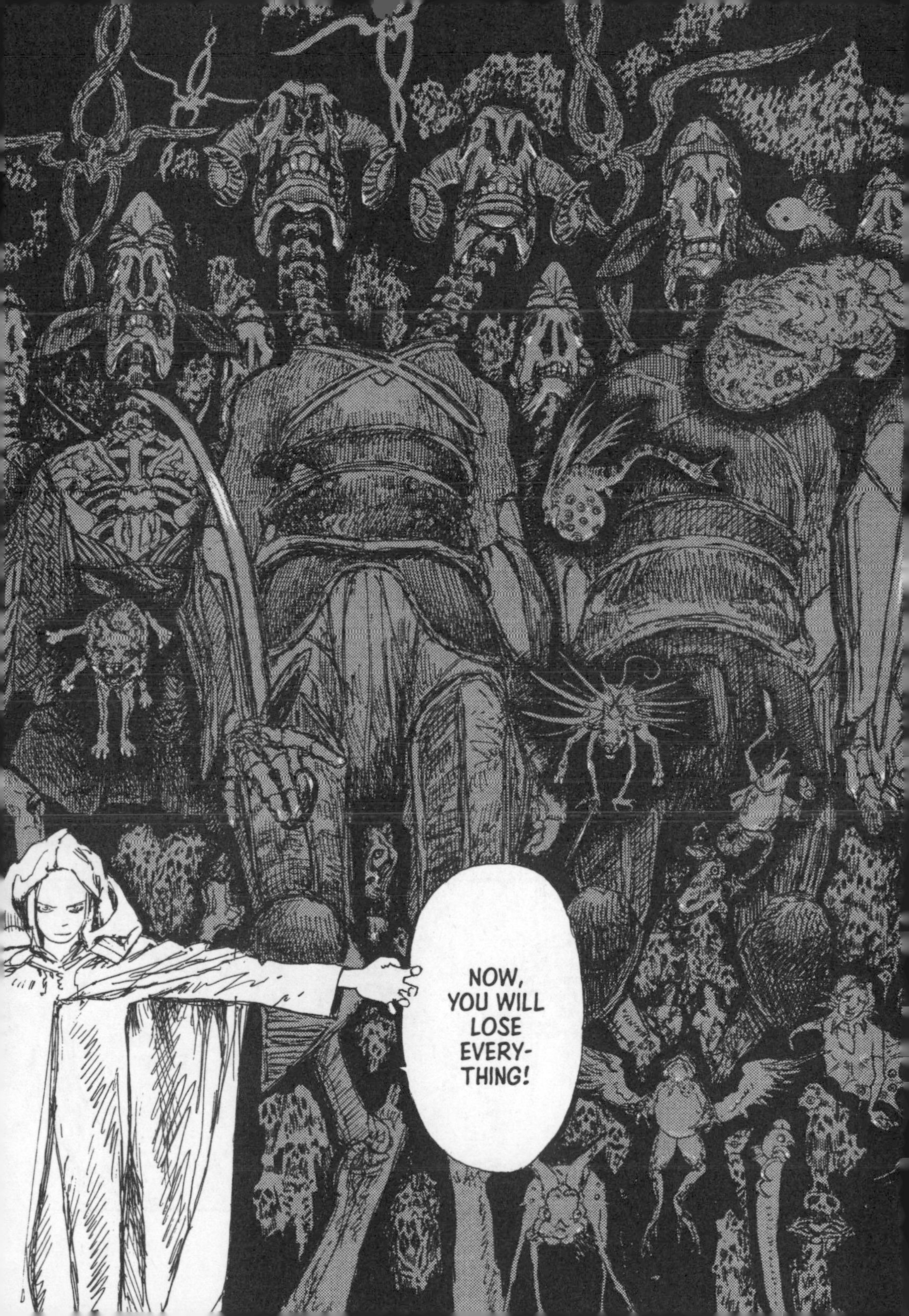
NOW, YOU WILL LOSE EVERY-THING!

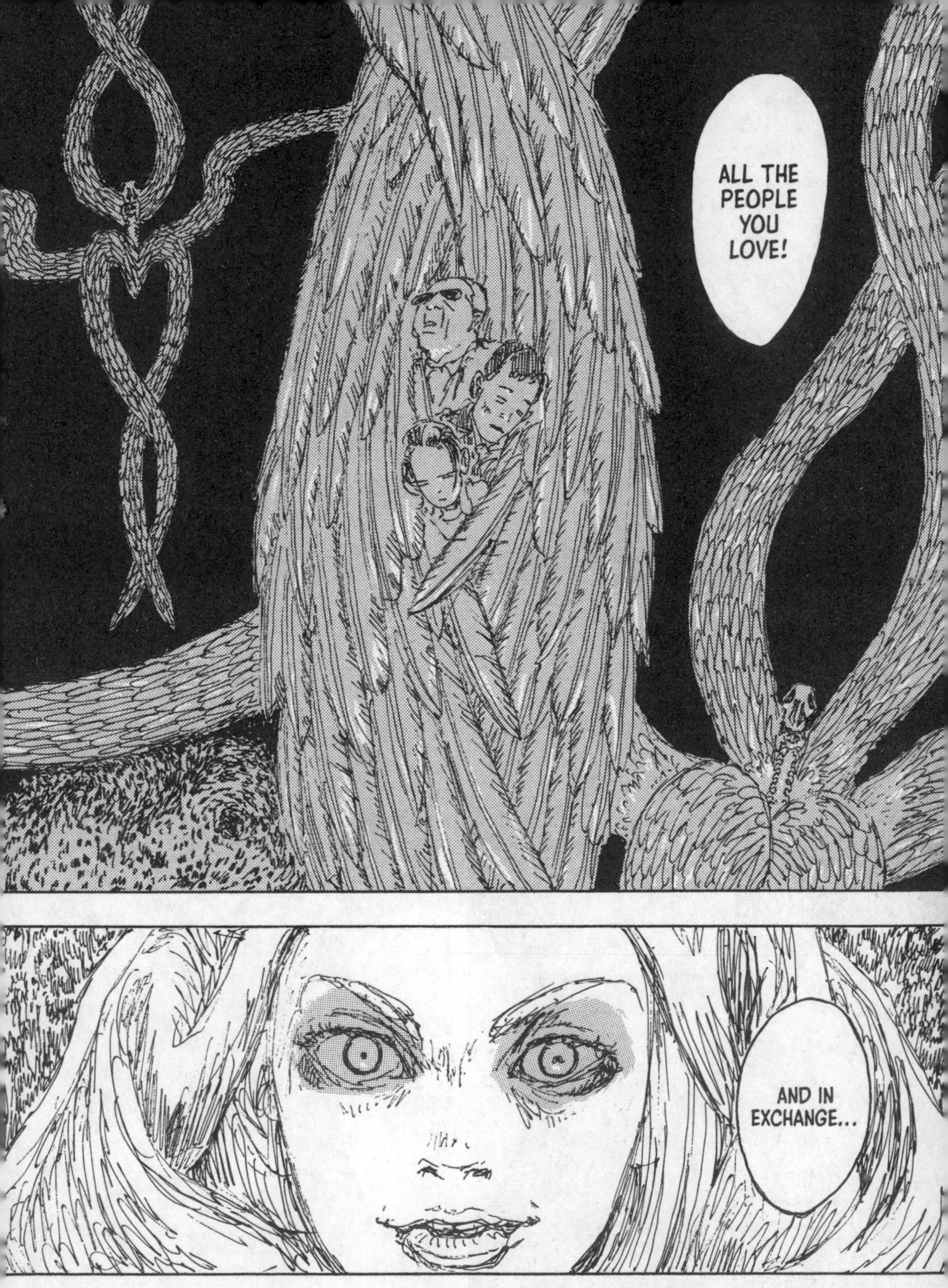
ALL THE PEOPLE YOU LOVE!
AND IN EXCHANGE...

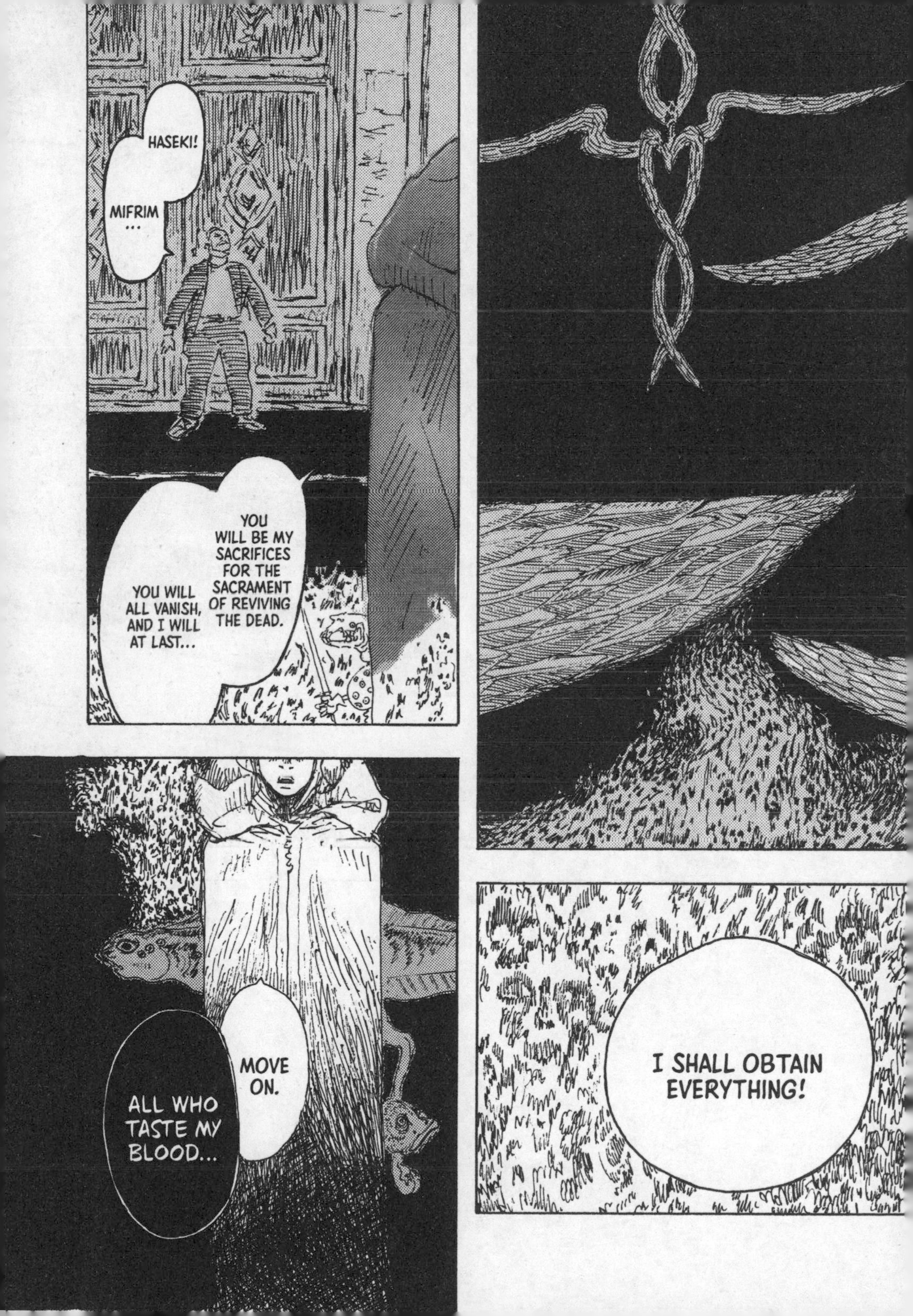
HASEKI!
MIFRIM...
YOU WILL BE MY SACRIFICES FOR THE SACRAMENT OF REVIVING THE DEAD.
YOU WILL ALL VANISH, AND I WILL AT LAST...
I SHALL OBTAIN EVERYTHING!
MOVE ON.
ALL WHO TASTE MY BLOOD...

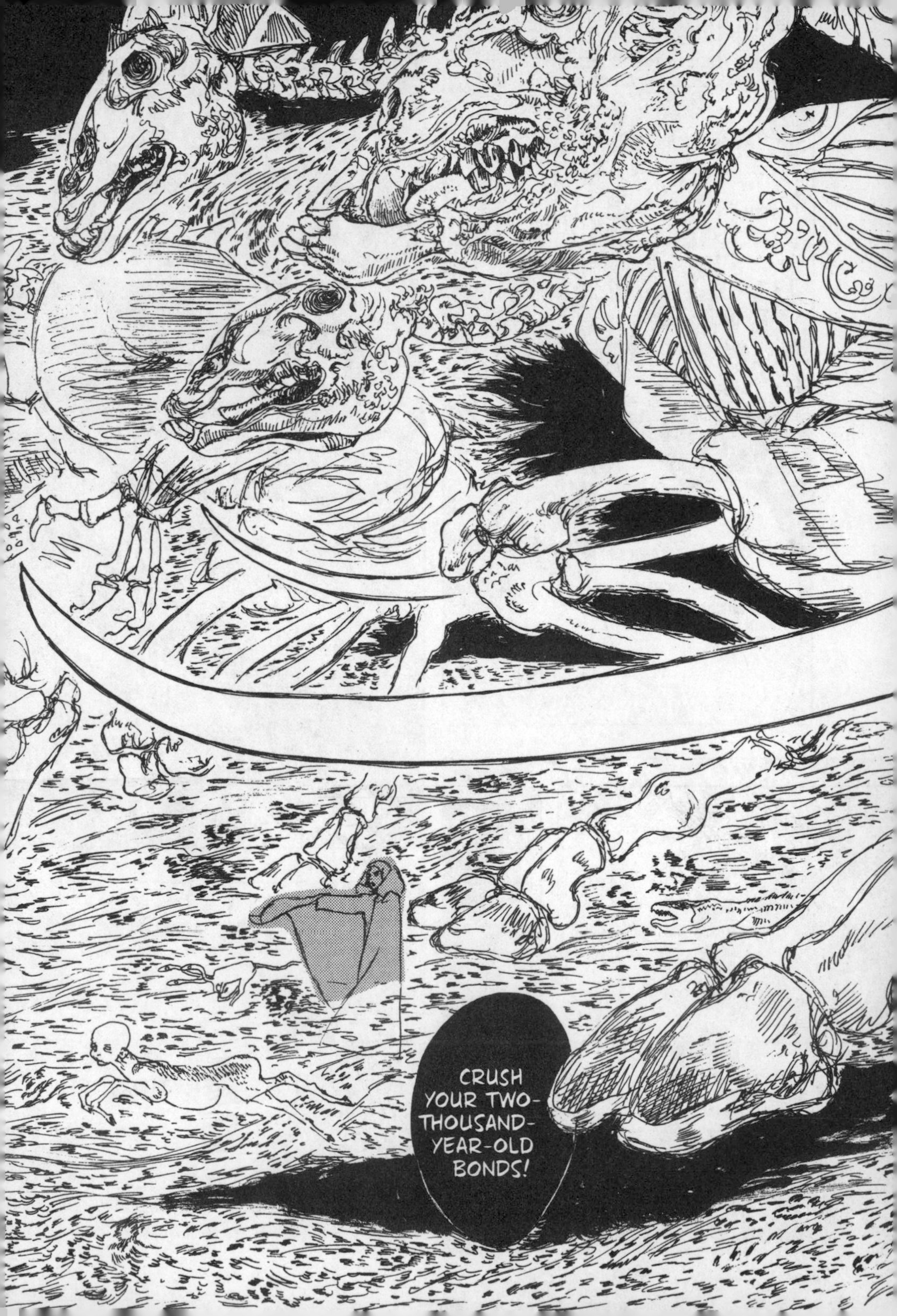
CRUSH YOUR TWO-THOUSAND-YEAR-OLD BONDS!

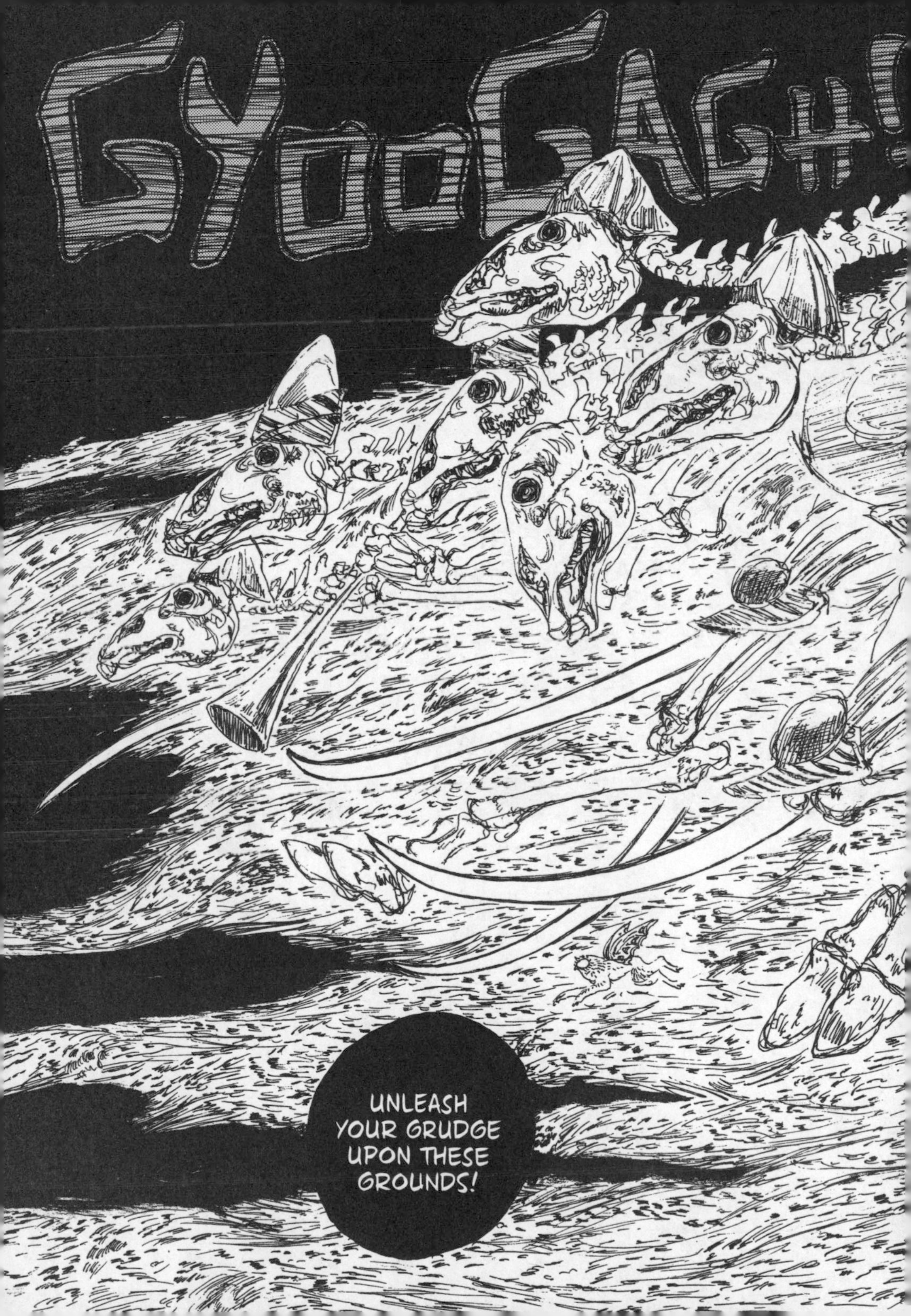
GYOOGAGH!
UNLEASH YOUR GRUDGE UPON THESE GROUNDS!

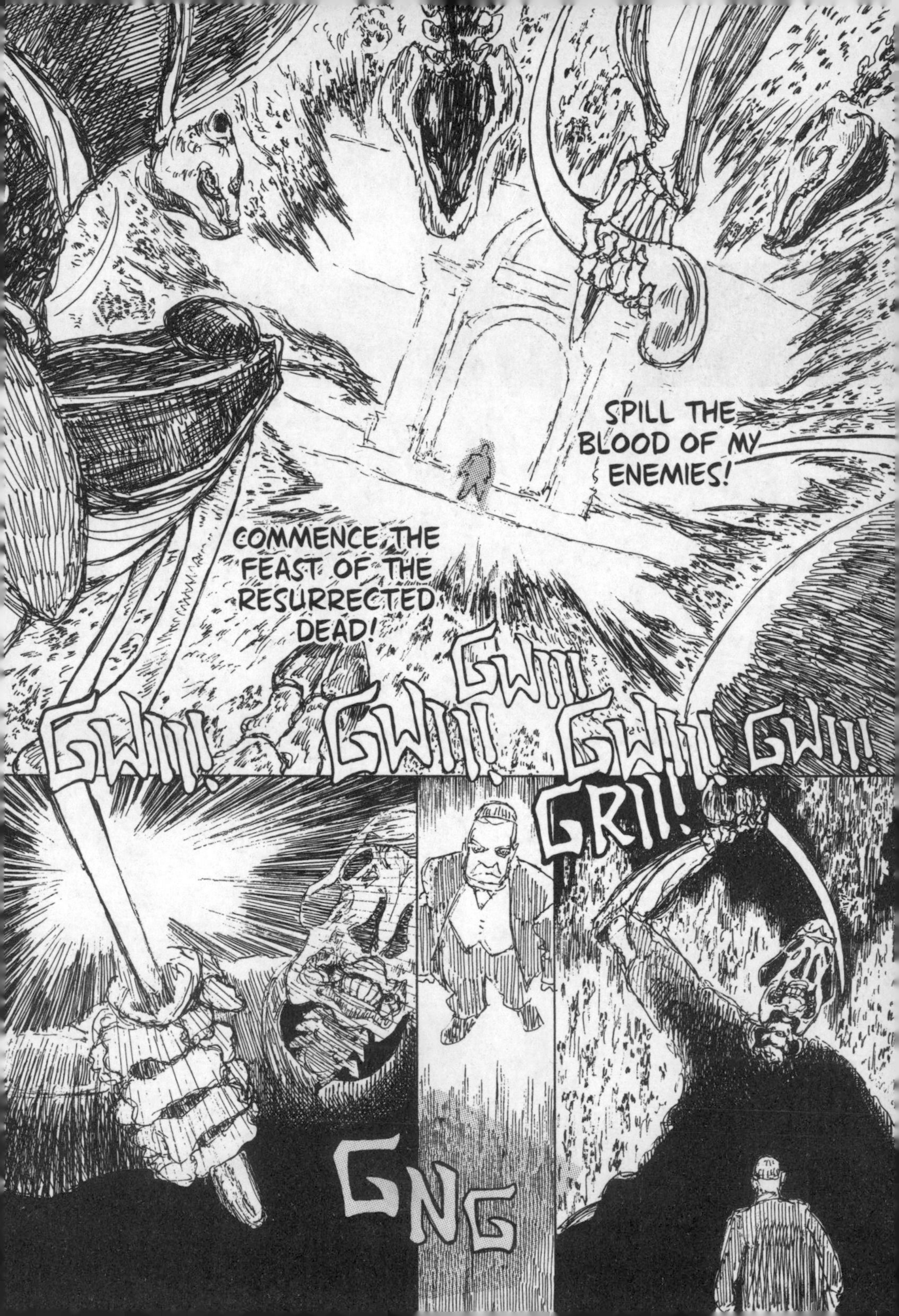
SPILL THE BLOOD OF MY ENEMIES!
COMMENCE THE FEAST OF THE RESURRECTED DEAD!
GWII! GWII!
GWII
GWII! GWII!
GRII!
GNG

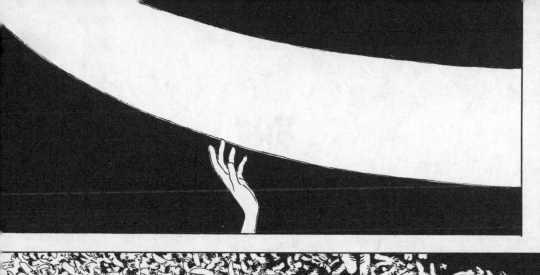

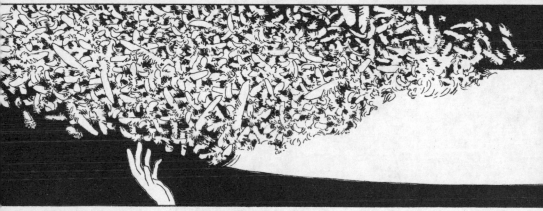

BWSSH

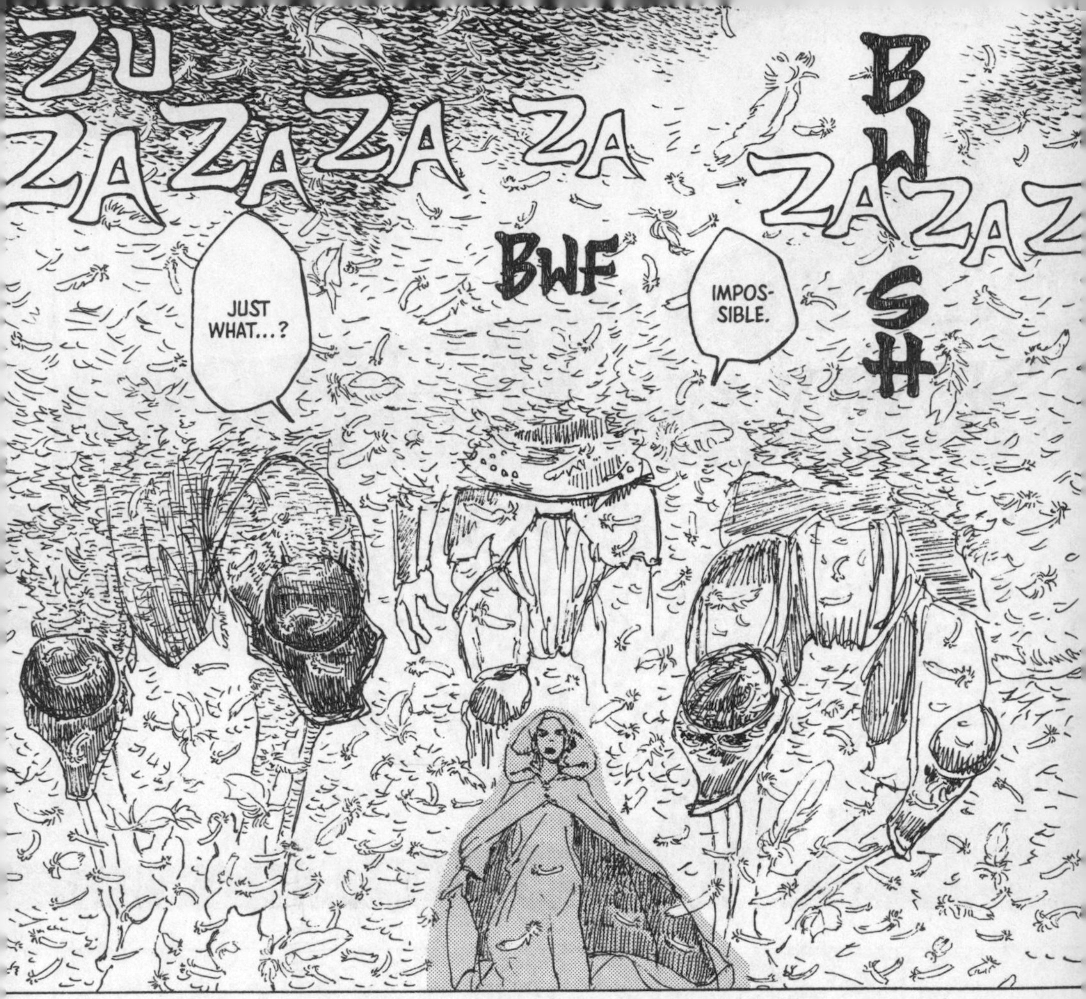
BWSH
ZAZAZ
IMPOS-
SIBLE.
BWF
ZU ZAZAZA ZA
JUST WHAT...?

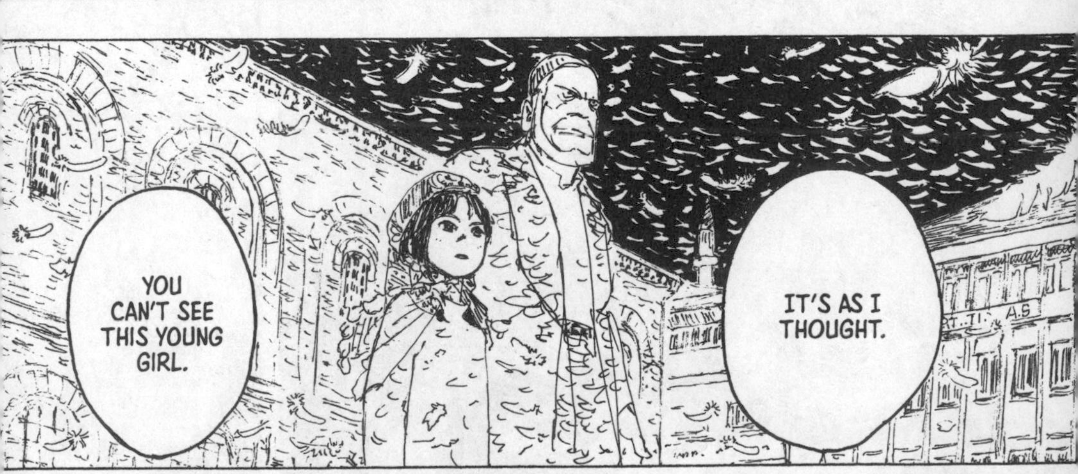
IT'S AS I THOUGHT.
YOU CAN'T SEE THIS YOUNG GIRL.

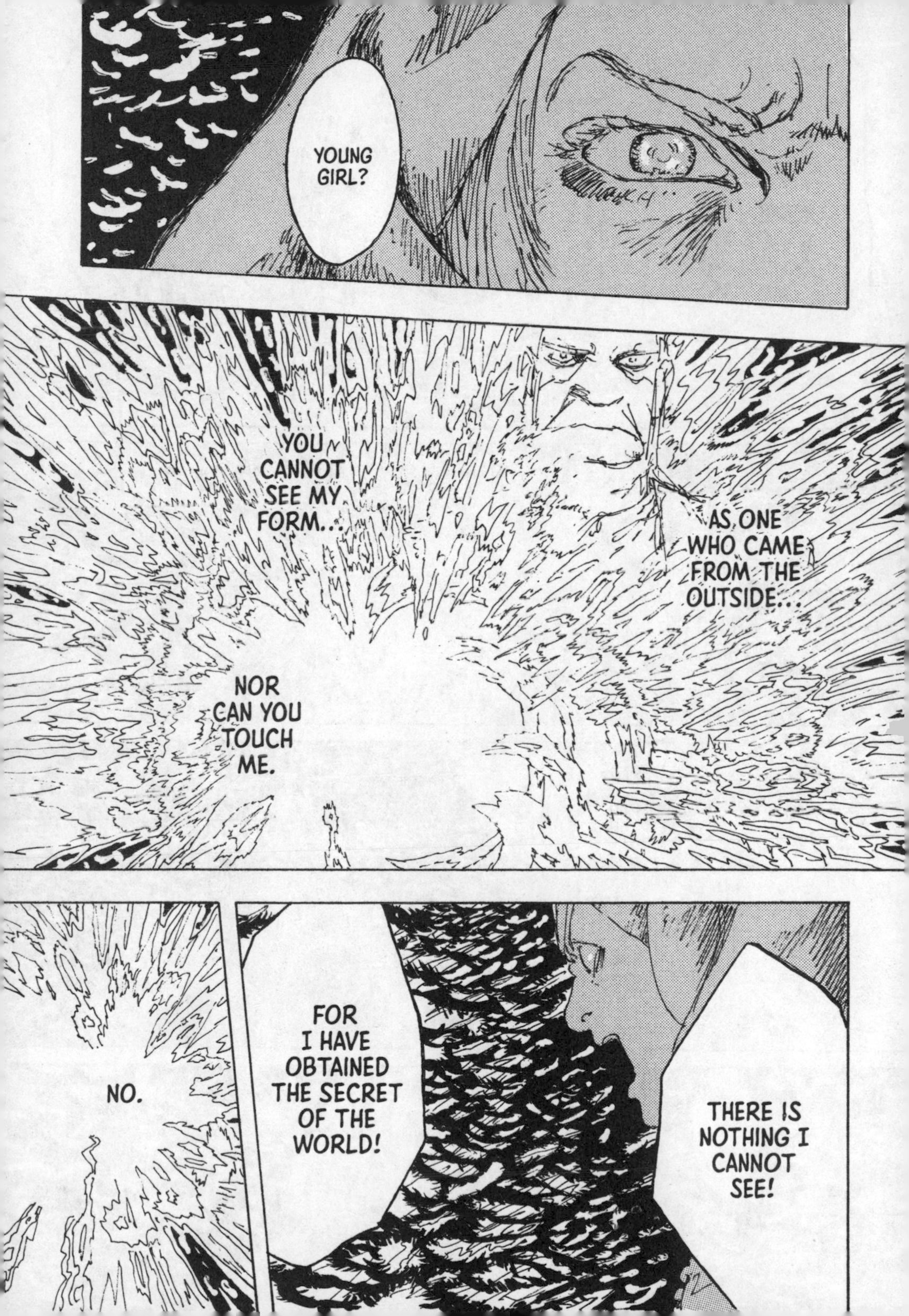
YOUNG GIRL?
AS ONE WHO CAME FROM THE OUTSIDE...
YOU CANNOT SEE MY FORM...
NOR CAN YOU TOUCH ME.
THERE IS NOTHING I CANNOT SEE!
FOR I HAVE OBTAINED THE SECRET OF THE WORLD!
NO.

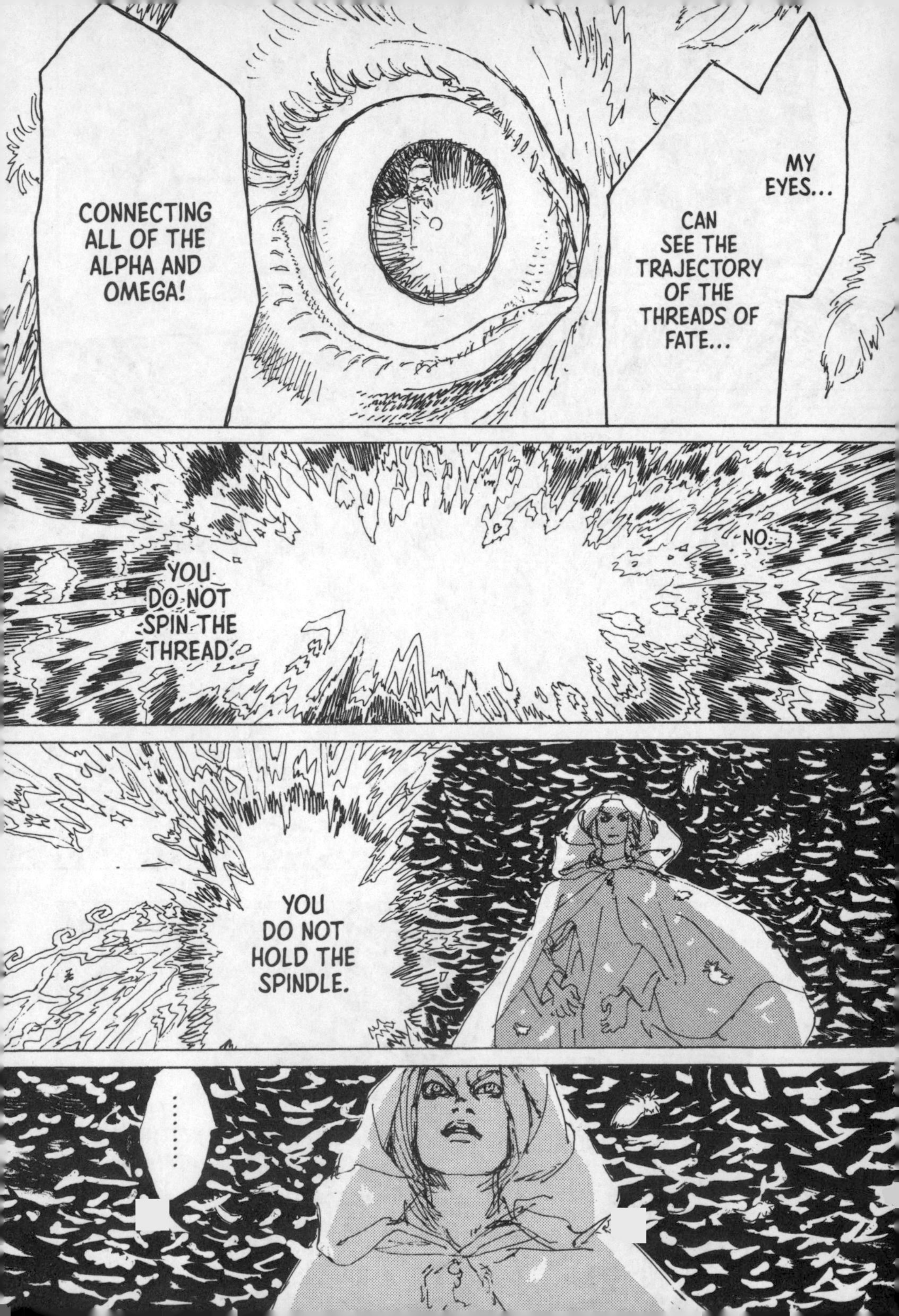
MY EYES...
CAN SEE THE TRAJECTORY OF THE THREADS OF FATE...
CONNECTING ALL OF THE ALPHA AND OMEGA!
NO.
YOU DO NOT SPIN THE THREAD.
YOU DO NOT HOLD THE SPINDLE.
......

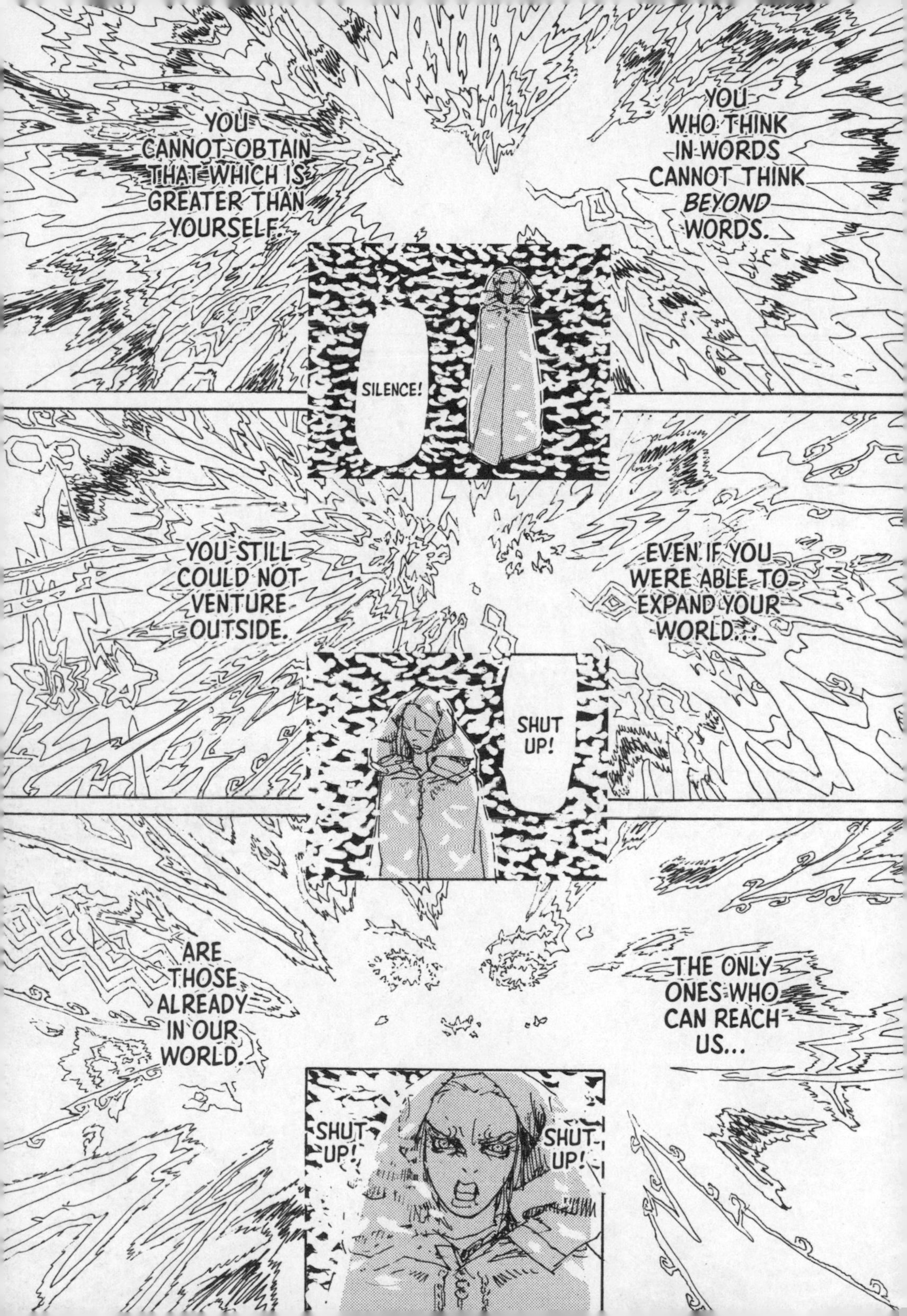
YOU WHO THINK IN WORDS CANNOT THINK *BEYOND* WORDS.
YOU CANNOT OBTAIN THAT WHICH IS GREATER THAN YOURSELF.
SILENCE!
EVEN IF YOU WERE ABLE TO EXPAND YOUR WORLD...
YOU STILL COULD NOT VENTURE OUTSIDE.
SHUT UP!
THE ONLY ONES WHO CAN REACH US...
ARE THOSE ALREADY IN OUR WORLD.
SHUT UP!
SHUT UP!

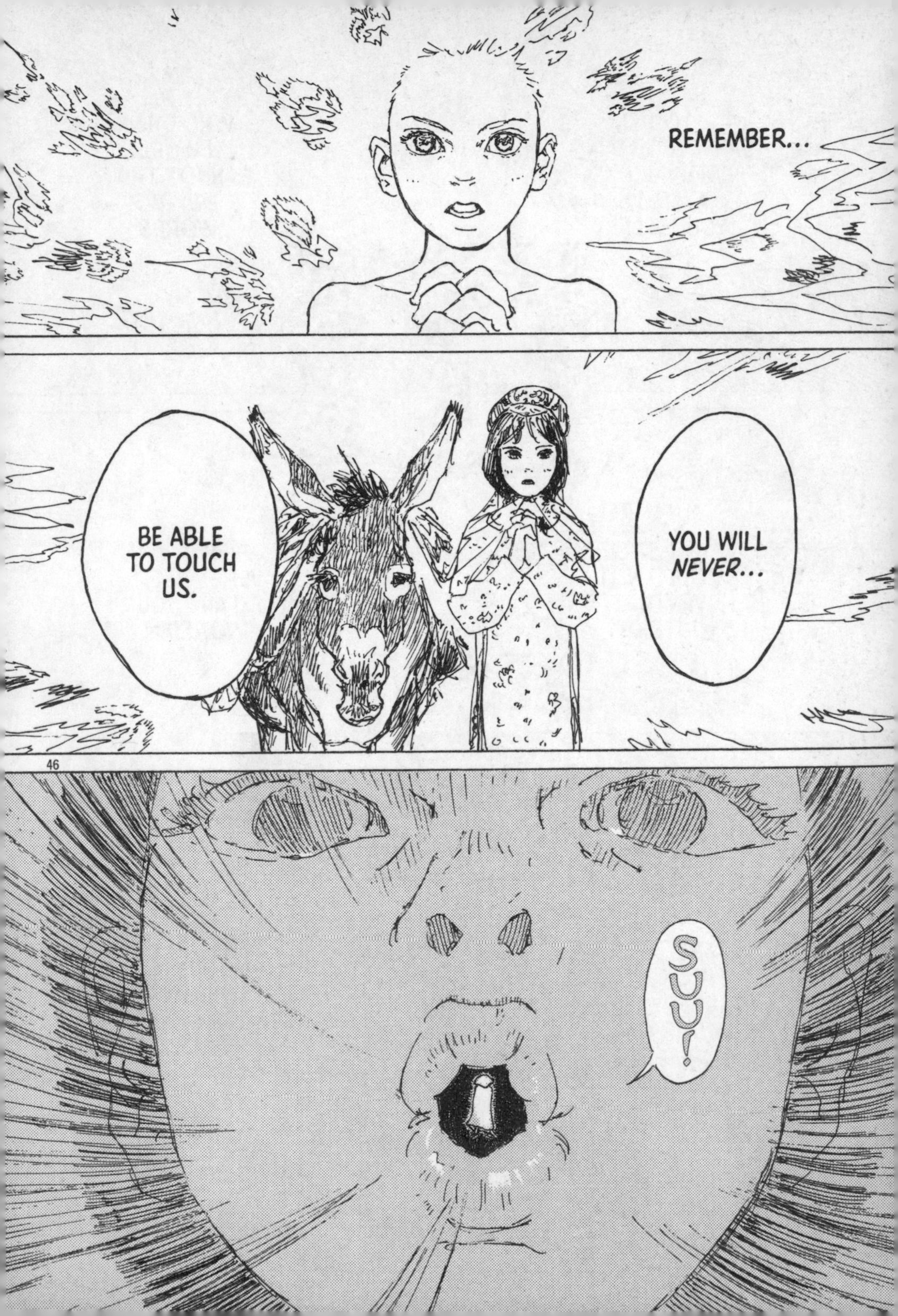
REMEMBER...
YOU WILL NEVER...
BE ABLE TO TOUCH US.
SUU!

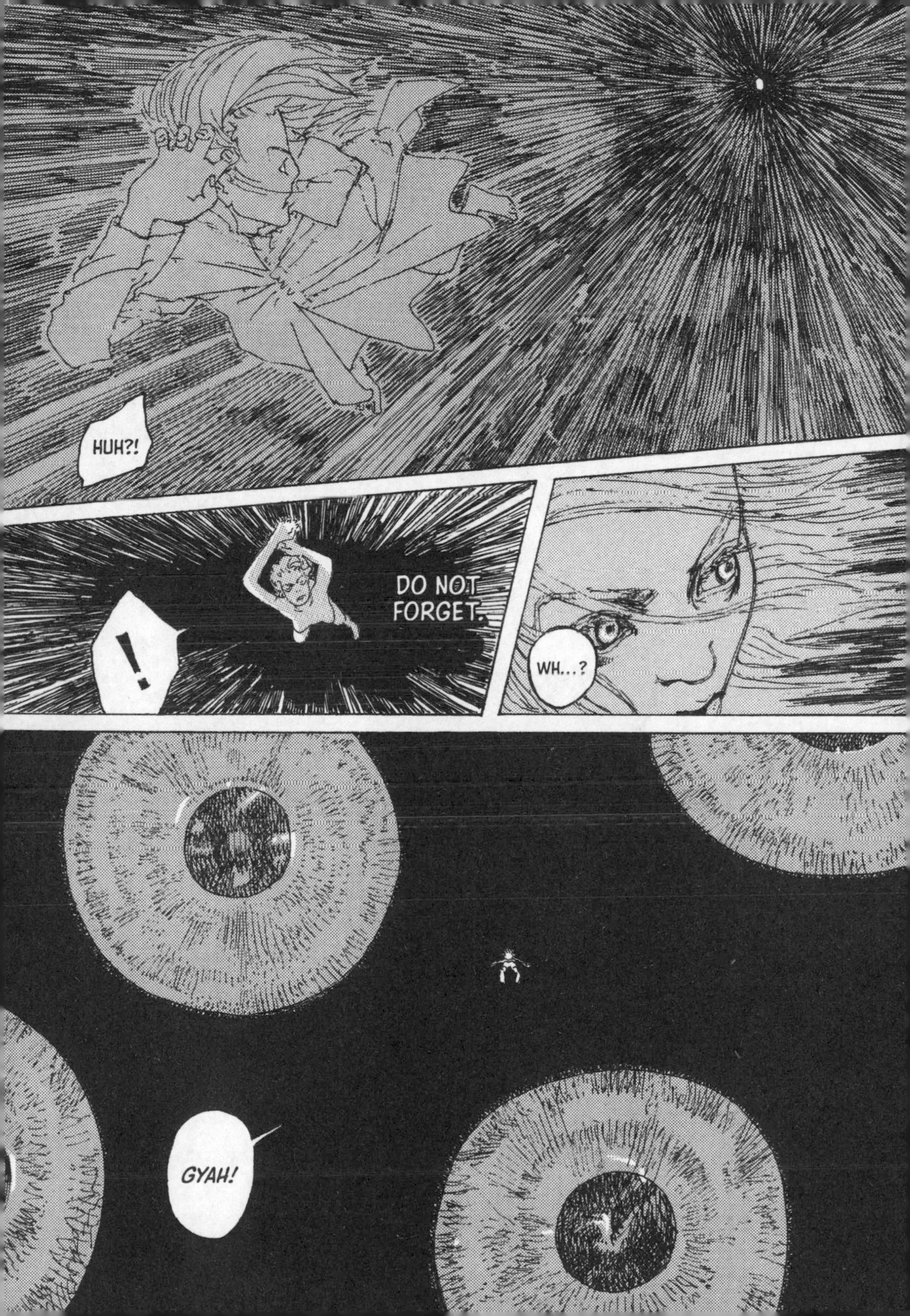
HUH?!
WH...?
DO NOT FORGET.
!
GYAH!

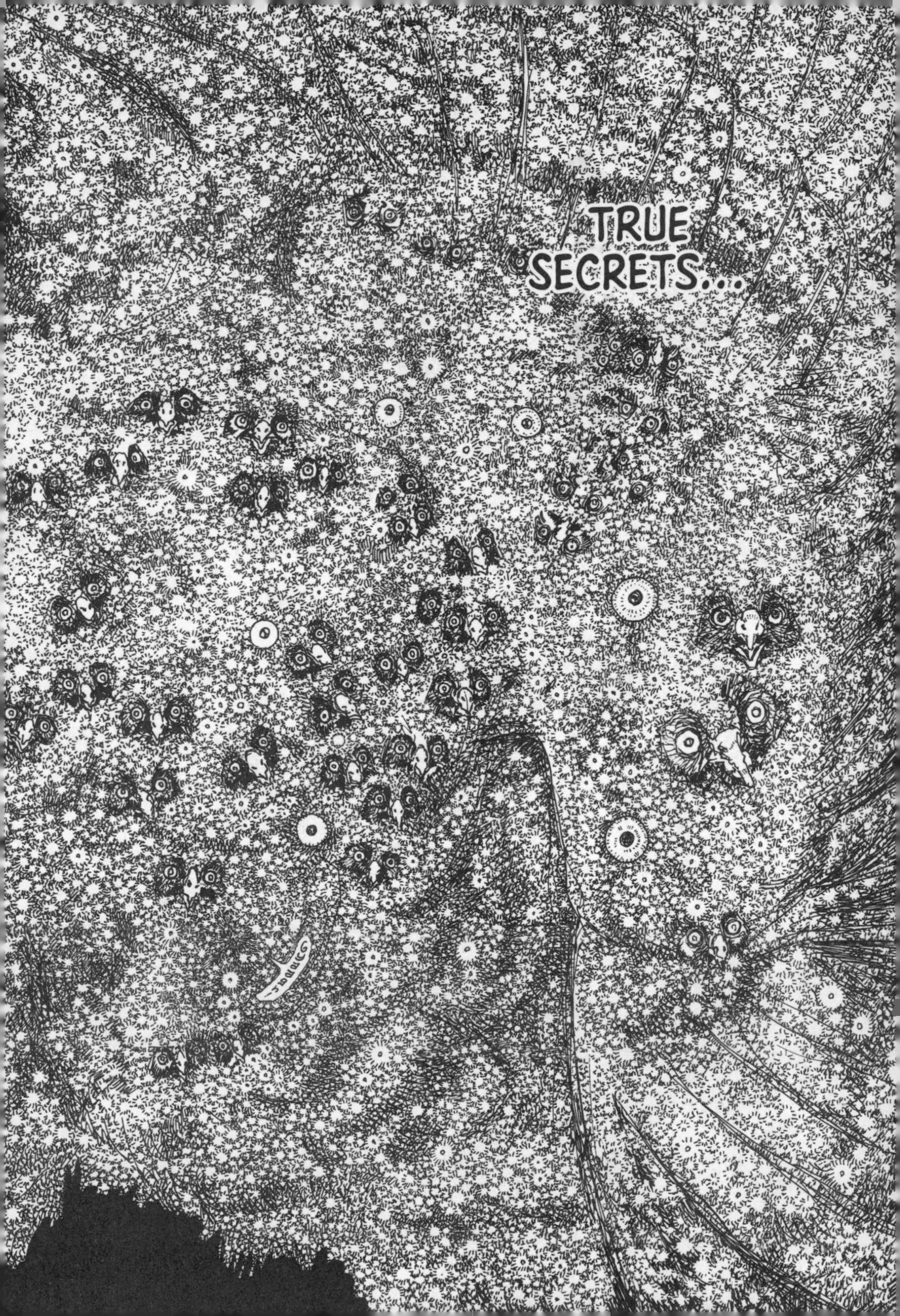
TRUE SECRETS...

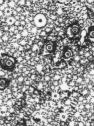

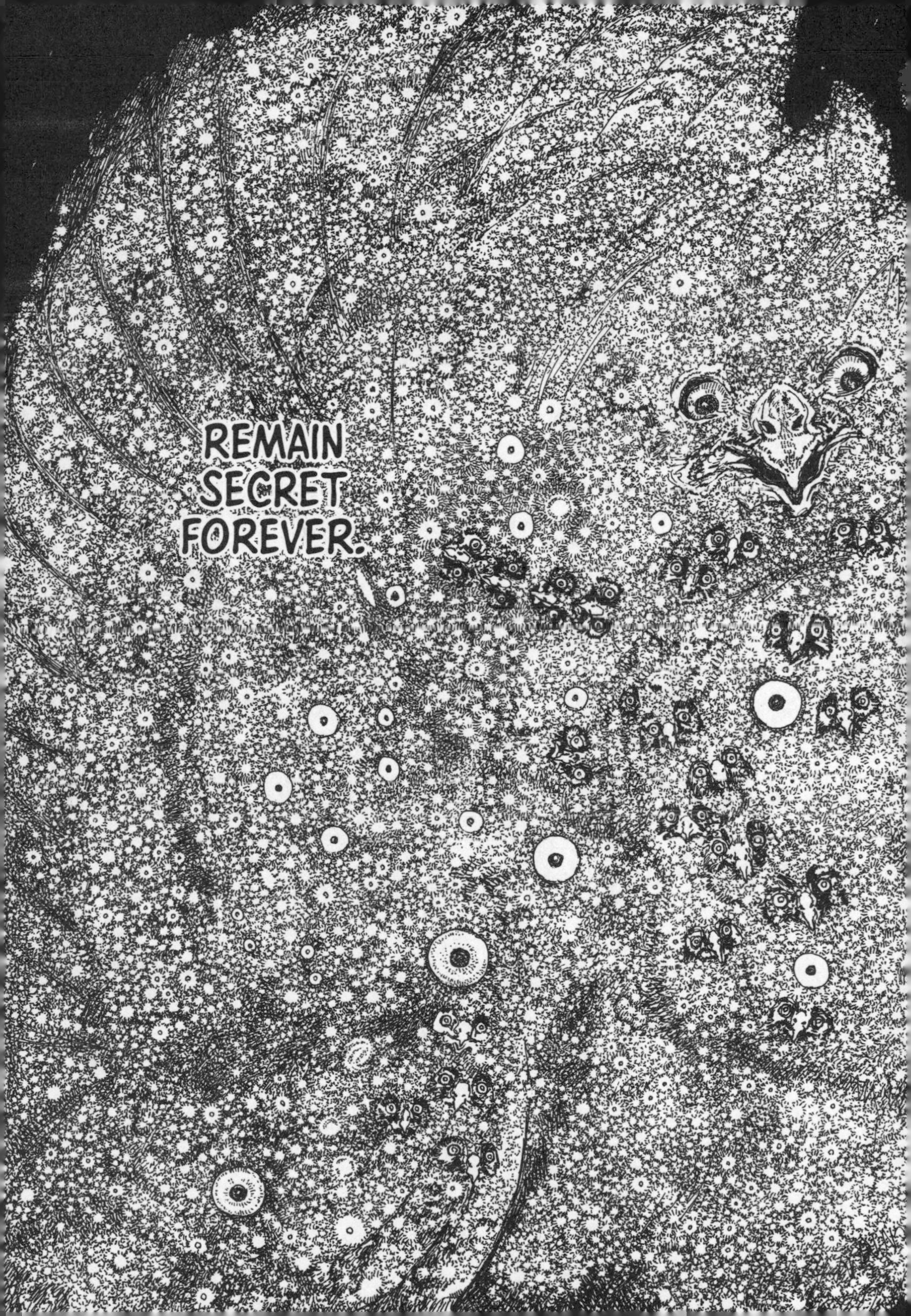

REMAIN
SECRET
FOREVER.

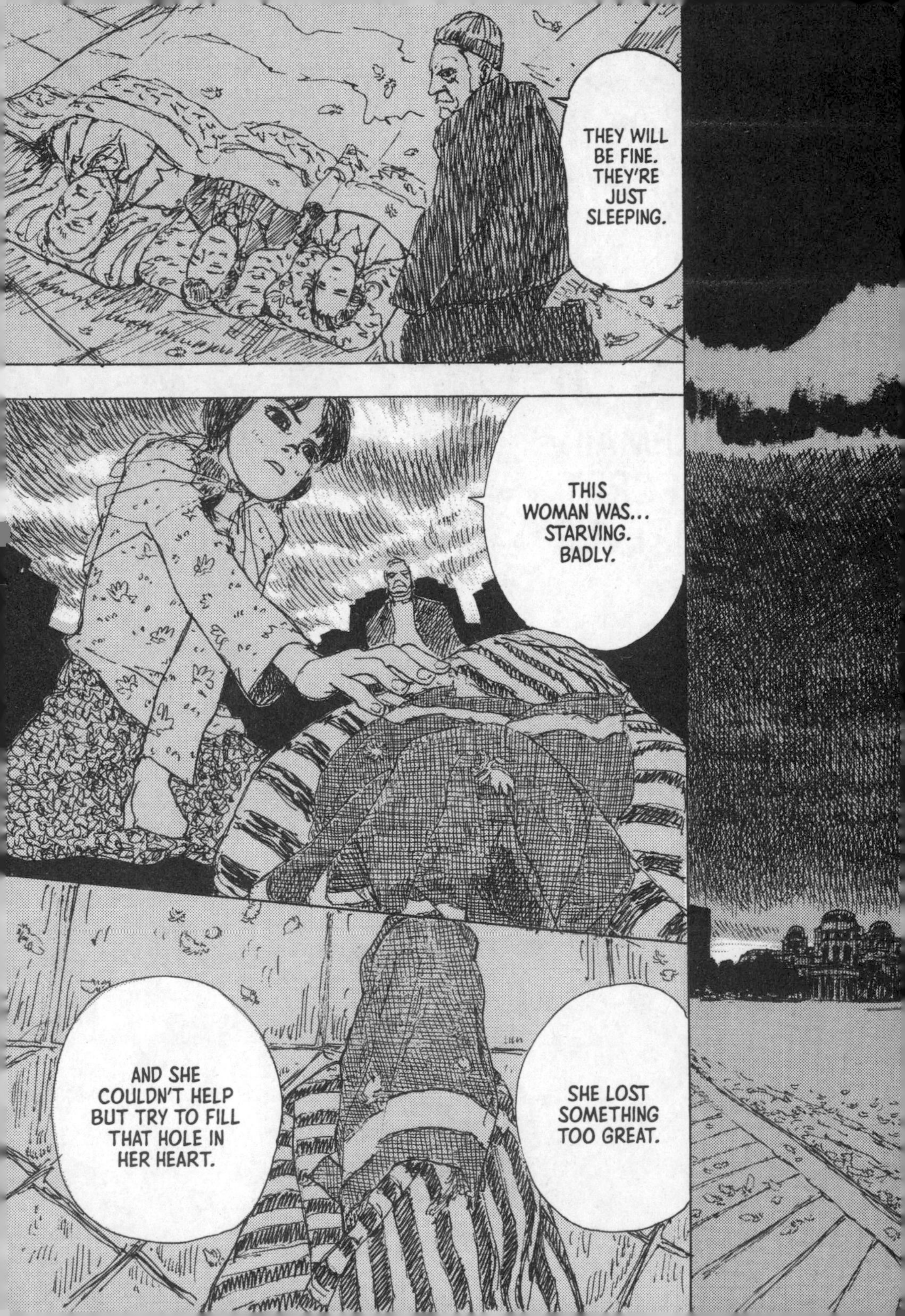
THEY WILL BE FINE. THEY'RE JUST SLEEPING.
THIS WOMAN WAS... STARVING. BADLY.
SHE LOST SOMETHING TOO GREAT.
AND SHE COULDN'T HELP BUT TRY TO FILL THAT HOLE IN HER HEART.

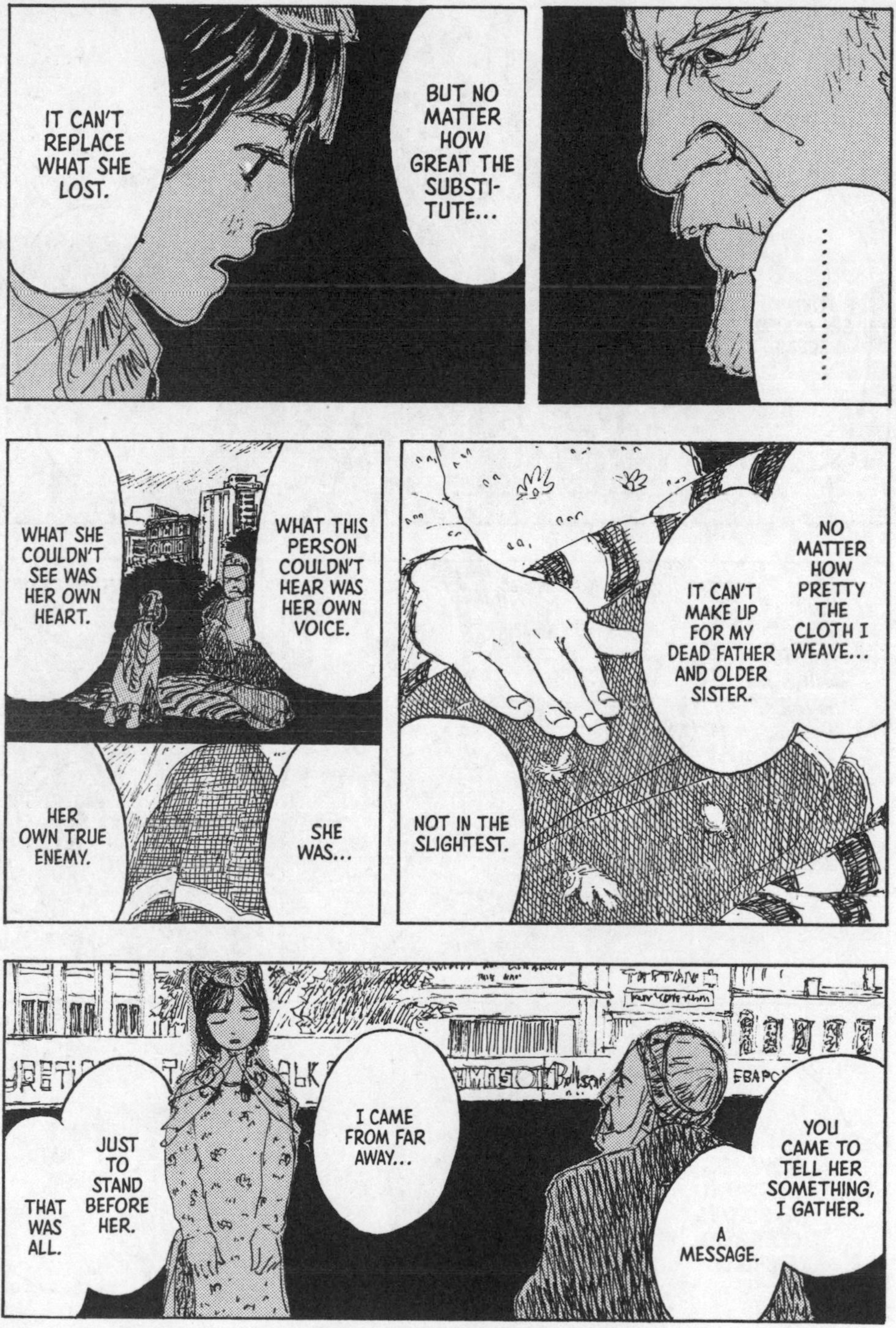
……
BUT NO MATTER HOW GREAT THE SUBSTITUTE…
IT CAN'T REPLACE WHAT SHE LOST.
NO MATTER HOW PRETTY THE CLOTH I WEAVE…
IT CAN'T MAKE UP FOR MY DEAD FATHER AND OLDER SISTER.
NOT IN THE SLIGHTEST.
WHAT THIS PERSON COULDN'T HEAR WAS HER OWN VOICE.
WHAT SHE COULDN'T SEE WAS HER OWN HEART.
SHE WAS…
HER OWN TRUE ENEMY.
YOU CAME TO TELL HER SOMETHING, I GATHER.
A MESSAGE.
I CAME FROM FAR AWAY…
JUST TO STAND BEFORE HER.
THAT WAS ALL.

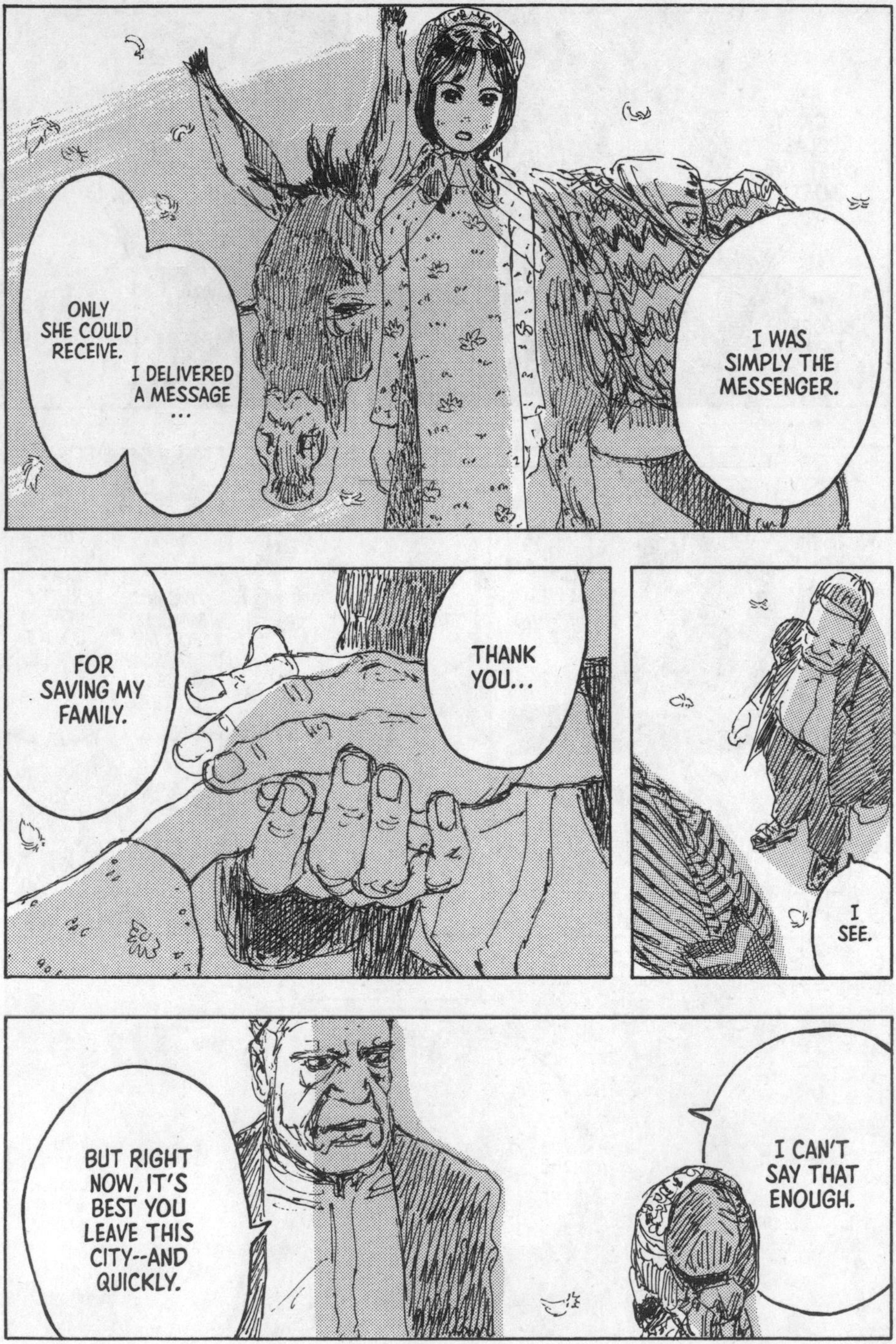
I WAS SIMPLY THE MESSENGER.
I DELIVERED A MESSAGE ...
ONLY SHE COULD RECEIVE.
I SEE.
THANK YOU...
FOR SAVING MY FAMILY.
I CAN'T SAY THAT ENOUGH.
BUT RIGHT NOW, IT'S BEST YOU LEAVE THIS CITY--AND QUICKLY.

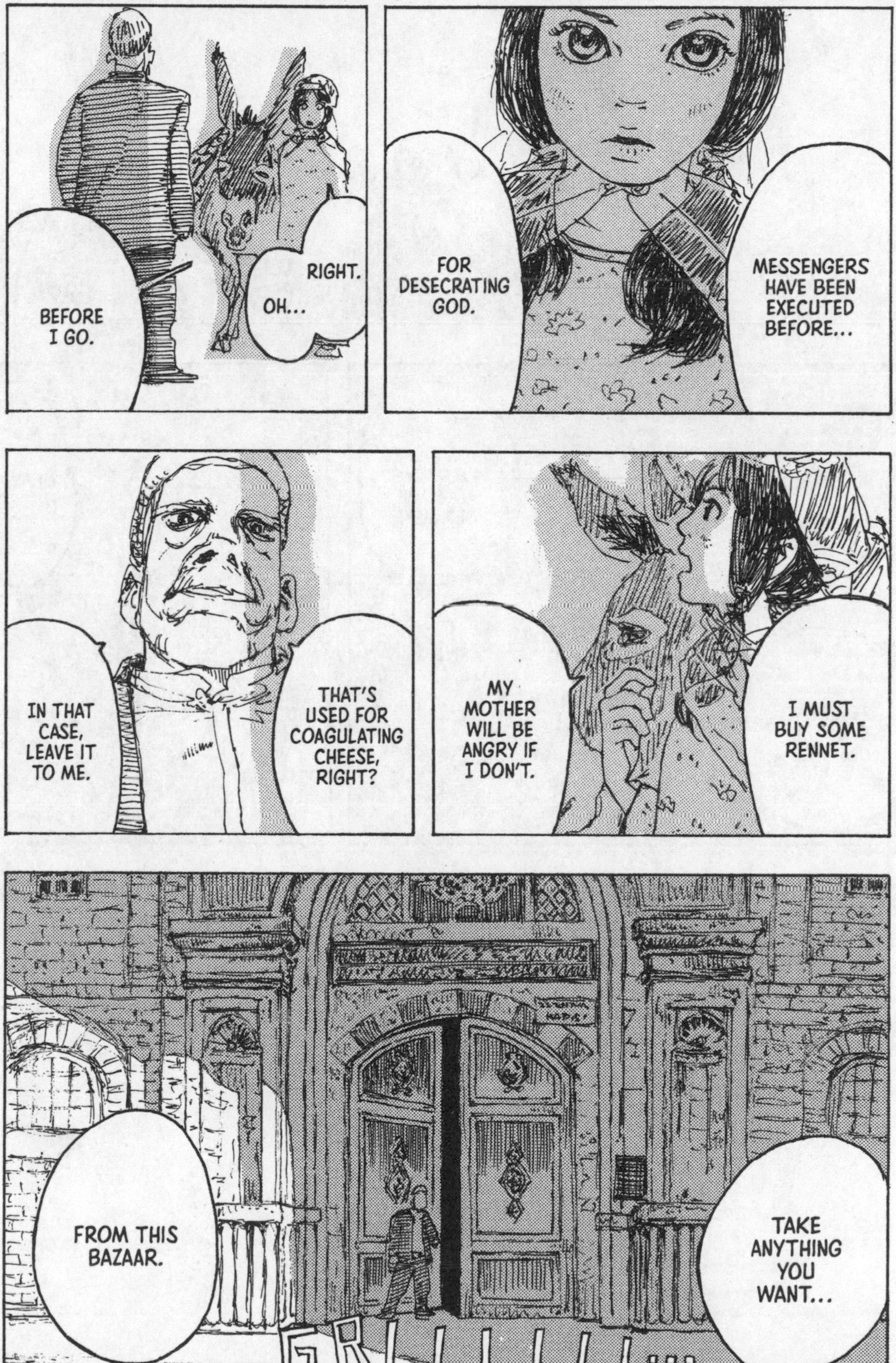
MESSENGERS HAVE BEEN EXECUTED BEFORE...
FOR DESECRATING GOD.
RIGHT.
OH...
BEFORE I GO.
I MUST BUY SOME RENNET.
MY MOTHER WILL BE ANGRY IF I DON'T.
THAT'S USED FOR COAGULATING CHEESE, RIGHT?
IN THAT CASE, LEAVE IT TO ME.
TAKE ANYTHING YOU WANT...
FROM THIS BAZAAR.
GRIIIIII...

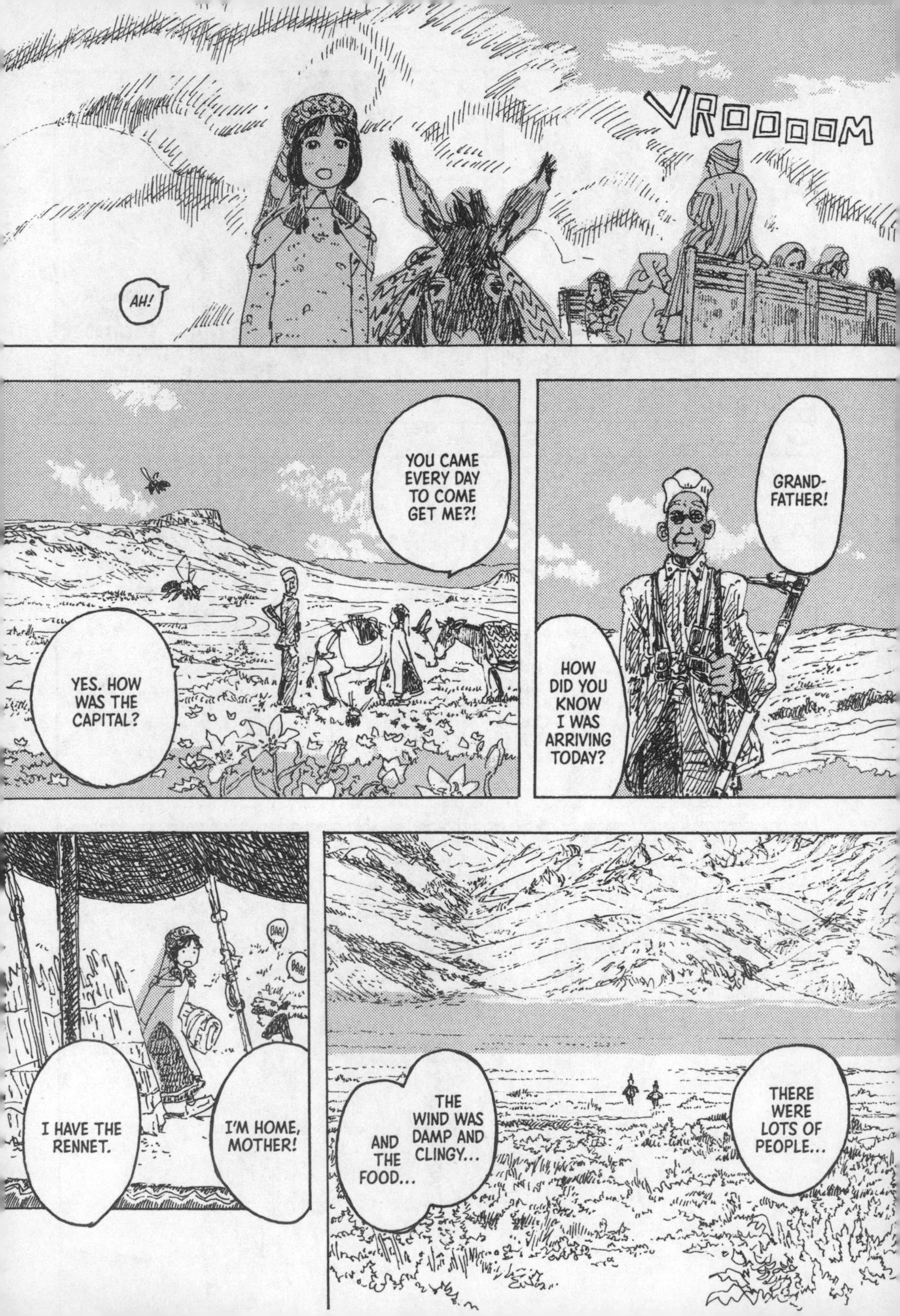
VROOOOOM
AH!
GRAND-FATHER!
HOW DID YOU KNOW I WAS ARRIVING TODAY?
YOU CAME EVERY DAY TO COME GET ME?!
YES. HOW WAS THE CAPITAL?
THERE WERE LOTS OF PEOPLE...
THE WIND WAS DAMP AND CLINGY...
AND THE FOOD...
BAA!
BAA!
I'M HOME, MOTHER!
I HAVE THE RENNET.

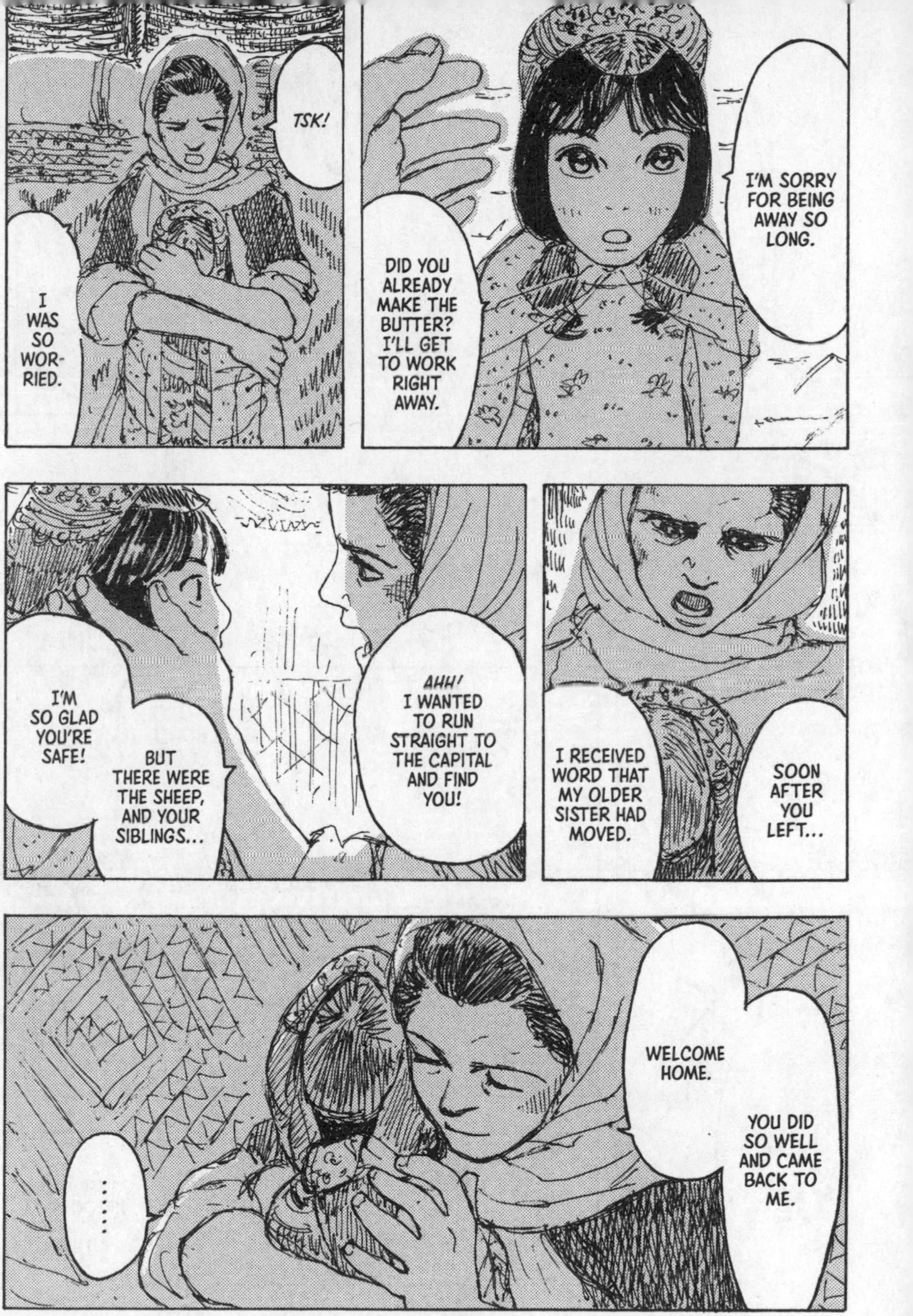
I'M SORRY FOR BEING AWAY SO LONG.
DID YOU ALREADY MAKE THE BUTTER? I'LL GET TO WORK RIGHT AWAY.
TSK!
I WAS SO WOR-RIED.
SOON AFTER YOU LEFT...
I RECEIVED WORD THAT MY OLDER SISTER HAD MOVED.
AHH! I WANTED TO RUN STRAIGHT TO THE CAPITAL AND FIND YOU!
BUT THERE WERE THE SHEEP, AND YOUR SIBLINGS...
I'M SO GLAD YOU'RE SAFE!
WELCOME HOME.
YOU DID SO WELL AND CAME BACK TO ME.
......

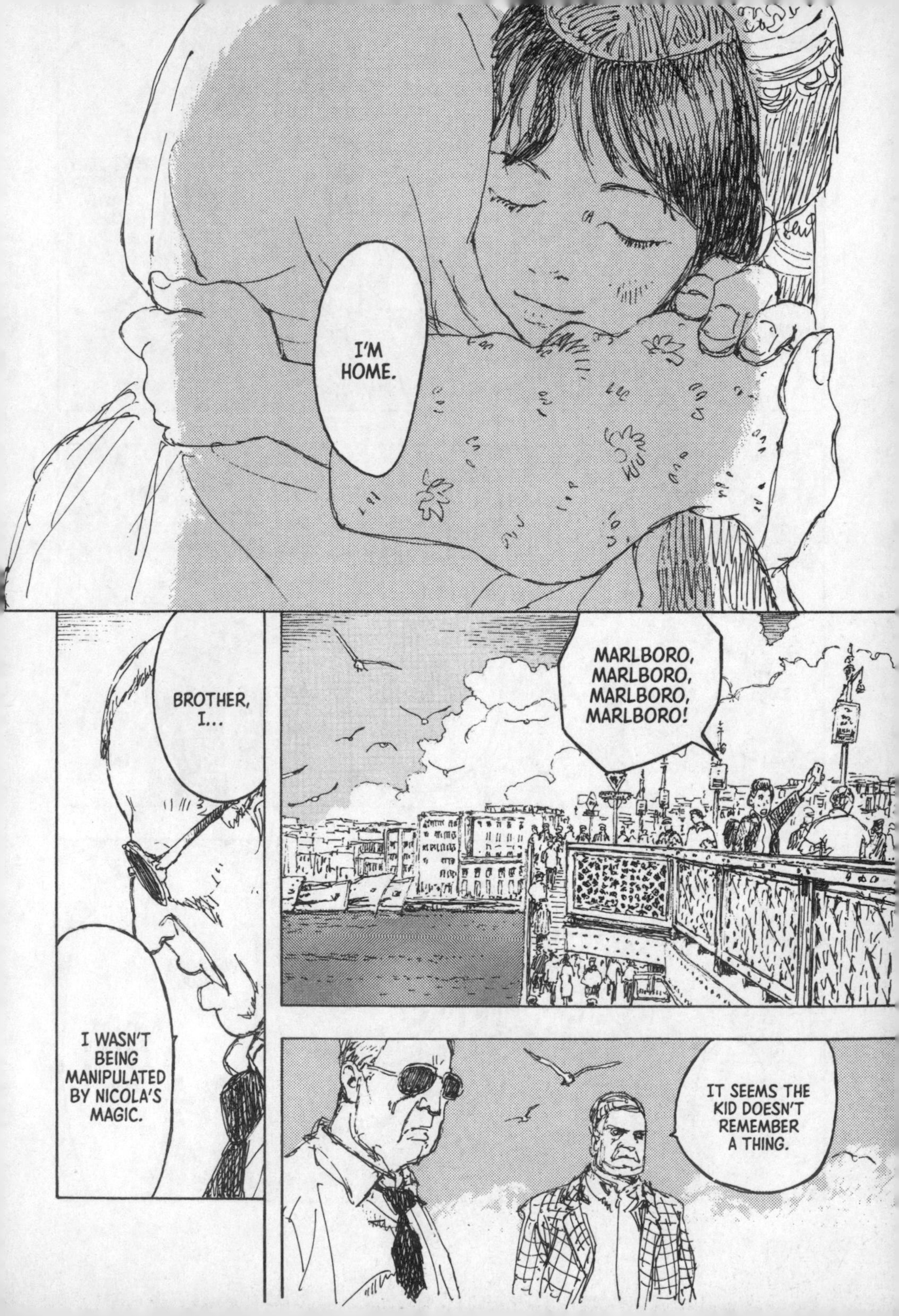
I'M HOME.
MARLBORO, MARLBORO, MARLBORO, MARLBORO!
IT SEEMS THE KID DOESN'T REMEMBER A THING.
BROTHER, I...
I WASN'T BEING MANIPULATED BY NICOLA'S MAGIC.

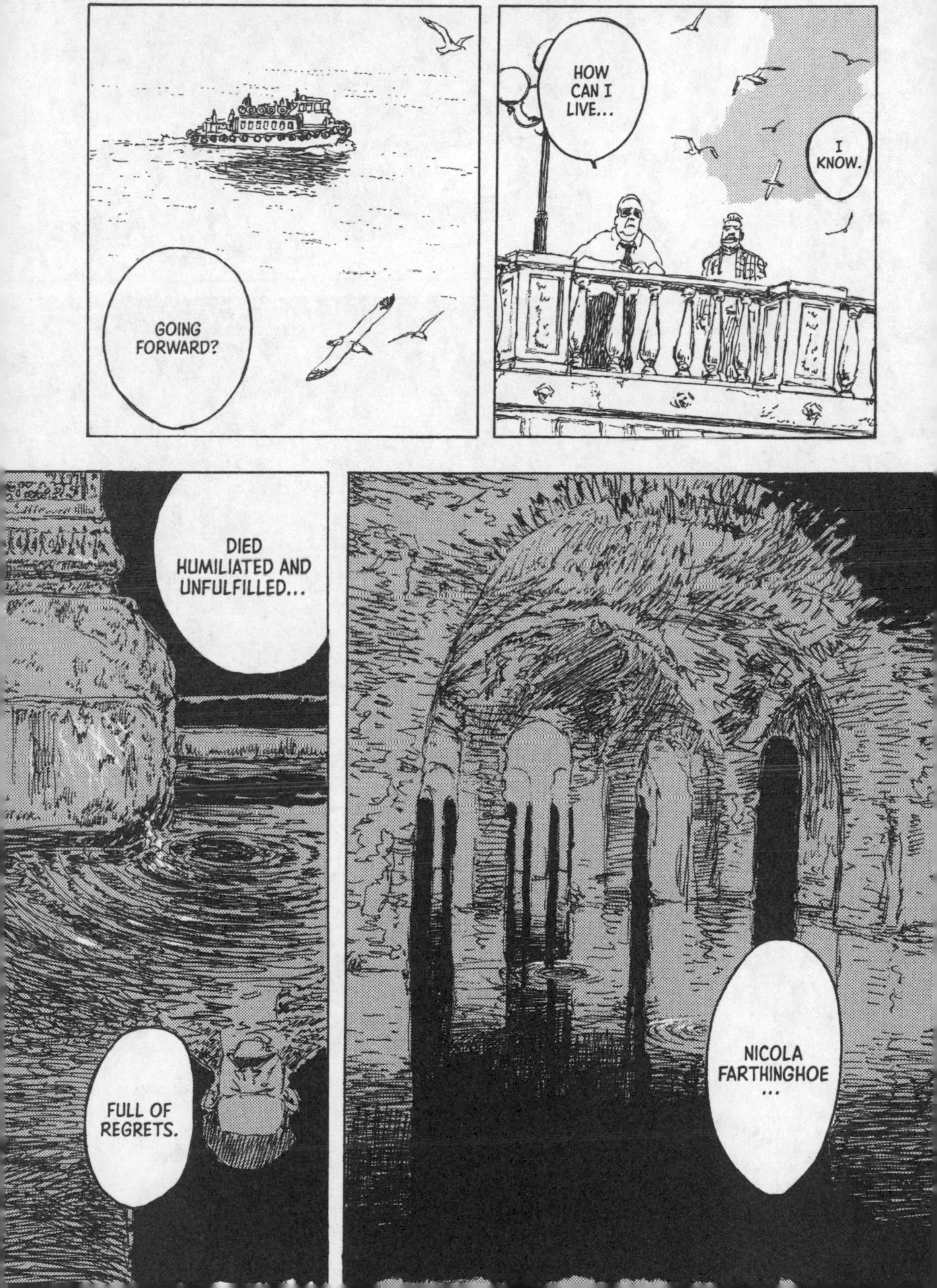
HOW CAN I LIVE...
I KNOW.
GOING FORWARD?
NICOLA FARTHINGHOE ...
DIED HUMILIATED AND UNFULFILLED...
FULL OF REGRETS.

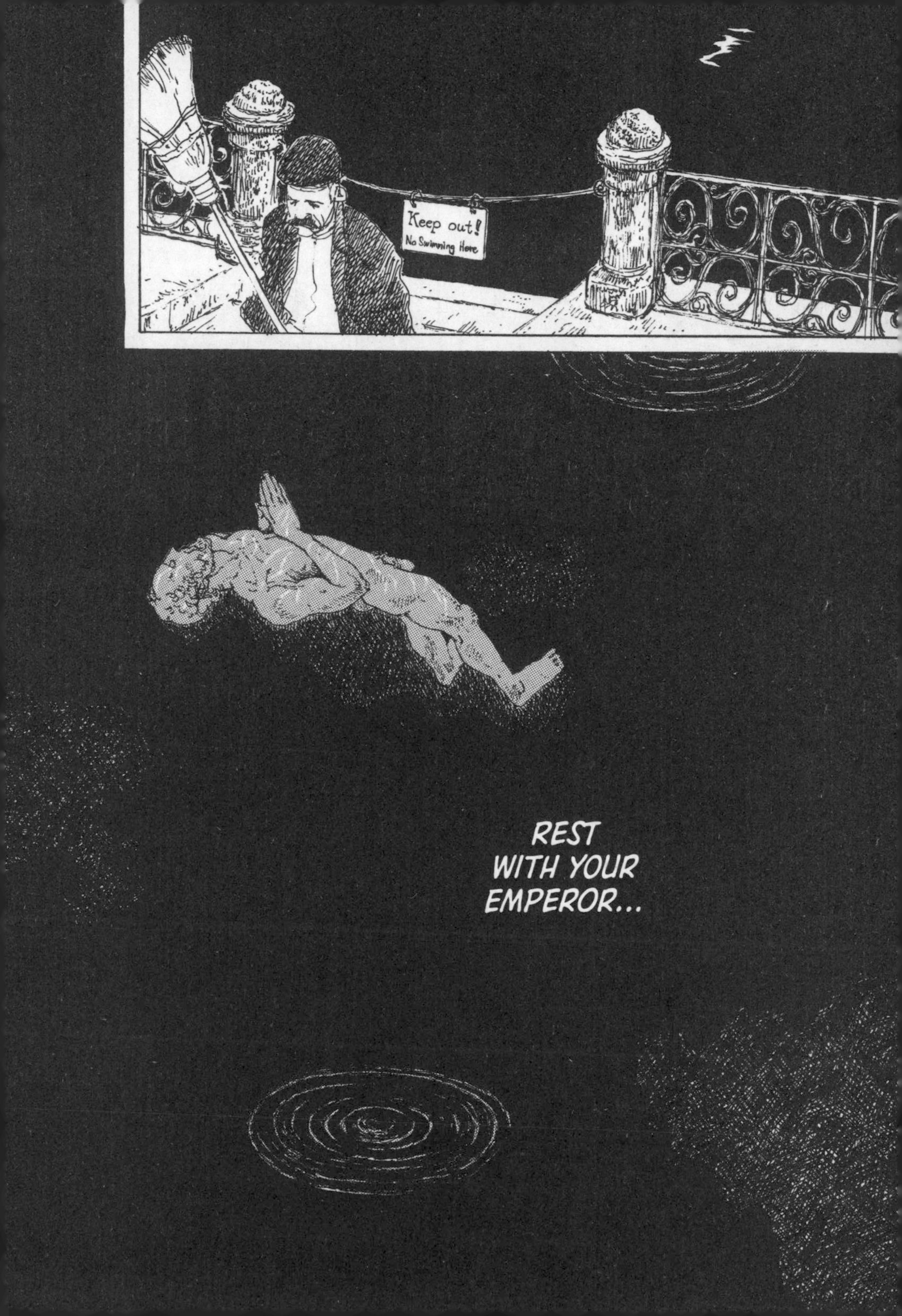
Keep out!
No Swimming Here
REST WITH YOUR EMPEROR...

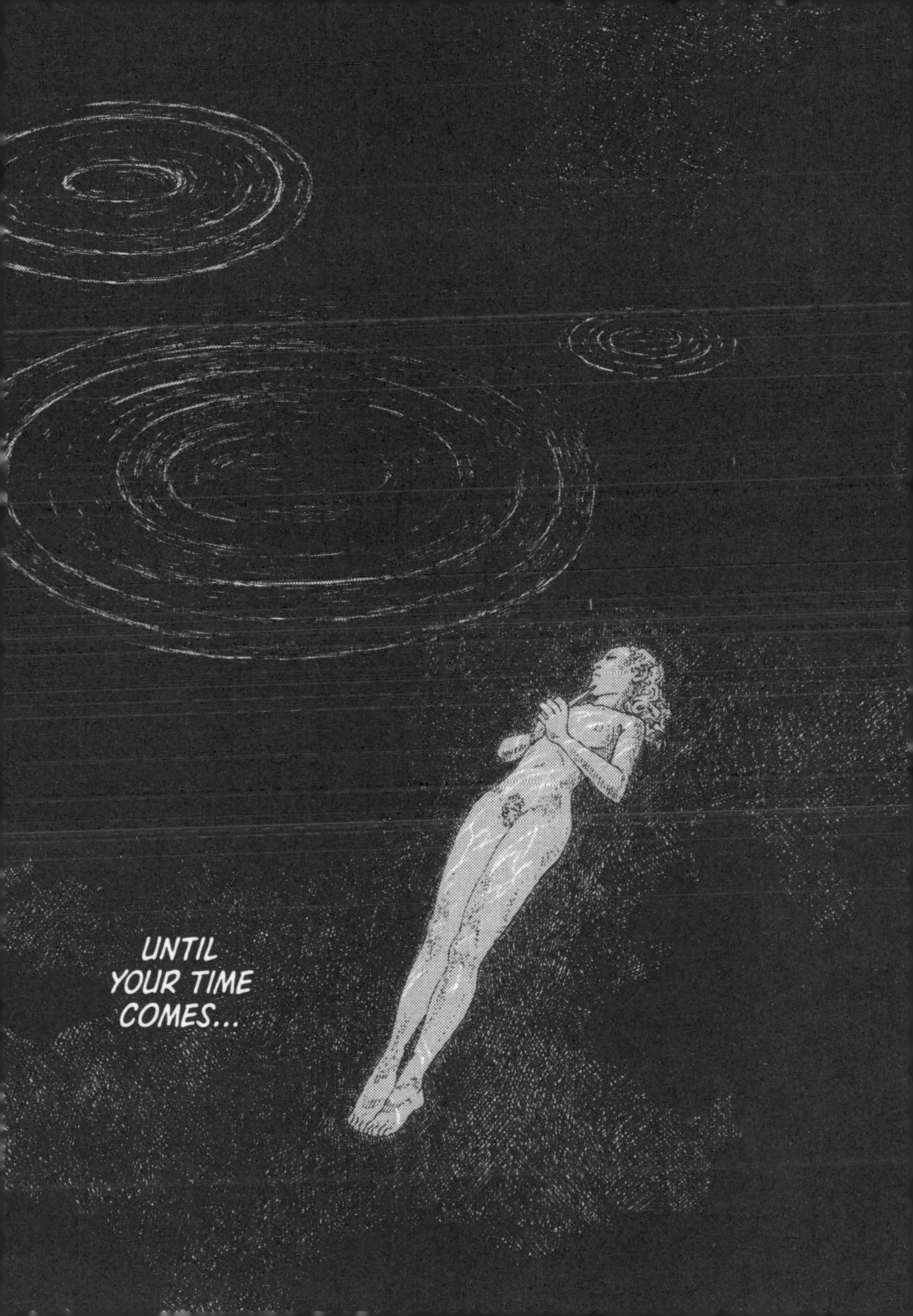
UNTIL YOUR TIME COMES...

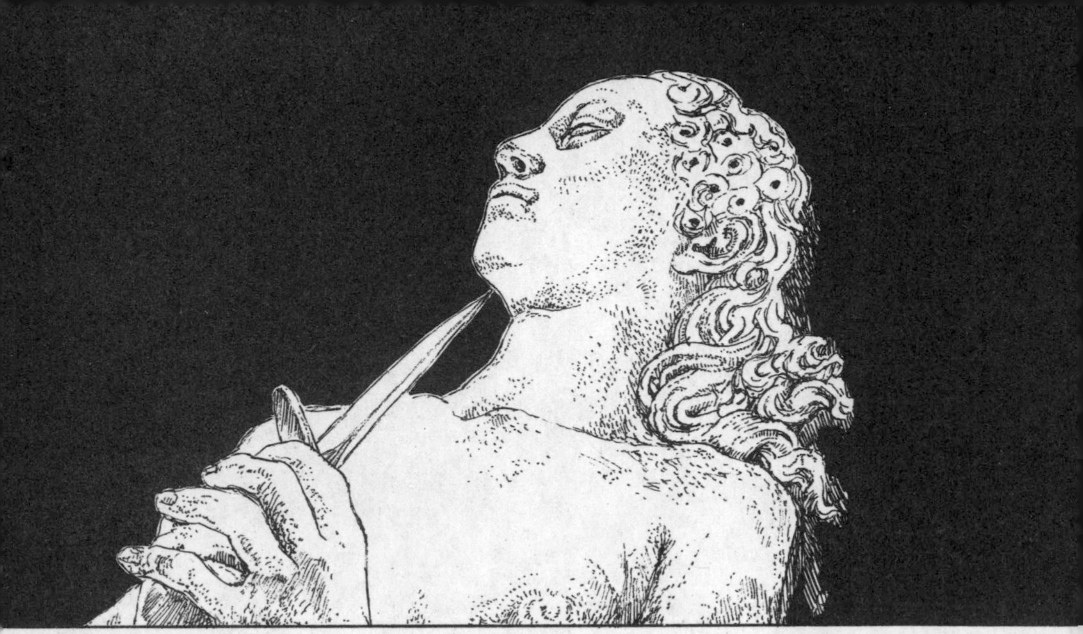

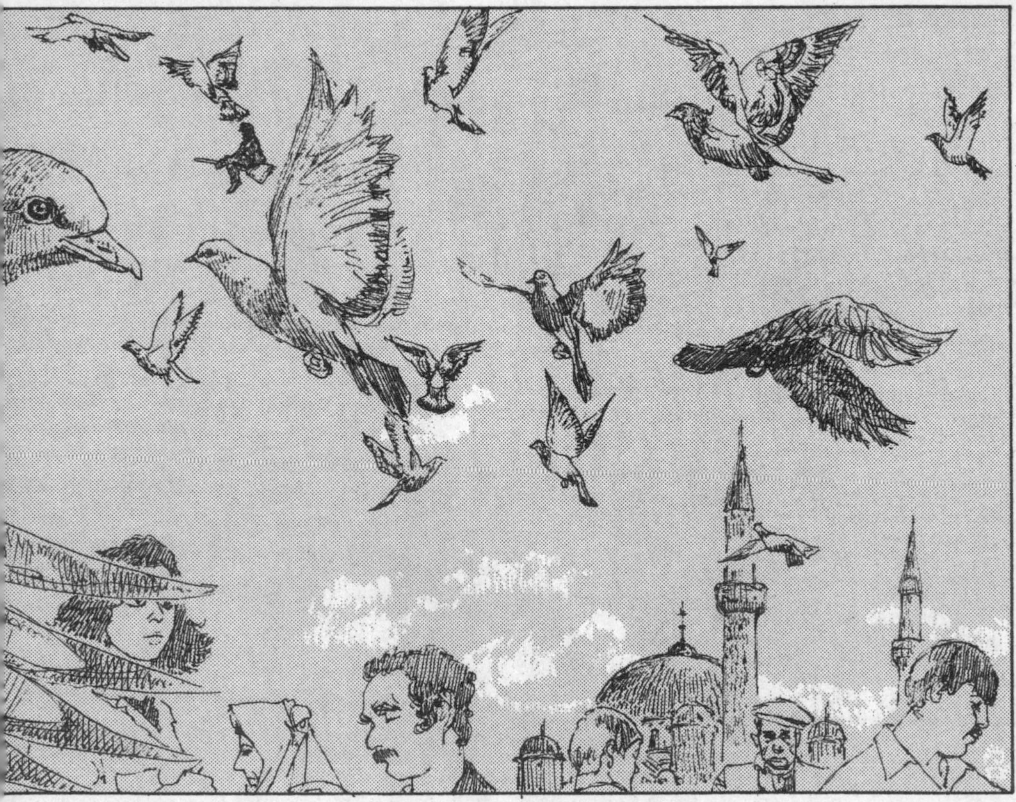

SPINDLE ~ End

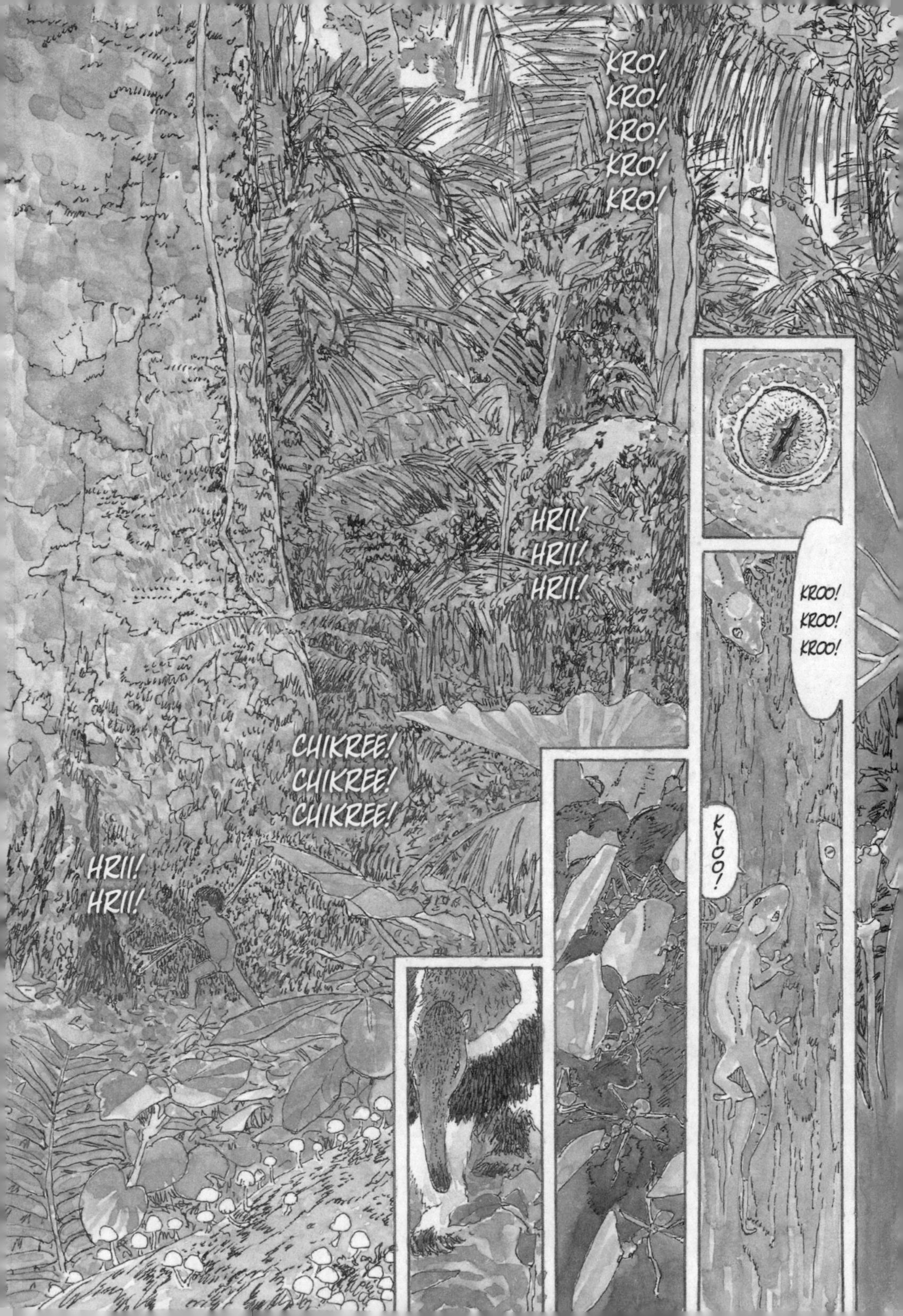
KRO! KRO! KRO! KRO! KRO!
KROO! KROO! KROO!
HRII! HRII! HRII!
KYOO!
CHIKREE! CHIKREE! CHIKREE!
HRII! HRII!

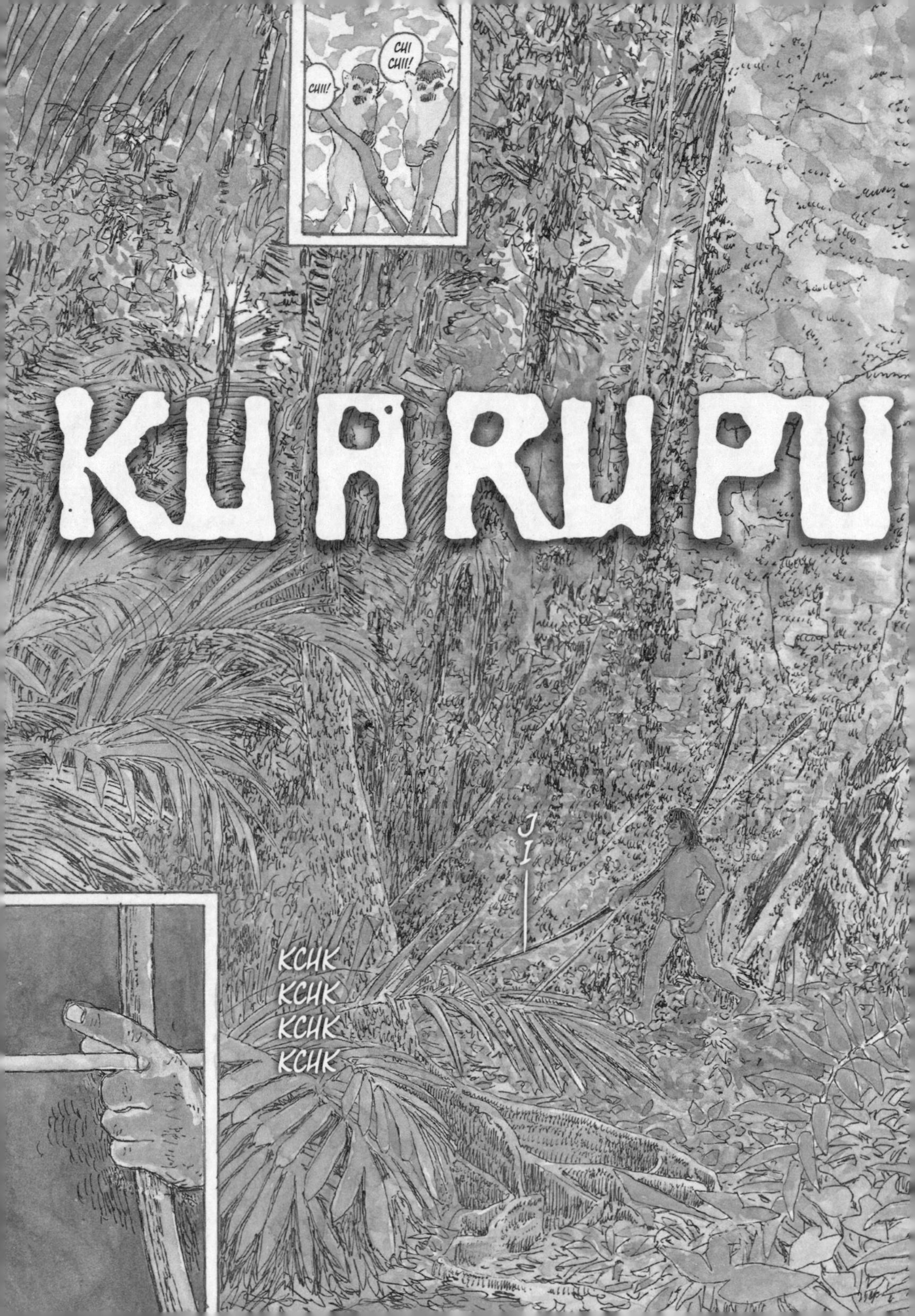
CHII!
CHI CHII!
KUARUPU
JI
KCHK
KCHK
KCHK
KCHK

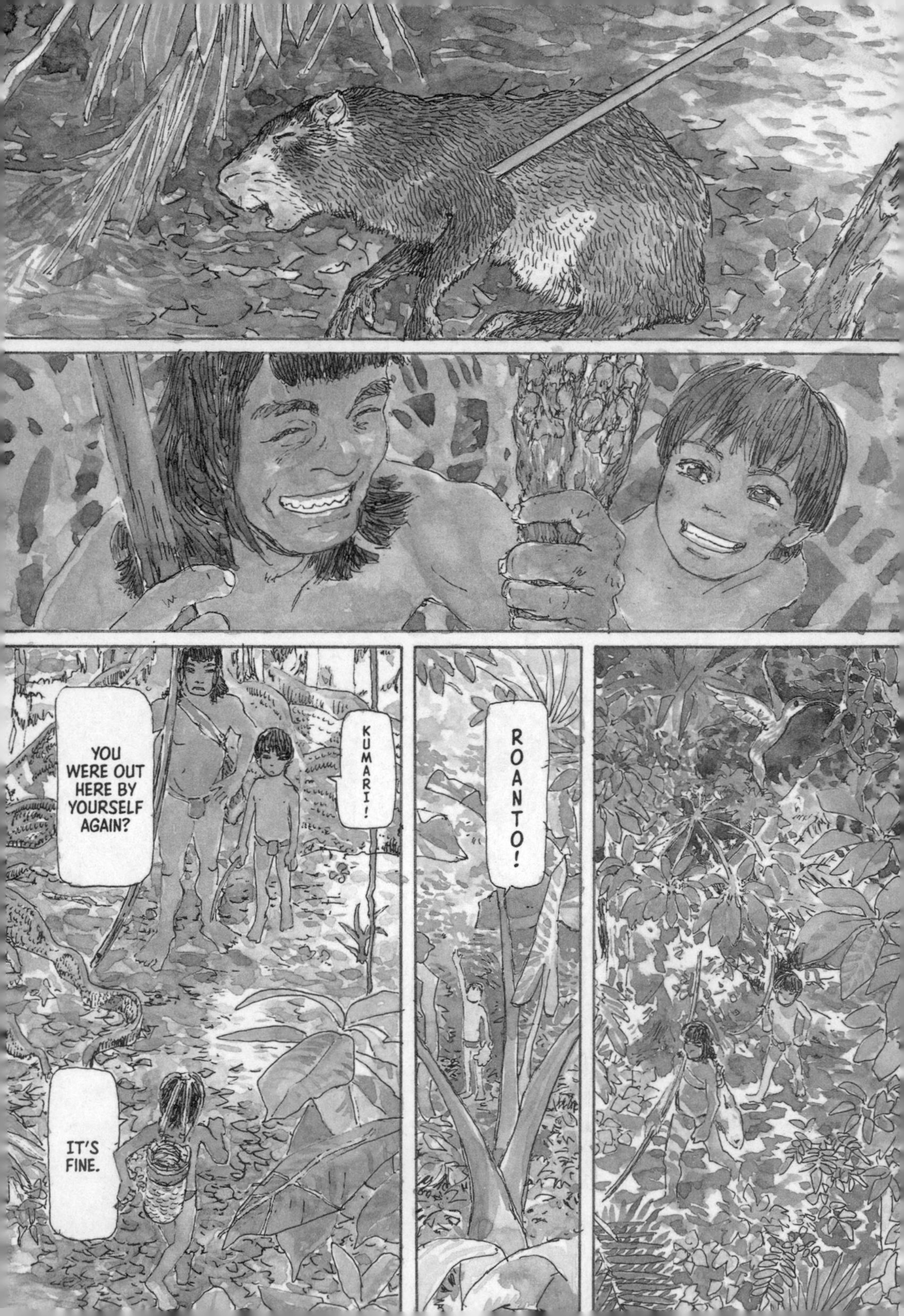
ROANTO!
KUMARI!
YOU WERE OUT HERE BY YOURSELF AGAIN?
IT'S FINE.

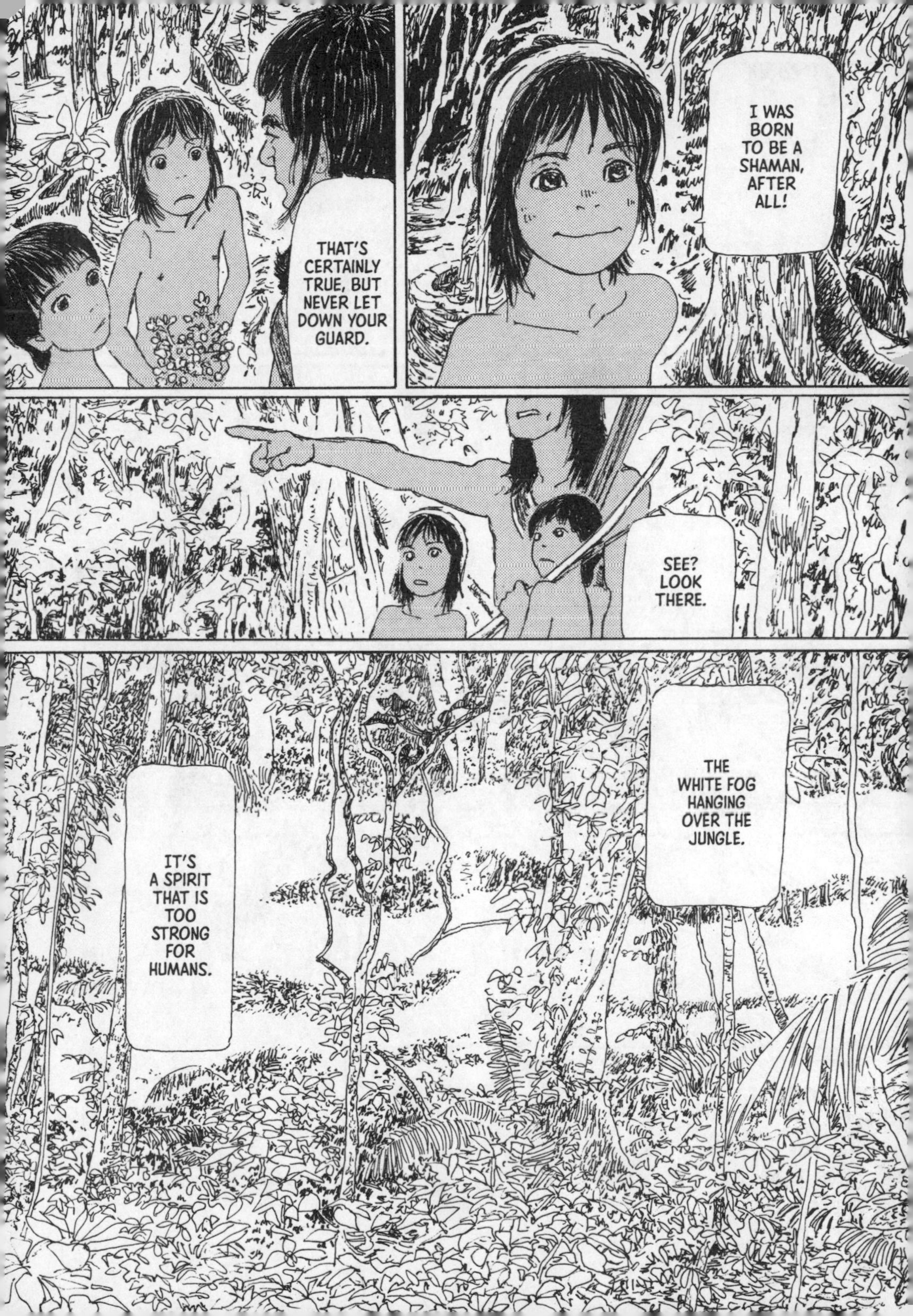
I WAS BORN TO BE A SHAMAN, AFTER ALL!
THAT'S CERTAINLY TRUE, BUT NEVER LET DOWN YOUR GUARD.
SEE? LOOK THERE.
THE WHITE FOG HANGING OVER THE JUNGLE.
IT'S A SPIRIT THAT IS TOO STRONG FOR HUMANS.

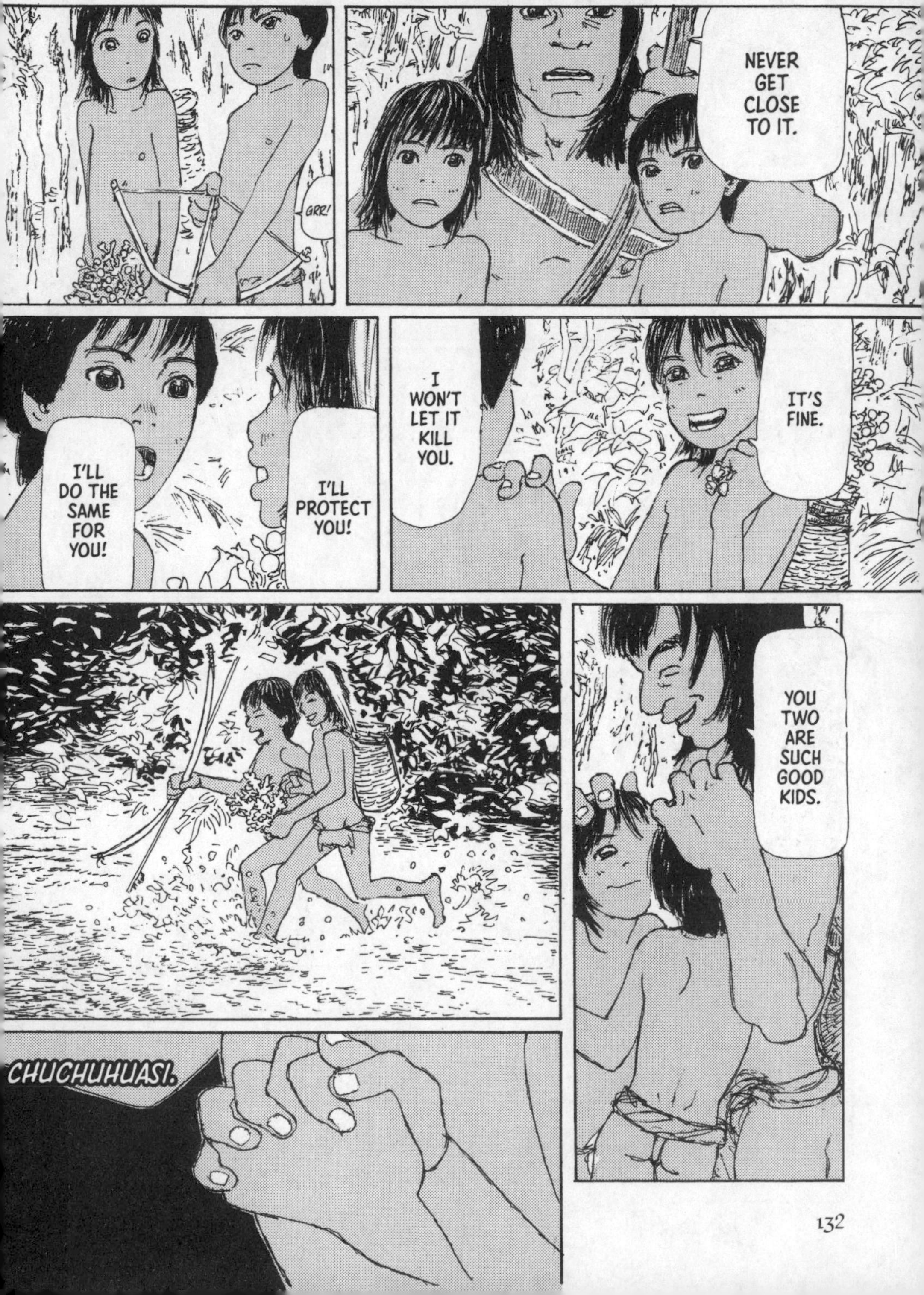
NEVER GET CLOSE TO IT.
GRR!
IT'S FINE.
I WON'T LET IT KILL YOU.
I'LL PROTECT YOU!
I'LL DO THE SAME FOR YOU!
YOU TWO ARE SUCH GOOD KIDS.
CHUCHUHUASI.

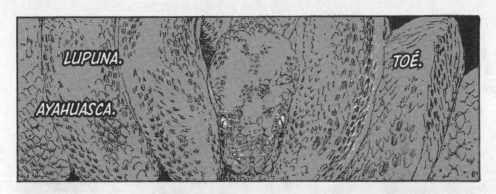

TOÉ.
LUPUNA.
AYAHUASCA.
LORD OF THE PLANTS...
KING OF THE SPIRITS...
LEND ME YOUR POWER.
GIVE SHAMAN KUMARI THE SOULS OF ALL SPIRITS...
FOR HER REVENGE.

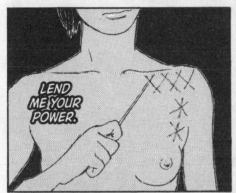

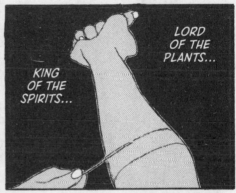

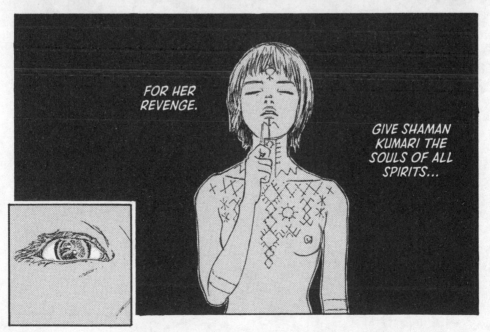

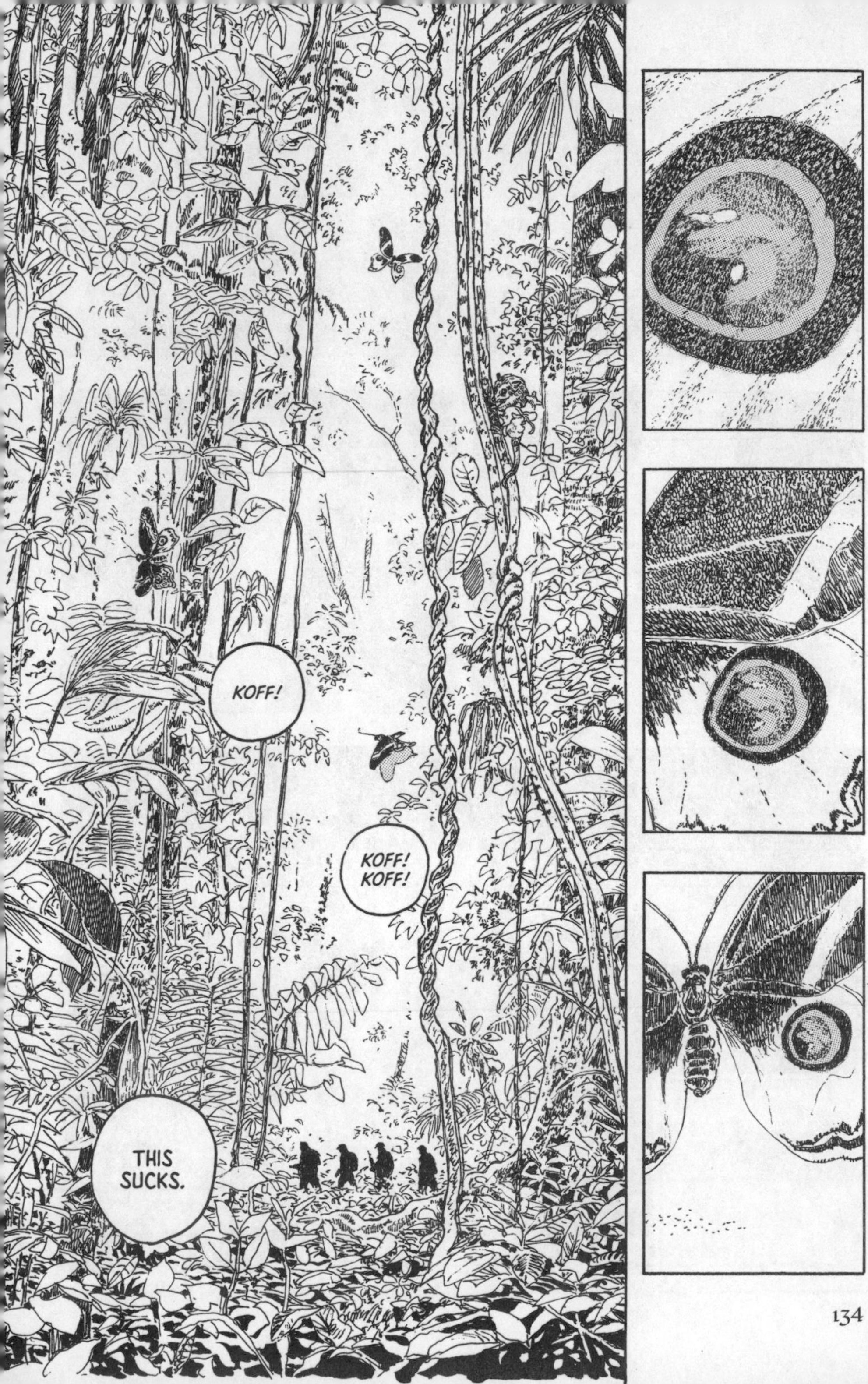
KOFF!
KOFF! KOFF!
THIS SUCKS.

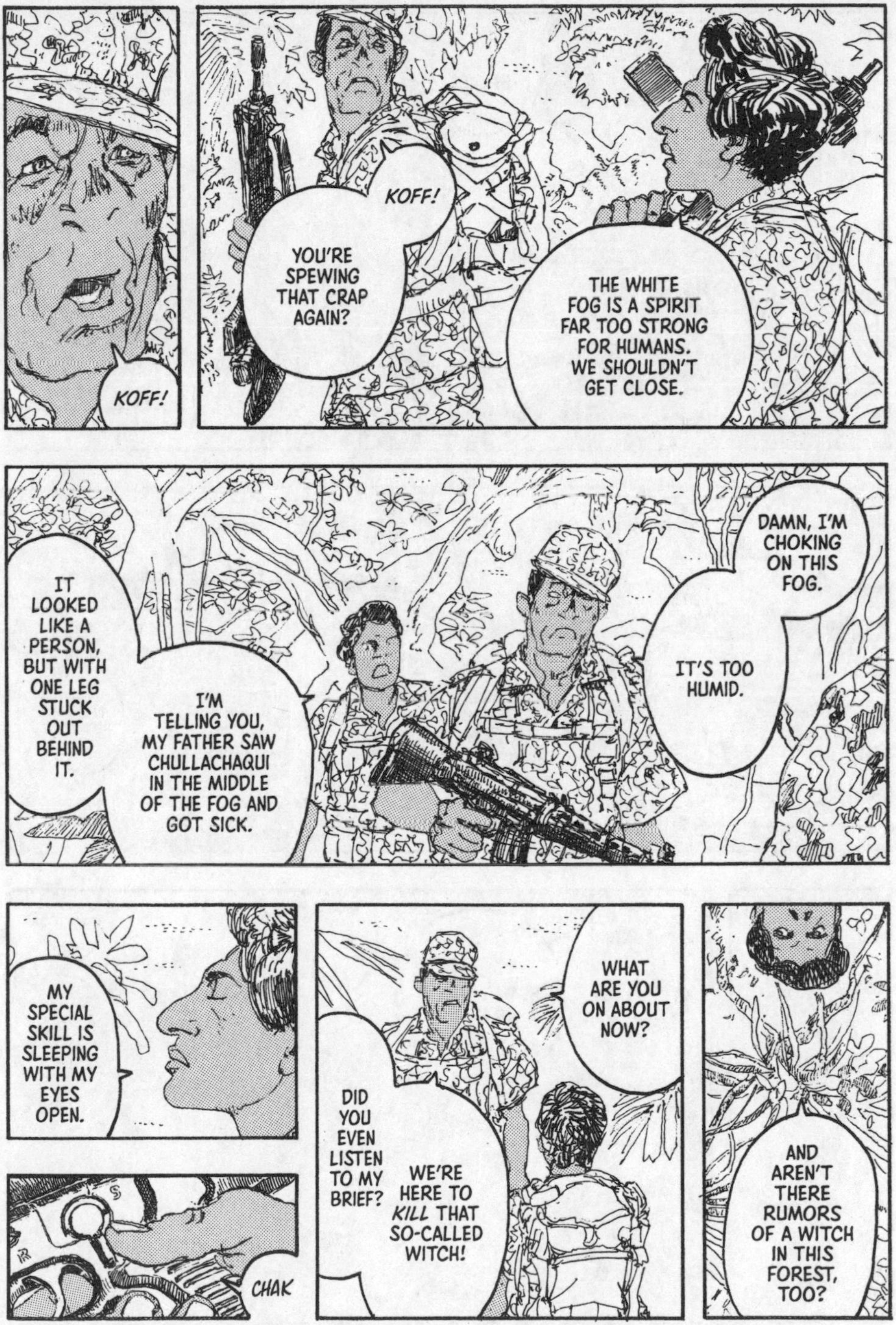
THE WHITE FOG IS A SPIRIT FAR TOO STRONG FOR HUMANS. WE SHOULDN'T GET CLOSE.
KOFF!
YOU'RE SPEWING THAT CRAP AGAIN?
KOFF!
DAMN, I'M CHOKING ON THIS FOG.
IT'S TOO HUMID.
I'M TELLING YOU, MY FATHER SAW CHULLACHAQUI IN THE MIDDLE OF THE FOG AND GOT SICK.
IT LOOKED LIKE A PERSON, BUT WITH ONE LEG STUCK OUT BEHIND IT.
AND AREN'T THERE RUMORS OF A WITCH IN THIS FOREST, TOO?
WHAT ARE YOU ON ABOUT NOW?
DID YOU EVEN LISTEN TO MY BRIEF?
WE'RE HERE TO *KILL* THAT SO-CALLED WITCH!
MY SPECIAL SKILL IS SLEEPING WITH MY EYES OPEN.
CHAK

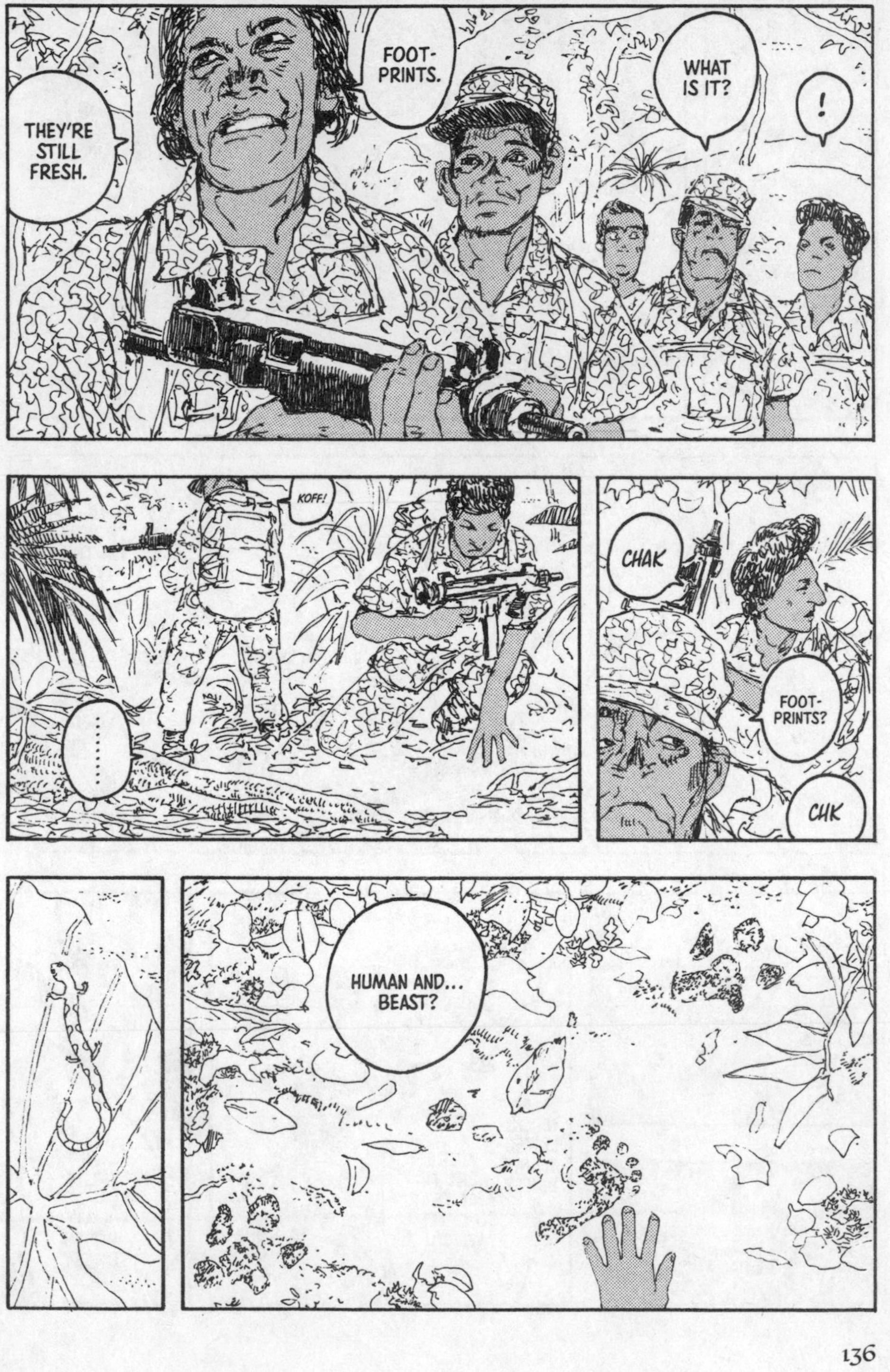
!
WHAT IS IT?
FOOT-PRINTS.
THEY'RE STILL FRESH.
CHAK
FOOT-PRINTS?
CHK
KOFF!
......
HUMAN AND... BEAST?

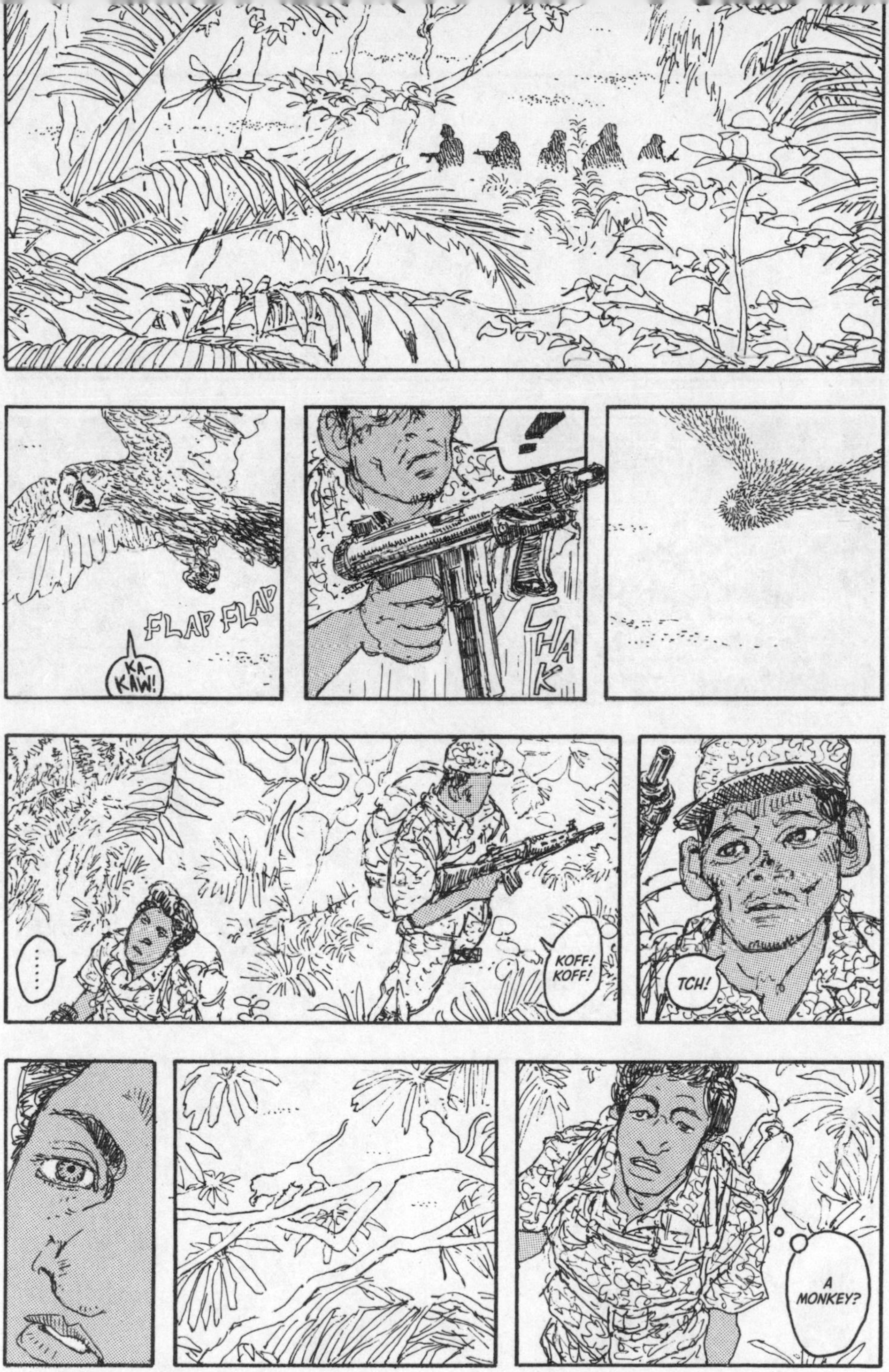
!
CHAK
FLAP FLAP
KA-KAW!
TCH!
KOFF! KOFF!
......
A MONKEY?

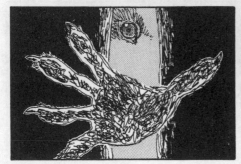

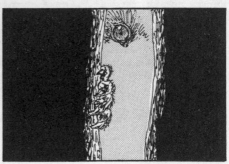

I'M BEING EATEN.

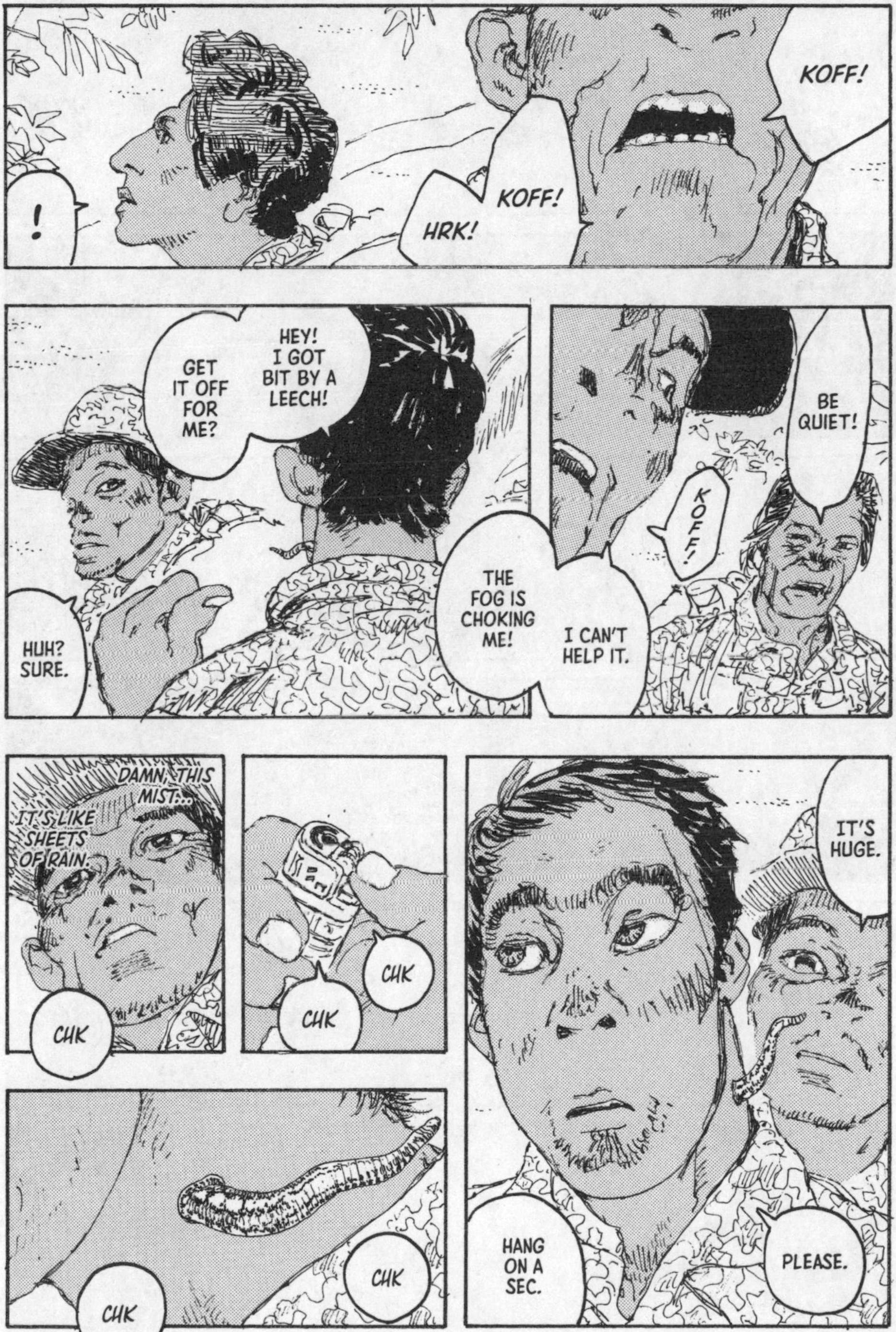
KOFF!
KOFF!
HRK!
!
BE QUIET!
KOFF!
I CAN'T HELP IT.
THE FOG IS CHOKING ME!
HEY! I GOT BIT BY A LEECH!
GET IT OFF FOR ME?
HUH? SURE.
IT'S HUGE.
PLEASE.
HANG ON A SEC.
CHK
CHK
DAMN, THIS MIST...
IT'S LIKE SHEETS OF RAIN.
CHK
CHK
CHK

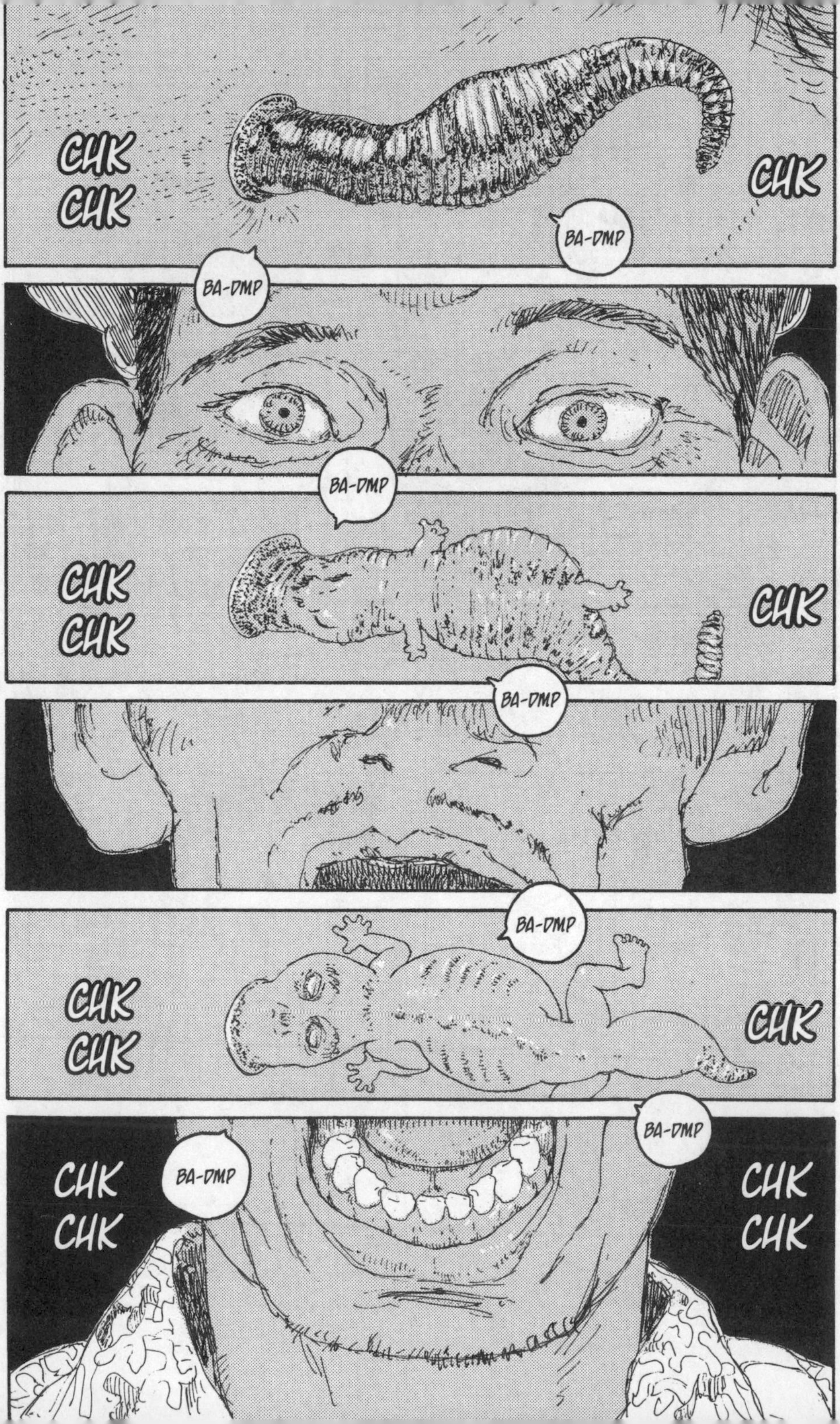
CHK
CHK CHK
BA-DMP
BA-DMP
BA-DMP
CHK
CHK CHK
BA-DMP
BA-DMP
CHK
CHK CHK
BA-DMP
CHK CHK
BA-DMP
CHK CHK

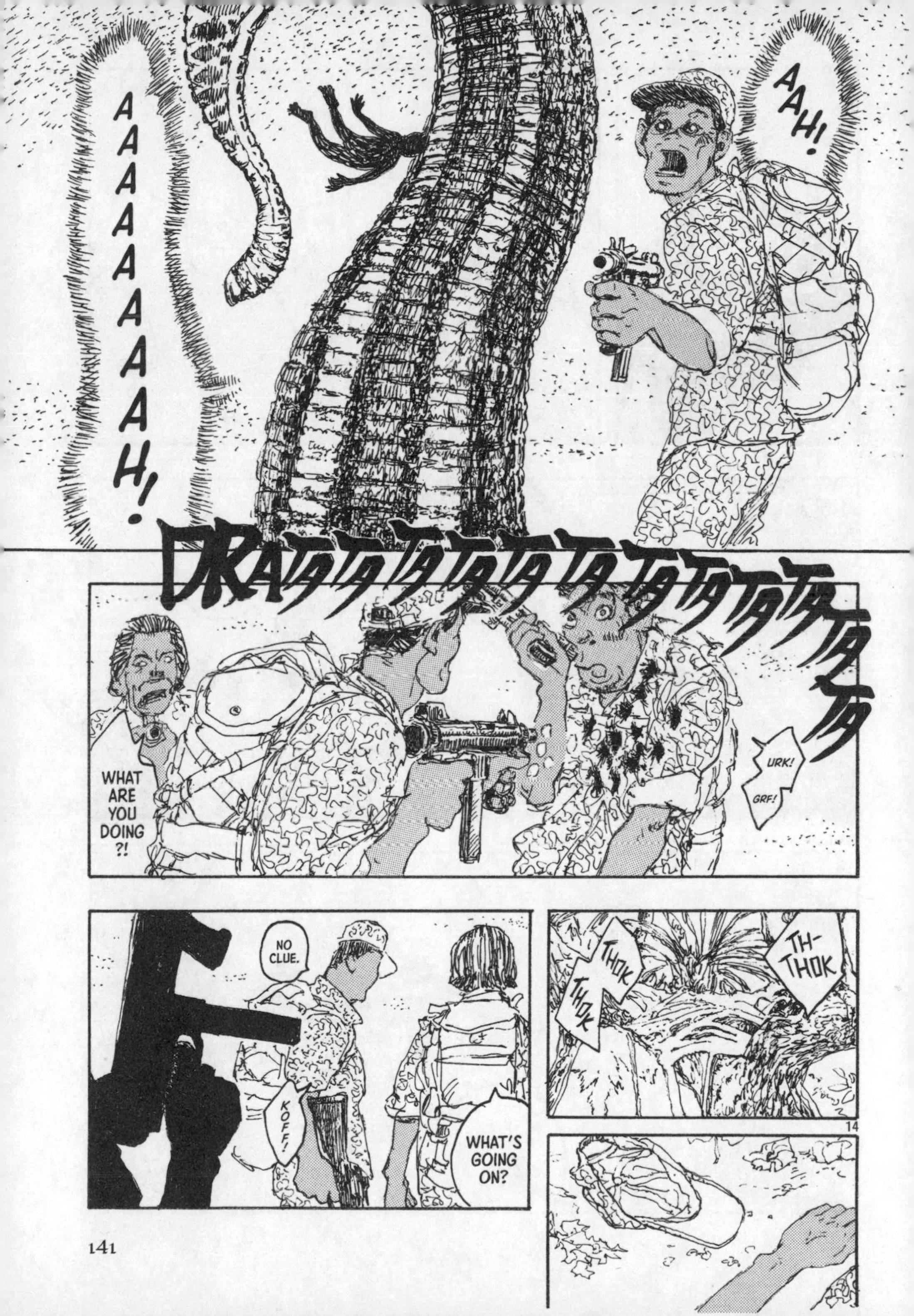
AAH!
AAAAAAAAH!
DRATATATATATATATATATATATATATA
URK!
GRF!
WHAT ARE YOU DOING ?!
TH-THOK
THOK THOK
NO CLUE.
WHAT'S GOING ON?
KOFF!
14

KOFF!
KOFF!
KOFF!
KOFF!
I'M BEING EATEN.
AS IF I'D GET MYSELF EATEN.

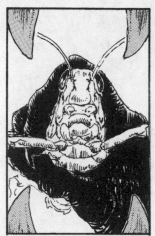

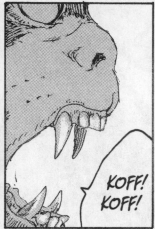

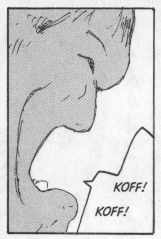

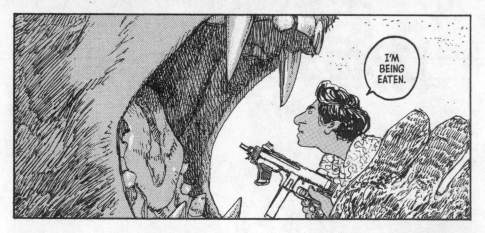

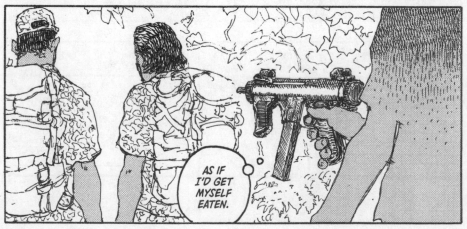

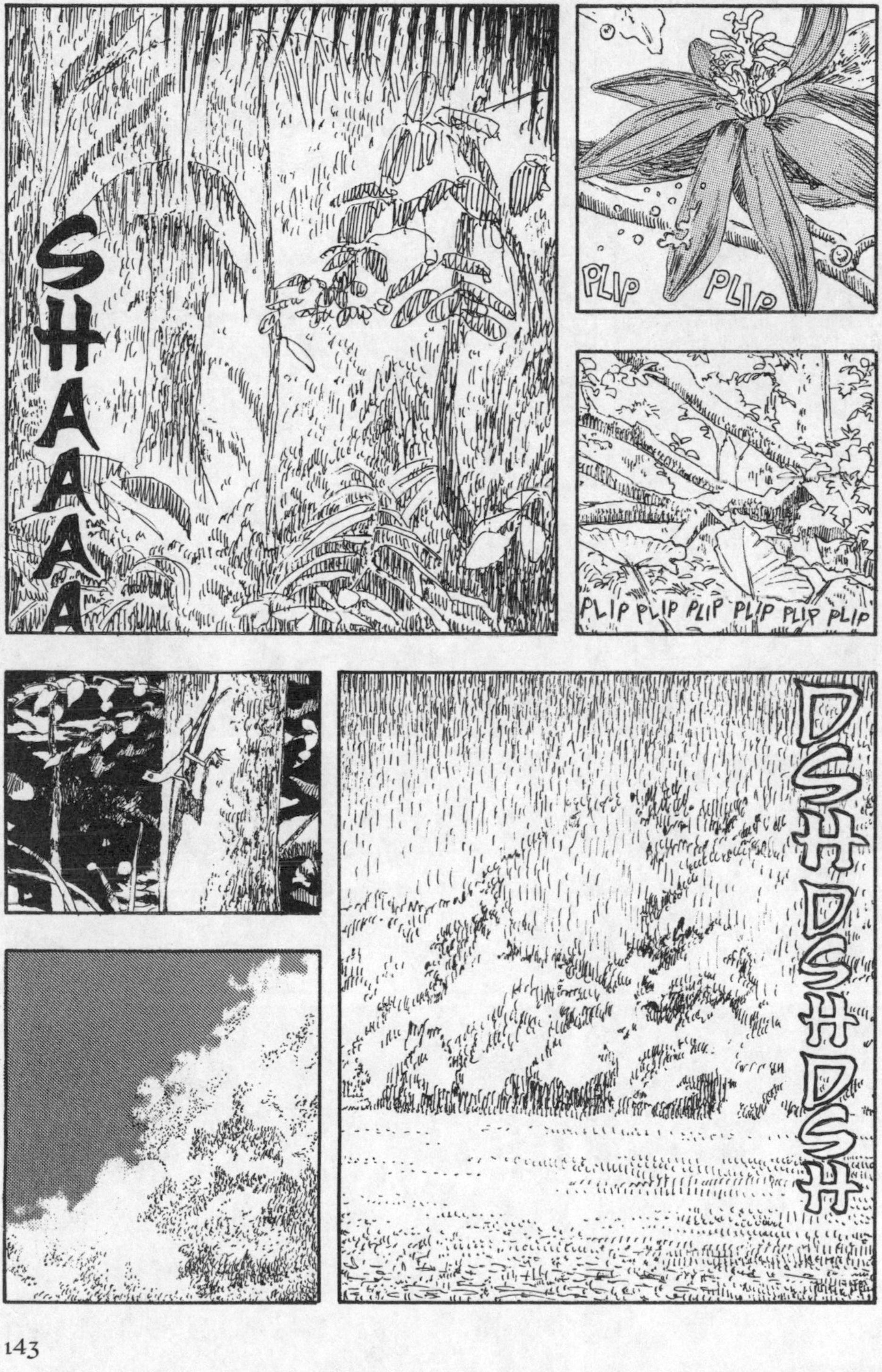
PLIP PLIP
PLIP PLIP PLIP PLIP PLIP PLIP
SHAAAA
DSHDSHDSH

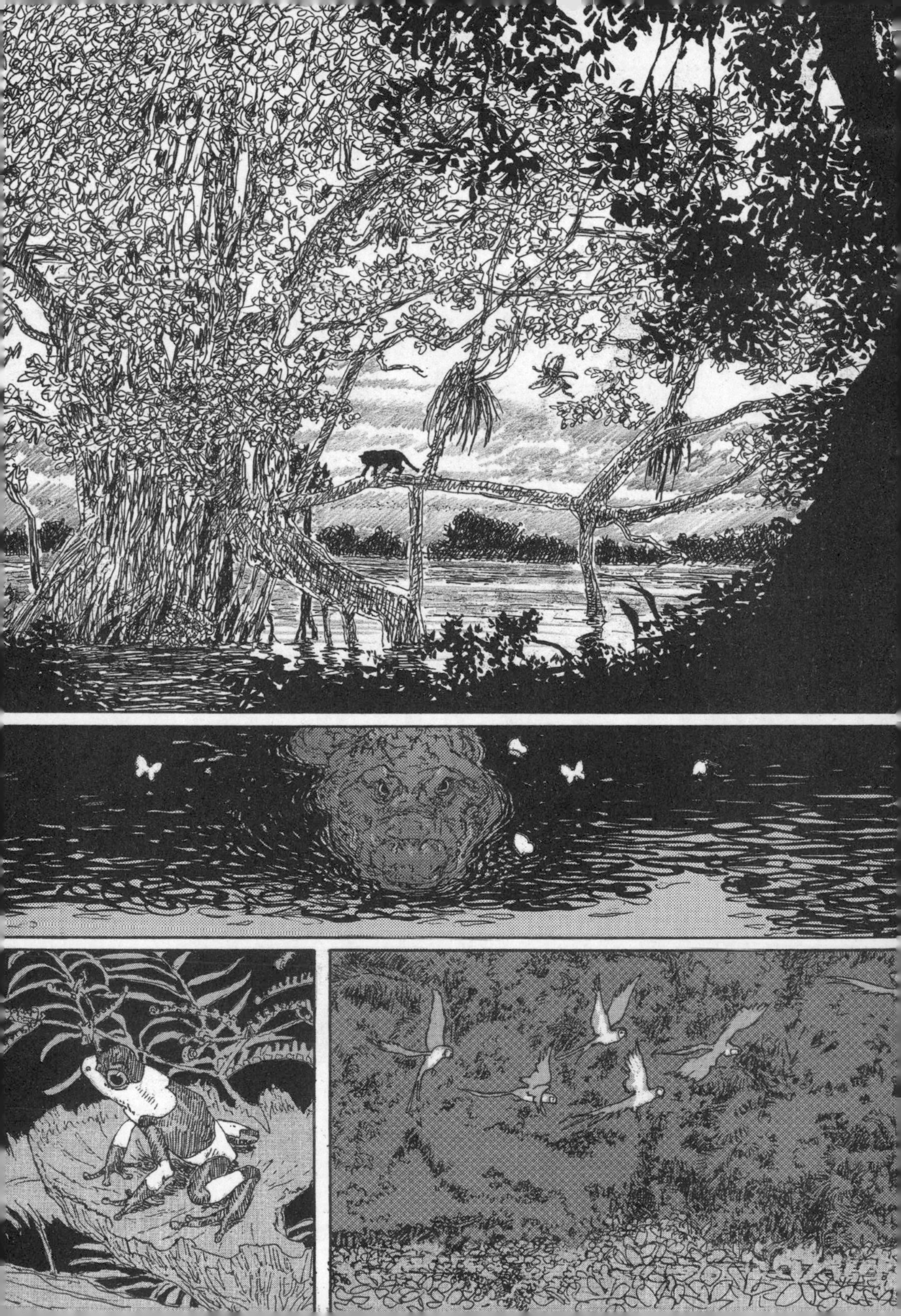

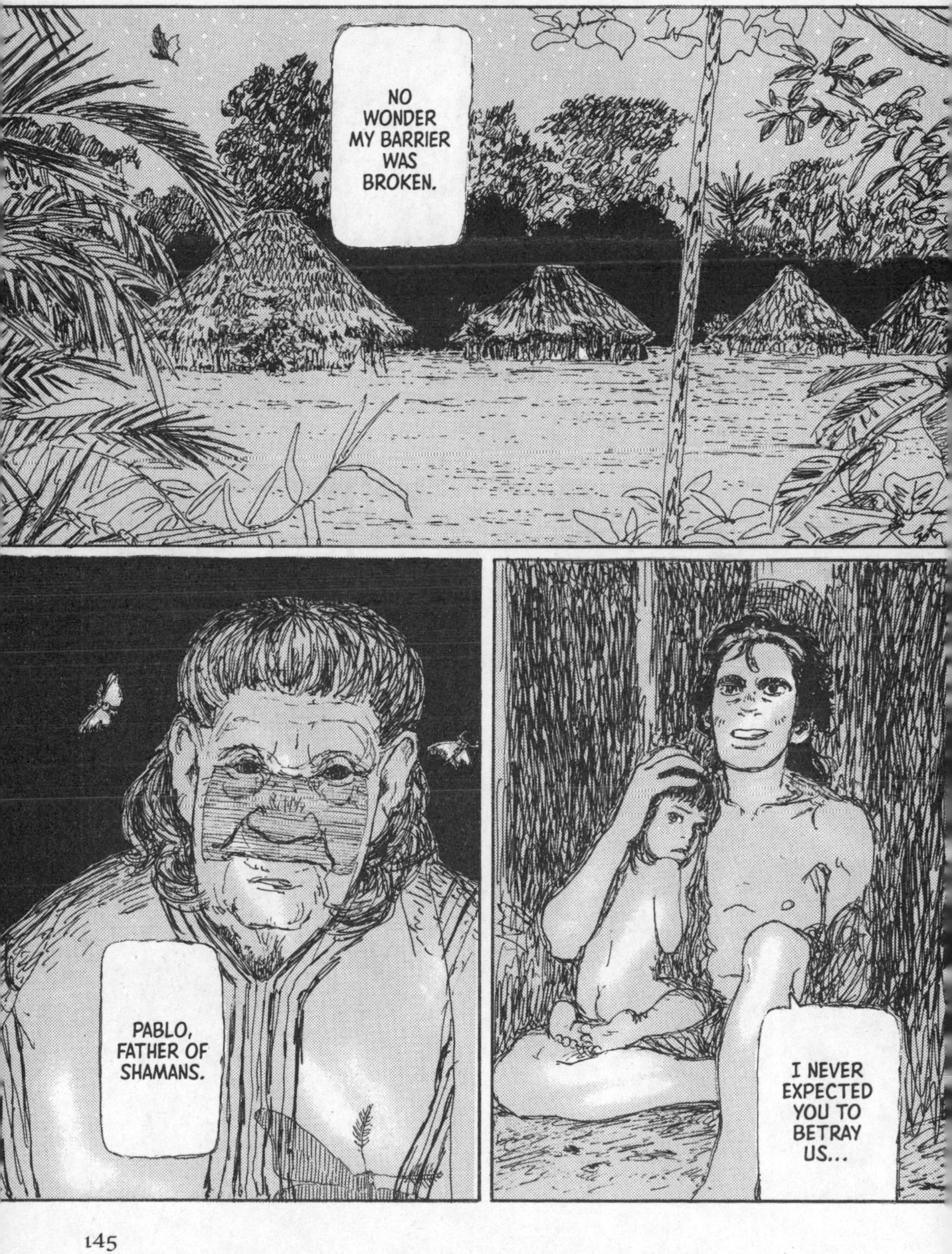
NO WONDER MY BARRIER WAS BROKEN.
I NEVER EXPECTED YOU TO BETRAY US...
PABLO, FATHER OF SHAMANS.

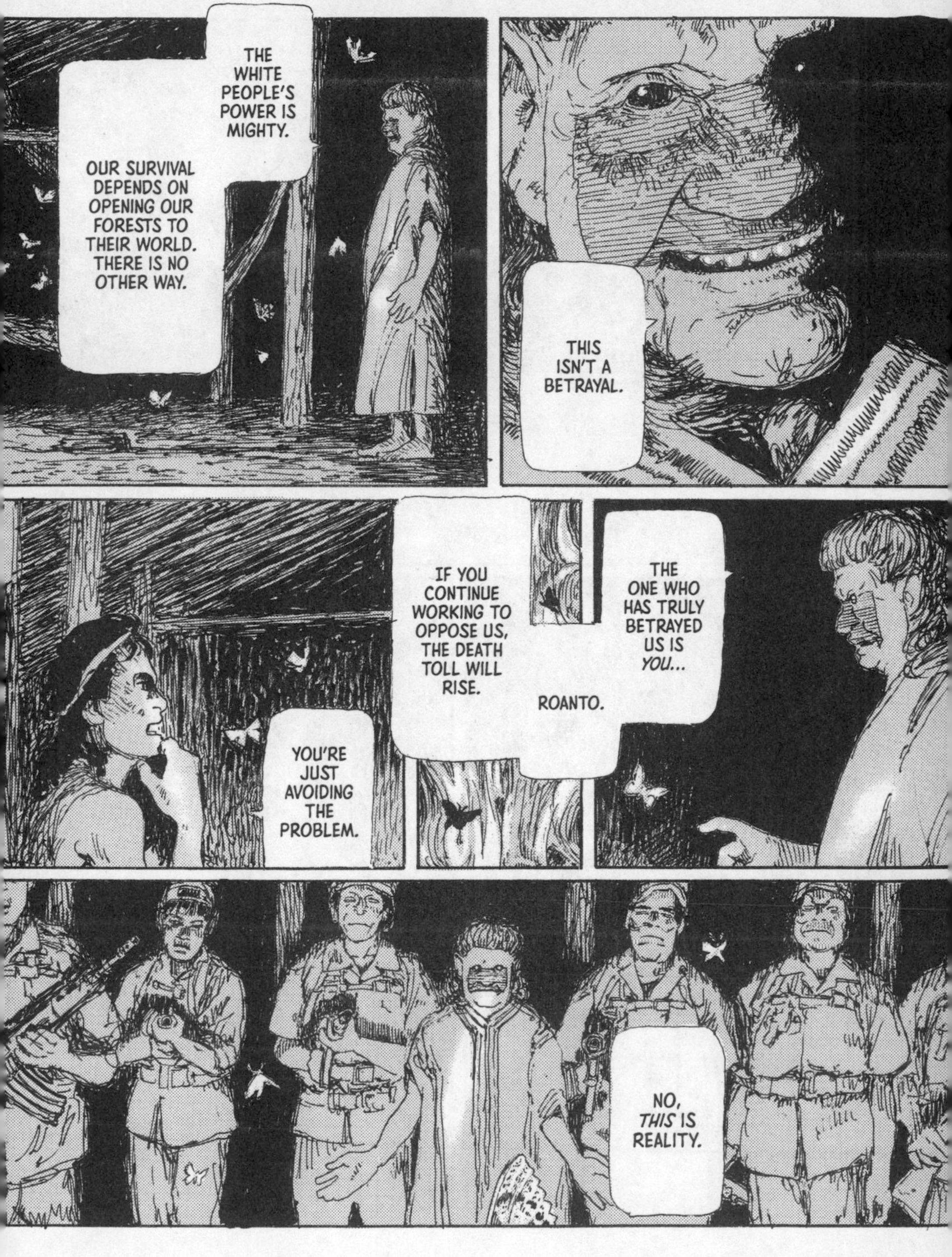
THIS ISN'T A BETRAYAL.
THE WHITE PEOPLE'S POWER IS MIGHTY.
OUR SURVIVAL DEPENDS ON OPENING OUR FORESTS TO THEIR WORLD. THERE IS NO OTHER WAY.
THE ONE WHO HAS TRULY BETRAYED US IS *YOU*...
ROANTO.
IF YOU CONTINUE WORKING TO OPPOSE US, THE DEATH TOLL WILL RISE.
YOU'RE JUST AVOIDING THE PROBLEM.
NO, *THIS* IS REALITY.

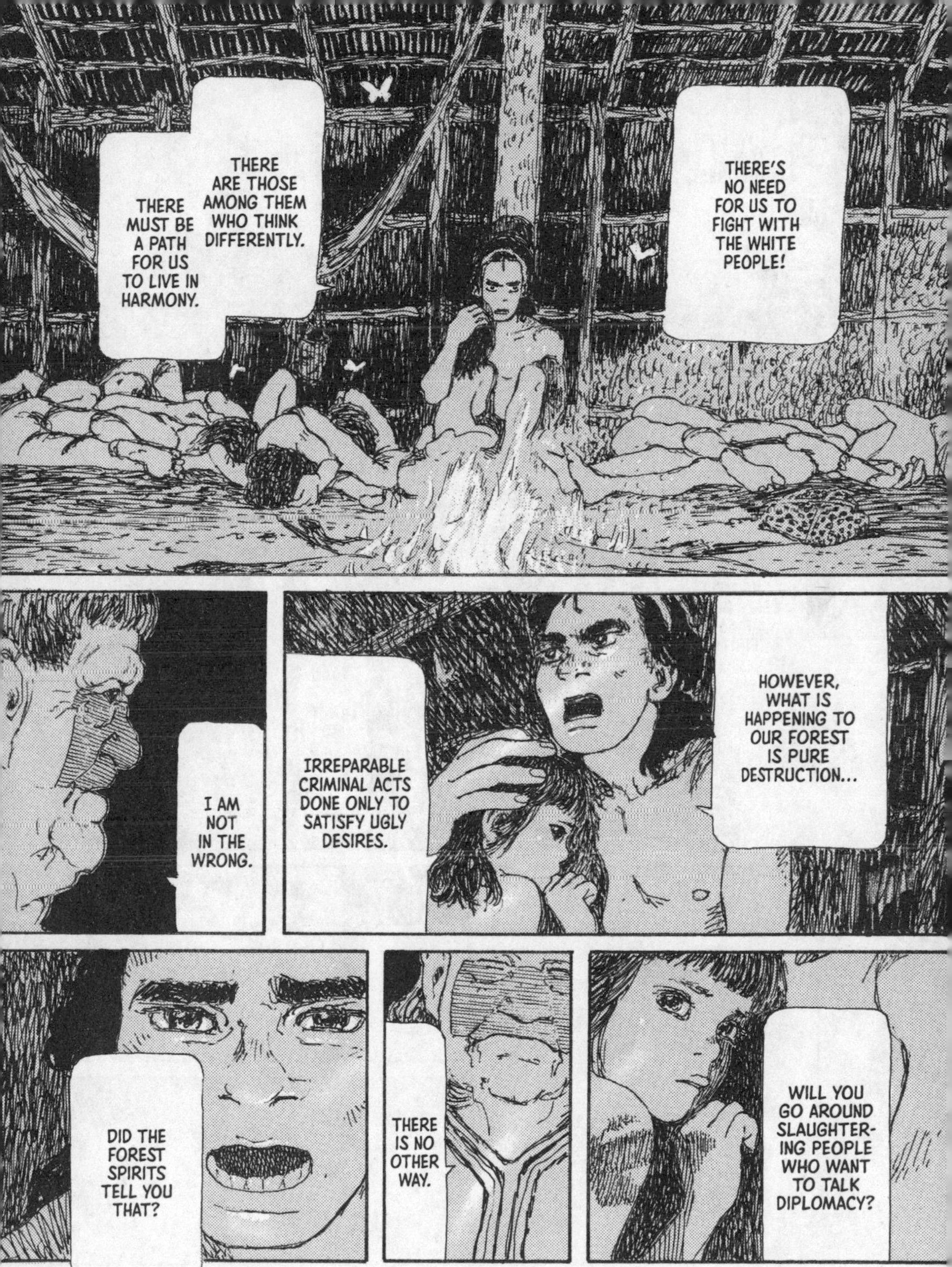
THERE'S NO NEED FOR US TO FIGHT WITH THE WHITE PEOPLE!
THERE ARE THOSE AMONG THEM WHO THINK DIFFERENTLY.
THERE MUST BE A PATH FOR US TO LIVE IN HARMONY.
HOWEVER, WHAT IS HAPPENING TO OUR FOREST IS PURE DESTRUCTION...
IRREPARABLE CRIMINAL ACTS DONE ONLY TO SATISFY UGLY DESIRES.
I AM NOT IN THE WRONG.
WILL YOU GO AROUND SLAUGHTERING PEOPLE WHO WANT TO TALK DIPLOMACY?
THERE IS NO OTHER WAY.
DID THE FOREST SPIRITS TELL YOU THAT?

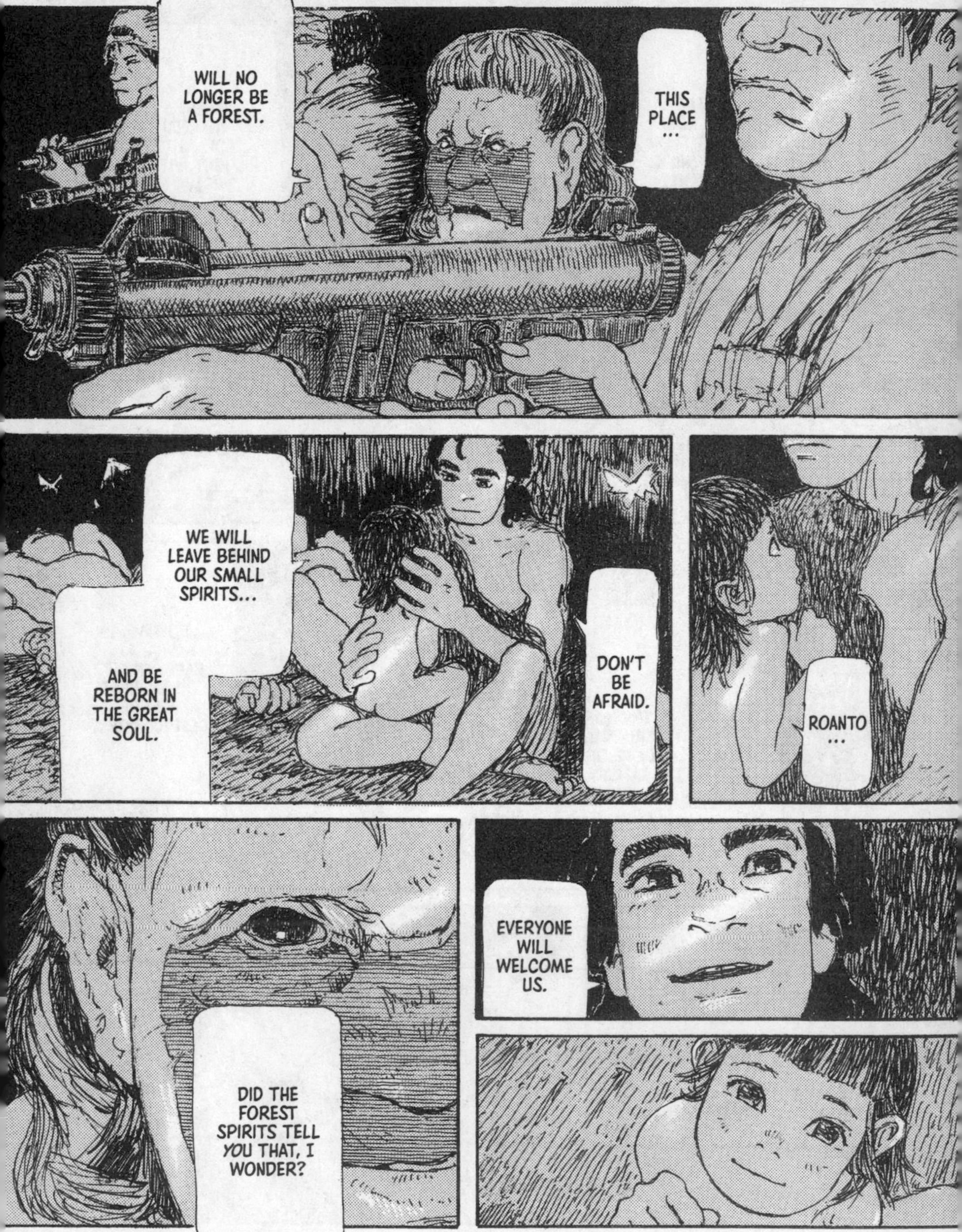
THIS PLACE ...
WILL NO LONGER BE A FOREST.
ROANTO ...
DON'T BE AFRAID.
WE WILL LEAVE BEHIND OUR SMALL SPIRITS...
AND BE REBORN IN THE GREAT SOUL.
EVERYONE WILL WELCOME US.
DID THE FOREST SPIRITS TELL *YOU* THAT, I WONDER?

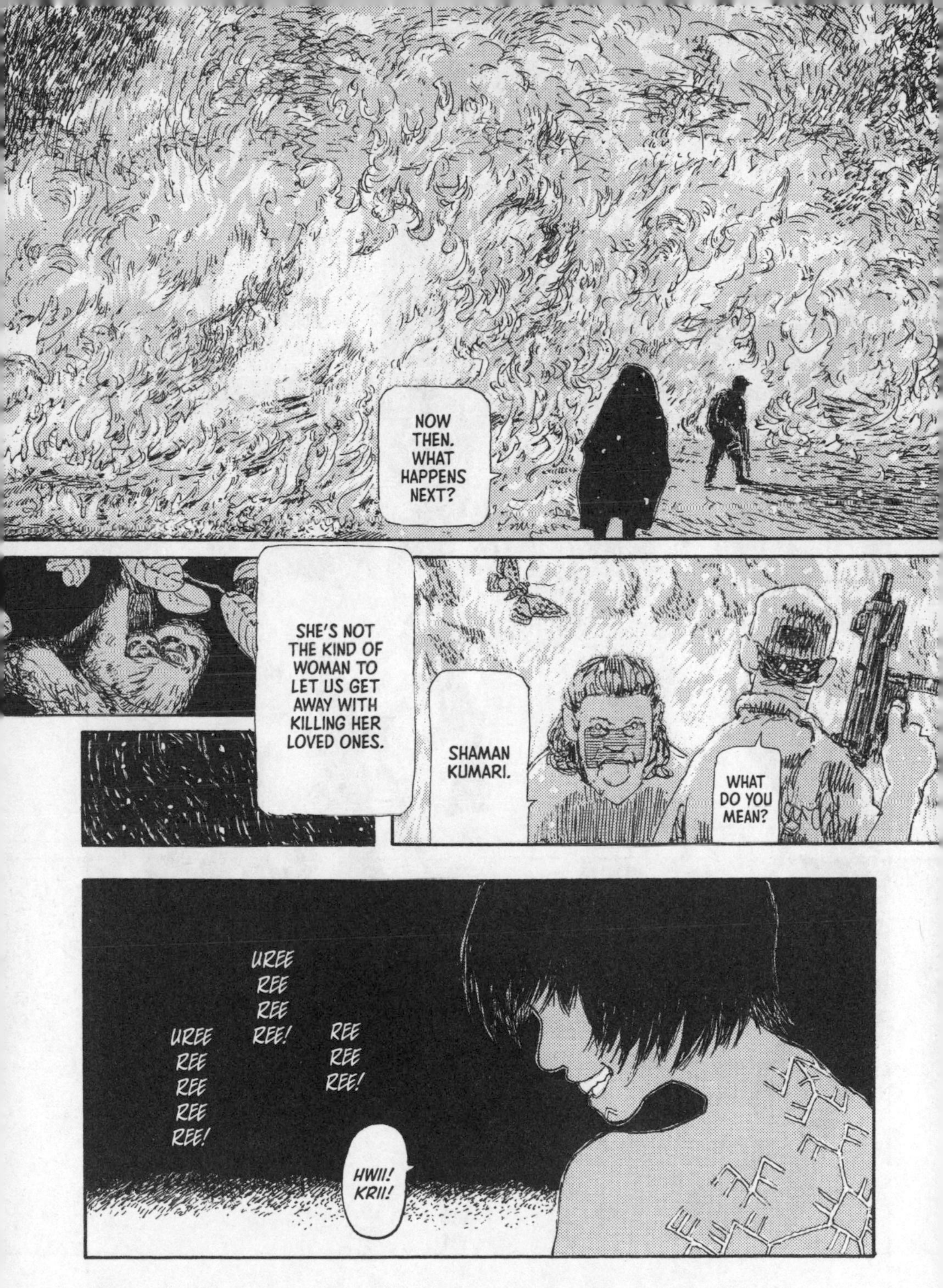
NOW THEN. WHAT HAPPENS NEXT?
SHAMAN KUMARI.
WHAT DO YOU MEAN?
SHE'S NOT THE KIND OF WOMAN TO LET US GET AWAY WITH KILLING HER LOVED ONES.
REE REE REE!
UREE REE REE REE!
UREE REE REE REE REE!
HWII! KRII!

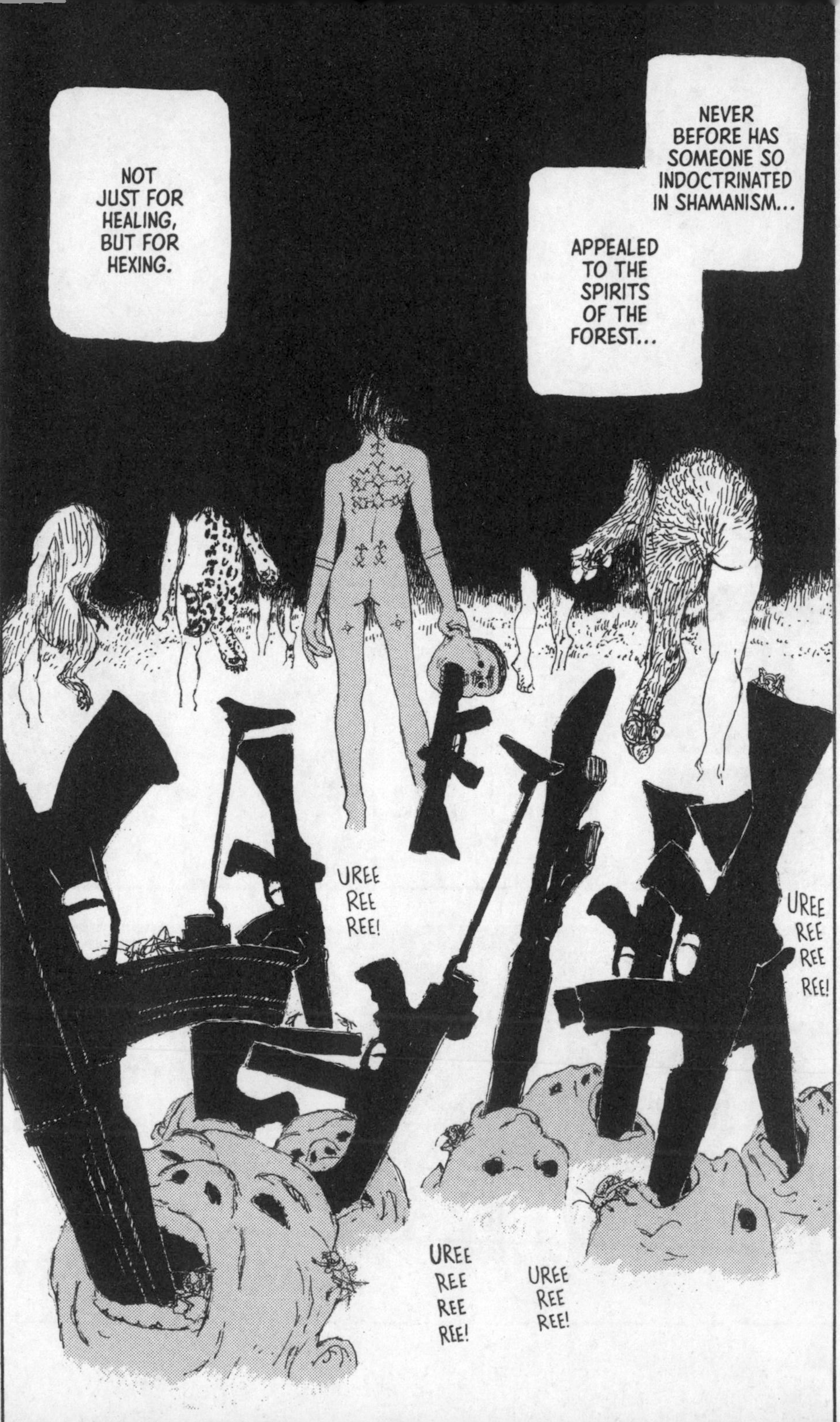
NEVER BEFORE HAS SOMEONE SO INDOCTRINATED IN SHAMANISM...
APPEALED TO THE SPIRITS OF THE FOREST...
NOT JUST FOR HEALING, BUT FOR HEXING.
UREE REE REE REE!
UREE REE REE!
UREE REE REE!
UREE REE REE REE!

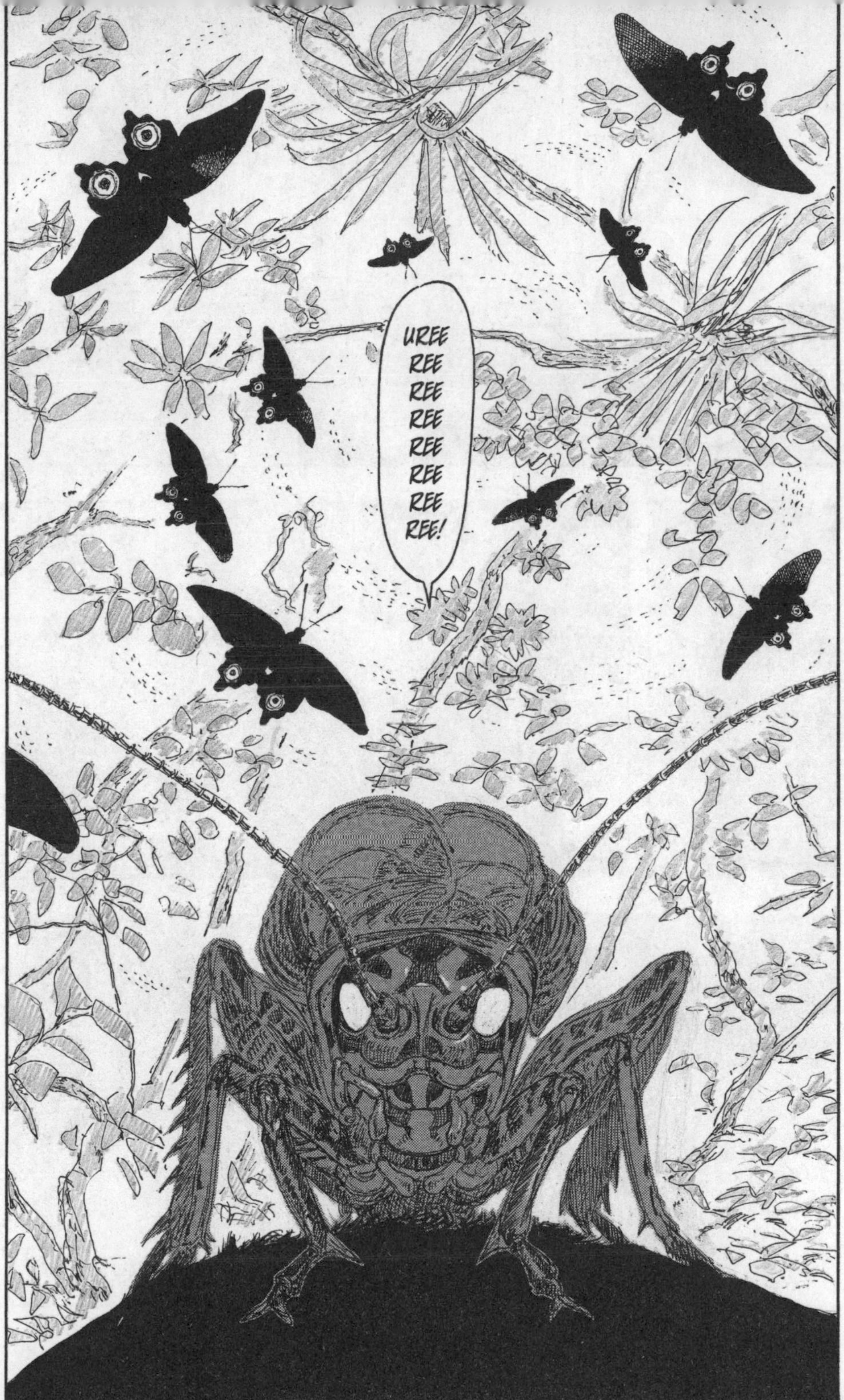
UREE REE REE REE REE REE REE REE REE!

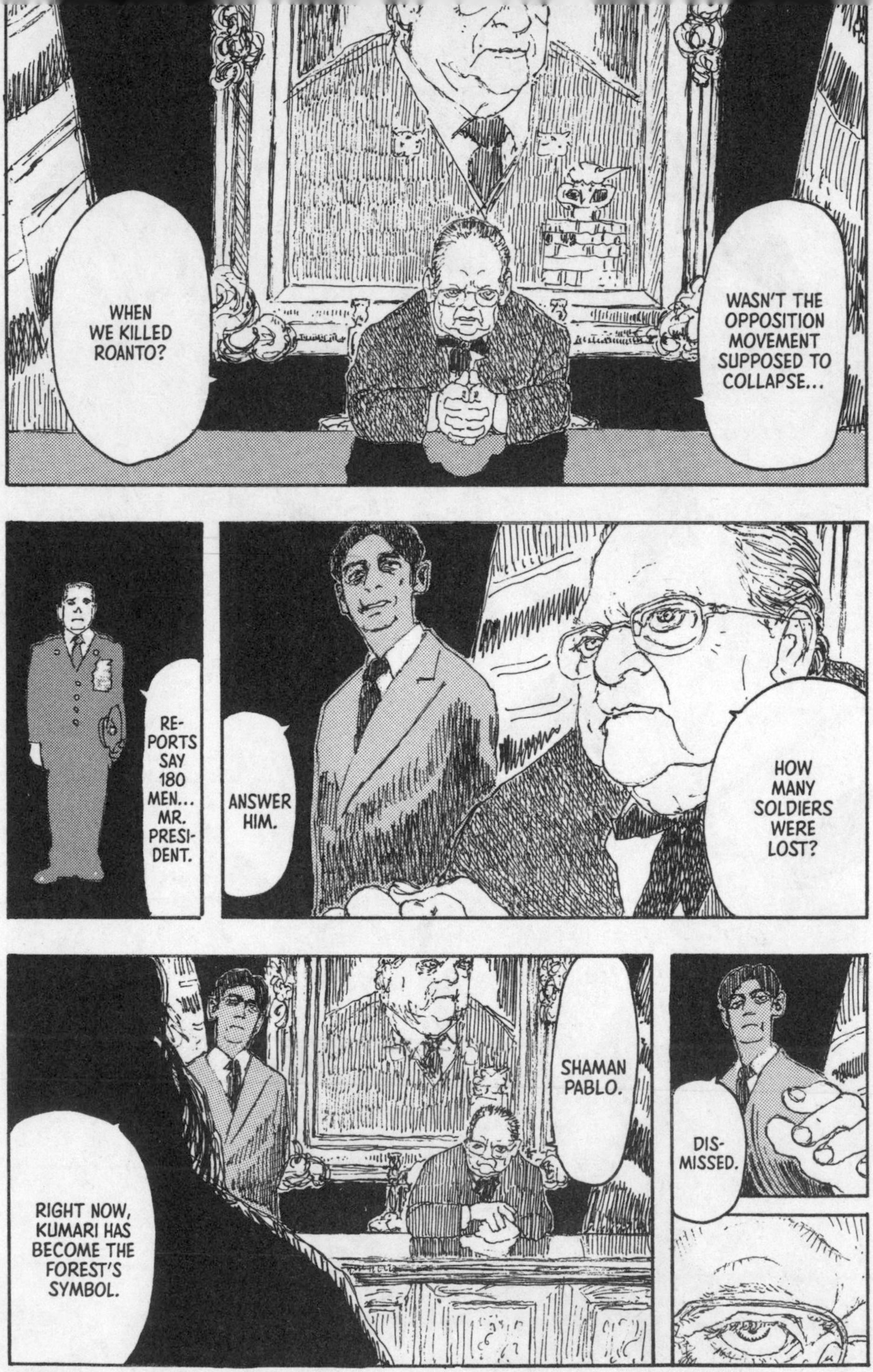
WASN'T THE OPPOSITION MOVEMENT SUPPOSED TO COLLAPSE...
WHEN WE KILLED ROANTO?
HOW MANY SOLDIERS WERE LOST?
ANSWER HIM.
RE-PORTS SAY 180 MEN... MR. PRESI-DENT.
DIS-MISSED.
SHAMAN PABLO.
RIGHT NOW, KUMARI HAS BECOME THE FOREST'S SYMBOL.

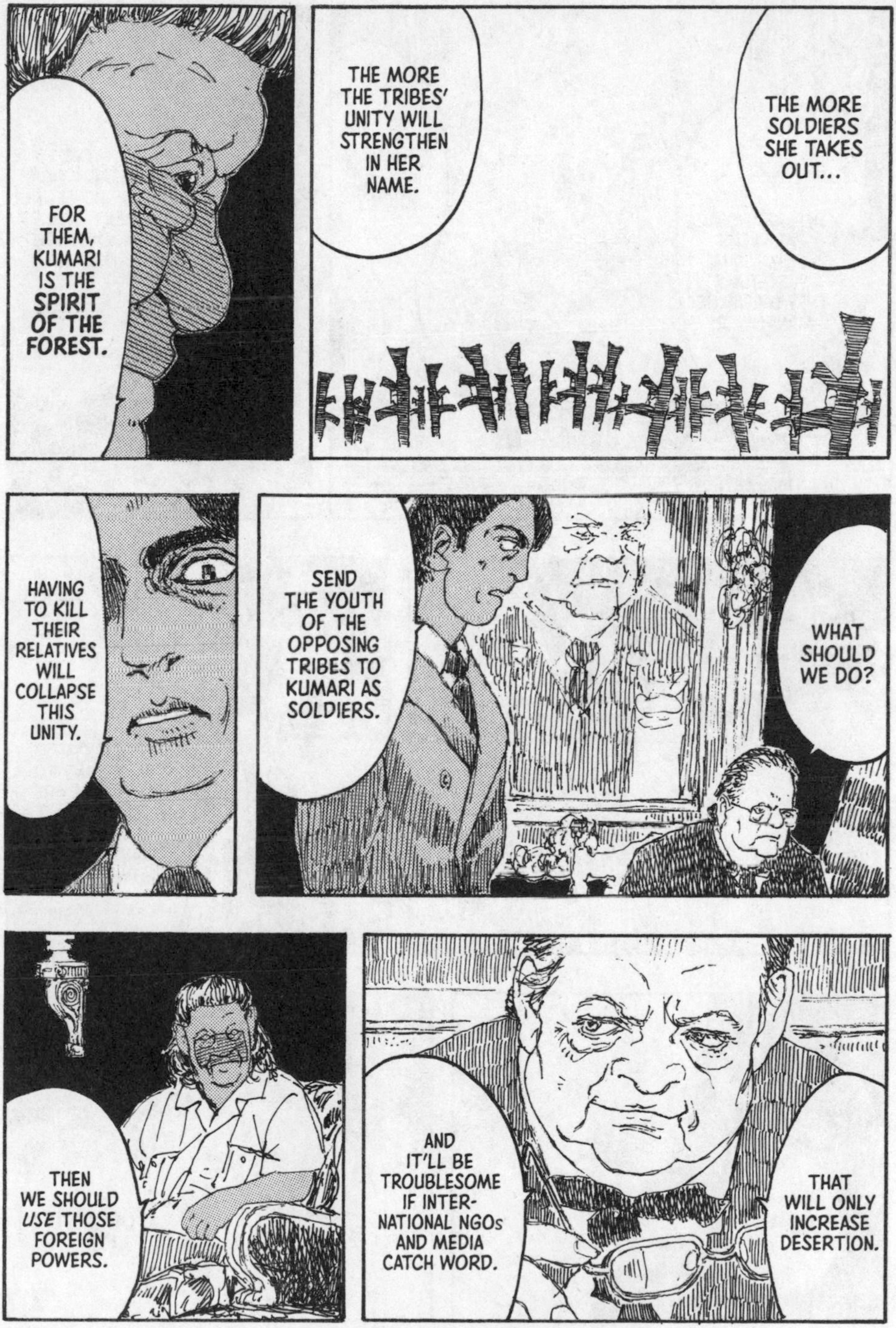
THE MORE SOLDIERS SHE TAKES OUT...
THE MORE THE TRIBES' UNITY WILL STRENGTHEN IN HER NAME.
FOR THEM, KUMARI IS THE SPIRIT OF THE FOREST.
WHAT SHOULD WE DO?
SEND THE YOUTH OF THE OPPOSING TRIBES TO KUMARI AS SOLDIERS.
HAVING TO KILL THEIR RELATIVES WILL COLLAPSE THIS UNITY.
THAT WILL ONLY INCREASE DESERTION.
AND IT'LL BE TROUBLESOME IF INTER-NATIONAL NGOs AND MEDIA CATCH WORD.
THEN WE SHOULD *USE* THOSE FOREIGN POWERS.

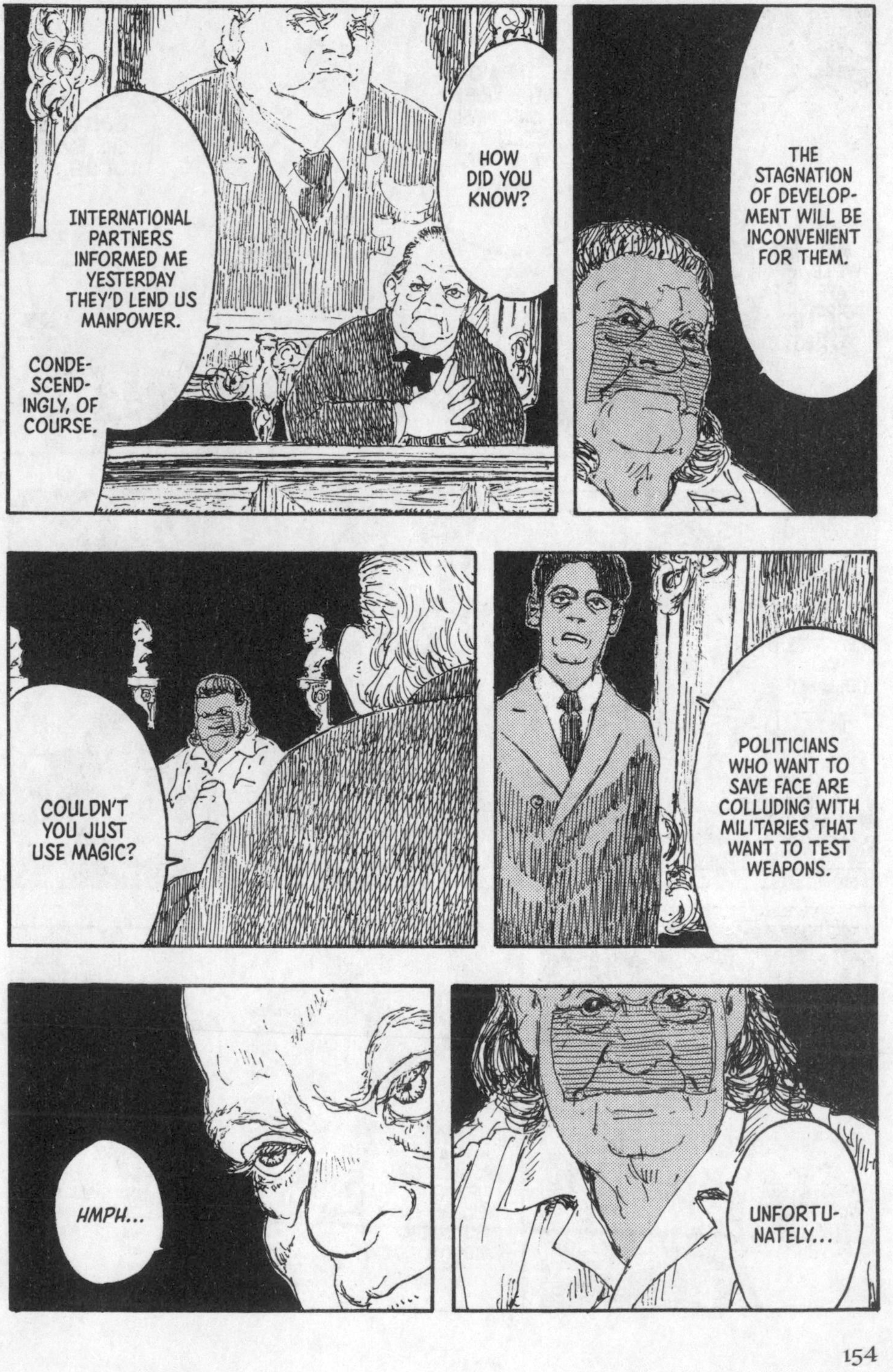
THE STAGNATION OF DEVELOPMENT WILL BE INCONVENIENT FOR THEM.
HOW DID YOU KNOW?
INTERNATIONAL PARTNERS INFORMED ME YESTERDAY THEY'D LEND US MANPOWER.
CONDESCENDINGLY, OF COURSE.
POLITICIANS WHO WANT TO SAVE FACE ARE COLLUDING WITH MILITARIES THAT WANT TO TEST WEAPONS.
COULDN'T YOU JUST USE MAGIC?
UNFORTUNATELY...
HMPH...

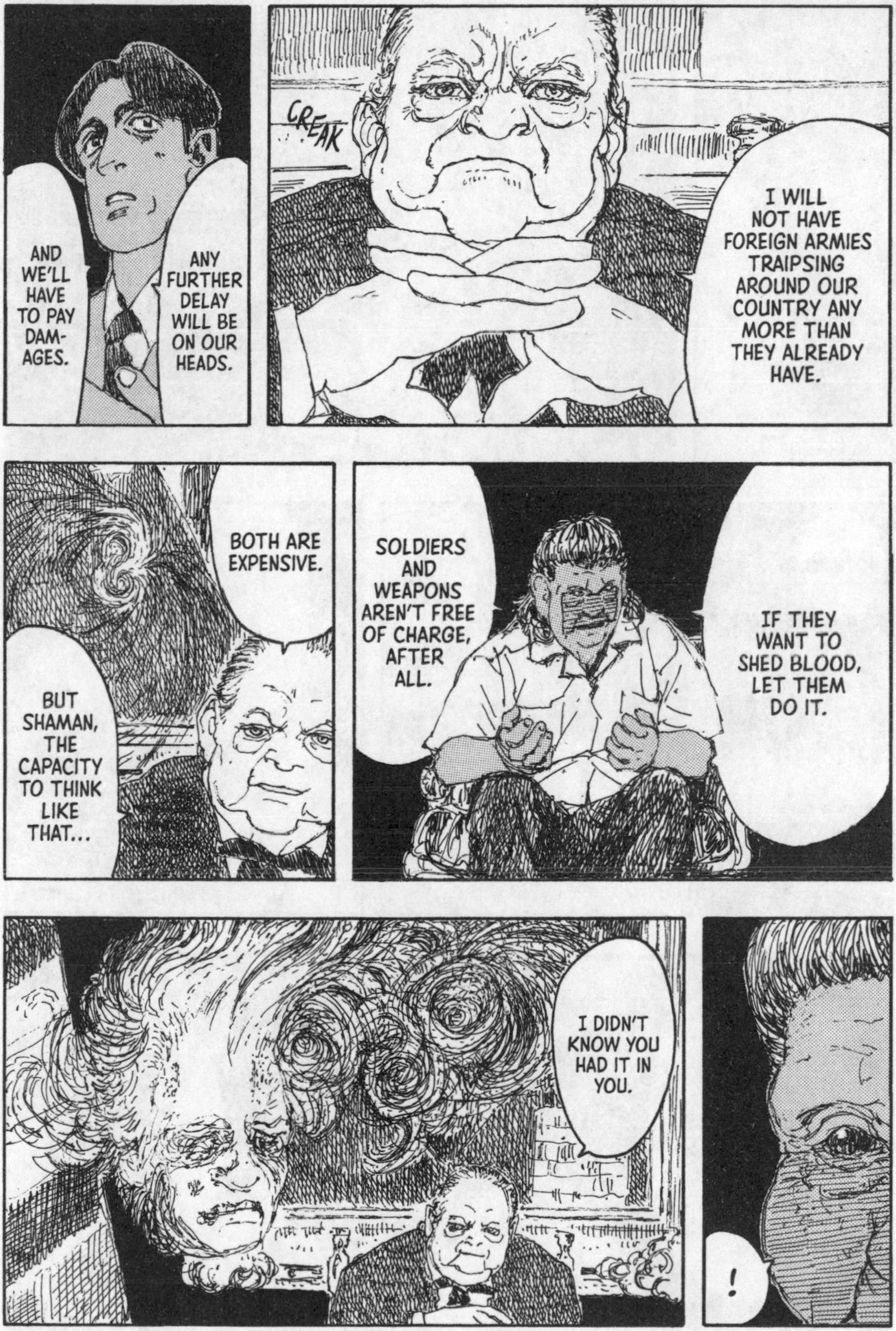
I WILL NOT HAVE FOREIGN ARMIES TRAIPSING AROUND OUR COUNTRY ANY MORE THAN THEY ALREADY HAVE.
CREAK
ANY FURTHER DELAY WILL BE ON OUR HEADS.
AND WE'LL HAVE TO PAY DAM-AGES.
IF THEY WANT TO SHED BLOOD, LET THEM DO IT.
SOLDIERS AND WEAPONS AREN'T FREE OF CHARGE, AFTER ALL.
BOTH ARE EXPENSIVE.
BUT SHAMAN, THE CAPACITY TO THINK LIKE THAT...
!
I DIDN'T KNOW YOU HAD IT IN YOU.

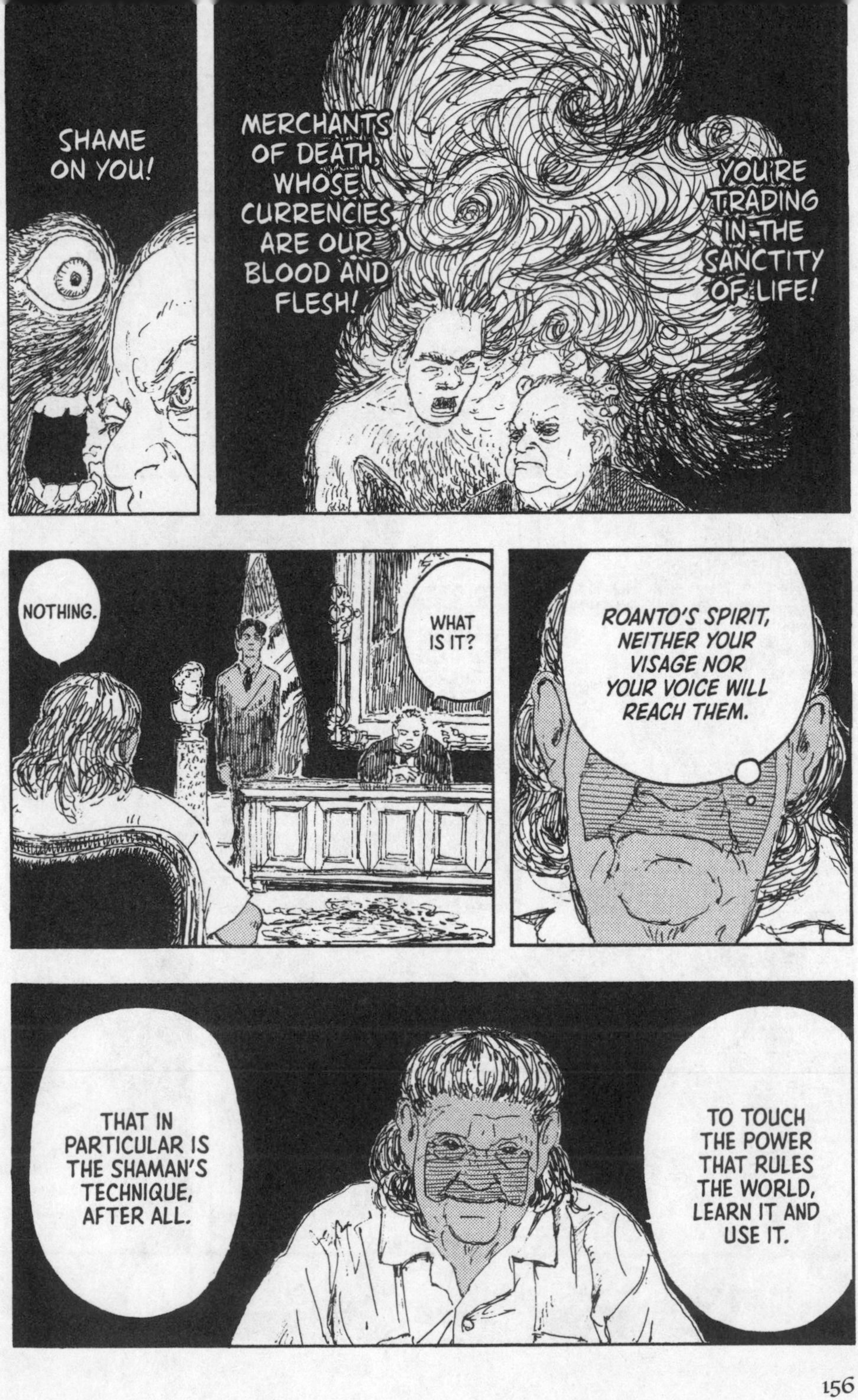
MERCHANTS OF DEATH, WHOSE CURRENCIES ARE OUR BLOOD AND FLESH!
YOU'RE TRADING IN THE SANCTITY OF LIFE!
SHAME ON YOU!
ROANTO'S SPIRIT, NEITHER YOUR VISAGE NOR YOUR VOICE WILL REACH THEM.
WHAT IS IT?
NOTHING.
TO TOUCH THE POWER THAT RULES THE WORLD, LEARN IT AND USE IT.
THAT IN PARTICULAR IS THE SHAMAN'S TECHNIQUE, AFTER ALL.

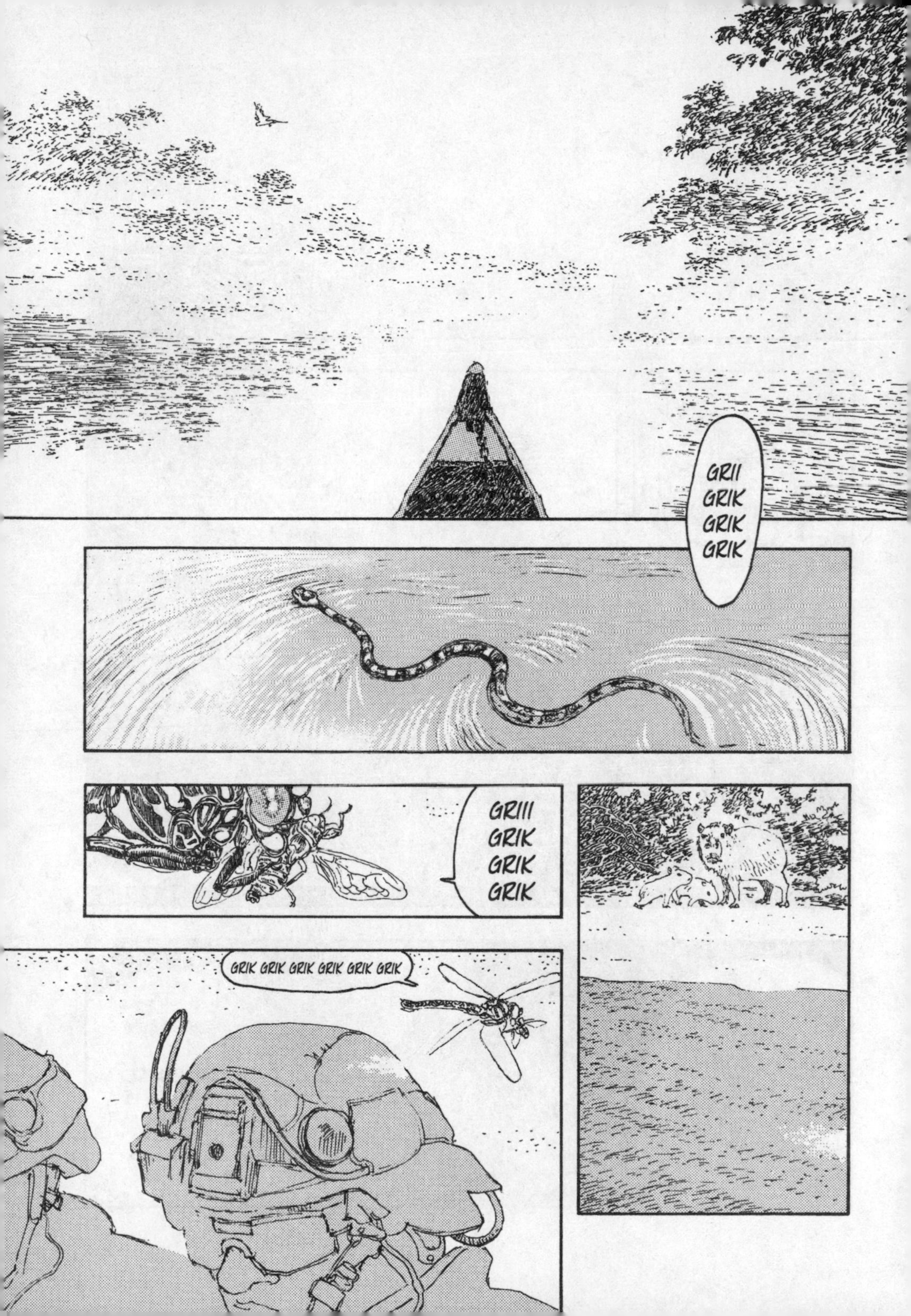
GRII GRIK GRIK GRIK
GRIII GRIK GRIK GRIK
GRIK GRIK GRIK GRIK GRIK GRIK

GRIK
GRIK
GRIK...

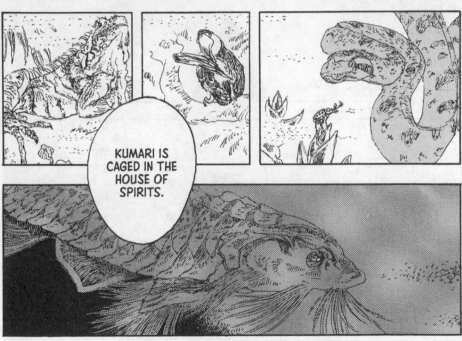

KUMARI IS CAGED IN THE HOUSE OF SPIRITS.

THEY CHANGE THEIR BODY ODOR TO A HONEYED SCENT ATTRACTIVE TO SPIRITS.

THE HOUSE OF SPIRITS IS A SHAMAN'S LAST RESORT.

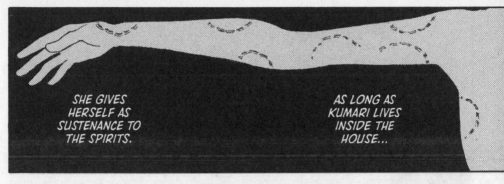

AS LONG AS KUMARI LIVES INSIDE THE HOUSE...
SHE GIVES HERSELF AS SUSTENANCE TO THE SPIRITS.
THOSE GREEDY SPIRITS...
WILL NOT ALLOW KUMARI TO LEAVE THE HOUSE.
IN EXCHANGE, BECAUSE THEY WANT TO EAT HER...
THE SPIRITS PROTECT KUMARI AND FOLLOW HER.
WE'VE ARRIVED.

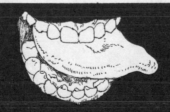

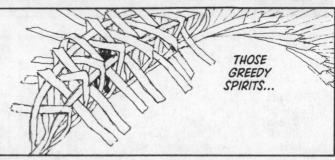

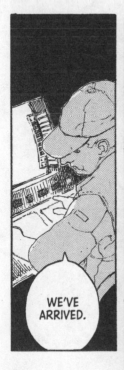

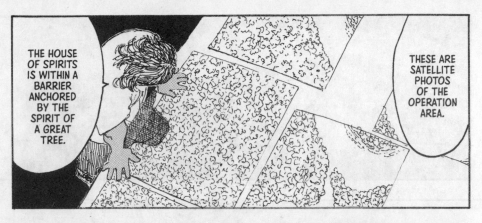

THESE ARE SATELLITE PHOTOS OF THE OPERATION AREA.
THE HOUSE OF SPIRITS IS WITHIN A BARRIER ANCHORED BY THE SPIRIT OF A GREAT TREE.
THE TREES THAT CAN USE IT ARE LIMITED.
HERE.
SHE WILL BE UNDER THIS GIANT LUPUNA TREE.

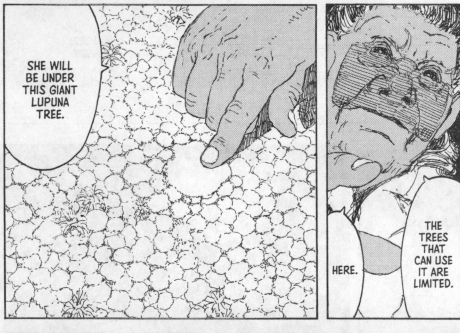

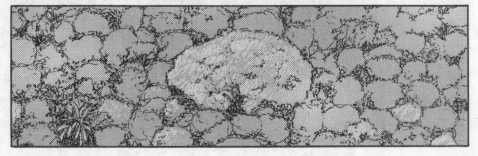

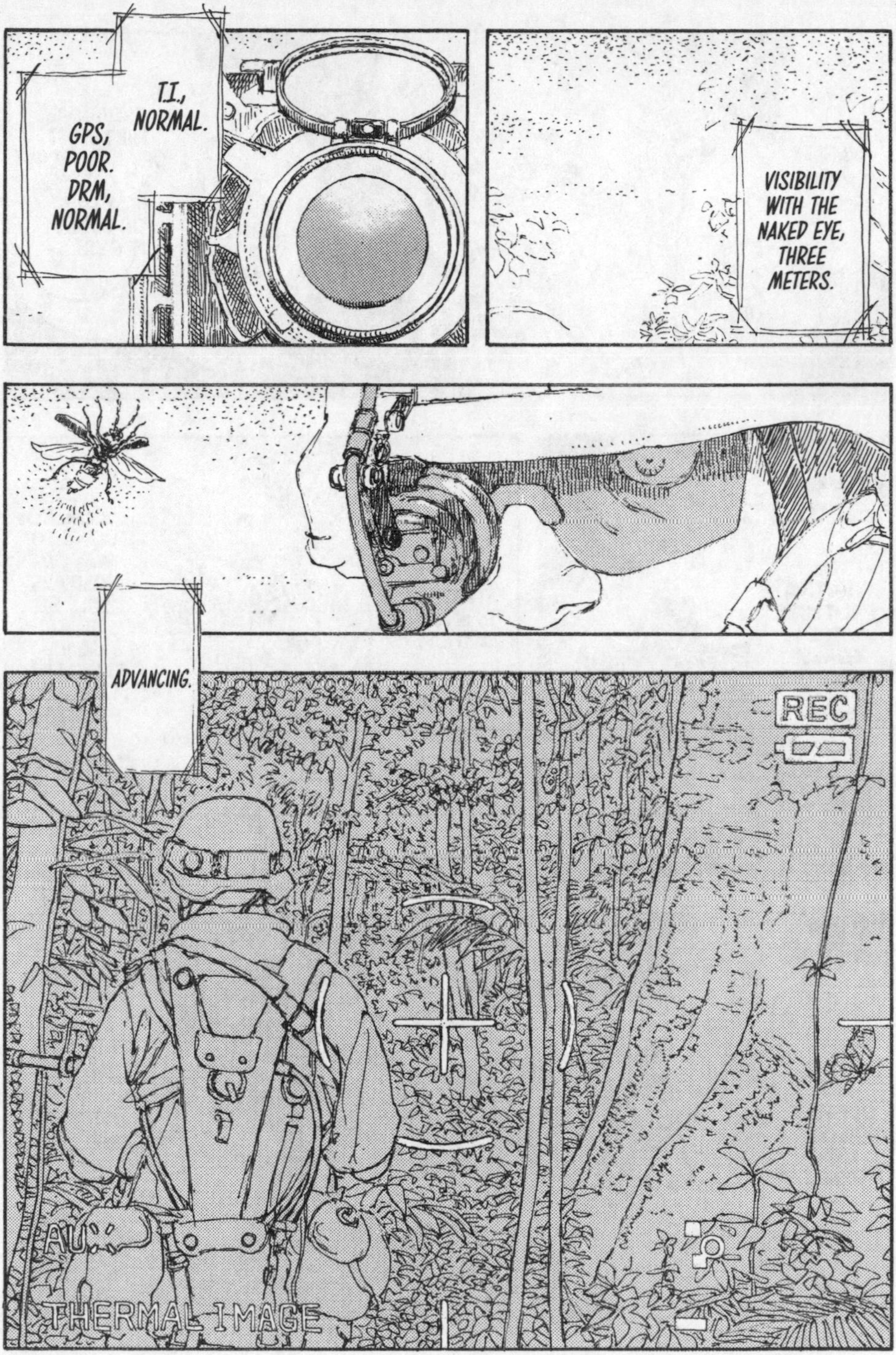
VISIBILITY WITH THE NAKED EYE, THREE METERS.
T.I., NORMAL.
GPS, POOR. DRM, NORMAL.
ADVANCING.
REC
AU
THERMAL IMAGE

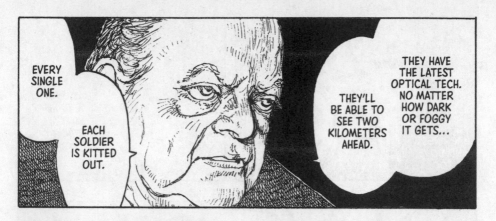

THEY HAVE THE LATEST OPTICAL TECH. NO MATTER HOW DARK OR FOGGY IT GETS...
THEY'LL BE ABLE TO SEE TWO KILOMETERS AHEAD.
EVERY SINGLE ONE.
EACH SOLDIER IS KITTED OUT.
IF IT COMES DOWN TO WAR, *OUR* SOLDIERS WILL BE BLIND, UNLIKE THE ENEMY. THEY WILL BE KILLED.
THE ENEMY'S STRATEGY IS INTIMI-DATION.
THEY HAVE BECOME RULERS OF THE NIGHT.
THE FOG THAT PROTECTS THE FOREST WILL BE USELESS.
I THINK THEY CAN KILL SHAMAN KUMARI.
WELL... THE WORLD ISN'T JUST MADE OF LIGHT AND HEAT.
IT HAS ODORS. TASTES AND SOUNDS, TOO.

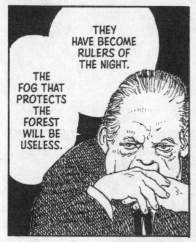

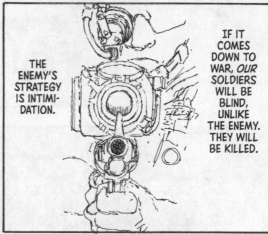

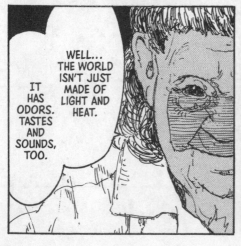

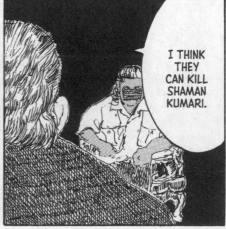

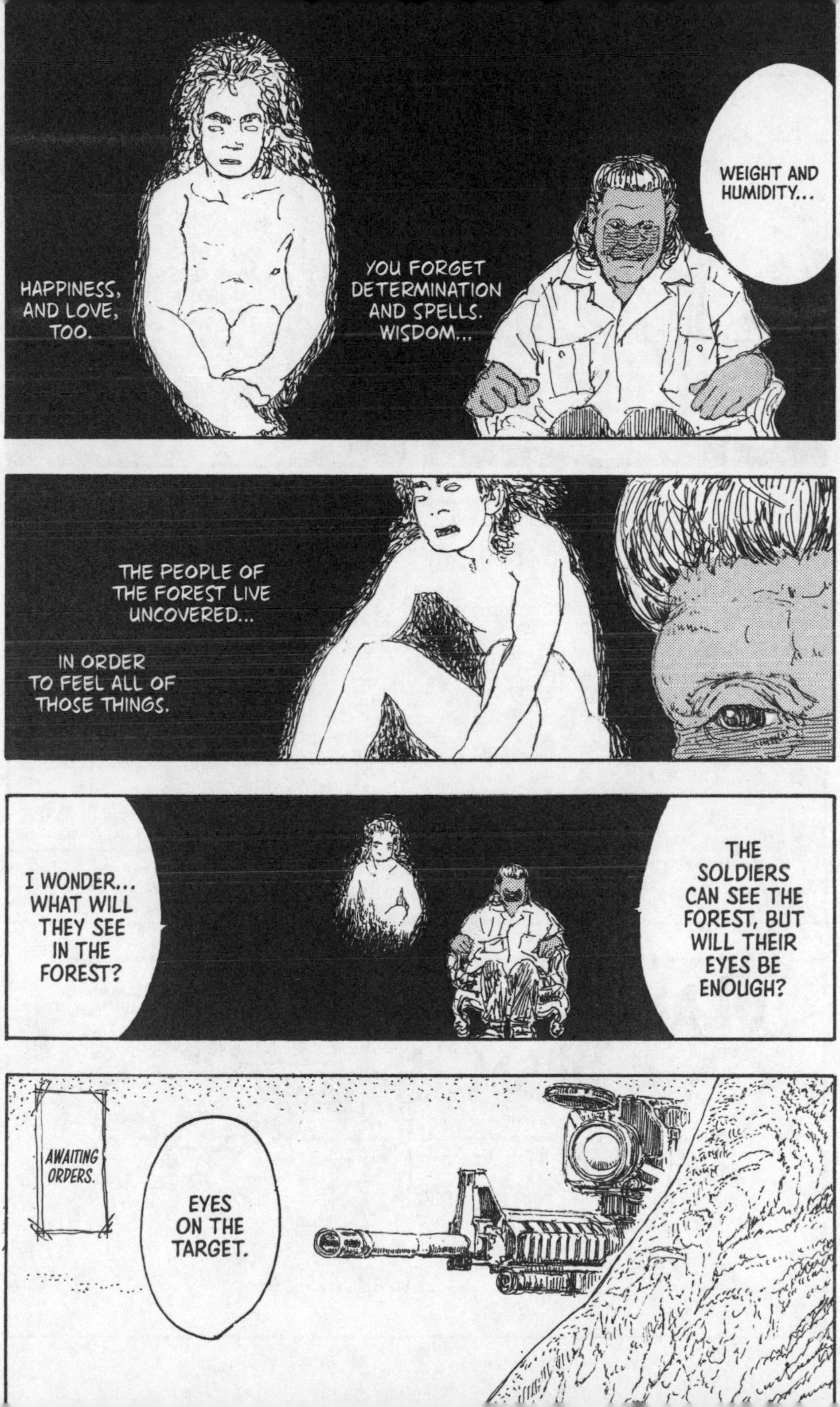
WEIGHT AND HUMIDITY...
YOU FORGET DETERMINATION AND SPELLS. WISDOM...
HAPPINESS, AND LOVE, TOO.
THE PEOPLE OF THE FOREST LIVE UNCOVERED...
IN ORDER TO FEEL ALL OF THOSE THINGS.
THE SOLDIERS CAN SEE THE FOREST, BUT WILL THEIR EYES BE ENOUGH?
I WONDER... WHAT WILL THEY SEE IN THE FOREST?
EYES ON THE TARGET.
AWAITING ORDERS.

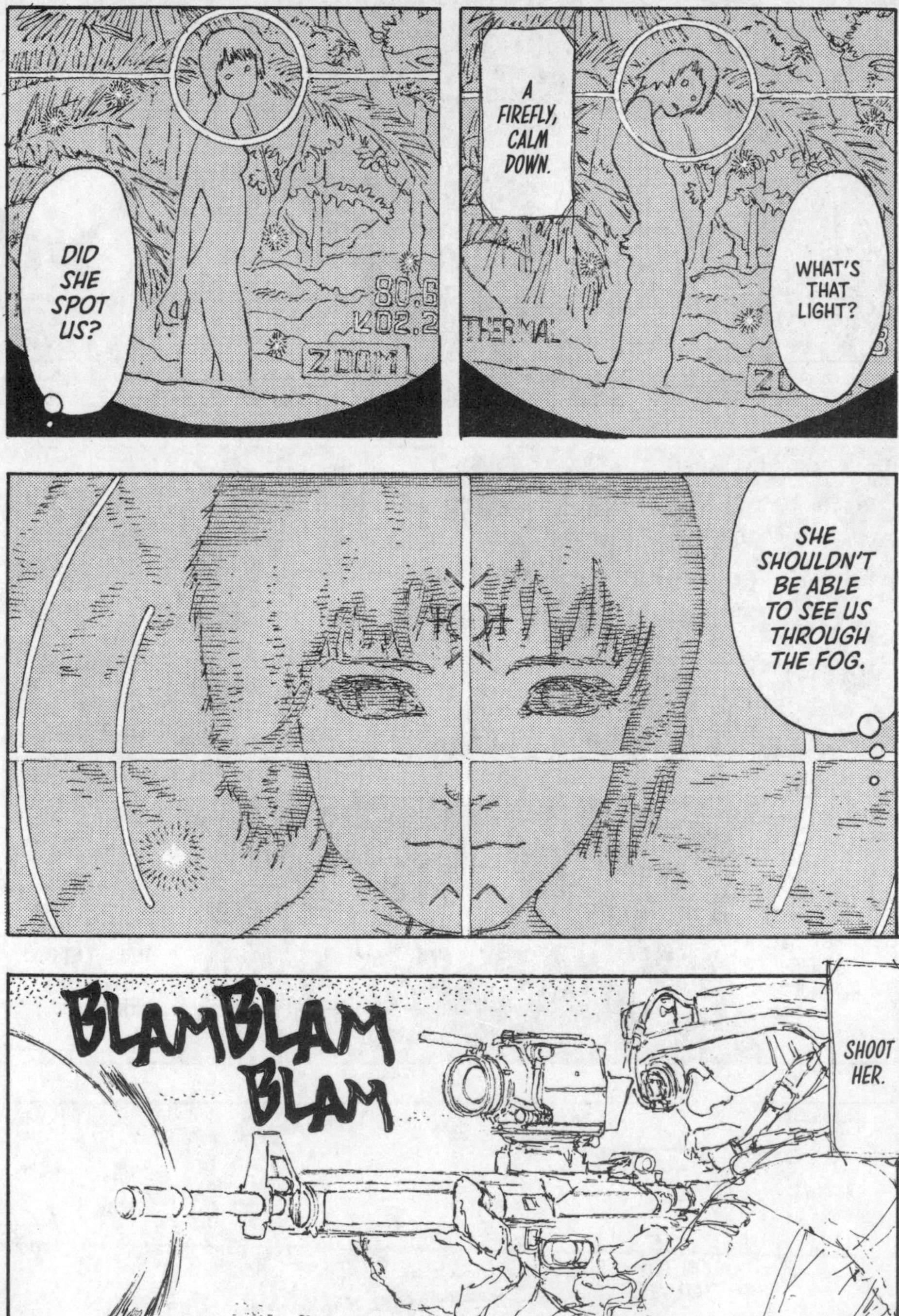
WHAT'S THAT LIGHT?
A FIREFLY, CALM DOWN.
THERMAL
DID SHE SPOT US?
ZOOM
SHE SHOULDN'T BE ABLE TO SEE US THROUGH THE FOG.
SHOOT HER.
BLAMBLAM BLAM

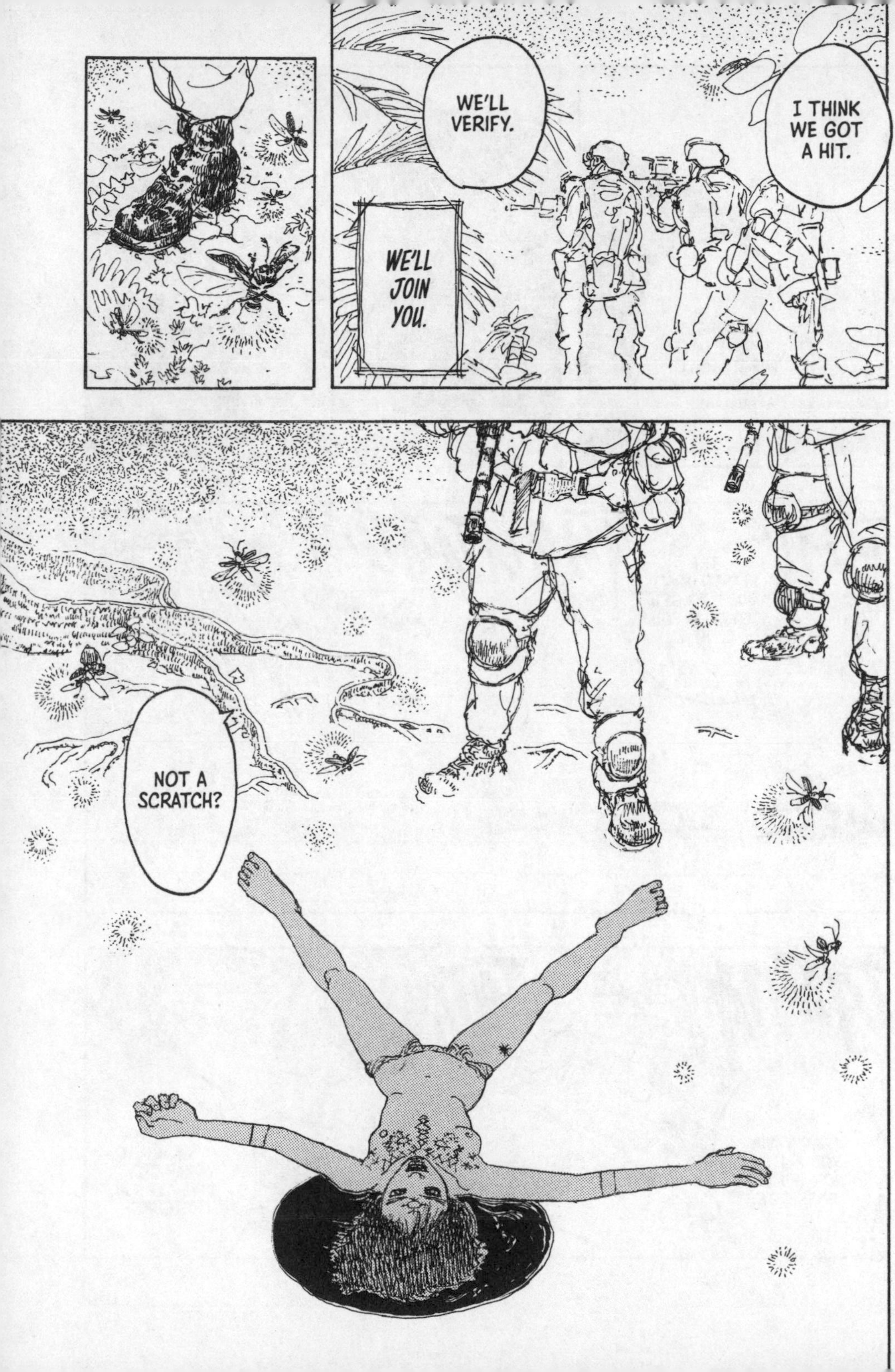
I THINK WE GOT A HIT.
WE'LL VERIFY.
WE'LL JOIN YOU.
NOT A SCRATCH?

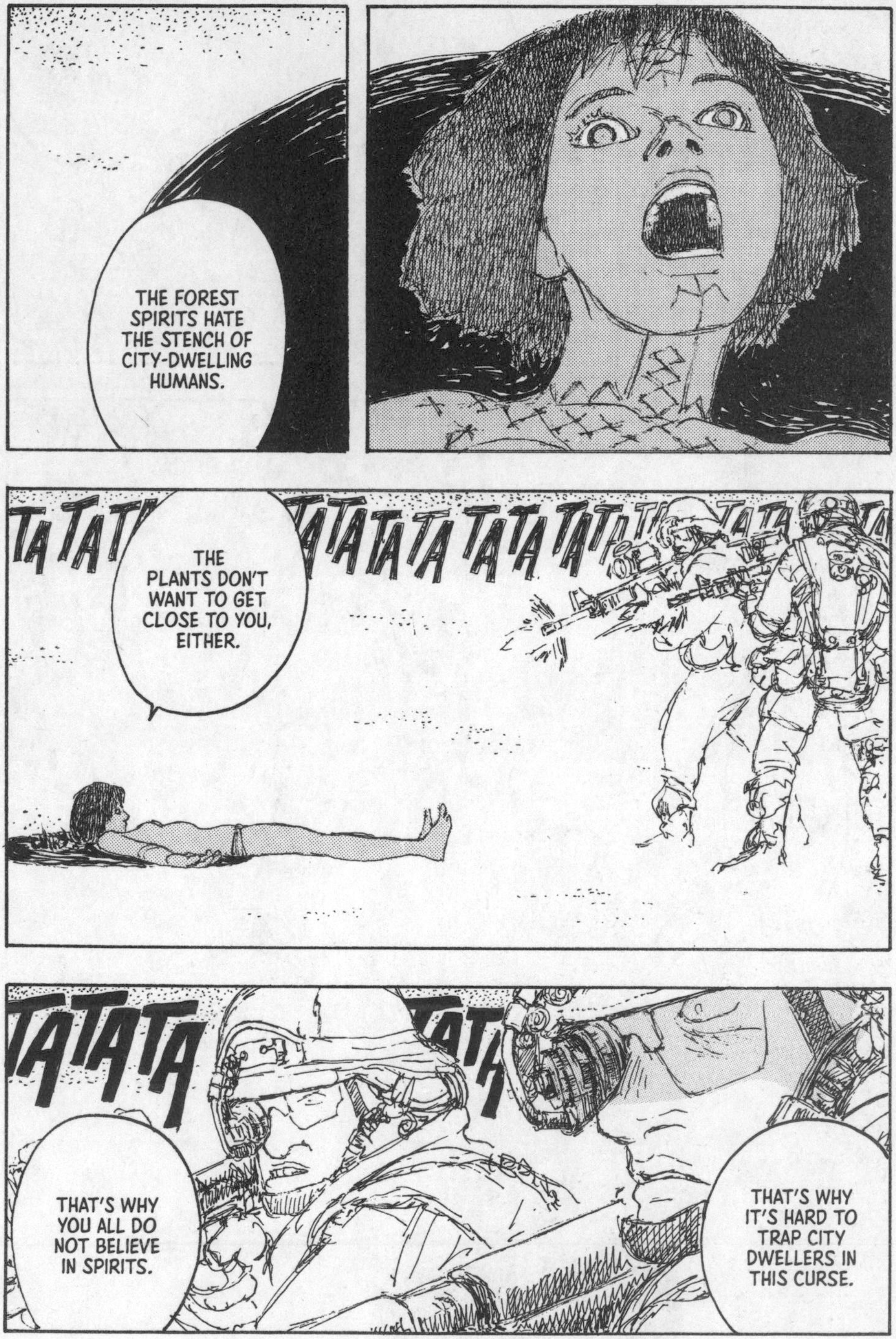
THE FOREST SPIRITS HATE THE STENCH OF CITY-DWELLING HUMANS.
THE PLANTS DON'T WANT TO GET CLOSE TO YOU, EITHER.
TATATA
THAT'S WHY IT'S HARD TO TRAP CITY DWELLERS IN THIS CURSE.
THAT'S WHY YOU ALL DO NOT BELIEVE IN SPIRITS.

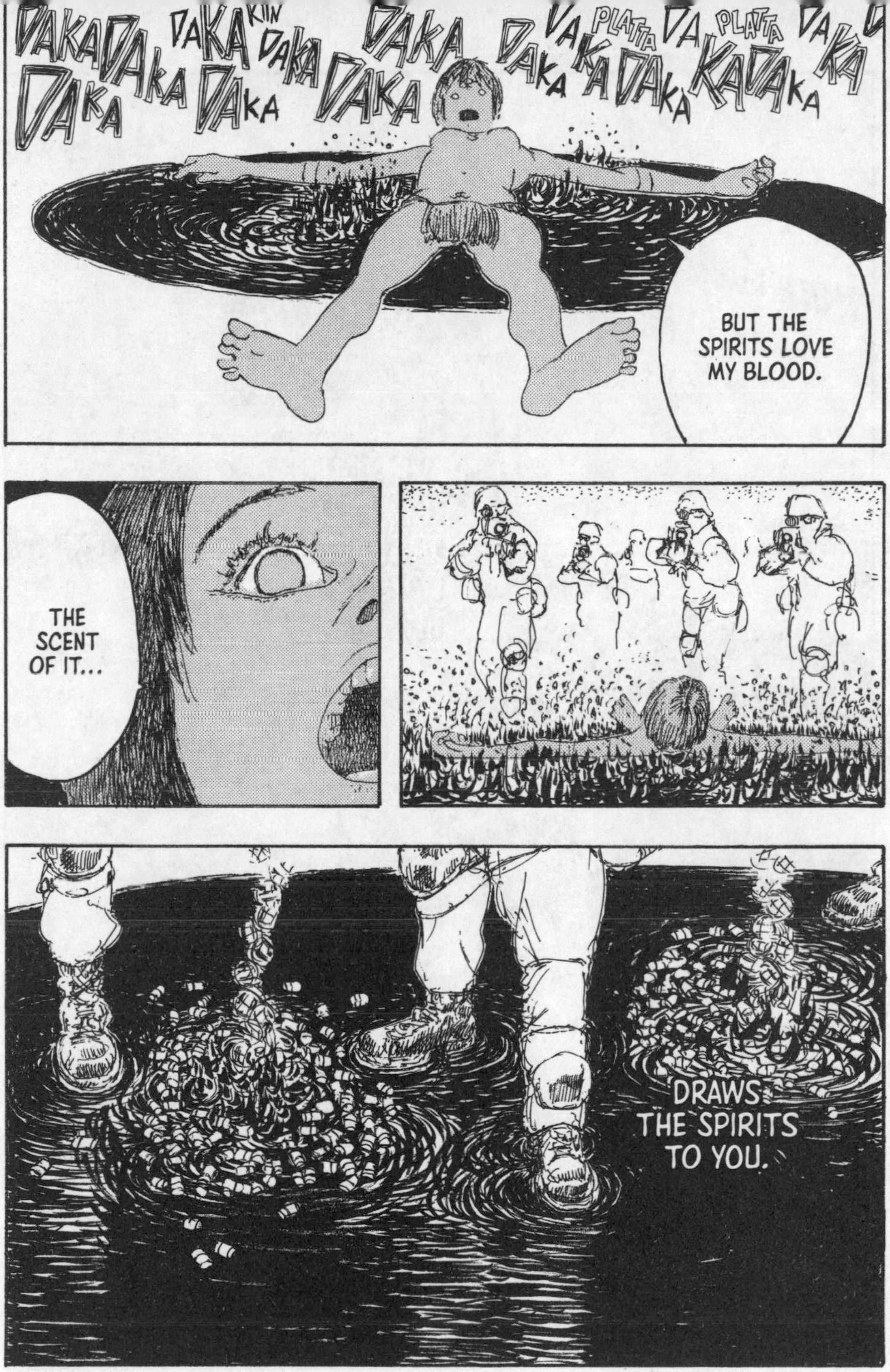
DAKA DAKA DAKA KIIN DAKA DAKA DAKA DAKA DAKA DAKA PLATTA DAKA PLATTA DAKA DAKA DAKA DAKA
BUT THE SPIRITS LOVE MY BLOOD.
THE SCENT OF IT...
DRAWS THE SPIRITS TO YOU.

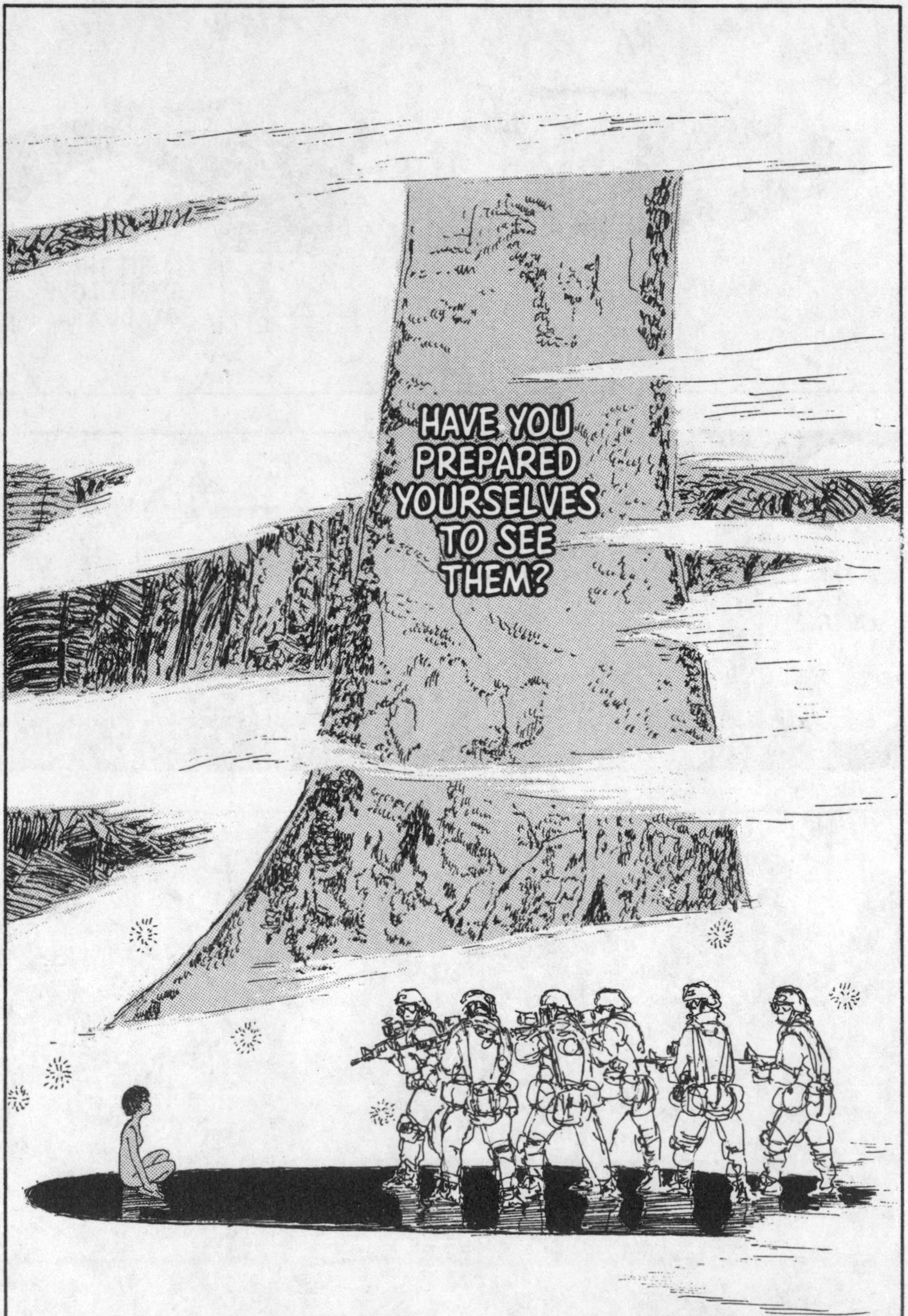
HAVE YOU PREPARED YOURSELVES TO SEE THEM?

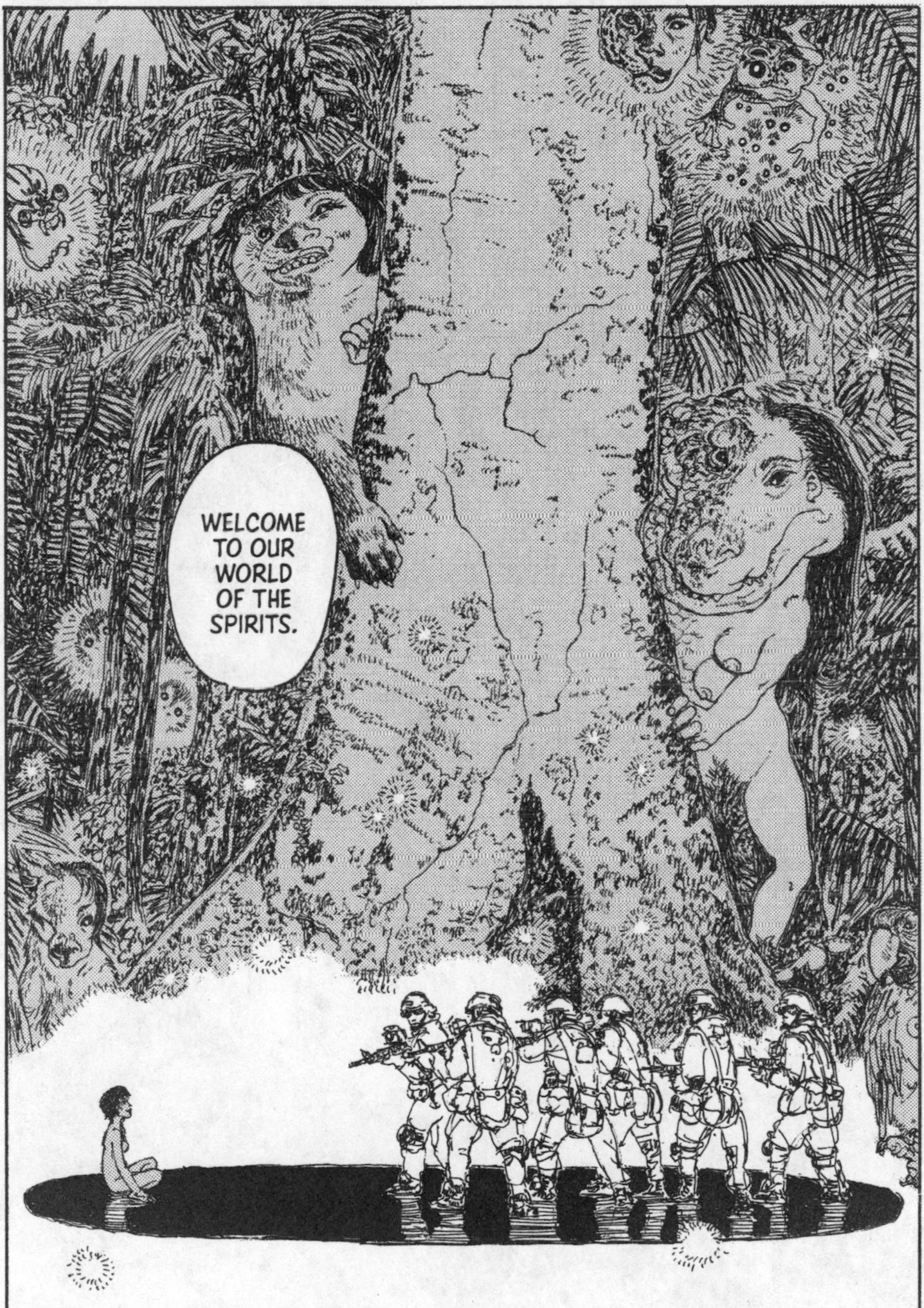
WELCOME TO OUR WORLD OF THE SPIRITS.

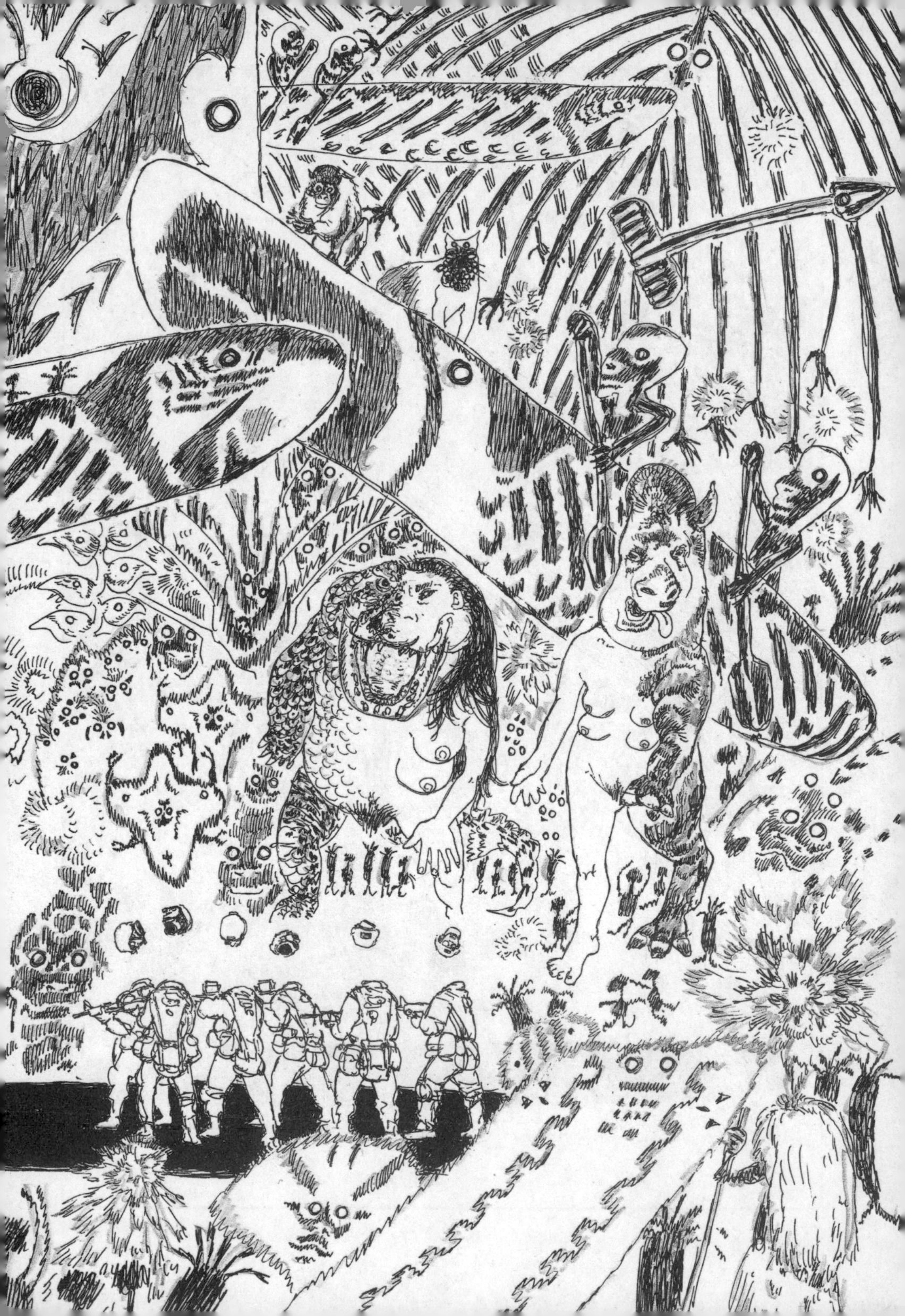

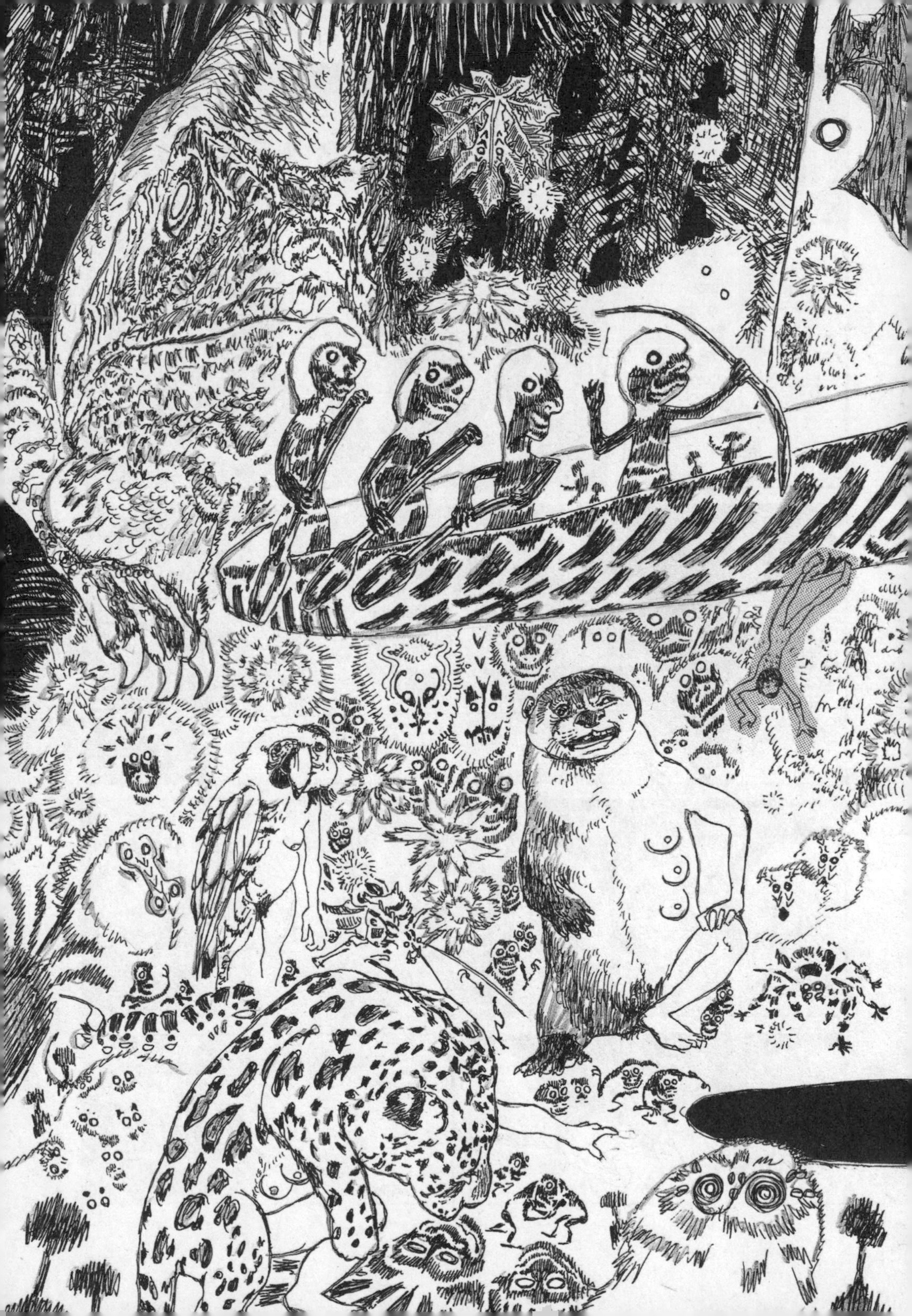

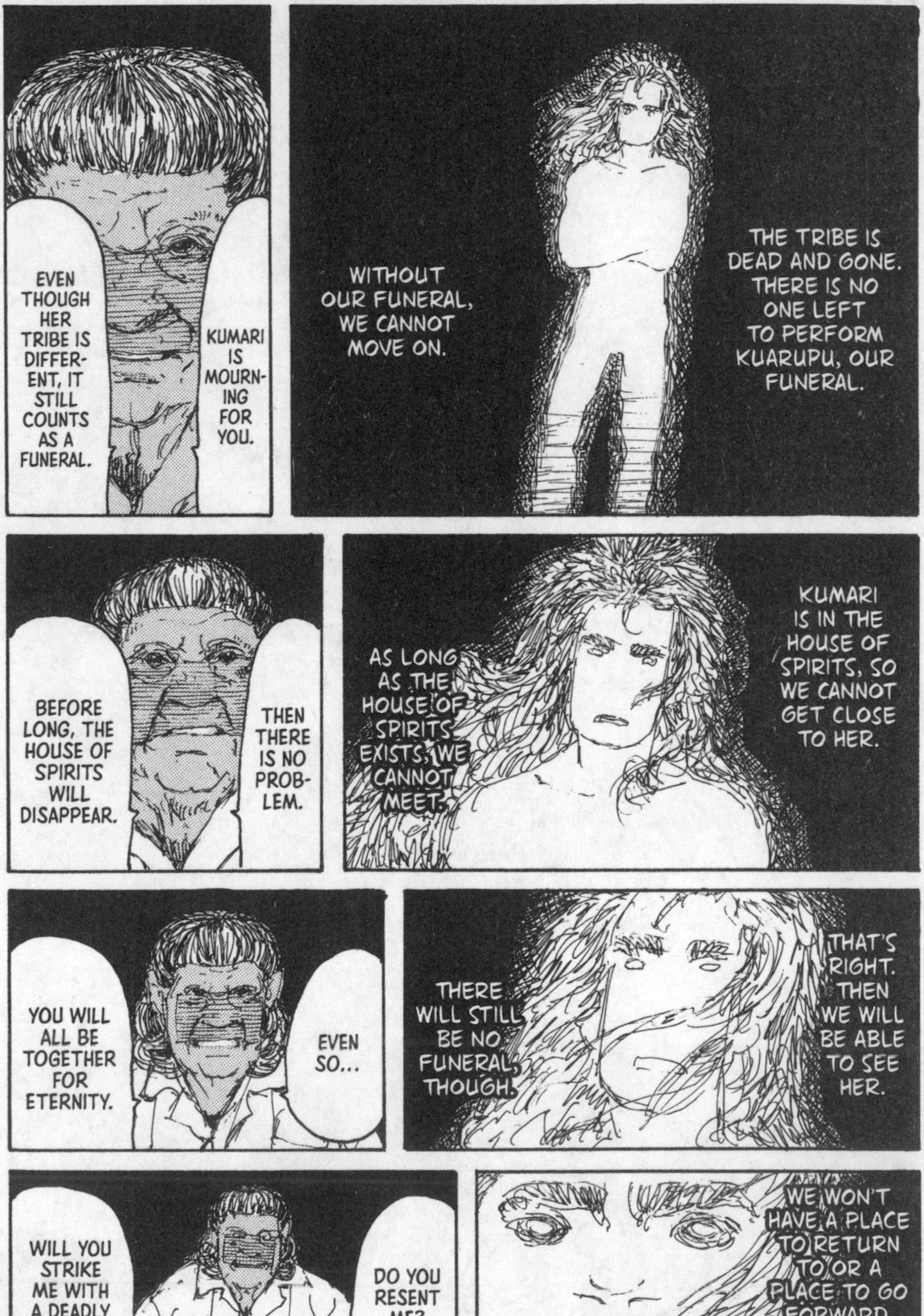
THE TRIBE IS DEAD AND GONE. THERE IS NO ONE LEFT TO PERFORM KUARUPU, OUR FUNERAL.
WITHOUT OUR FUNERAL, WE CANNOT MOVE ON.
KUMARI IS MOURNING FOR YOU.
EVEN THOUGH HER TRIBE IS DIFFERENT, IT STILL COUNTS AS A FUNERAL.
KUMARI IS IN THE HOUSE OF SPIRITS, SO WE CANNOT GET CLOSE TO HER.
AS LONG AS THE HOUSE OF SPIRITS EXISTS, WE CANNOT MEET.
THEN THERE IS NO PROBLEM.
BEFORE LONG, THE HOUSE OF SPIRITS WILL DISAPPEAR.
THAT'S RIGHT. THEN WE WILL BE ABLE TO SEE HER.
THERE WILL STILL BE NO FUNERAL, THOUGH.
EVEN SO...
YOU WILL ALL BE TOGETHER FOR ETERNITY.
WE WON'T HAVE A PLACE TO RETURN TO OR A PLACE TO GO FORWARD.
DO YOU RESENT ME?
WILL YOU STRIKE ME WITH A DEADLY CURSE?

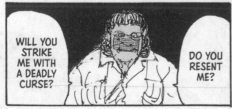

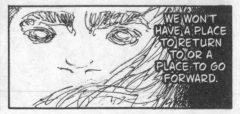

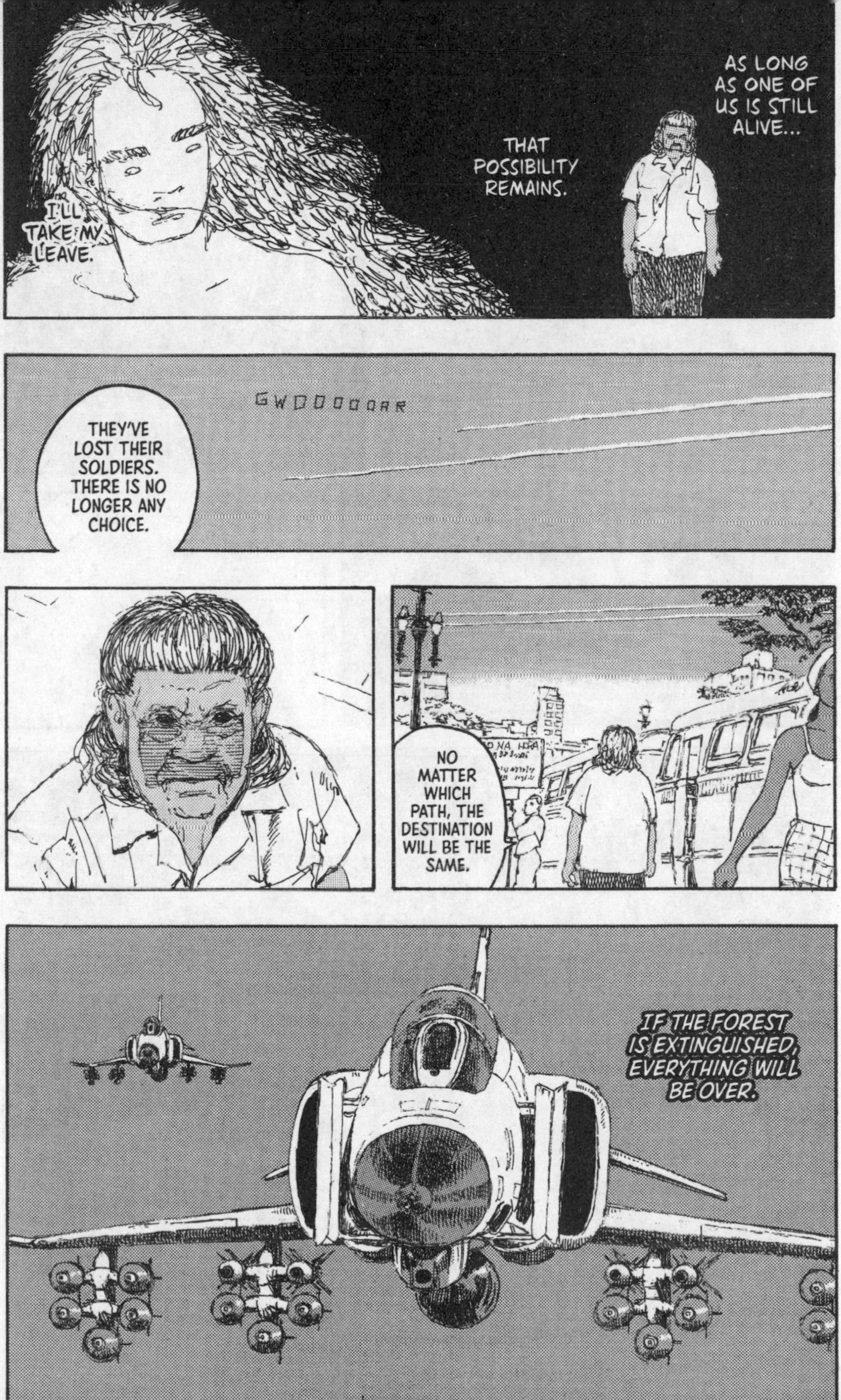
AS LONG AS ONE OF US IS STILL ALIVE...
THAT POSSIBILITY REMAINS.
I'LL TAKE MY LEAVE.
GWOOOOOAR
THEY'VE LOST THEIR SOLDIERS. THERE IS NO LONGER ANY CHOICE.
NO MATTER WHICH PATH, THE DESTINATION WILL BE THE SAME.
IF THE FOREST IS EXTINGUISHED, EVERYTHING WILL BE OVER.

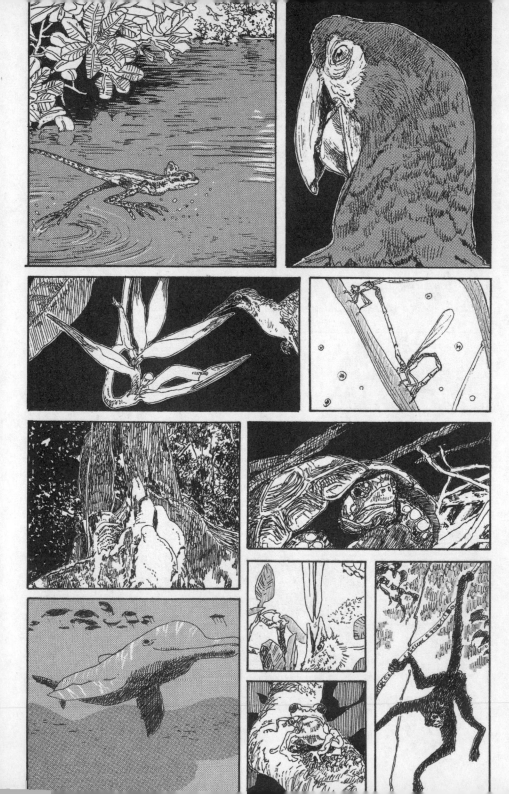

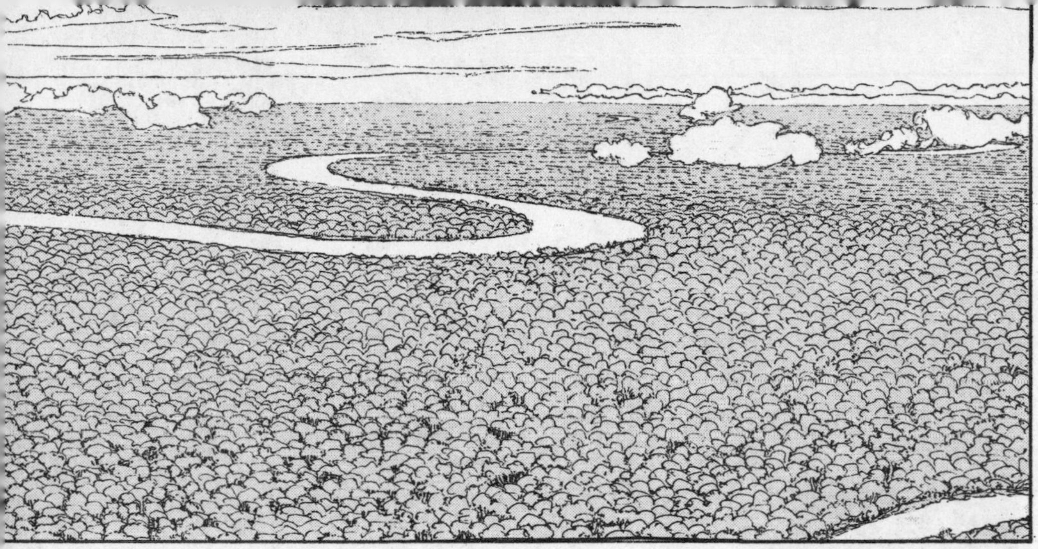
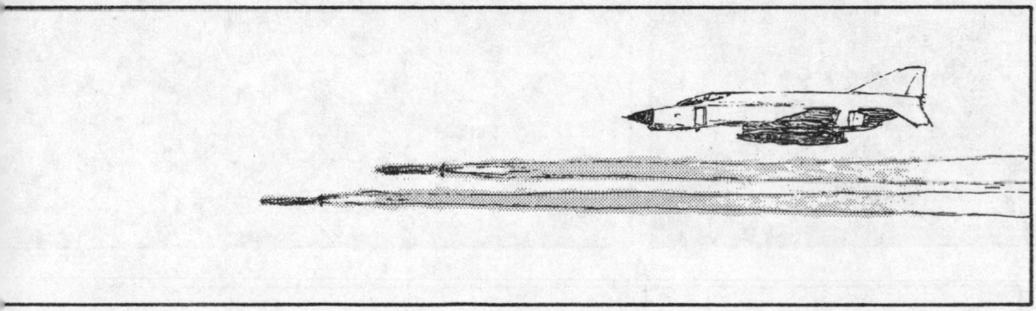
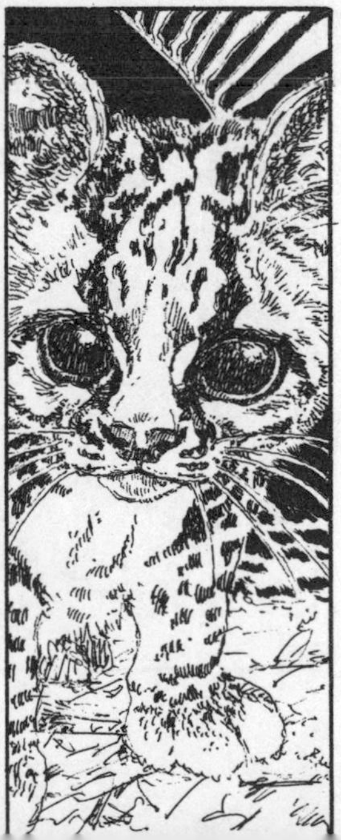
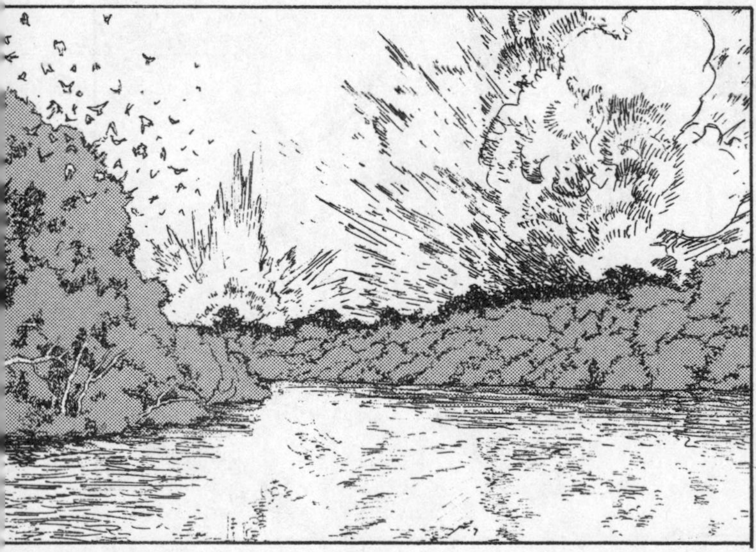

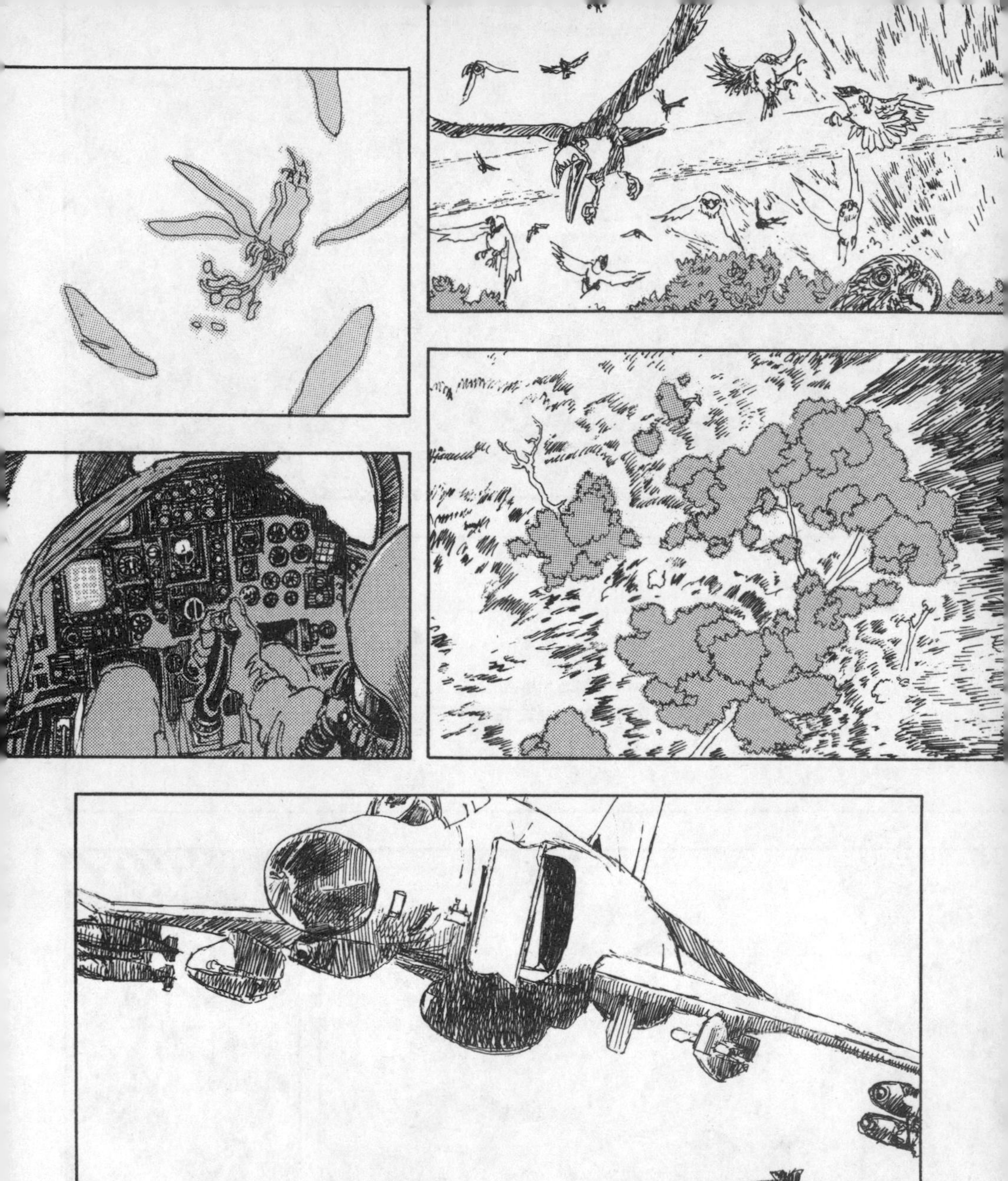

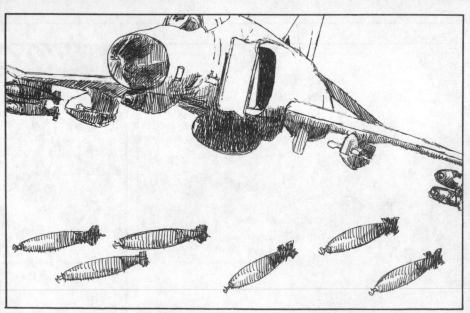

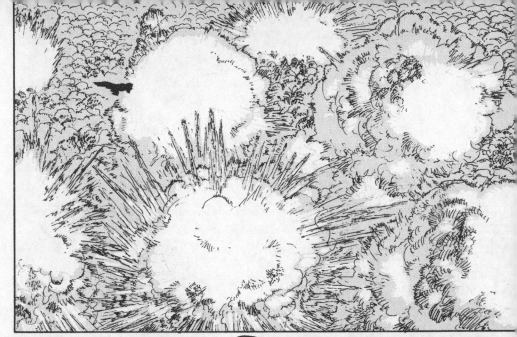

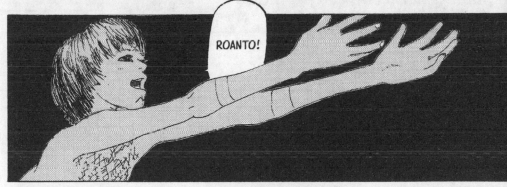

ROANTO!

I'M SORRY I COULDN'T PROTECT YOU.

I'M SORRY I COULDN'T GO SEE YOU.

ROANTO! ROANTO...

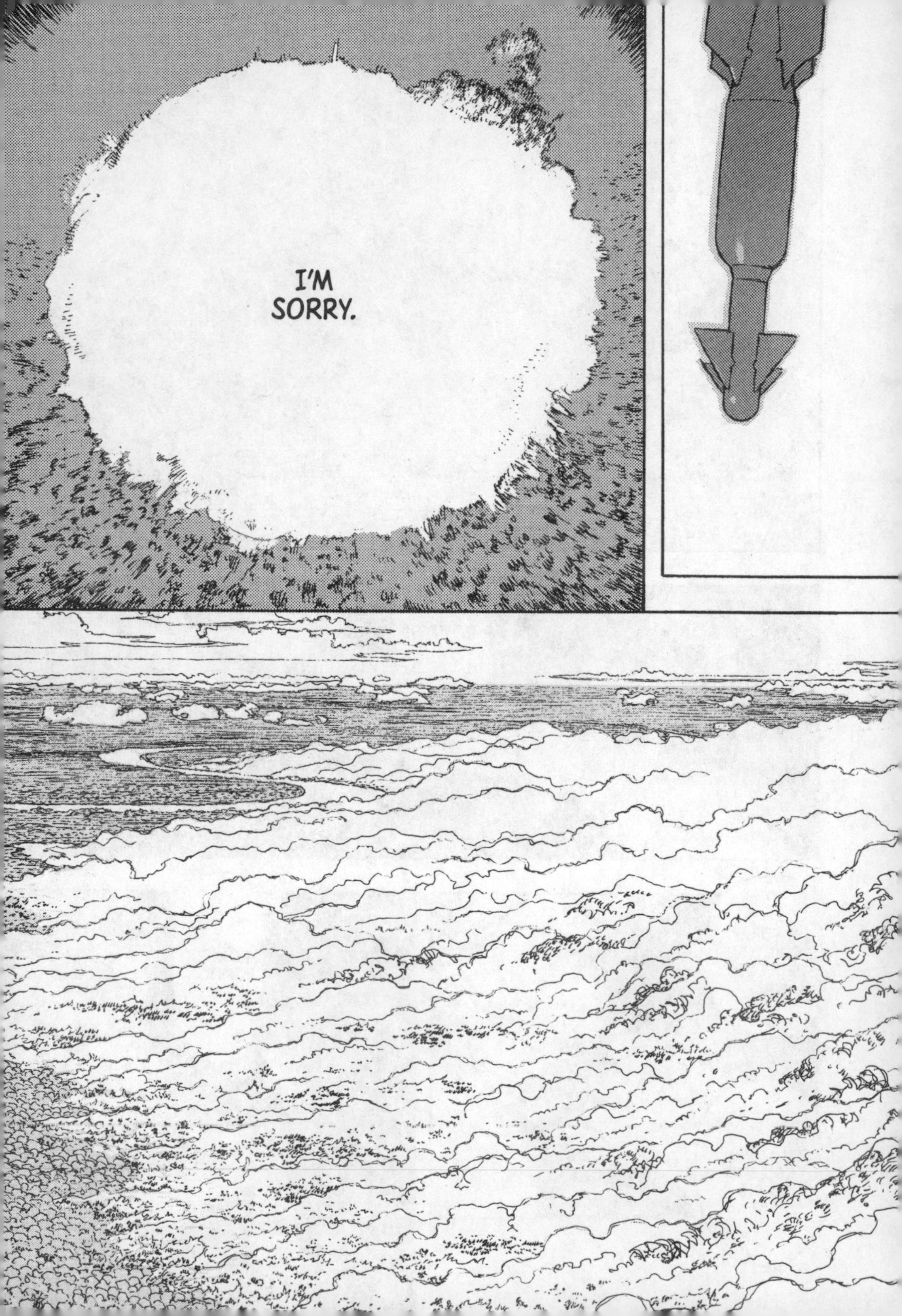
I'M SORRY.

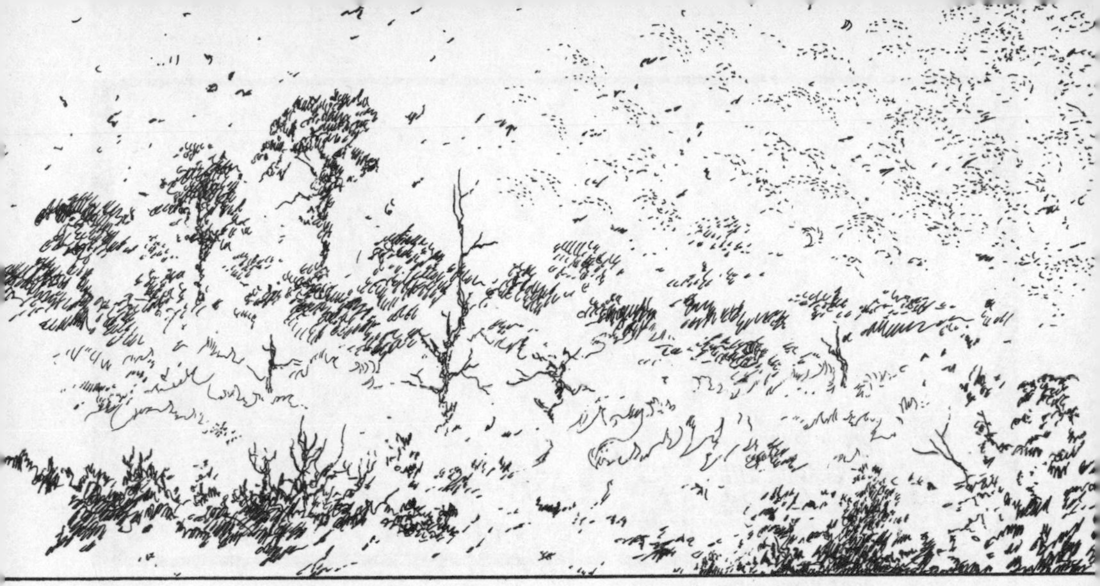

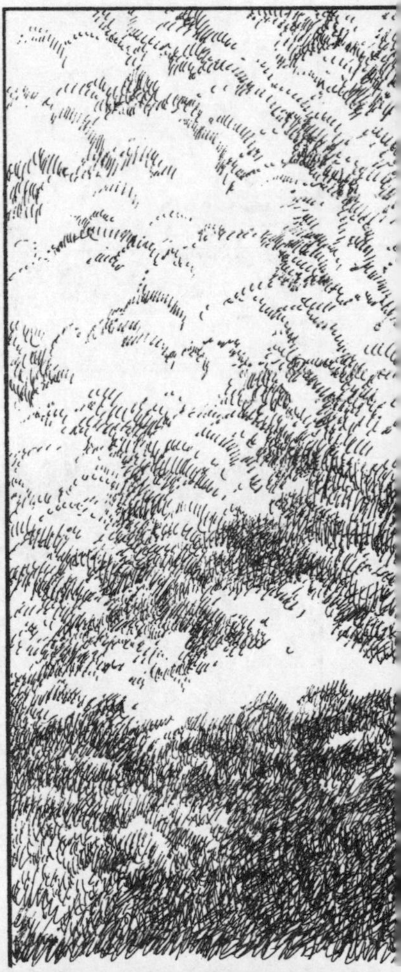

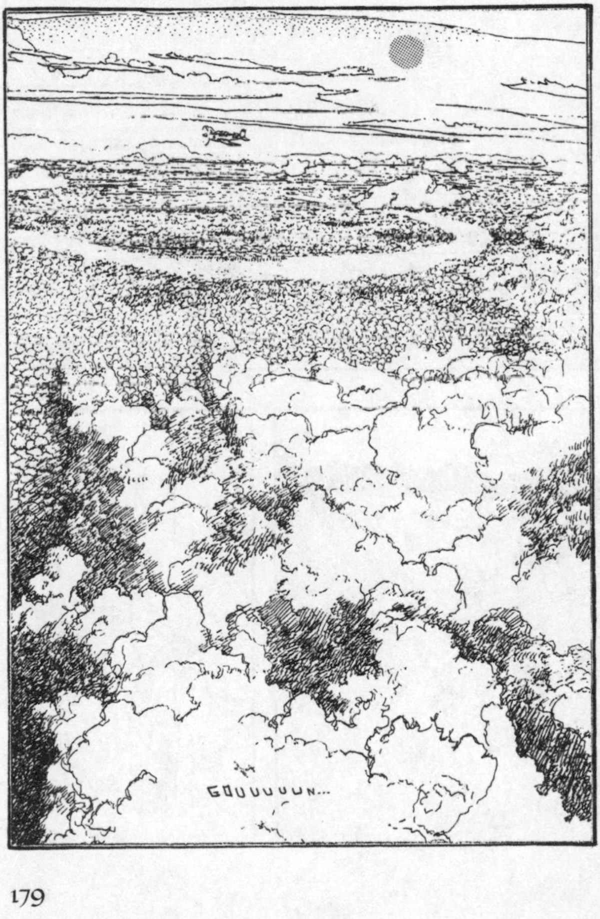
GOUUUUUN...

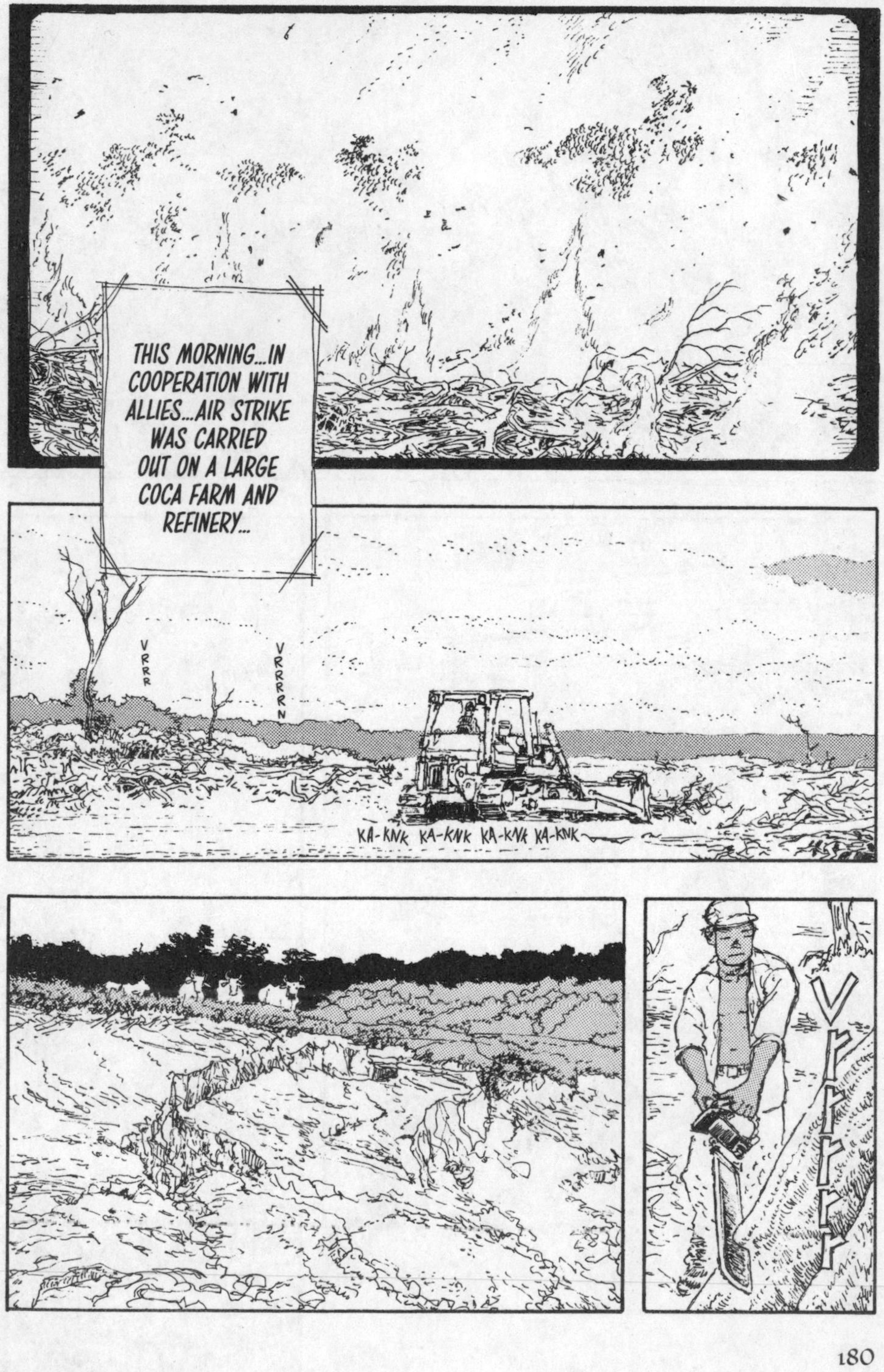
THIS MORNING...IN COOPERATION WITH ALLIES...AIR STRIKE WAS CARRIED OUT ON A LARGE COCA FARM AND REFINERY...
VRRRRN
VRRR
KA-KNK KA-KNK KA-KNK KA-KNK

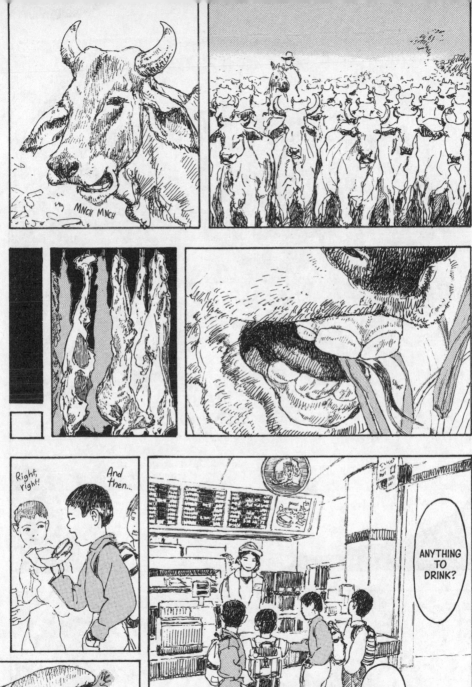

MNCH MNCH

Right, right!   And then...

ANYTHING TO DRINK?

NAH.

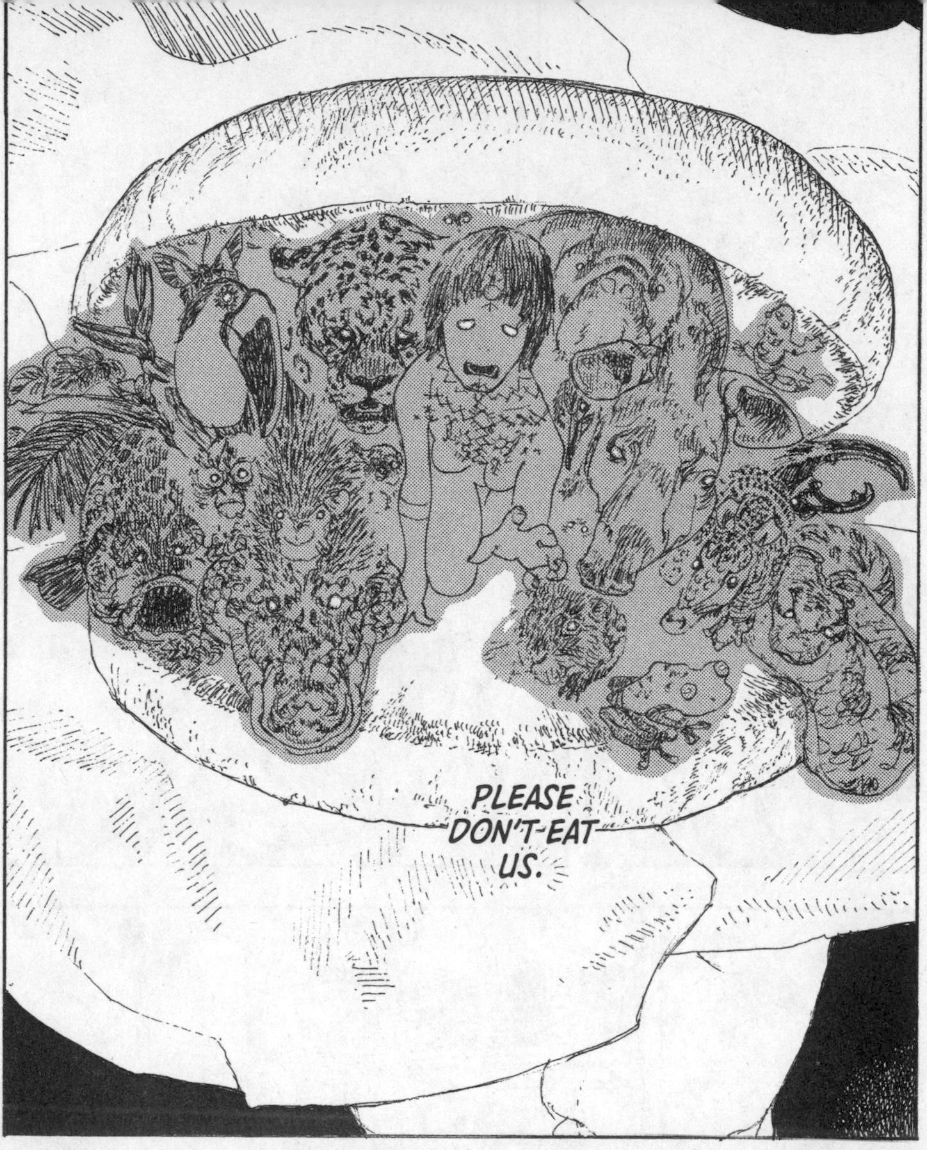
PLEASE DON'T EAT US.

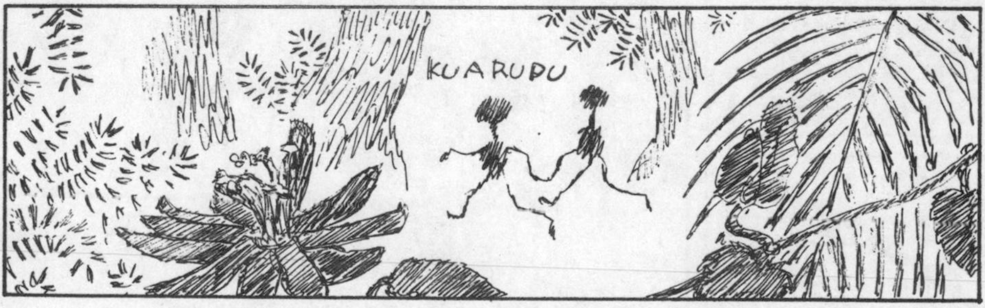
KUARUPU

Kuarupu ~ End

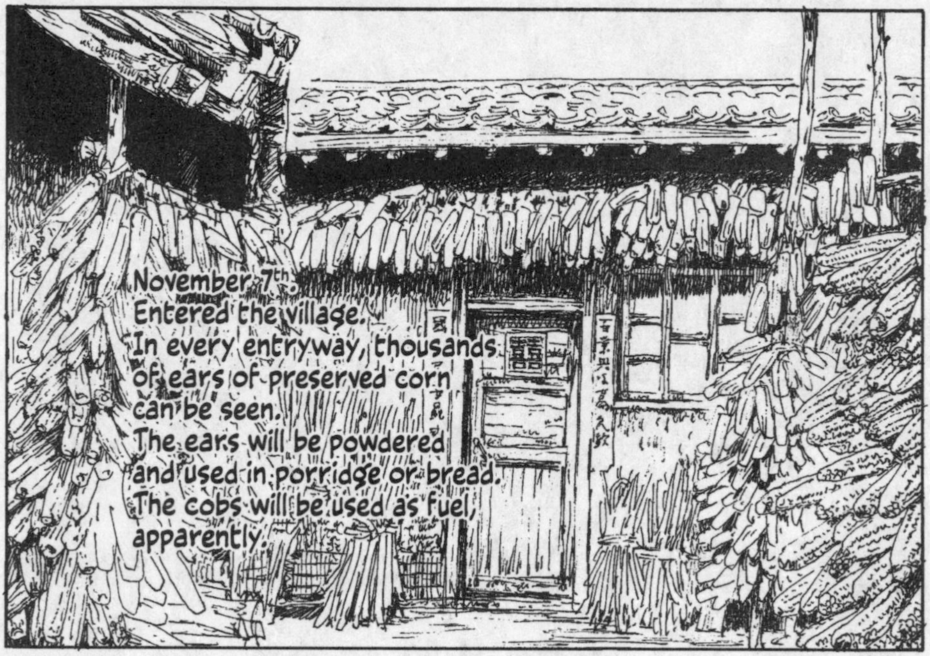
November 7th.
Entered the village.
In every entryway, thousands of ears of preserved corn can be seen.
The ears will be powdered and used in porridge or bread.
The cobs will be used as fuel, apparently.
囍
Character on door: Happiness

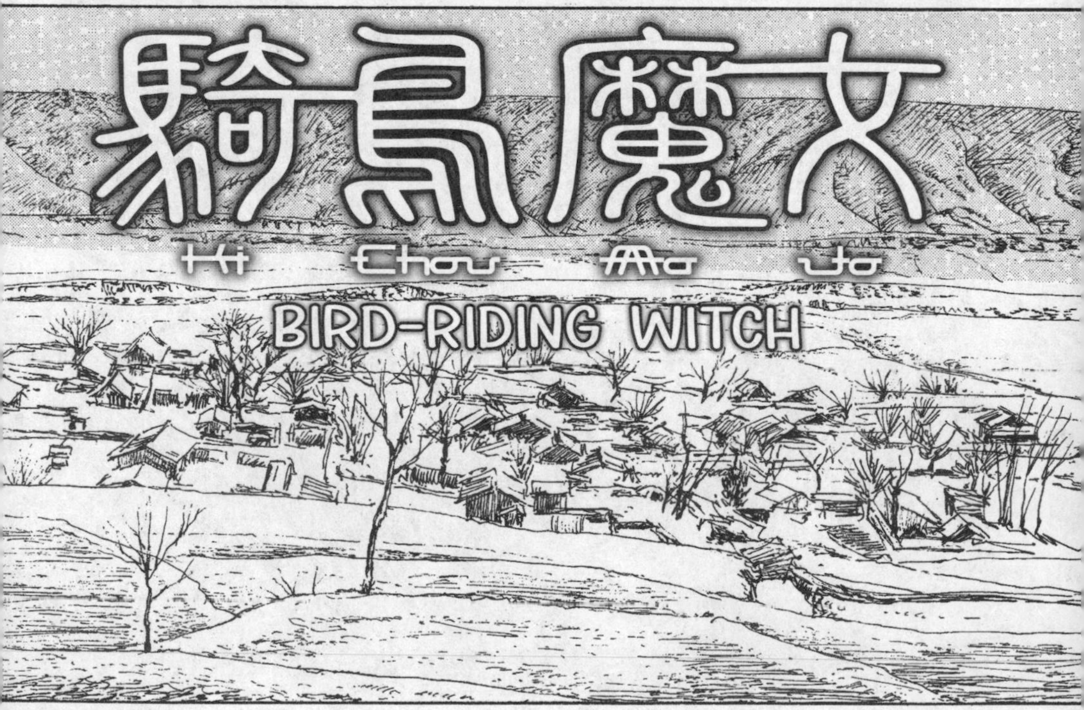
騎鳥魔女
Ki Chou Ma Jo
BIRD-RIDING WITCH

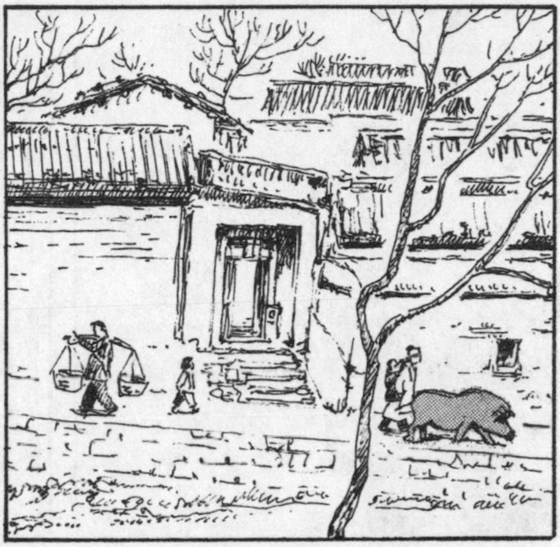

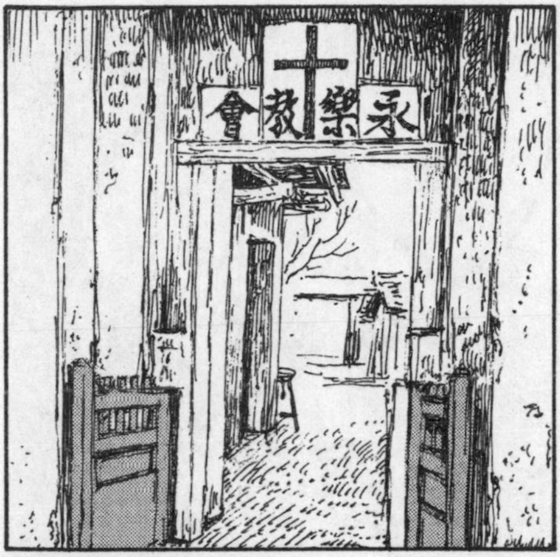
永樂教會

Sign: Church of Everlasting Peace

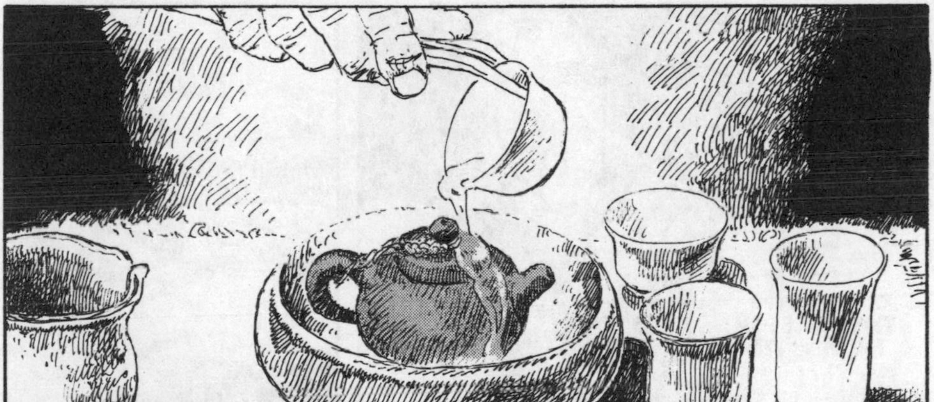

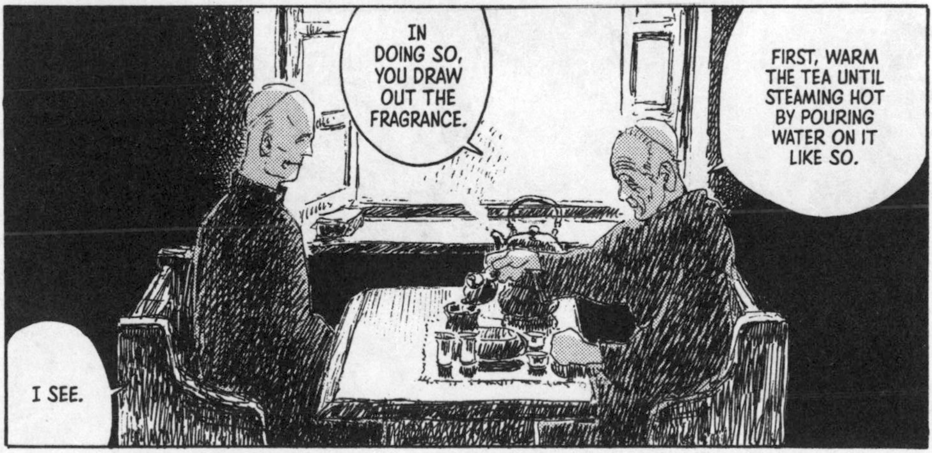
FIRST, WARM THE TEA UNTIL STEAMING HOT BY POURING WATER ON IT LIKE SO.
IN DOING SO, YOU DRAW OUT THE FRAGRANCE.
I SEE.

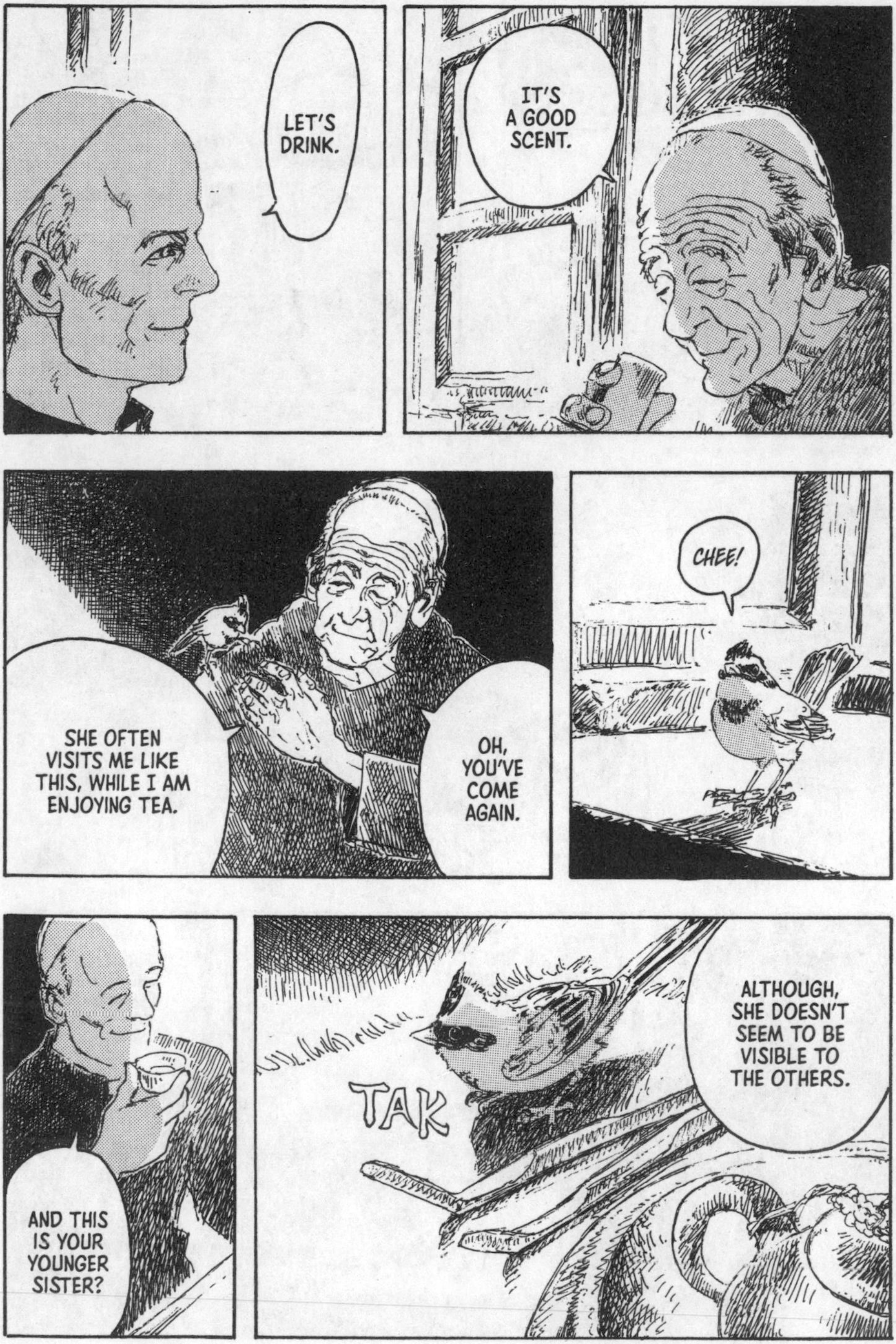
IT'S A GOOD SCENT.
LET'S DRINK.
CHEE!
OH, YOU'VE COME AGAIN.
SHE OFTEN VISITS ME LIKE THIS, WHILE I AM ENJOYING TEA.
ALTHOUGH, SHE DOESN'T SEEM TO BE VISIBLE TO THE OTHERS.
TAK
AND THIS IS YOUR YOUNGER SISTER?

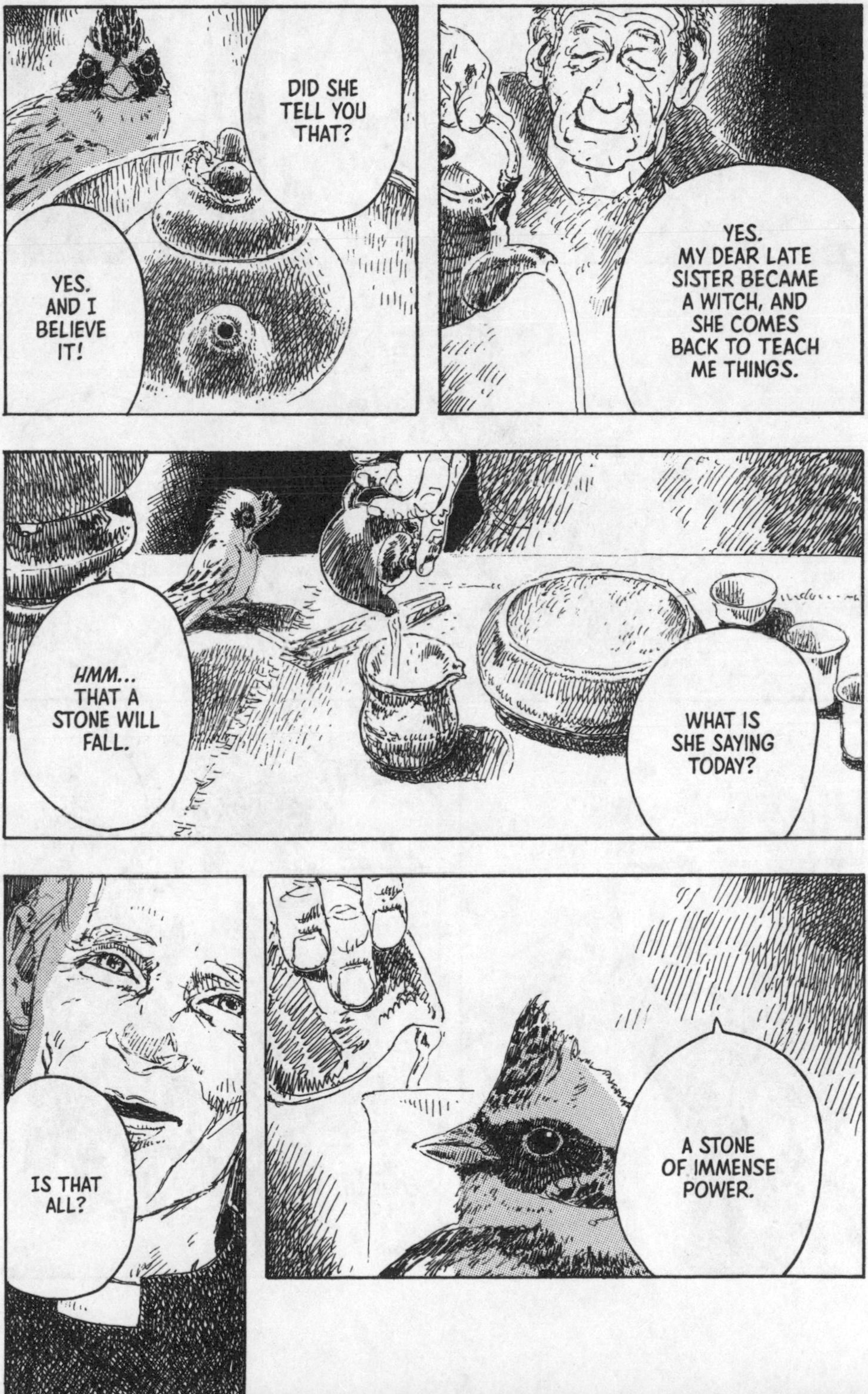
YES. MY DEAR LATE SISTER BECAME A WITCH, AND SHE COMES BACK TO TEACH ME THINGS.
DID SHE TELL YOU THAT?
YES. AND I BELIEVE IT!
WHAT IS SHE SAYING TODAY?
HMM... THAT A STONE WILL FALL.
A STONE OF IMMENSE POWER.
IS THAT ALL?

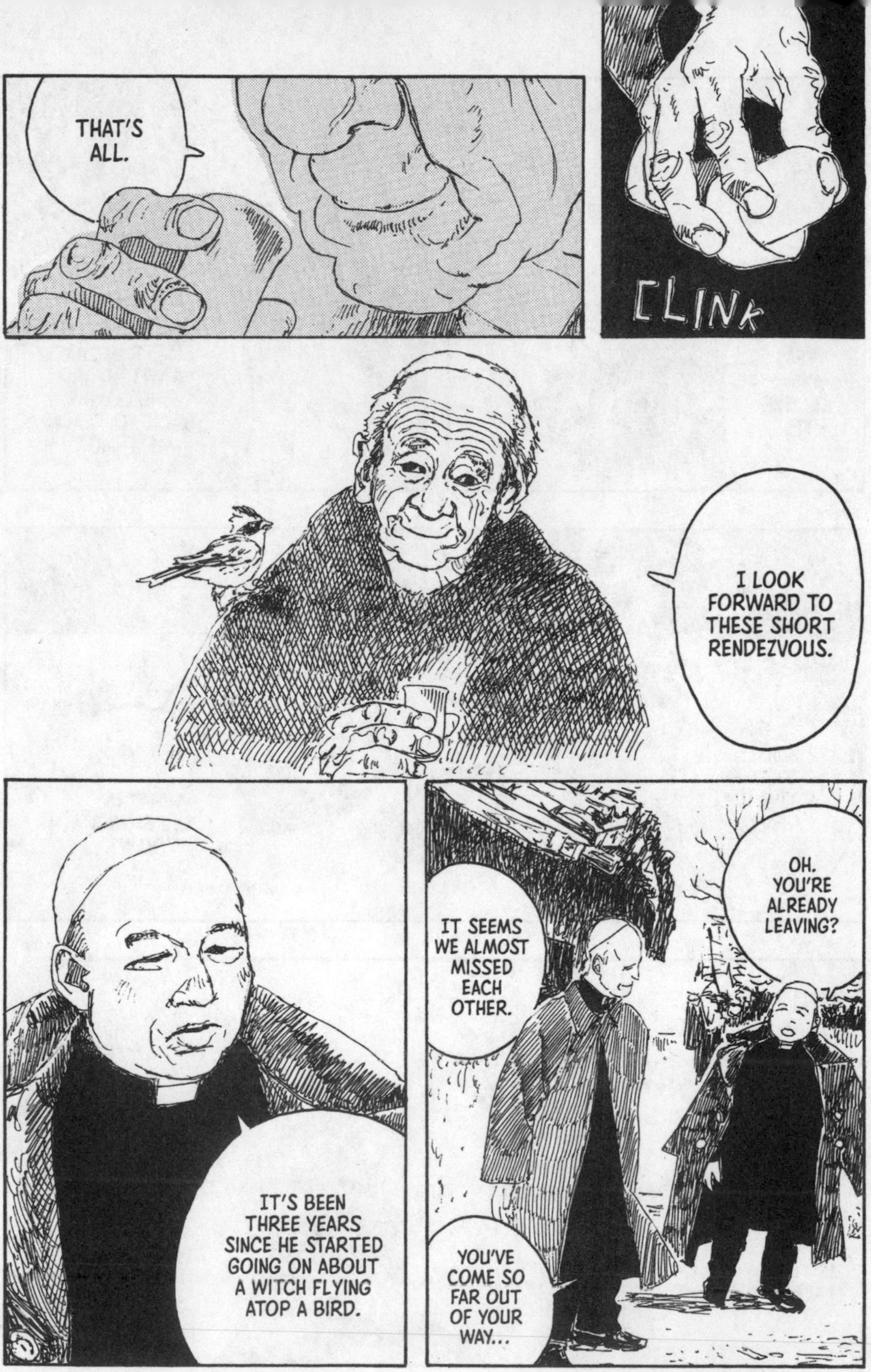
CLINK
THAT'S ALL.
I LOOK FORWARD TO THESE SHORT RENDEZVOUS.
OH. YOU'RE ALREADY LEAVING?
IT SEEMS WE ALMOST MISSED EACH OTHER.
YOU'VE COME SO FAR OUT OF YOUR WAY...
IT'S BEEN THREE YEARS SINCE HE STARTED GOING ON ABOUT A WITCH FLYING ATOP A BIRD.

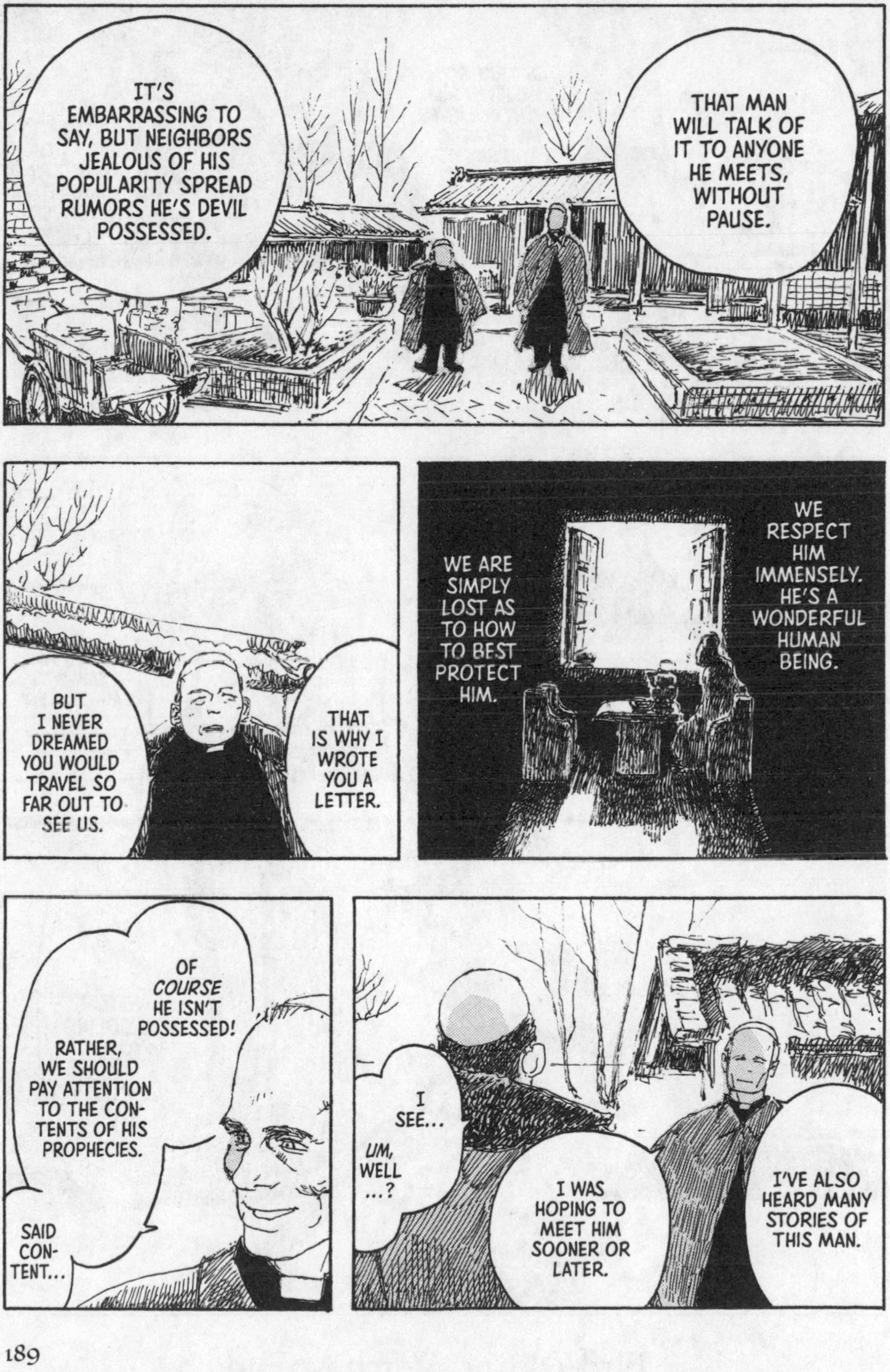
THAT MAN WILL TALK OF IT TO ANYONE HE MEETS, WITHOUT PAUSE.
IT'S EMBARRASSING TO SAY, BUT NEIGHBORS JEALOUS OF HIS POPULARITY SPREAD RUMORS HE'S DEVIL POSSESSED.
WE RESPECT HIM IMMENSELY. HE'S A WONDERFUL HUMAN BEING.
WE ARE SIMPLY LOST AS TO HOW TO BEST PROTECT HIM.
THAT IS WHY I WROTE YOU A LETTER.
BUT I NEVER DREAMED YOU WOULD TRAVEL SO FAR OUT TO SEE US.
I'VE ALSO HEARD MANY STORIES OF THIS MAN.
I WAS HOPING TO MEET HIM SOONER OR LATER.
I SEE...
UM, WELL ...?
OF *COURSE* HE ISN'T POSSESSED!
RATHER, WE SHOULD PAY ATTENTION TO THE CONTENTS OF HIS PROPHECIES.
SAID CONTENT...

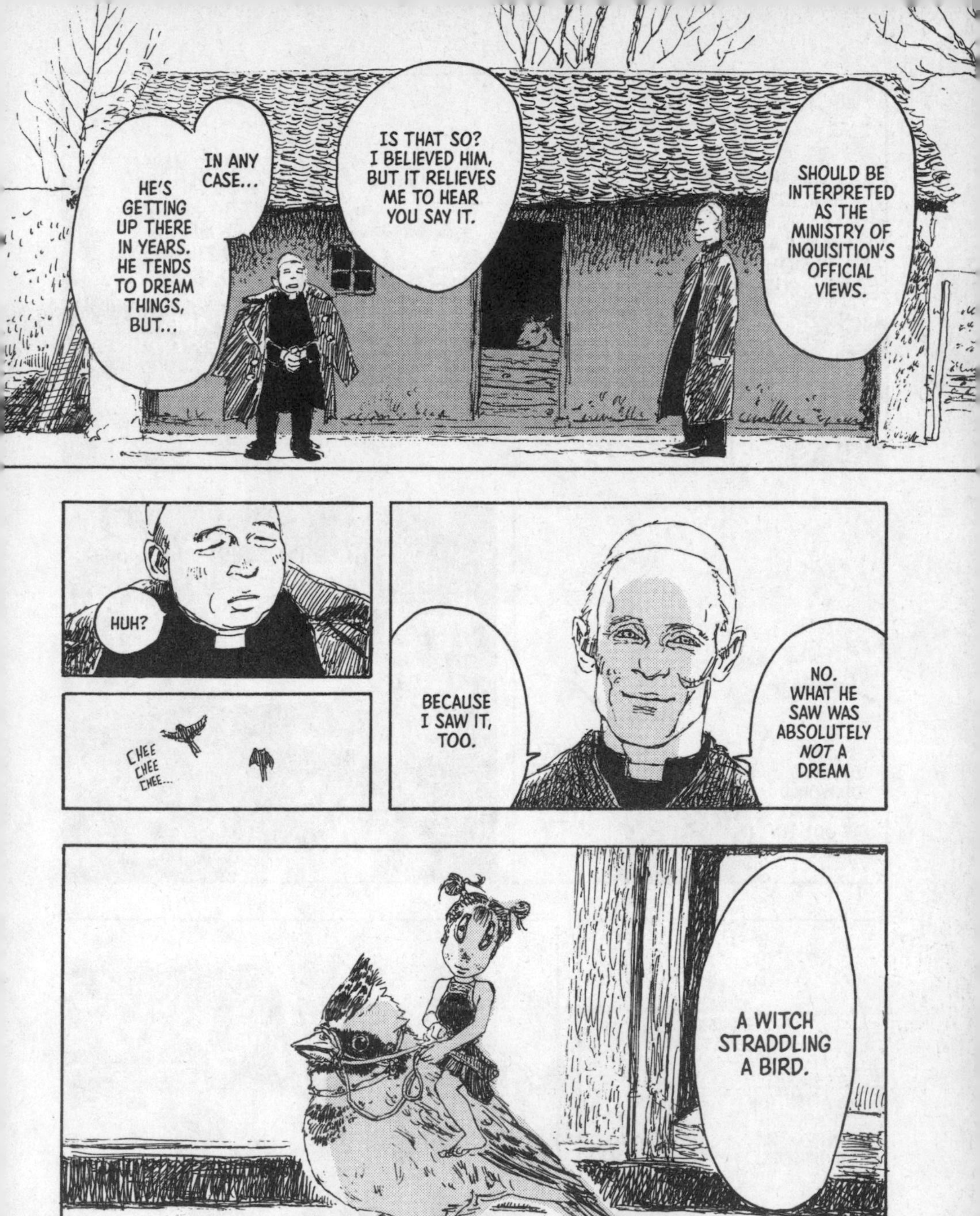
SHOULD BE INTERPRETED AS THE MINISTRY OF INQUISITION'S OFFICIAL VIEWS.
IS THAT SO? I BELIEVED HIM, BUT IT RELIEVES ME TO HEAR YOU SAY IT.
IN ANY CASE...
HE'S GETTING UP THERE IN YEARS. HE TENDS TO DREAM THINGS, BUT...
NO. WHAT HE SAW WAS ABSOLUTELY *NOT* A DREAM
BECAUSE I SAW IT, TOO.
HUH?
CHEE CHEE CHEE...
A WITCH STRADDLING A BIRD.

Bird-Riding Witch ~ End

LIFE IS BORN IN THE STARS. PLANETS DIE AND BECOME DUST.

SOMEWHERE, THEY ARE GATHERED AGAIN AND MIXED ANEW.
THEY ARE REBORN AS A NEW PLANET. AND AGAIN, THEY DIE.

THE MEMORY OF LIFE IS ENGRAVED IN ALL THINGS...

AMIDST THAT REPETITION.

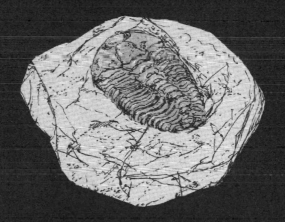

PETRA
GENITALIX

TWO HUNDRED METERS FROM THE MOTHER SHIP.

CONGRATS! THAT'S A *GUINNESS* RECORD!

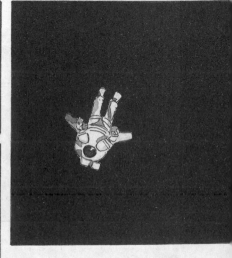

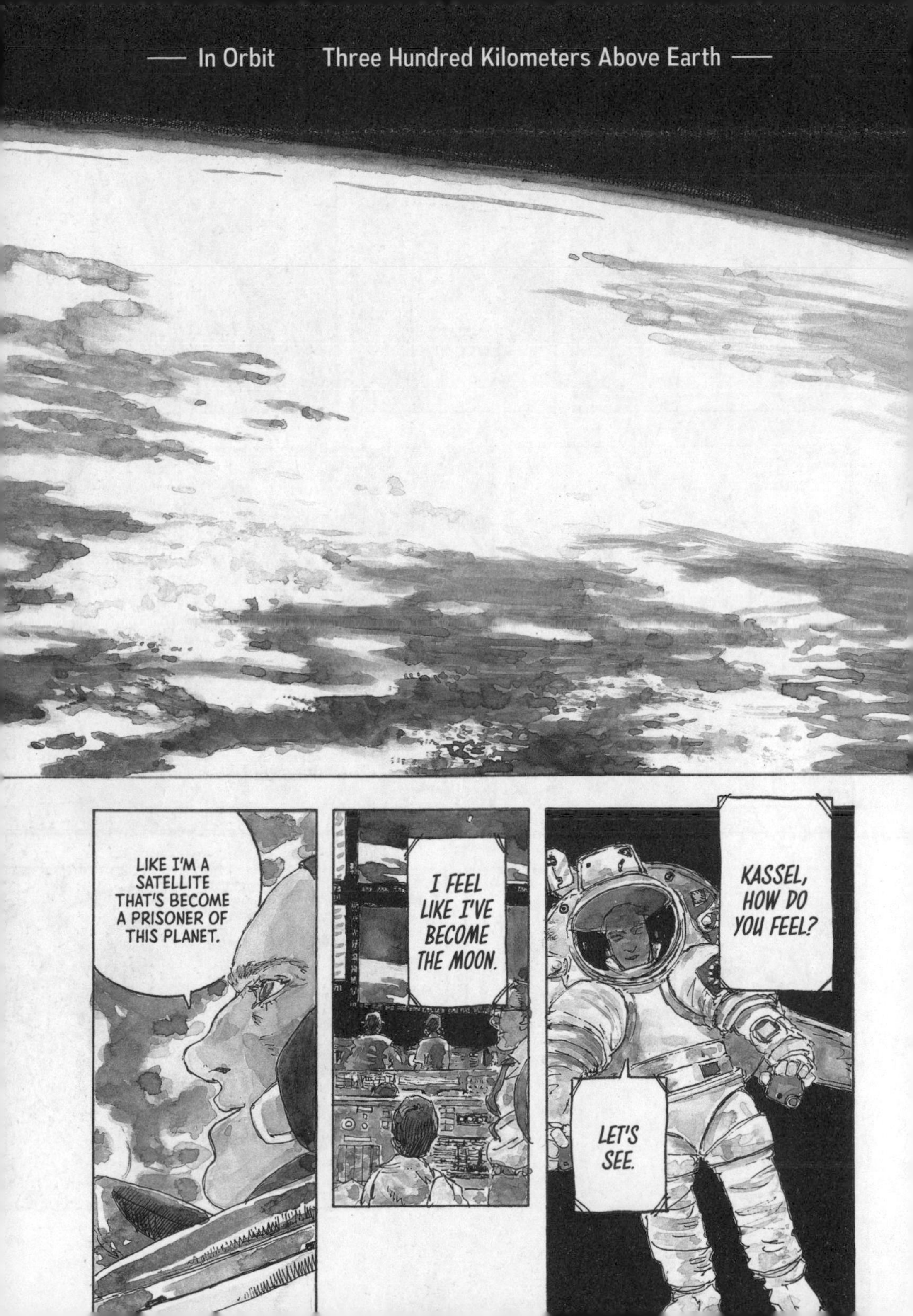
In Orbit Three Hundred Kilometers Above Earth
KASSEL, HOW DO YOU FEEL?
LET'S SEE.
I FEEL LIKE I'VE BECOME THE MOON.
LIKE I'M A SATELLITE THAT'S BECOME A PRISONER OF THIS PLANET.

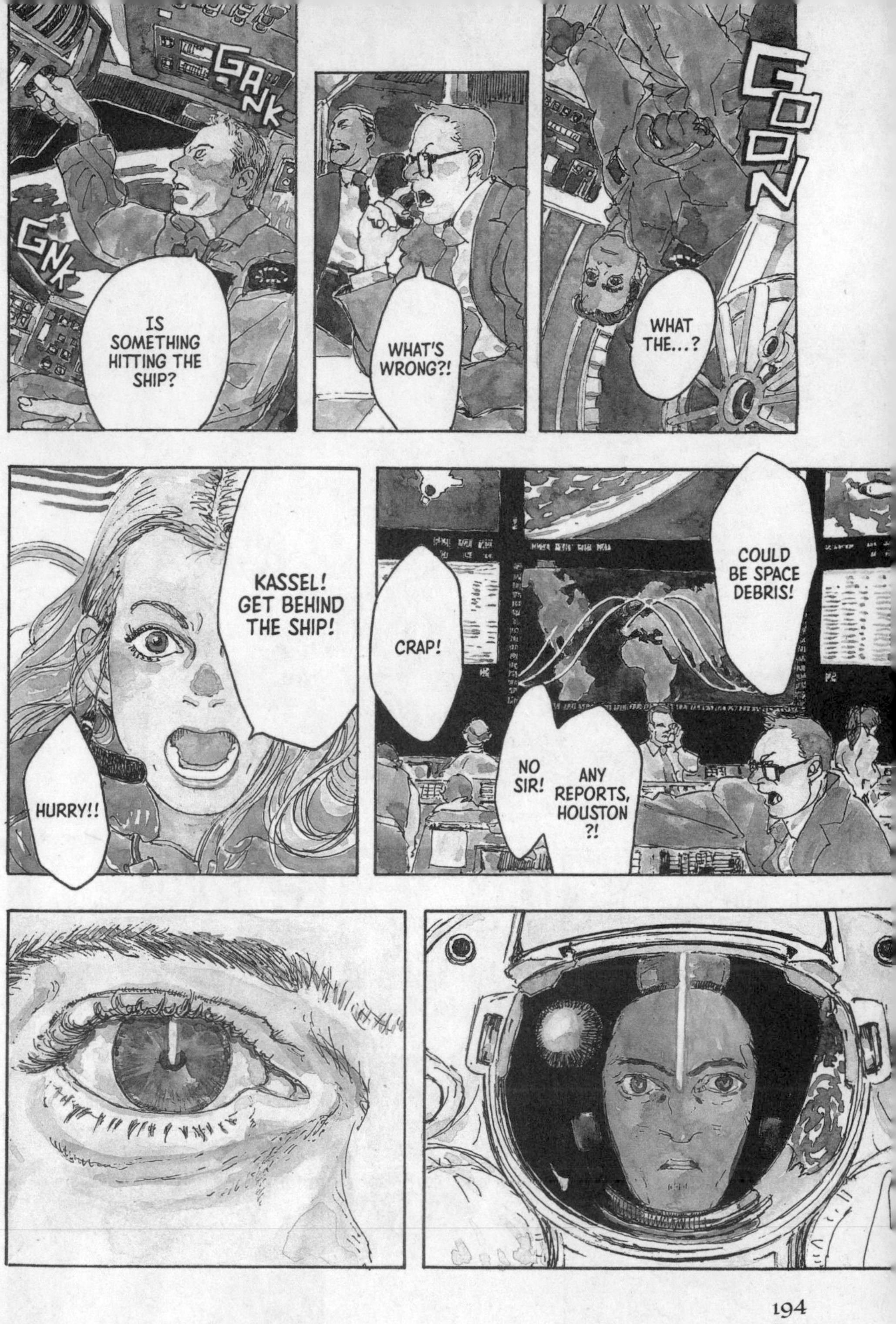
GOON
WHAT THE...?
WHAT'S WRONG?!
GANK
GNK
IS SOMETHING HITTING THE SHIP?
COULD BE SPACE DEBRIS!
CRAP!
ANY REPORTS, HOUSTON ?!
NO SIR!
KASSEL! GET BEHIND THE SHIP!
HURRY!!

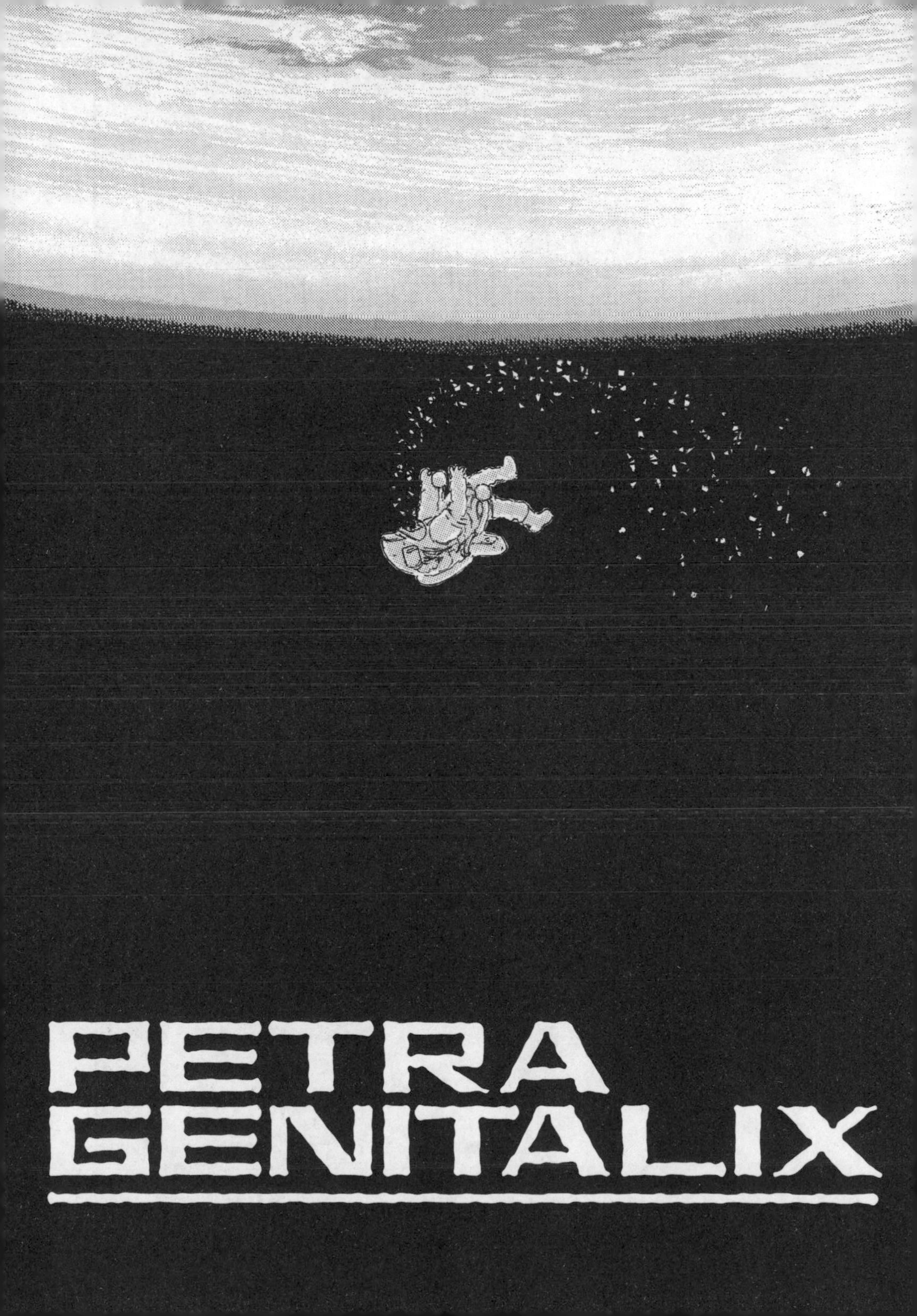
PETRA
GENITALIX

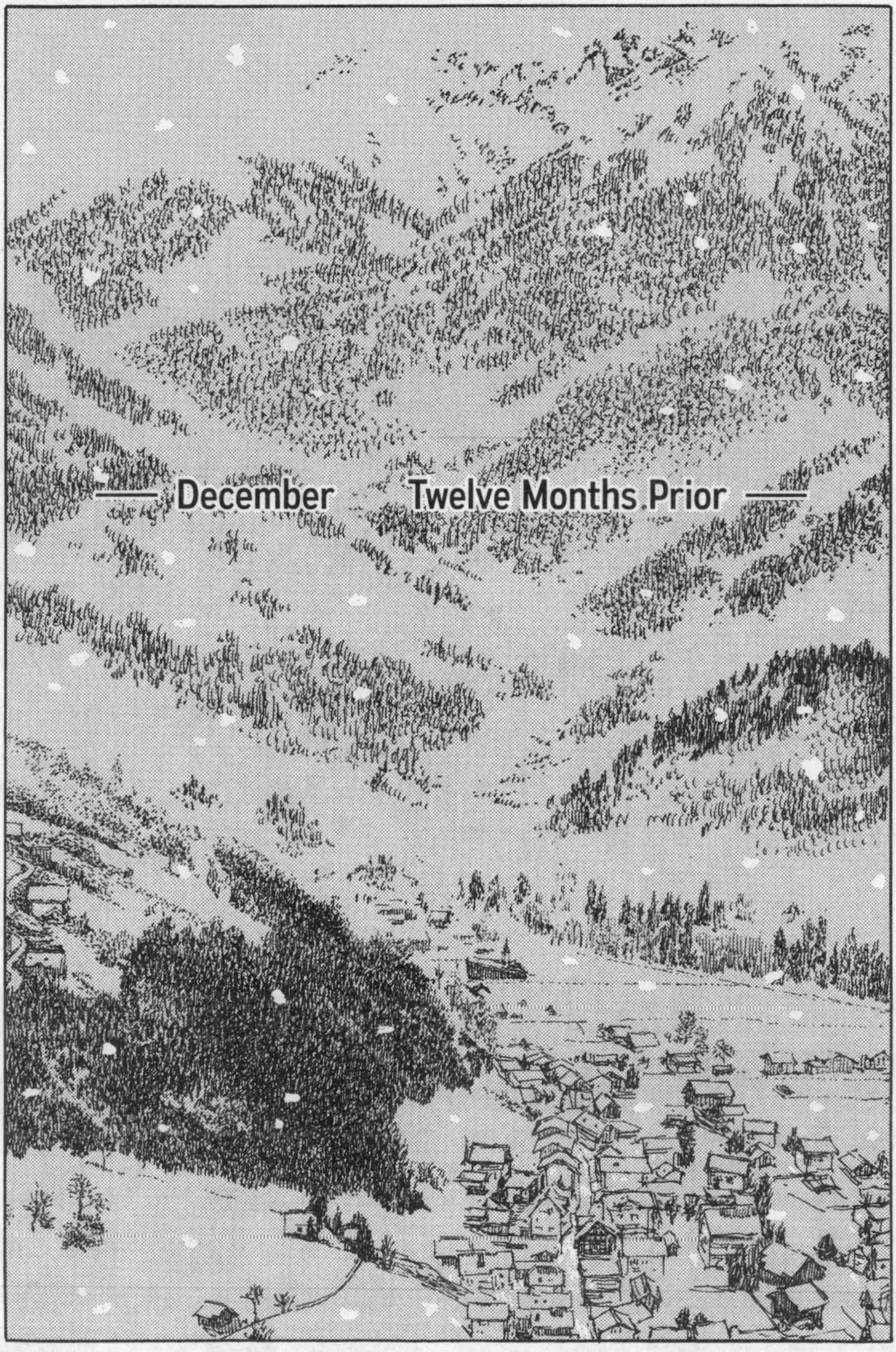
— December Twelve Months Prior —

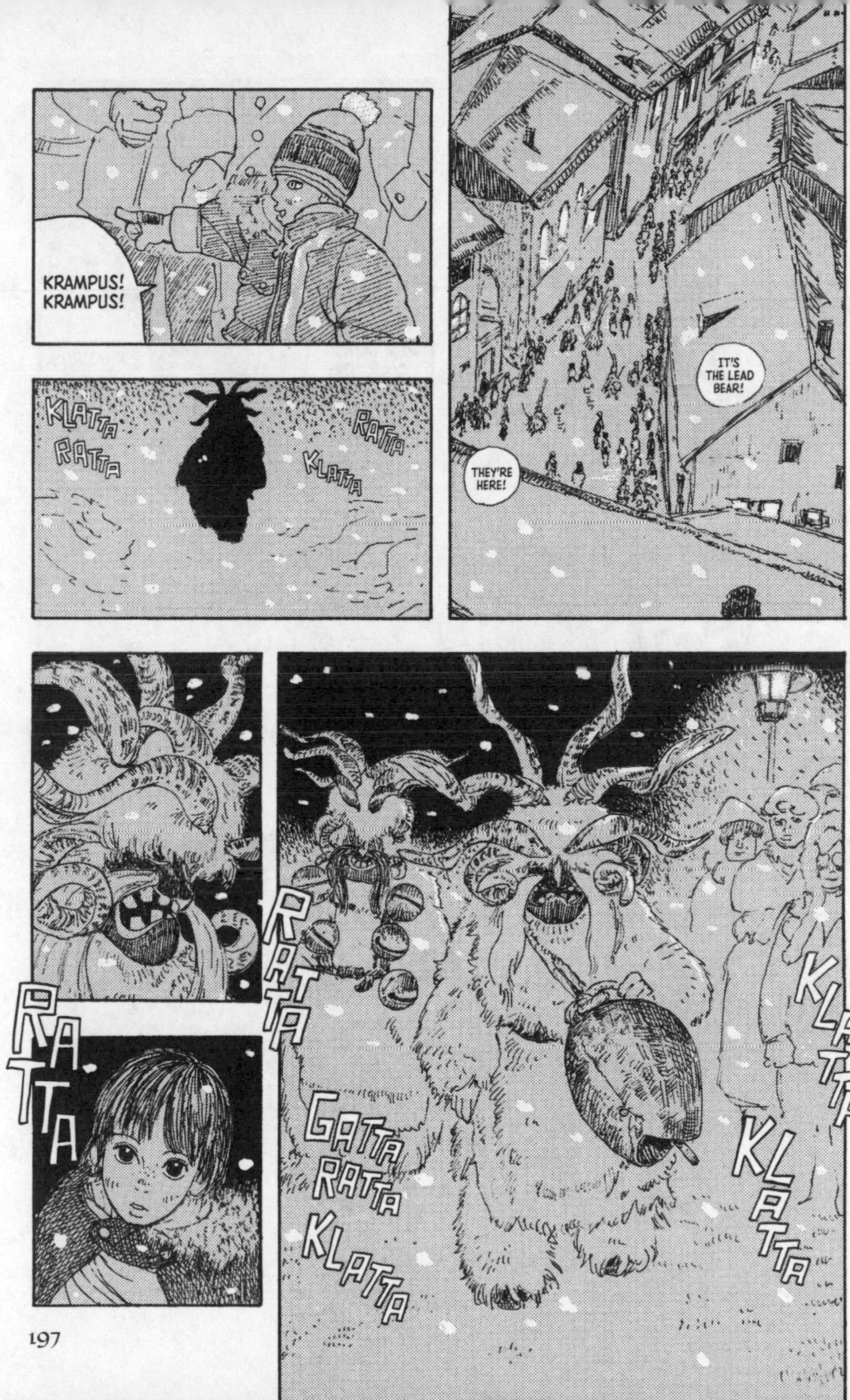
IT'S THE LEAD BEAR!
THEY'RE HERE!
KRAMPUS! KRAMPUS!
RATTA
KLATTA
KLATTA
RATTA
KLATTA
KLATTA
RATTA
GATTA RATTA KLATTA
RATTA
RATTA

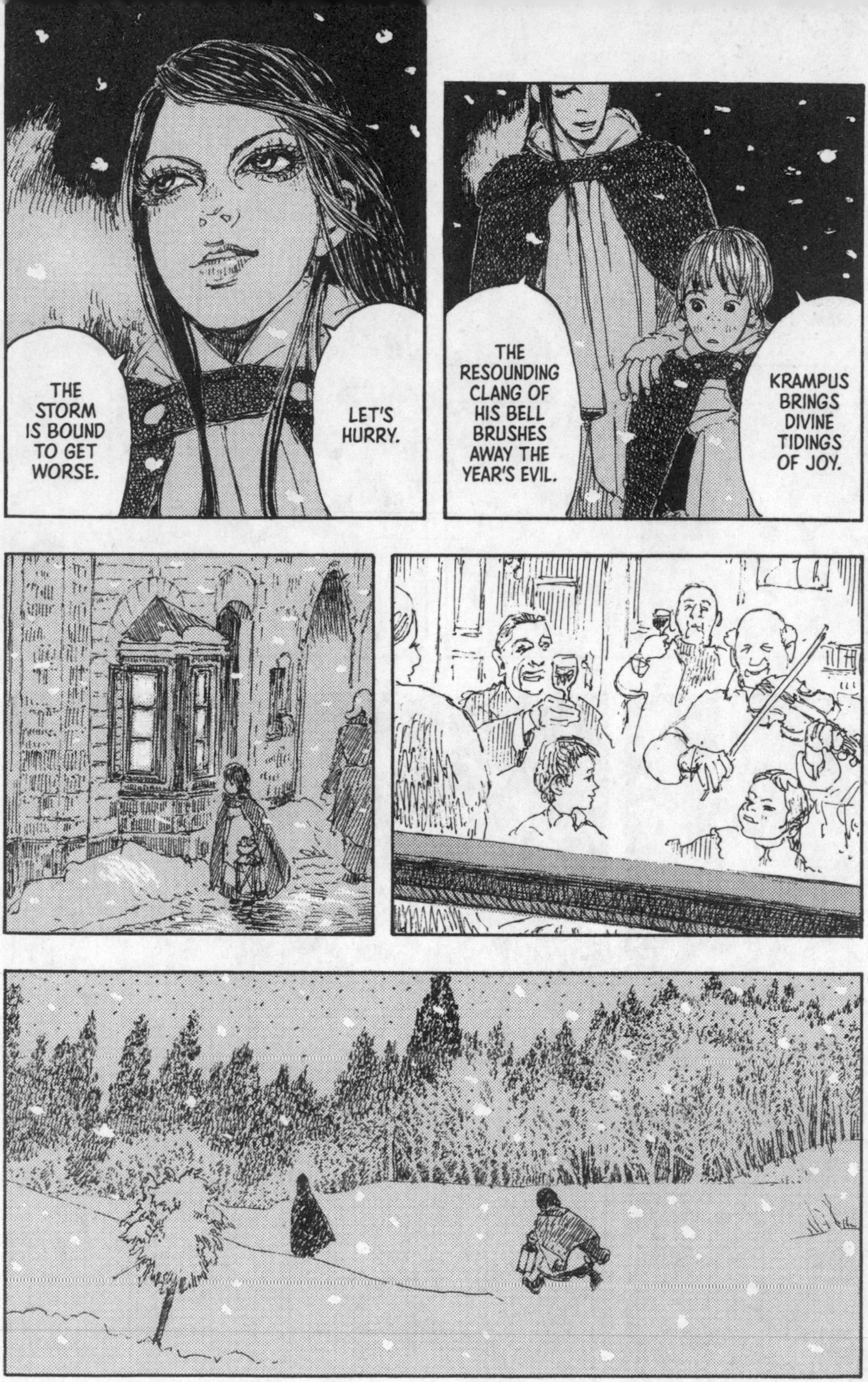
KRAMPUS BRINGS DIVINE TIDINGS OF JOY.
THE RESOUNDING CLANG OF HIS BELL BRUSHES AWAY THE YEAR'S EVIL.
LET'S HURRY.
THE STORM IS BOUND TO GET WORSE.

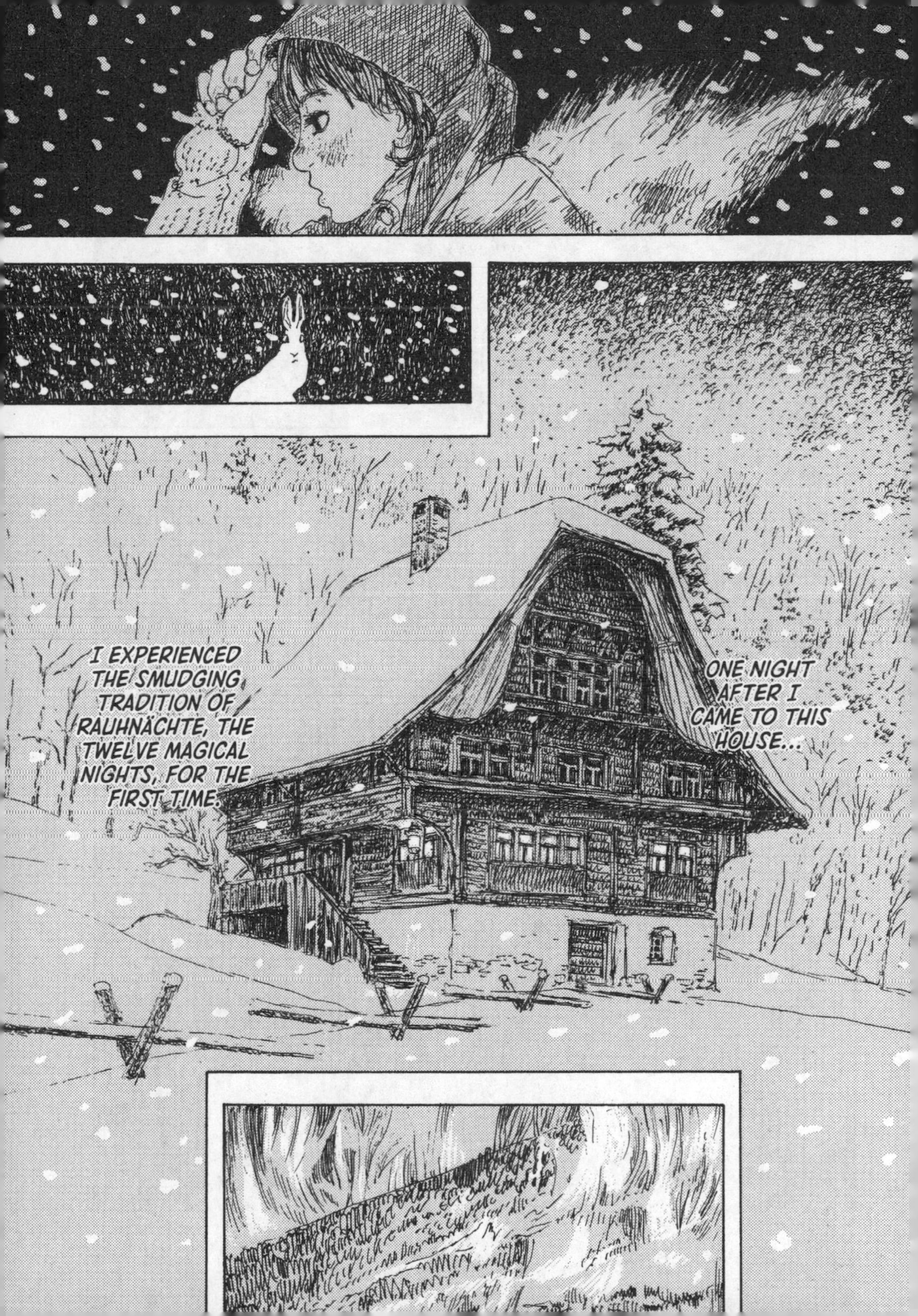
ONE NIGHT AFTER I CAME TO THIS HOUSE...
I EXPERIENCED THE SMUDGING TRADITION OF RAUHNÄCHTE, THE TWELVE MAGICAL NIGHTS, FOR THE FIRST TIME.

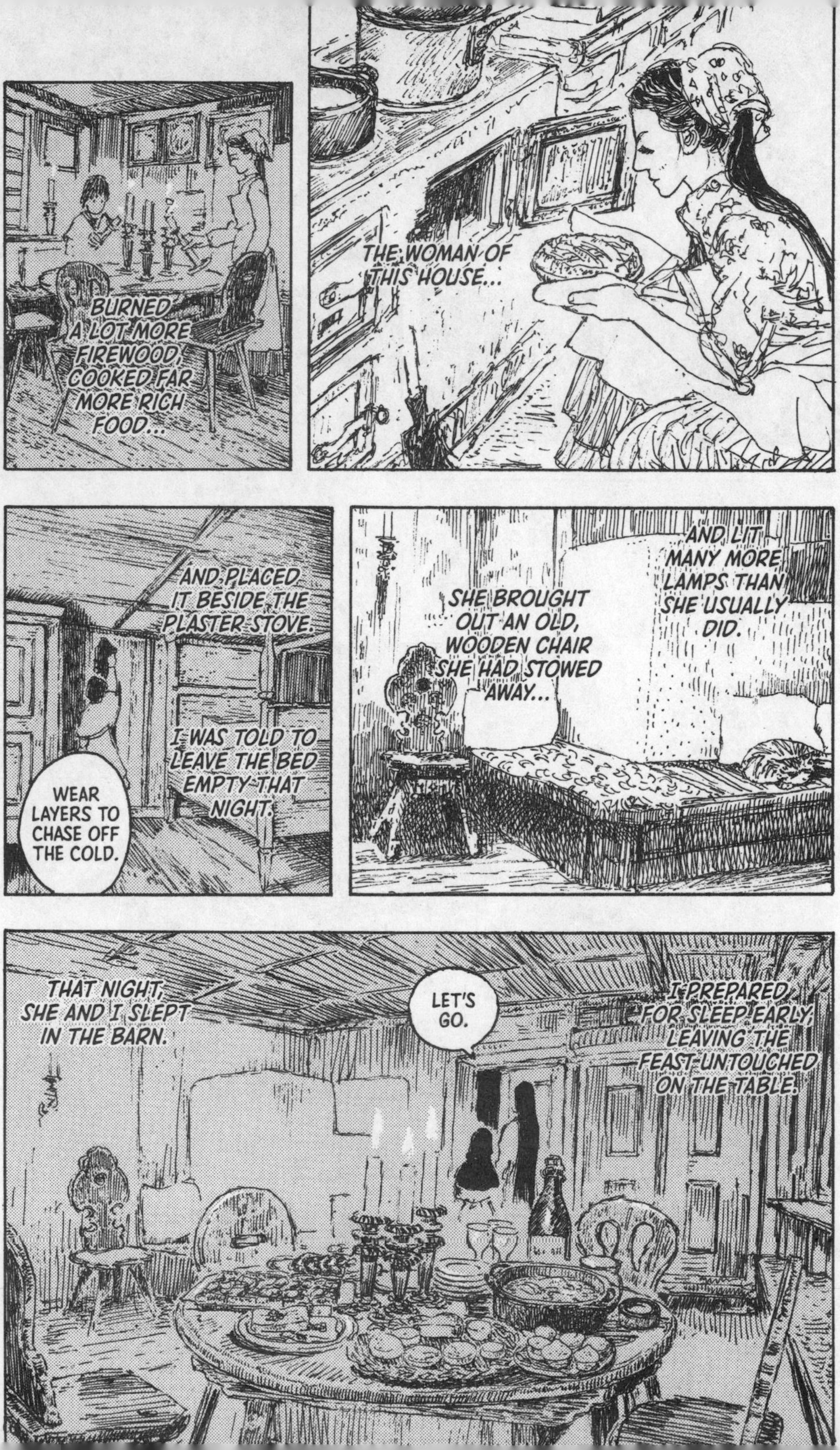
THE WOMAN OF THIS HOUSE...
BURNED A LOT MORE FIREWOOD, COOKED FAR MORE RICH FOOD...
AND LIT MANY MORE LAMPS THAN SHE USUALLY DID.
SHE BROUGHT OUT AN OLD, WOODEN CHAIR SHE HAD STOWED AWAY...
AND PLACED IT BESIDE THE PLASTER STOVE.
I WAS TOLD TO LEAVE THE BED EMPTY THAT NIGHT.
WEAR LAYERS TO CHASE OFF THE COLD.
I PREPARED FOR SLEEP EARLY, LEAVING THE FEAST UNTOUCHED ON THE TABLE.
LET'S GO.
THAT NIGHT, SHE AND I SLEPT IN THE BARN.

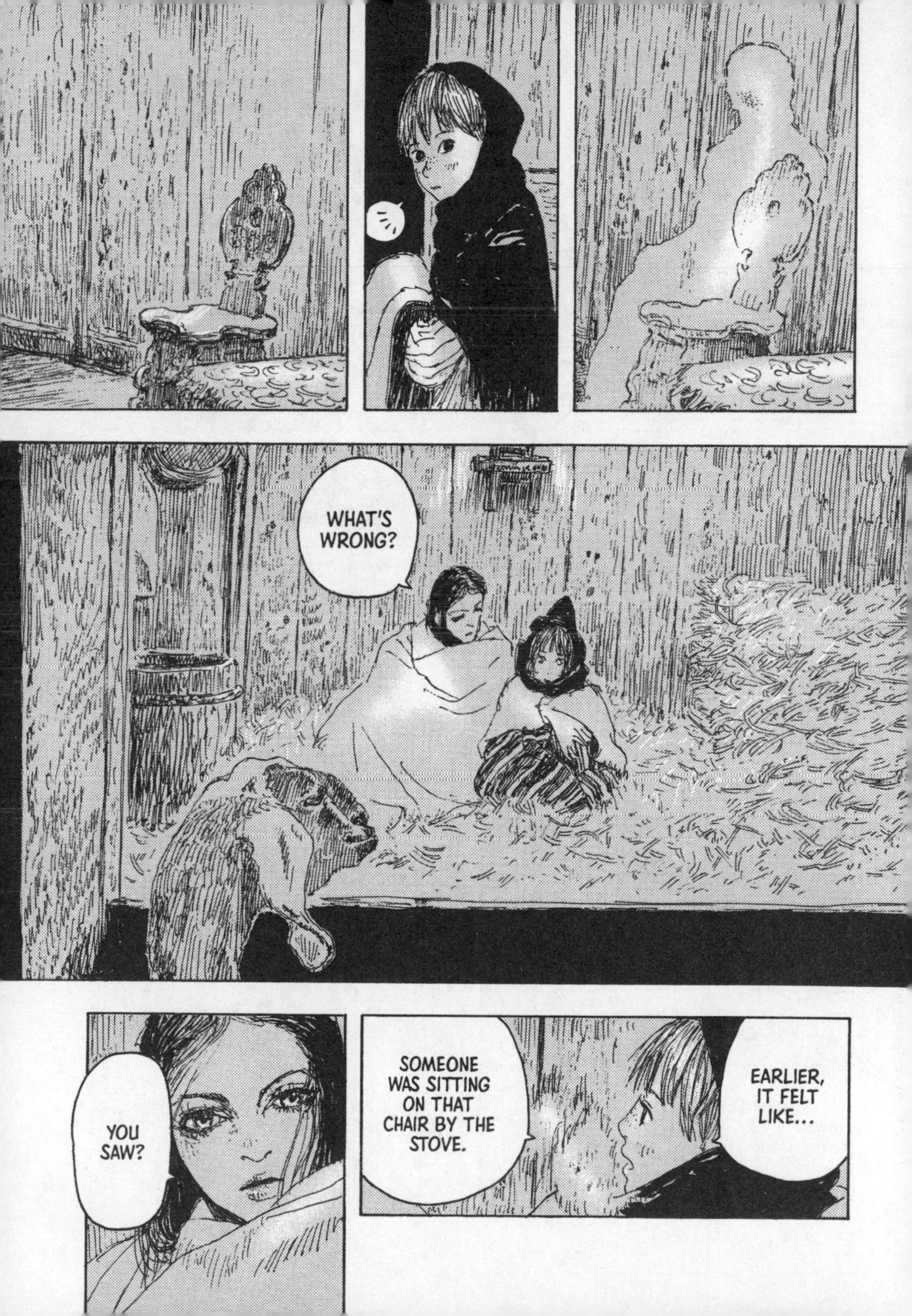
WHAT'S WRONG?
EARLIER, IT FELT LIKE...
SOMEONE WAS SITTING ON THAT CHAIR BY THE STOVE.
YOU SAW?

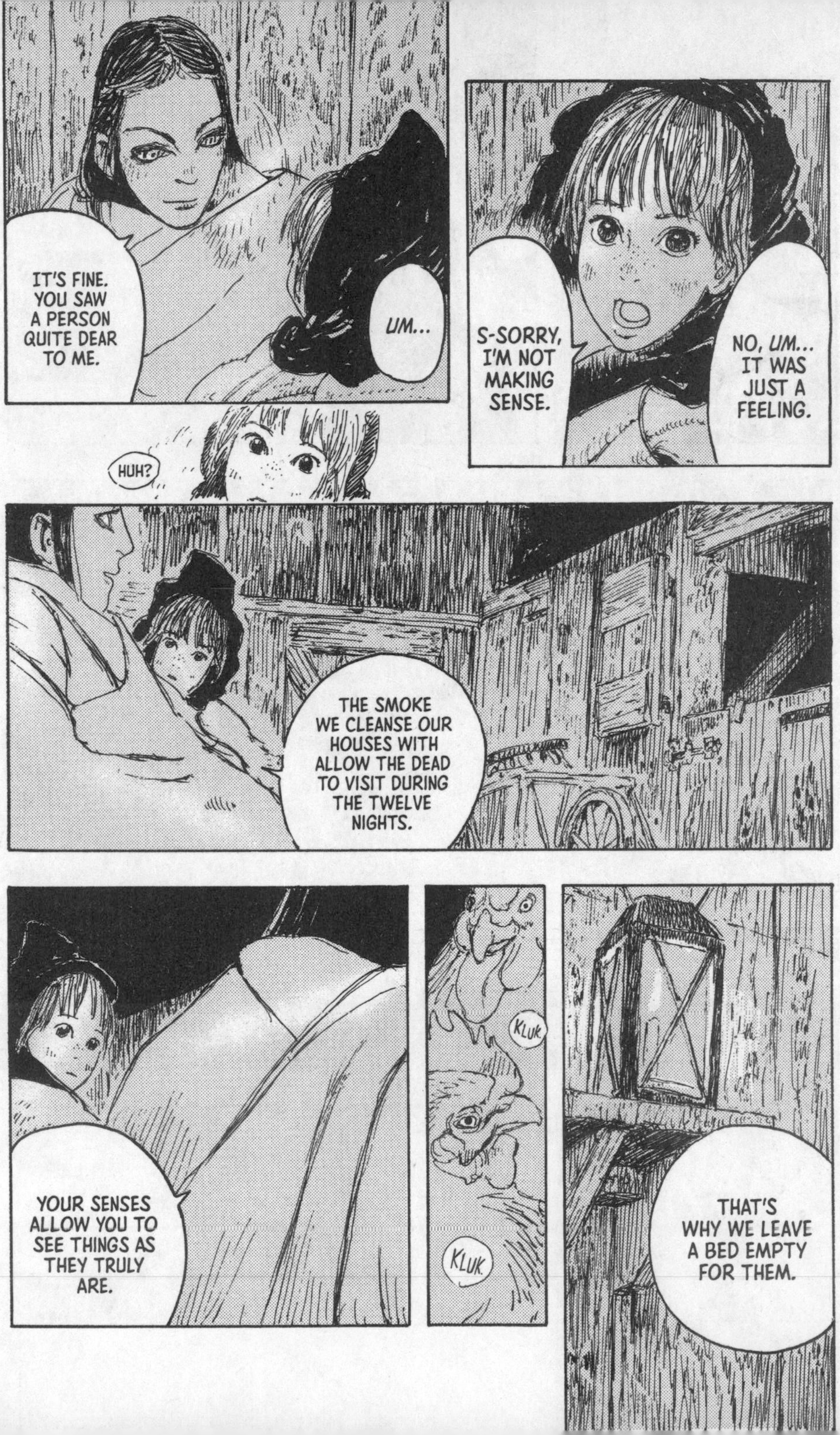
NO, UM... IT WAS JUST A FEELING.
S-SORRY, I'M NOT MAKING SENSE.
UM...
IT'S FINE. YOU SAW A PERSON QUITE DEAR TO ME.
HUH?
THE SMOKE WE CLEANSE OUR HOUSES WITH ALLOW THE DEAD TO VISIT DURING THE TWELVE NIGHTS.
THAT'S WHY WE LEAVE A BED EMPTY FOR THEM.
KLUK.
KLUK.
YOUR SENSES ALLOW YOU TO SEE THINGS AS THEY TRULY ARE.

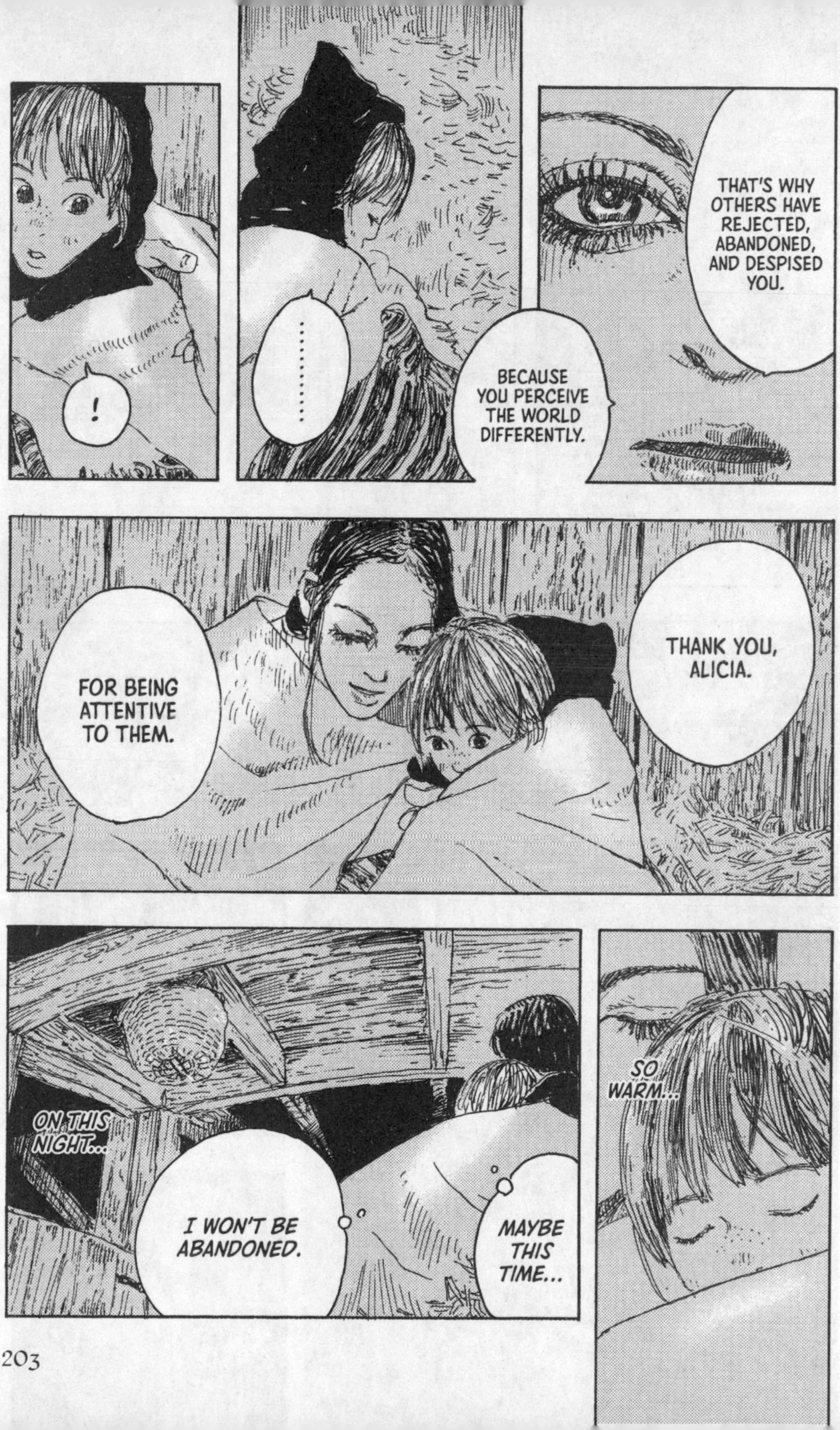
THAT'S WHY OTHERS HAVE REJECTED, ABANDONED, AND DESPISED YOU.
BECAUSE YOU PERCEIVE THE WORLD DIFFERENTLY.
......
!
THANK YOU, ALICIA.
FOR BEING ATTENTIVE TO THEM.
SO WARM...
MAYBE THIS TIME...
I WON'T BE ABANDONED.
ON THIS NIGHT...

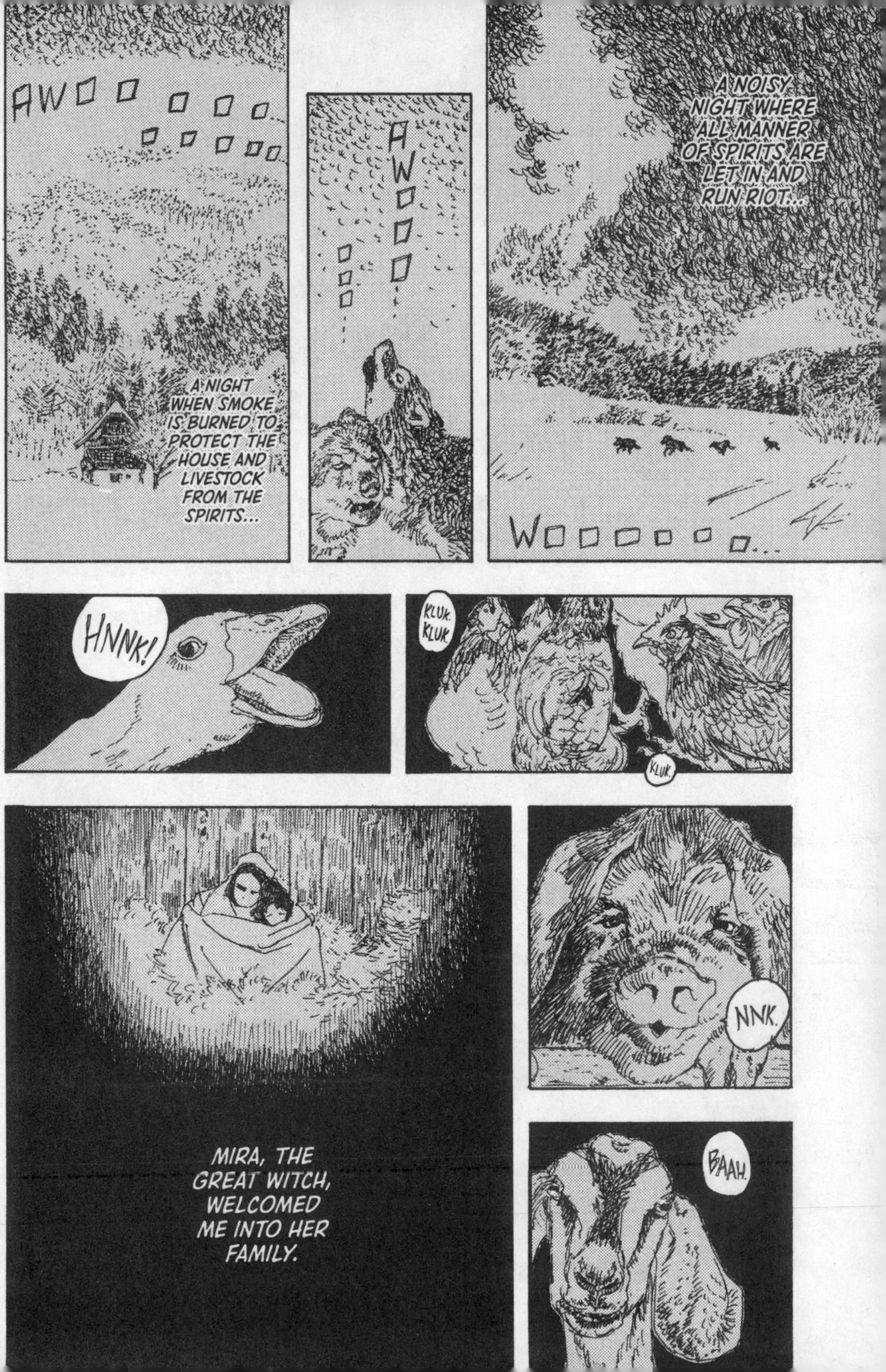
A NOISY NIGHT WHERE ALL MANNER OF SPIRITS ARE LET IN AND RUN RIOT...
WOOOOOOO...
AWOOOO
OOO
AWOOOOOO OOOO...
A NIGHT WHEN SMOKE IS BURNED TO PROTECT THE HOUSE AND LIVESTOCK FROM THE SPIRITS...
KLUK. KLUK.
KLUK.
HNNK!
NNK.
BAAH.
MIRA, THE GREAT WITCH, WELCOMED ME INTO HER FAMILY.

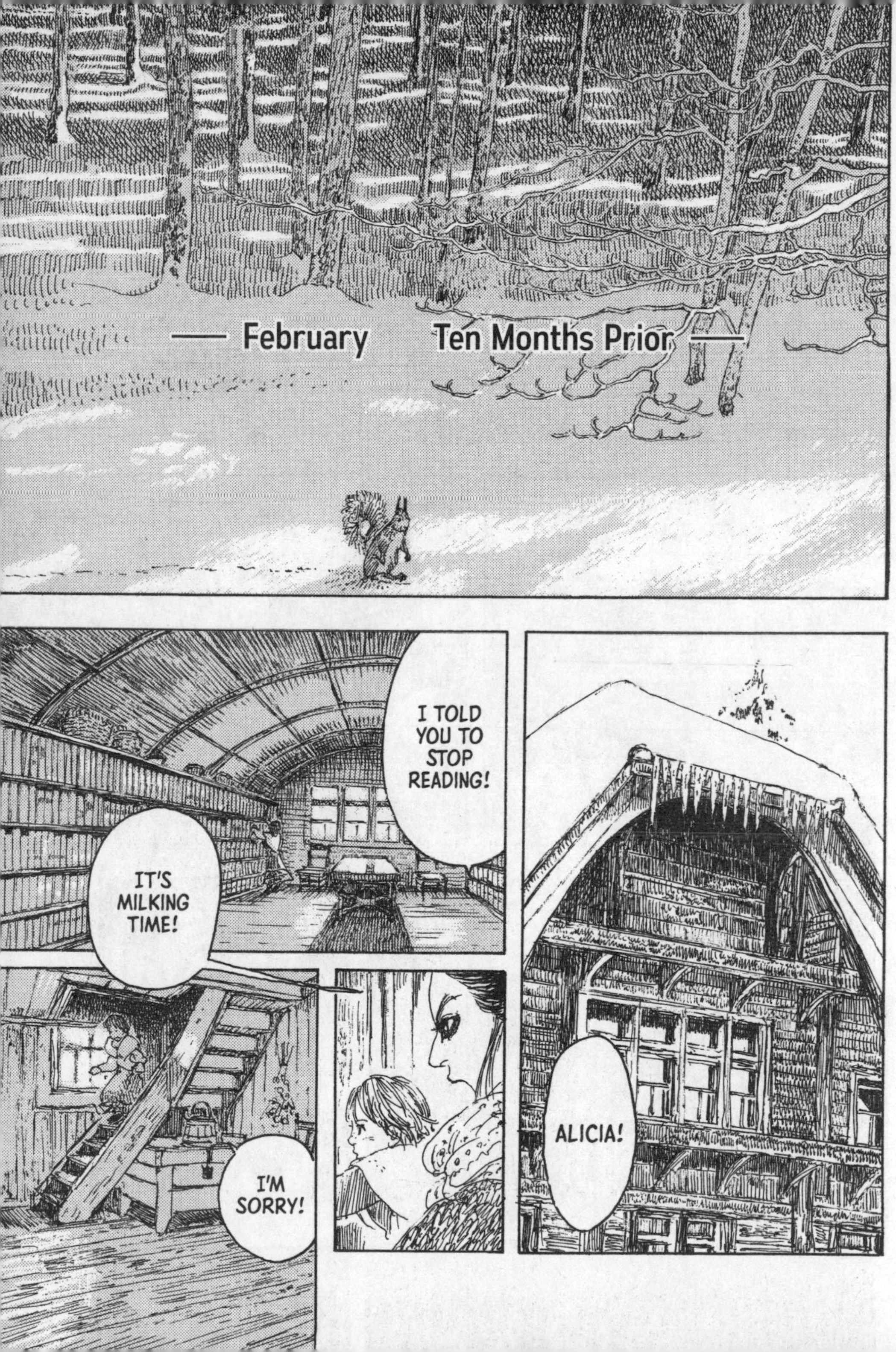
— February Ten Months Prior —
ALICIA!
I TOLD YOU TO STOP READING!
IT'S MILKING TIME!
I'M SORRY!

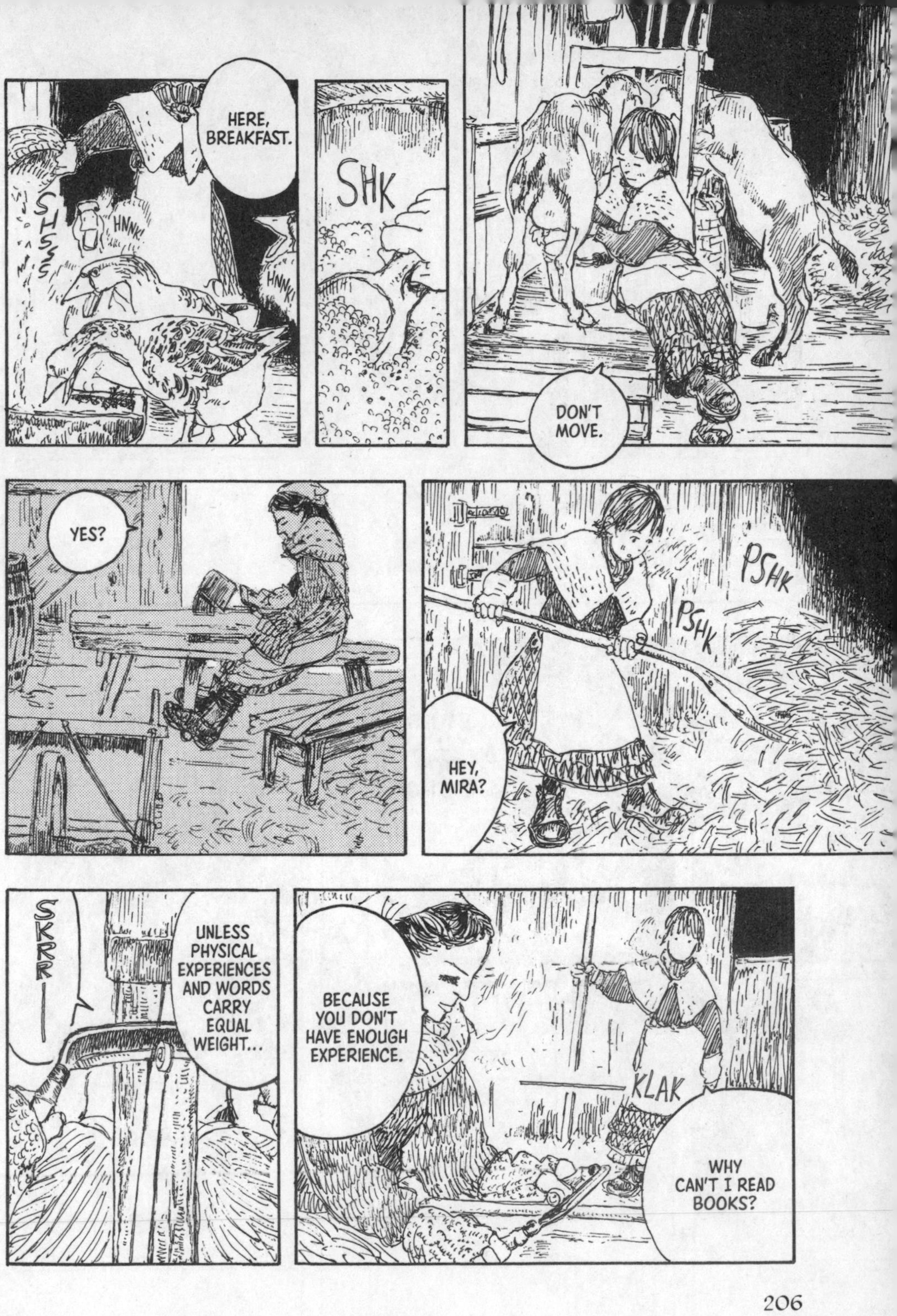
DON'T MOVE.
SHK
HERE, BREAKFAST.
HNNK!
SHSSS
HNNK!
PSHK
PSHK
HEY, MIRA?
YES?
KLAK
WHY CAN'T I READ BOOKS?
BECAUSE YOU DON'T HAVE ENOUGH EXPERIENCE.
UNLESS PHYSICAL EXPERIENCES AND WORDS CARRY EQUAL WEIGHT...
SKRR—

MORE IMPORTANTLY, NOW THAT IT'S SNOWED...

YOUR SPIRIT WON'T ACHIEVE BALANCE.

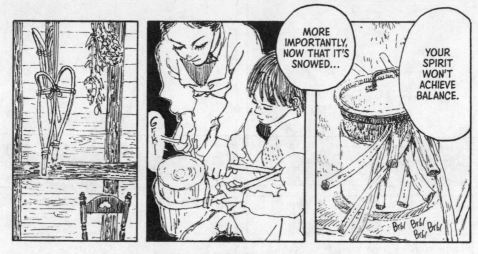

GriKi

Brbl Brbl Brbl Brbl

"READ THE FOOTPRINTS," SHE SAID...

KNCH

KNCH

FRAU HANNAH!

A BIG ONE.

HE'S HEADED TOWARDS FRAU HANNAH'S HOUSE.

IT'S A FOX.

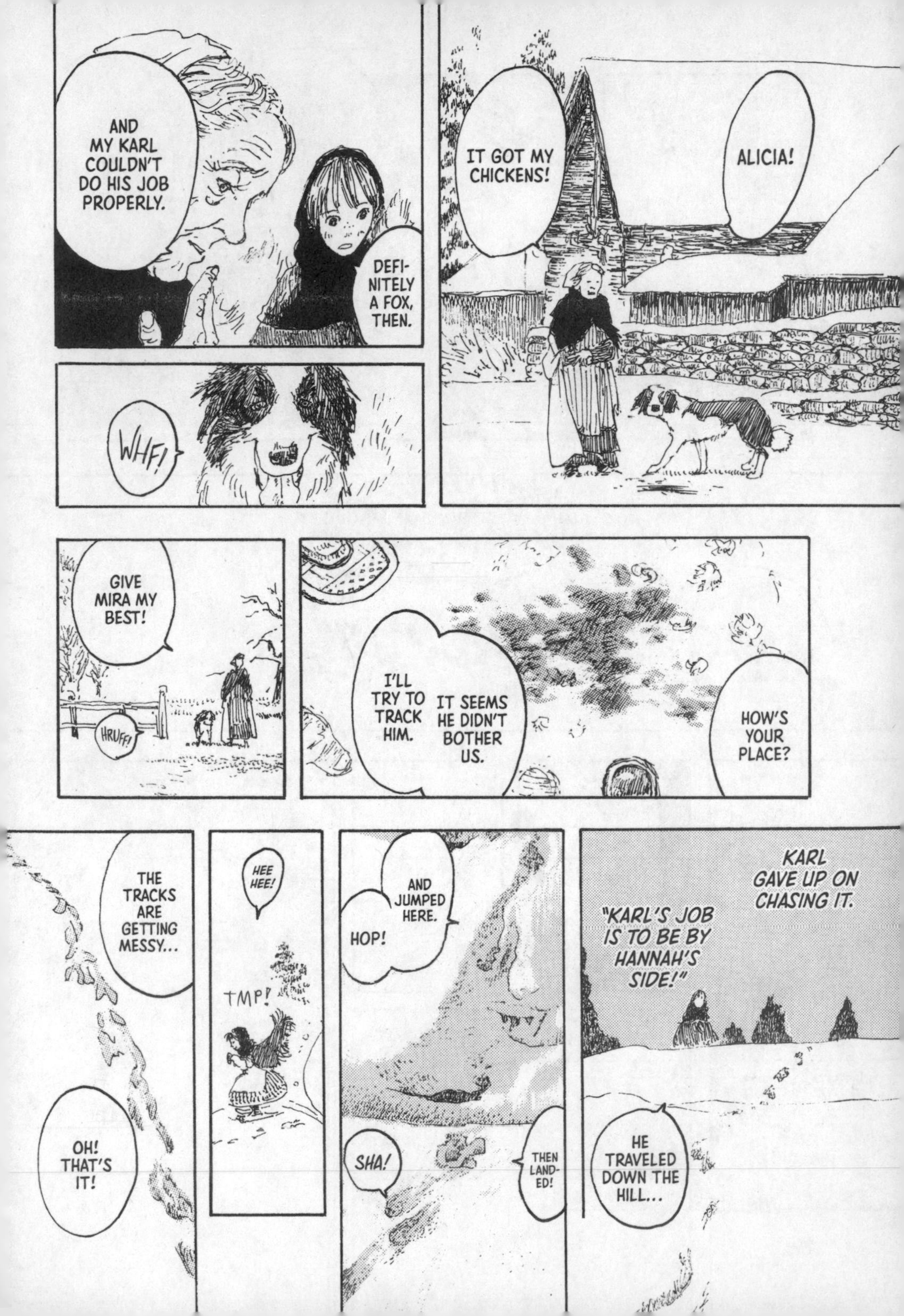
ALICIA!
IT GOT MY CHICKENS!
AND MY KARL COULDN'T DO HIS JOB PROPERLY.
DEFINITELY A FOX, THEN.
WHF!
HOW'S YOUR PLACE?
IT SEEMS HE DIDN'T BOTHER US.
I'LL TRY TO TRACK HIM.
GIVE MIRA MY BEST!
HRUFF!
KARL GAVE UP ON CHASING IT.
"KARL'S JOB IS TO BE BY HANNAH'S SIDE!"
HE TRAVELED DOWN THE HILL...
AND JUMPED HERE.
HOP!
THEN LANDED!
SHA!
HEE HEE!
TMP!
THE TRACKS ARE GETTING MESSY...
OH! THAT'S IT!

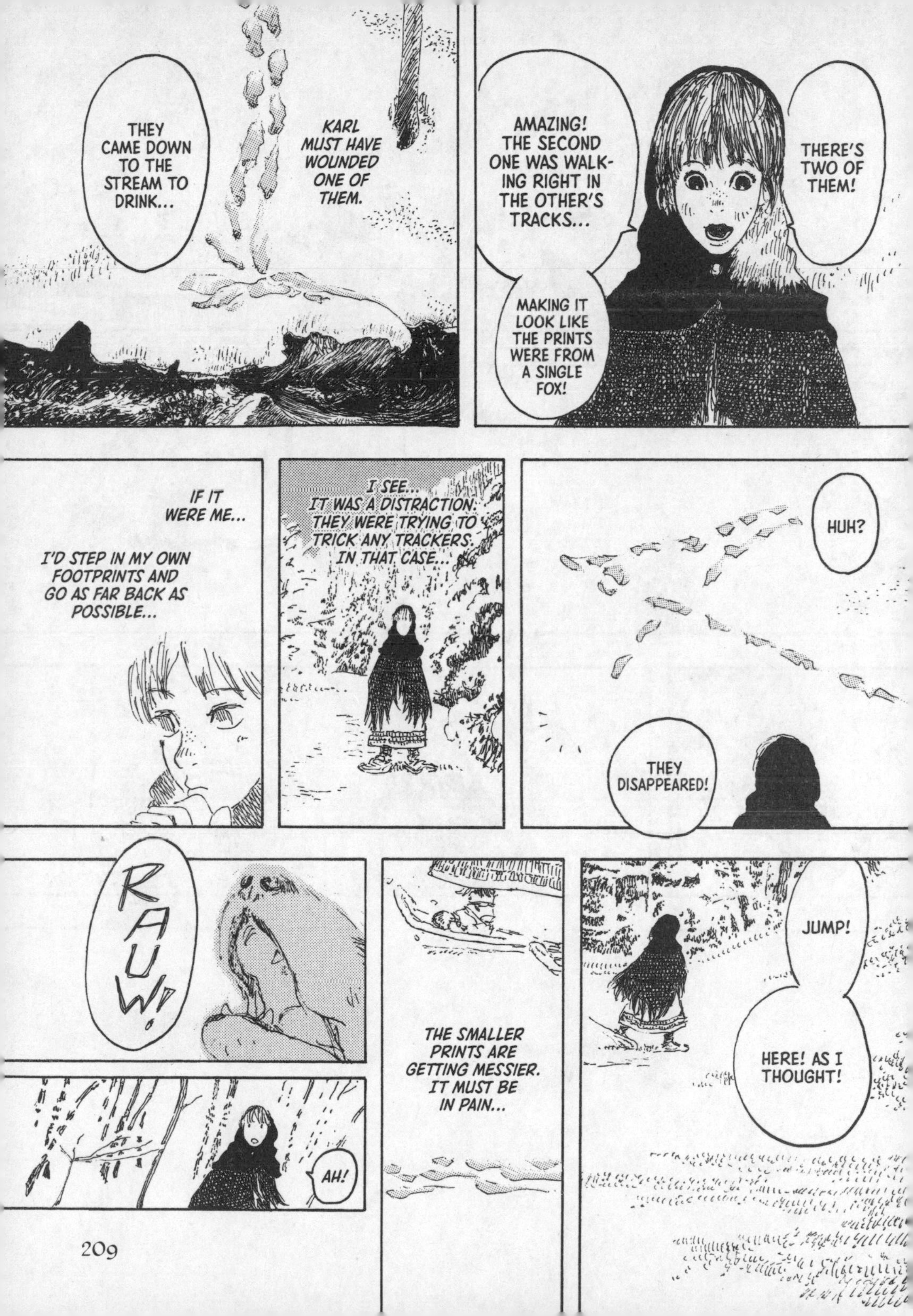
THERE'S TWO OF THEM!
AMAZING! THE SECOND ONE WAS WALKING RIGHT IN THE OTHER'S TRACKS...
MAKING IT LOOK LIKE THE PRINTS WERE FROM A SINGLE FOX!
KARL MUST HAVE WOUNDED ONE OF THEM.
THEY CAME DOWN TO THE STREAM TO DRINK...
HUH?
THEY DISAPPEARED!
I SEE... IT WAS A DISTRACTION: THEY WERE TRYING TO TRICK ANY TRACKERS. IN THAT CASE...
IF IT WERE ME...
I'D STEP IN MY OWN FOOTPRINTS AND GO AS FAR BACK AS POSSIBLE...
JUMP!
HERE! AS I THOUGHT!
THE SMALLER PRINTS ARE GETTING MESSIER. IT MUST BE IN PAIN...
RAUW!
AH!

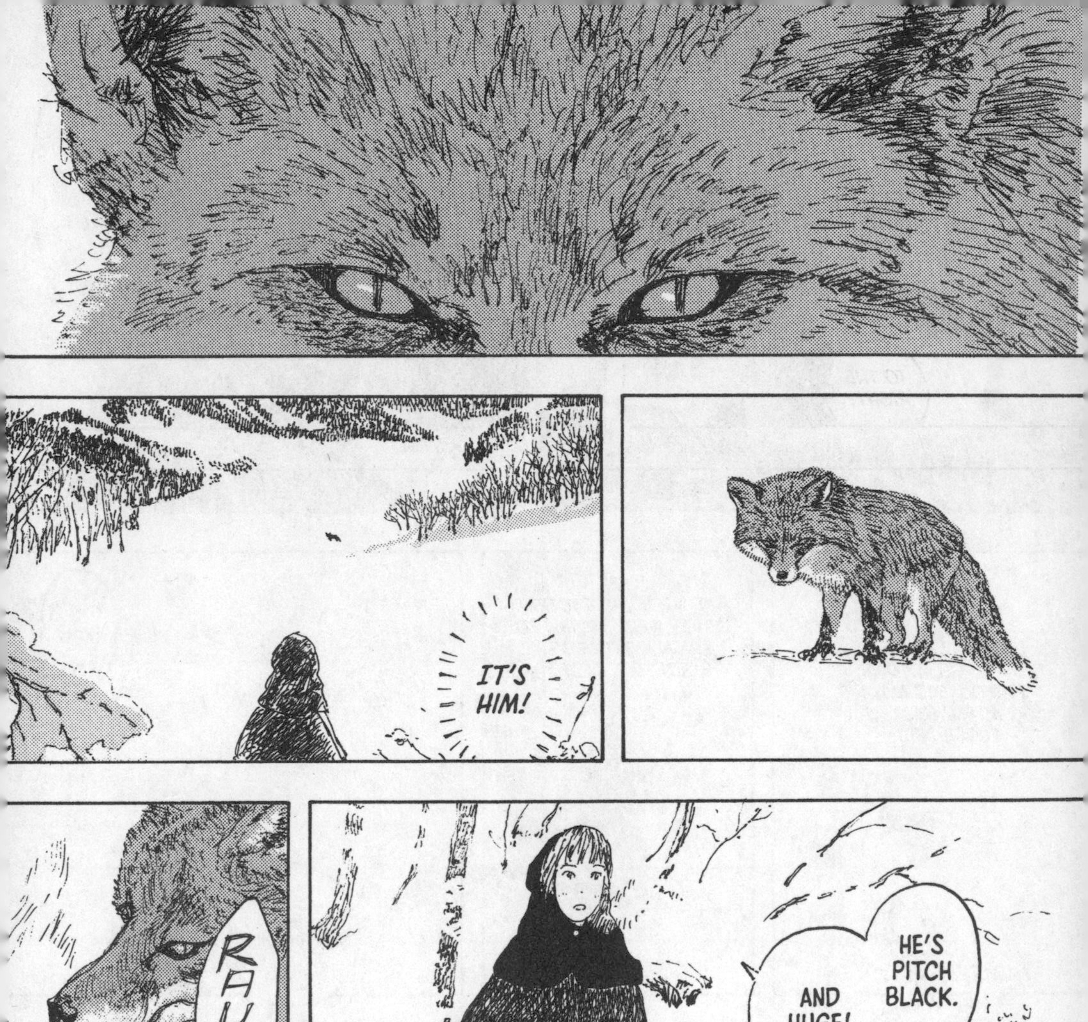
IT'S HIM!
HE'S PITCH BLACK.
AND HUGE!
RAUW!
RHH!
RHH!
RHH!
IS HE TRYING TO DISTRACT ME?

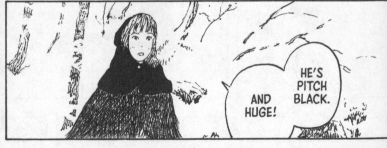

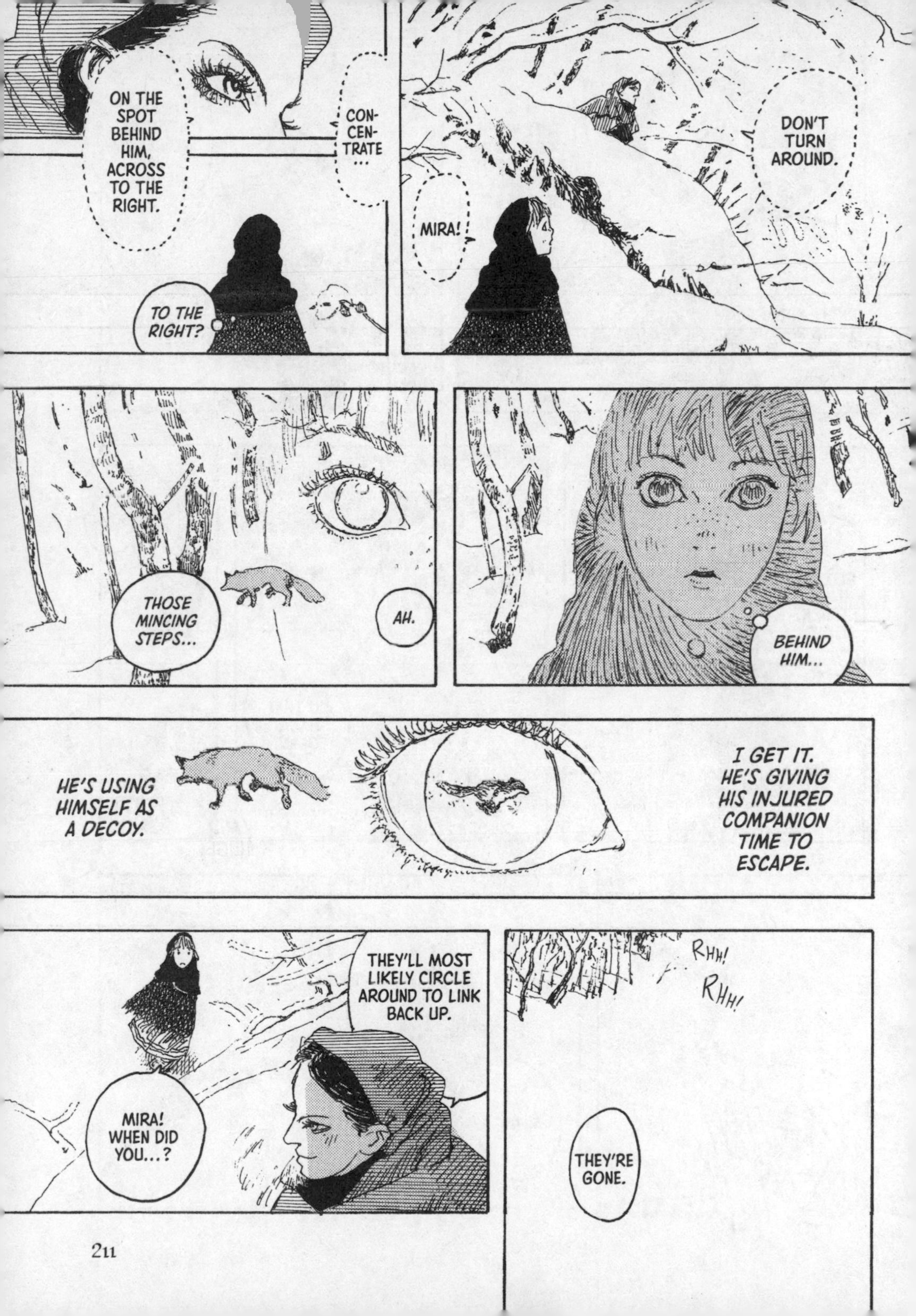
DON'T TURN AROUND.
MIRA!
CON-CEN-TRATE...
ON THE SPOT BEHIND HIM, ACROSS TO THE RIGHT.
TO THE RIGHT?
BEHIND HIM...
AH.
THOSE MINCING STEPS...
I GET IT. HE'S GIVING HIS INJURED COMPANION TIME TO ESCAPE.
HE'S USING HIMSELF AS A DECOY.
RHH!
RHH!
THEY'RE GONE.
THEY'LL MOST LIKELY CIRCLE AROUND TO LINK BACK UP.
MIRA! WHEN DID YOU...?

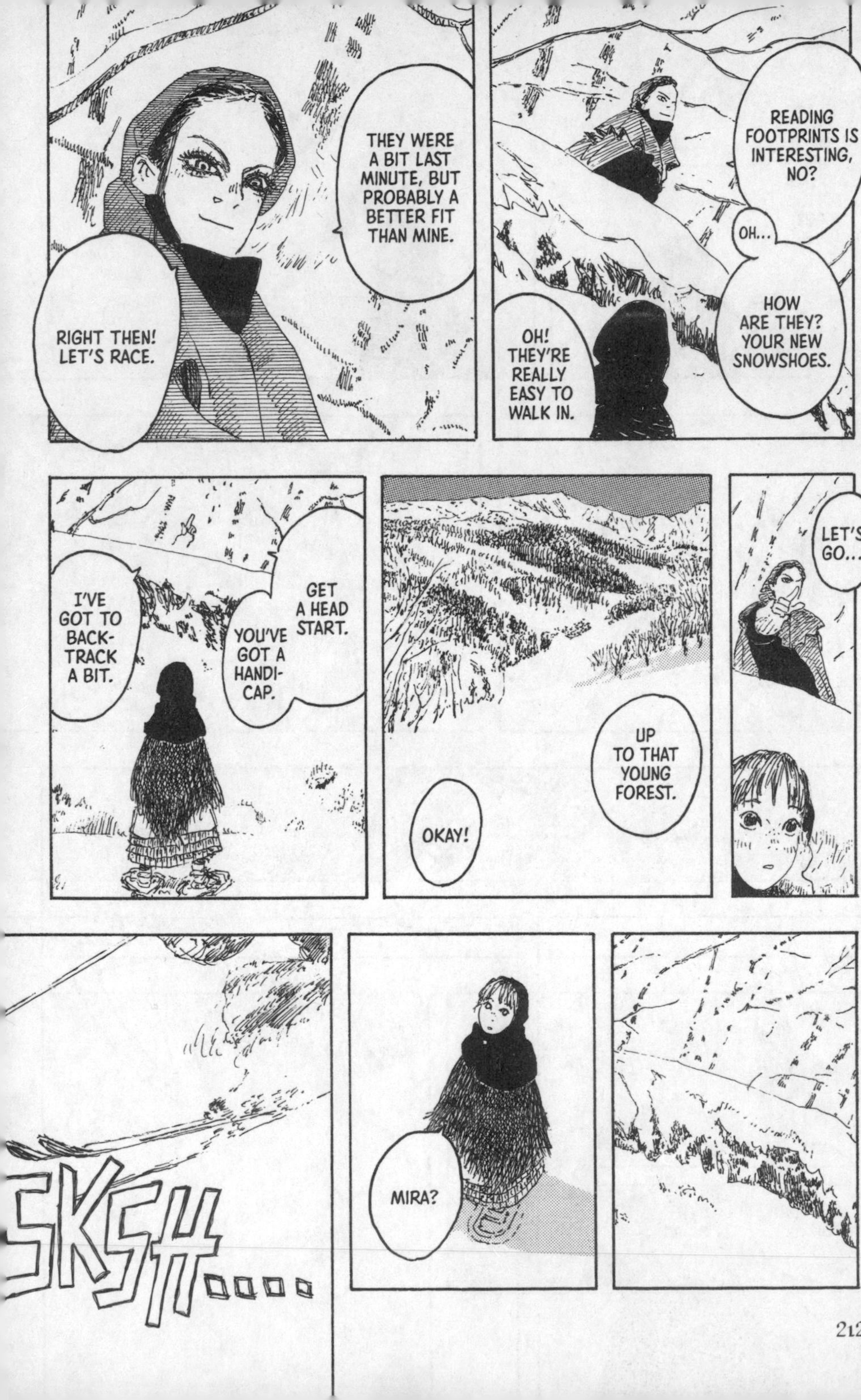
READING FOOTPRINTS IS INTERESTING, NO?
OH...
HOW ARE THEY? YOUR NEW SNOWSHOES.
OH! THEY'RE REALLY EASY TO WALK IN.
THEY WERE A BIT LAST MINUTE, BUT PROBABLY A BETTER FIT THAN MINE.
RIGHT THEN! LET'S RACE.
LET'S GO...
UP TO THAT YOUNG FOREST.
OKAY!
GET A HEAD START.
YOU'VE GOT A HANDI-CAP.
I'VE GOT TO BACK-TRACK A BIT.
MIRA?
SKSH.....

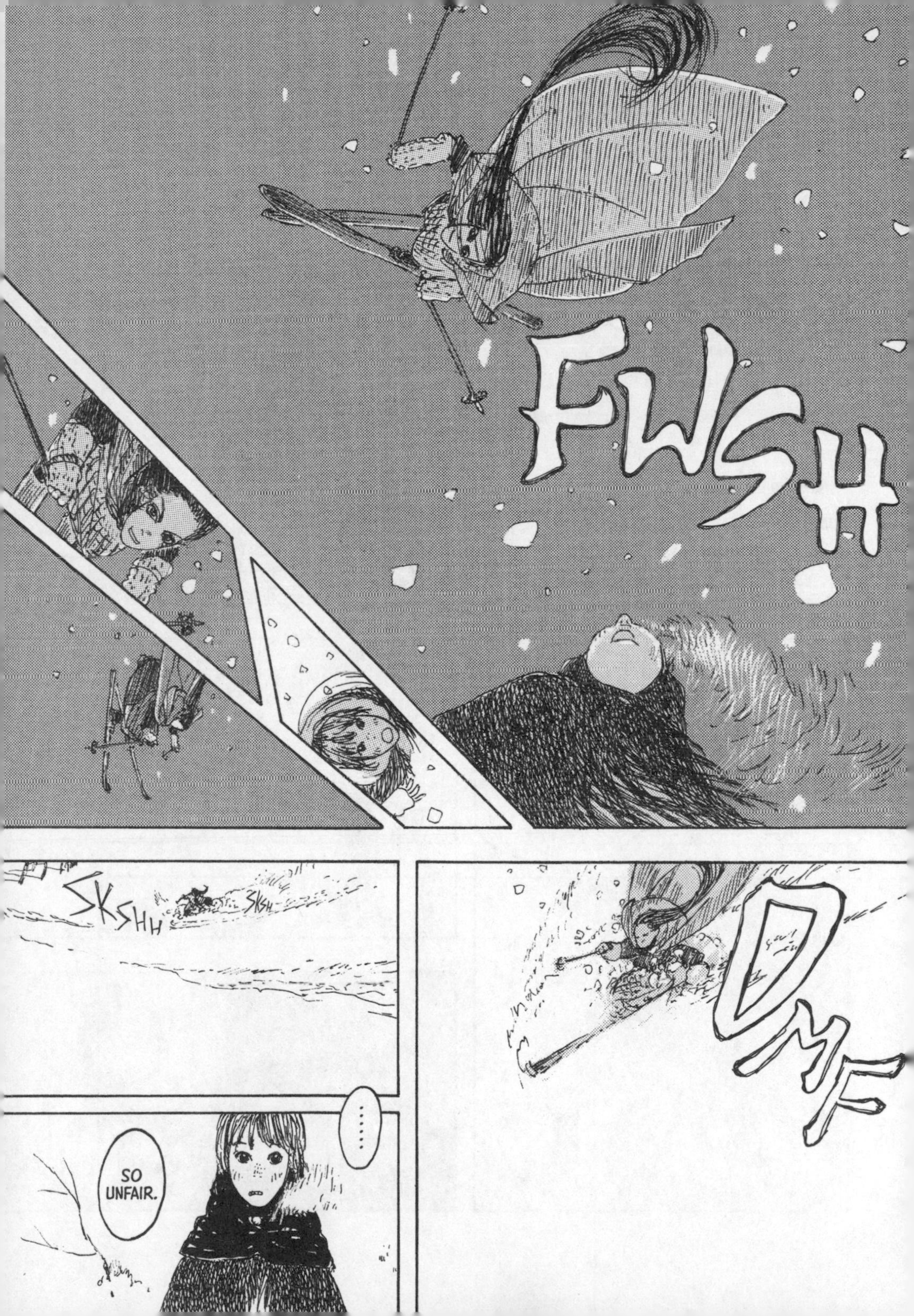
FWSH
DMF
SKSHH
SKSH
......
SO UNFAIR.

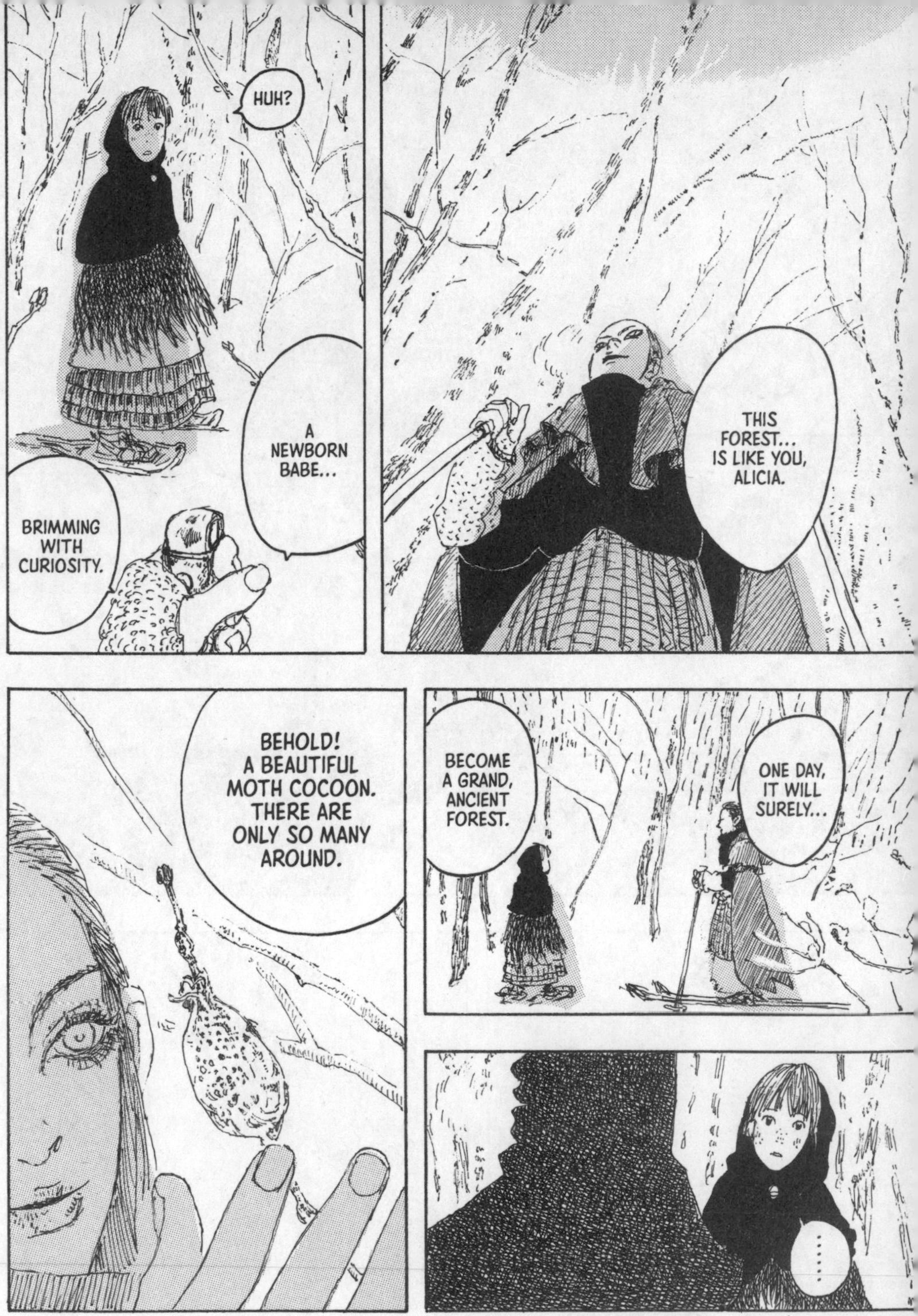
THIS FOREST... IS LIKE YOU, ALICIA.
HUH?
A NEWBORN BABE...
BRIMMING WITH CURIOSITY.
ONE DAY, IT WILL SURELY...
BECOME A GRAND, ANCIENT FOREST.
......
BEHOLD! A BEAUTIFUL MOTH COCOON. THERE ARE ONLY SO MANY AROUND.

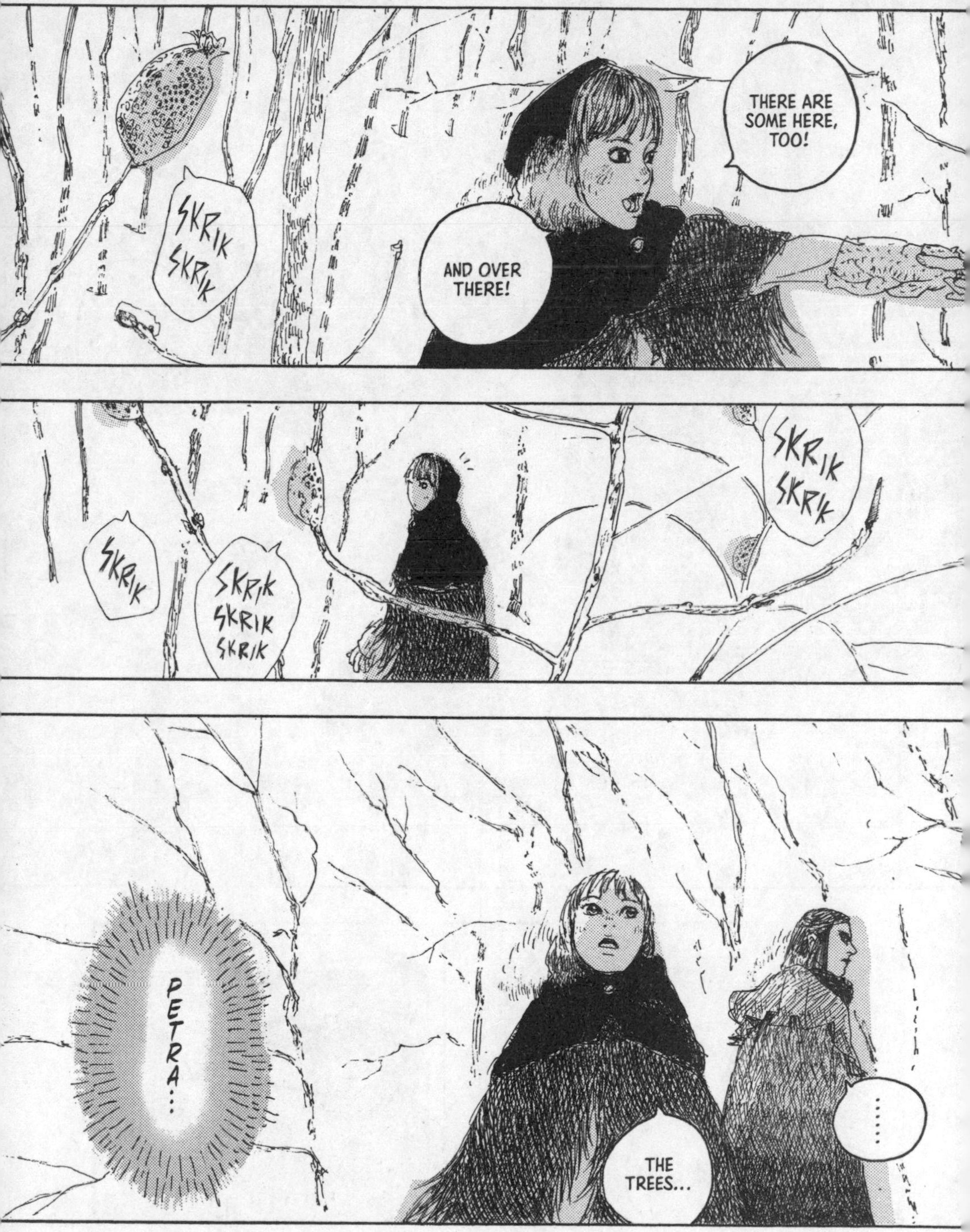

THERE ARE SOME HERE, TOO!
AND OVER THERE!
SKRIK SKRIK
SKRIK SKRIK
SKRIK SKRIK SKRIK
SKRIK
......
THE TREES...
PETRA...

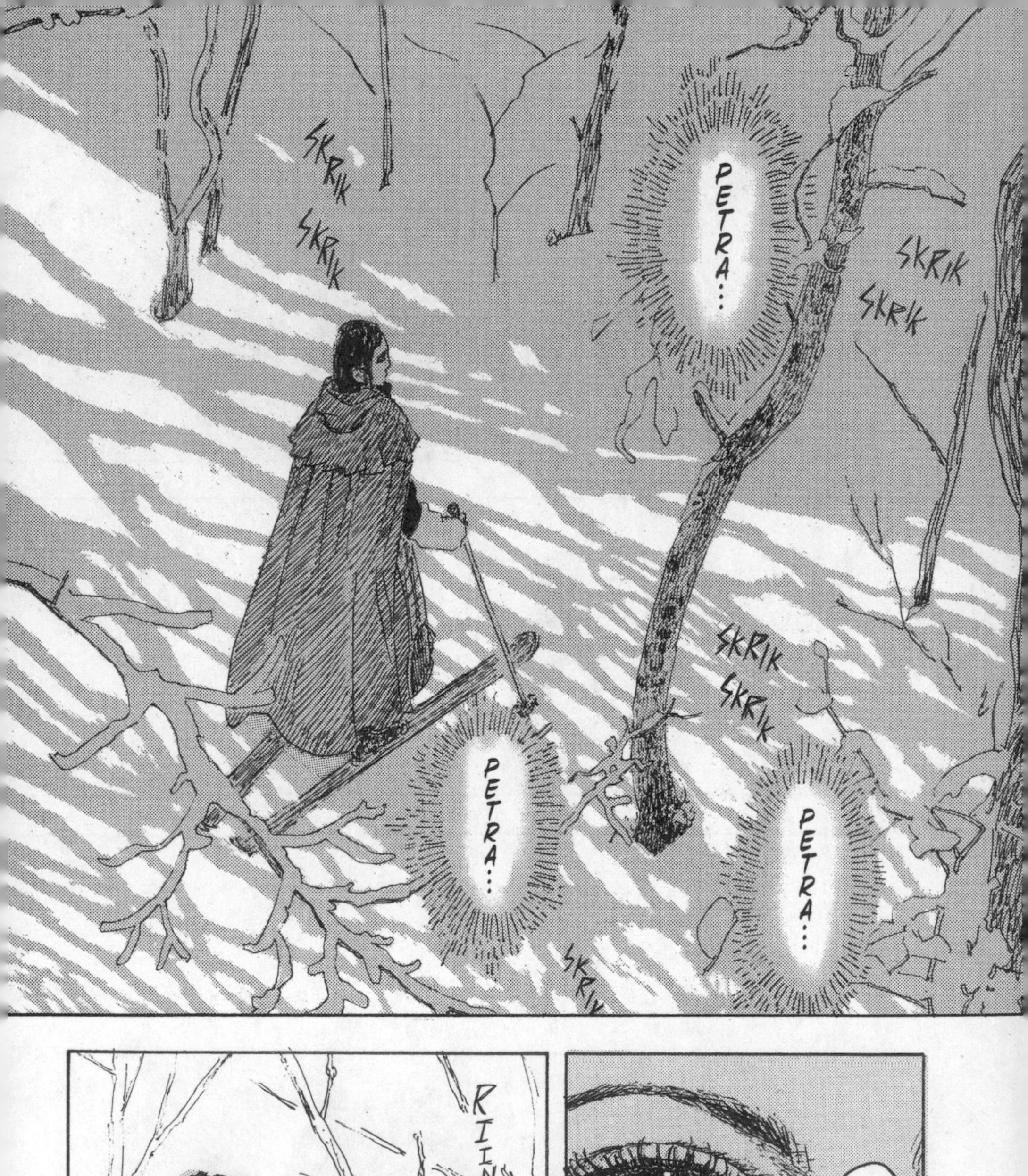
PETRA...
SKRIK
SKRIK
SKRIK
SKRIK
SKRIK
SKRIK
PETRA...
PETRA...
PETRA...
RIIN...
OH... THEY STOPPED.

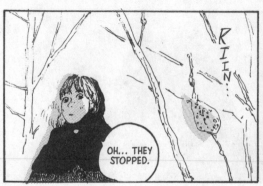

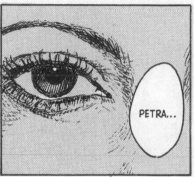

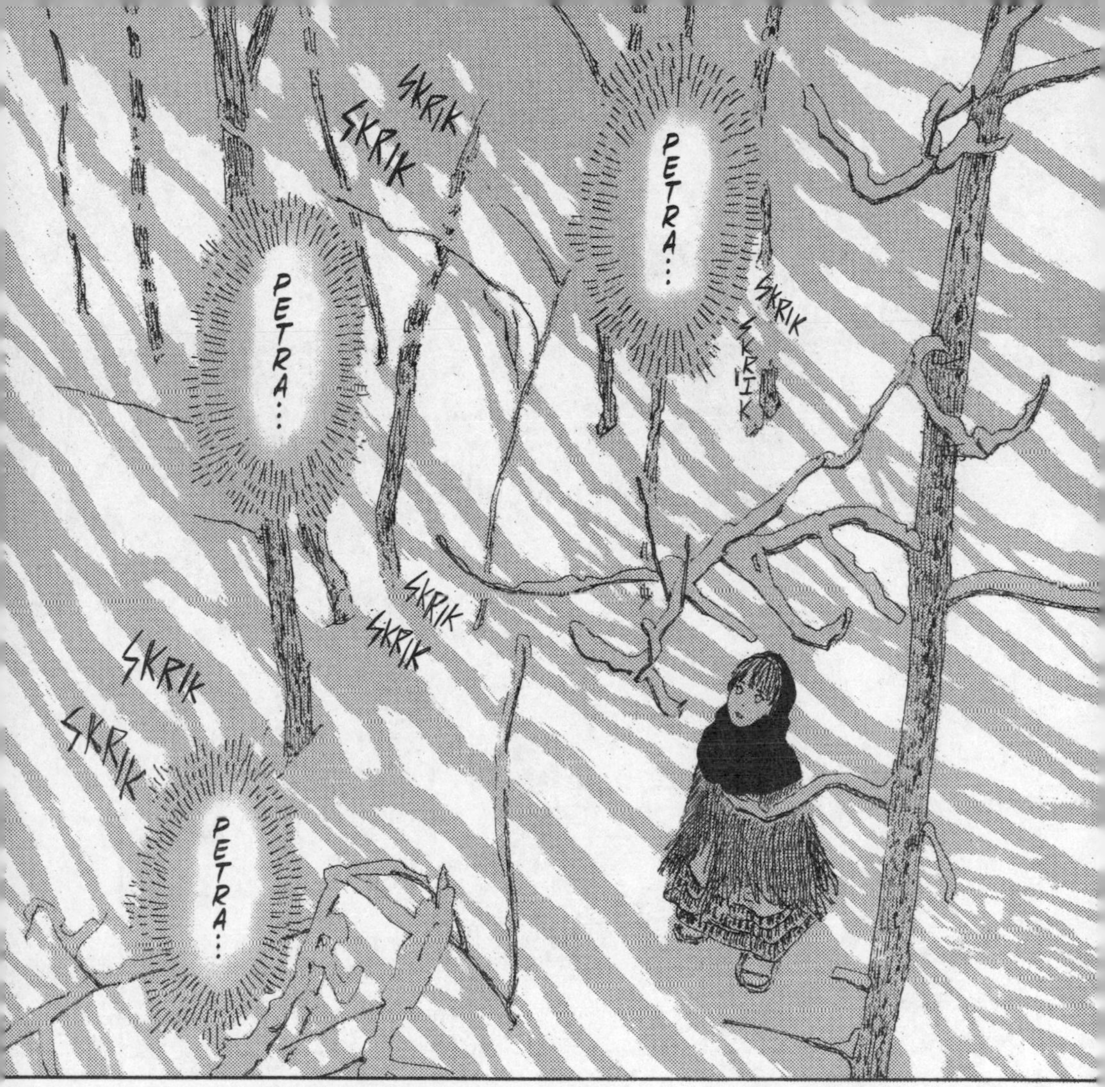
PETRA...
SKRIK
SKRIK
SKRIK
SKRIK
PETRA...
SKRIK
SKRIK
SKRIK
SKRIK
PETRA...
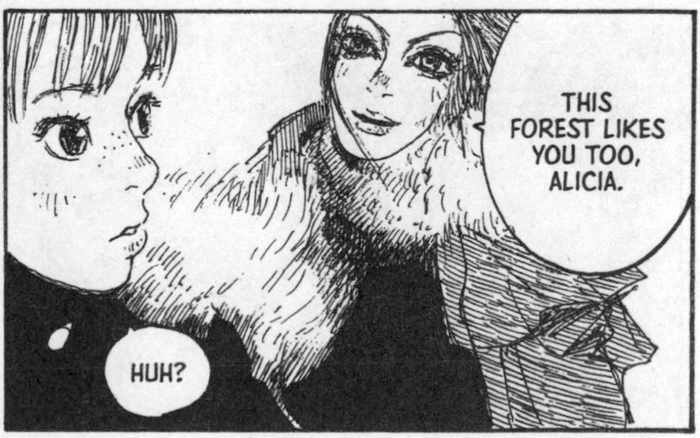
THIS FOREST LIKES YOU TOO, ALICIA.
HUH?
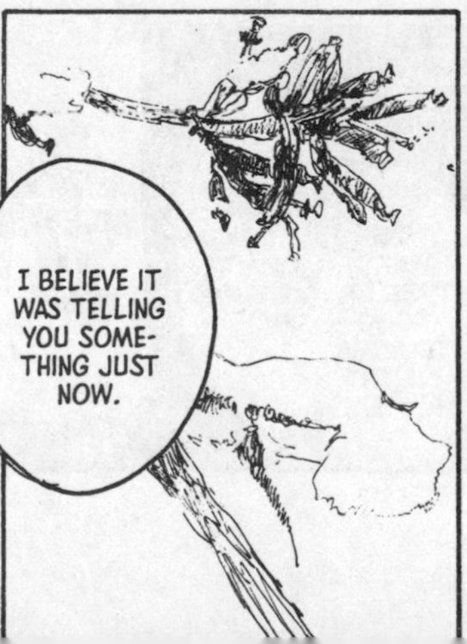
I BELIEVE IT WAS TELLING YOU SOMETHING JUST NOW.

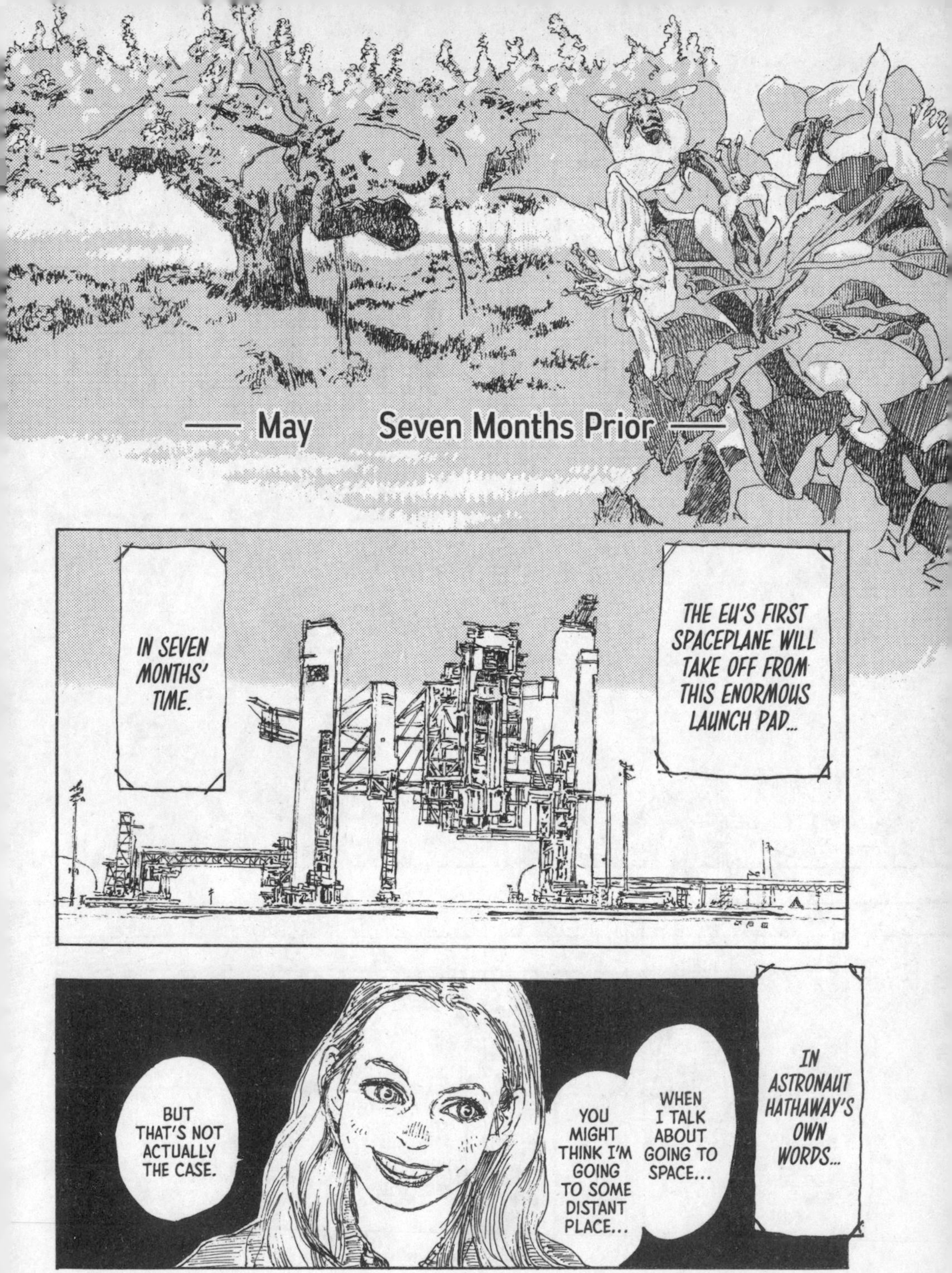
— May Seven Months Prior —
THE EU'S FIRST SPACEPLANE WILL TAKE OFF FROM THIS ENORMOUS LAUNCH PAD...
IN SEVEN MONTHS' TIME.
IN ASTRONAUT HATHAWAY'S OWN WORDS...
WHEN I TALK ABOUT GOING TO SPACE...
YOU MIGHT THINK I'M GOING TO SOME DISTANT PLACE...
BUT THAT'S NOT ACTUALLY THE CASE.

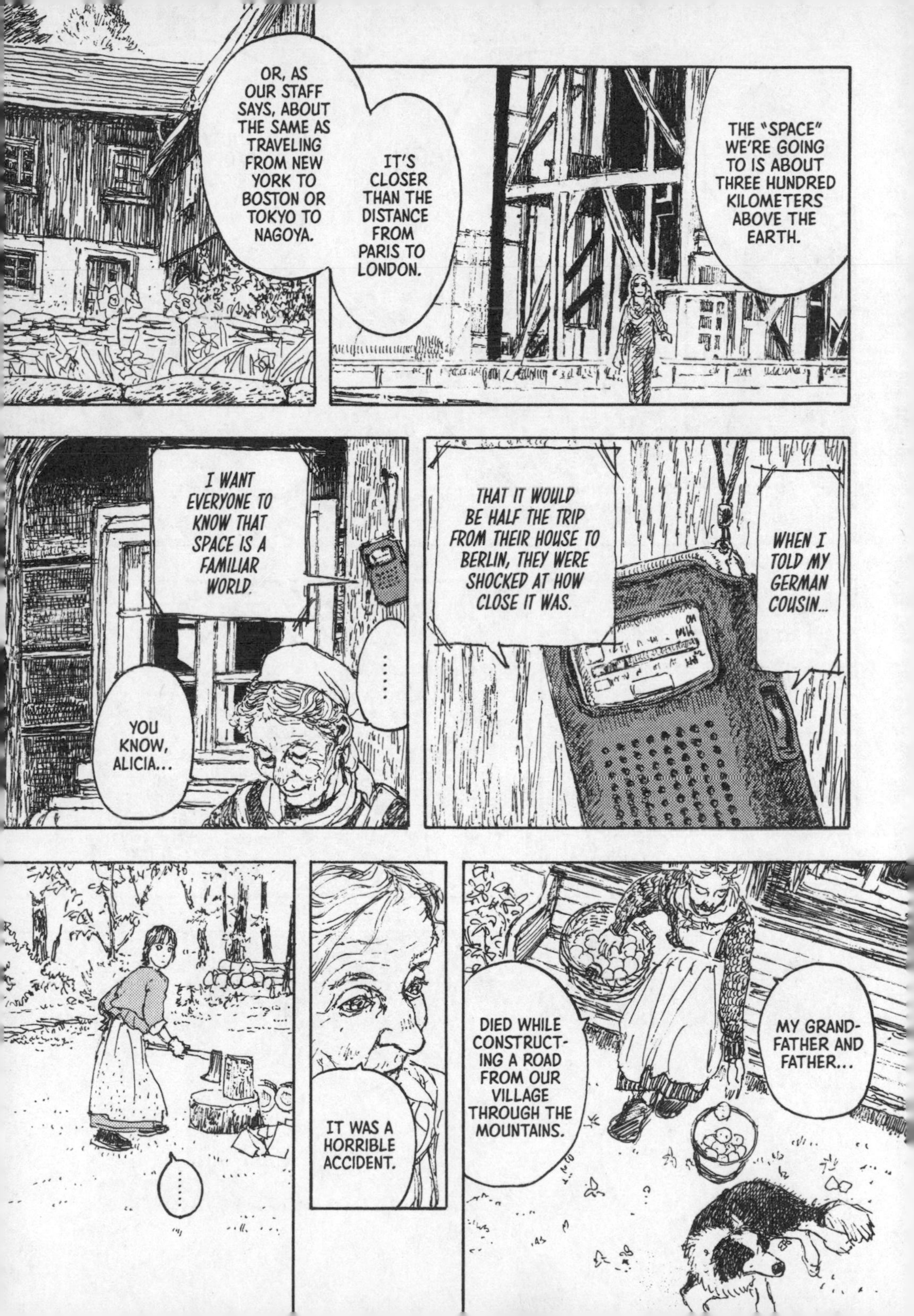
THE "SPACE" WE'RE GOING TO IS ABOUT THREE HUNDRED KILOMETERS ABOVE THE EARTH.
IT'S CLOSER THAN THE DISTANCE FROM PARIS TO LONDON.
OR, AS OUR STAFF SAYS, ABOUT THE SAME AS TRAVELING FROM NEW YORK TO BOSTON OR TOKYO TO NAGOYA.
WHEN I TOLD MY GERMAN COUSIN...
THAT IT WOULD BE HALF THE TRIP FROM THEIR HOUSE TO BERLIN, THEY WERE SHOCKED AT HOW CLOSE IT WAS.
I WANT EVERYONE TO KNOW THAT SPACE IS A FAMILIAR WORLD.
......
YOU KNOW, ALICIA...
MY GRAND-FATHER AND FATHER...
DIED WHILE CONSTRUCT-ING A ROAD FROM OUR VILLAGE THROUGH THE MOUNTAINS.
IT WAS A HORRIBLE ACCIDENT.
......

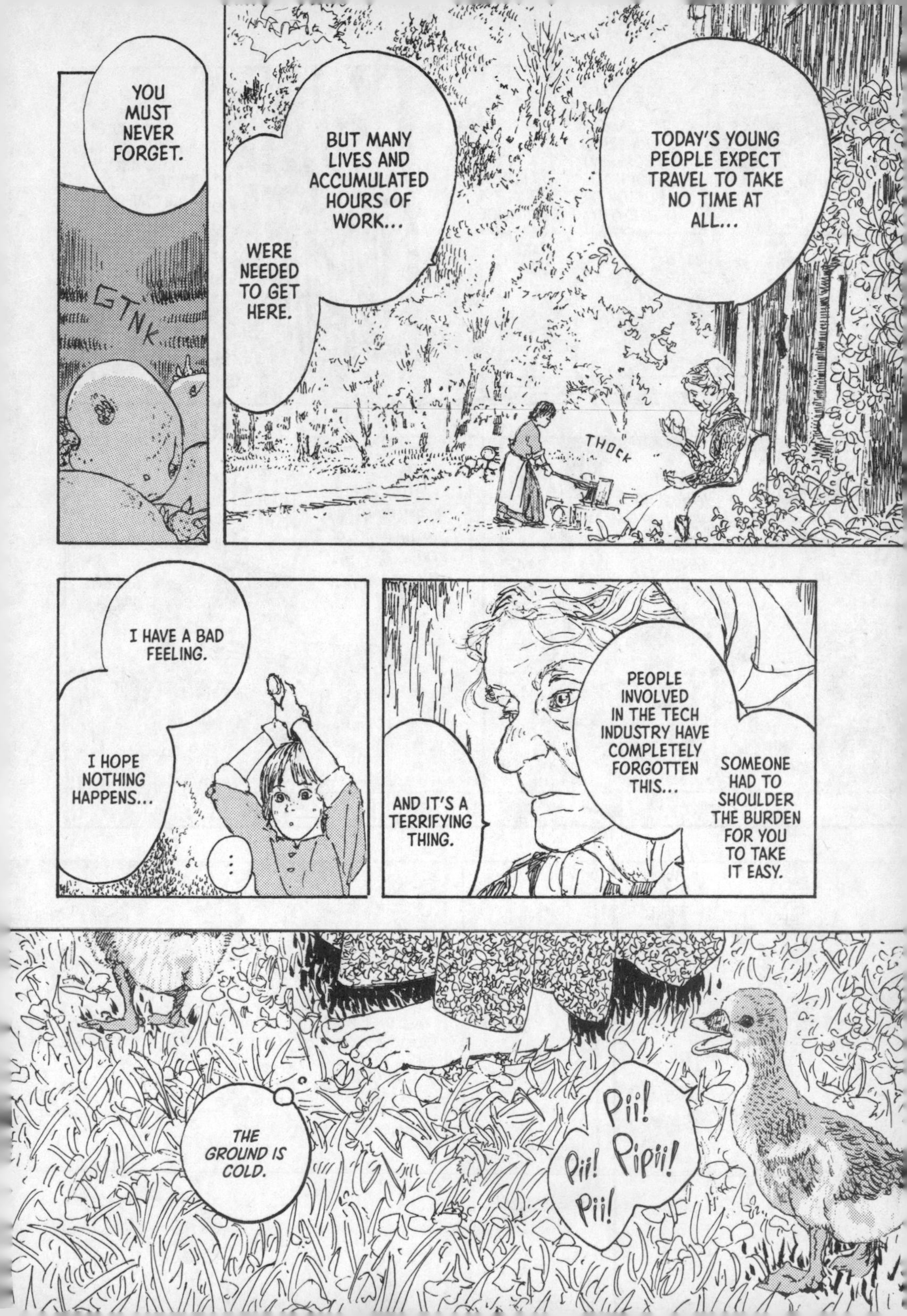
TODAY'S YOUNG PEOPLE EXPECT TRAVEL TO TAKE NO TIME AT ALL...
BUT MANY LIVES AND ACCUMULATED HOURS OF WORK...
WERE NEEDED TO GET HERE.
THOCK
YOU MUST NEVER FORGET.
GTNK
SOMEONE HAD TO SHOULDER THE BURDEN FOR YOU TO TAKE IT EASY.
PEOPLE INVOLVED IN THE TECH INDUSTRY HAVE COMPLETELY FORGOTTEN THIS...
AND IT'S A TERRIFYING THING.
I HAVE A BAD FEELING.
I HOPE NOTHING HAPPENS...
...
Pii! Pipii!
Pii!
Pii!
THE GROUND IS COLD.

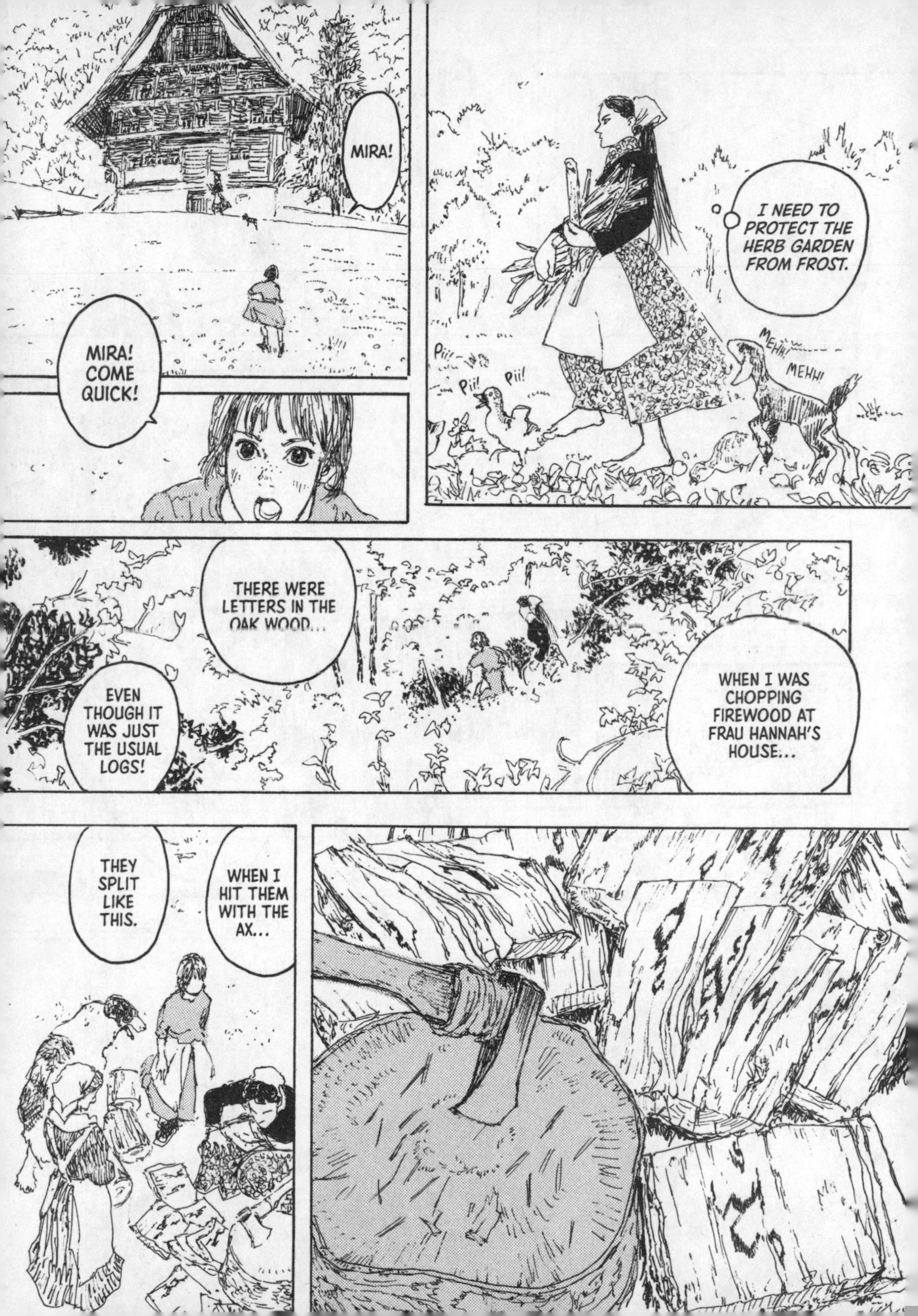
I NEED TO PROTECT THE HERB GARDEN FROM FROST.
MEHH!
MEHH!
Pii!
Pii!
Pii!
MIRA!
MIRA! COME QUICK!
WHEN I WAS CHOPPING FIREWOOD AT FRAU HANNAH'S HOUSE...
THERE WERE LETTERS IN THE OAK WOOD...
EVEN THOUGH IT WAS JUST THE USUAL LOGS!
WHEN I HIT THEM WITH THE AX...
THEY SPLIT LIKE THIS.

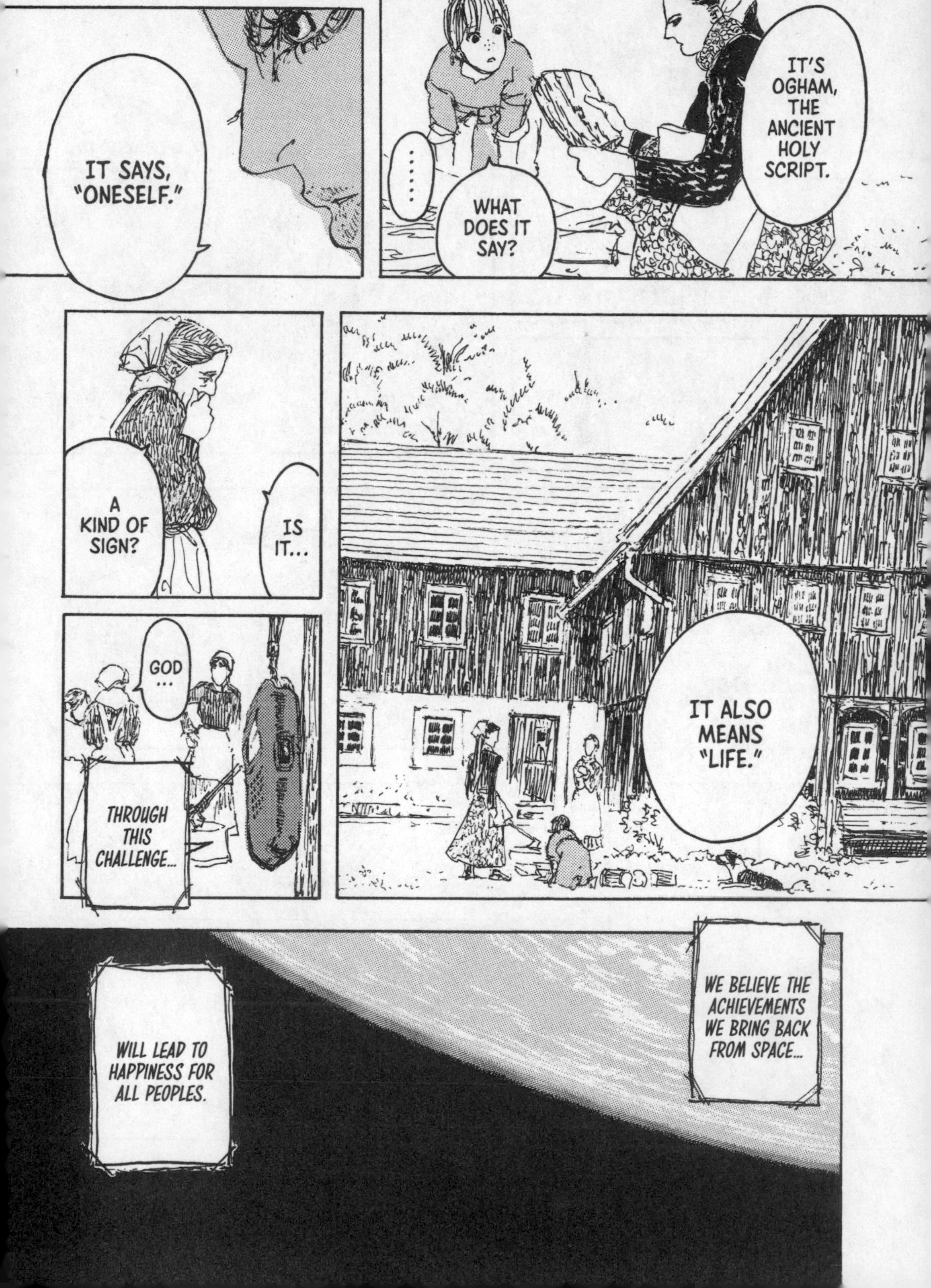
IT'S OGHAM, THE ANCIENT HOLY SCRIPT.
......
WHAT DOES IT SAY?
IT SAYS, "ONESELF."
IT ALSO MEANS "LIFE."
IS IT...
A KIND OF SIGN?
GOD...
THROUGH THIS CHALLENGE...
WE BELIEVE THE ACHIEVEMENTS WE BRING BACK FROM SPACE...
WILL LEAD TO HAPPINESS FOR ALL PEOPLES.

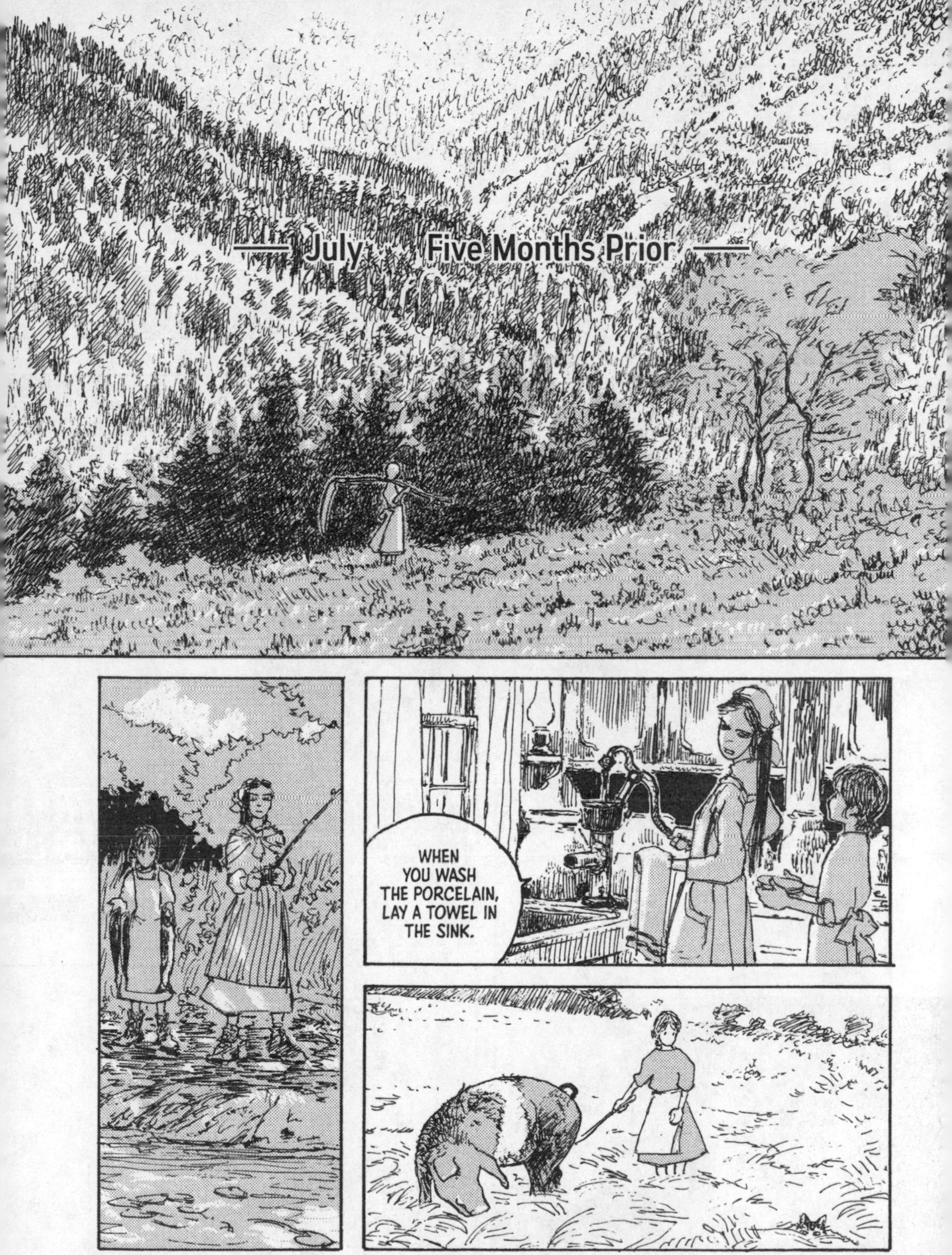
—— July Five Months Prior ——
WHEN YOU WASH THE PORCELAIN, LAY A TOWEL IN THE SINK.

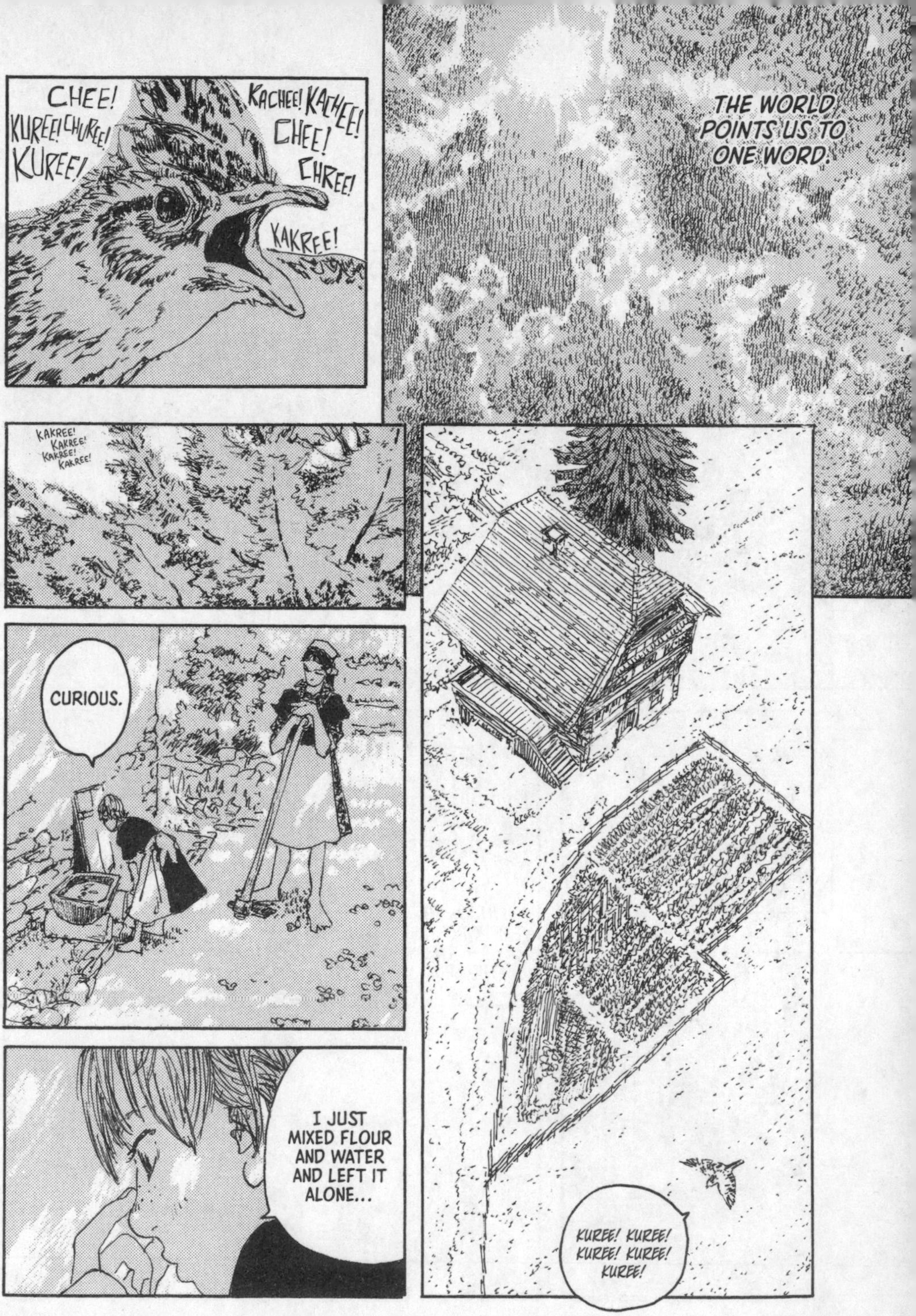
THE WORLD POINTS US TO ONE WORD.
KACHEE! KACHEE!
CHEE!
CHREE!
KAKREE!
CHEE!
KUREE! CHUREE!
KUREE!
KUREE! KUREE! KUREE! KUREE! KUREE!
KAKREE! KAKREE! KAKREE! KAKREE!
CURIOUS.
I JUST MIXED FLOUR AND WATER AND LEFT IT ALONE...

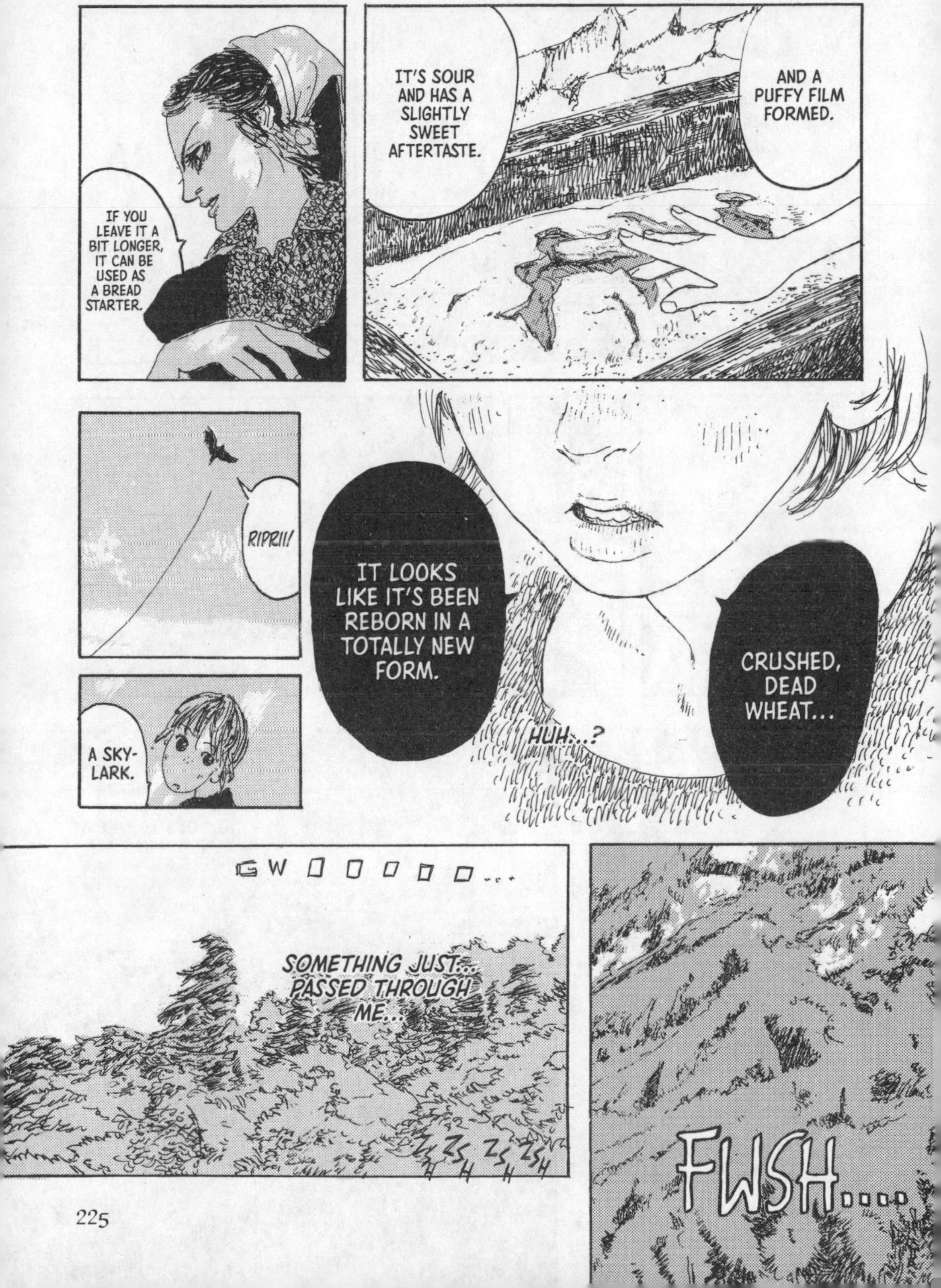
AND A PUFFY FILM FORMED.
IT'S SOUR AND HAS A SLIGHTLY SWEET AFTERTASTE.
IF YOU LEAVE IT A BIT LONGER, IT CAN BE USED AS A BREAD STARTER.
CRUSHED, DEAD WHEAT...
IT LOOKS LIKE IT'S BEEN REBORN IN A TOTALLY NEW FORM.
HUH...?
RIPRII!
A SKY-LARK.
FWSH....
GWOOOOOO...
SOMETHING JUST... PASSED THROUGH ME...
ZSH ZSH ZSH ZSH

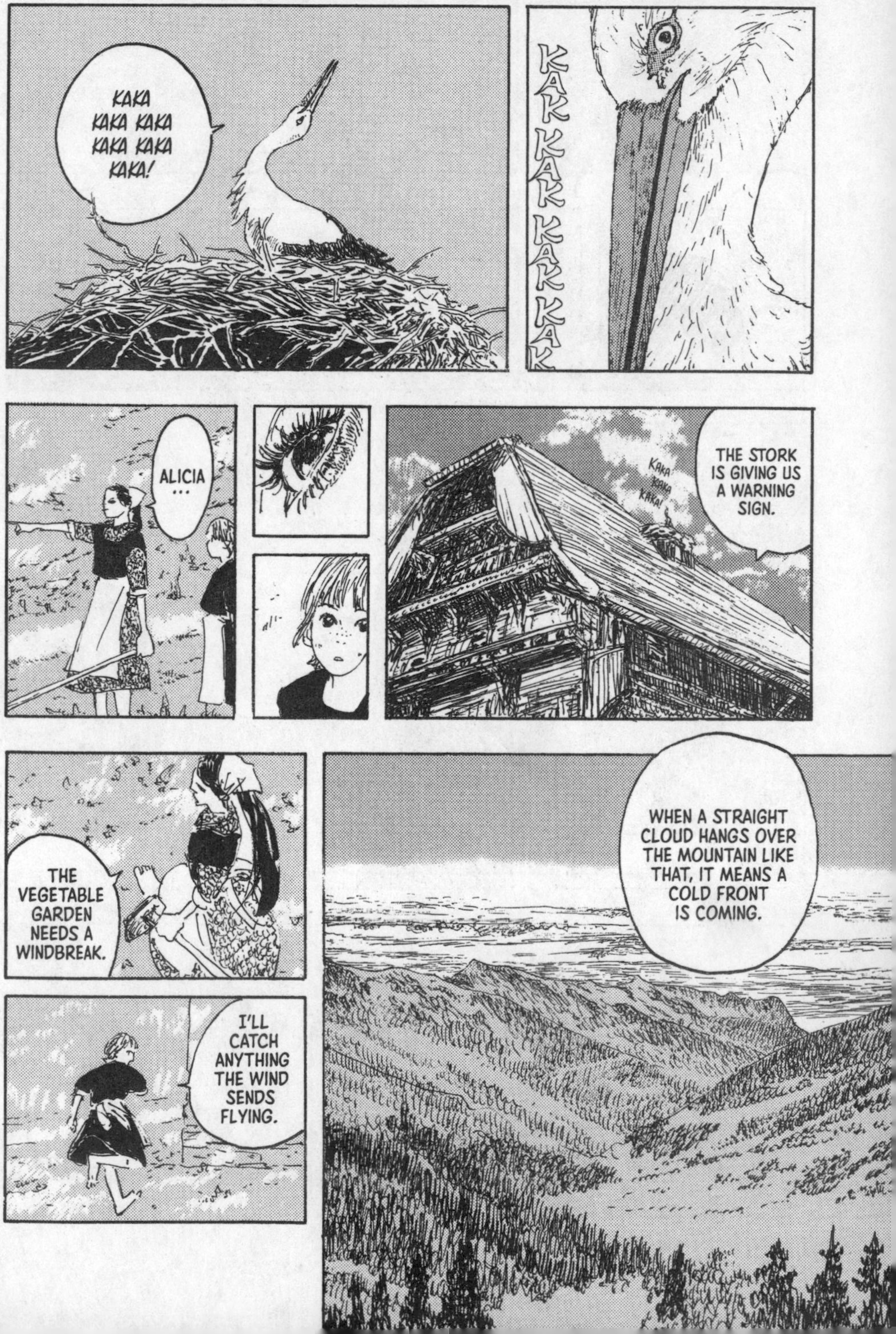
KAK KAK KAK KAK KAK
KAKA KAKA KAKA KAKA KAKA KAKA!
THE STORK IS GIVING US A WARNING SIGN.
Kaka kaka kaka!
ALICIA ...
WHEN A STRAIGHT CLOUD HANGS OVER THE MOUNTAIN LIKE THAT, IT MEANS A COLD FRONT IS COMING.
THE VEGETABLE GARDEN NEEDS A WINDBREAK.
I'LL CATCH ANYTHING THE WIND SENDS FLYING.

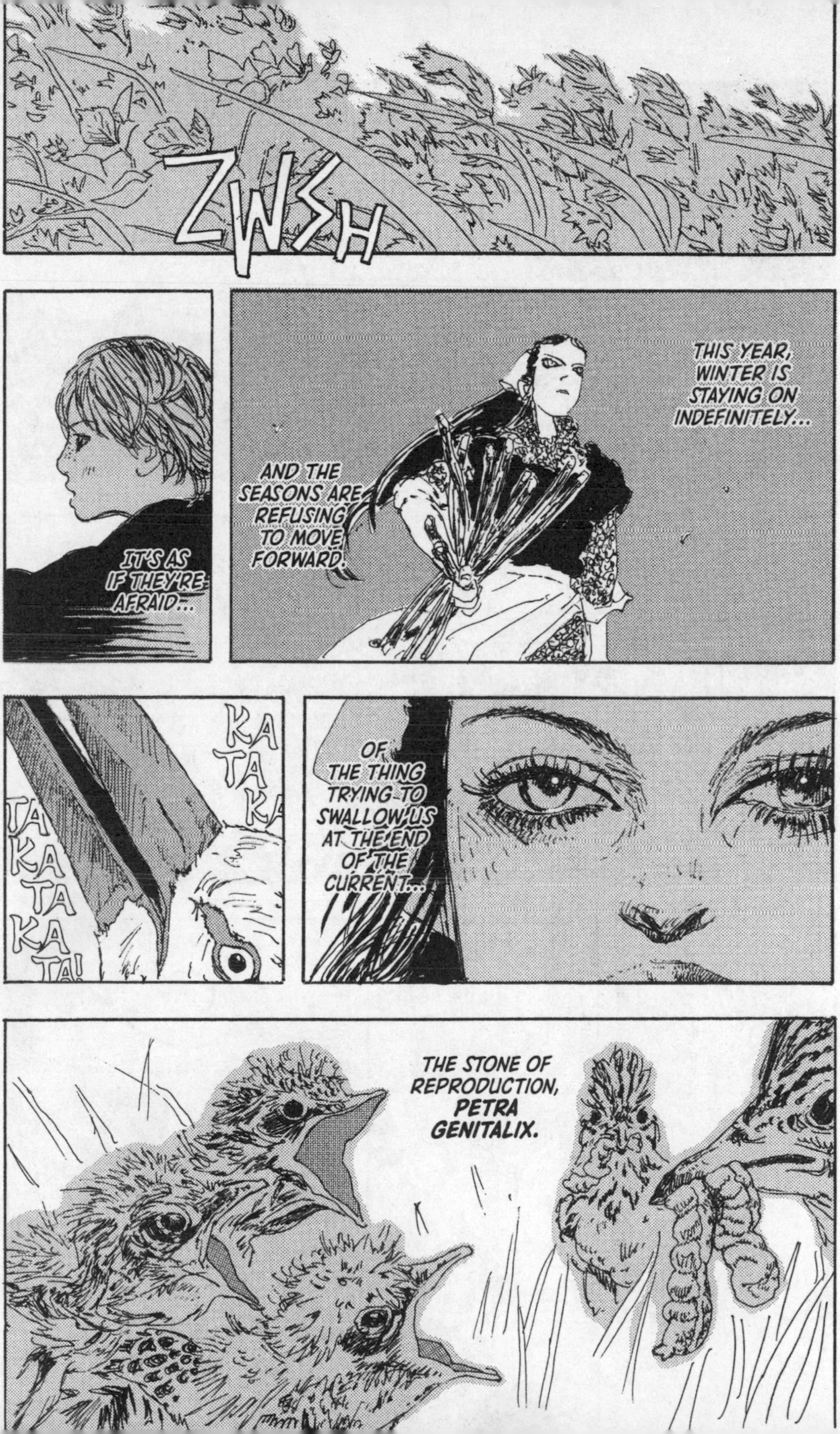
ZWSH
THIS YEAR, WINTER IS STAYING ON INDEFINITELY...
AND THE SEASONS ARE REFUSING TO MOVE FORWARD.
IT'S AS IF THEY'RE AFRAID...
OF THE THING TRYING TO SWALLOW US AT THE END OF THE CURRENT...
KATAKA
TAKATATAKATA!
THE STONE OF REPRODUCTION, **PETRA GENITALIX.**

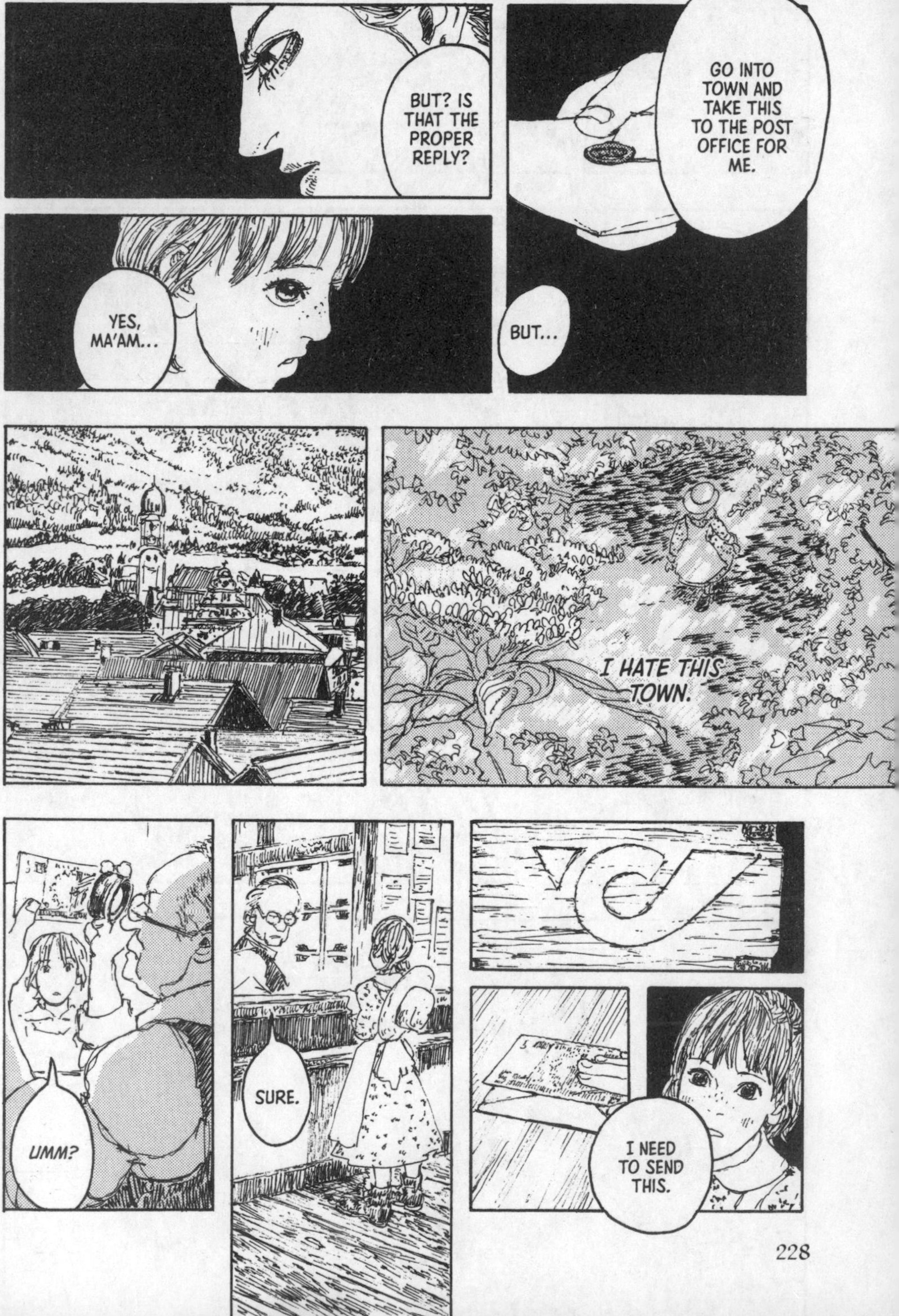

GO INTO TOWN AND TAKE THIS TO THE POST OFFICE FOR ME.
BUT? IS THAT THE PROPER REPLY?
BUT...
YES, MA'AM...
I HATE THIS TOWN.
I NEED TO SEND THIS.
SURE.
UMM?

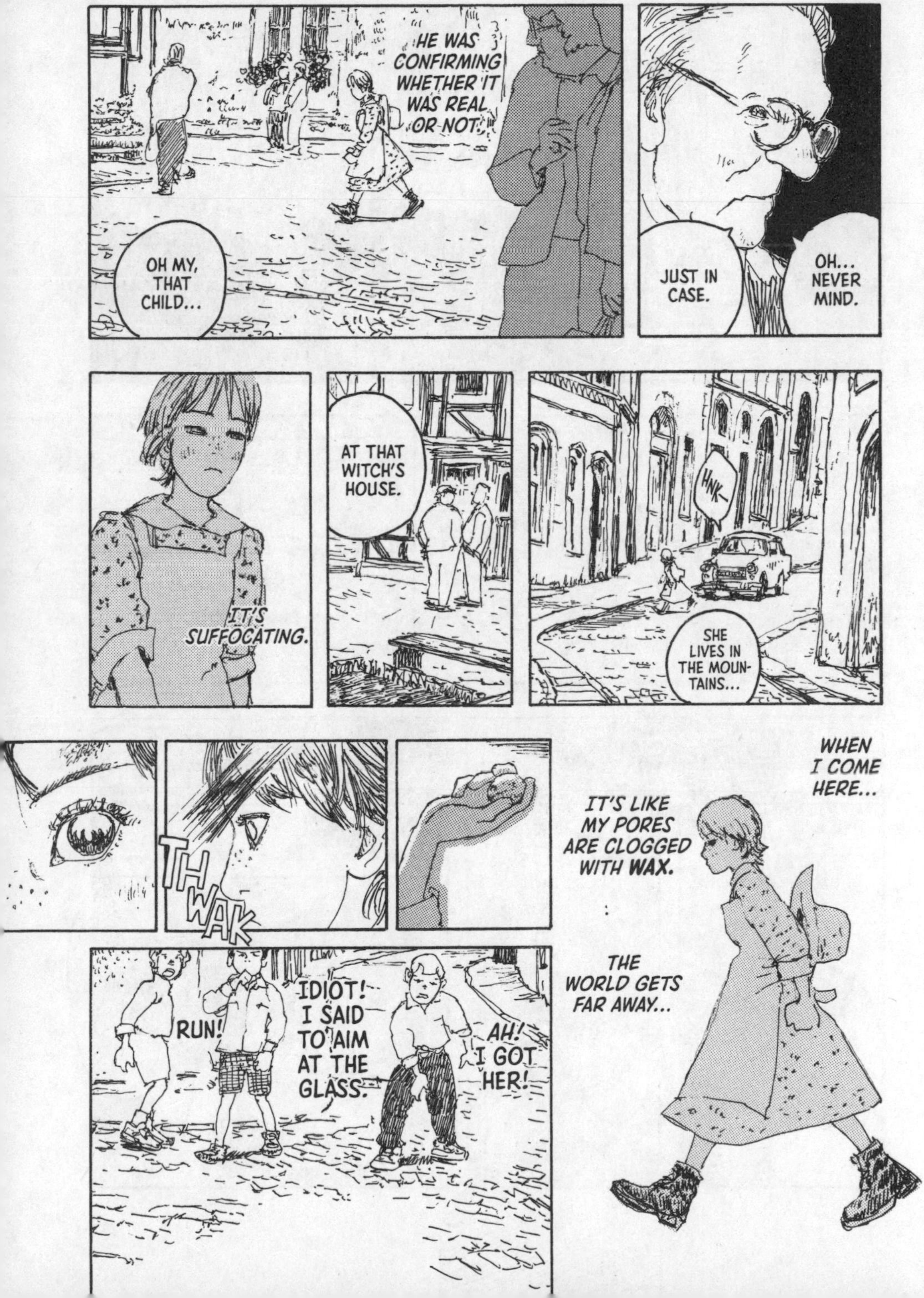
OH... NEVER MIND.
JUST IN CASE.
HE WAS CONFIRMING WHETHER IT WAS REAL OR NOT.
OH MY, THAT CHILD...
HNK-
SHE LIVES IN THE MOUNTAINS...
AT THAT WITCH'S HOUSE.
IT'S SUFFOCATING.
WHEN I COME HERE...
IT'S LIKE MY PORES ARE CLOGGED WITH **WAX.**
THE WORLD GETS FAR AWAY...
THWAK
AH! I GOT HER!
IDIOT! I SAID TO AIM AT THE GLASS.
RUN!

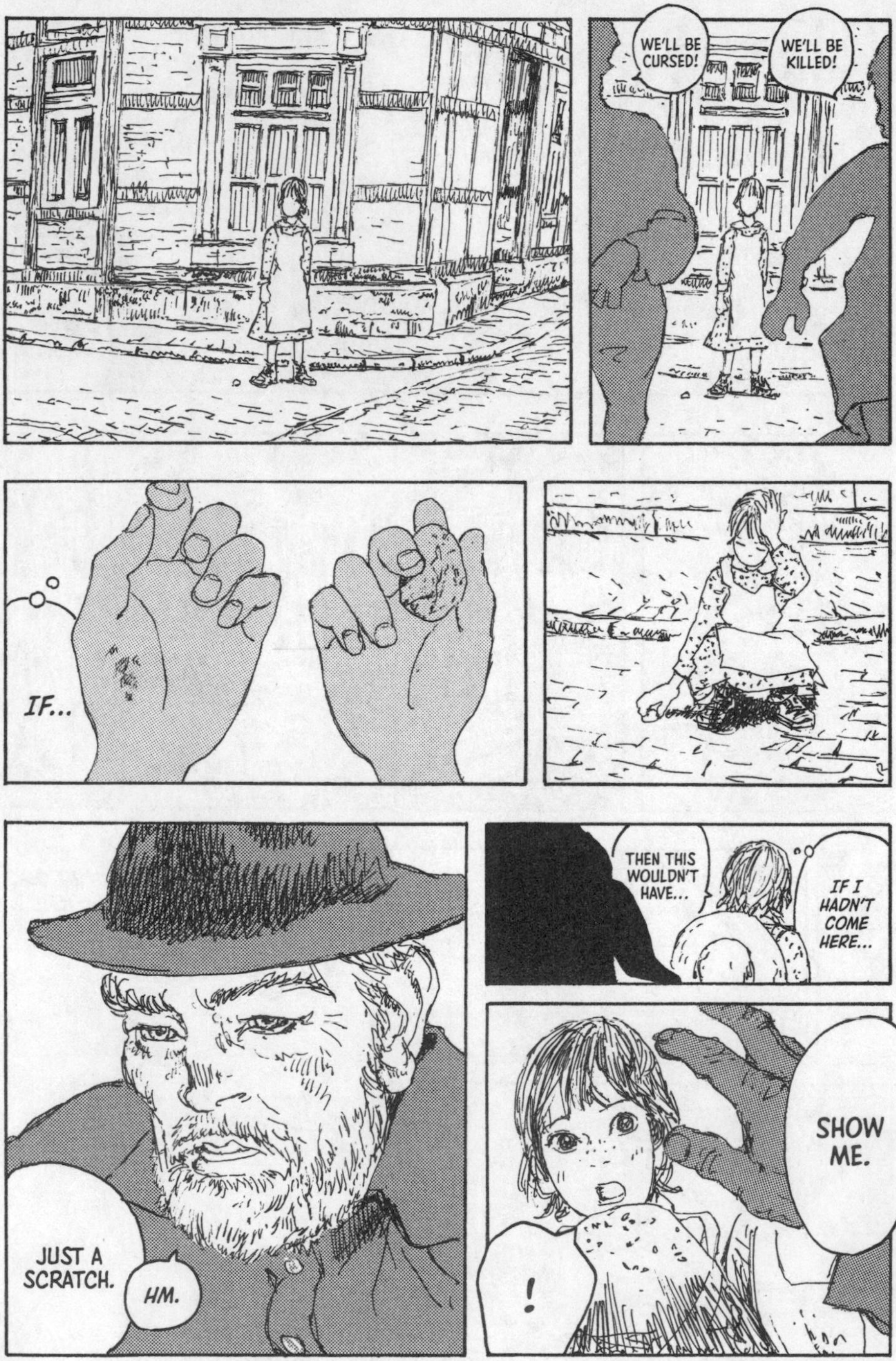
WE'LL BE KILLED!
WE'LL BE CURSED!
IF...
IF I HADN'T COME HERE...
THEN THIS WOULDN'T HAVE...
SHOW ME.
!
HM.
JUST A SCRATCH.

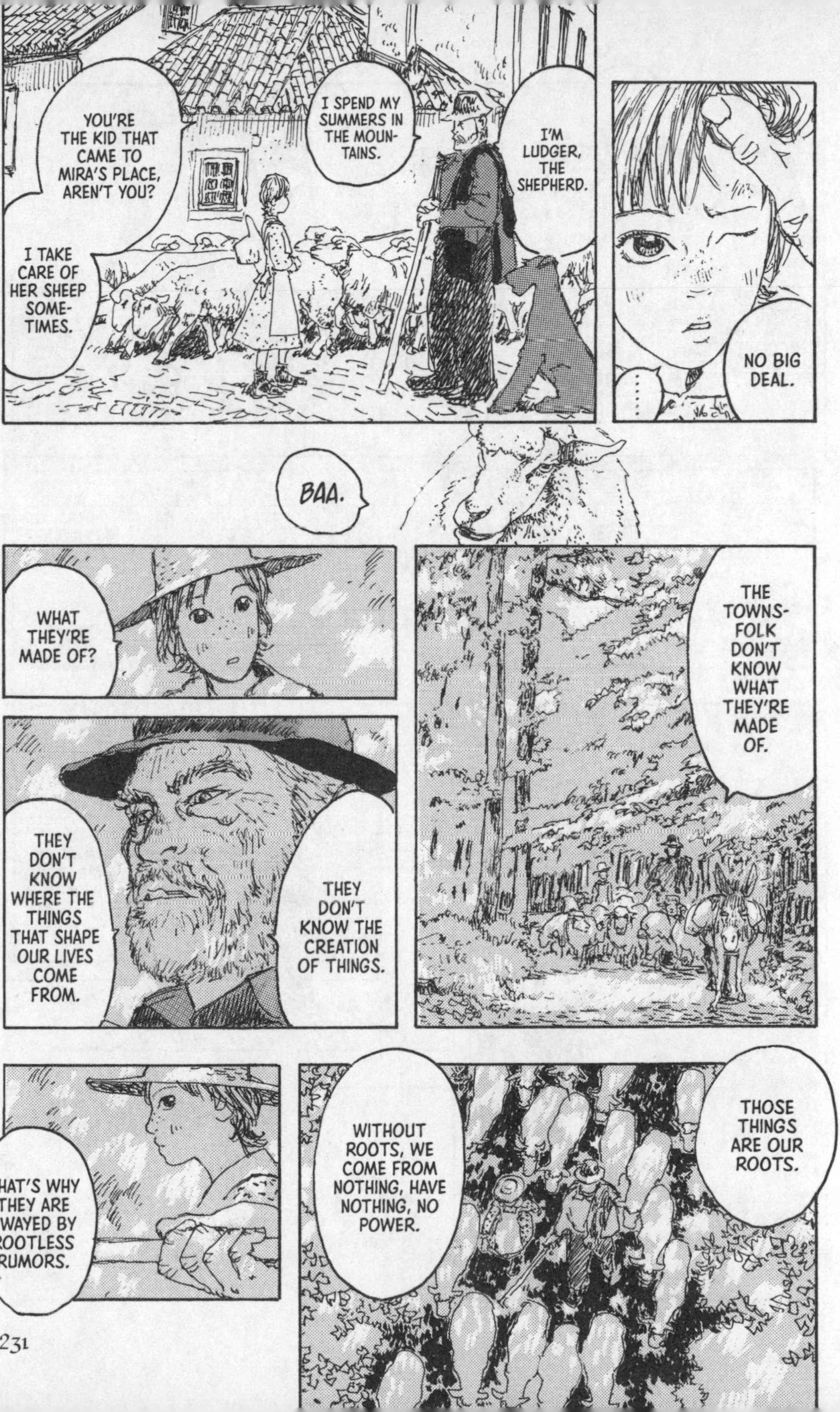
...
NO BIG DEAL.
I'M LUDGER, THE SHEPHERD.
I SPEND MY SUMMERS IN THE MOUNTAINS.
YOU'RE THE KID THAT CAME TO MIRA'S PLACE, AREN'T YOU?
I TAKE CARE OF HER SHEEP SOMETIMES.
BAA.
THE TOWNSFOLK DON'T KNOW WHAT THEY'RE MADE OF.
WHAT THEY'RE MADE OF?
THEY DON'T KNOW THE CREATION OF THINGS.
THEY DON'T KNOW WHERE THE THINGS THAT SHAPE OUR LIVES COME FROM.
THOSE THINGS ARE OUR ROOTS.
WITHOUT ROOTS, WE COME FROM NOTHING, HAVE NOTHING, NO POWER.
THAT'S WHY THEY ARE SWAYED BY ROOTLESS RUMORS.

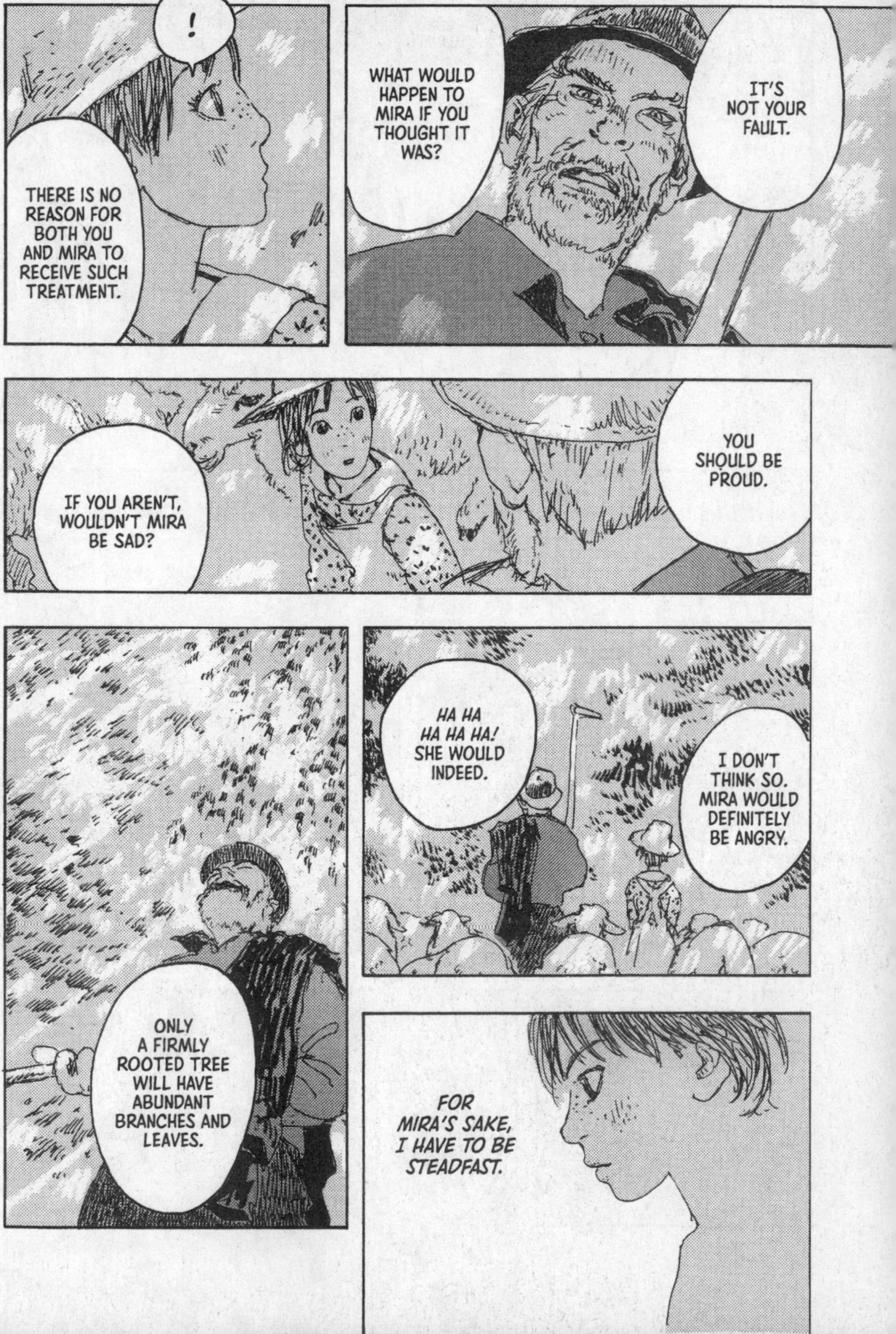
IT'S NOT YOUR FAULT.
WHAT WOULD HAPPEN TO MIRA IF YOU THOUGHT IT WAS?
!
THERE IS NO REASON FOR BOTH YOU AND MIRA TO RECEIVE SUCH TREATMENT.
YOU SHOULD BE PROUD.
IF YOU AREN'T, WOULDN'T MIRA BE SAD?
I DON'T THINK SO. MIRA WOULD DEFINITELY BE ANGRY.
HA HA HA HA HA! SHE WOULD INDEED.
FOR MIRA'S SAKE, I HAVE TO BE STEADFAST.
ONLY A FIRMLY ROOTED TREE WILL HAVE ABUNDANT BRANCHES AND LEAVES.

—— December   The Present ——

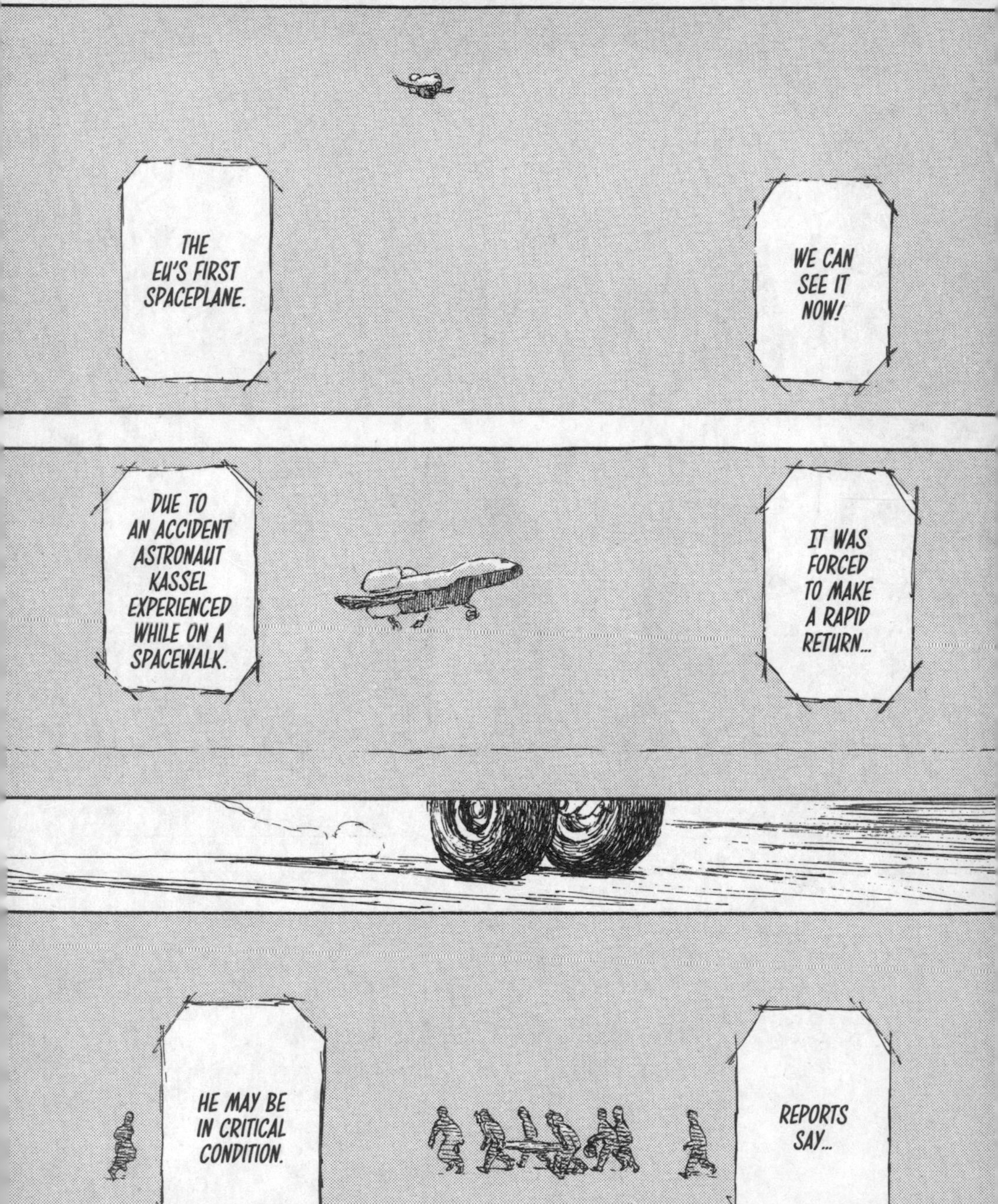
WE CAN SEE IT NOW!
THE EU'S FIRST SPACEPLANE.
IT WAS FORCED TO MAKE A RAPID RETURN...
DUE TO AN ACCIDENT ASTRONAUT KASSEL EXPERIENCED WHILE ON A SPACEWALK.
REPORTS SAY...
HE MAY BE IN CRITICAL CONDITION.

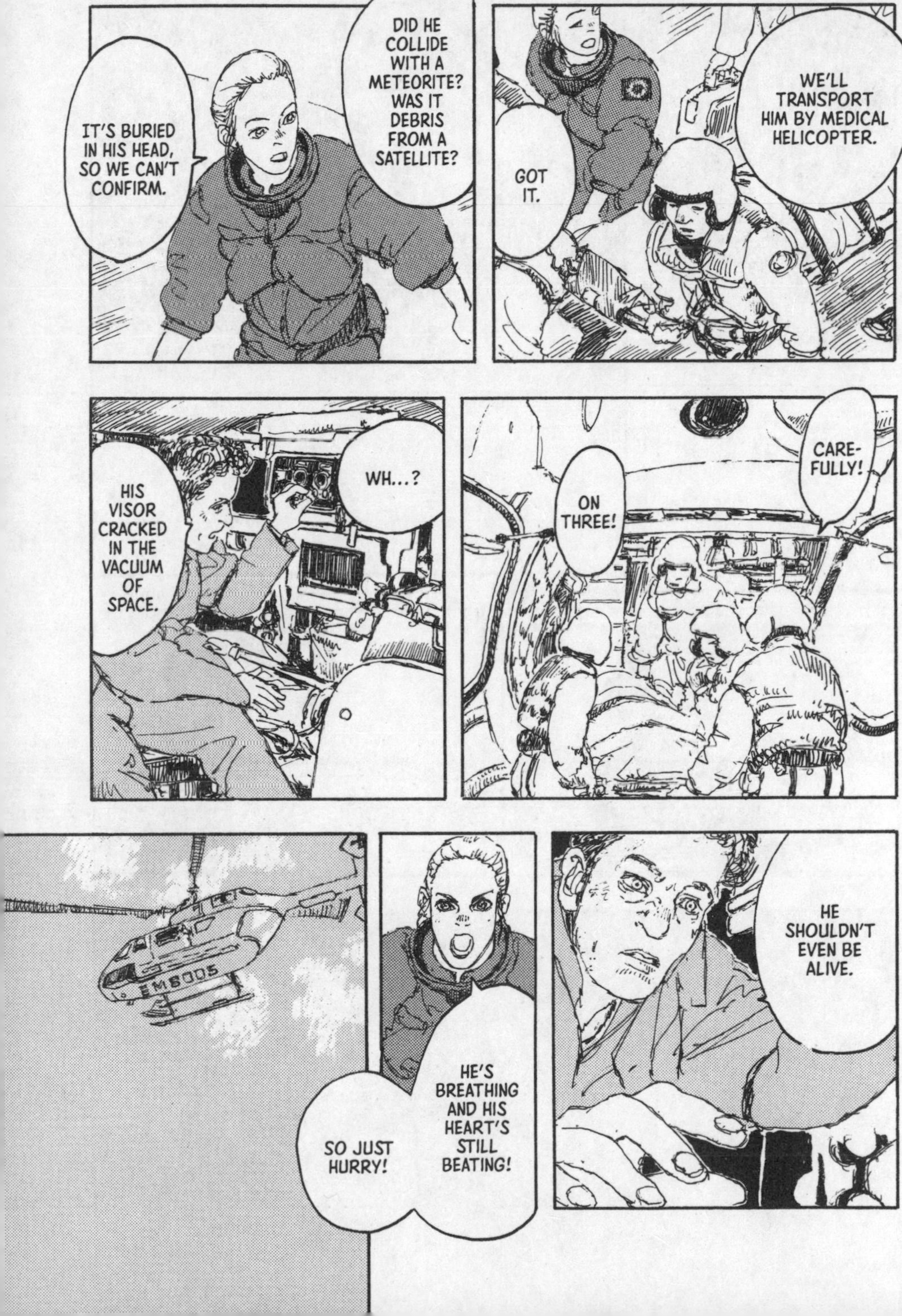
WE'LL TRANSPORT HIM BY MEDICAL HELICOPTER.
GOT IT.
DID HE COLLIDE WITH A METEORITE? WAS IT DEBRIS FROM A SATELLITE?
IT'S BURIED IN HIS HEAD, SO WE CAN'T CONFIRM.
CARE-FULLY!
ON THREE!
WH...?
HIS VISOR CRACKED IN THE VACUUM OF SPACE.
HE SHOULDN'T EVEN BE ALIVE.
HE'S BREATHING AND HIS HEART'S STILL BEATING!
SO JUST HURRY!

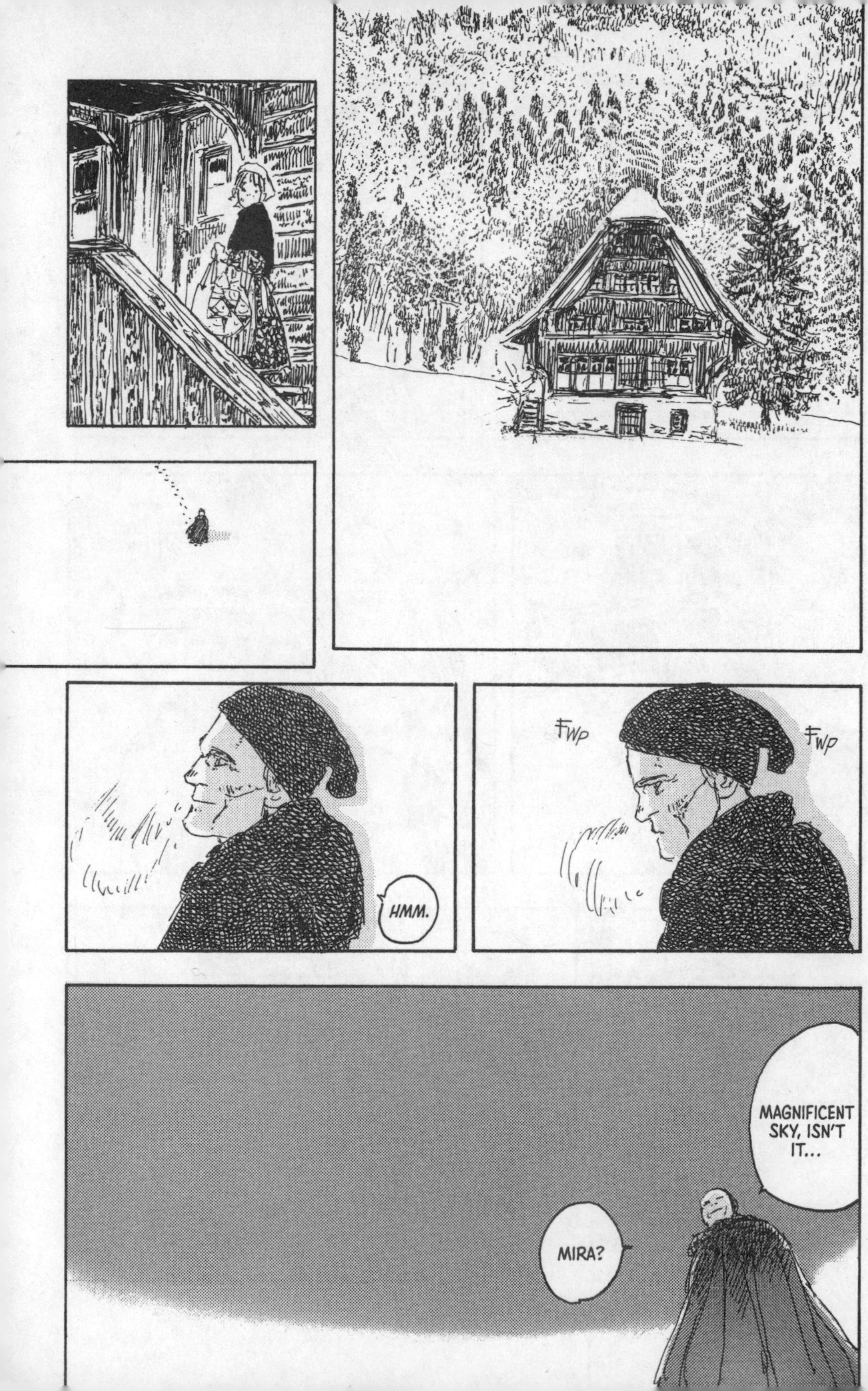
FWP
FWP
HMM.
MAGNIFICENT SKY, ISN'T IT...
MIRA?

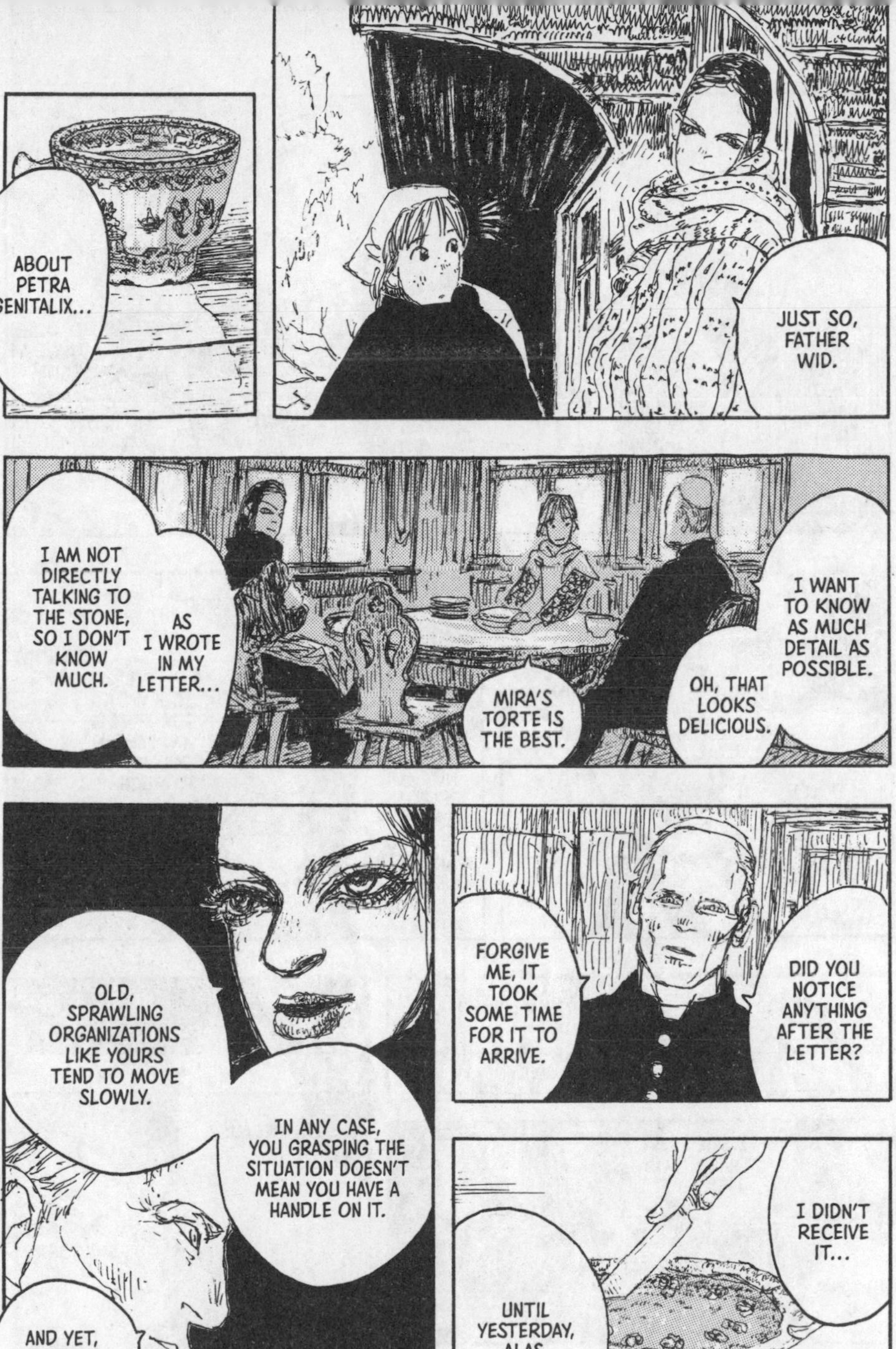
JUST SO, FATHER WID.
ABOUT PETRA GENITALIX...
I WANT TO KNOW AS MUCH DETAIL AS POSSIBLE.
OH, THAT LOOKS DELICIOUS.
MIRA'S TORTE IS THE BEST.
AS I WROTE IN MY LETTER...
I AM NOT DIRECTLY TALKING TO THE STONE, SO I DON'T KNOW MUCH.
DID YOU NOTICE ANYTHING AFTER THE LETTER?
FORGIVE ME, IT TOOK SOME TIME FOR IT TO ARRIVE.
I DIDN'T RECEIVE IT...
UNTIL YESTERDAY, ALAS.
OLD, SPRAWLING ORGANIZATIONS LIKE YOURS TEND TO MOVE SLOWLY.
IN ANY CASE, YOU GRASPING THE SITUATION DOESN'T MEAN YOU HAVE A HANDLE ON IT.
AND YET, YOU STILL SENT ME A LETTER.

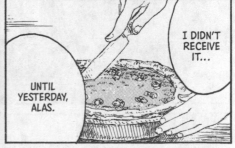

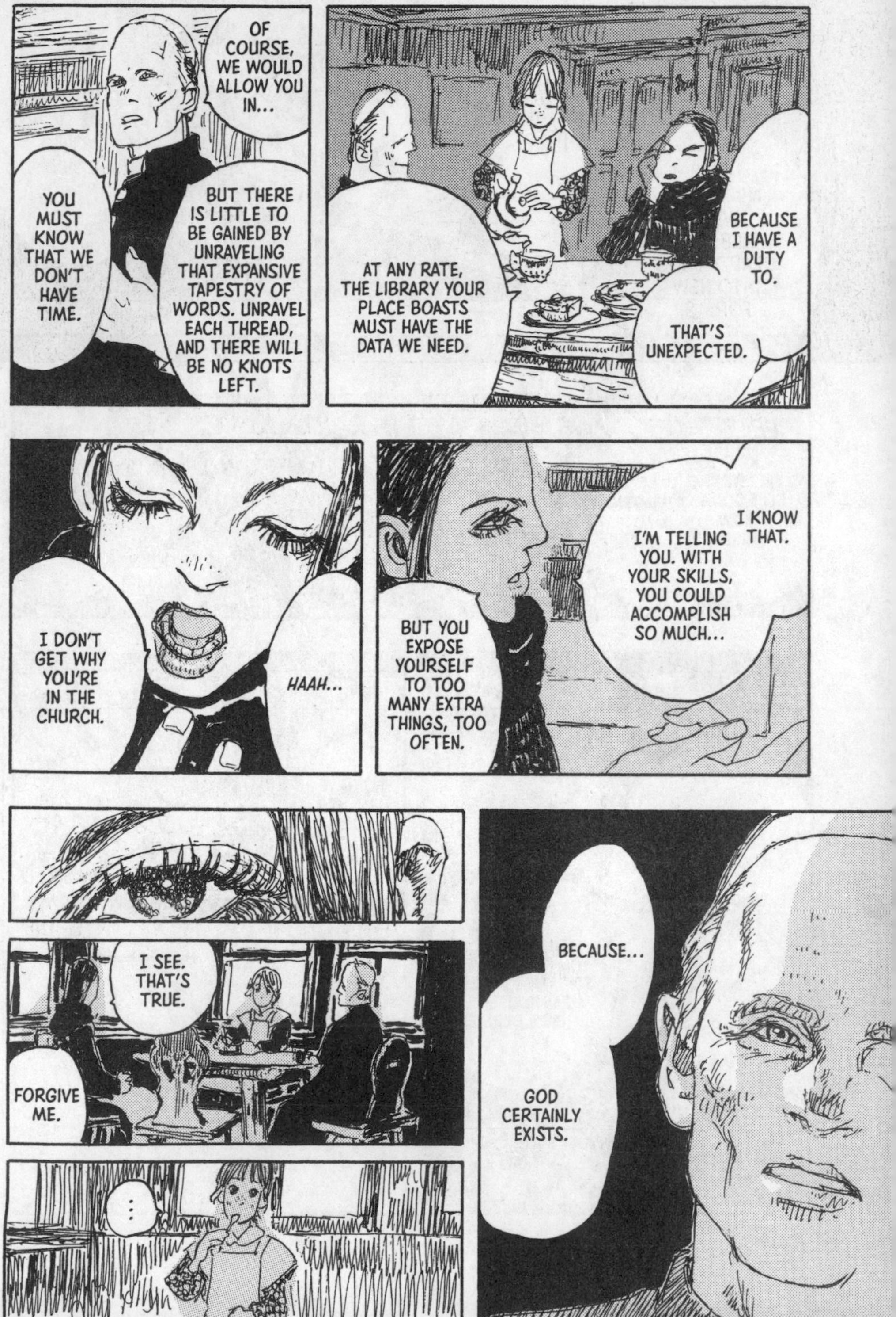
BECAUSE I HAVE A DUTY TO.
THAT'S UNEXPECTED.
AT ANY RATE, THE LIBRARY YOUR PLACE BOASTS MUST HAVE THE DATA WE NEED.
OF COURSE, WE WOULD ALLOW YOU IN...
BUT THERE IS LITTLE TO BE GAINED BY UNRAVELING THAT EXPANSIVE TAPESTRY OF WORDS. UNRAVEL EACH THREAD, AND THERE WILL BE NO KNOTS LEFT.
YOU MUST KNOW THAT WE DON'T HAVE TIME.
I KNOW THAT.
I'M TELLING YOU. WITH YOUR SKILLS, YOU COULD ACCOMPLISH SO MUCH...
BUT YOU EXPOSE YOURSELF TO TOO MANY EXTRA THINGS, TOO OFTEN.
HAAH...
I DON'T GET WHY YOU'RE IN THE CHURCH.
BECAUSE...
GOD CERTAINLY EXISTS.
I SEE. THAT'S TRUE.
FORGIVE ME.
...

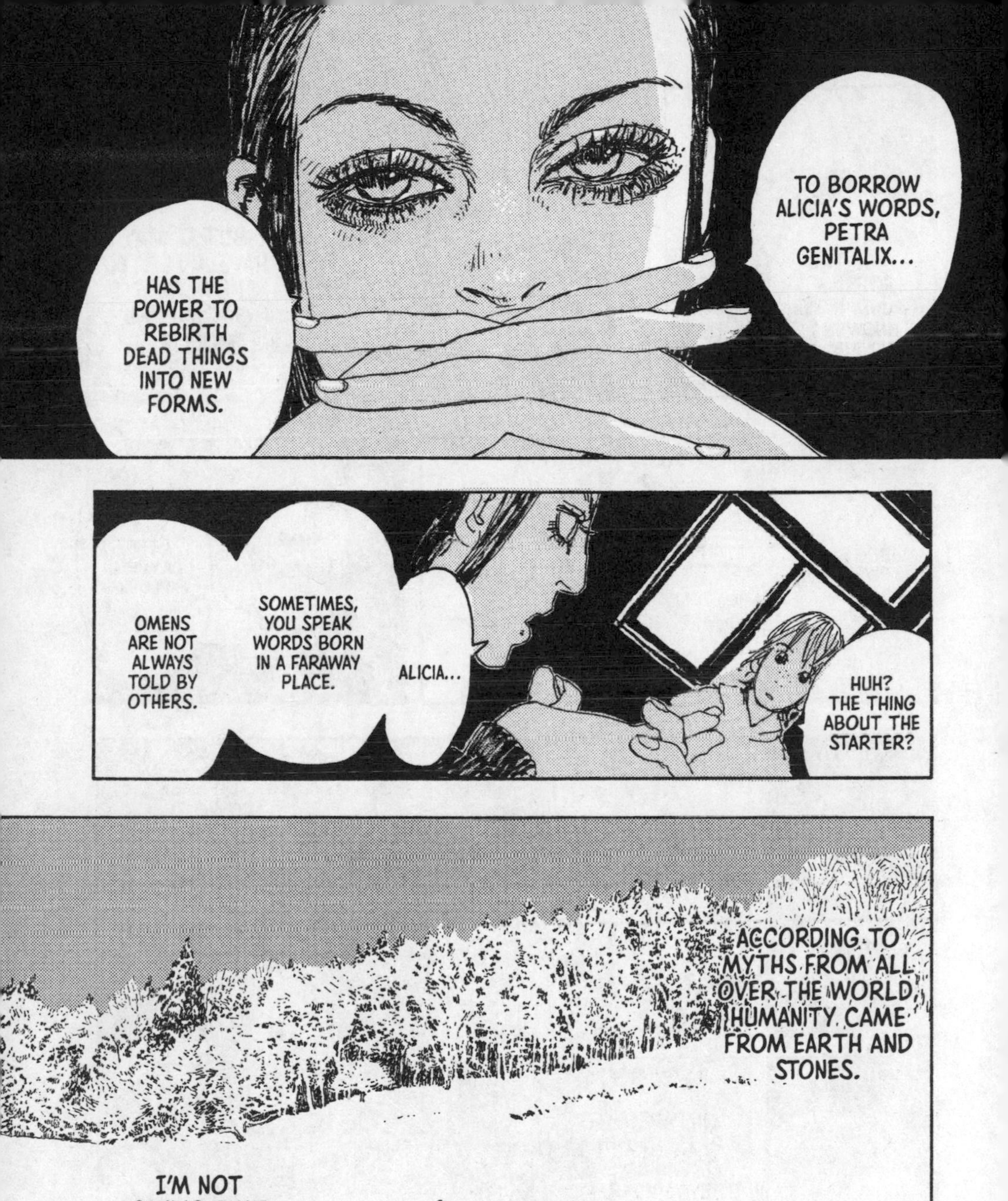
TO BORROW ALICIA'S WORDS, PETRA GENITALIX...
HAS THE POWER TO REBIRTH DEAD THINGS INTO NEW FORMS.
HUH? THE THING ABOUT THE STARTER?
ALICIA...
SOMETIMES, YOU SPEAK WORDS BORN IN A FARAWAY PLACE.
OMENS ARE NOT ALWAYS TOLD BY OTHERS.
ACCORDING TO MYTHS FROM ALL OVER THE WORLD, HUMANITY CAME FROM EARTH AND STONES.
I'M NOT SAYING THAT PETRA GENITALIX IS THE SEED OF LIFE...

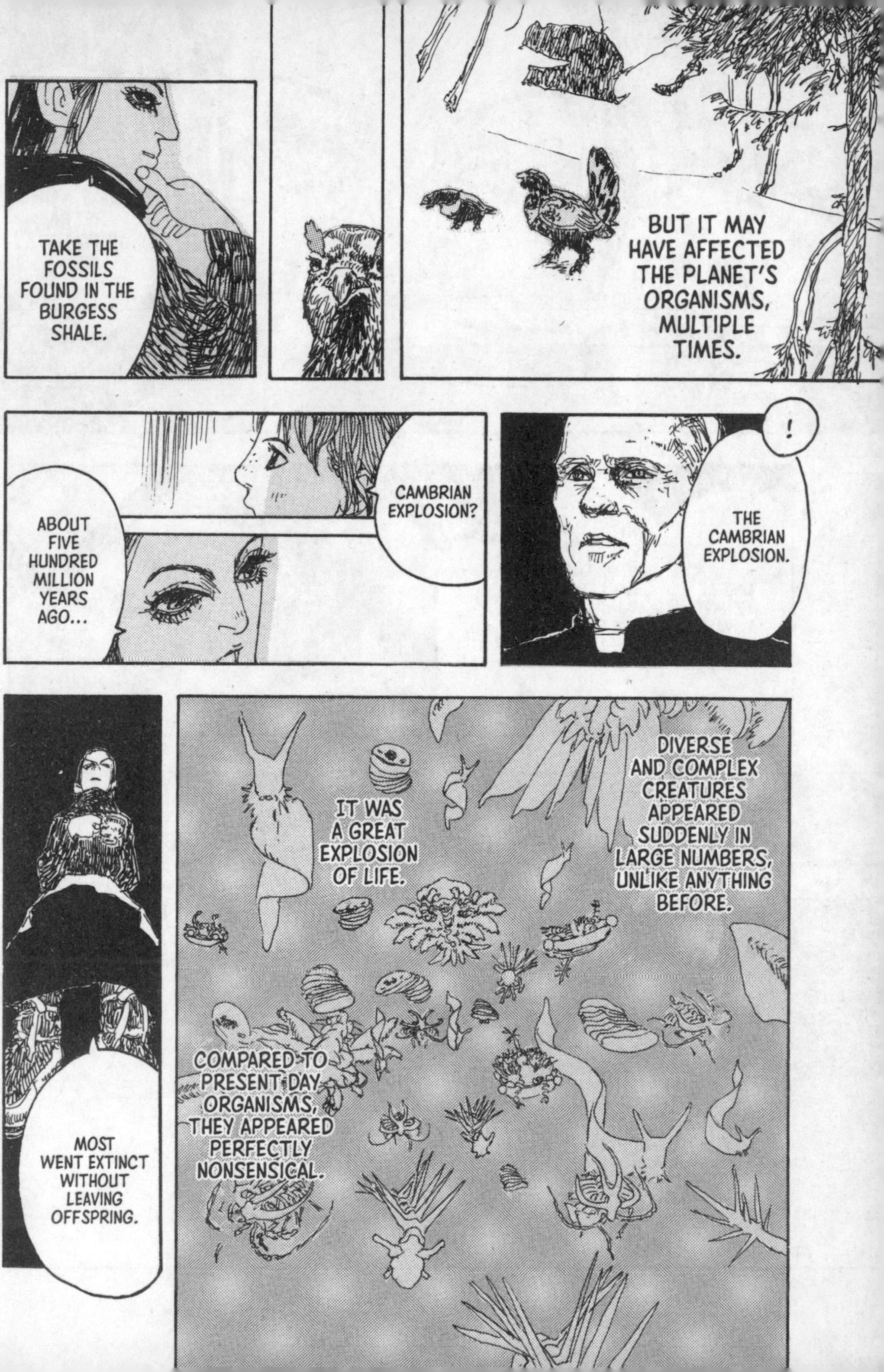
BUT IT MAY HAVE AFFECTED THE PLANET'S ORGANISMS, MULTIPLE TIMES.
TAKE THE FOSSILS FOUND IN THE BURGESS SHALE.
!
THE CAMBRIAN EXPLOSION.
CAMBRIAN EXPLOSION?
ABOUT FIVE HUNDRED MILLION YEARS AGO...
DIVERSE AND COMPLEX CREATURES APPEARED SUDDENLY IN LARGE NUMBERS, UNLIKE ANYTHING BEFORE.
IT WAS A GREAT EXPLOSION OF LIFE.
COMPARED TO PRESENT DAY ORGANISMS, THEY APPEARED PERFECTLY NONSENSICAL.
MOST WENT EXTINCT WITHOUT LEAVING OFFSPRING.

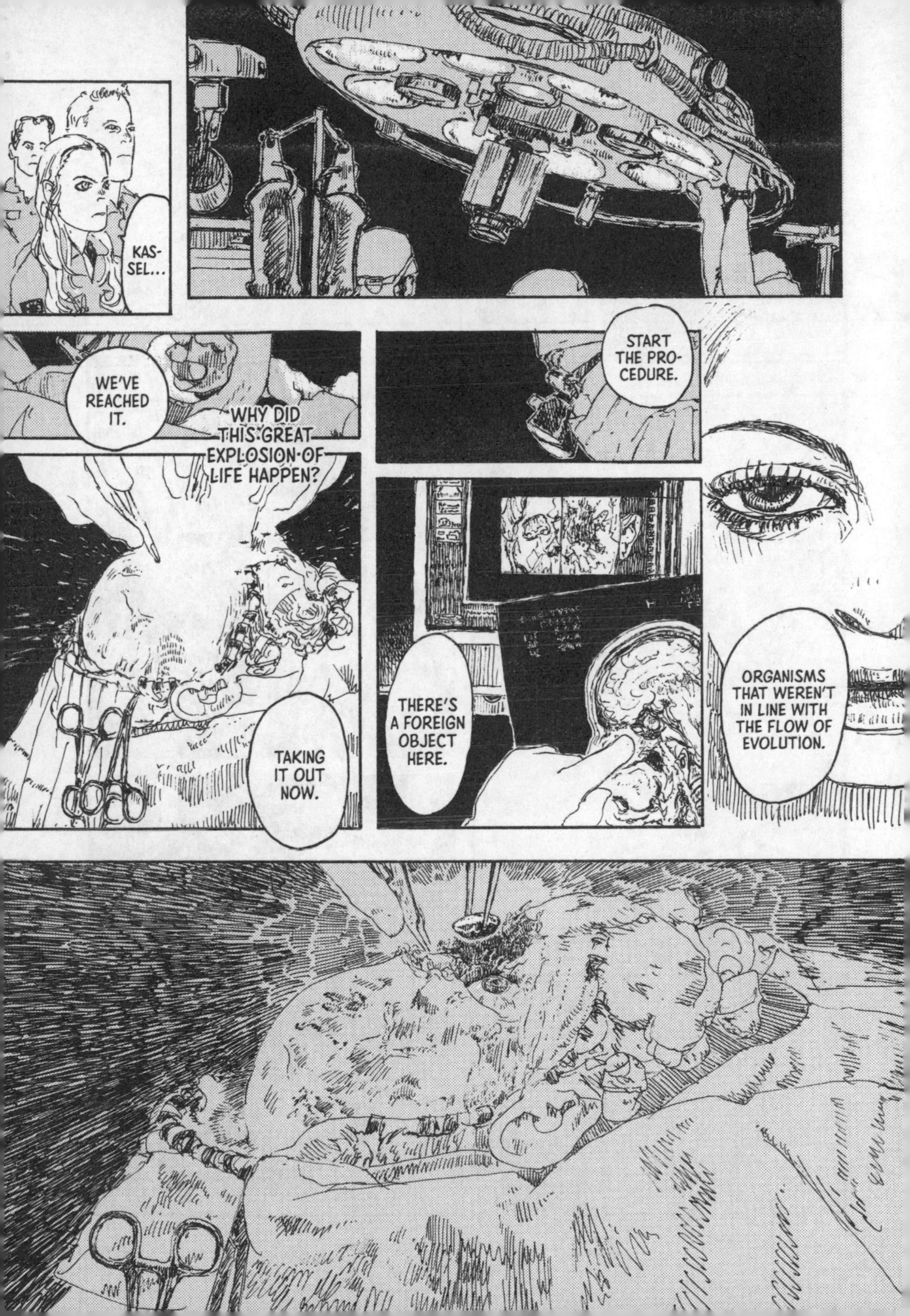
KAS-SEL...
START THE PRO-CEDURE.
WE'VE REACHED IT.
WHY DID THIS GREAT EXPLOSION OF LIFE HAPPEN?
ORGANISMS THAT WEREN'T IN LINE WITH THE FLOW OF EVOLUTION.
THERE'S A FOREIGN OBJECT HERE.
TAKING IT OUT NOW.

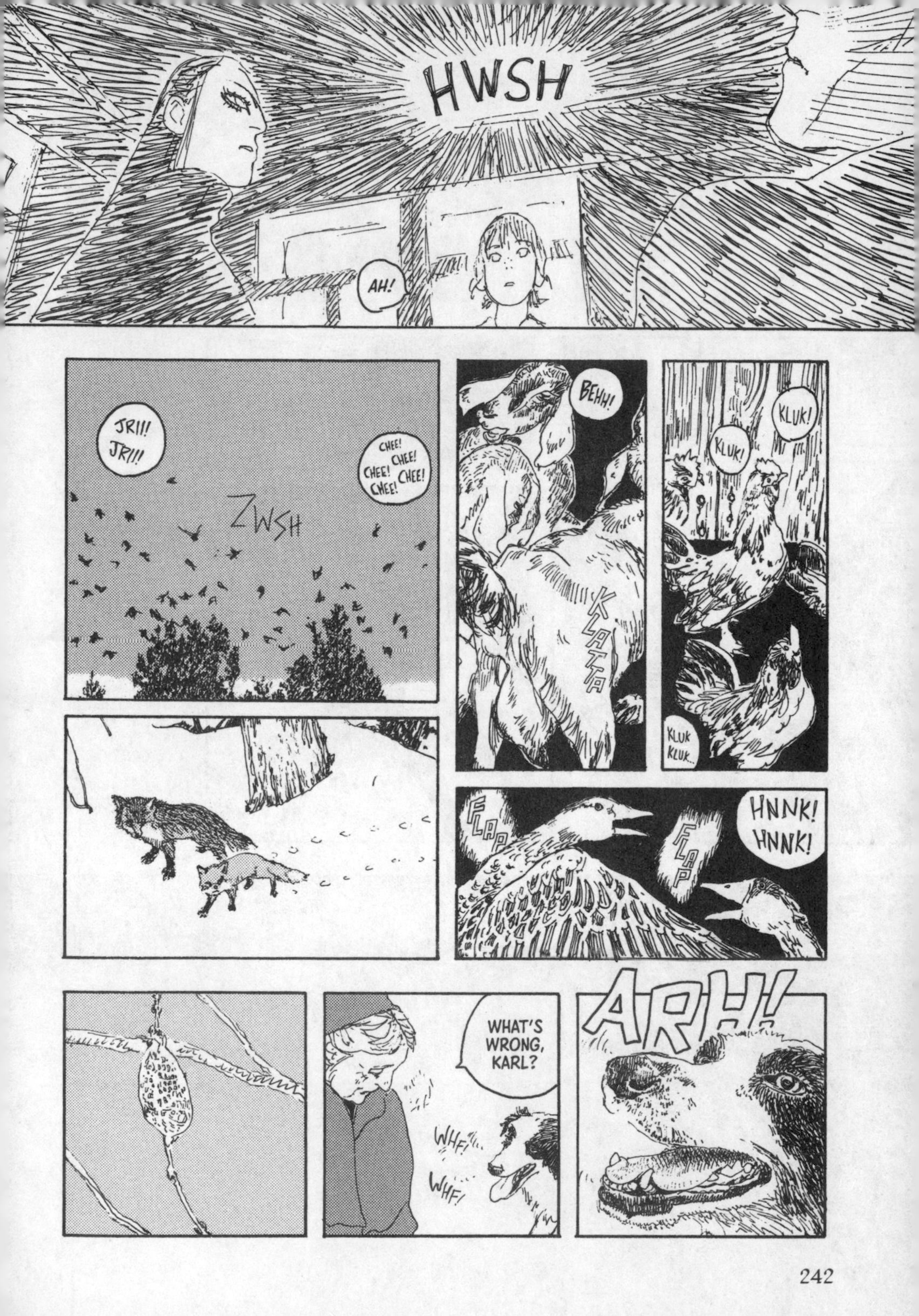
HWSH
AH!
KLUK!
KLUK!
KLUK KLUK...
BEHH!
KLATTA
HNNK! HNNK!
FLAP
FLAP
JRII! JRII!
CHEE! CHEE! CHEE! CHEE! CHEE!
ZWSH
ARH!
WHAT'S WRONG, KARL?
WHF!
WHF!

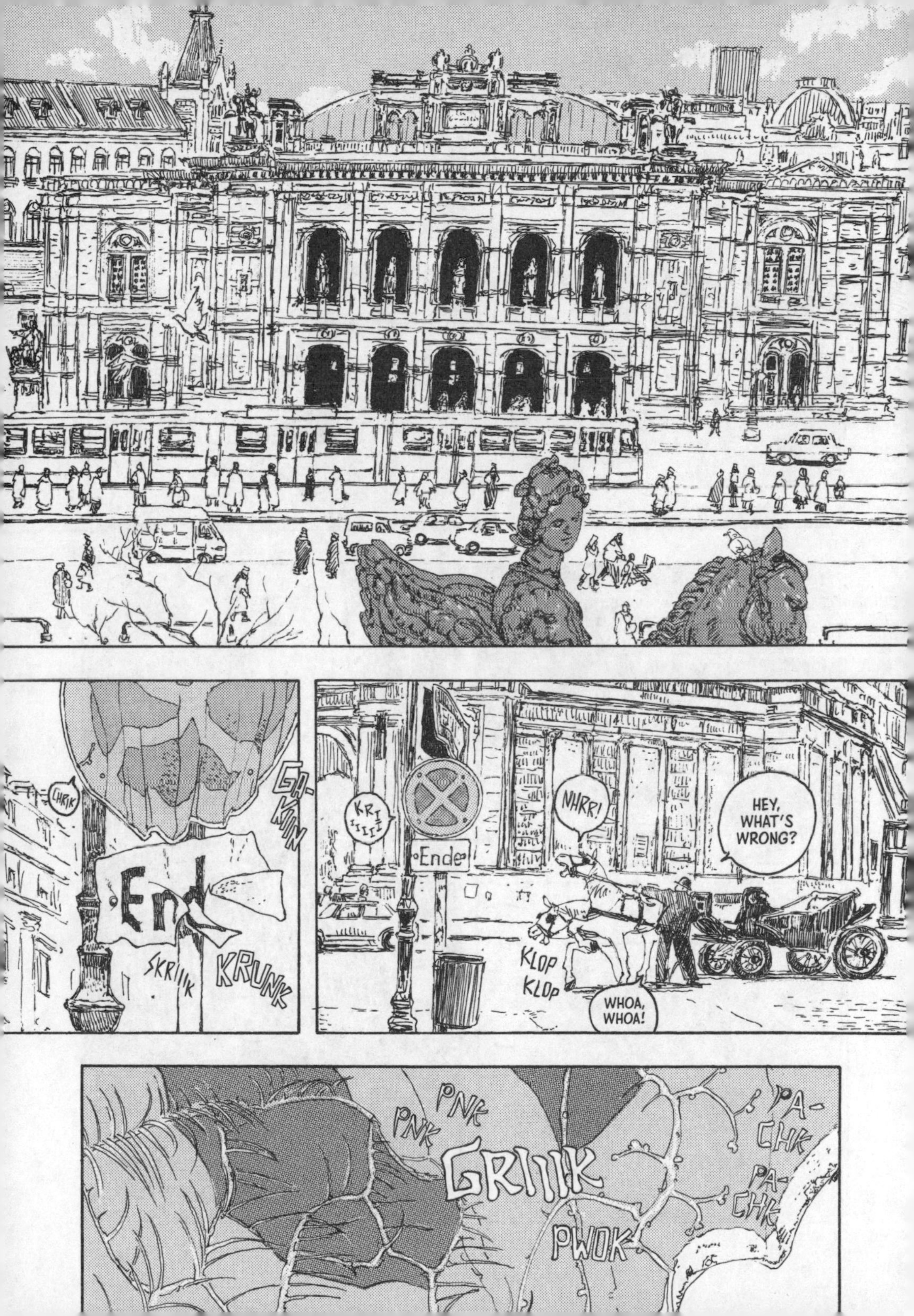
HEY, WHAT'S WRONG?
NHRR!
KRI IIIII
Ende
KLOP KLOP
WHOA, WHOA!
GA-KIIN
CHRIK
End
KRUNK
SKRIIIK
PA-CHK
PA-CHK
PNK
PNK
GRIIIK
PWOK

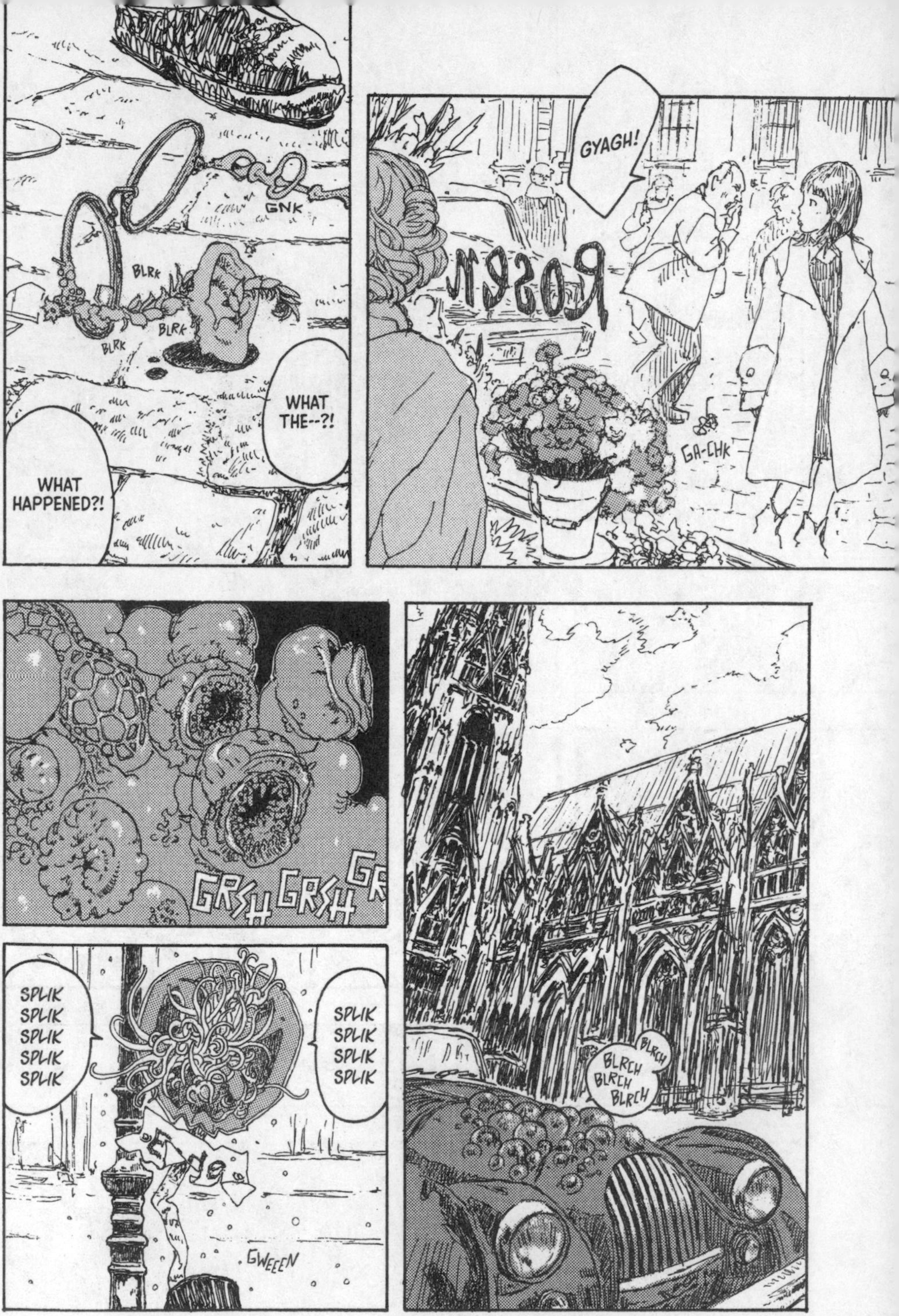
GYAGH!
GA-CHK
GNK
BLRK
BLRK
BLRK
WHAT THE--?!
WHAT HAPPENED?!
BLRCH
BLRCH
BLRCH
BLRCH
GRSH GRSH GR
SPLIK SPLIK SPLIK SPLIK
SPLIK SPLIK SPLIK SPLIK SPLIK
GWEEEN

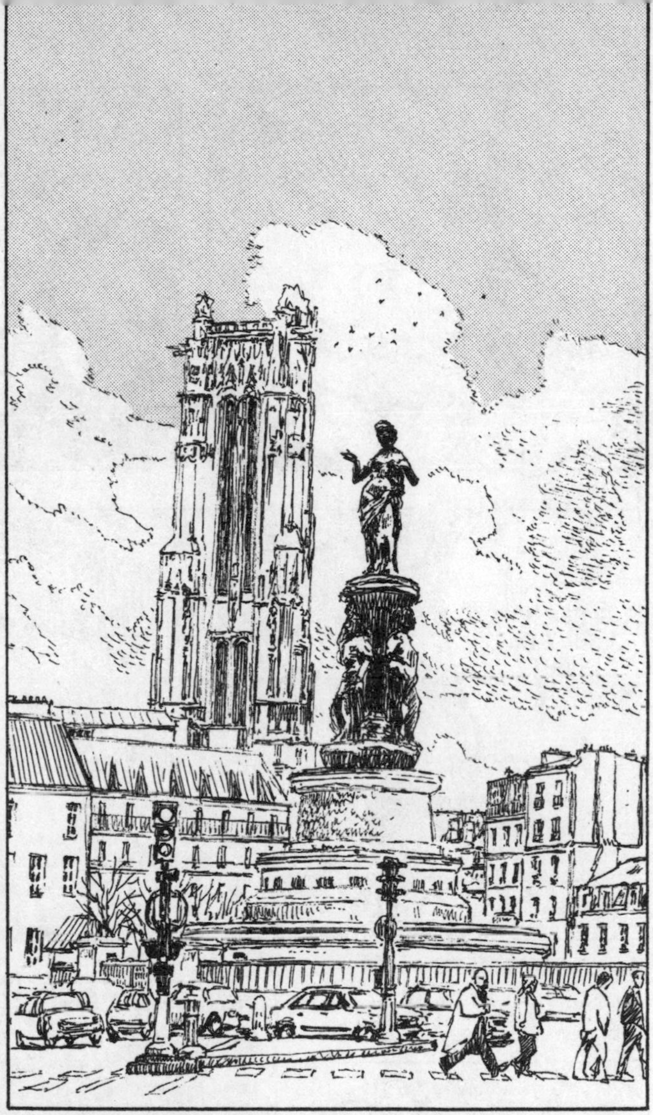

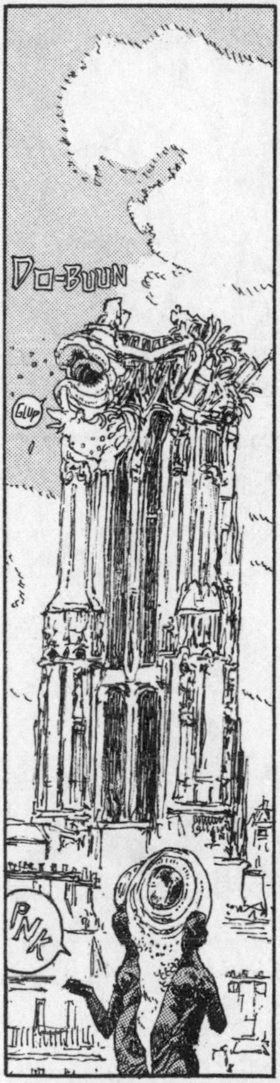
DO-BUUN
GLUP
PNK

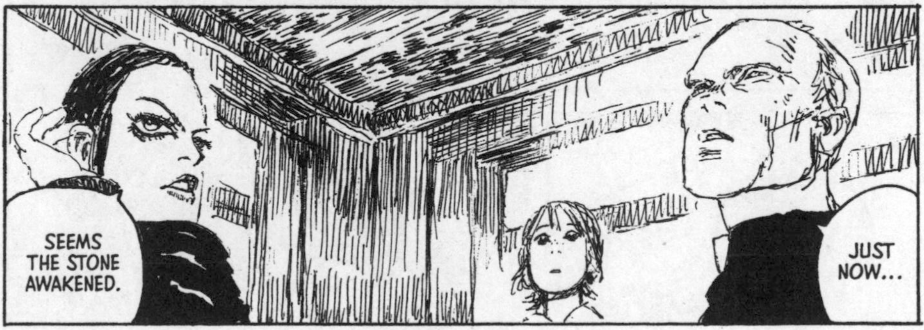
JUST NOW...
SEEMS THE STONE AWAKENED.

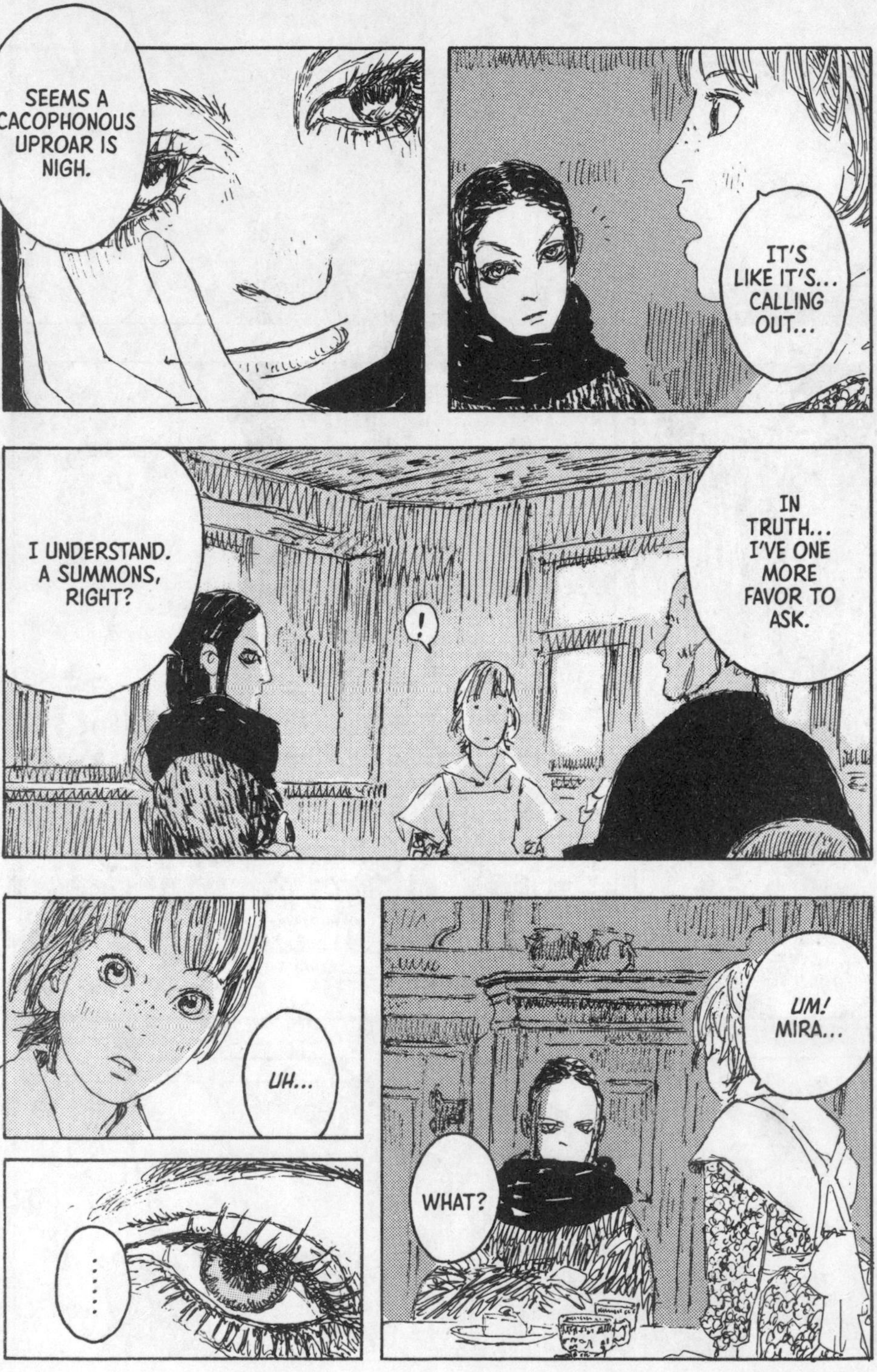
IT'S LIKE IT'S... CALLING OUT...
SEEMS A CACOPHONOUS UPROAR IS NIGH.
IN TRUTH... I'VE ONE MORE FAVOR TO ASK.
!
I UNDERSTAND. A SUMMONS, RIGHT?
UM! MIRA...
WHAT?
UH...
......

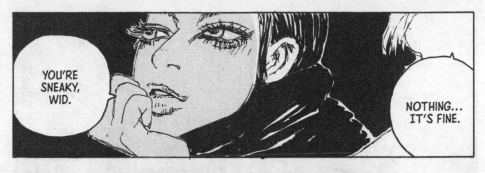

NOTHING... IT'S FINE.
YOU'RE SNEAKY, WID.
YOU BLESSED ME WITH YOUR PRESENCE...
SO I COULDN'T REFUSE FACE-TO-FACE.
I WON'T APOLOGIZE.
"IF YOU'RE GOING TO APOLOGIZE, DON'T DO IT IN THE FIRST PLACE," AYE?
THERE IS A CONDITION.
LET ALICIA COME.
!

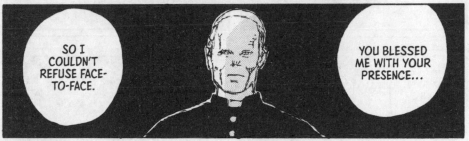

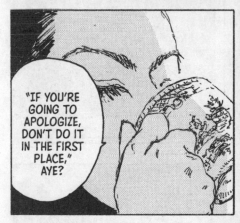

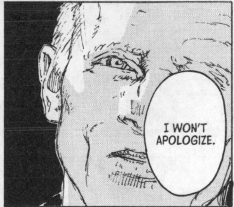

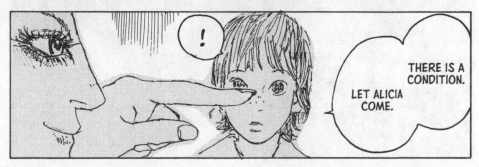

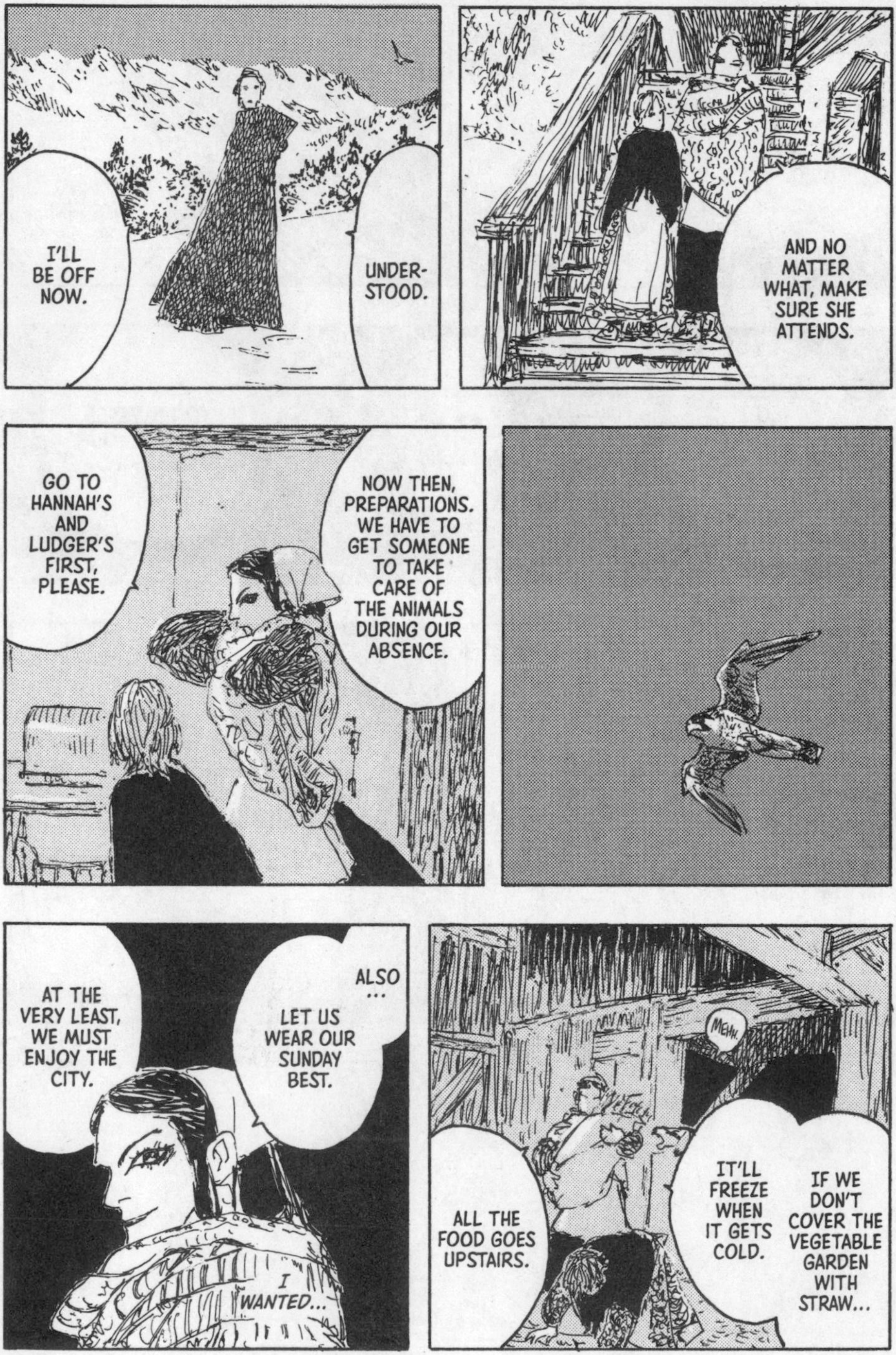
AND NO MATTER WHAT, MAKE SURE SHE ATTENDS.
UNDER-STOOD.
I'LL BE OFF NOW.
NOW THEN, PREPARATIONS. WE HAVE TO GET SOMEONE TO TAKE CARE OF THE ANIMALS DURING OUR ABSENCE.
GO TO HANNAH'S AND LUDGER'S FIRST, PLEASE.
MEHH.
IF WE DON'T COVER THE VEGETABLE GARDEN WITH STRAW...
IT'LL FREEZE WHEN IT GETS COLD.
ALL THE FOOD GOES UPSTAIRS.
ALSO...
LET US WEAR OUR SUNDAY BEST.
AT THE VERY LEAST, WE MUST ENJOY THE CITY.
I WANTED...

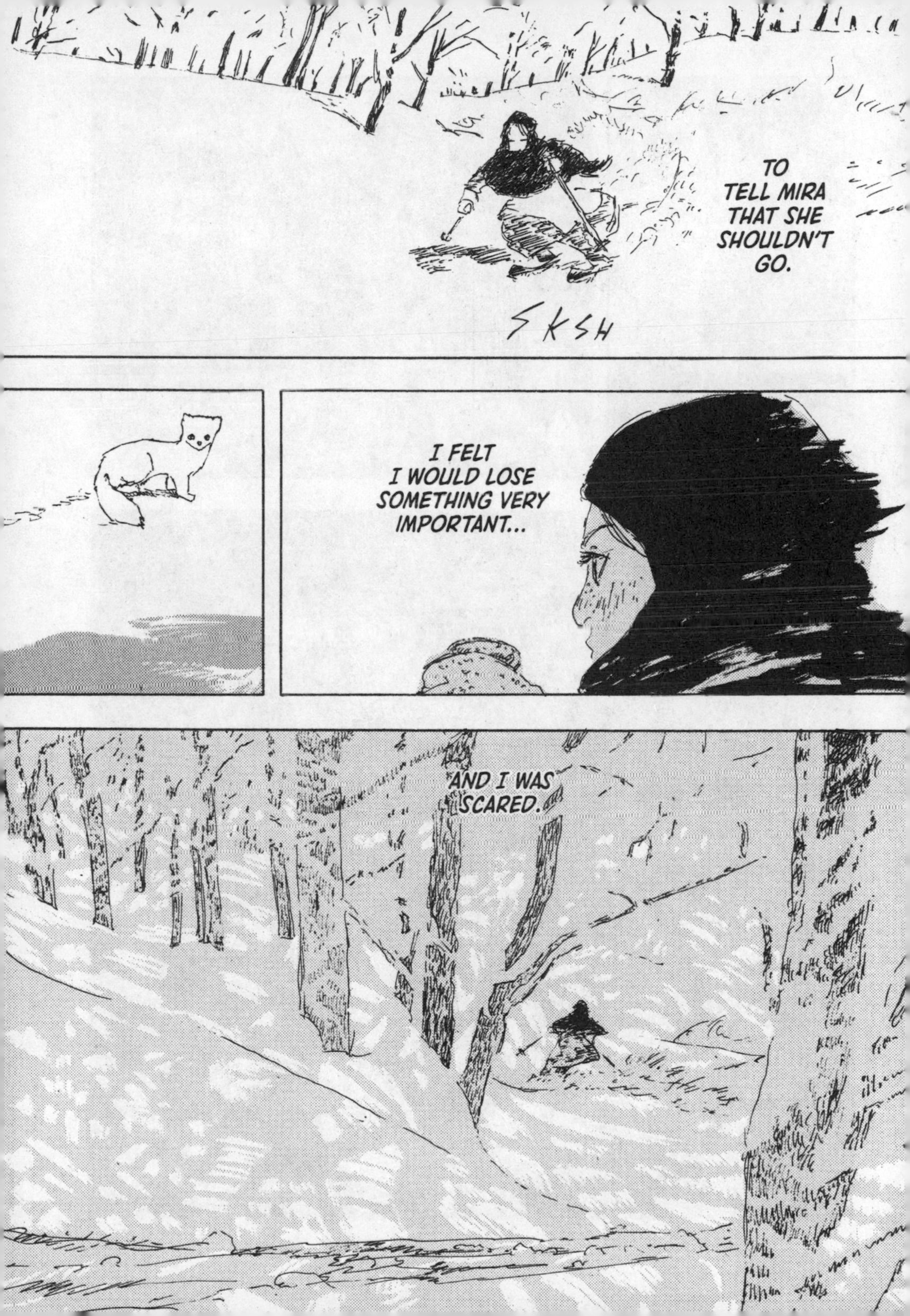
TO TELL MIRA THAT SHE SHOULDN'T GO.
SKSH
I FELT I WOULD LOSE SOMETHING VERY IMPORTANT...
AND I WAS SCARED.

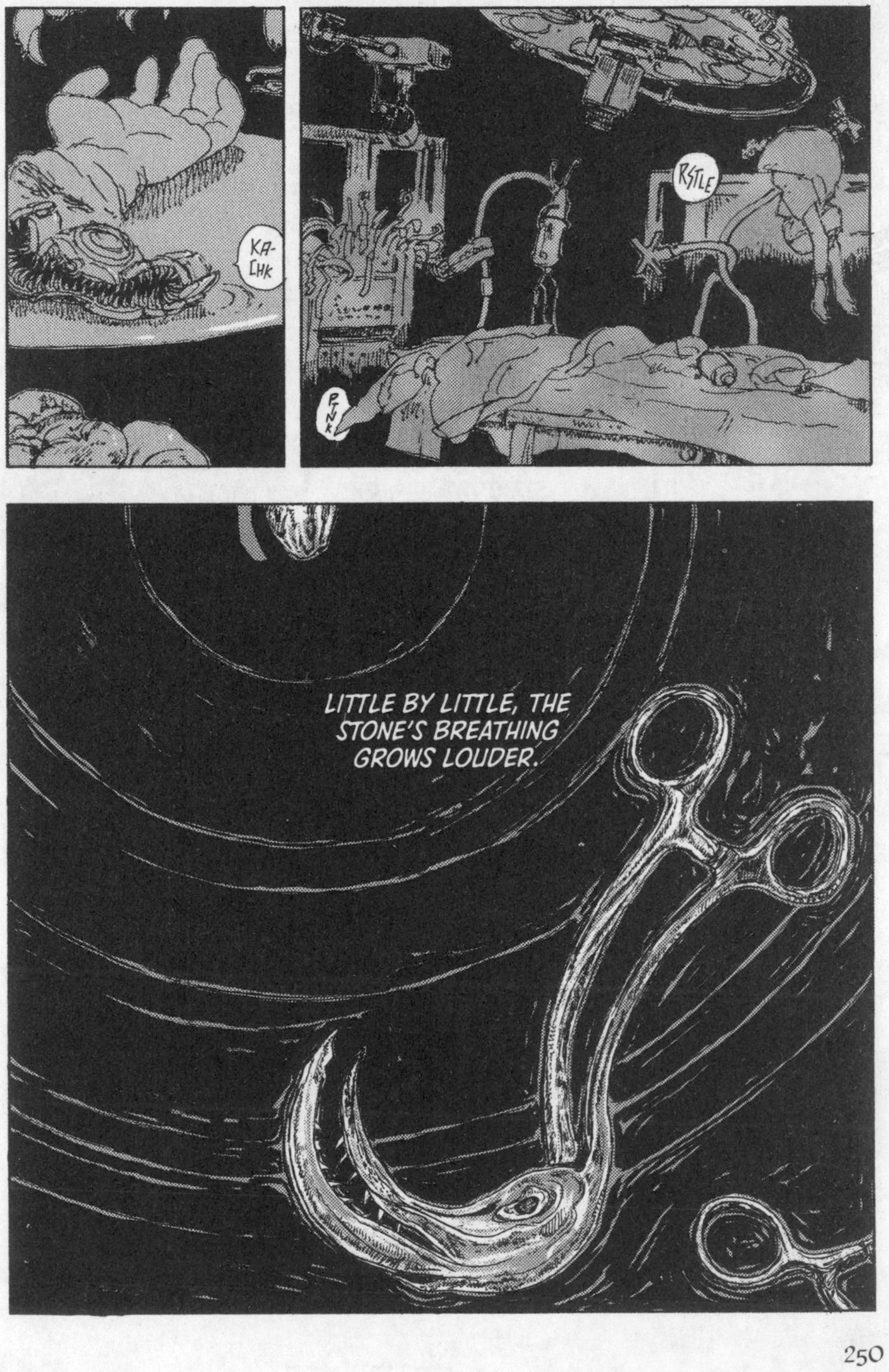
RSTLE
PINK
KA-CHK
LITTLE BY LITTLE, THE STONE'S BREATHING GROWS LOUDER.

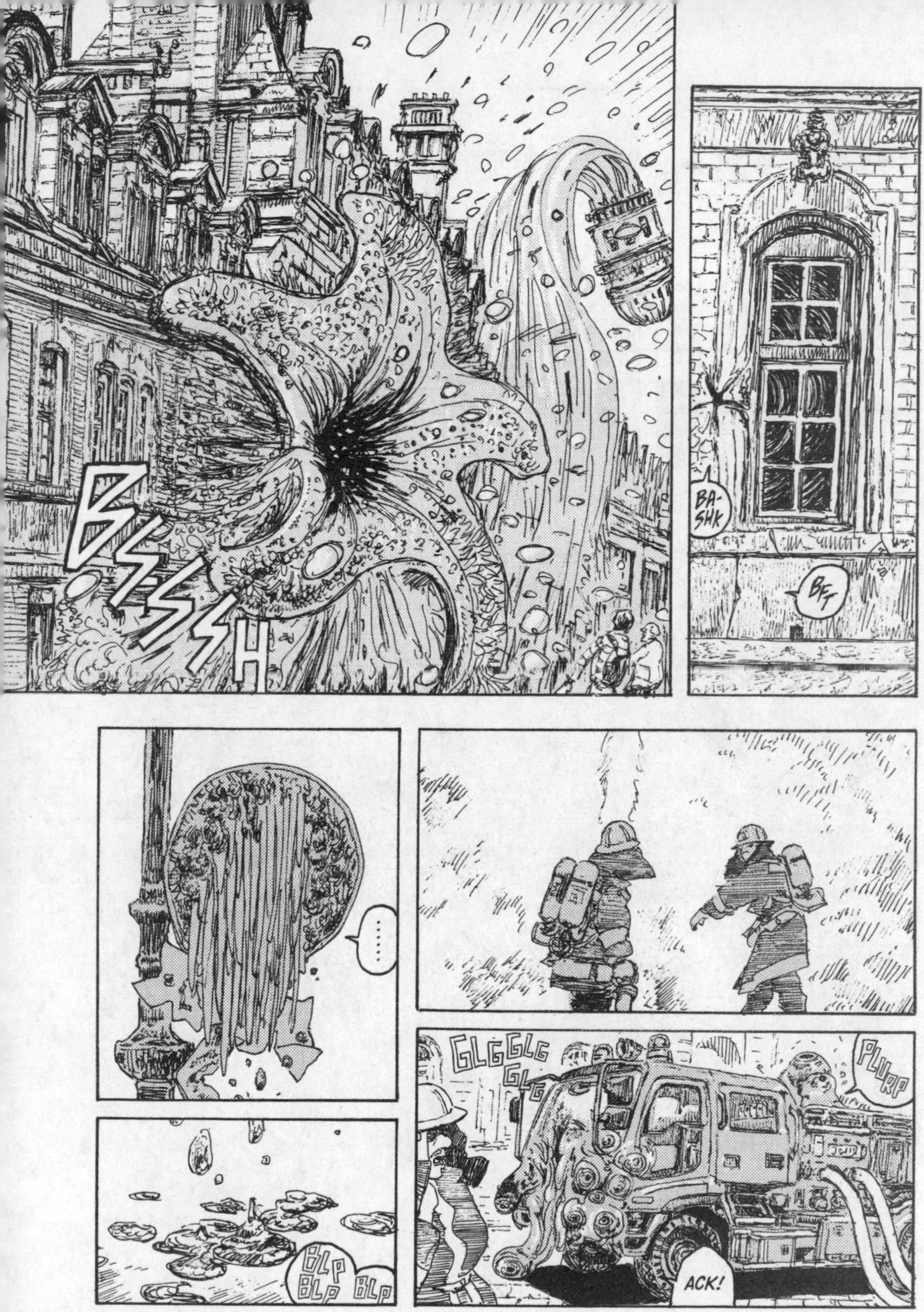
BA-SHK
BFT
BSSSSH
......
PLURP
GLGGLG GLG
ACK!
BLP BLP BLP

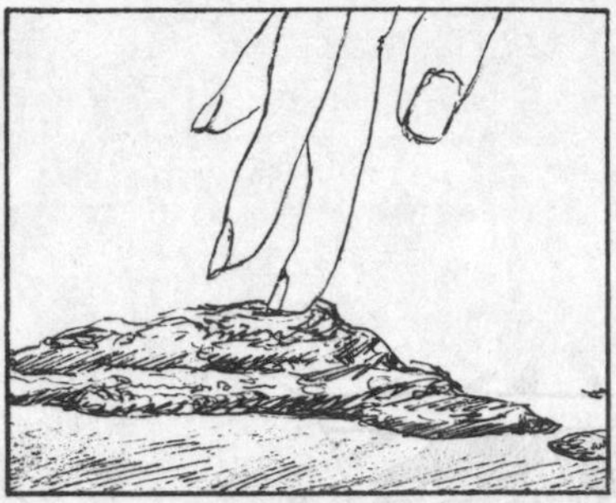

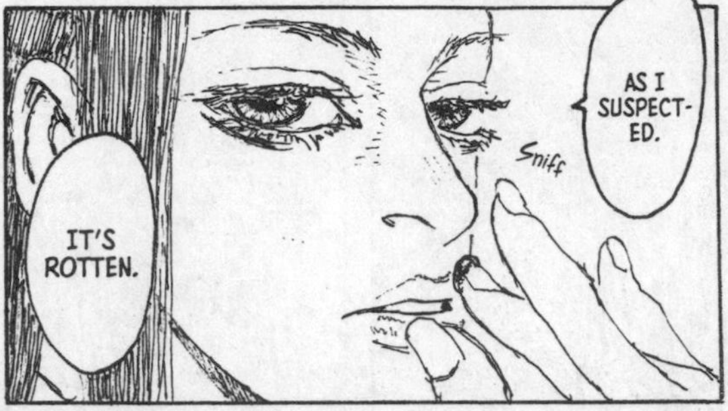

AS I SUSPECTED.
Sniff
IT'S ROTTEN.

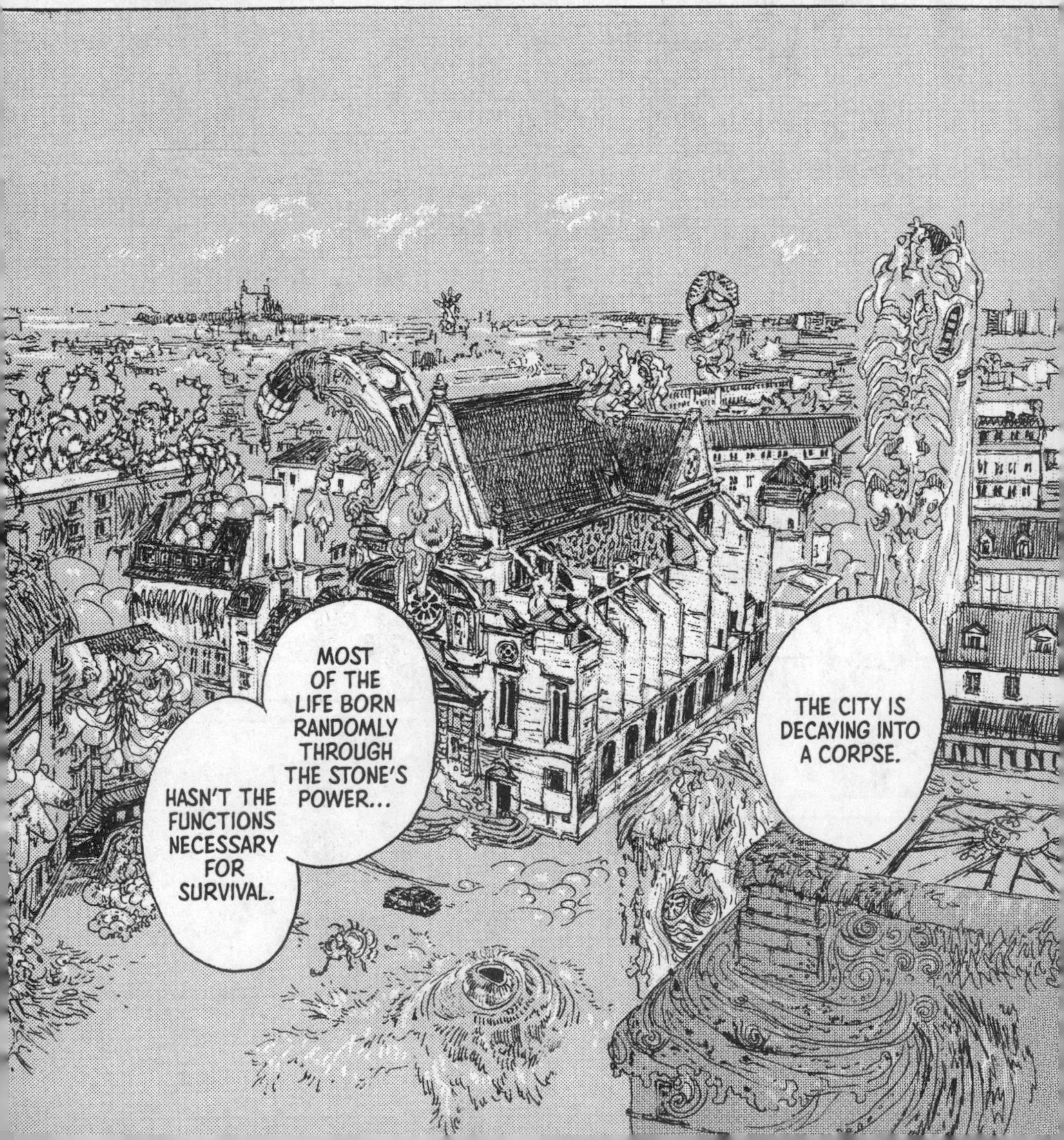

THE CITY IS DECAYING INTO A CORPSE.
MOST OF THE LIFE BORN RANDOMLY THROUGH THE STONE'S POWER...
HASN'T THE FUNCTIONS NECESSARY FOR SURVIVAL.

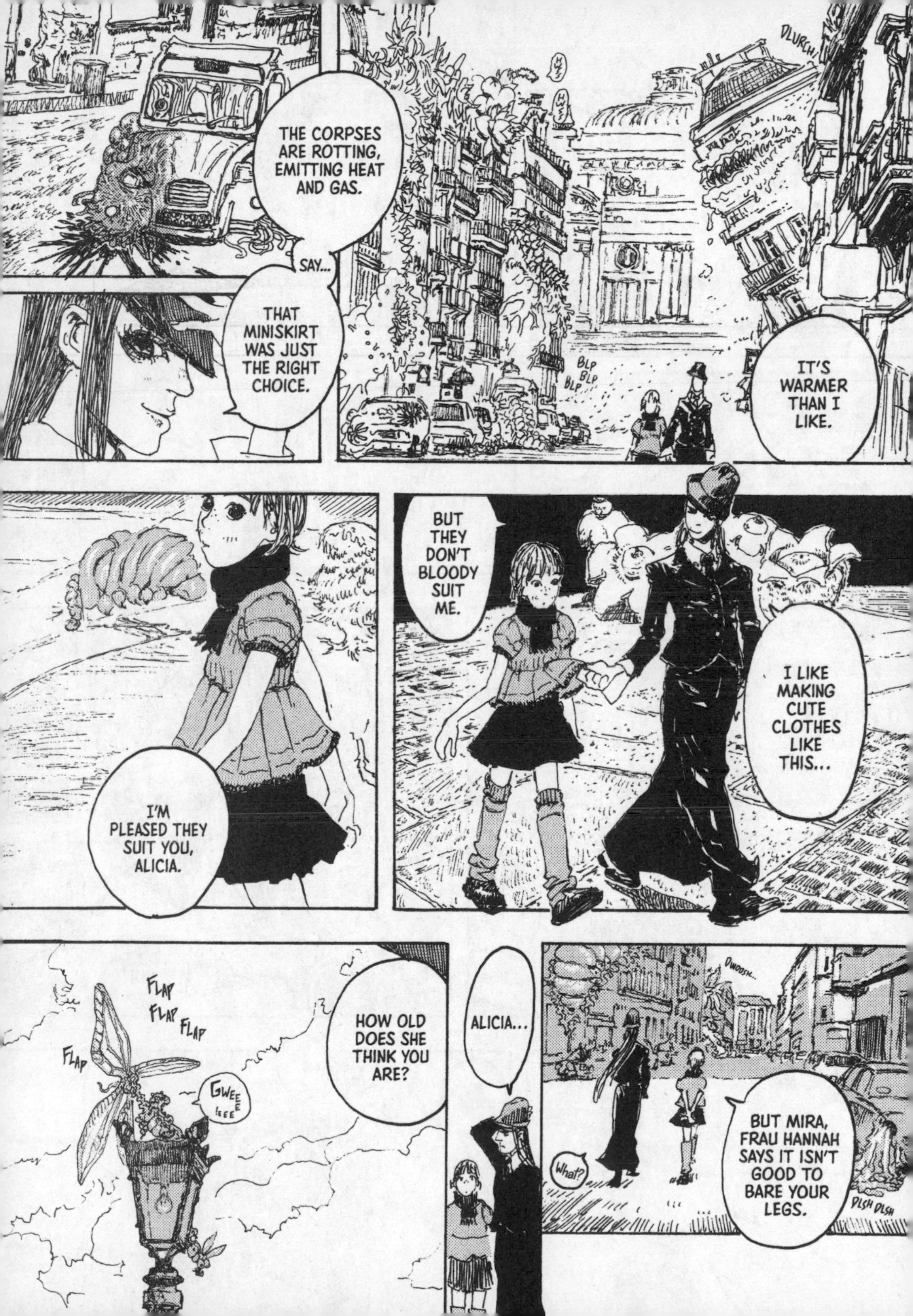
DLURCH
BLP BLP BLP
IT'S WARMER THAN I LIKE.
THE CORPSES ARE ROTTING, EMITTING HEAT AND GAS.
SAY...
THAT MINISKIRT WAS JUST THE RIGHT CHOICE.
I LIKE MAKING CUTE CLOTHES LIKE THIS...
BUT THEY DON'T BLOODY SUIT ME.
I'M PLEASED THEY SUIT YOU, ALICIA.
DWOOSH...
BUT MIRA, FRAU HANNAH SAYS IT ISN'T GOOD TO BARE YOUR LEGS.
What?
...
DLSH DLSH
ALICIA...
HOW OLD DOES SHE THINK YOU ARE?
FLAP FLAP FLAP FLAP
GWEEE !EEE

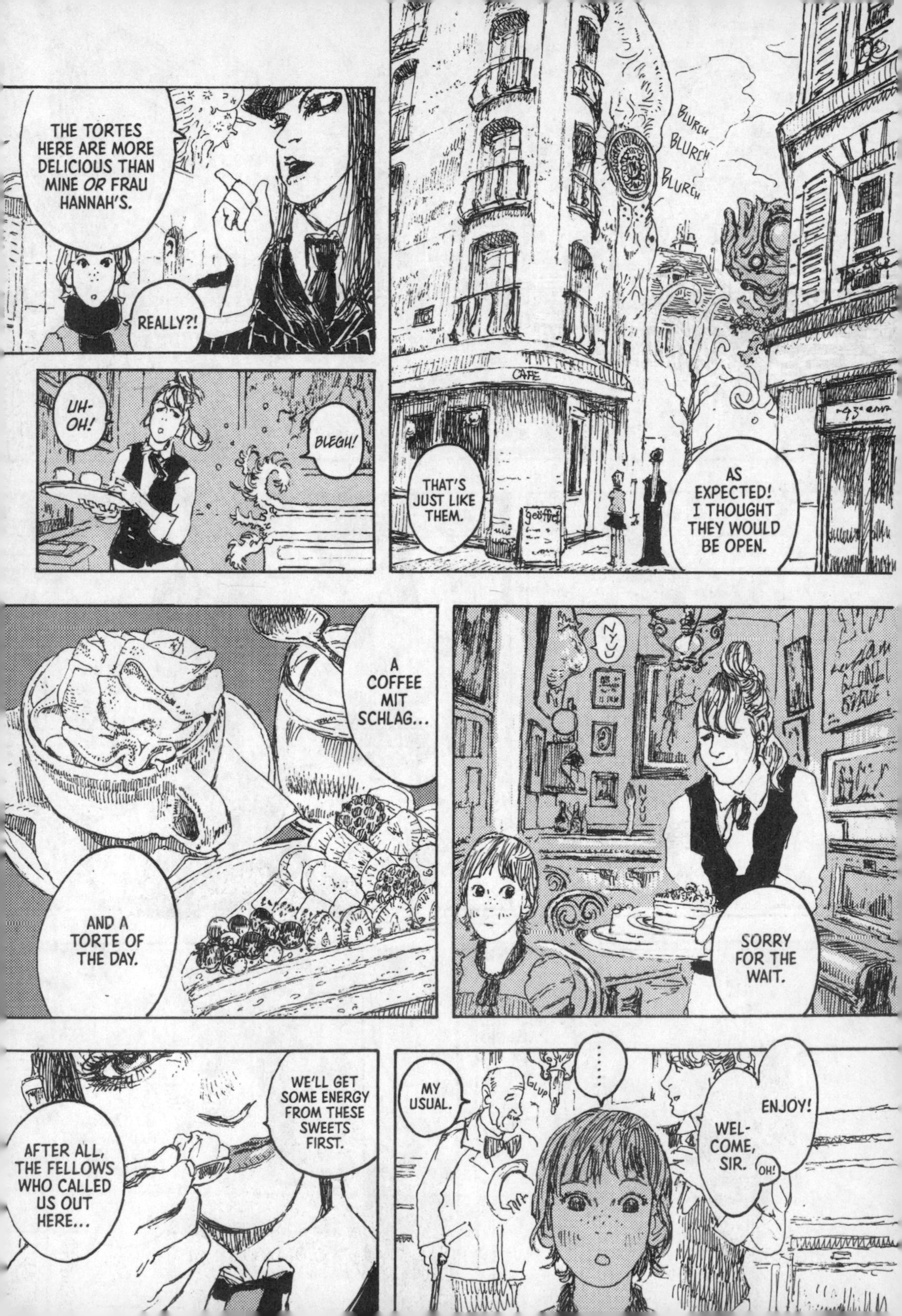
BLURCH
BLURCH
BLURCH
CAFE
AS EXPECTED! I THOUGHT THEY WOULD BE OPEN.
THAT'S JUST LIKE THEM.
THE TORTES HERE ARE MORE DELICIOUS THAN MINE *OR* FRAU HANNAH'S.
REALLY?!
BLEGH!
UH-OH!
NYUU
SORRY FOR THE WAIT.
NYUU
A COFFEE MIT SCHLAG...
AND A TORTE OF THE DAY.
...
ENJOY!
WEL-COME, SIR.
OH!
GLUP
MY USUAL.
WE'LL GET SOME ENERGY FROM THESE SWEETS FIRST.
AFTER ALL, THE FELLOWS WHO CALLED US OUT HERE...

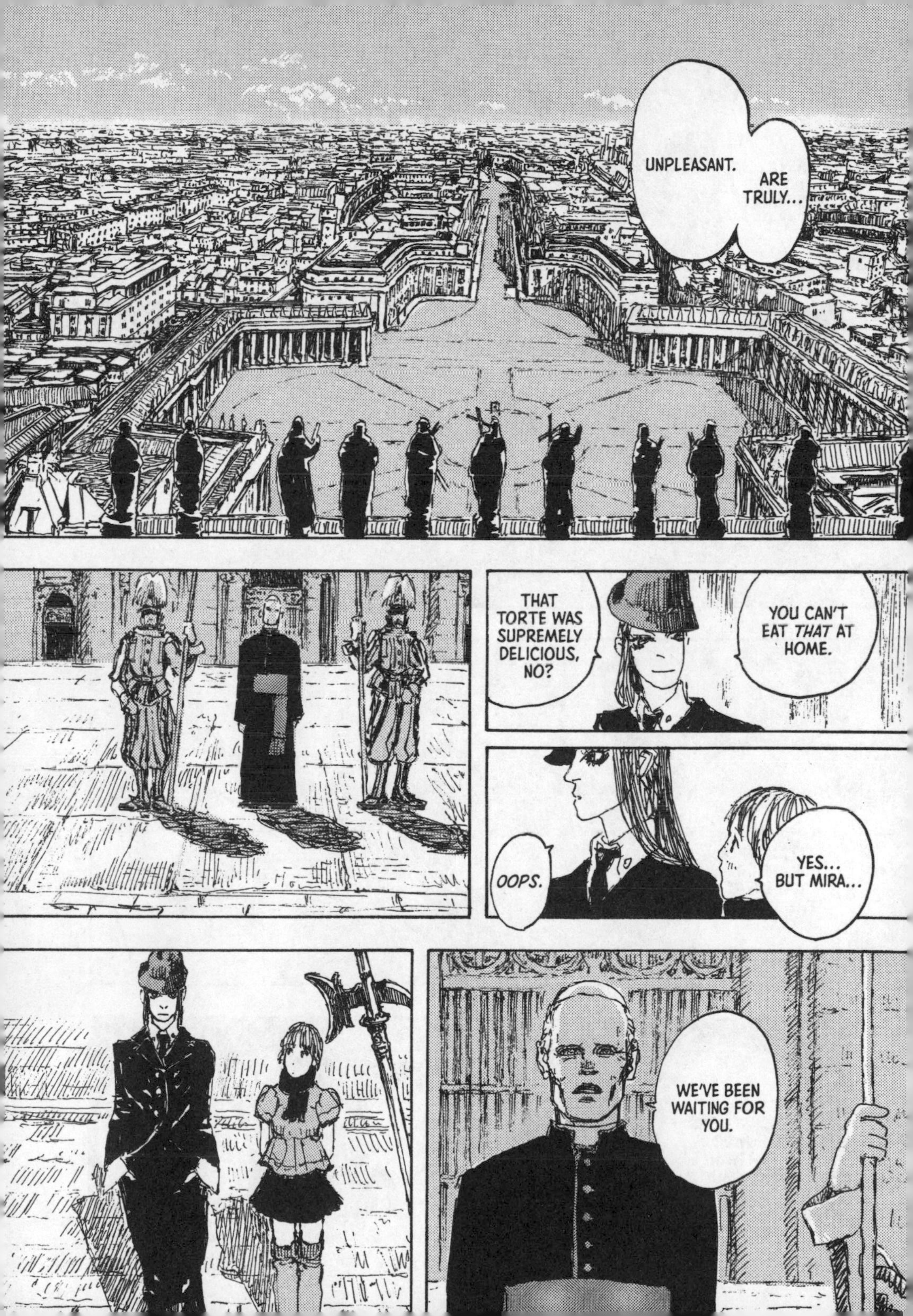
UNPLEASANT. ARE TRULY...
YOU CAN'T EAT *THAT* AT HOME.
THAT TORTE WAS SUPREMELY DELICIOUS, NO?
YES... BUT MIRA...
OOPS.
WE'VE BEEN WAITING FOR YOU.

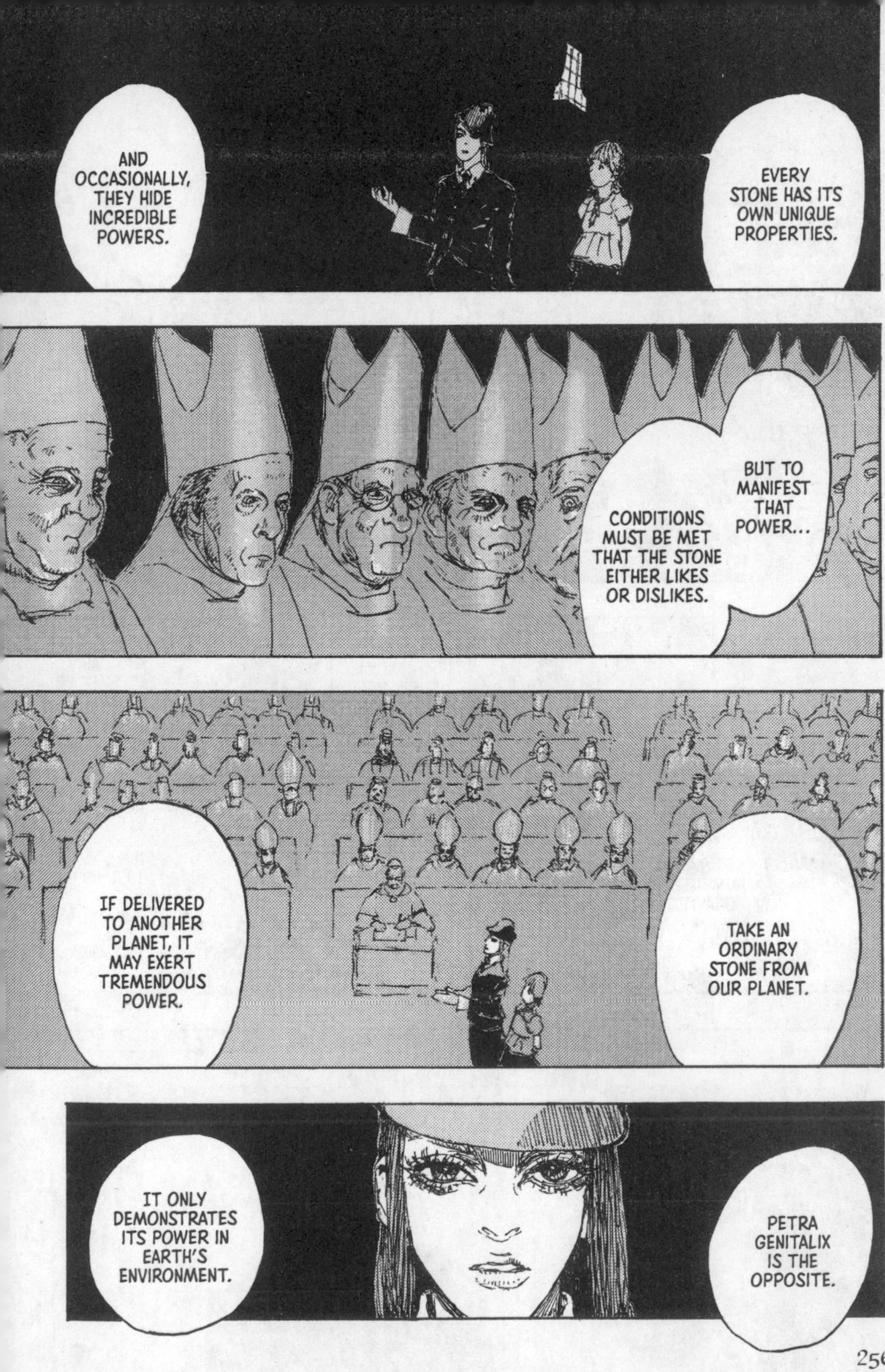
EVERY STONE HAS ITS OWN UNIQUE PROPERTIES.
AND OCCASIONALLY, THEY HIDE INCREDIBLE POWERS.
BUT TO MANIFEST THAT POWER...
CONDITIONS MUST BE MET THAT THE STONE EITHER LIKES OR DISLIKES.
TAKE AN ORDINARY STONE FROM OUR PLANET.
IF DELIVERED TO ANOTHER PLANET, IT MAY EXERT TREMENDOUS POWER.
PETRA GENITALIX IS THE OPPOSITE.
IT ONLY DEMONSTRATES ITS POWER IN EARTH'S ENVIRONMENT.

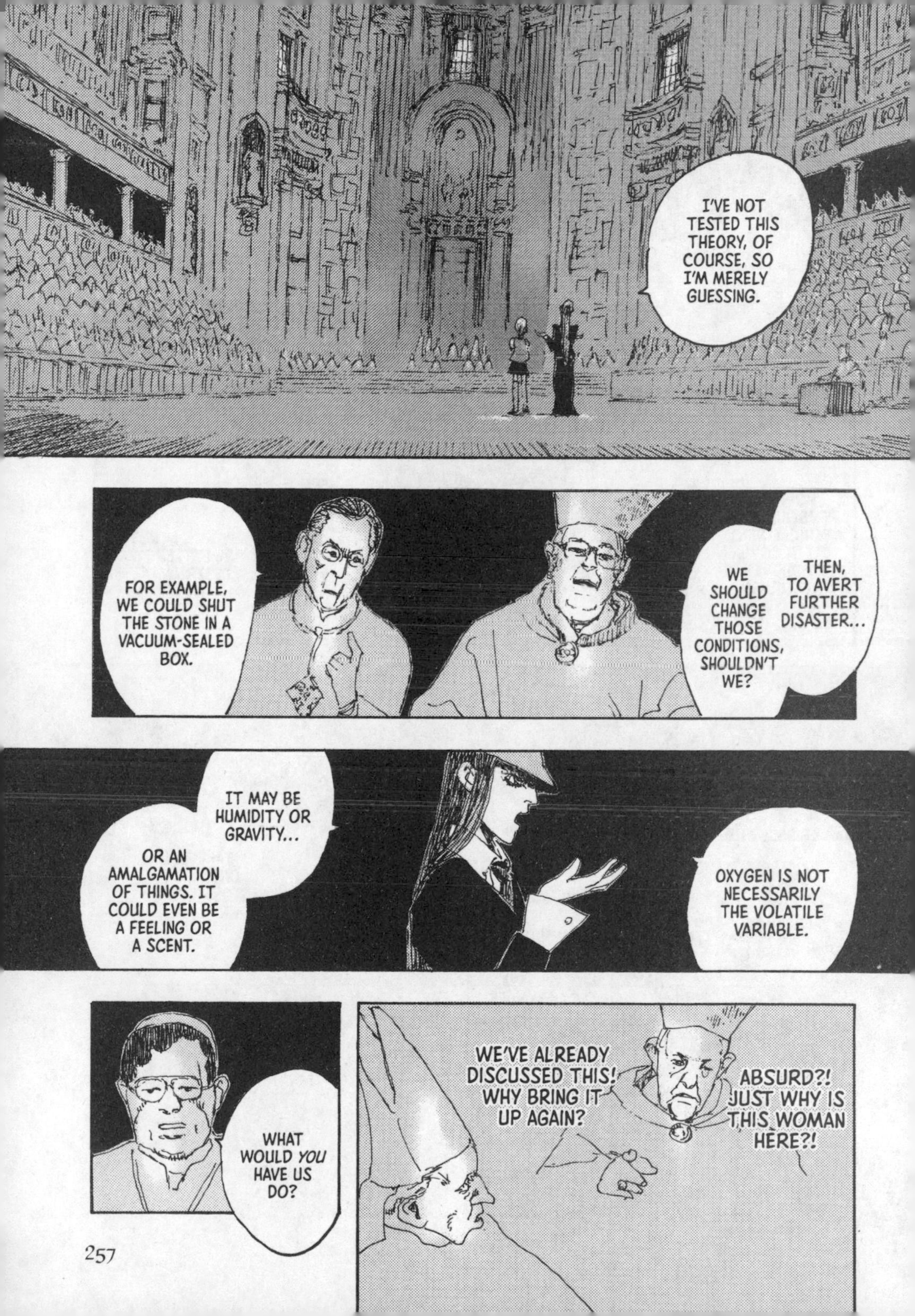

I'VE NOT TESTED THIS THEORY, OF COURSE, SO I'M MERELY GUESSING.
THEN, TO AVERT FURTHER DISASTER...
WE SHOULD CHANGE THOSE CONDITIONS, SHOULDN'T WE?
FOR EXAMPLE, WE COULD SHUT THE STONE IN A VACUUM-SEALED BOX.
OXYGEN IS NOT NECESSARILY THE VOLATILE VARIABLE.
IT MAY BE HUMIDITY OR GRAVITY...
OR AN AMALGAMATION OF THINGS. IT COULD EVEN BE A FEELING OR A SCENT.
ABSURD?! JUST WHY IS THIS WOMAN HERE?!
WE'VE ALREADY DISCUSSED THIS! WHY BRING IT UP AGAIN?
WHAT WOULD *YOU* HAVE US DO?

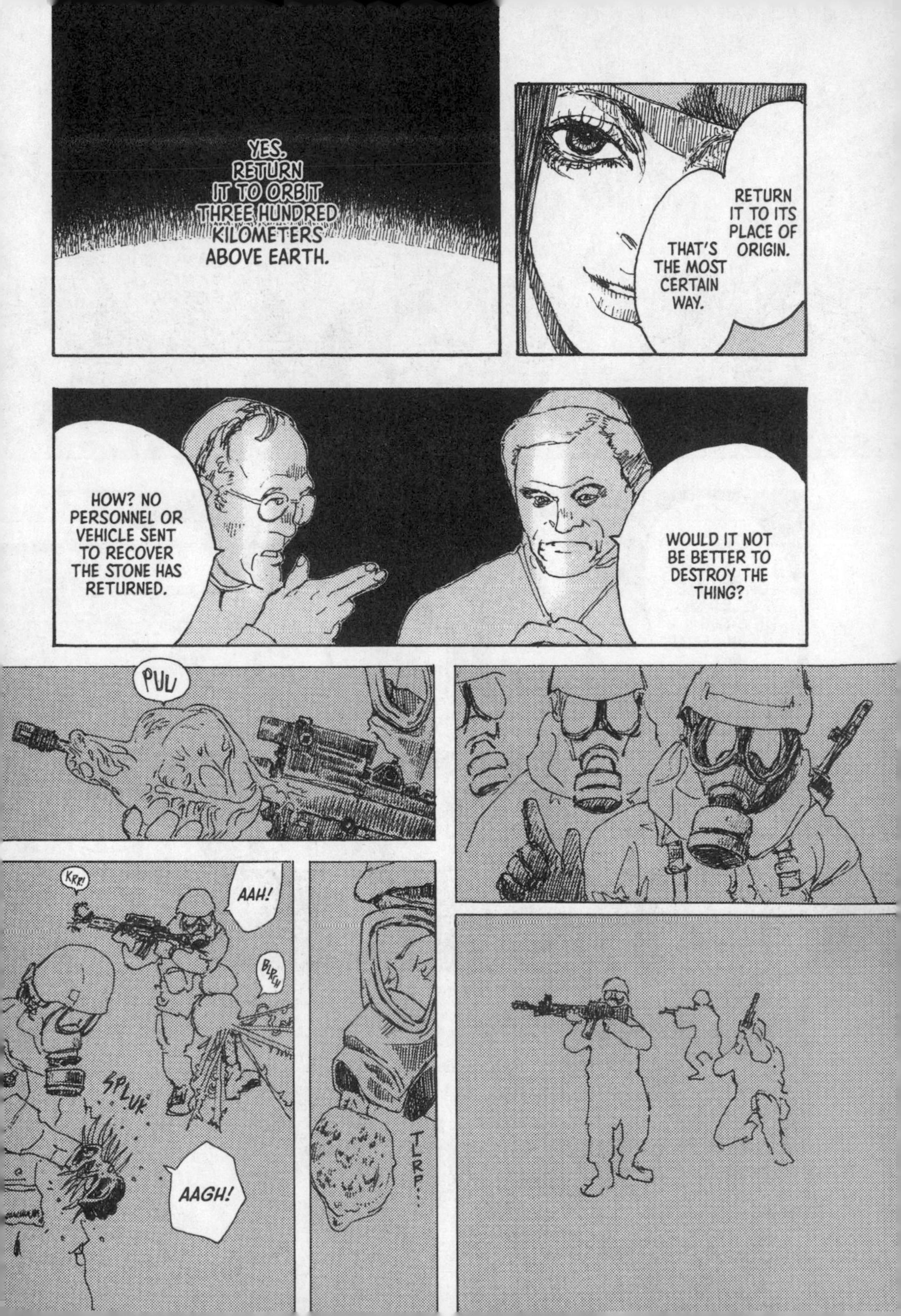
RETURN IT TO ITS PLACE OF ORIGIN.
THAT'S THE MOST CERTAIN WAY.
YES. RETURN IT TO ORBIT THREE HUNDRED KILOMETERS ABOVE EARTH.
WOULD IT NOT BE BETTER TO DESTROY THE THING?
HOW? NO PERSONNEL OR VEHICLE SENT TO RECOVER THE STONE HAS RETURNED.
PUU
TLRP...
KRR!
AAH!
BLRCH
SPLUK
AAGH!

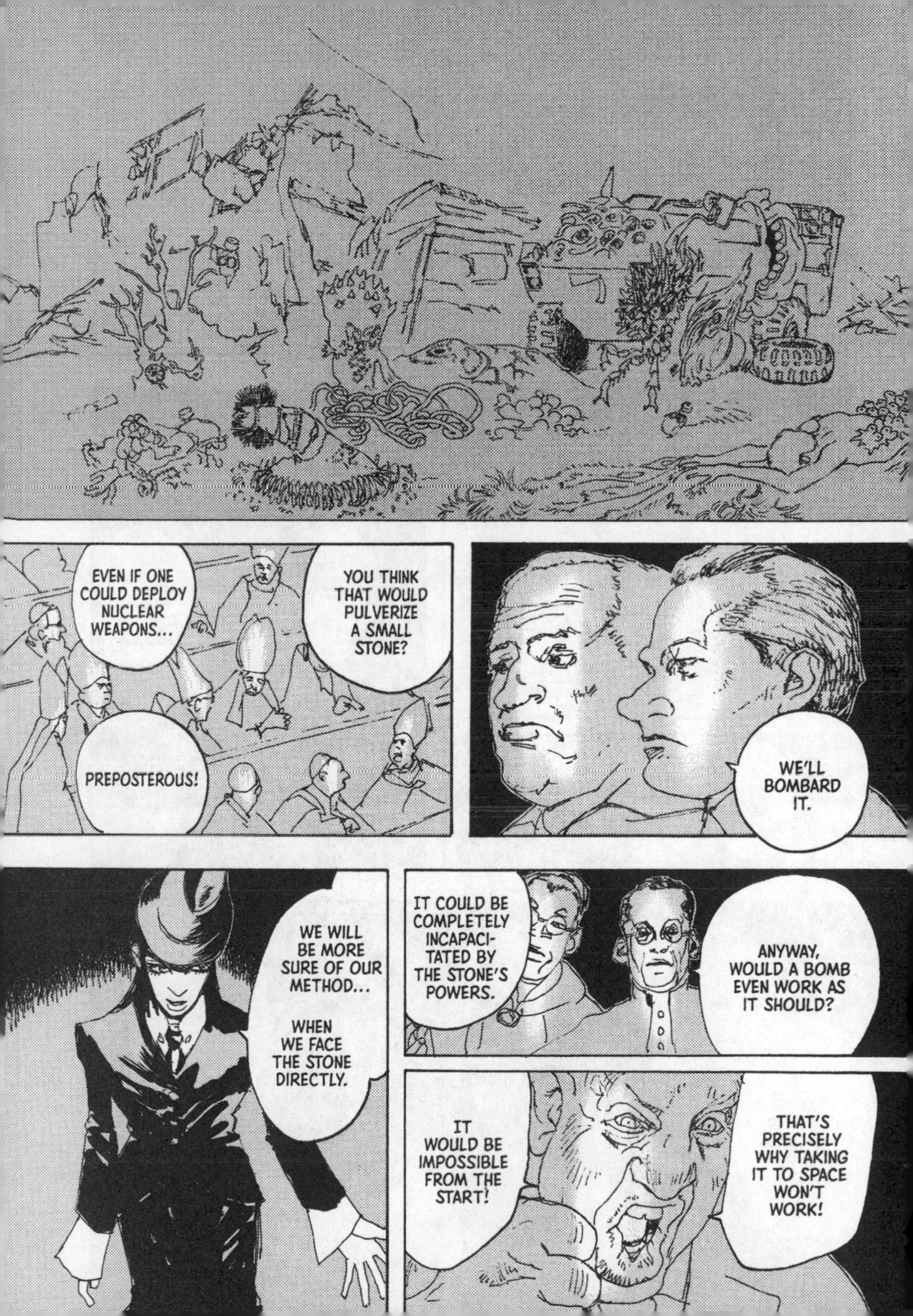
WE'LL BOMBARD IT.
YOU THINK THAT WOULD PULVERIZE A SMALL STONE?
EVEN IF ONE COULD DEPLOY NUCLEAR WEAPONS...
PREPOSTEROUS!
ANYWAY, WOULD A BOMB EVEN WORK AS IT SHOULD?
IT COULD BE COMPLETELY INCAPACI-TATED BY THE STONE'S POWERS.
THAT'S PRECISELY WHY TAKING IT TO SPACE WON'T WORK!
IT WOULD BE IMPOSSIBLE FROM THE START!
WE WILL BE MORE SURE OF OUR METHOD...
WHEN WE FACE THE STONE DIRECTLY.

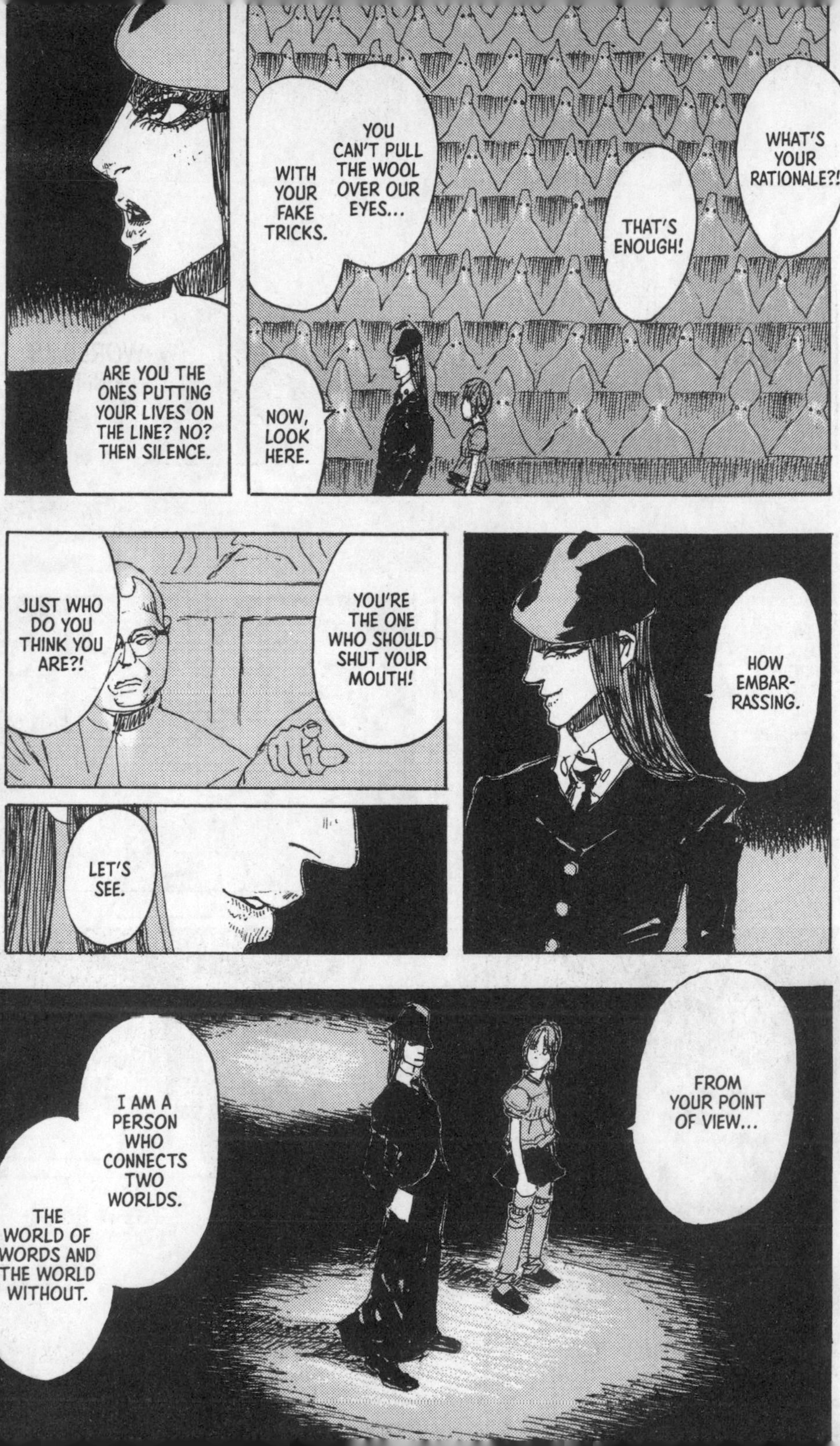
WHAT'S YOUR RATIONALE?!
THAT'S ENOUGH!
YOU CAN'T PULL THE WOOL OVER OUR EYES...
WITH YOUR FAKE TRICKS.
NOW, LOOK HERE.
ARE YOU THE ONES PUTTING YOUR LIVES ON THE LINE? NO? THEN SILENCE.
HOW EMBAR-RASSING.
YOU'RE THE ONE WHO SHOULD SHUT YOUR MOUTH!
JUST WHO DO YOU THINK YOU ARE?!
LET'S SEE.
FROM YOUR POINT OF VIEW...
I AM A PERSON WHO CONNECTS TWO WORLDS.
THE WORLD OF WORDS AND THE WORLD WITHOUT.

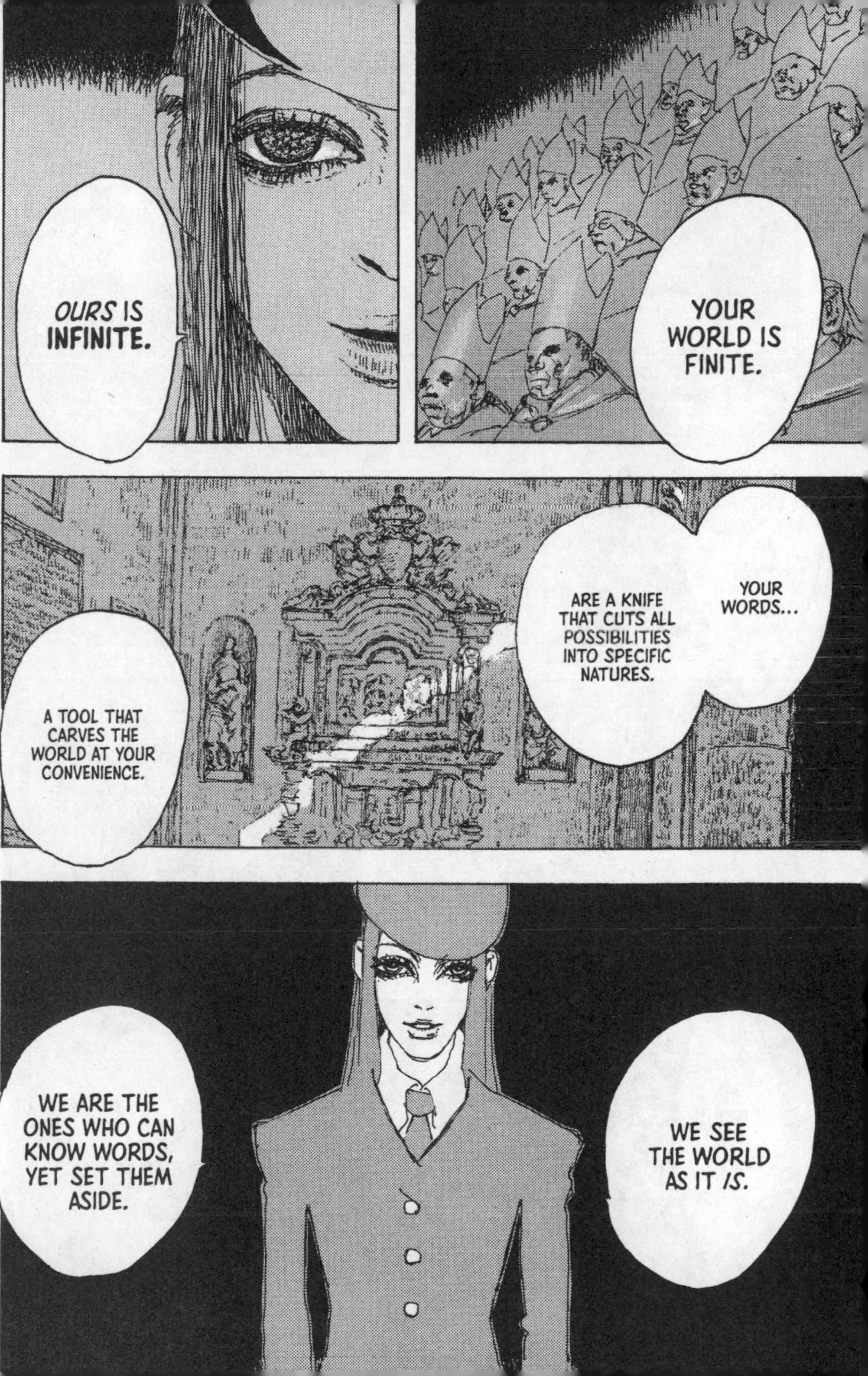
YOUR WORLD IS FINITE.
OURS IS **INFINITE.**
YOUR WORDS...
ARE A KNIFE THAT CUTS ALL POSSIBILITIES INTO SPECIFIC NATURES.
A TOOL THAT CARVES THE WORLD AT YOUR CONVENIENCE.
WE SEE THE WORLD AS IT *IS*.
WE ARE THE ONES WHO CAN KNOW WORDS, YET SET THEM ASIDE.

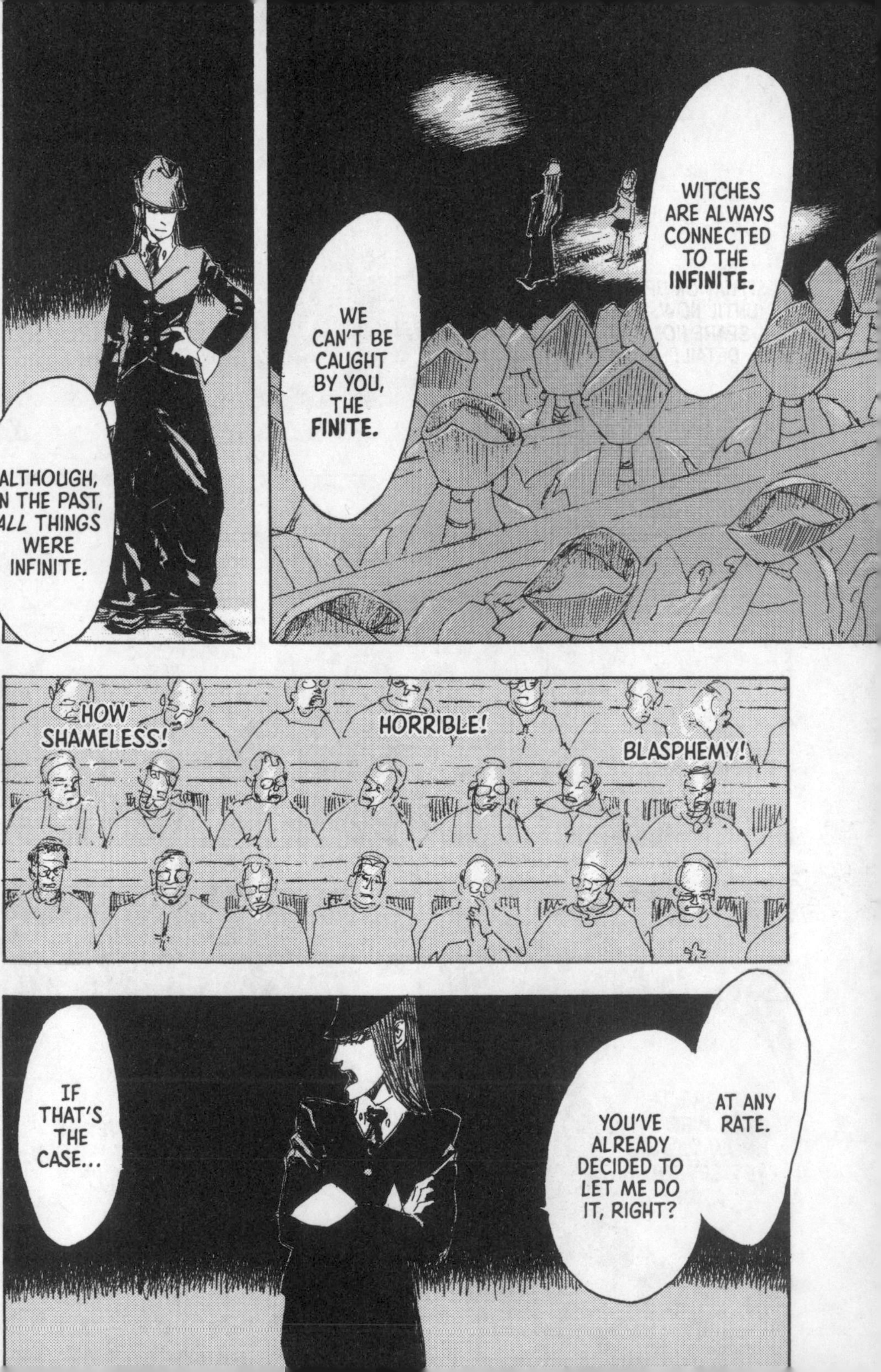
WITCHES ARE ALWAYS CONNECTED TO THE **INFINITE.**
WE CAN'T BE CAUGHT BY YOU, THE **FINITE.**
ALTHOUGH, IN THE PAST, *ALL* THINGS WERE INFINITE.
BLASPHEMY!
HORRIBLE!
HOW SHAMELESS!
AT ANY RATE.
YOU'VE ALREADY DECIDED TO LET ME DO IT, RIGHT?
IF THAT'S THE CASE...

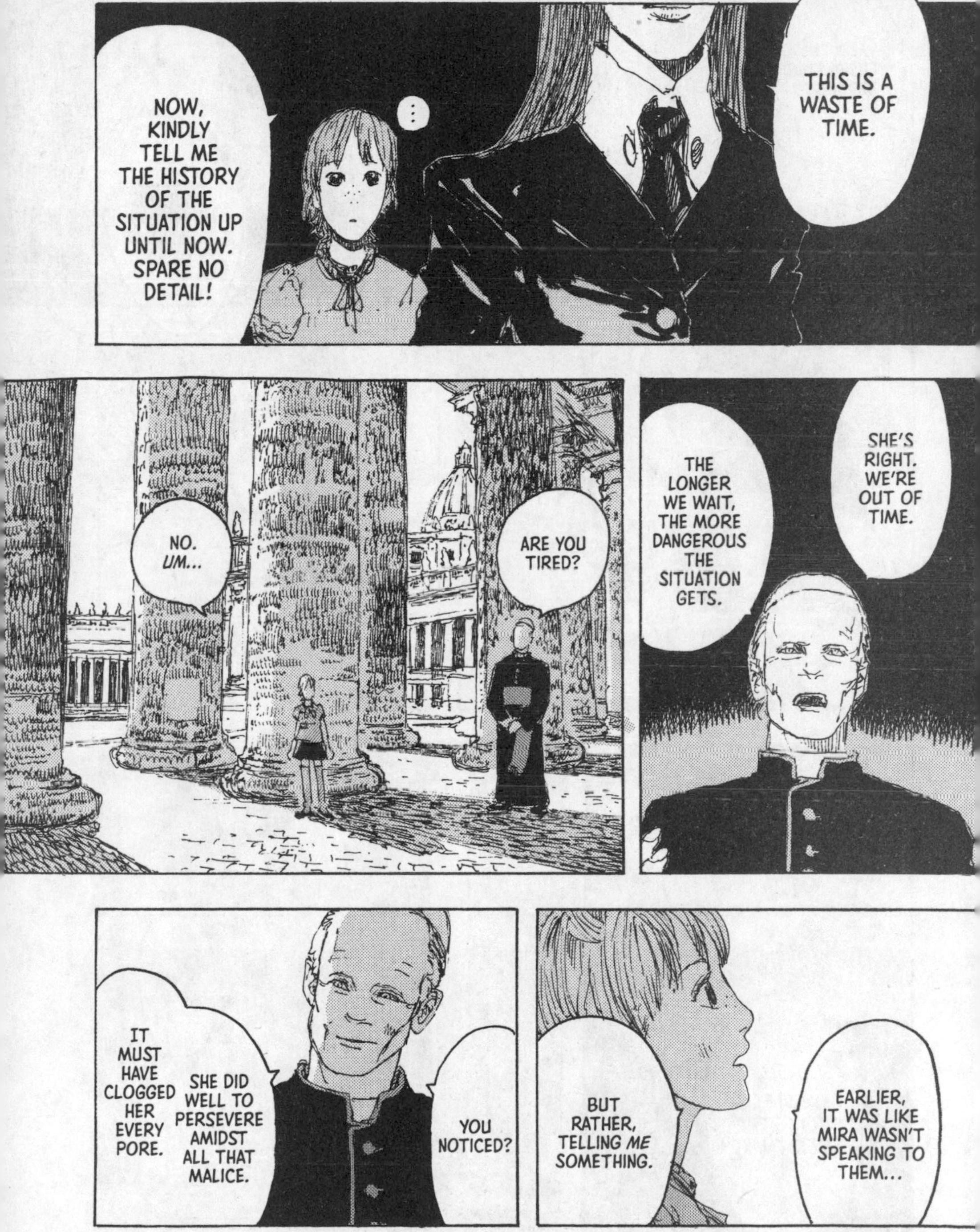
THIS IS A WASTE OF TIME.
…
NOW, KINDLY TELL ME THE HISTORY OF THE SITUATION UP UNTIL NOW. SPARE NO DETAIL!
SHE'S RIGHT. WE'RE OUT OF TIME.
THE LONGER WE WAIT, THE MORE DANGEROUS THE SITUATION GETS.
ARE YOU TIRED?
NO. *UM...*
EARLIER, IT WAS LIKE MIRA WASN'T SPEAKING TO THEM...
BUT RATHER, TELLING *ME* SOMETHING.
YOU NOTICED?
SHE DID WELL TO PERSEVERE AMIDST ALL THAT MALICE.
IT MUST HAVE CLOGGED HER EVERY PORE.

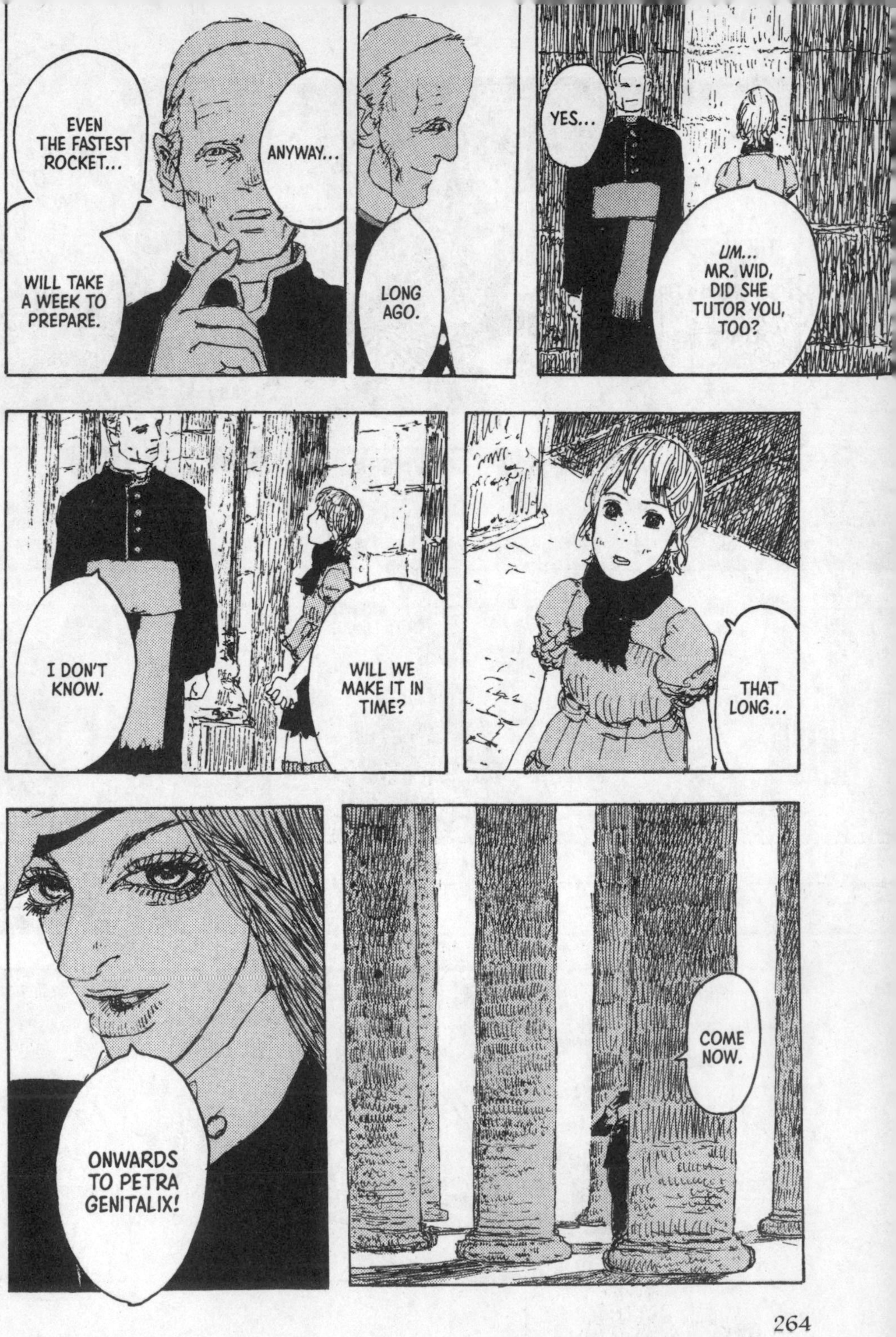
UM... MR. WID, DID SHE TUTOR YOU, TOO?
YES...
LONG AGO.
ANYWAY...
EVEN THE FASTEST ROCKET...
WILL TAKE A WEEK TO PREPARE.
THAT LONG...
WILL WE MAKE IT IN TIME?
I DON'T KNOW.
COME NOW.
ONWARDS TO PETRA GENITALIX!

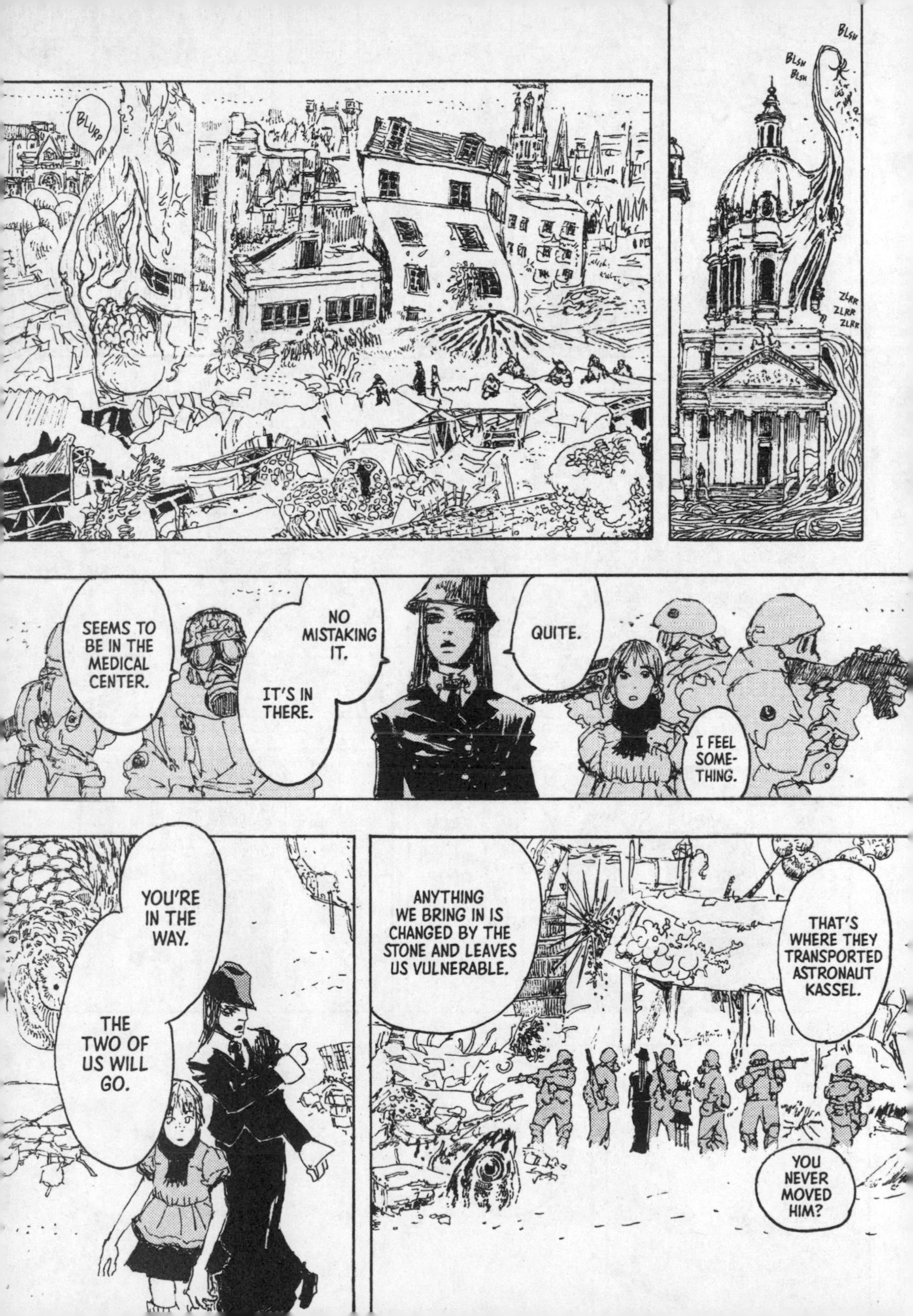
BLSH
BLSH
BLSH
ZLRR
ZLRR
ZLRR
BLURP
I FEEL SOME-THING.
QUITE.
NO MISTAKING IT.
IT'S IN THERE.
SEEMS TO BE IN THE MEDICAL CENTER.
THAT'S WHERE THEY TRANSPORTED ASTRONAUT KASSEL.
YOU NEVER MOVED HIM?
ANYTHING WE BRING IN IS CHANGED BY THE STONE AND LEAVES US VULNERABLE.
YOU'RE IN THE WAY.
THE TWO OF US WILL GO.

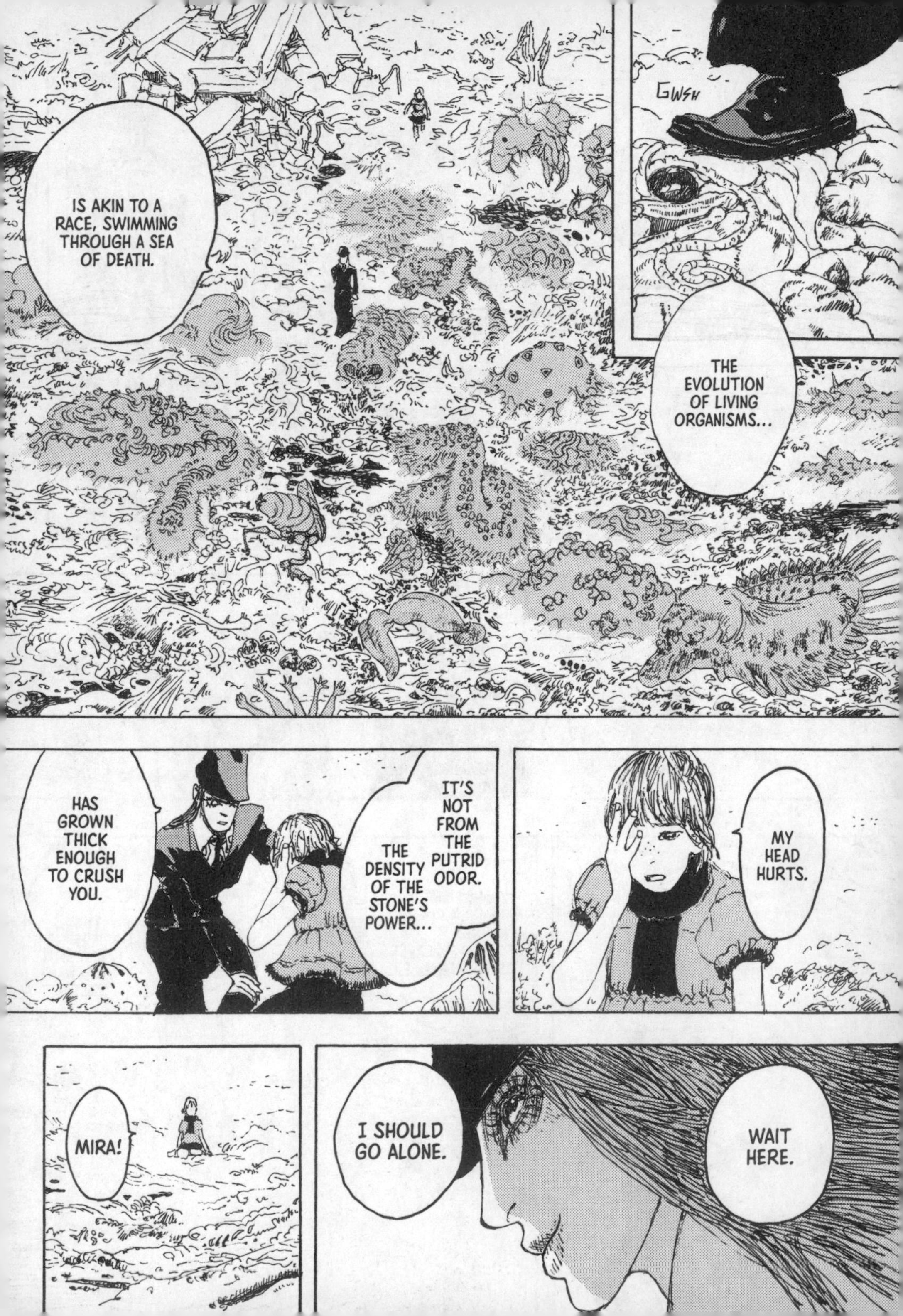
GWSH
THE EVOLUTION OF LIVING ORGANISMS...
IS AKIN TO A RACE, SWIMMING THROUGH A SEA OF DEATH.
MY HEAD HURTS.
IT'S NOT FROM THE PUTRID ODOR.
THE DENSITY OF THE STONE'S POWER...
HAS GROWN THICK ENOUGH TO CRUSH YOU.
WAIT HERE.
I SHOULD GO ALONE.
MIRA!

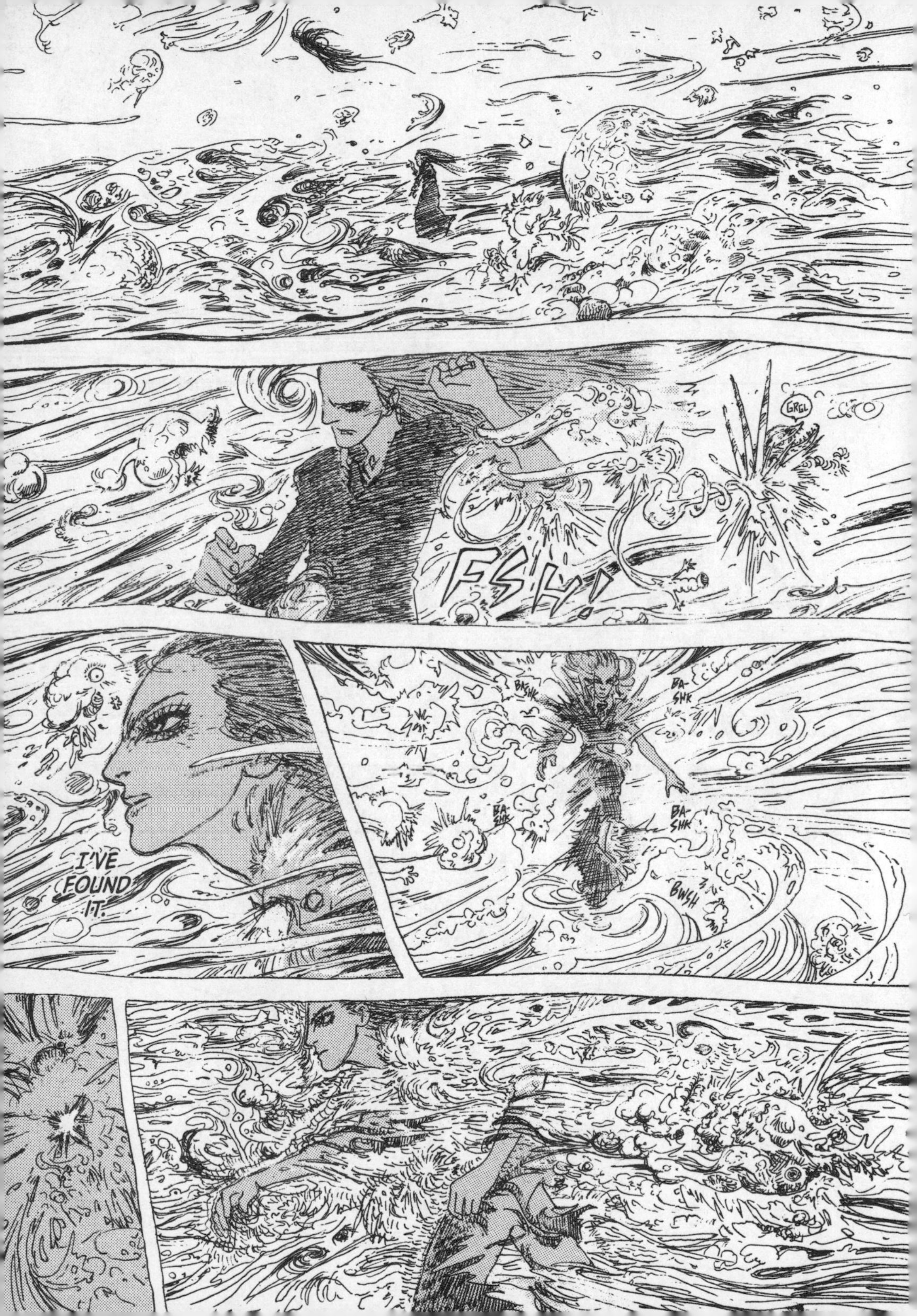
GRGL
FSH!
BA-SHK
BASHK
BA-SHK
BA-SHK
BWSH
I'VE FOUND IT.

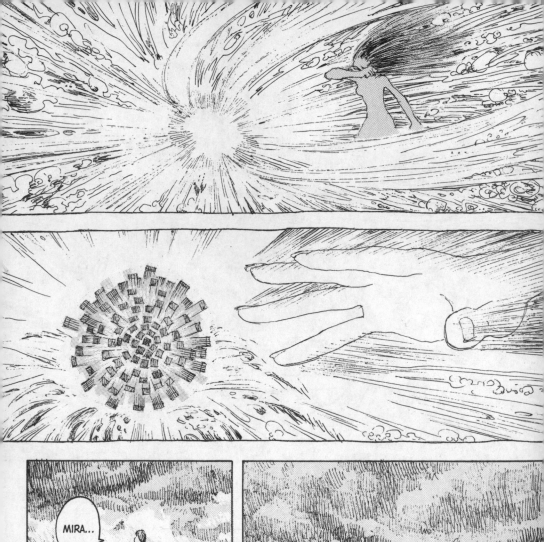

MIRA...

!

THE STONE'S POWER HAS...

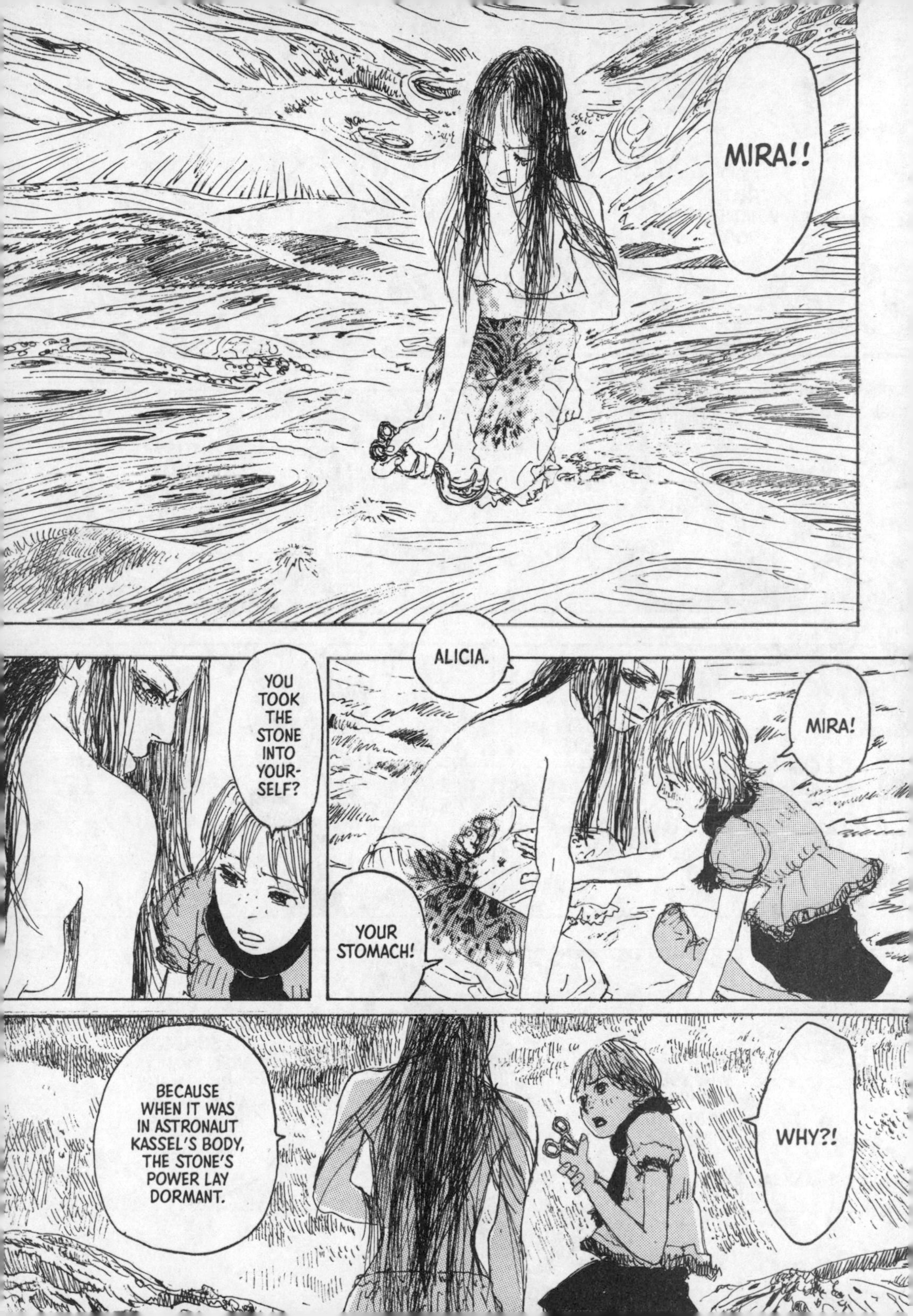
MIRA!!
MIRA!
ALICIA.
YOUR STOMACH!
YOU TOOK THE STONE INTO YOUR-SELF?
WHY?!
BECAUSE WHEN IT WAS IN ASTRONAUT KASSEL'S BODY, THE STONE'S POWER LAY DORMANT.

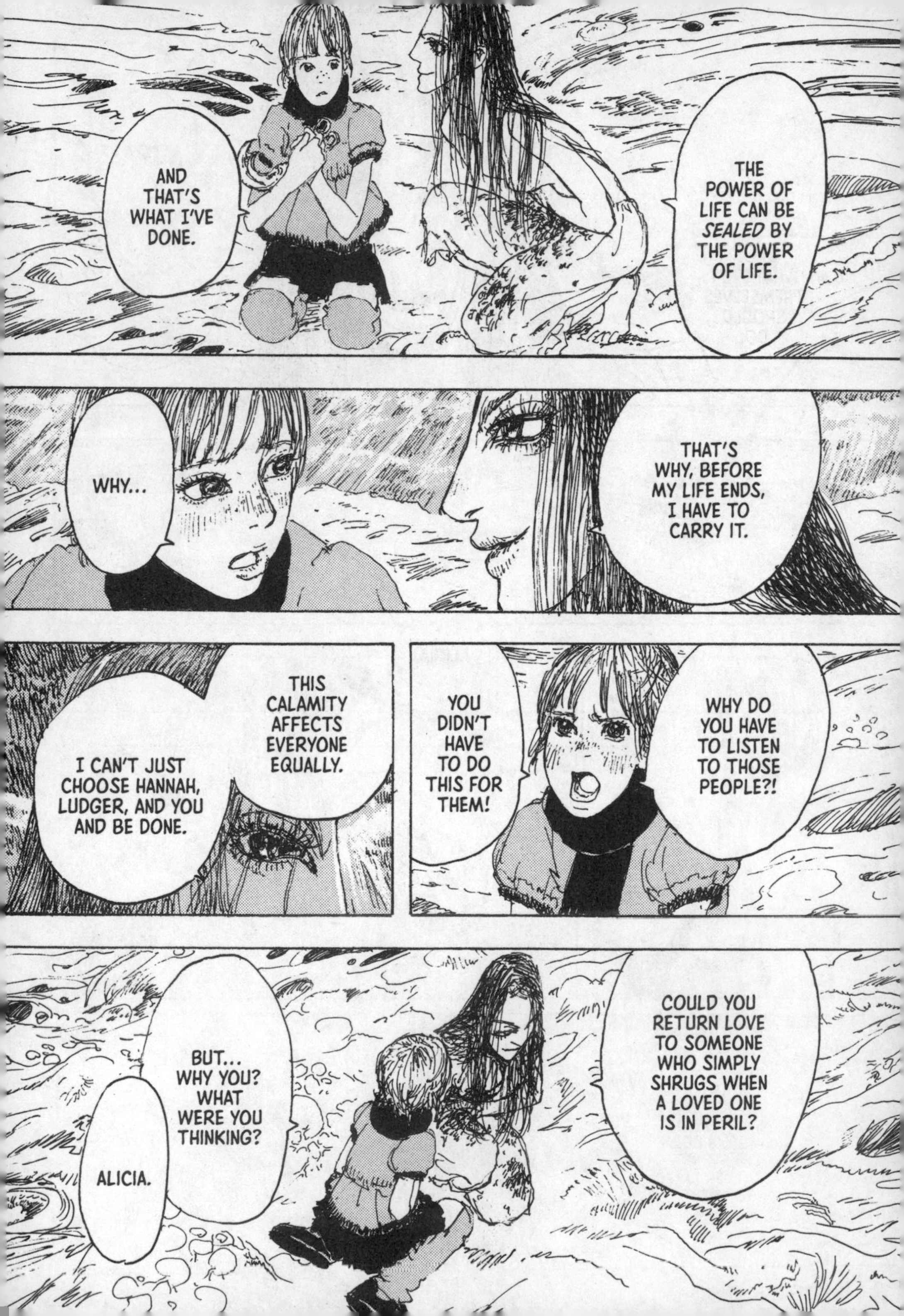
THE POWER OF LIFE CAN BE *SEALED* BY THE POWER OF LIFE.
AND THAT'S WHAT I'VE DONE.
THAT'S WHY, BEFORE MY LIFE ENDS, I HAVE TO CARRY IT.
WHY...
WHY DO YOU HAVE TO LISTEN TO THOSE PEOPLE?!
YOU DIDN'T HAVE TO DO THIS FOR THEM!
THIS CALAMITY AFFECTS EVERYONE EQUALLY.
I CAN'T JUST CHOOSE HANNAH, LUDGER, AND YOU AND BE DONE.
COULD YOU RETURN LOVE TO SOMEONE WHO SIMPLY SHRUGS WHEN A LOVED ONE IS IN PERIL?
BUT... WHY YOU? WHAT WERE YOU THINKING?
ALICIA.

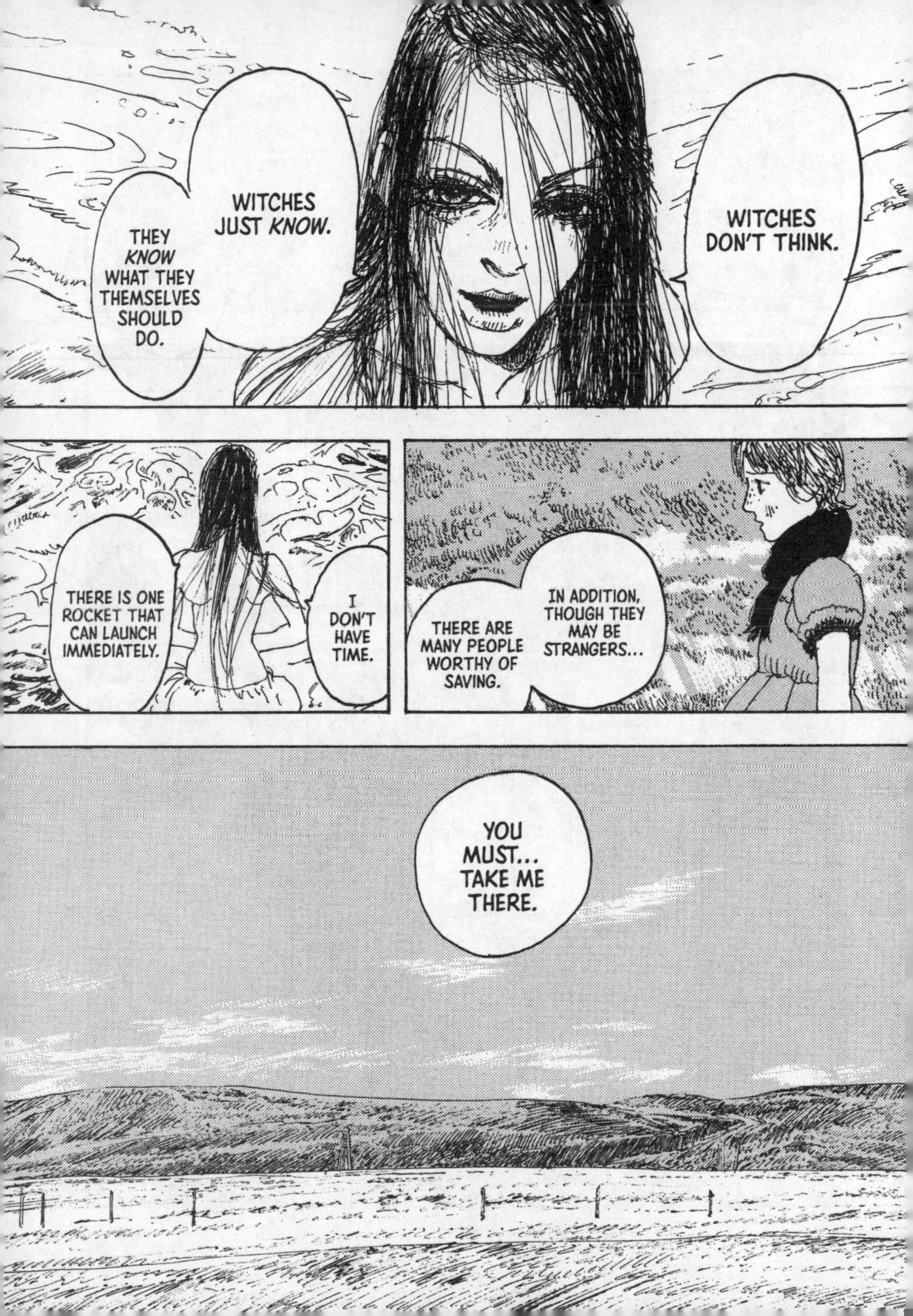
WITCHES DON'T THINK.
WITCHES JUST *KNOW*.
THEY *KNOW* WHAT THEY THEMSELVES SHOULD DO.
IN ADDITION, THOUGH THEY MAY BE STRANGERS...
THERE ARE MANY PEOPLE WORTHY OF SAVING.
I DON'T HAVE TIME.
THERE IS ONE ROCKET THAT CAN LAUNCH IMMEDIATELY.
YOU MUST... TAKE ME THERE.

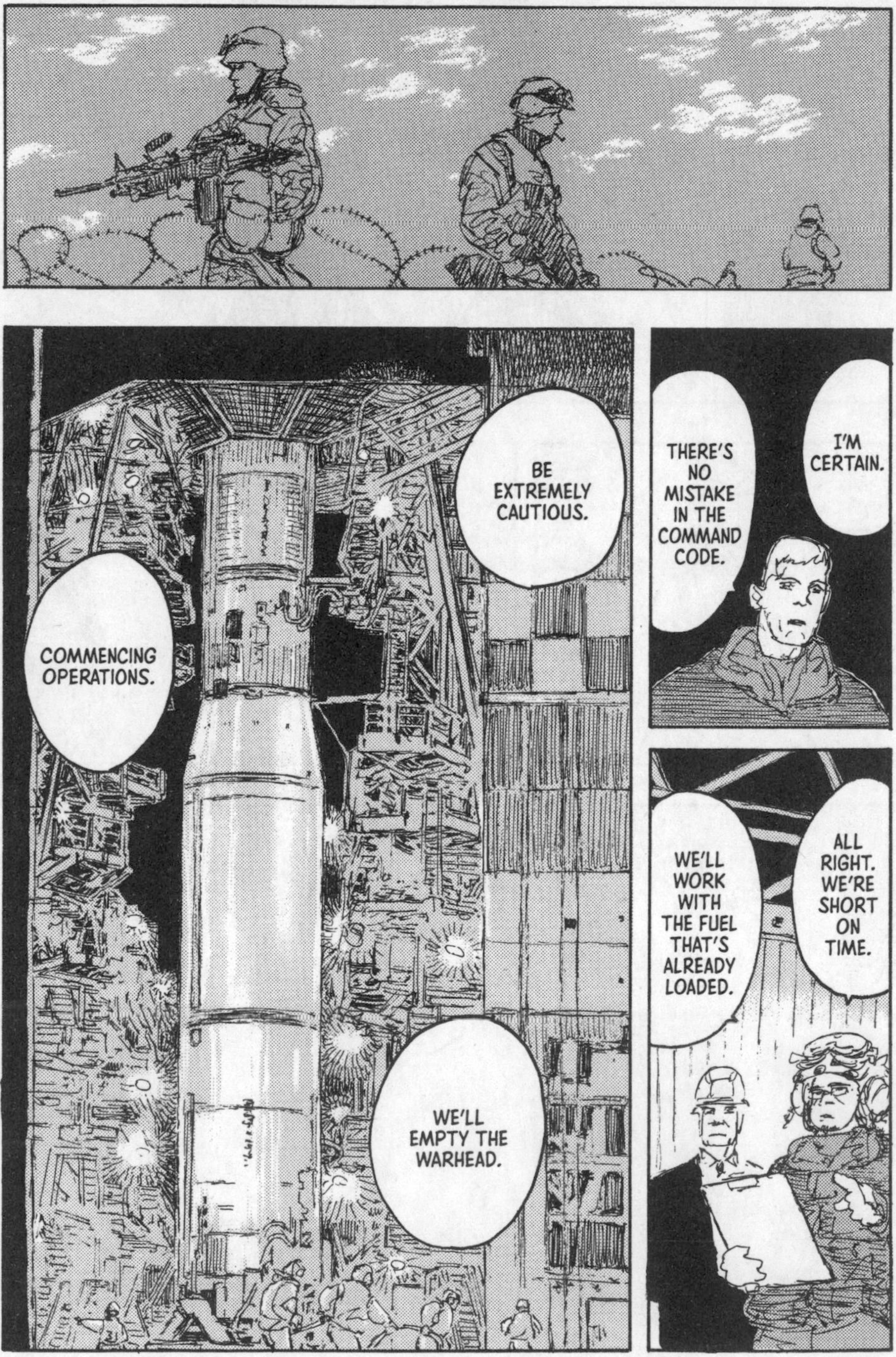
I'M CERTAIN.
THERE'S NO MISTAKE IN THE COMMAND CODE.
ALL RIGHT. WE'RE SHORT ON TIME.
WE'LL WORK WITH THE FUEL THAT'S ALREADY LOADED.
BE EXTREMELY CAUTIOUS.
COMMENCING OPERATIONS.
WE'LL EMPTY THE WARHEAD.

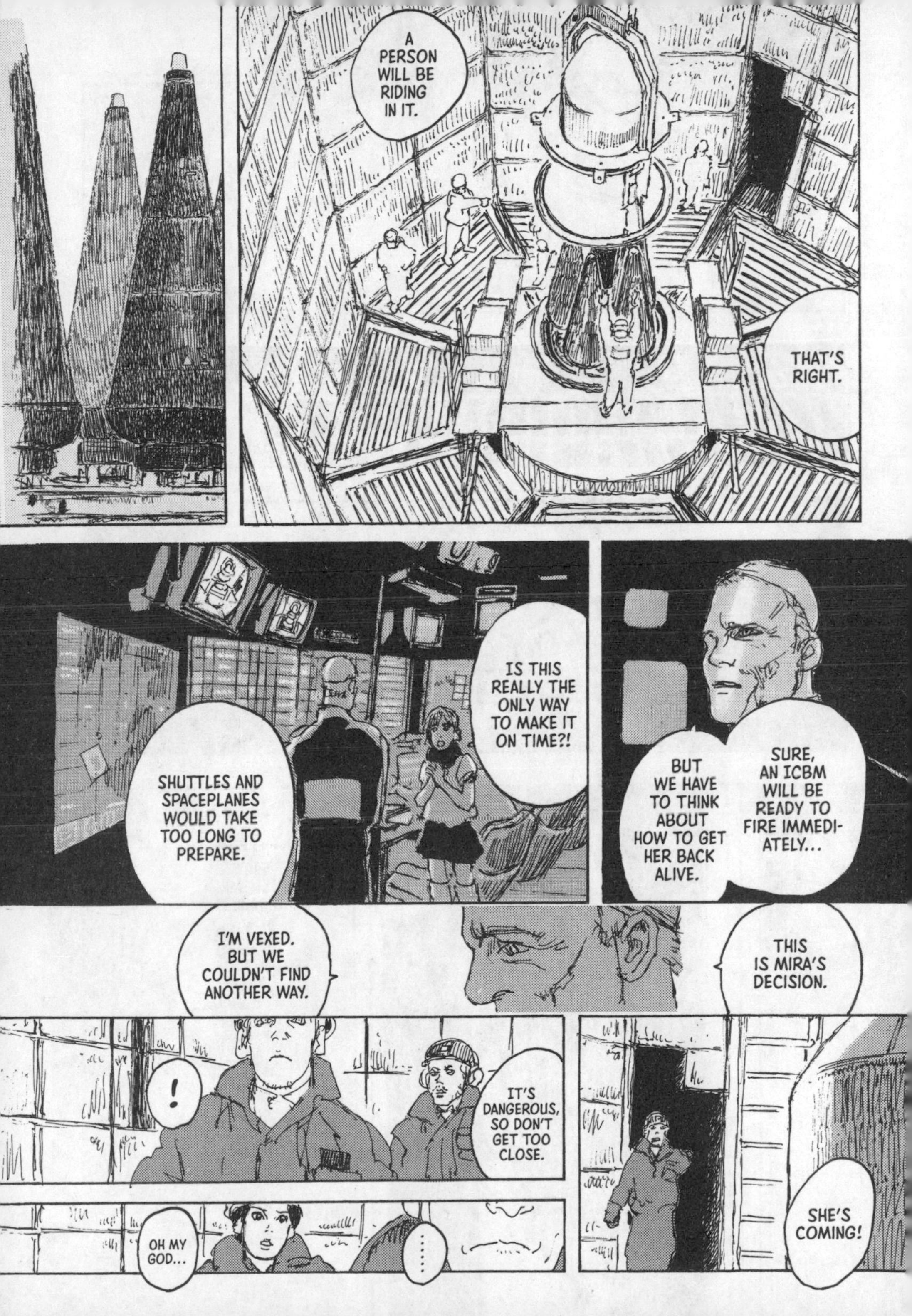
A PERSON WILL BE RIDING IN IT.
THAT'S RIGHT.
SURE, AN ICBM WILL BE READY TO FIRE IMMEDI-ATELY...
BUT WE HAVE TO THINK ABOUT HOW TO GET HER BACK ALIVE.
IS THIS REALLY THE ONLY WAY TO MAKE IT ON TIME?!
SHUTTLES AND SPACEPLANES WOULD TAKE TOO LONG TO PREPARE.
THIS IS MIRA'S DECISION.
I'M VEXED. BUT WE COULDN'T FIND ANOTHER WAY.
SHE'S COMING!
IT'S DANGEROUS, SO DON'T GET TOO CLOSE.
!
......
OH MY GOD...

PLp

PLp

PLp

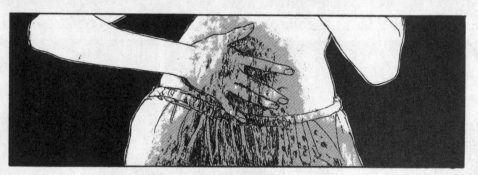

A WITCH...

SHE'S THE WITCH...

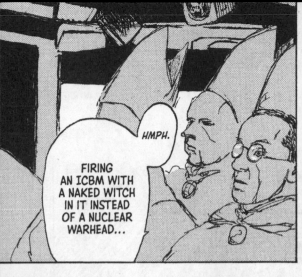

HOW INDECENT.
HMPH.
FIRING AN ICBM WITH A NAKED WITCH IN IT INSTEAD OF A NUCLEAR WARHEAD...
IT'S QUITE ABSURD.
BUT SHE'S UNEXPECTEDLY USEFUL FOR SUCH A TROUBLESOME PERSON.
OF COURSE.
THEIR EXISTENCE ITSELF IS BLASPHEMY.
BUT IT'S BECAUSE OF MO-MENTS LIKE THESE...
THAT WE DON'T ELIMINATE THEM.
CAN I SPEAK TO HER?!
THIS IS FOR MONITORING. YOU CAN'T SPEAK THROUGH IT.
MIRA!

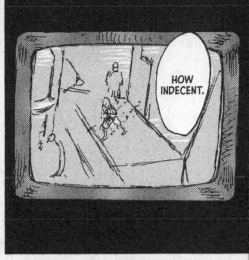

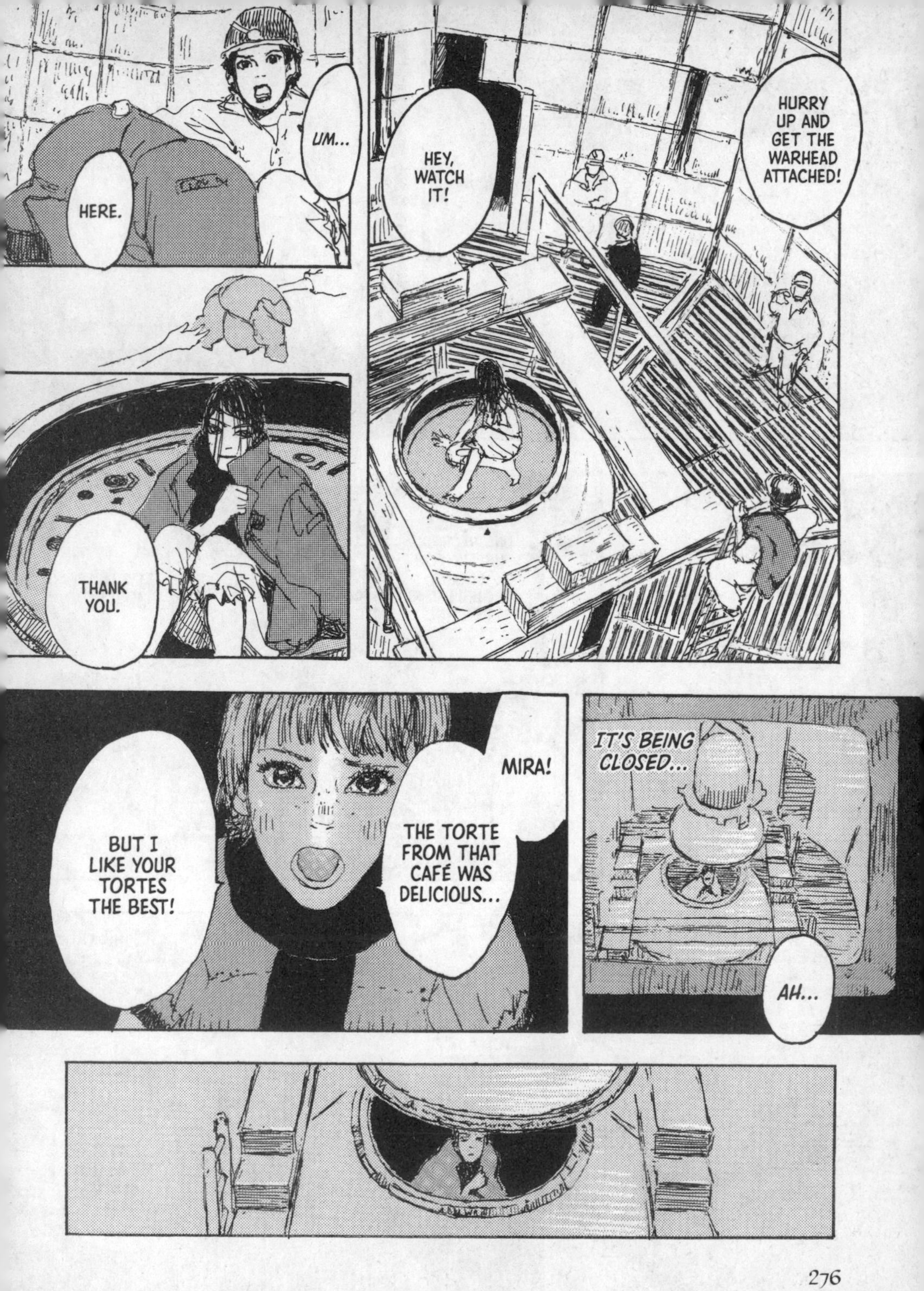
HURRY UP AND GET THE WARHEAD ATTACHED!
HEY, WATCH IT!
UM...
HERE.
THANK YOU.
IT'S BEING CLOSED...
AH...
MIRA!
THE TORTE FROM THAT CAFÉ WAS DELICIOUS...
BUT I LIKE YOUR TORTES THE BEST!

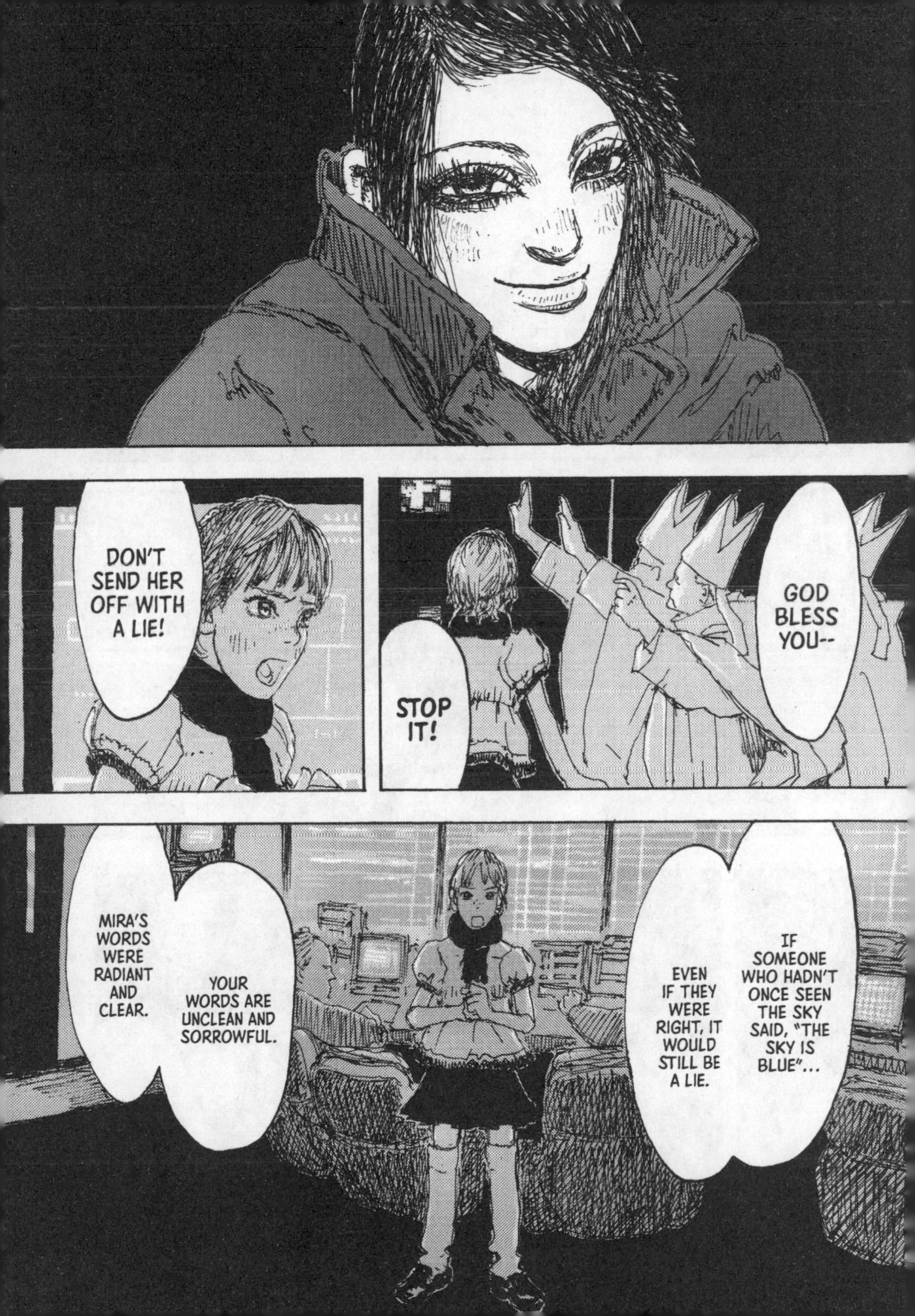
GOD BLESS YOU--
STOP IT!
DON'T SEND HER OFF WITH A LIE!
IF SOMEONE WHO HADN'T ONCE SEEN THE SKY SAID, "THE SKY IS BLUE"...
EVEN IF THEY WERE RIGHT, IT WOULD STILL BE A LIE.
MIRA'S WORDS WERE RADIANT AND CLEAR.
YOUR WORDS ARE UNCLEAN AND SORROWFUL.

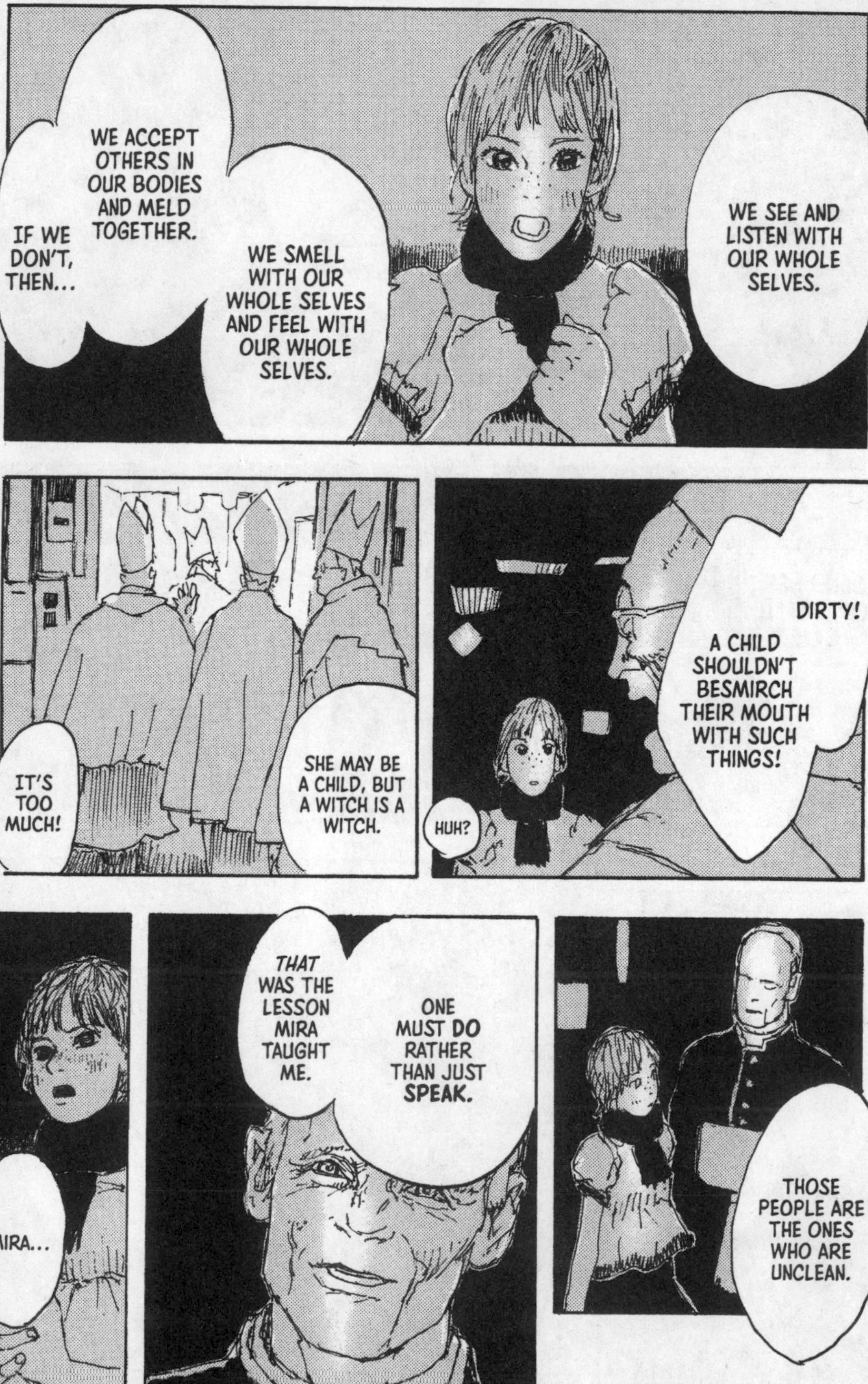
WE SEE AND LISTEN WITH OUR WHOLE SELVES.
WE SMELL WITH OUR WHOLE SELVES AND FEEL WITH OUR WHOLE SELVES.
WE ACCEPT OTHERS IN OUR BODIES AND MELD TOGETHER.
IF WE DON'T, THEN...
DIRTY!
A CHILD SHOULDN'T BESMIRCH THEIR MOUTH WITH SUCH THINGS!
HUH?
SHE MAY BE A CHILD, BUT A WITCH IS A WITCH.
IT'S TOO MUCH!
THOSE PEOPLE ARE THE ONES WHO ARE UNCLEAN.
ONE MUST **DO** RATHER THAN JUST **SPEAK.**
THAT WAS THE LESSON MIRA TAUGHT ME.
MIRA...

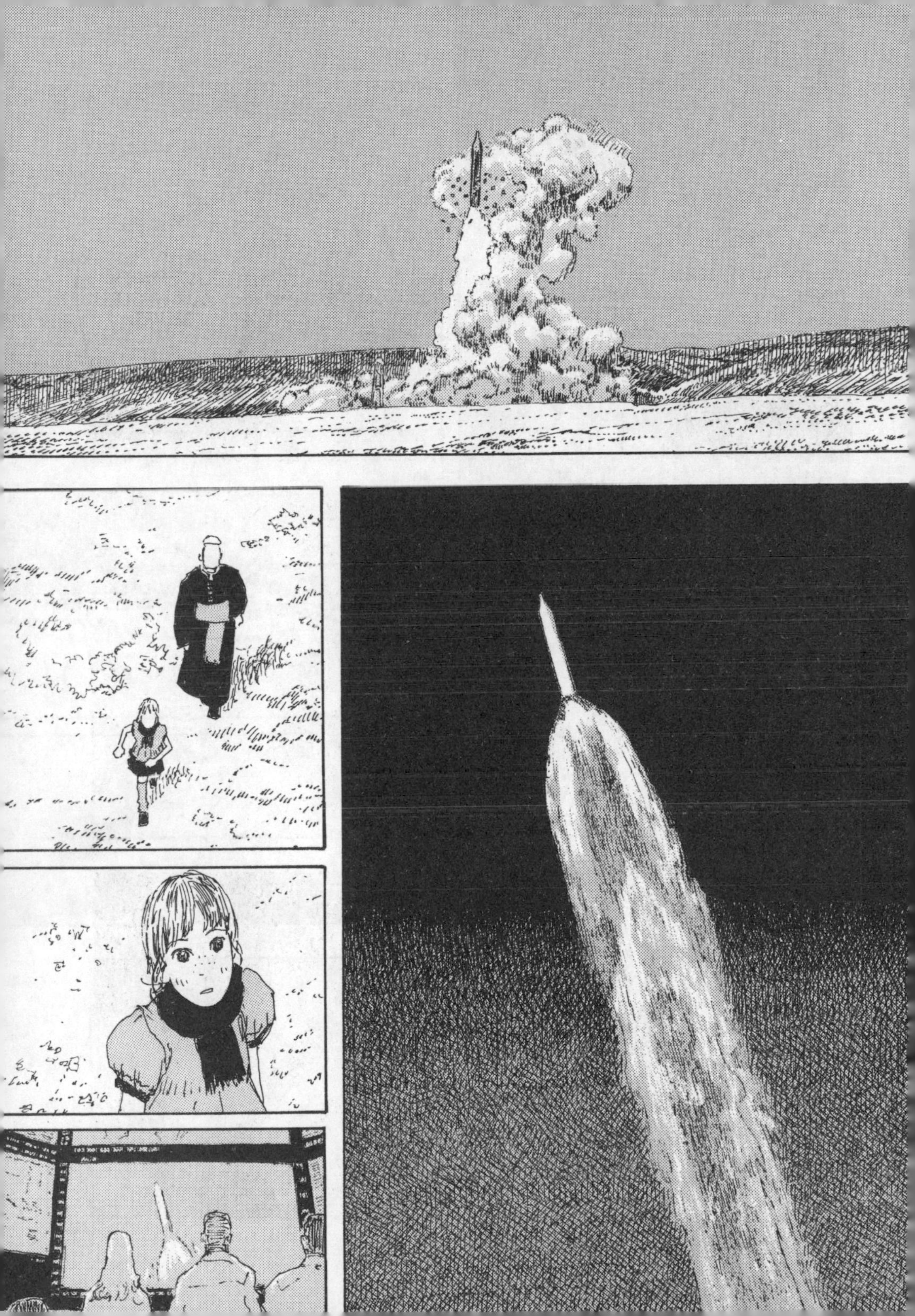

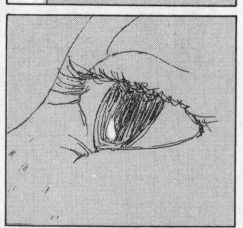

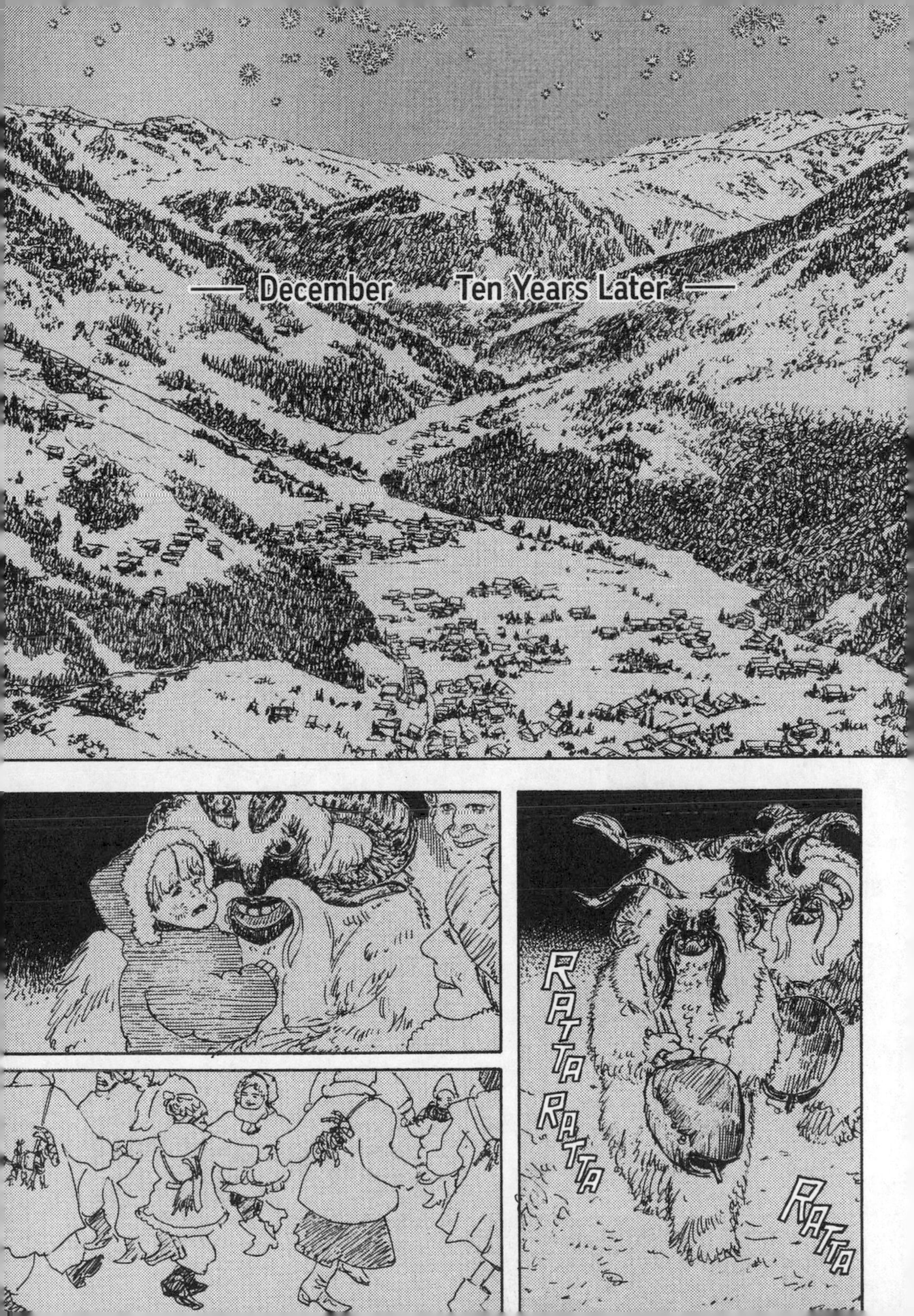
December Ten Years Later
RATTA RATTA RATTA
RATTA

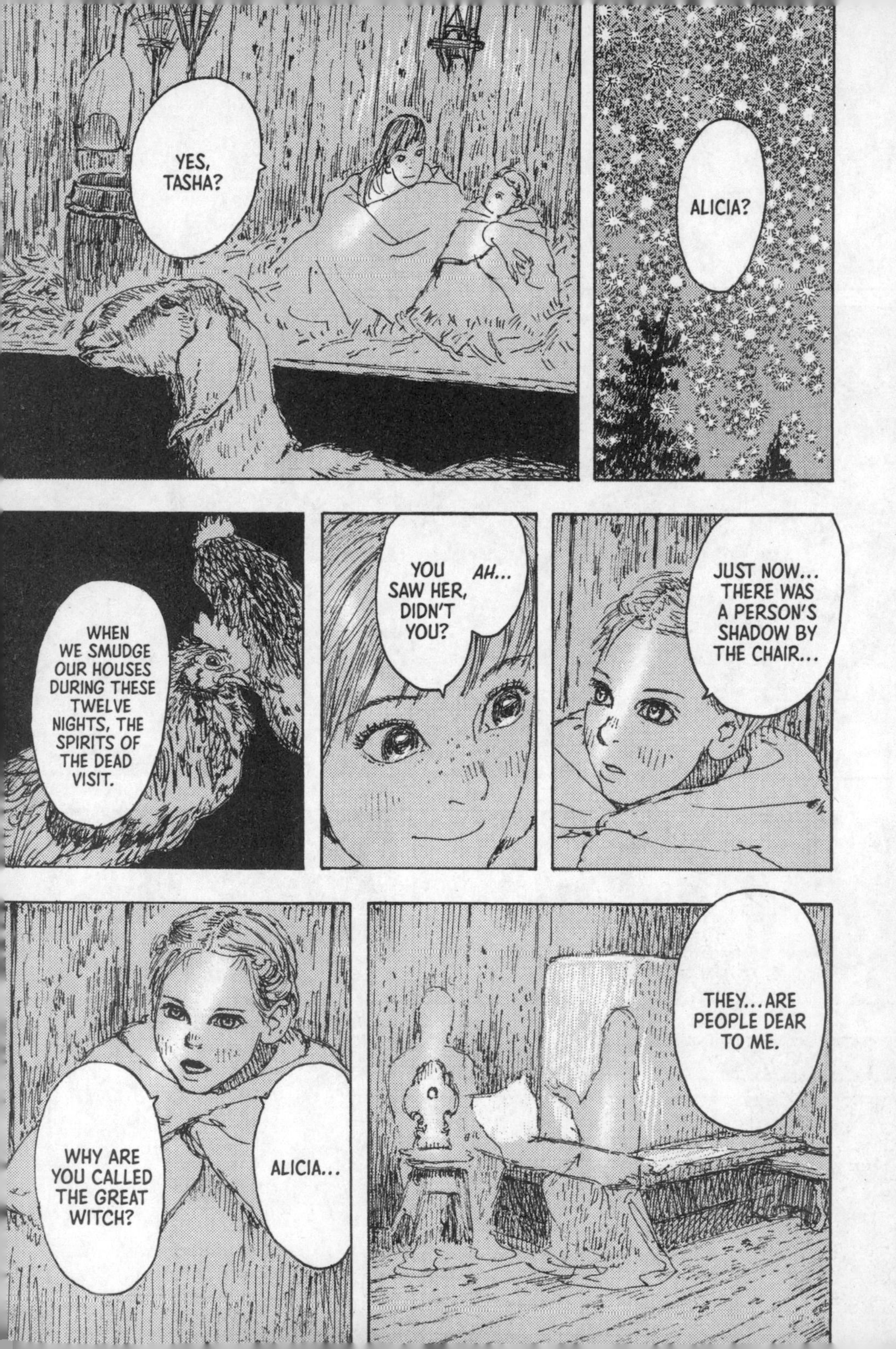
ALICIA?
YES, TASHA?
JUST NOW... THERE WAS A PERSON'S SHADOW BY THE CHAIR...
AH...
YOU SAW HER, DIDN'T YOU?
WHEN WE SMUDGE OUR HOUSES DURING THESE TWELVE NIGHTS, THE SPIRITS OF THE DEAD VISIT.
THEY...ARE PEOPLE DEAR TO ME.
ALICIA...
WHY ARE YOU CALLED THE GREAT WITCH?

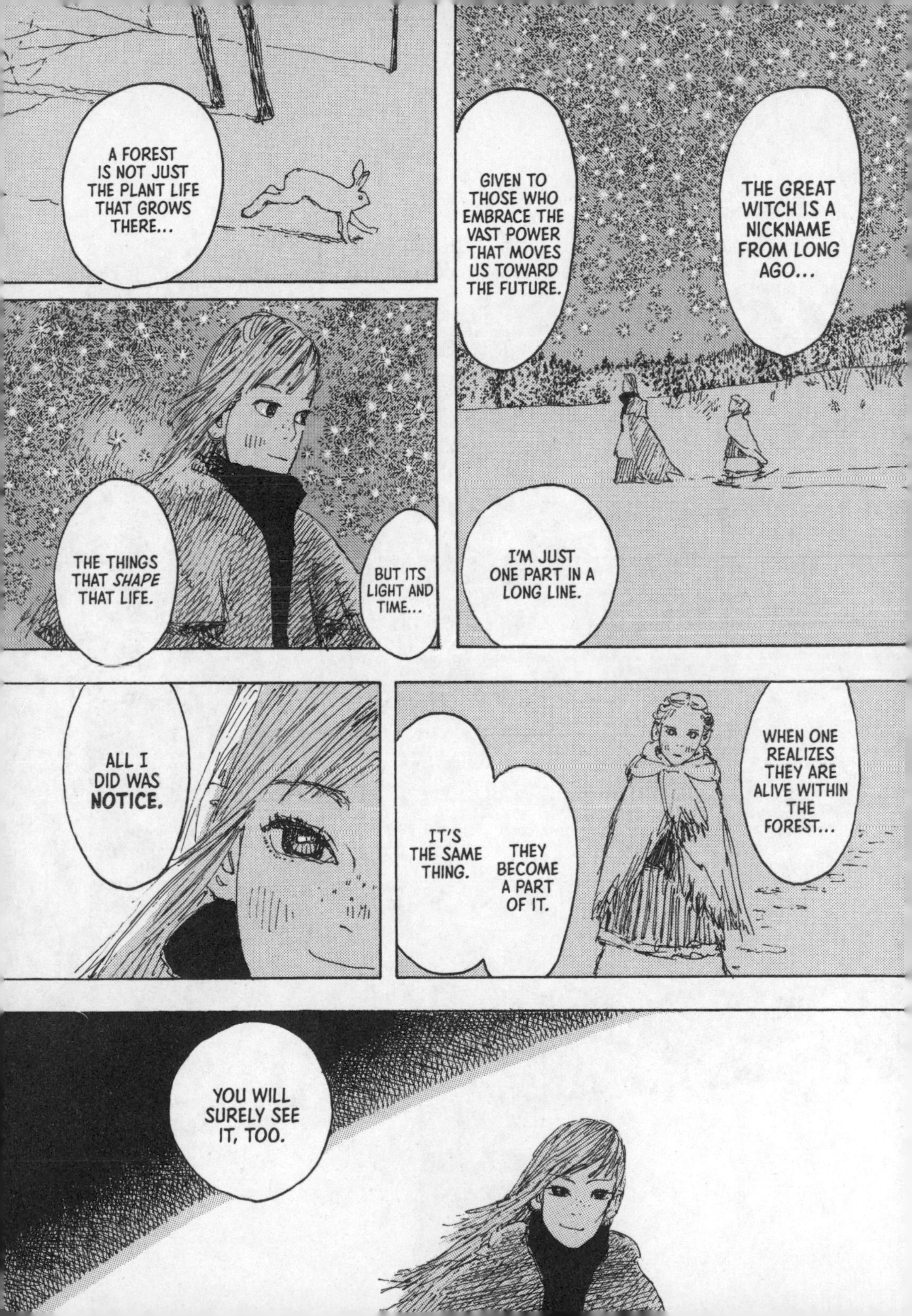
THE GREAT WITCH IS A NICKNAME FROM LONG AGO...
GIVEN TO THOSE WHO EMBRACE THE VAST POWER THAT MOVES US TOWARD THE FUTURE.
I'M JUST ONE PART IN A LONG LINE.
A FOREST IS NOT JUST THE PLANT LIFE THAT GROWS THERE...
BUT ITS LIGHT AND TIME...
THE THINGS THAT *SHAPE* THAT LIFE.
WHEN ONE REALIZES THEY ARE ALIVE WITHIN THE FOREST...
THEY BECOME A PART OF IT.
IT'S THE SAME THING.
ALL I DID WAS **NOTICE.**
YOU WILL SURELY SEE IT, TOO.

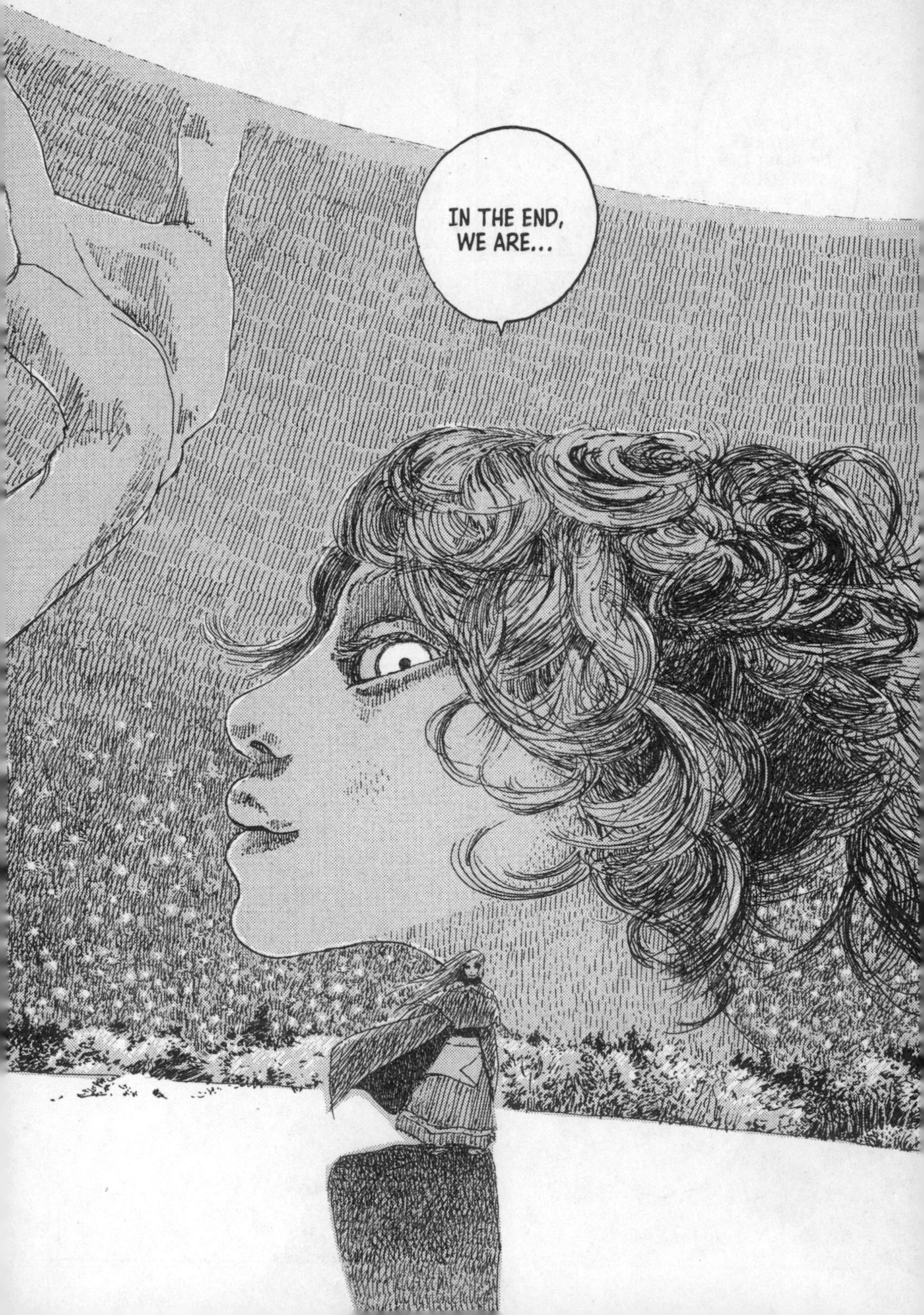
IN THE END, WE ARE...

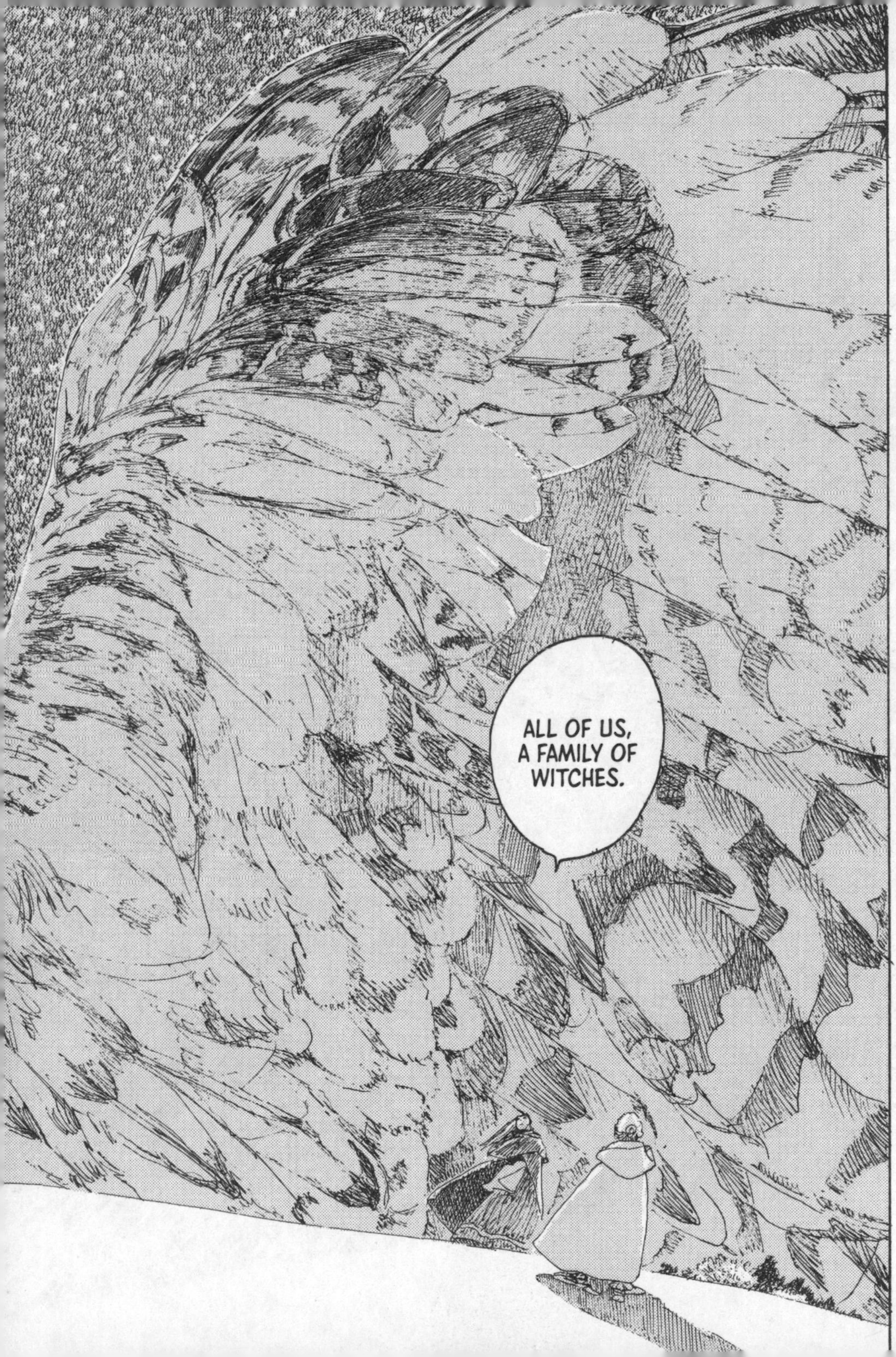
ALL OF US, A FAMILY OF WITCHES.

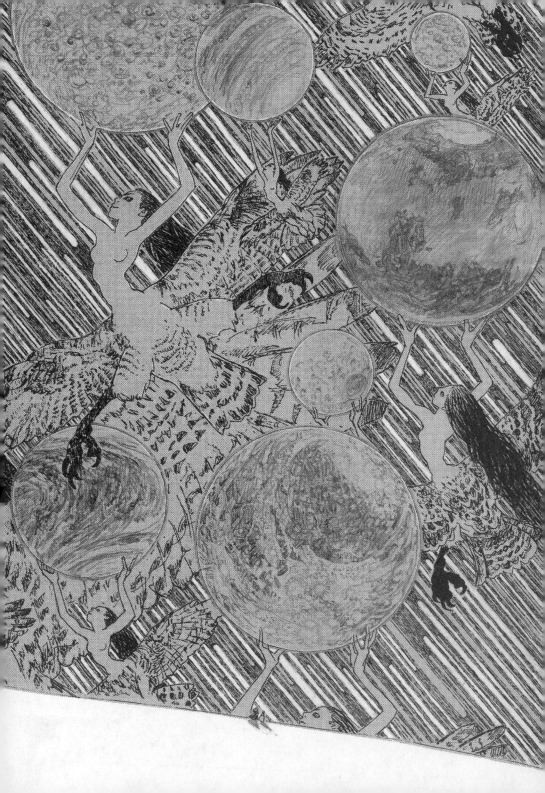

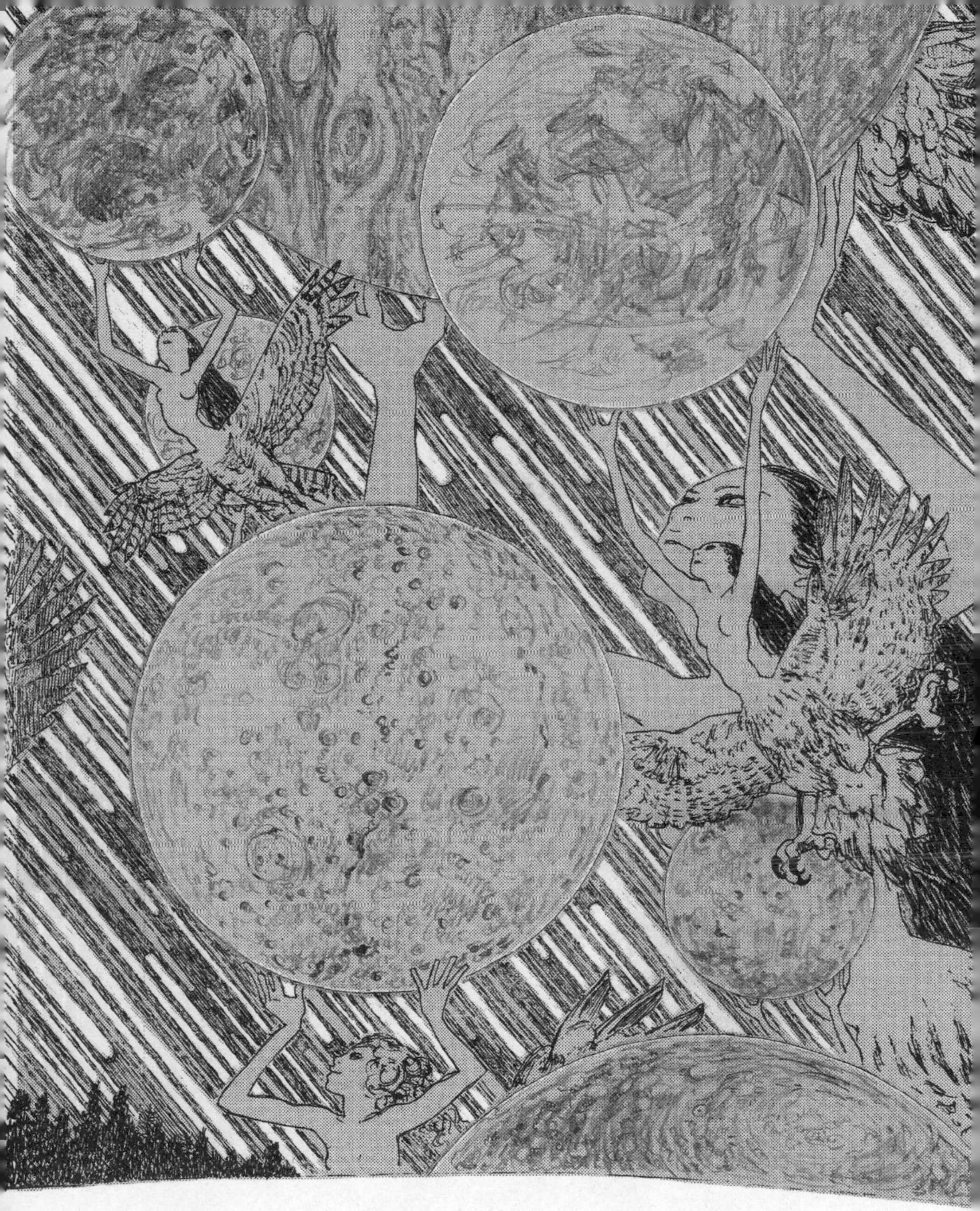

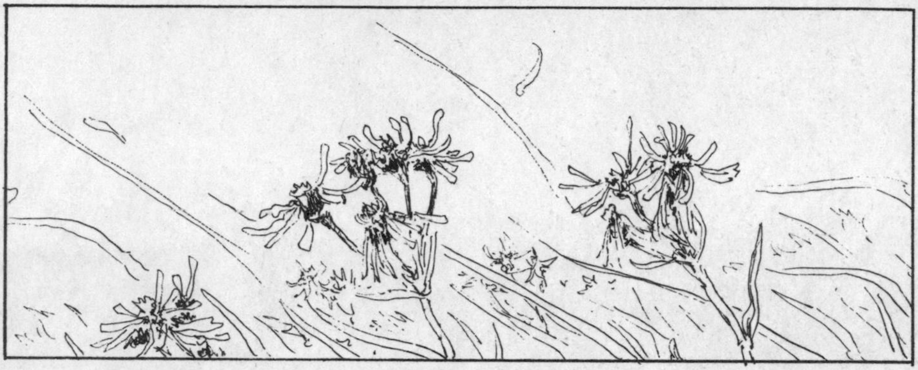

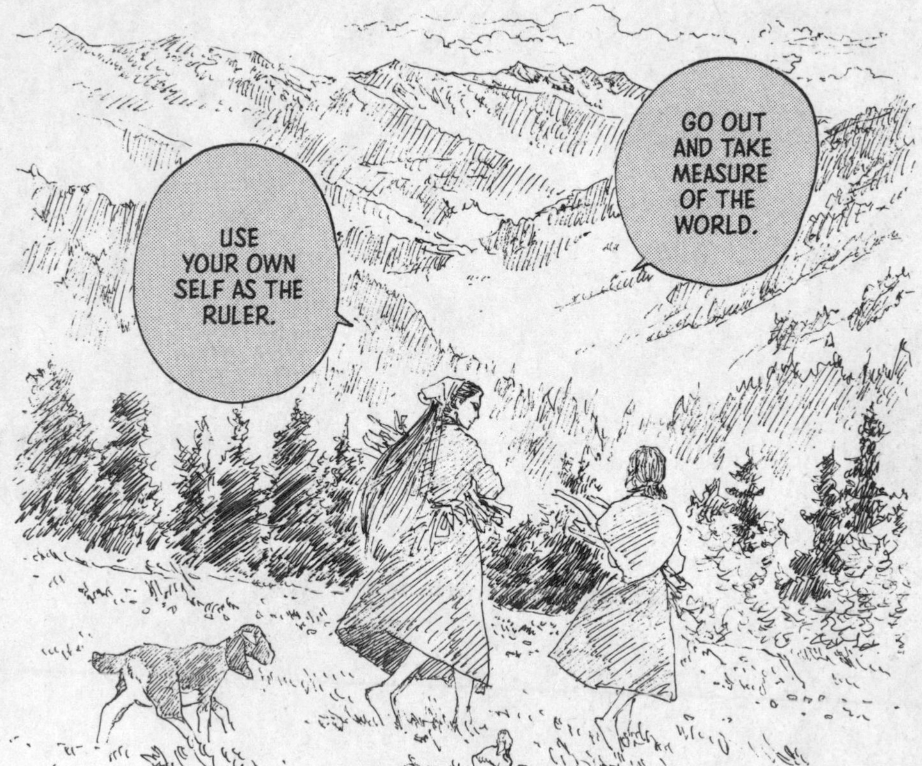
GO OUT AND TAKE MEASURE OF THE WORLD.
USE YOUR OWN SELF AS THE RULER.

Petra Genitalix ~ End

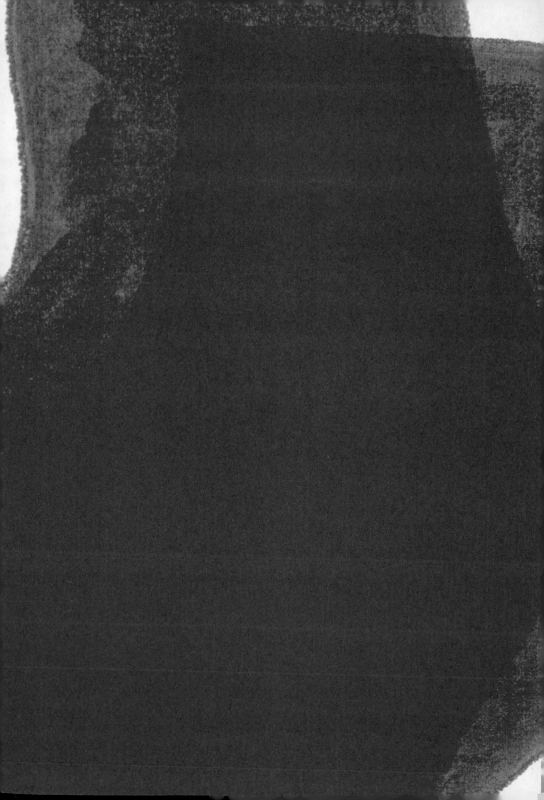

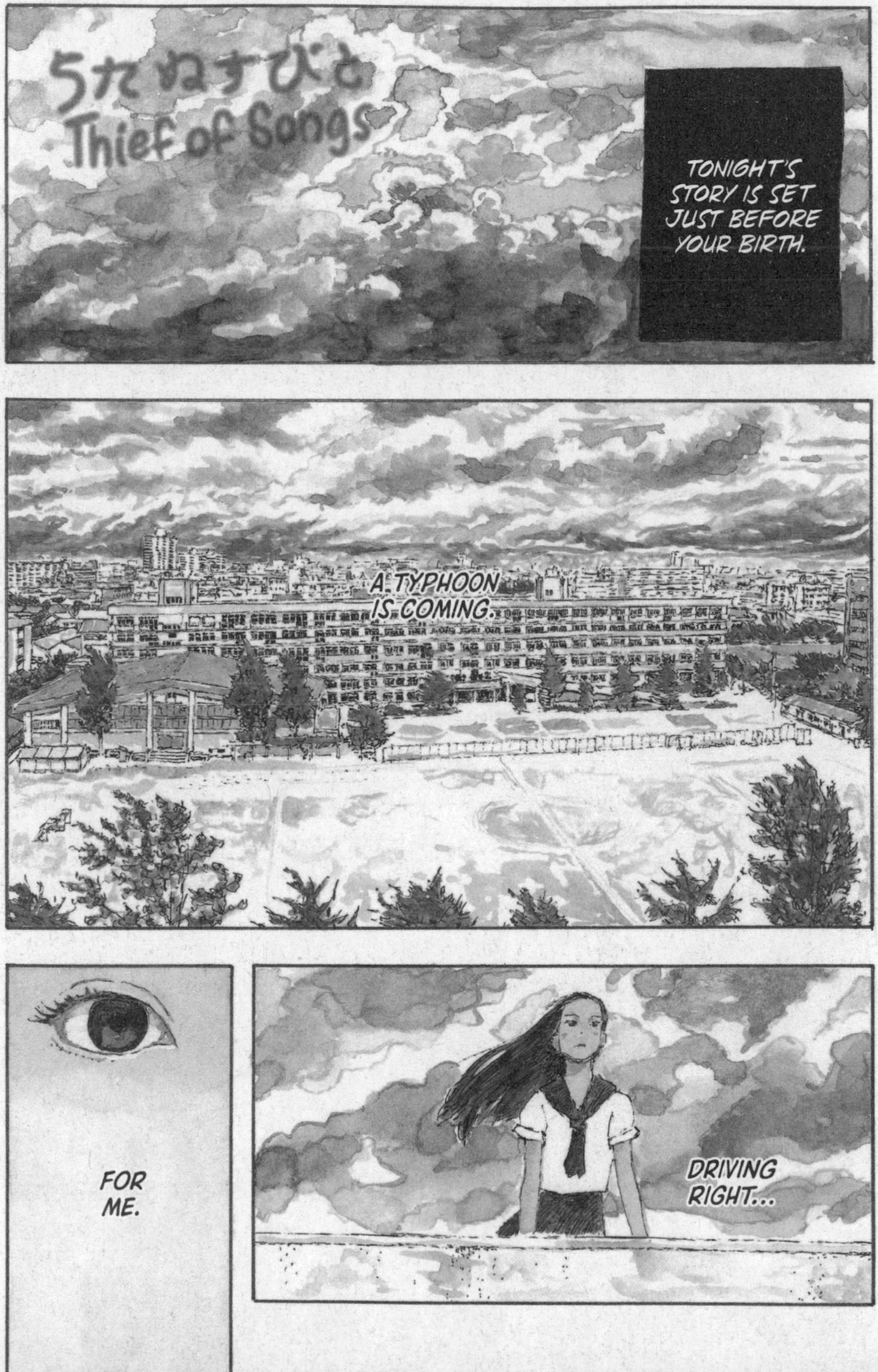

うたぬすびと
Thief of Songs
TONIGHT'S STORY IS SET JUST BEFORE YOUR BIRTH.
A TYPHOON IS COMING.
DRIVING RIGHT...
FOR ME.

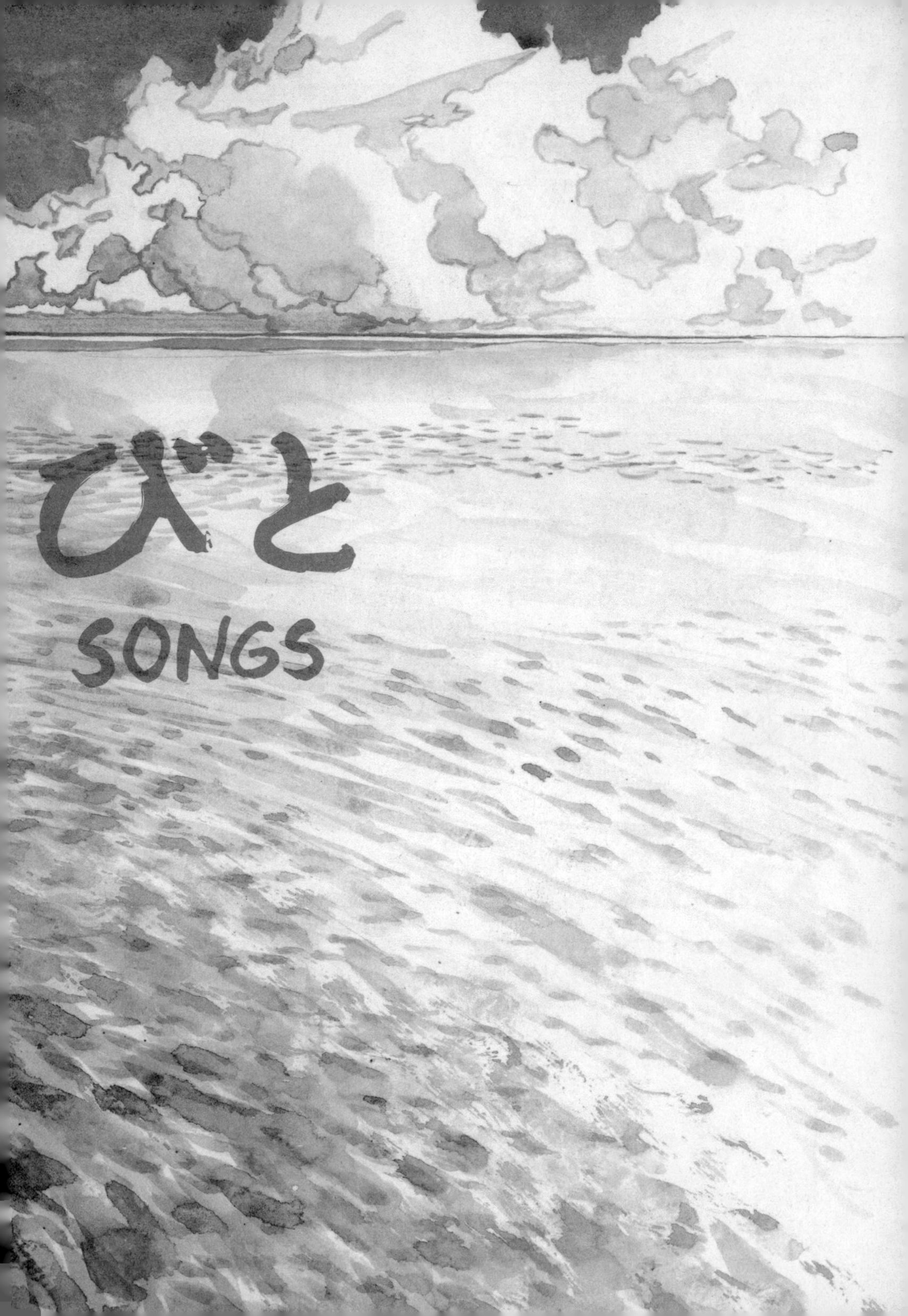
びと
SONGS

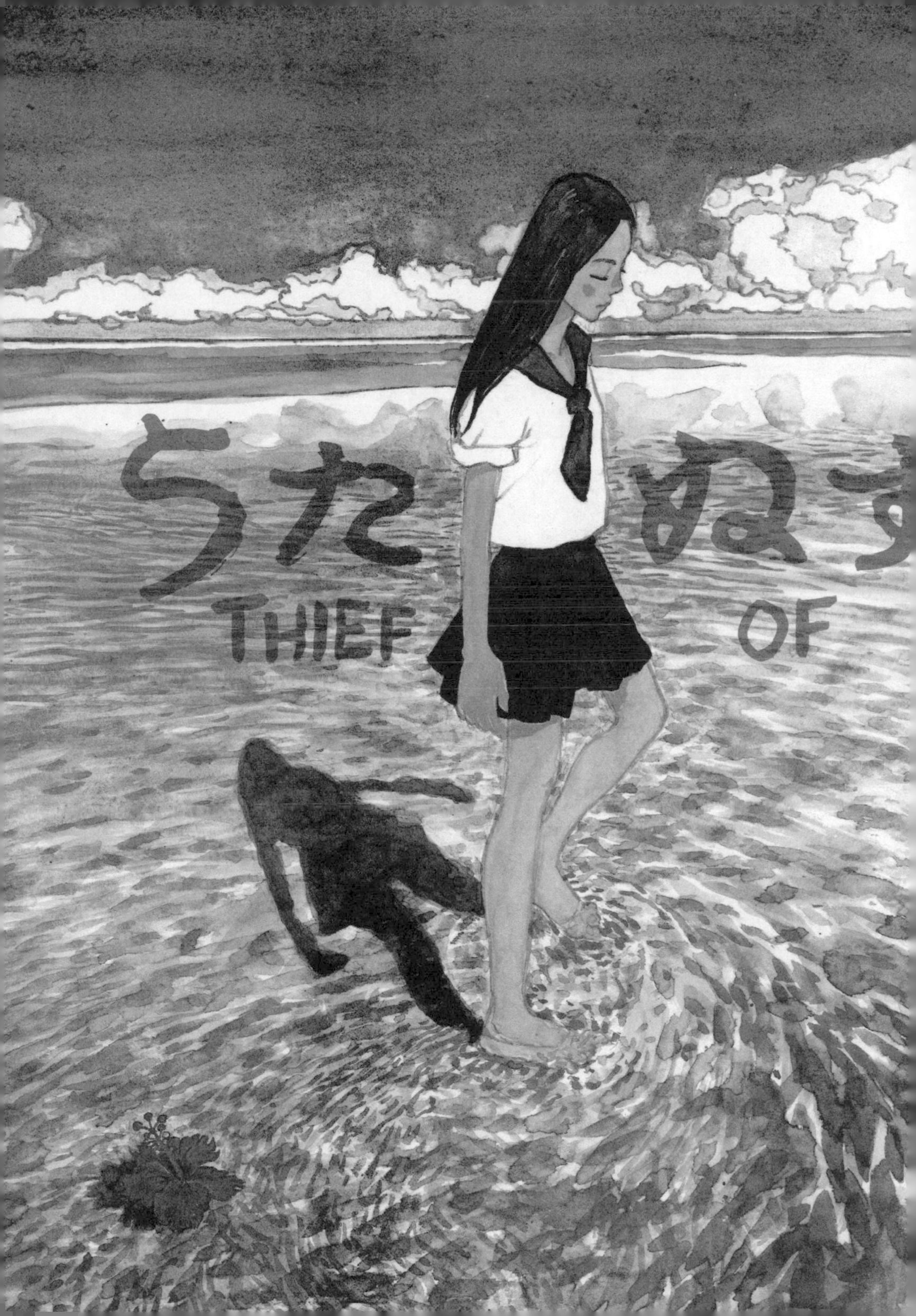
うた
ぬ
THIEF
OF

SKRIIK

PA-
CHK

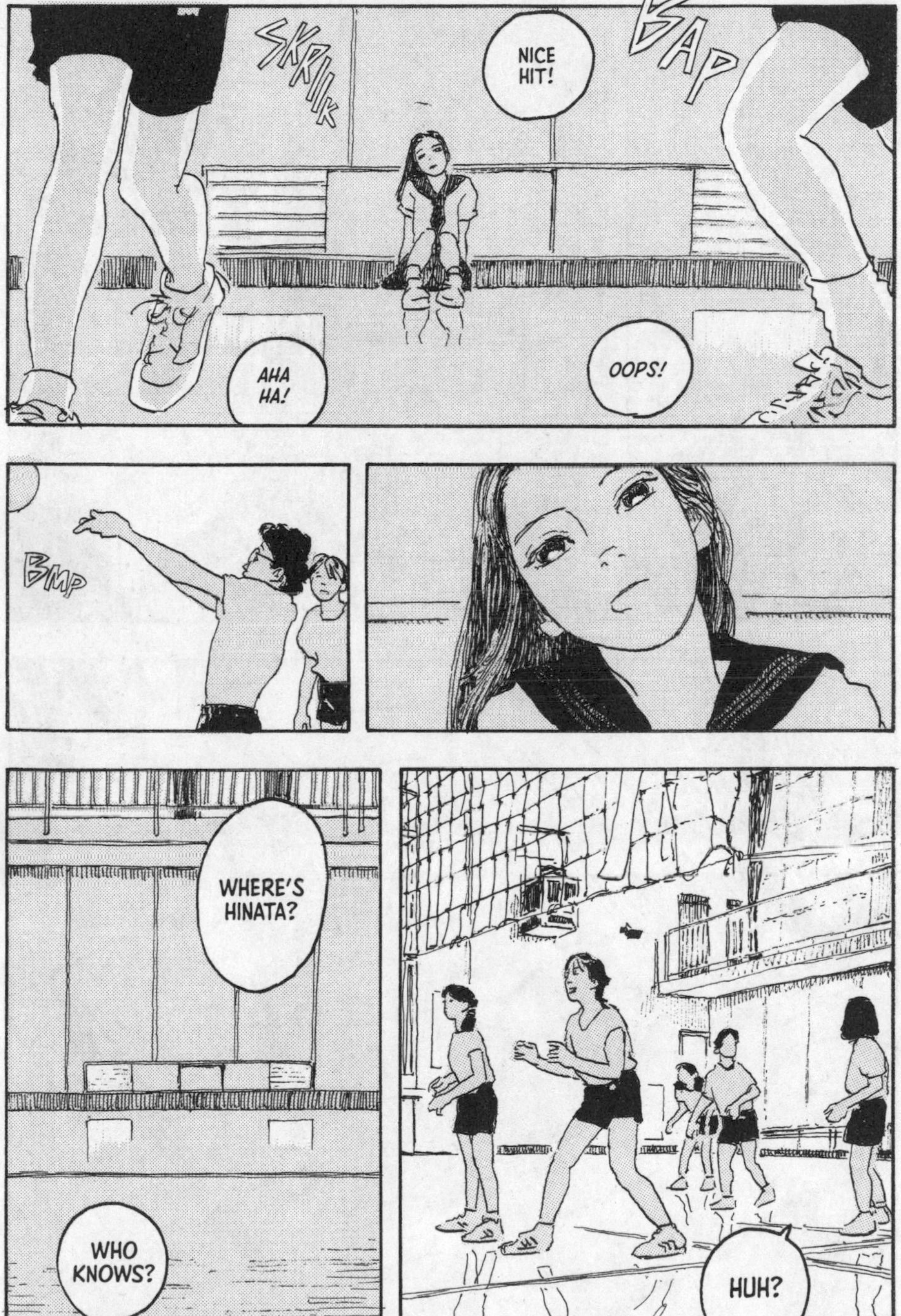
BAP
NICE HIT!
SKRIIK
OOPS!
AHA HA!
BMP
HUH?
WHERE'S HINATA?
WHO KNOWS?

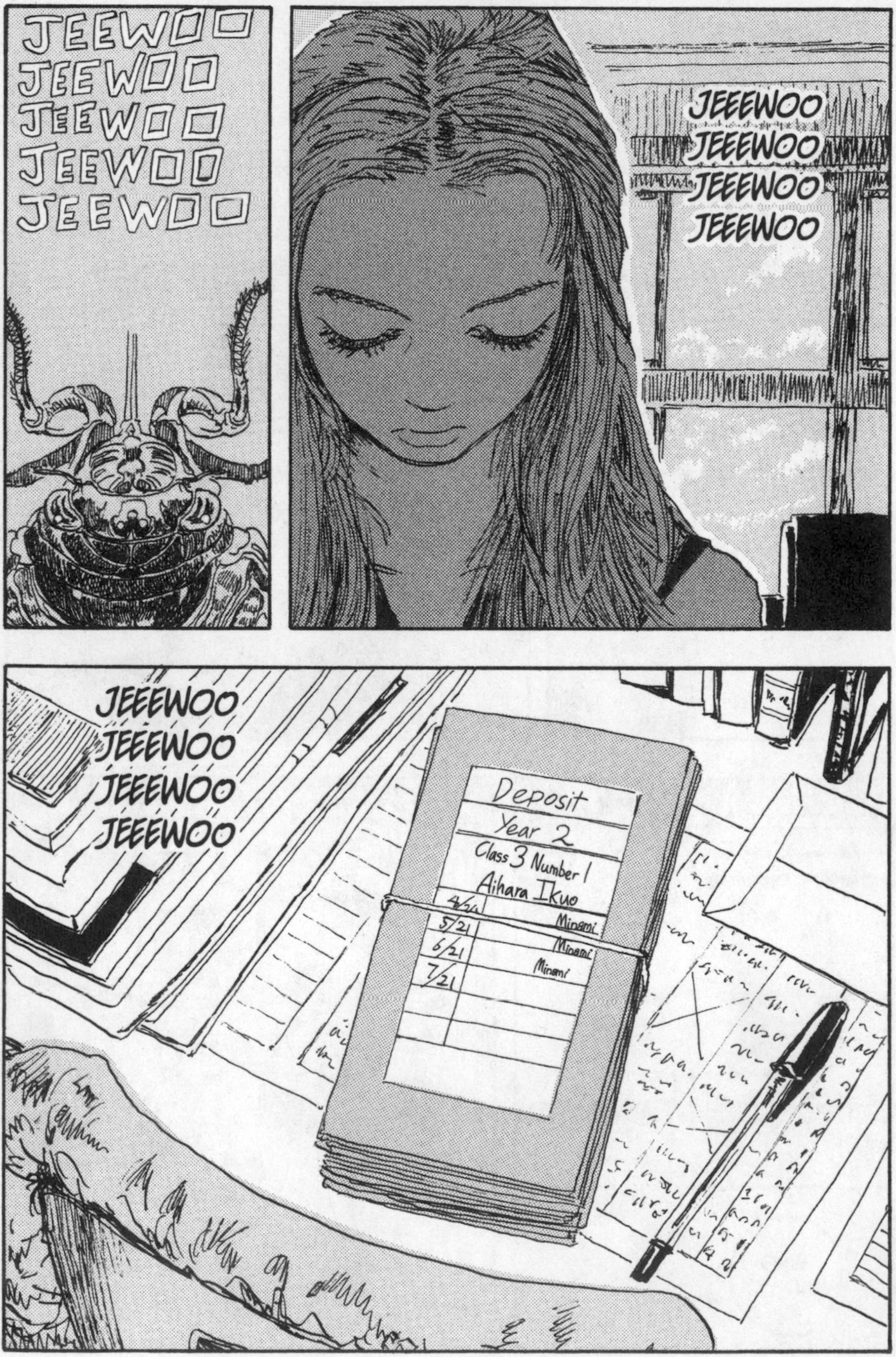
JEEEWOO
JEEEWOO
JEEEWOO
JEEEWOO
JEEWOO
JEEWOO
JEEWOO
JEEWOO
JEEWOO
JEEEWOO
JEEEWOO
JEEEWOO
JEEEWOO
Deposit
Year 2
Class 3 Number 1
Aihara Ikuo
4/21
5/21 Minami
6/21 Minami
Minami
7/21

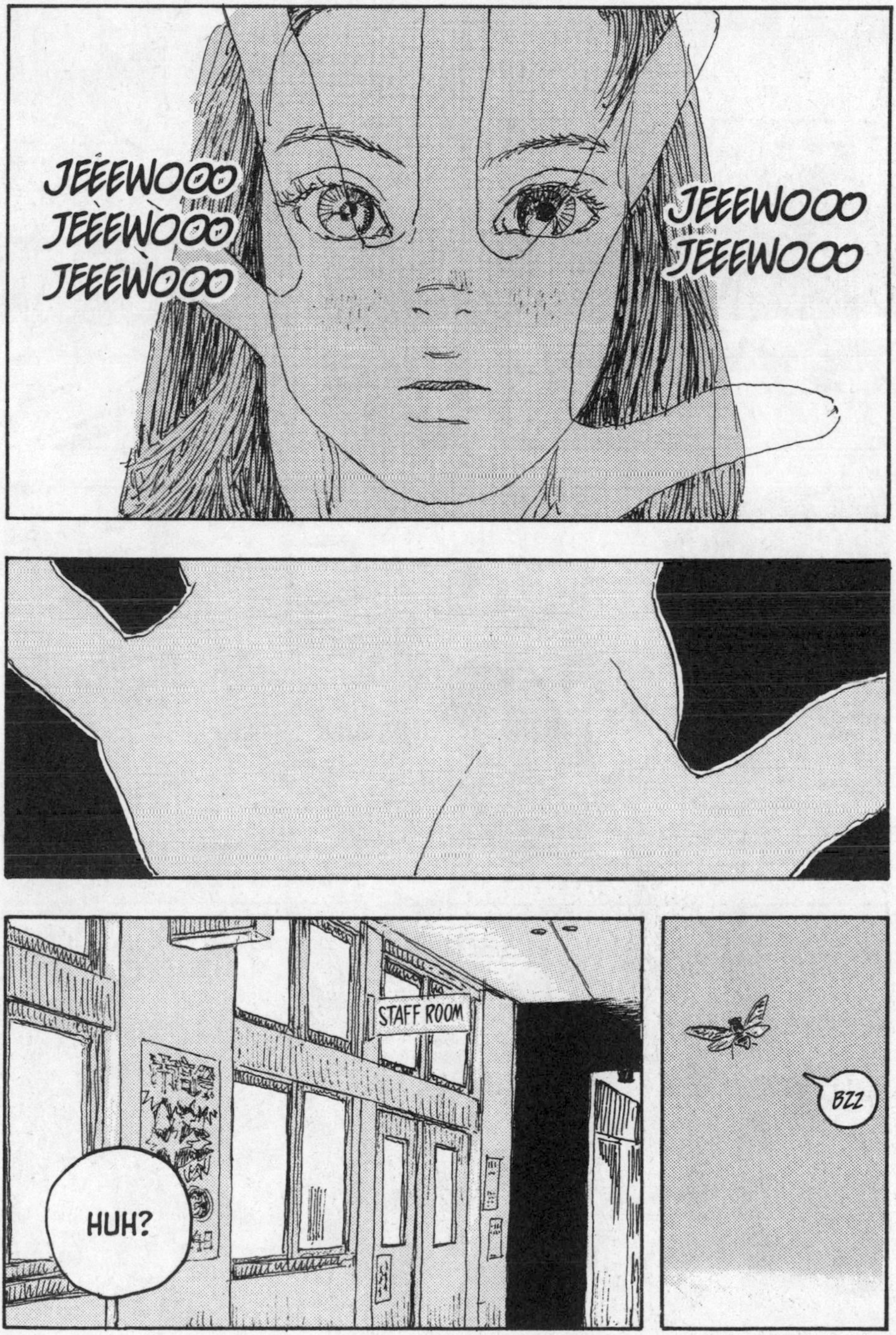
JEEEWOOO
JEEEWOOO
JEEEWOOO
JEEEWOOO
JEEEWOOO
BZZ
STAFF ROOM
HUH?

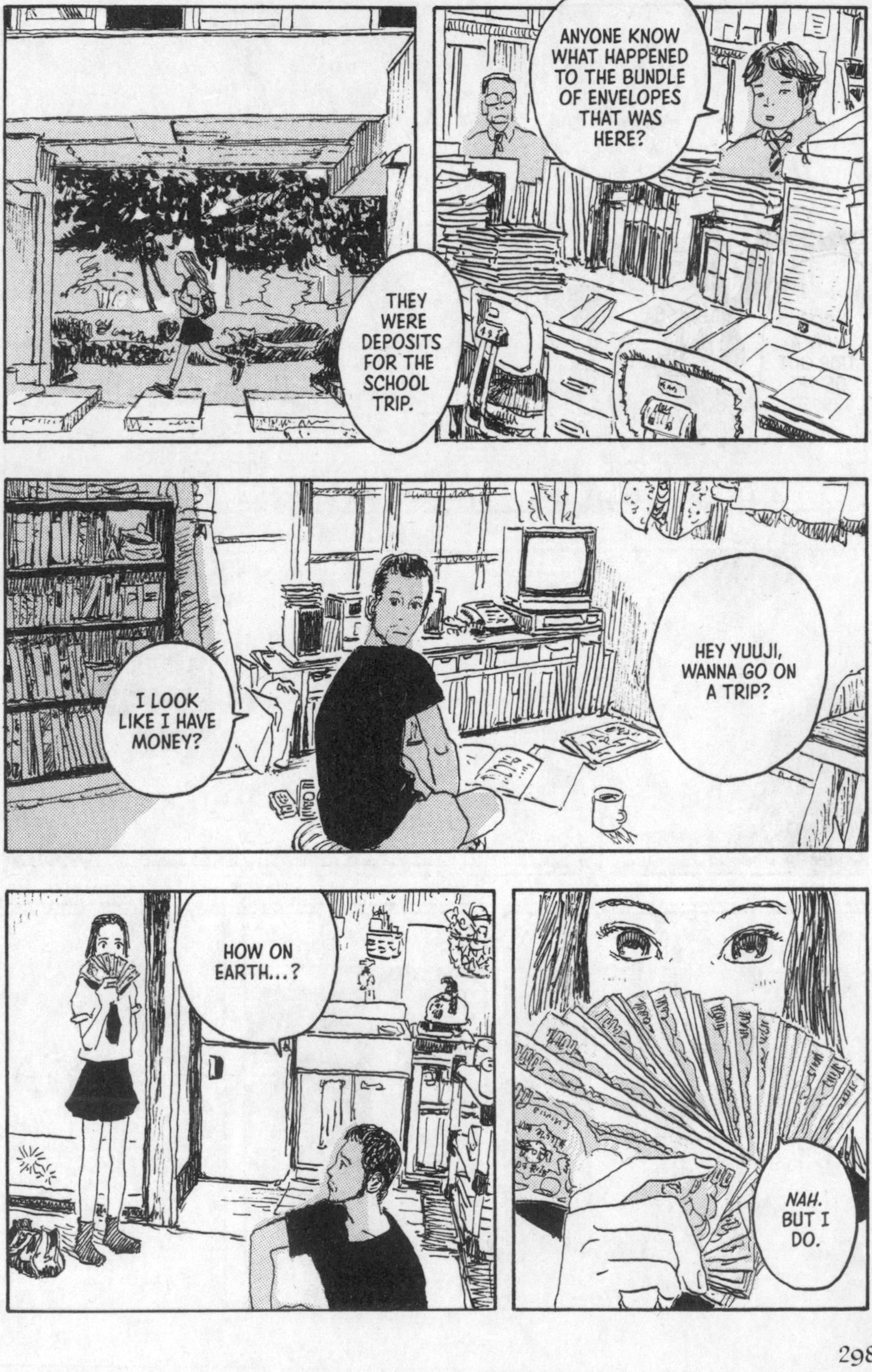
ANYONE KNOW WHAT HAPPENED TO THE BUNDLE OF ENVELOPES THAT WAS HERE?
THEY WERE DEPOSITS FOR THE SCHOOL TRIP.
HEY YUUJI, WANNA GO ON A TRIP?
I LOOK LIKE I HAVE MONEY?
NAH. BUT I DO.
HOW ON EARTH...?

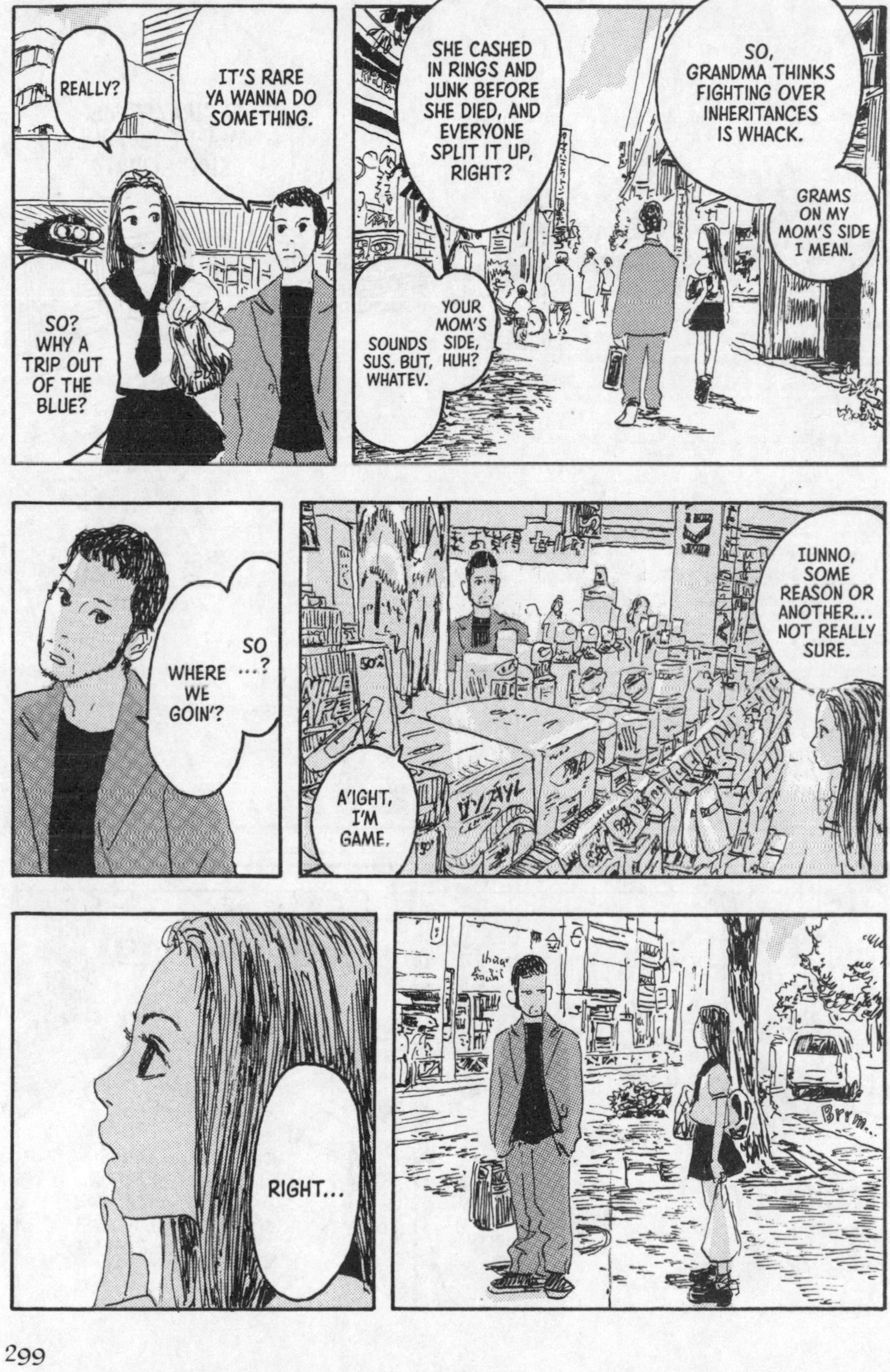
SO, GRANDMA THINKS FIGHTING OVER INHERITANCES IS WHACK.
GRAMS ON MY MOM'S SIDE I MEAN.
SHE CASHED IN RINGS AND JUNK BEFORE SHE DIED, AND EVERYONE SPLIT IT UP, RIGHT?
YOUR MOM'S SIDE, HUH?
SOUNDS SUS. BUT, WHATEV.
IT'S RARE YA WANNA DO SOMETHING.
REALLY?
SO? WHY A TRIP OUT OF THE BLUE?
IUNNO, SOME REASON OR ANOTHER... NOT REALLY SURE.
A'IGHT, I'M GAME.
SO ...?
WHERE WE GOIN'?
Brrm...
RIGHT...

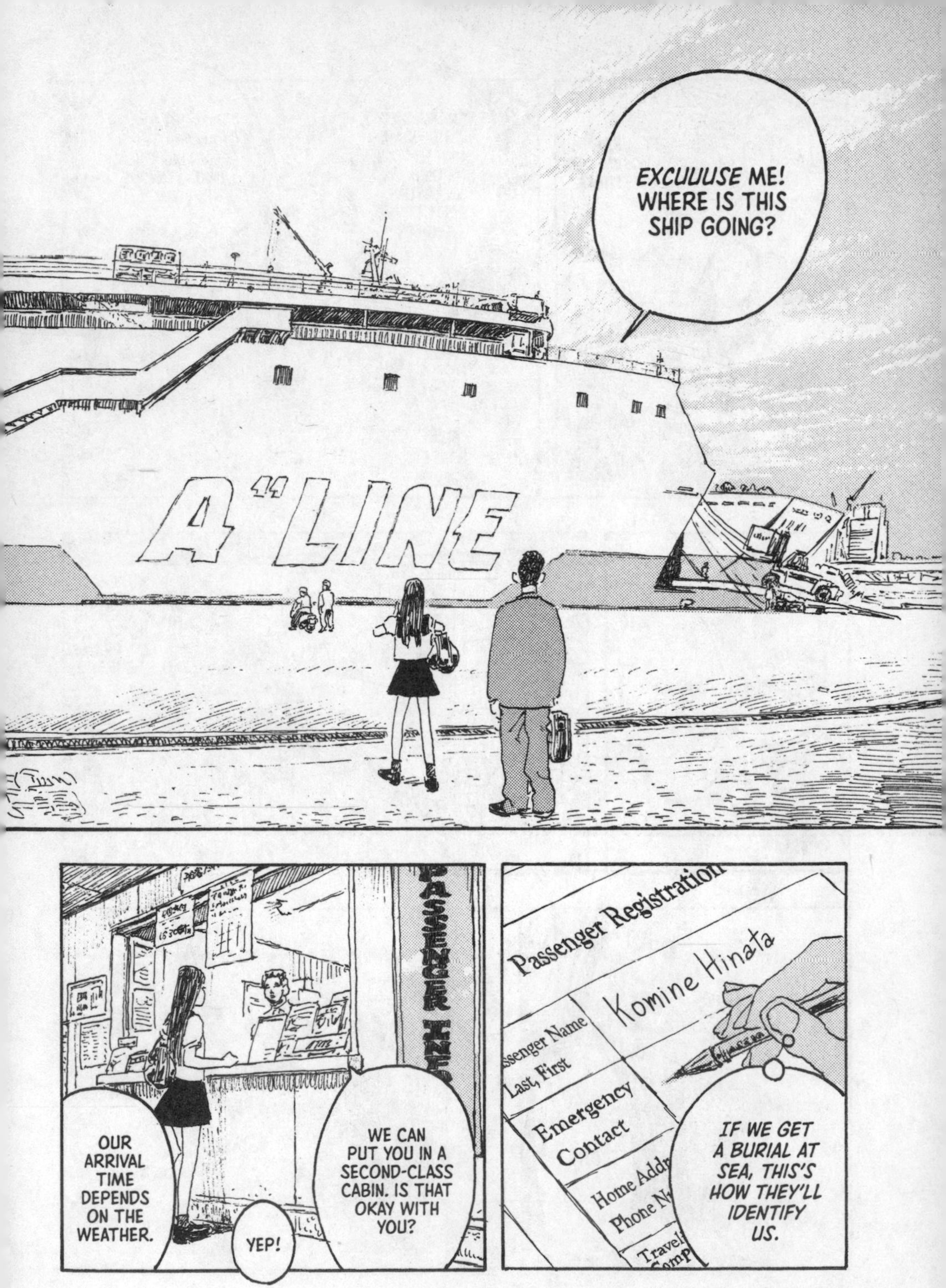
EXCUUUSE ME! WHERE IS THIS SHIP GOING?
A LINE
Passenger Registration
Komine Hinata
assenger Name Last, First
Emergency Contact
Home Addr
Phone N
IF WE GET A BURIAL AT SEA, THIS'S HOW THEY'LL IDENTIFY US.
PASSENGER
WE CAN PUT YOU IN A SECOND-CLASS CABIN. IS THAT OKAY WITH YOU?
YEP!
OUR ARRIVAL TIME DEPENDS ON THE WEATHER.

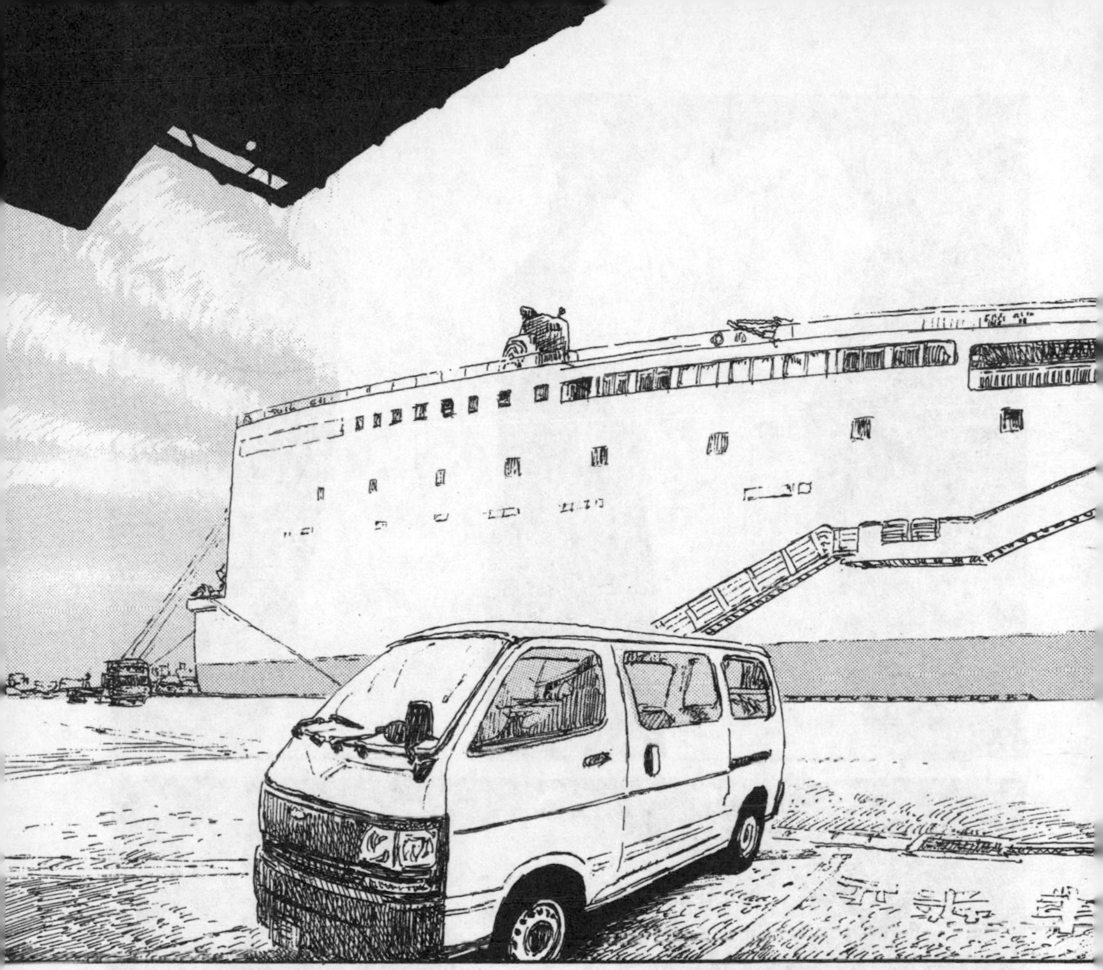

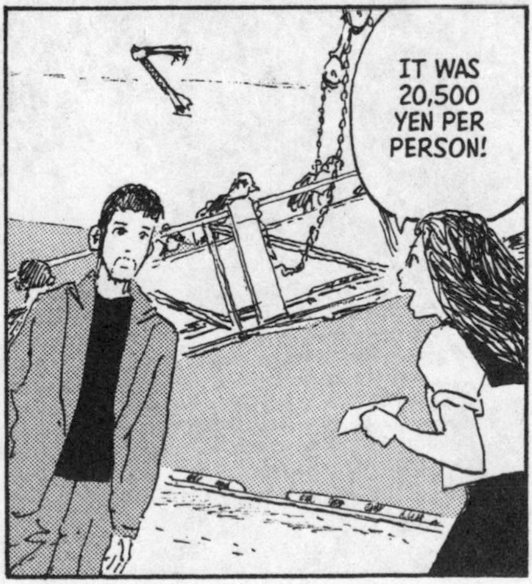
IT WAS 20,500 YEN PER PERSON!

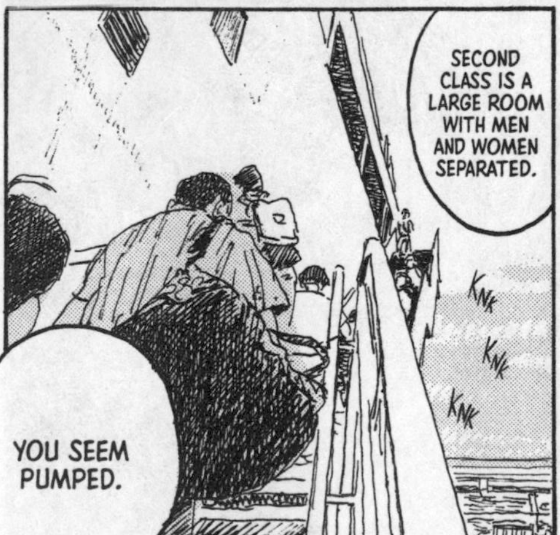
SECOND CLASS IS A LARGE ROOM WITH MEN AND WOMEN SEPARATED.
KNK
KNK
KNK
YOU SEEM PUMPED.

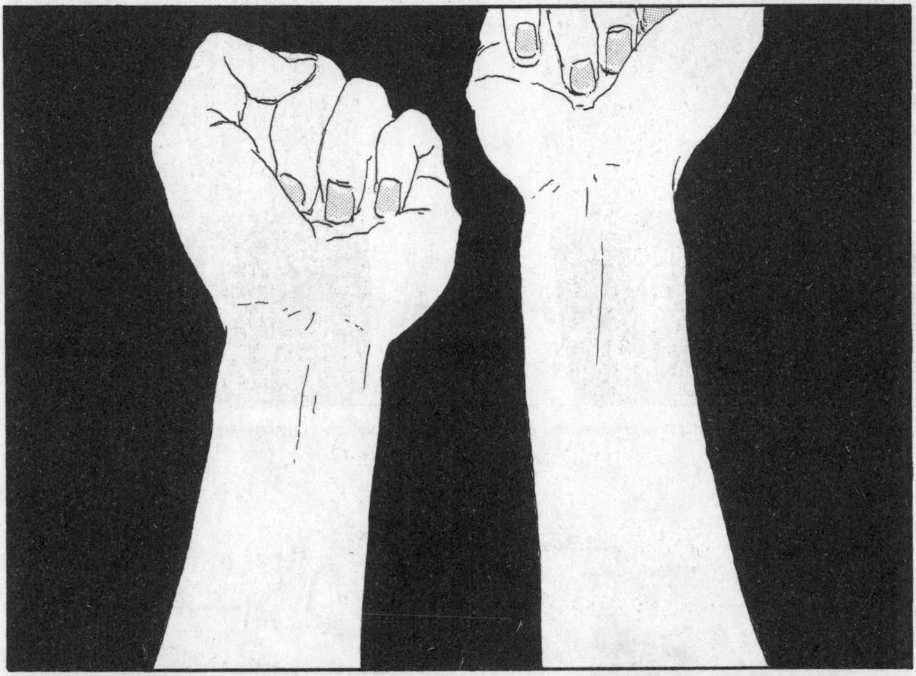

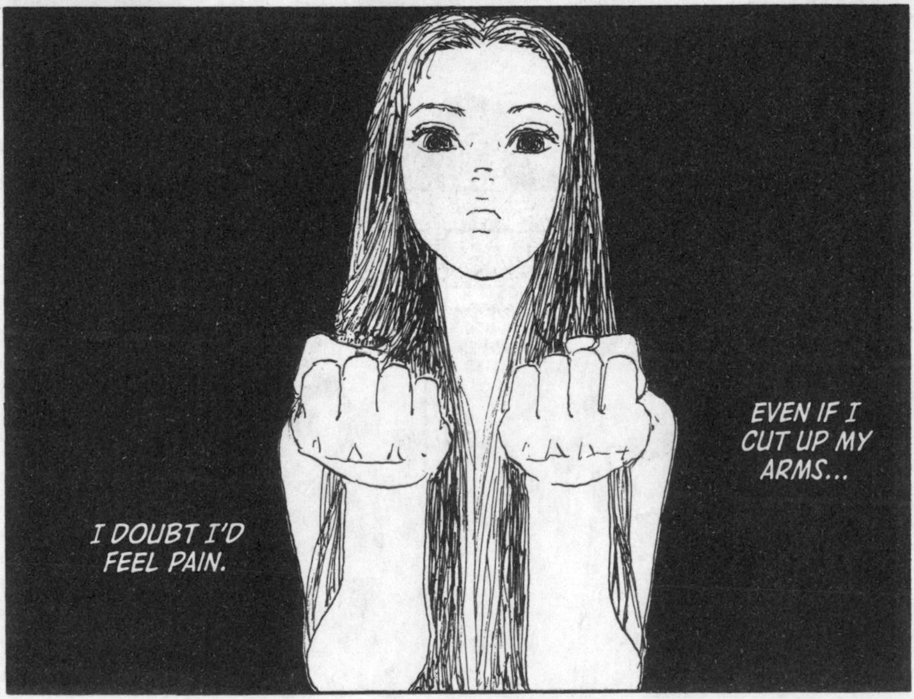
EVEN IF I CUT UP MY ARMS...
I DOUBT I'D FEEL PAIN.

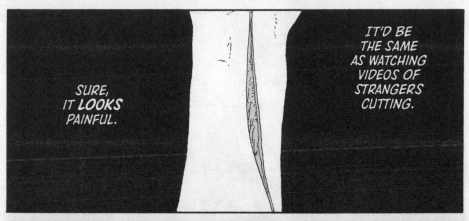

IT'D BE THE SAME AS WATCHING VIDEOS OF STRANGERS CUTTING.
SURE, IT **LOOKS** PAINFUL.
BUT I'M REALLY IN A ROOM SOMEWHERE FAR AWAY...
WATCHING A VIDEO CALLED "MY DAILY LIFE."
JUST WATCHING.

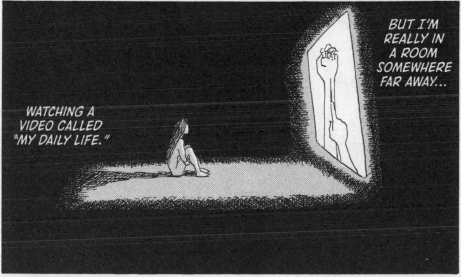

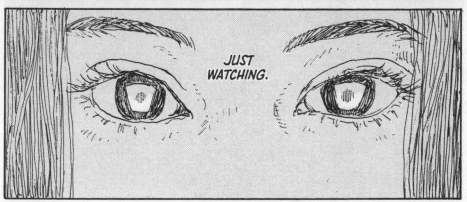

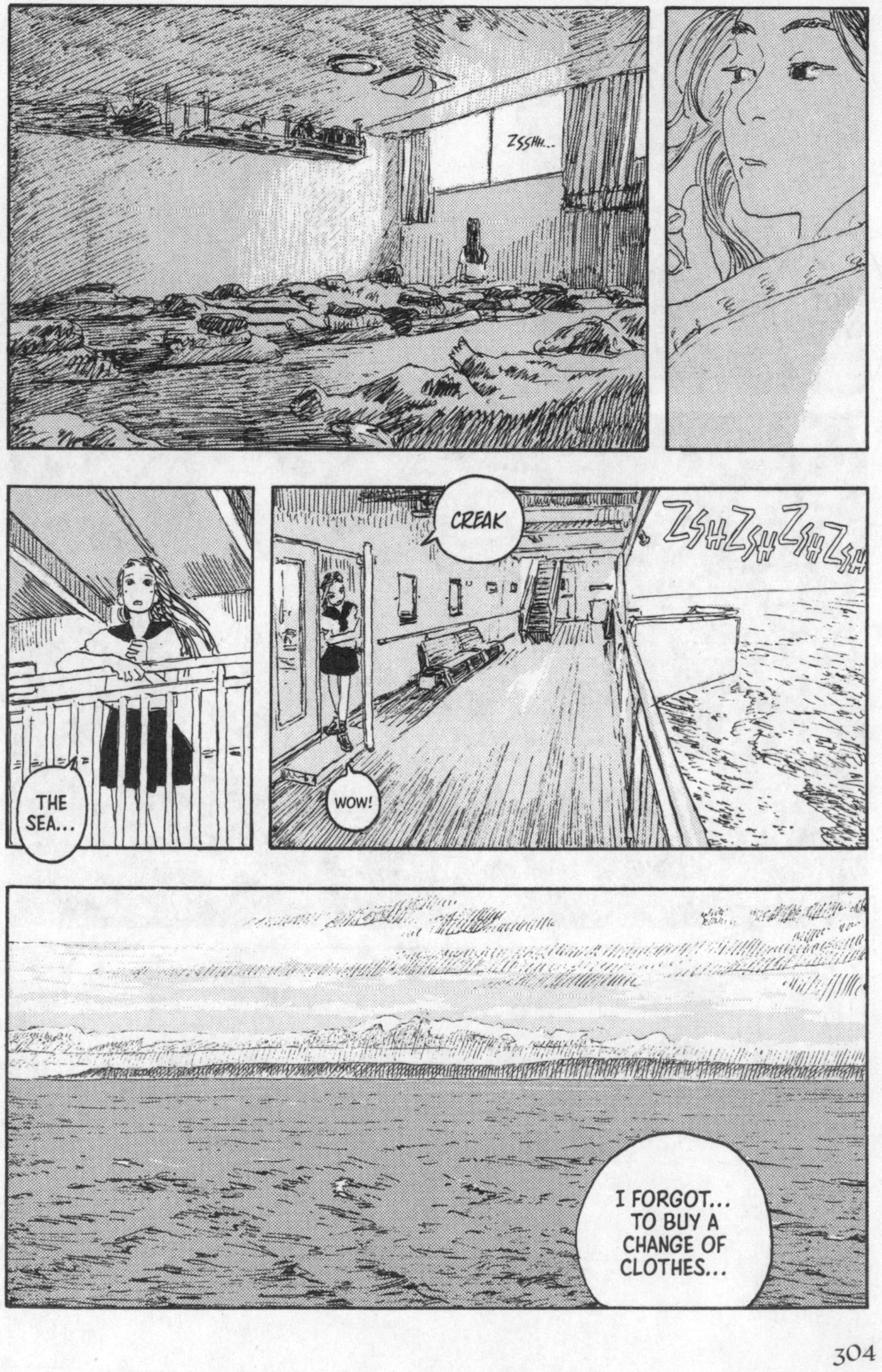
ZSSHH...
CREAK
ZSHZSHZSHZSH
WOW!
THE SEA...
I FORGOT... TO BUY A CHANGE OF CLOTHES...

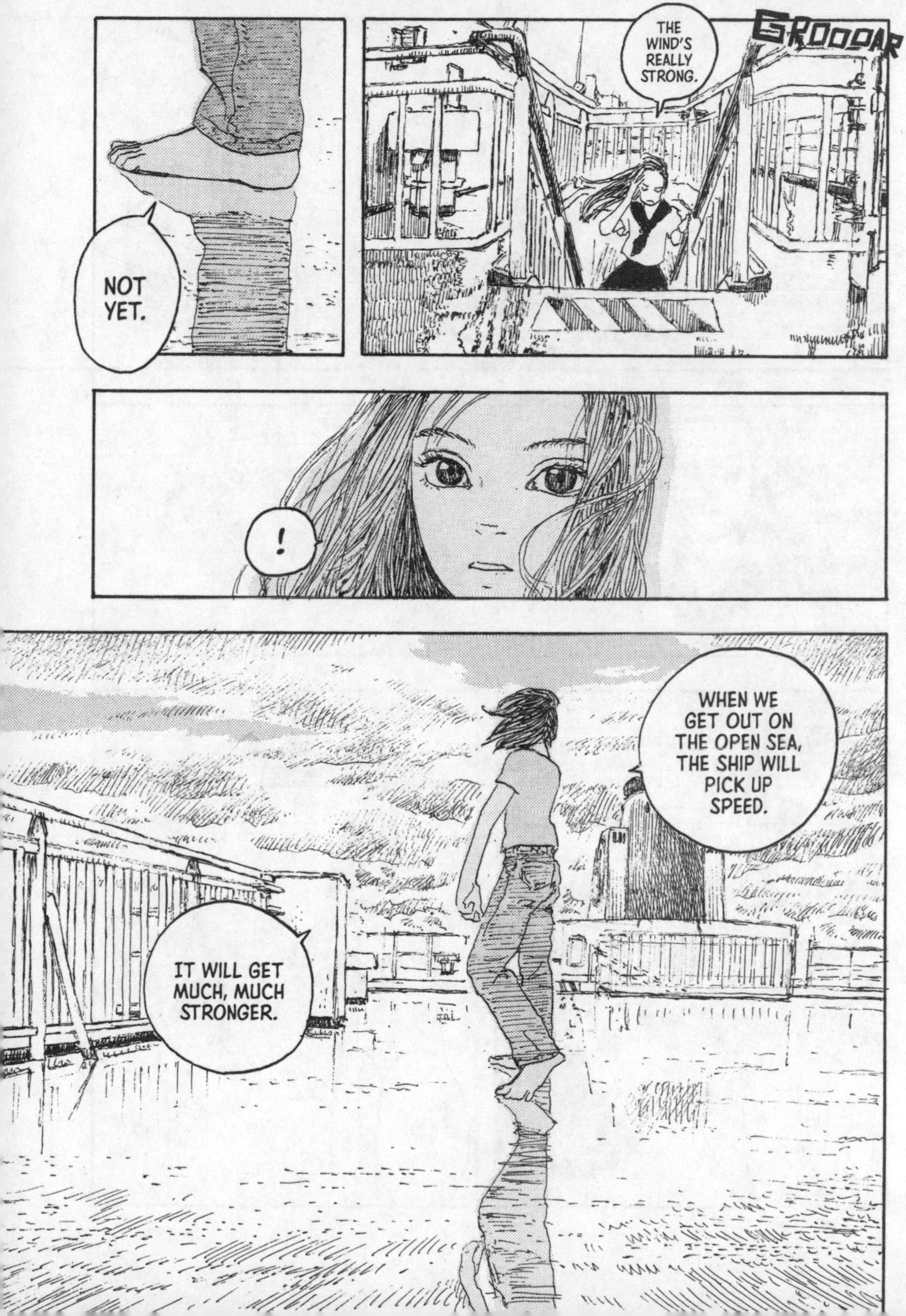
GROOOAR
THE WIND'S REALLY STRONG.
NOT YET.
!
WHEN WE GET OUT ON THE OPEN SEA, THE SHIP WILL PICK UP SPEED.
IT WILL GET MUCH, MUCH STRONGER.

THE WIND...

I MEAN.

HER PUPILS...

AMAZING.

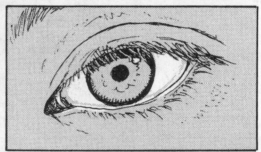

HUH?

I'M CHITARU.

AREN'T AWAKE, YOU KNOW.

YOU...

306

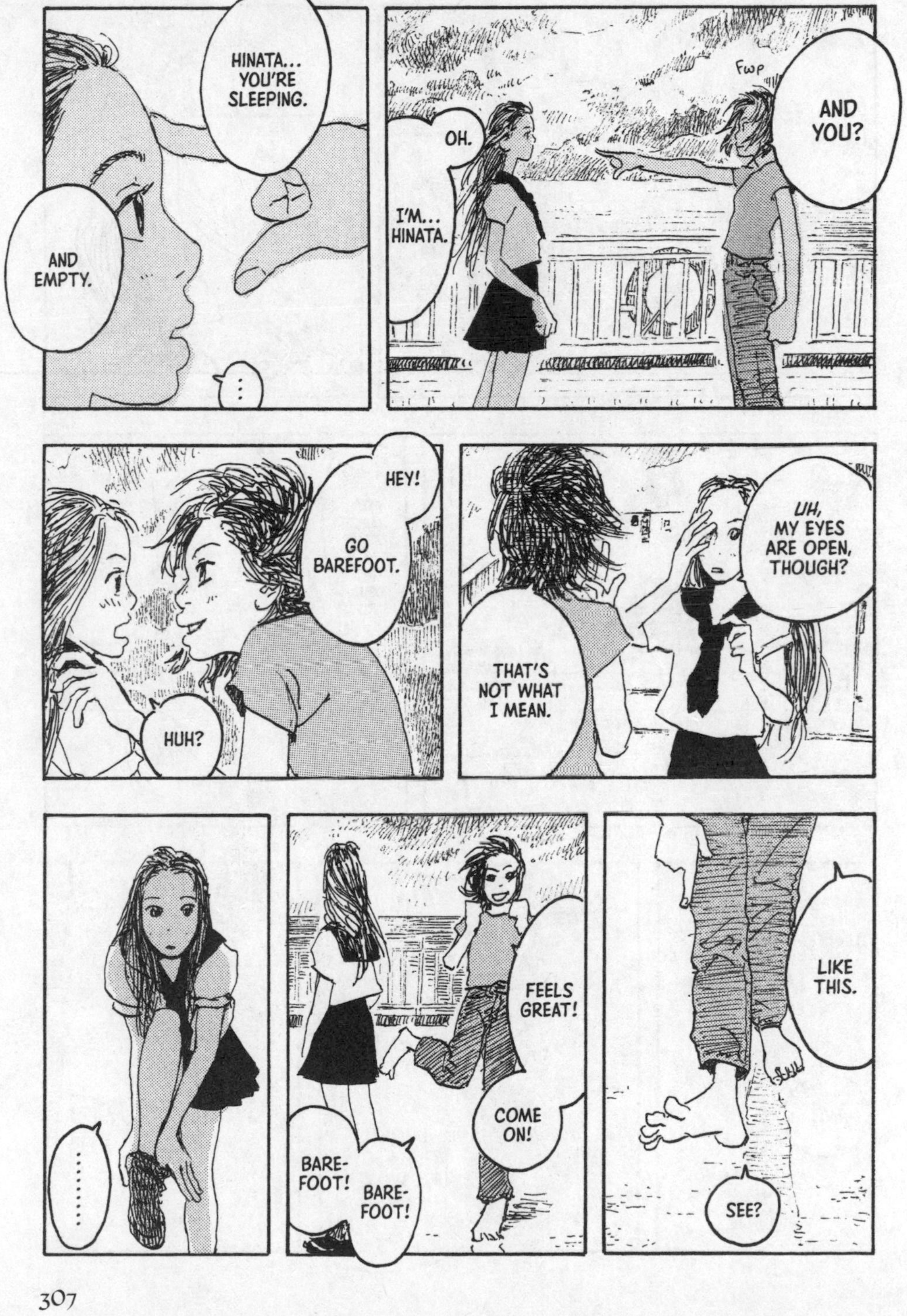

Fwp
AND YOU?
OH.
I'M... HINATA.
HINATA... YOU'RE SLEEPING.
AND EMPTY.
...
UH, MY EYES ARE OPEN, THOUGH?
THAT'S NOT WHAT I MEAN.
HEY!
GO BAREFOOT.
HUH?
LIKE THIS.
SEE?
FEELS GREAT!
COME ON!
BARE-FOOT!
BARE-FOOT!
......

WOW...
AND COLD...
AND WET.
IT'S ROUGH...
C'MON!
WALK, WALK!
IT HURTS. THE ROUGHNESS BITES INTO MY FEET.
IT'S HARD TO SLIP EVEN IF IT GETS WET.
I SEE...
THE WIND... IS WHIPPING AGAINST MY LEGS...
THIS FEELS... GREAT...
RIGHT?
LOOK! YOUR LEGS HAVE WOKEN UP.
AH...

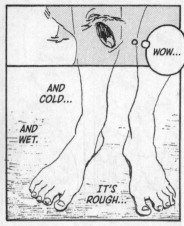

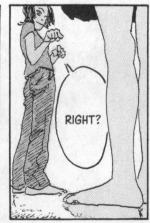

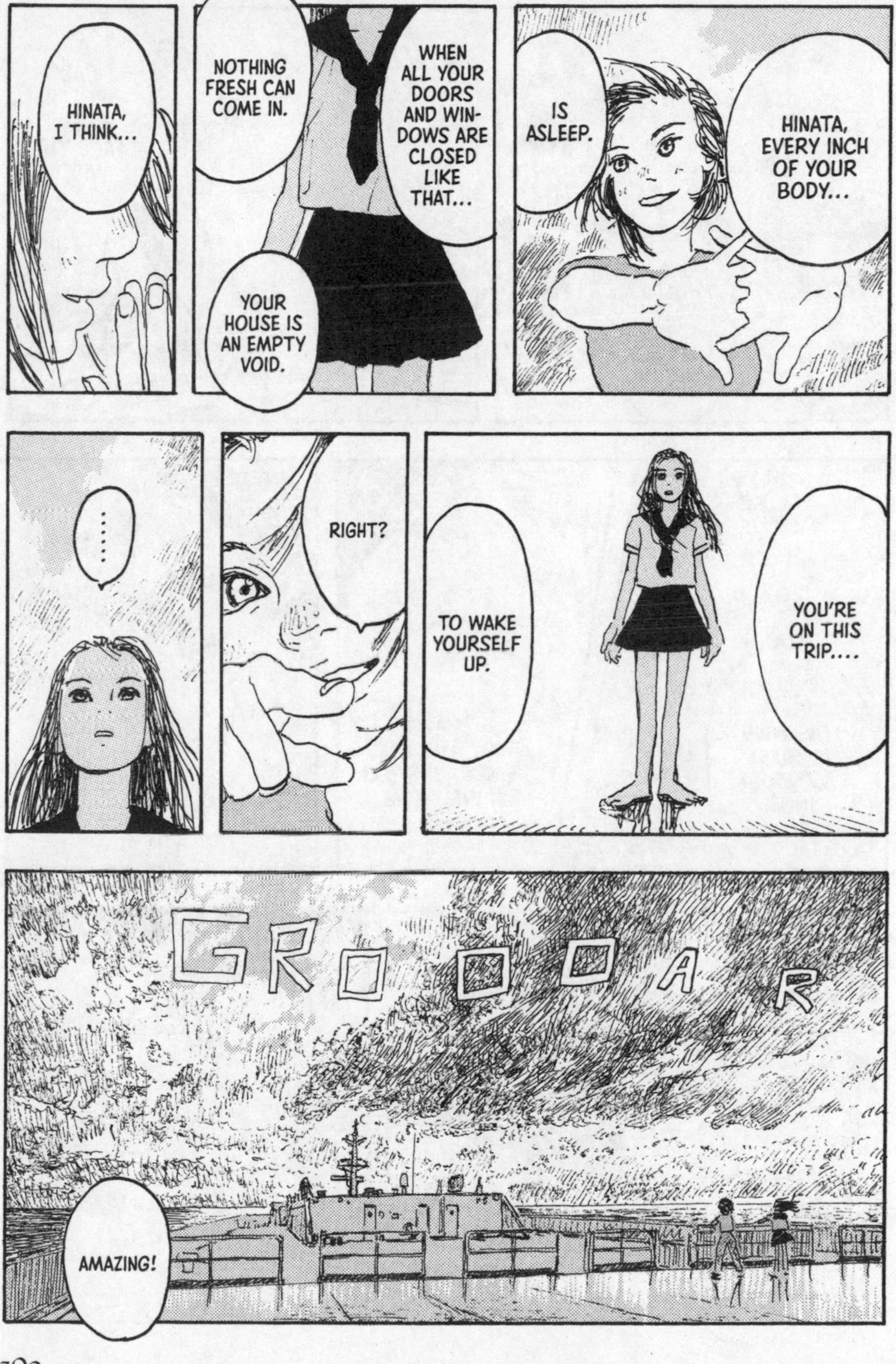
HINATA, EVERY INCH OF YOUR BODY...
IS ASLEEP.
WHEN ALL YOUR DOORS AND WINDOWS ARE CLOSED LIKE THAT...
NOTHING FRESH CAN COME IN.
YOUR HOUSE IS AN EMPTY VOID.
HINATA, I THINK...
YOU'RE ON THIS TRIP....
TO WAKE YOURSELF UP.
RIGHT?
......
GROOOOAR
AMAZING!

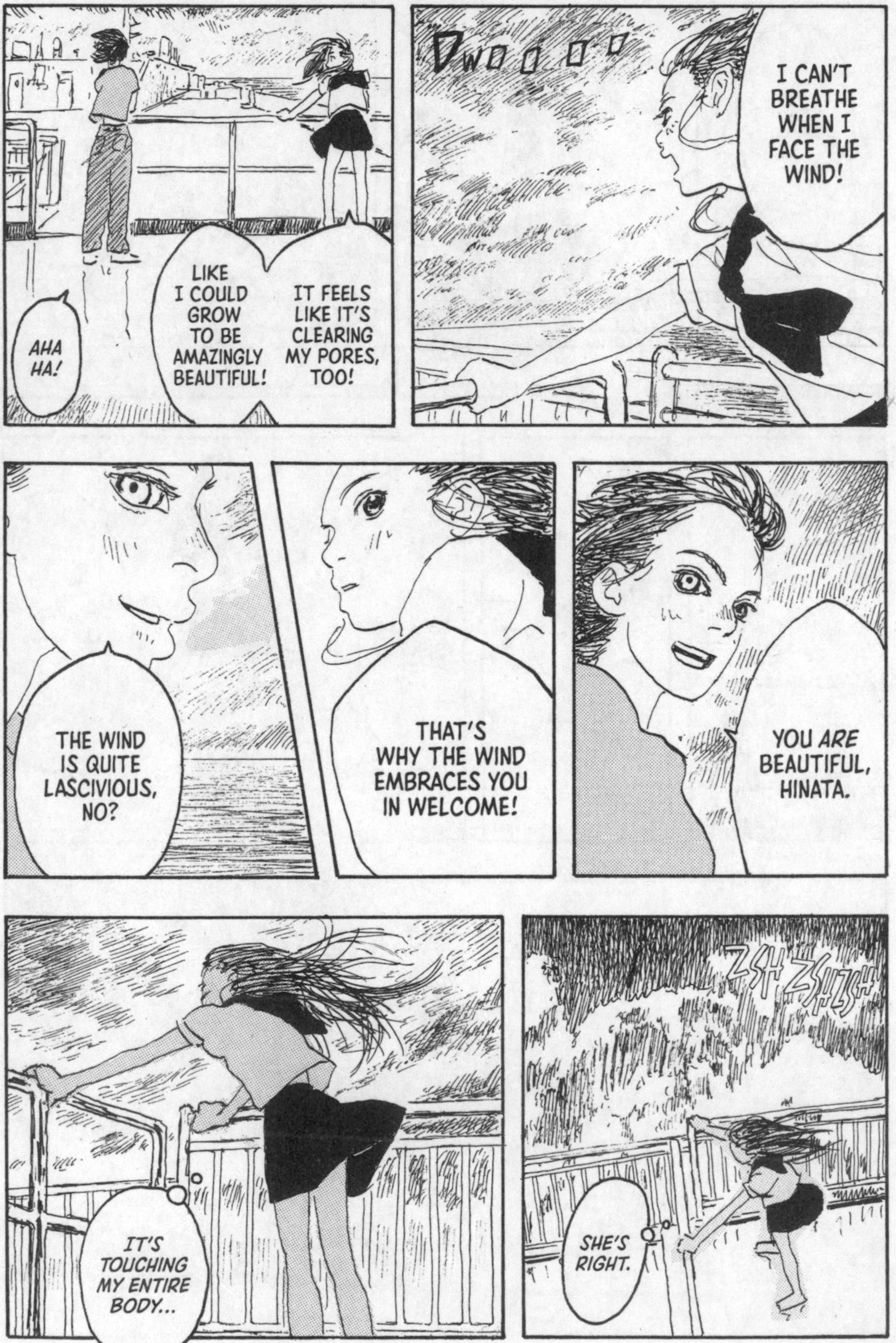
DWOOOOO
I CAN'T BREATHE WHEN I FACE THE WIND!
IT FEELS LIKE IT'S CLEARING MY PORES, TOO!
LIKE I COULD GROW TO BE AMAZINGLY BEAUTIFUL!
AHA HA!
YOU *ARE* BEAUTIFUL, HINATA.
THAT'S WHY THE WIND EMBRACES YOU IN WELCOME!
THE WIND IS QUITE LASCIVIOUS, NO?
ZSH ZSHZSH
SHE'S RIGHT.
IT'S TOUCHING MY ENTIRE BODY...

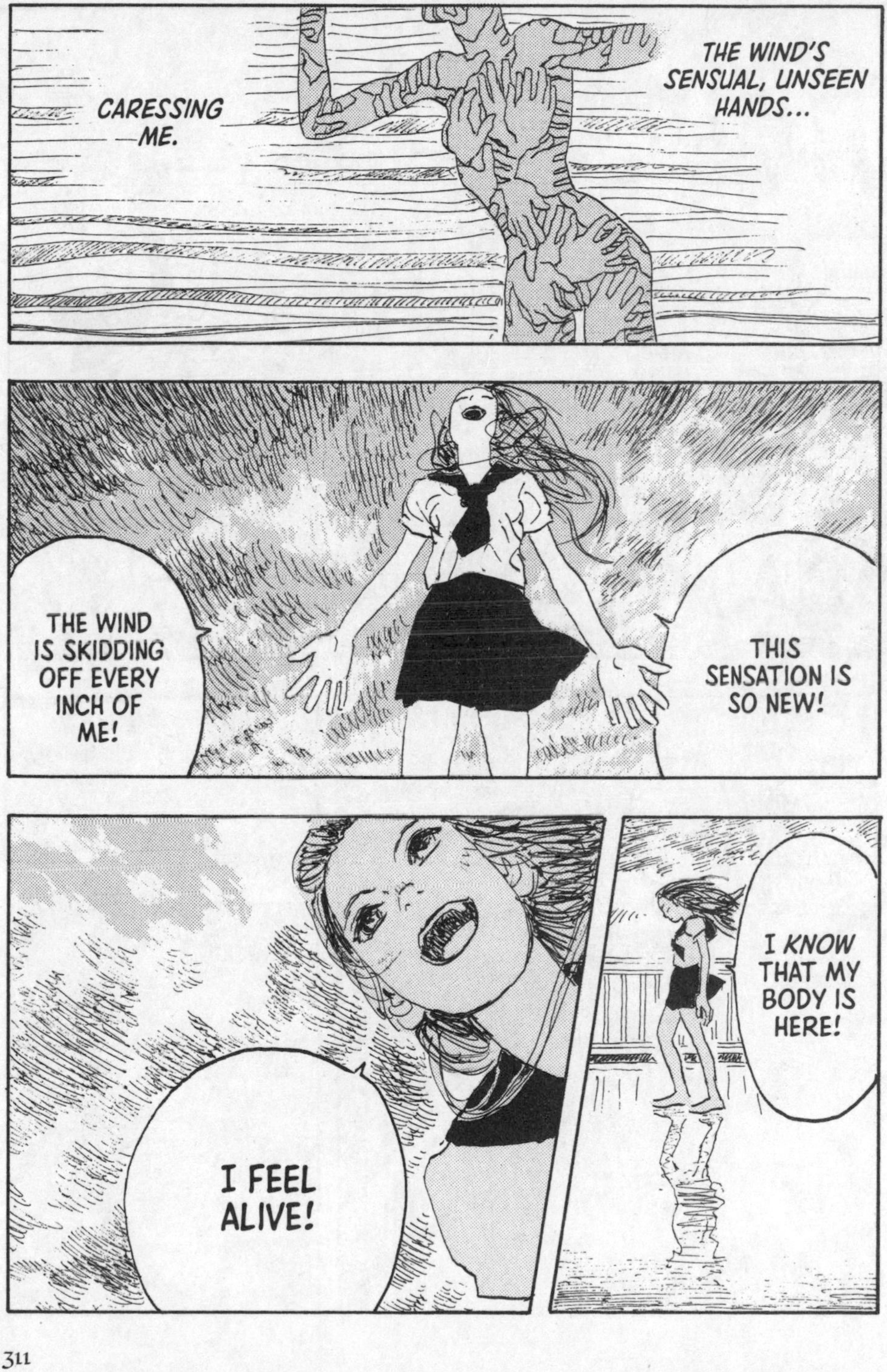
THE WIND'S SENSUAL, UNSEEN HANDS...
CARESSING ME.
THIS SENSATION IS SO NEW!
THE WIND IS SKIDDING OFF EVERY INCH OF ME!
I *KNOW* THAT MY BODY IS HERE!
I FEEL ALIVE!

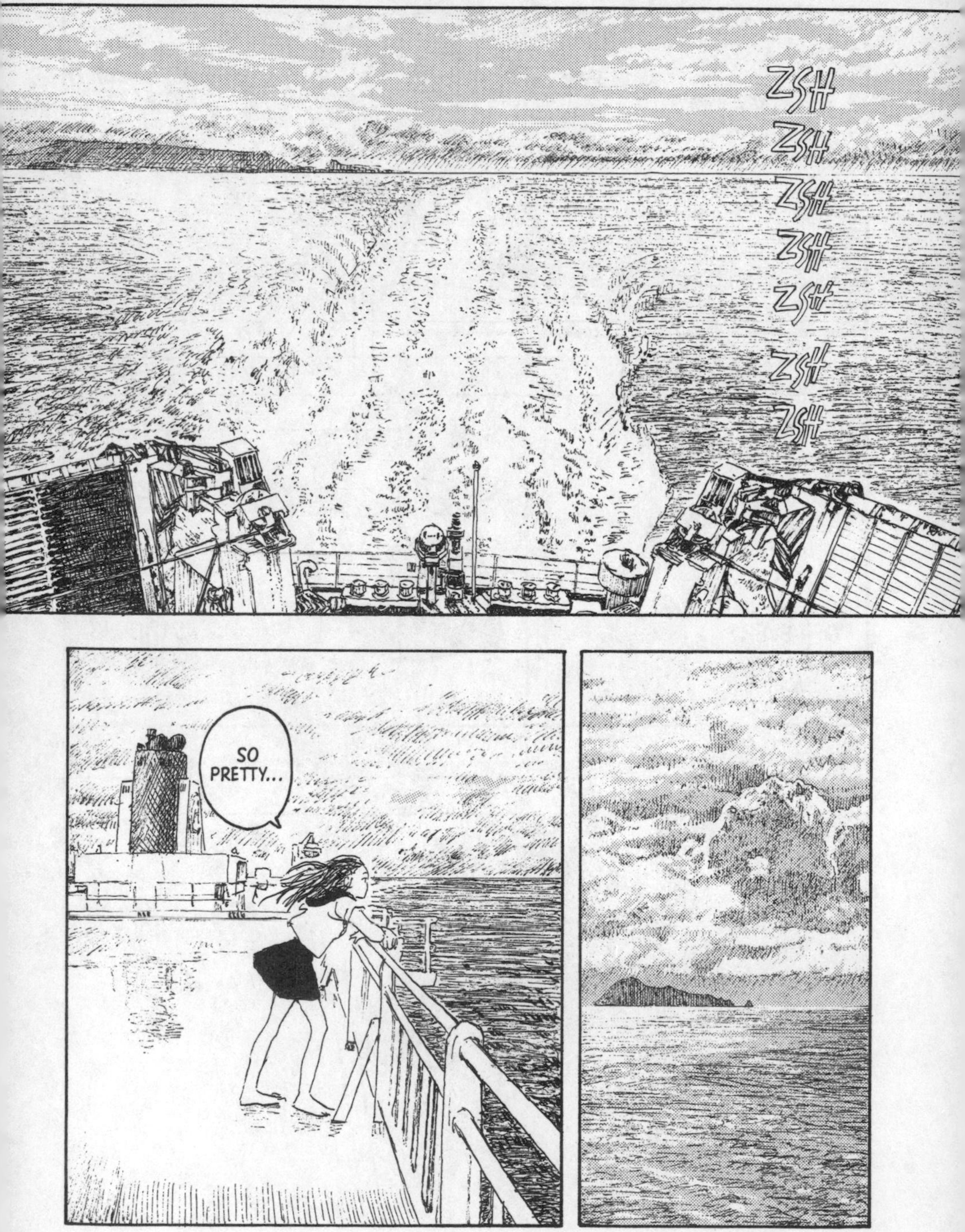
ZSH
ZSH
ZSH
ZSH
ZSH
ZSH
ZSH
SO PRETTY...

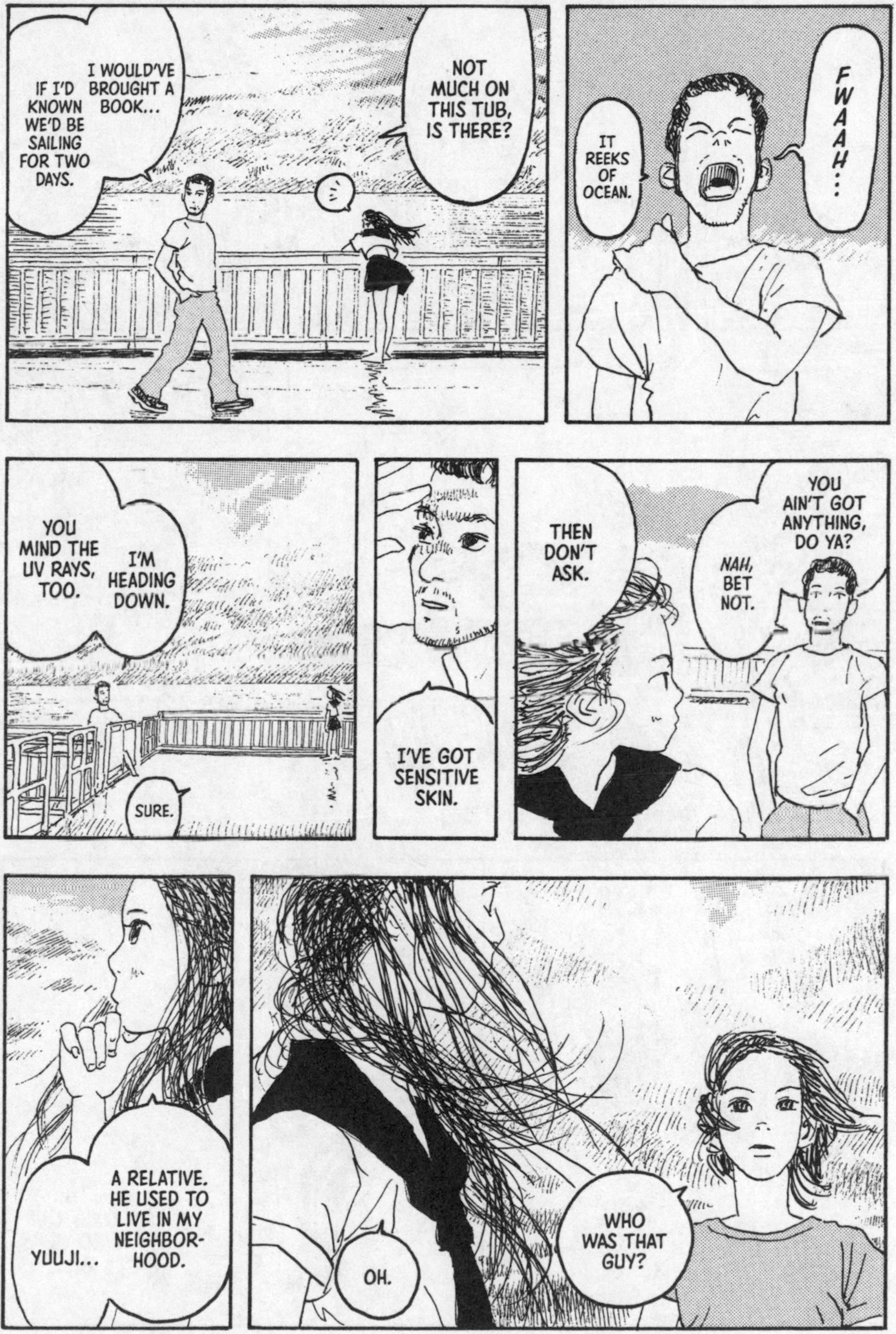
FWAAH...
IT REEKS OF OCEAN.
NOT MUCH ON THIS TUB, IS THERE?
I WOULD'VE BROUGHT A BOOK...
IF I'D KNOWN WE'D BE SAILING FOR TWO DAYS.
YOU AIN'T GOT ANYTHING, DO YA?
NAH, BET NOT.
THEN DON'T ASK.
I'VE GOT SENSITIVE SKIN.
YOU MIND THE UV RAYS, TOO.
I'M HEADING DOWN.
SURE.
WHO WAS THAT GUY?
OH.
A RELATIVE. HE USED TO LIVE IN MY NEIGHBOR-HOOD.
YUUJI...

WHEN ONE CUTS THEIR ARMS...

BUT...

DUNNO...

SO?

YOU LIKE HIM?

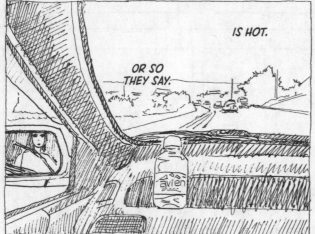

IS HOT.

OR SO THEY SAY.

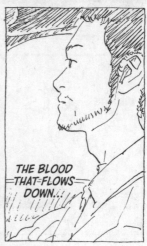

THE BLOOD THAT FLOWS DOWN...

HMM.

IS YUUJI.

THE ONLY ONE WHO GETS ME...

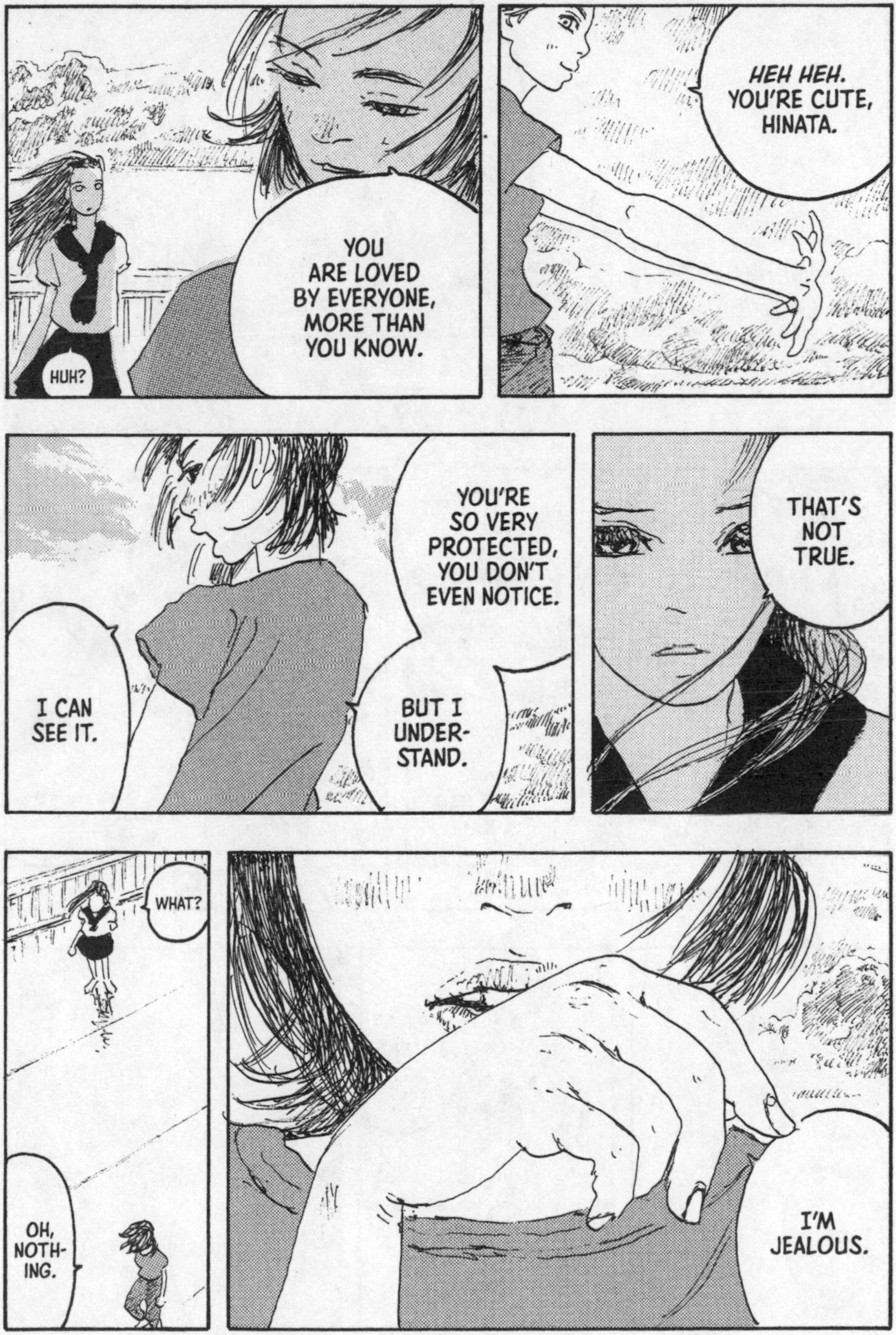
HEH HEH. YOU'RE CUTE, HINATA.
YOU ARE LOVED BY EVERYONE, MORE THAN YOU KNOW.
HUH?
THAT'S NOT TRUE.
YOU'RE SO VERY PROTECTED, YOU DON'T EVEN NOTICE.
BUT I UNDER-STAND.
I CAN SEE IT.
I'M JEALOUS.
WHAT?
OH, NOTH-ING.

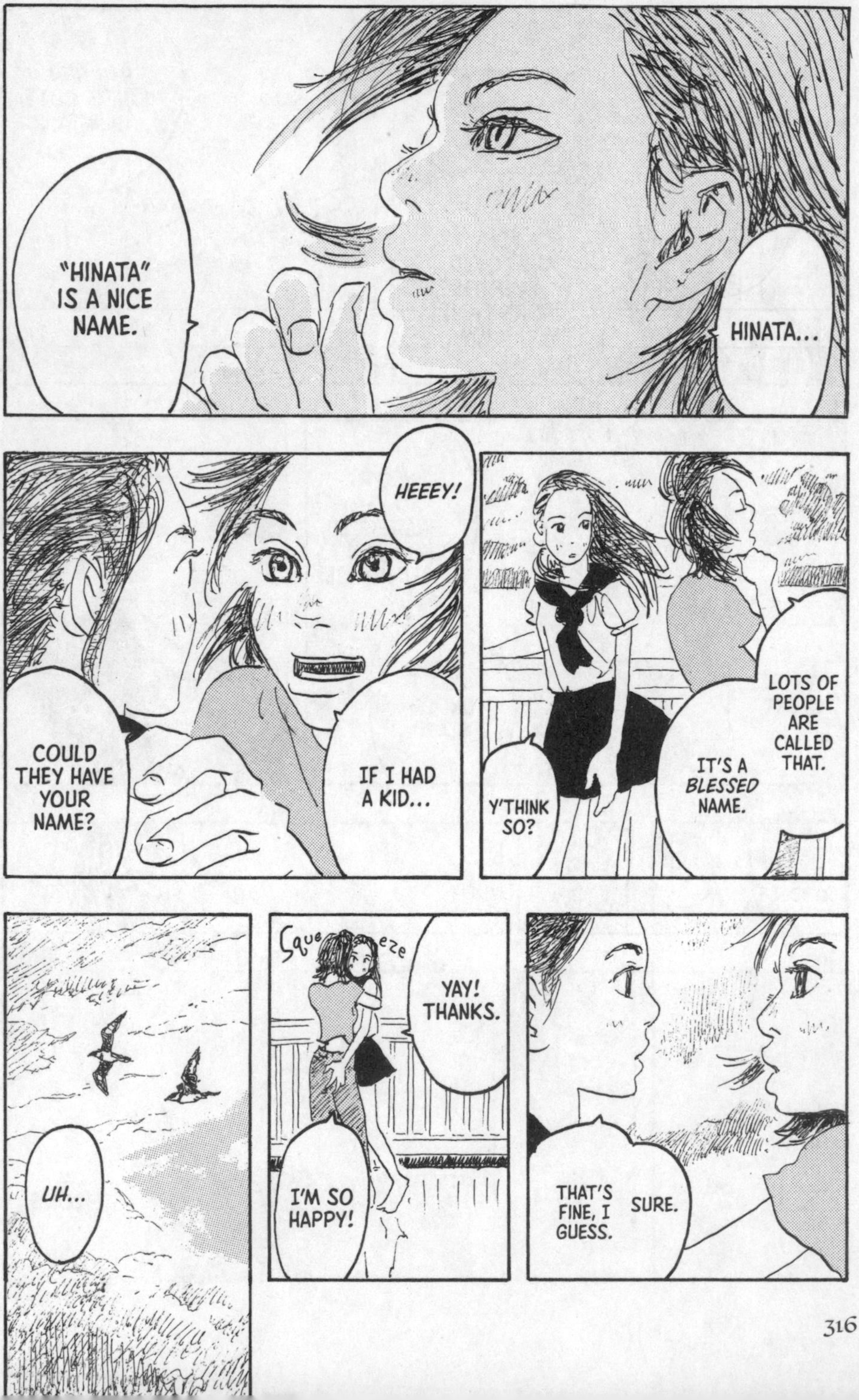
HINATA...
"HINATA" IS A NICE NAME.
LOTS OF PEOPLE ARE CALLED THAT.
IT'S A *BLESSED* NAME.
Y'THINK SO?
HEEEY!
IF I HAD A KID...
COULD THEY HAVE YOUR NAME?
SURE.
THAT'S FINE, I GUESS.
Sque eze
YAY! THANKS.
I'M SO HAPPY!
UH...

HM?
WHERE ARE YOU GOING, CHITARU-SAN?
AHH.
TO A SPECIAL PLACE.
THE HOUSE I WAS BORN IN.
WHERE ARE *YOU* GOING, HINATA? HAVE YOU DECIDED?
NOT REALLY...
IN THAT CASE!
LET ME RECOMMEND THIS ISLAND TO YOU!
YOU'LL HAVE TO MAKE A BUNCH OF BOAT TRANSFERS, BUT...
LET'S SEE, MAYBE IT'S IN THIS BOOK...
FLIP FLIP FLIP

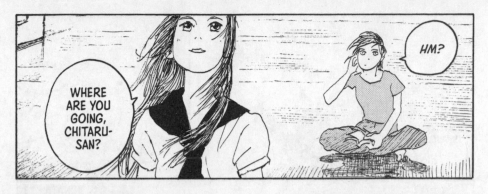

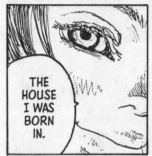

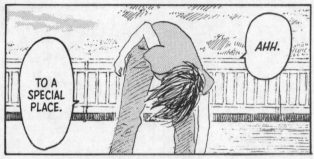

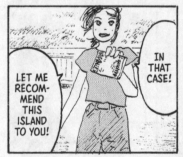

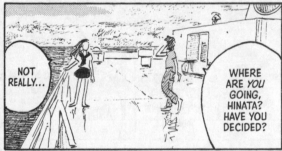

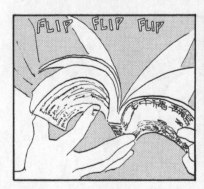

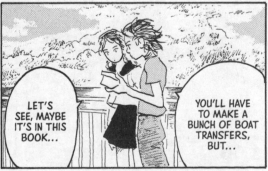

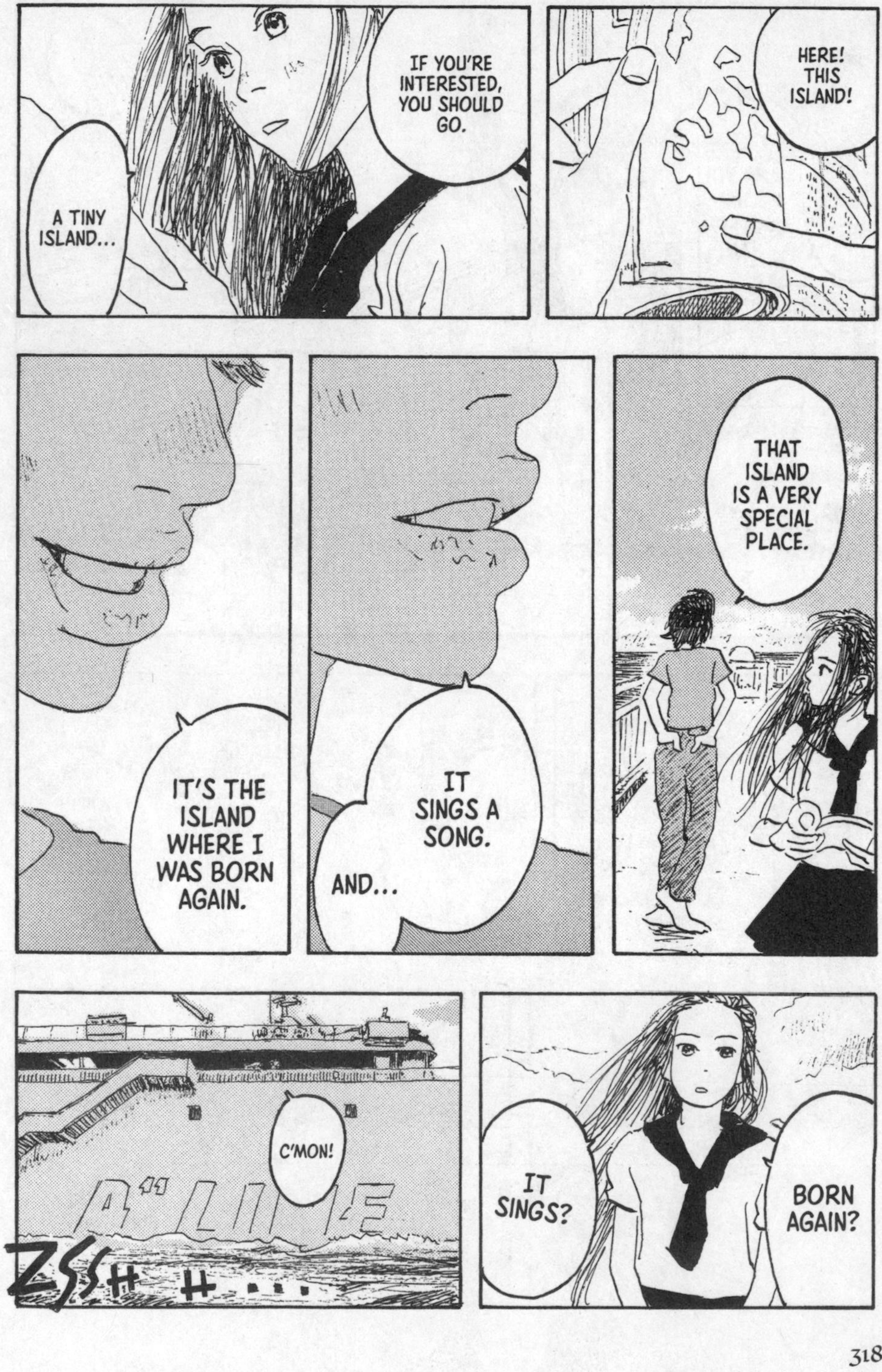
HERE! THIS ISLAND!
IF YOU'RE INTERESTED, YOU SHOULD GO.
A TINY ISLAND...
THAT ISLAND IS A VERY SPECIAL PLACE.
IT SINGS A SONG.
AND...
IT'S THE ISLAND WHERE I WAS BORN AGAIN.
BORN AGAIN?
IT SINGS?
C'MON!
ZSSHH H...

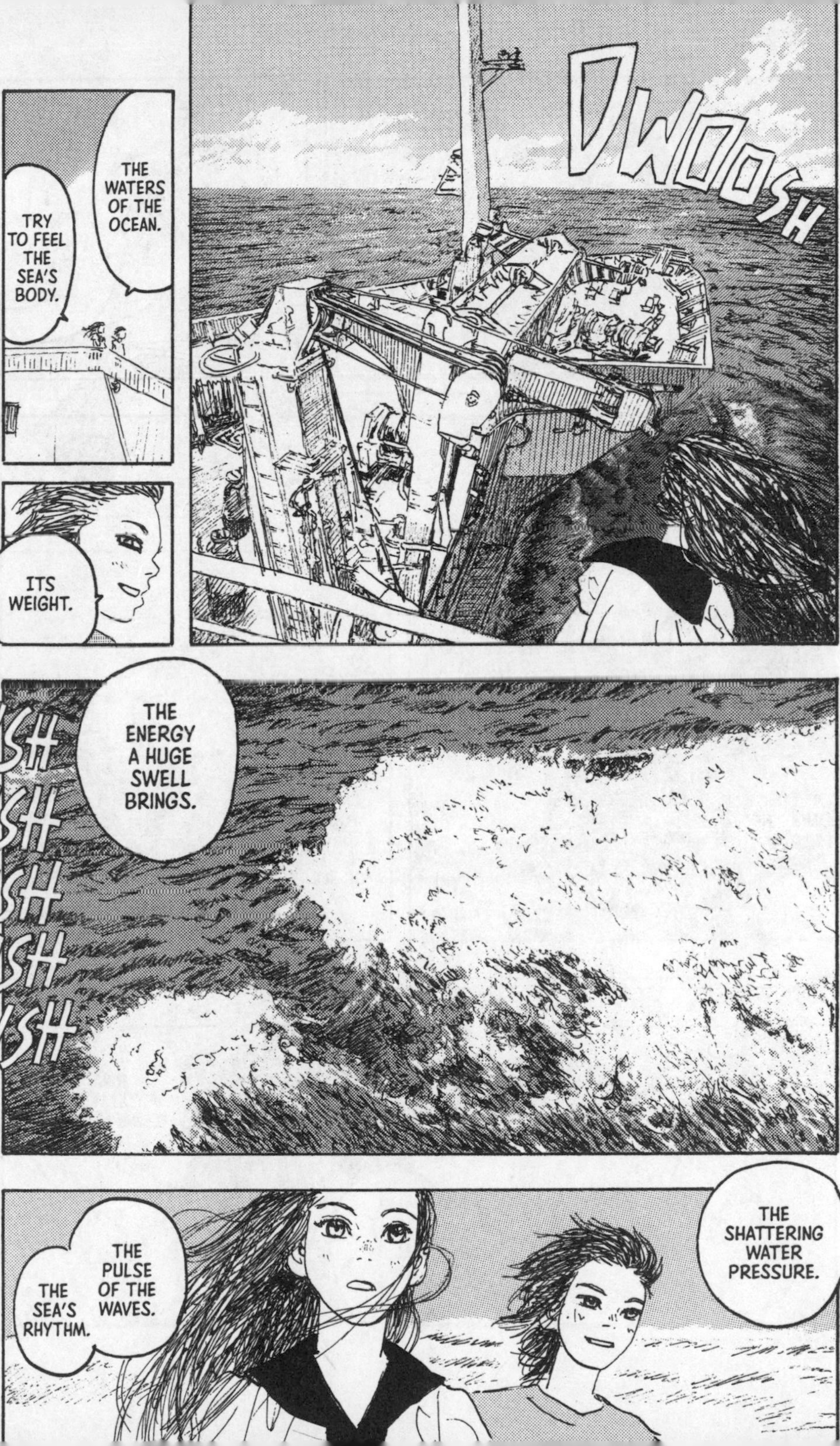
DWOOSH
THE WATERS OF THE OCEAN.
TRY TO FEEL THE SEA'S BODY.
ITS WEIGHT.
THE ENERGY A HUGE SWELL BRINGS.
VSH VSH VSH VSH VSH
THE SHATTERING WATER PRESSURE.
THE PULSE OF THE WAVES.
THE SEA'S RHYTHM.

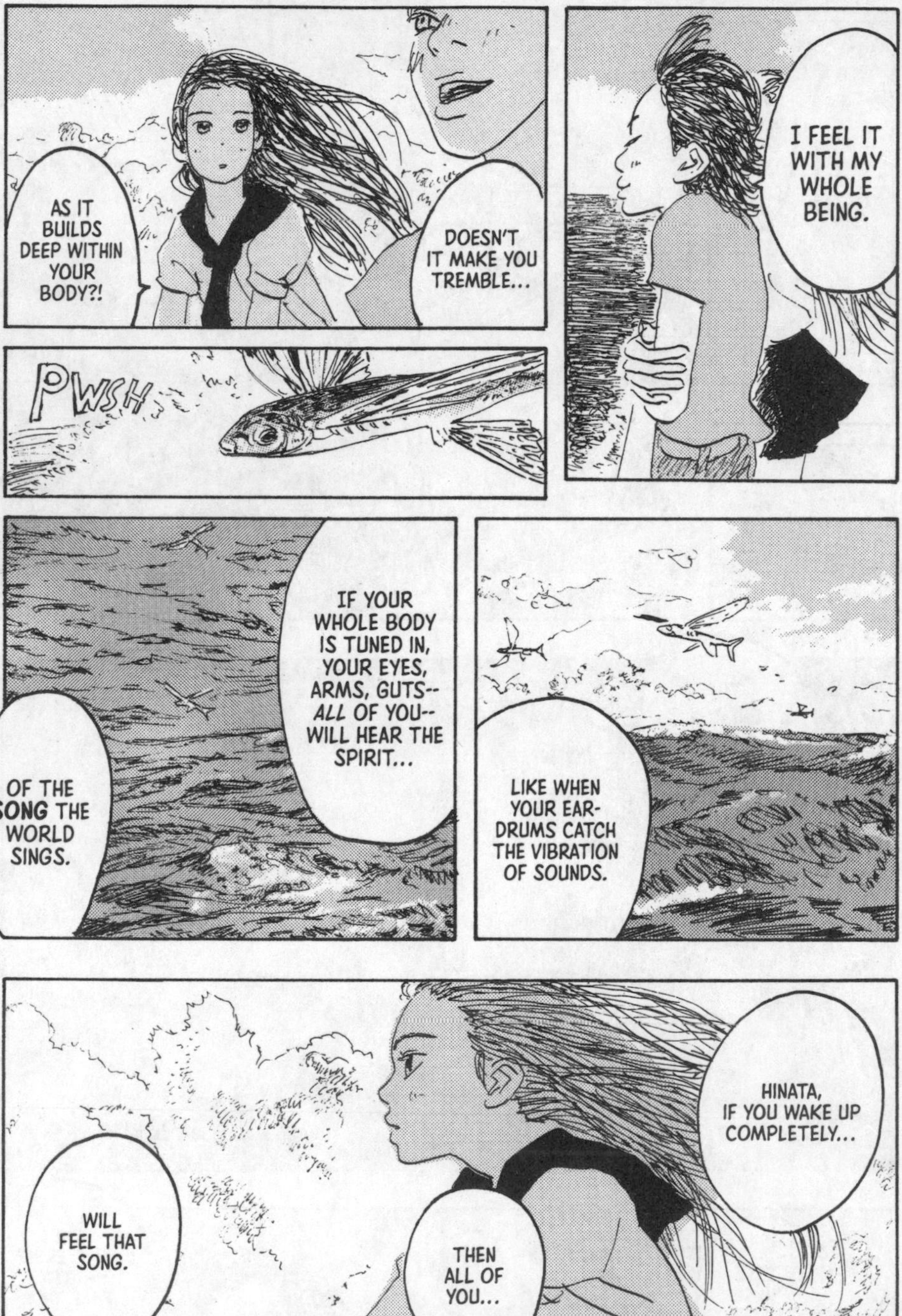
I FEEL IT WITH MY WHOLE BEING.
DOESN'T IT MAKE YOU TREMBLE...
AS IT BUILDS DEEP WITHIN YOUR BODY?!
PWSH
LIKE WHEN YOUR EAR-DRUMS CATCH THE VIBRATION OF SOUNDS.
IF YOUR WHOLE BODY IS TUNED IN, YOUR EYES, ARMS, GUTS-- *ALL* OF YOU-- WILL HEAR THE SPIRIT...
OF THE **SONG** THE WORLD SINGS.
HINATA, IF YOU WAKE UP COMPLETELY...
THEN ALL OF YOU...
WILL FEEL THAT SONG.

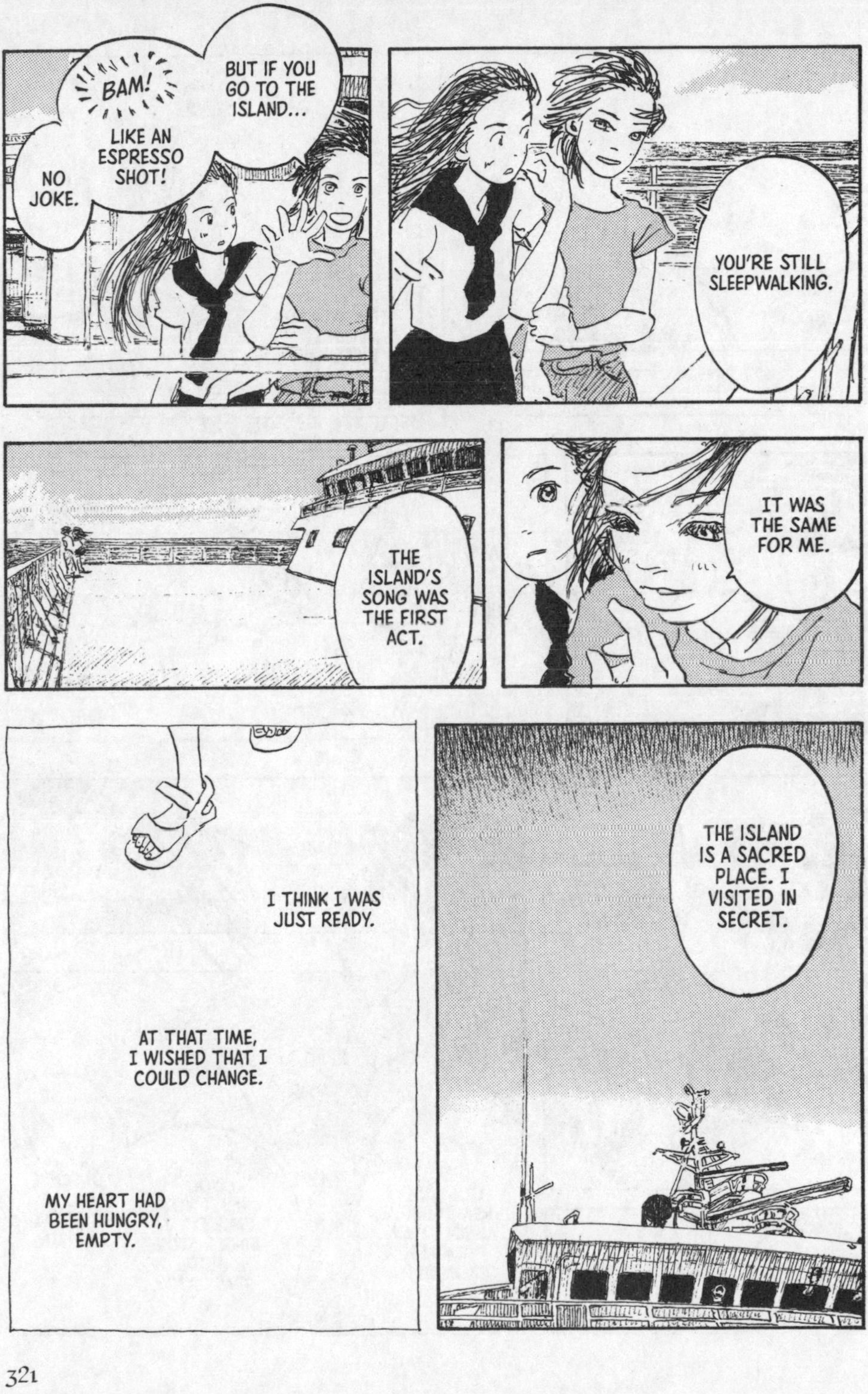
YOU'RE STILL SLEEPWALKING.
BUT IF YOU GO TO THE ISLAND...
BAM!
LIKE AN ESPRESSO SHOT!
NO JOKE.
IT WAS THE SAME FOR ME.
THE ISLAND'S SONG WAS THE FIRST ACT.
THE ISLAND IS A SACRED PLACE. I VISITED IN SECRET.
I THINK I WAS JUST READY.
AT THAT TIME, I WISHED THAT I COULD CHANGE.
MY HEART HAD BEEN HUNGRY, EMPTY.

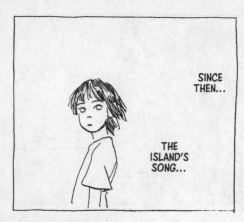

MY BODY...
FILLED WITH SONG.
THE WORLD LOOKED DIFFERENT.
SINCE THEN...
THE ISLAND'S SONG...
AND THE BEATING OF MY HEART...
HAVE FORMED A PERFECT DUET.
PERHAPS... IT'S BECAUSE IT IS A SACRED PLACE.
OH, RIGHT!
BECAUSE THE ISLAND IS SO, SO SACRED...
YOU MUST NOT TAKE EVEN A SINGLE STONE OR BLADE OF GRASS AWAY.
IF YOU GO, JUST REMEMBER. ABSOLUTELY PROMISE! PROMISE!!
STEAL WHAT YOU LIKE ELSEWHERE, THOUGH.
BA-DMP
THAT'S RIGHT.

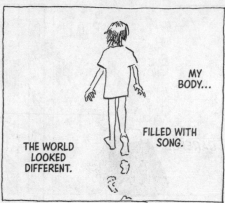

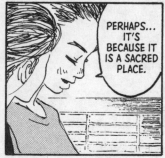

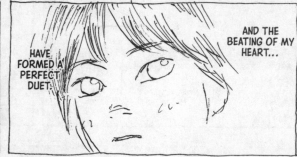

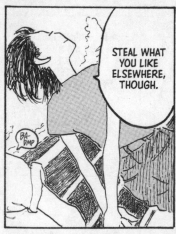

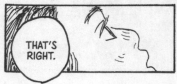

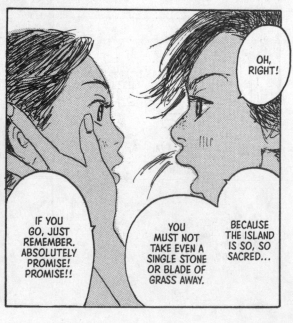

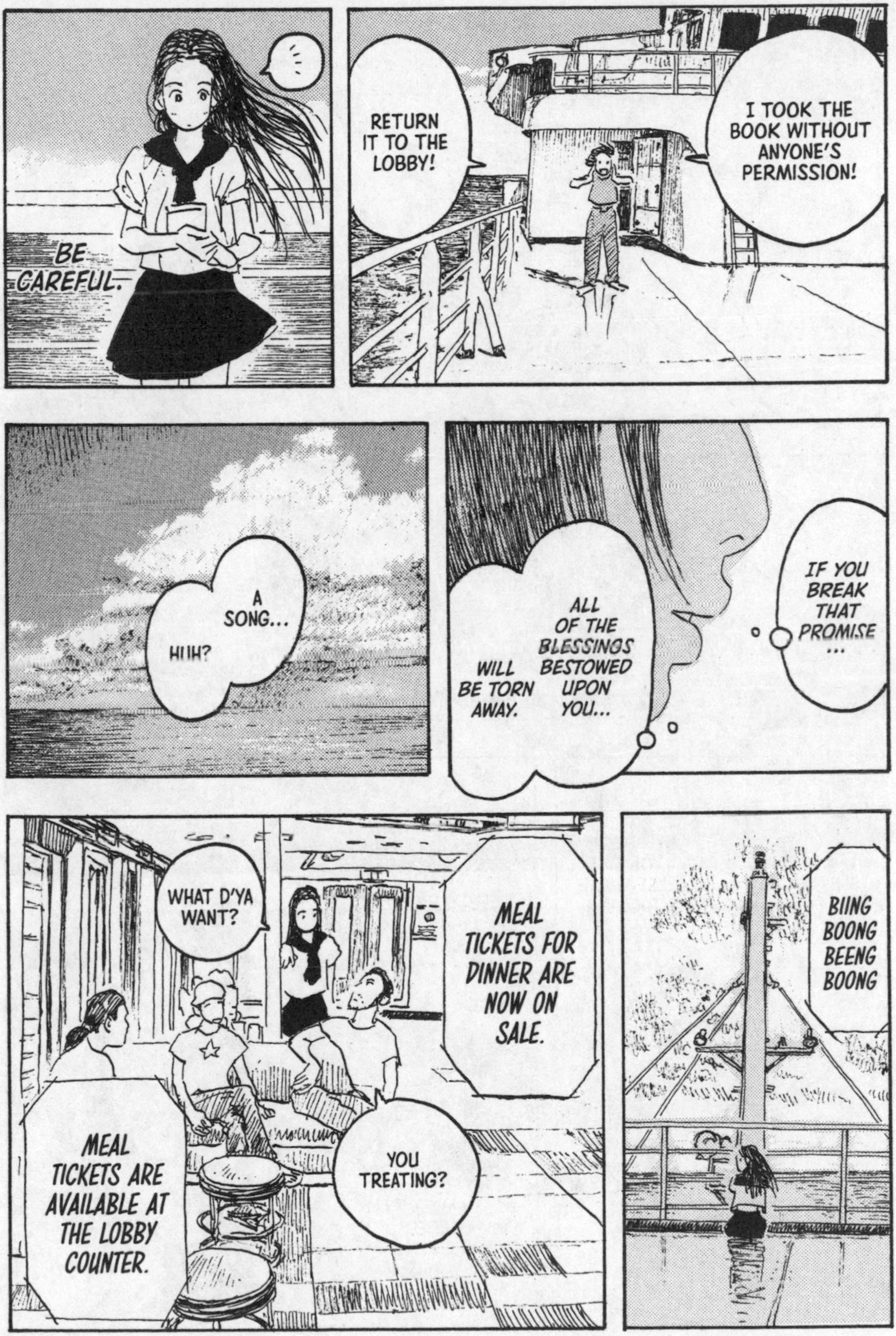
I TOOK THE BOOK WITHOUT ANYONE'S PERMISSION!
RETURN IT TO THE LOBBY!
BE CAREFUL.
IF YOU BREAK THAT PROMISE...
ALL OF THE BLESSINGS BESTOWED UPON YOU...
WILL BE TORN AWAY.
A SONG...
HUH?
BIING BOONG BEENG BOONG
MEAL TICKETS FOR DINNER ARE NOW ON SALE.
WHAT D'YA WANT?
YOU TREATING?
MEAL TICKETS ARE AVAILABLE AT THE LOBBY COUNTER.

IT'S COOL. I'D FEEL BAD IF I USED ALL THE MONEY ON MYSELF.

WHAT'S THAT MEAN?

!

WHAT?

I SAID HEY!

HEY...

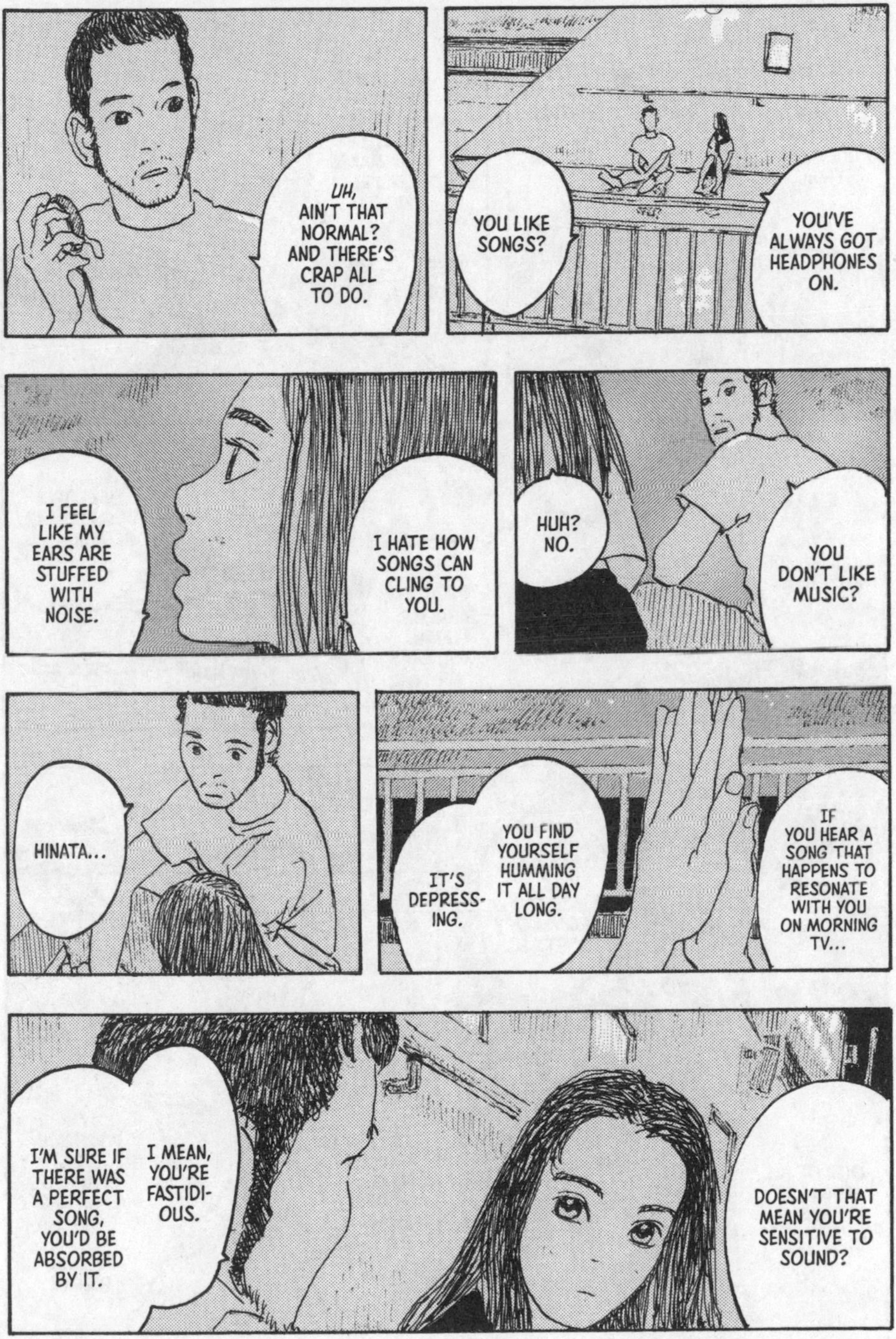
YOU'VE ALWAYS GOT HEADPHONES ON.
YOU LIKE SONGS?
UH, AIN'T THAT NORMAL? AND THERE'S CRAP ALL TO DO.
YOU DON'T LIKE MUSIC?
HUH? NO.
I HATE HOW SONGS CAN CLING TO YOU.
I FEEL LIKE MY EARS ARE STUFFED WITH NOISE.
IF YOU HEAR A SONG THAT HAPPENS TO RESONATE WITH YOU ON MORNING TV...
YOU FIND YOURSELF HUMMING IT ALL DAY LONG.
IT'S DEPRESS-ING.
HINATA...
DOESN'T THAT MEAN YOU'RE SENSITIVE TO SOUND?
I MEAN, YOU'RE FASTIDI-OUS.
I'M SURE IF THERE WAS A PERFECT SONG, YOU'D BE ABSORBED BY IT.

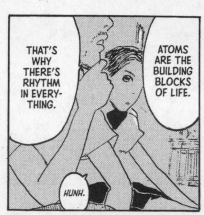

GET THIS.
"RHYTHM" WAS ORIGINALLY AN ANCIENT GREEK WORD.
IT DESCRIBES THE MOVEMENT OF THE STUFF THAT MAKES UP THE WORLD.
LIKE, ATOMS.
ATOMS ARE THE BUILDING BLOCKS OF LIFE.
THAT'S WHY THERE'S RHYTHM IN EVERYTHING.
HUNH.
SON
IN PEOPLE, DOGS, CHERRY BLOSSOMS...
CARROTS, SUGAR, WATER, AIR...
PROBABLY EVEN IN PLASTIC.
THEY'VE ALL GOT UNIQUE RHYTHMS.
EVEN WHEN YOU LOOK AT A PICTURE OR A PAINTING, THERE'S A POETIC FEELING, RIGHT?
YOU'RE PROBABLY UNCONSCIOUSLY FEELING ITS RHYTHM.
SAY YOU PICK UP A STONE FROM A DRY RIVERBED.
WHY, OUT OF ALL THE MANY STONES, DID YOU CHOOSE THAT EXACT ONE?

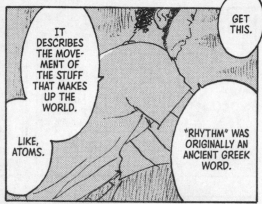

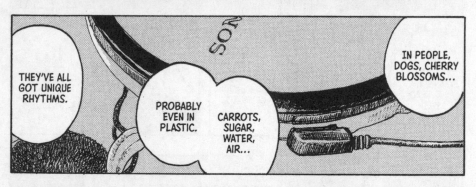

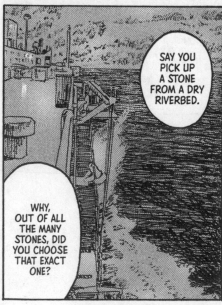

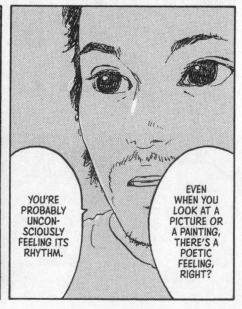

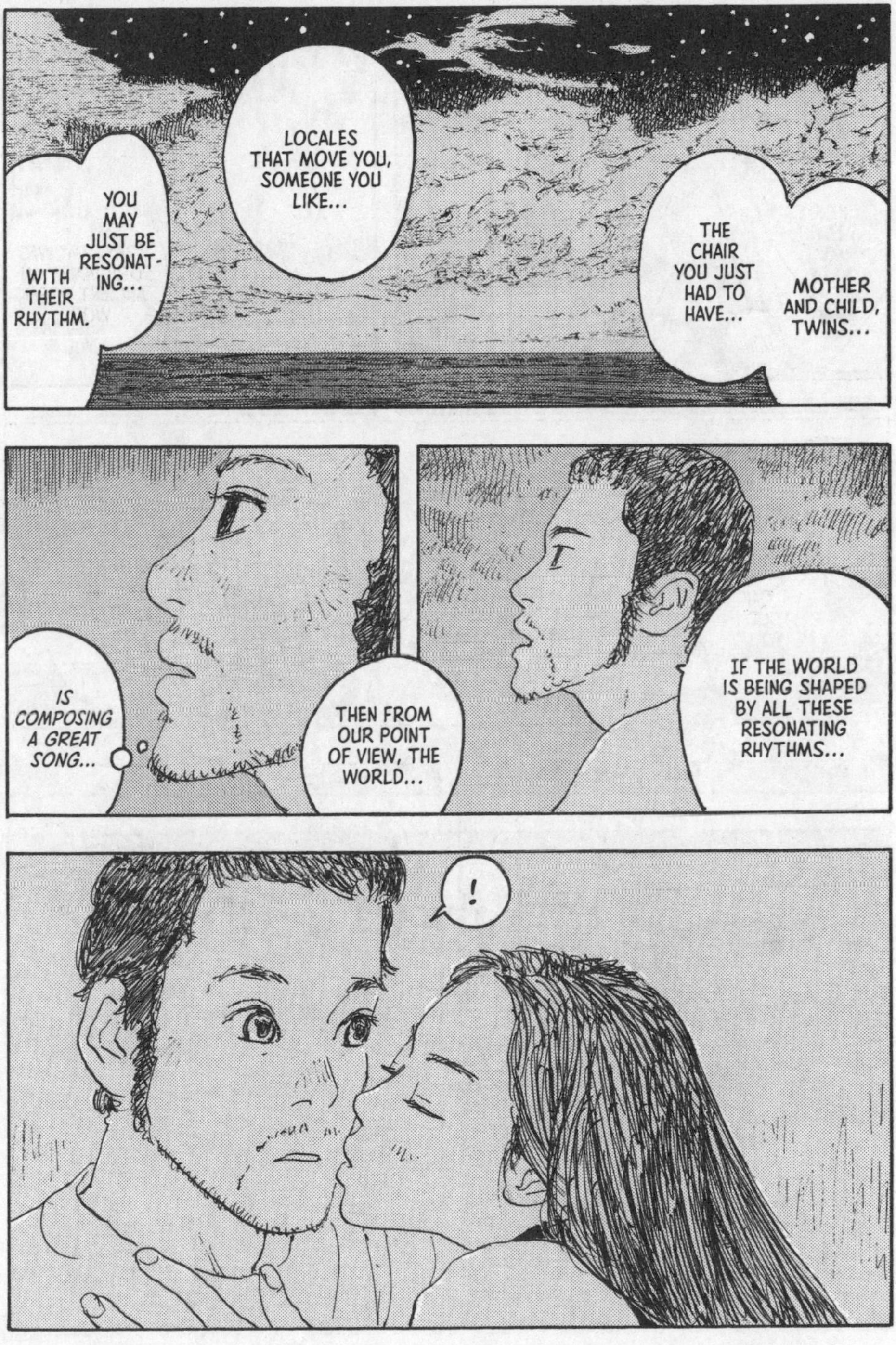
MOTHER AND CHILD, TWINS...
THE CHAIR YOU JUST HAD TO HAVE...
LOCALES THAT MOVE YOU, SOMEONE YOU LIKE...
YOU MAY JUST BE RESONATING...
WITH THEIR RHYTHM.
IF THE WORLD IS BEING SHAPED BY ALL THESE RESONATING RHYTHMS...
THEN FROM OUR POINT OF VIEW, THE WORLD...
IS COMPOSING A GREAT SONG...
!

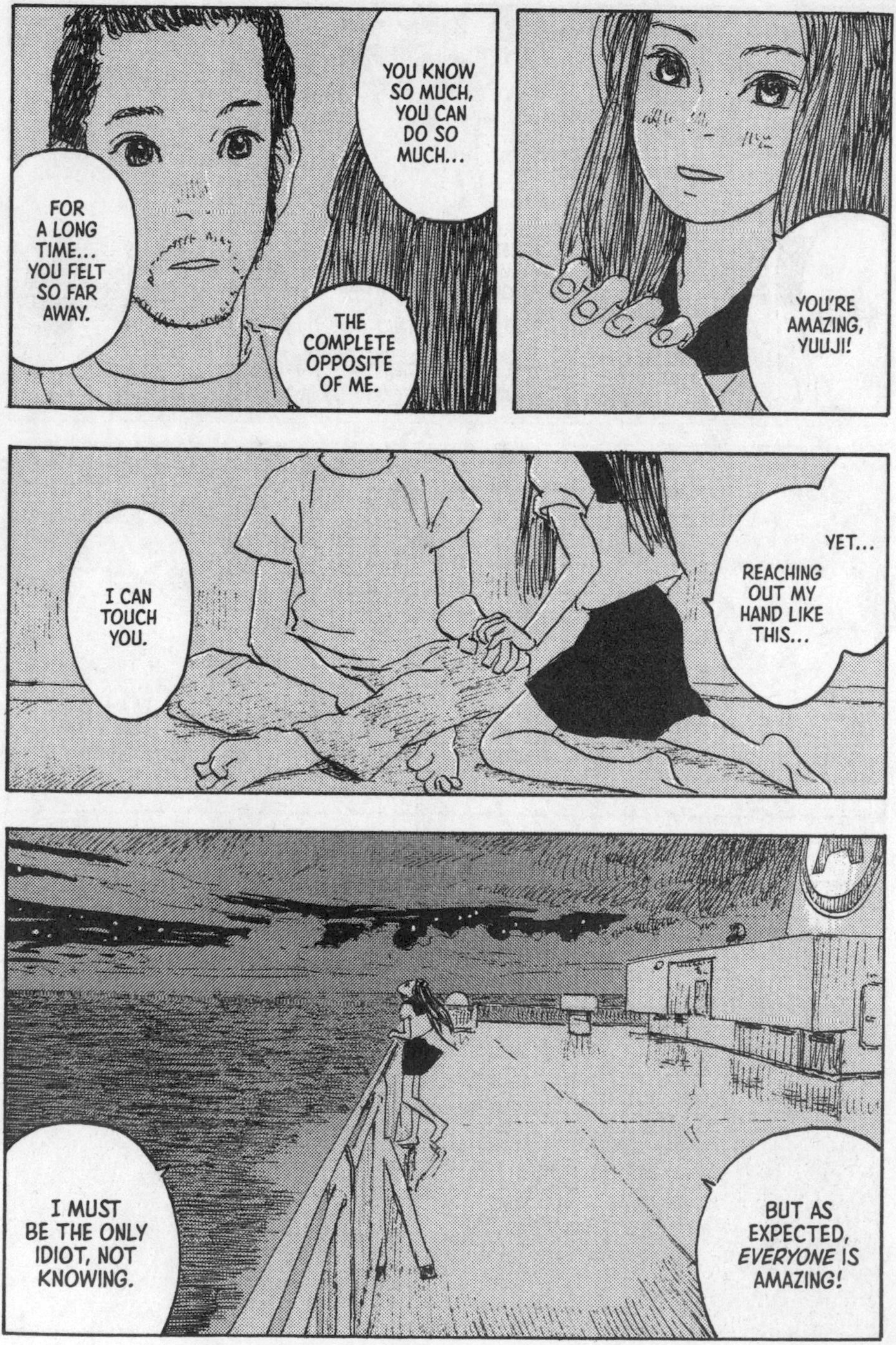
YOU'RE AMAZING, YUUJI!
YOU KNOW SO MUCH, YOU CAN DO SO MUCH...
THE COMPLETE OPPOSITE OF ME.
FOR A LONG TIME... YOU FELT SO FAR AWAY.
YET... REACHING OUT MY HAND LIKE THIS...
I CAN TOUCH YOU.
BUT AS EXPECTED, *EVERYONE* IS AMAZING!
I MUST BE THE ONLY IDIOT, NOT KNOWING.

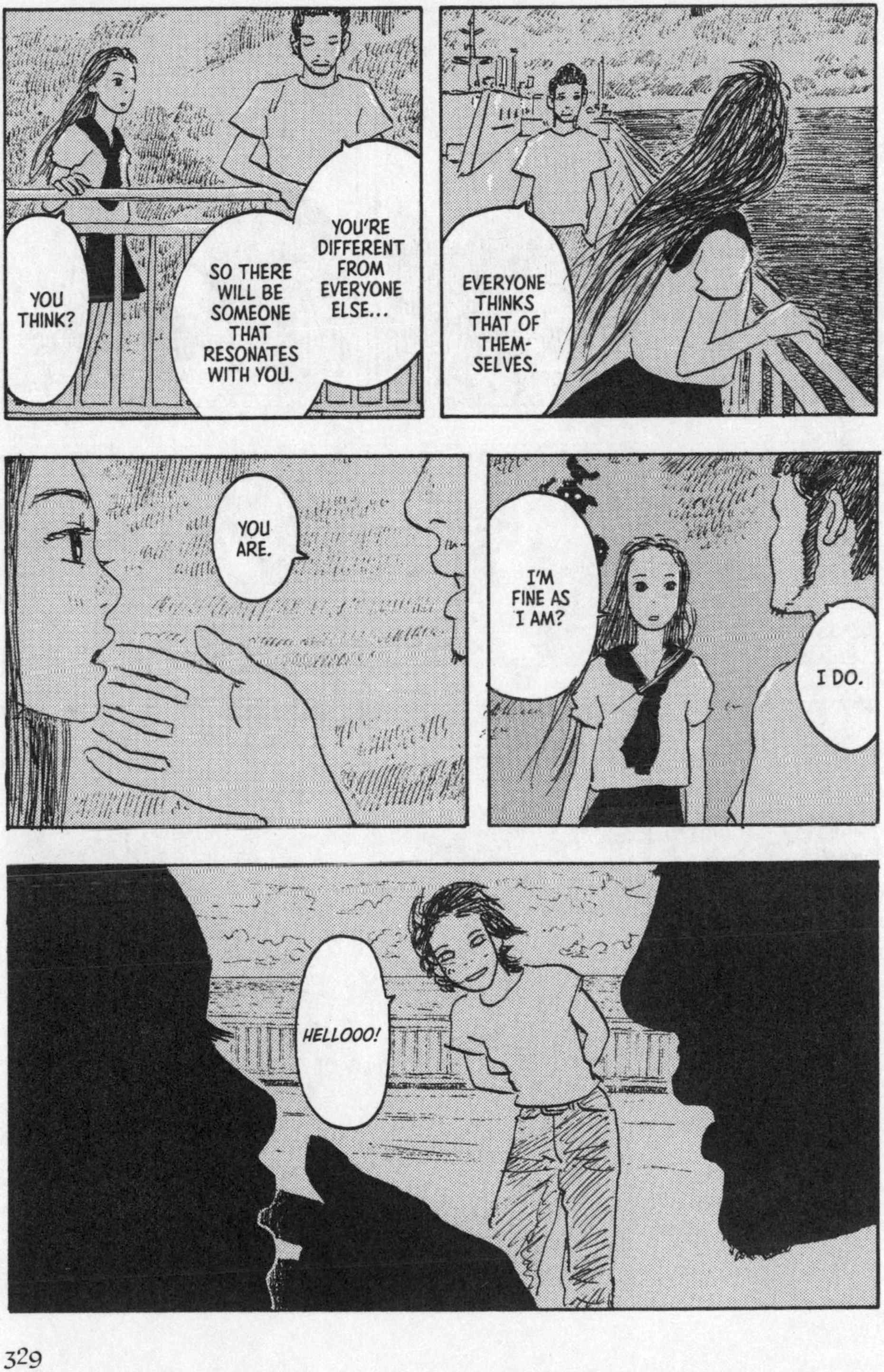
EVERYONE THINKS THAT OF THEM-SELVES.
YOU'RE DIFFERENT FROM EVERYONE ELSE...
SO THERE WILL BE SOMEONE THAT RESONATES WITH YOU.
YOU THINK?
I'M FINE AS I AM?
I DO.
YOU ARE.
HELLOOO!

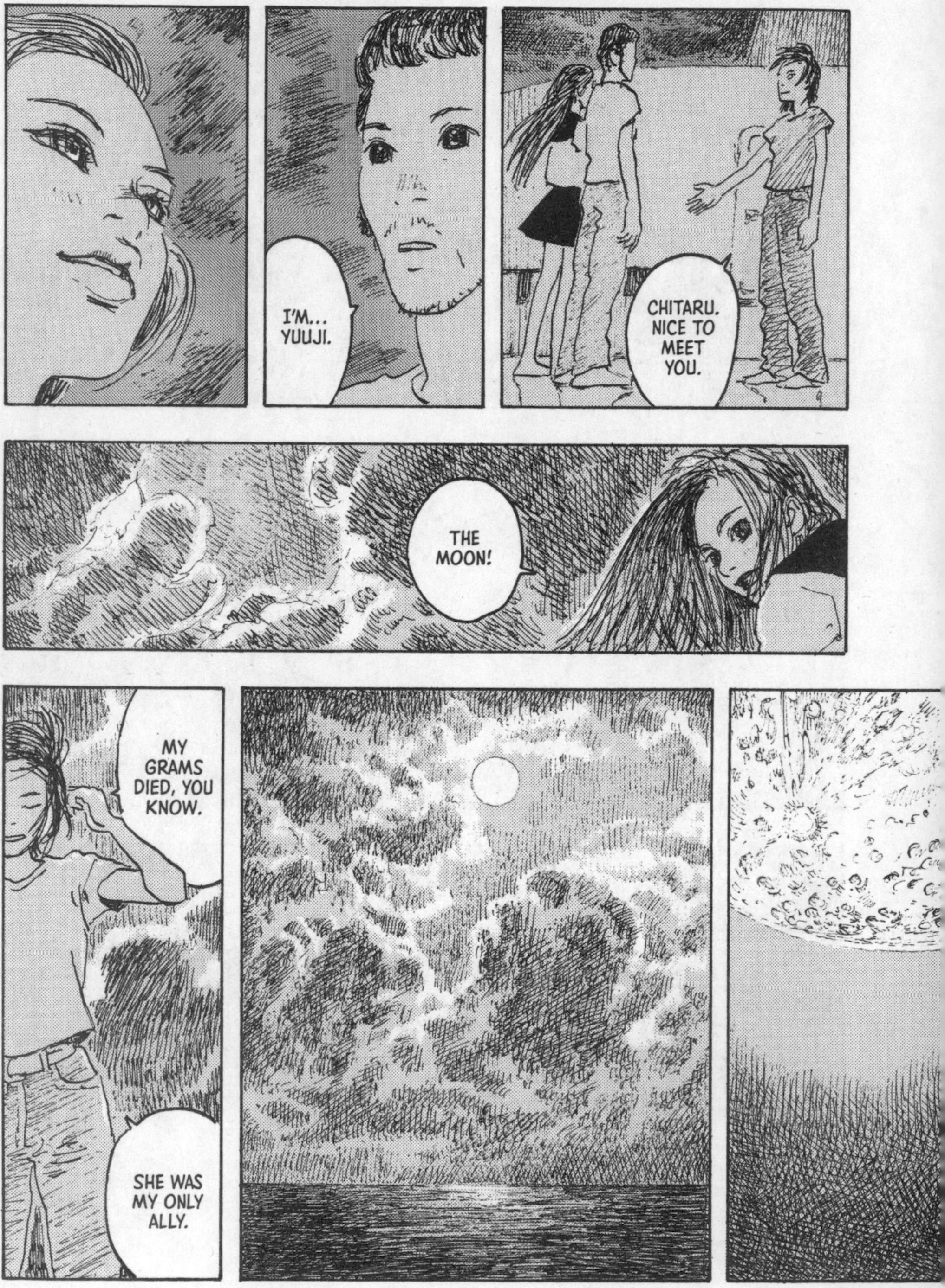
CHITARU. NICE TO MEET YOU.
I'M... YUUJI.
THE MOON!
MY GRAMS DIED, YOU KNOW.
SHE WAS MY ONLY ALLY.

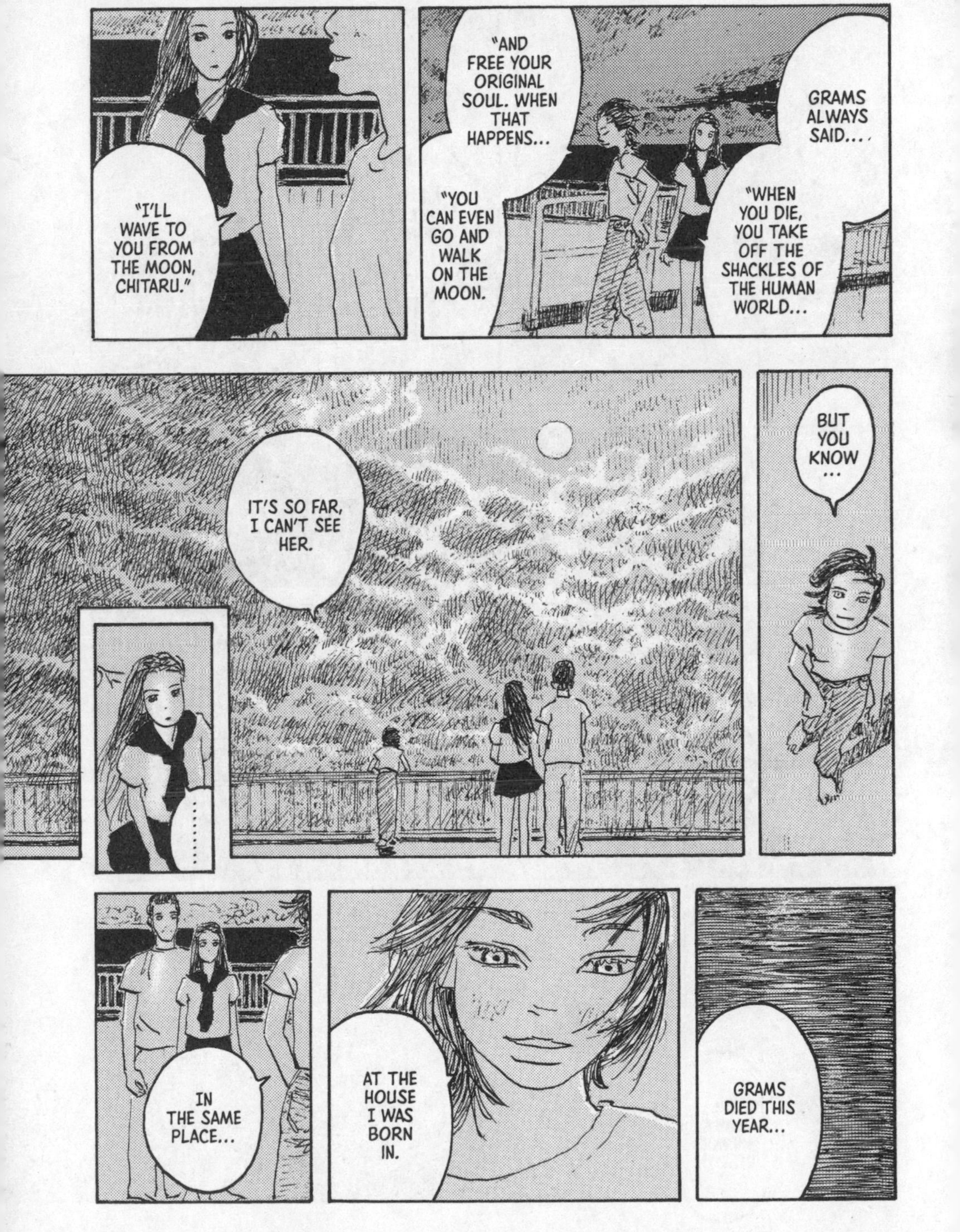
GRAMS ALWAYS SAID...
"WHEN YOU DIE, YOU TAKE OFF THE SHACKLES OF THE HUMAN WORLD...
"AND FREE YOUR ORIGINAL SOUL. WHEN THAT HAPPENS...
"YOU CAN EVEN GO AND WALK ON THE MOON.
"I'LL WAVE TO YOU FROM THE MOON, CHITARU."
BUT YOU KNOW ...
IT'S SO FAR, I CAN'T SEE HER.
......
GRAMS DIED THIS YEAR...
AT THE HOUSE I WAS BORN IN.
IN THE SAME PLACE...

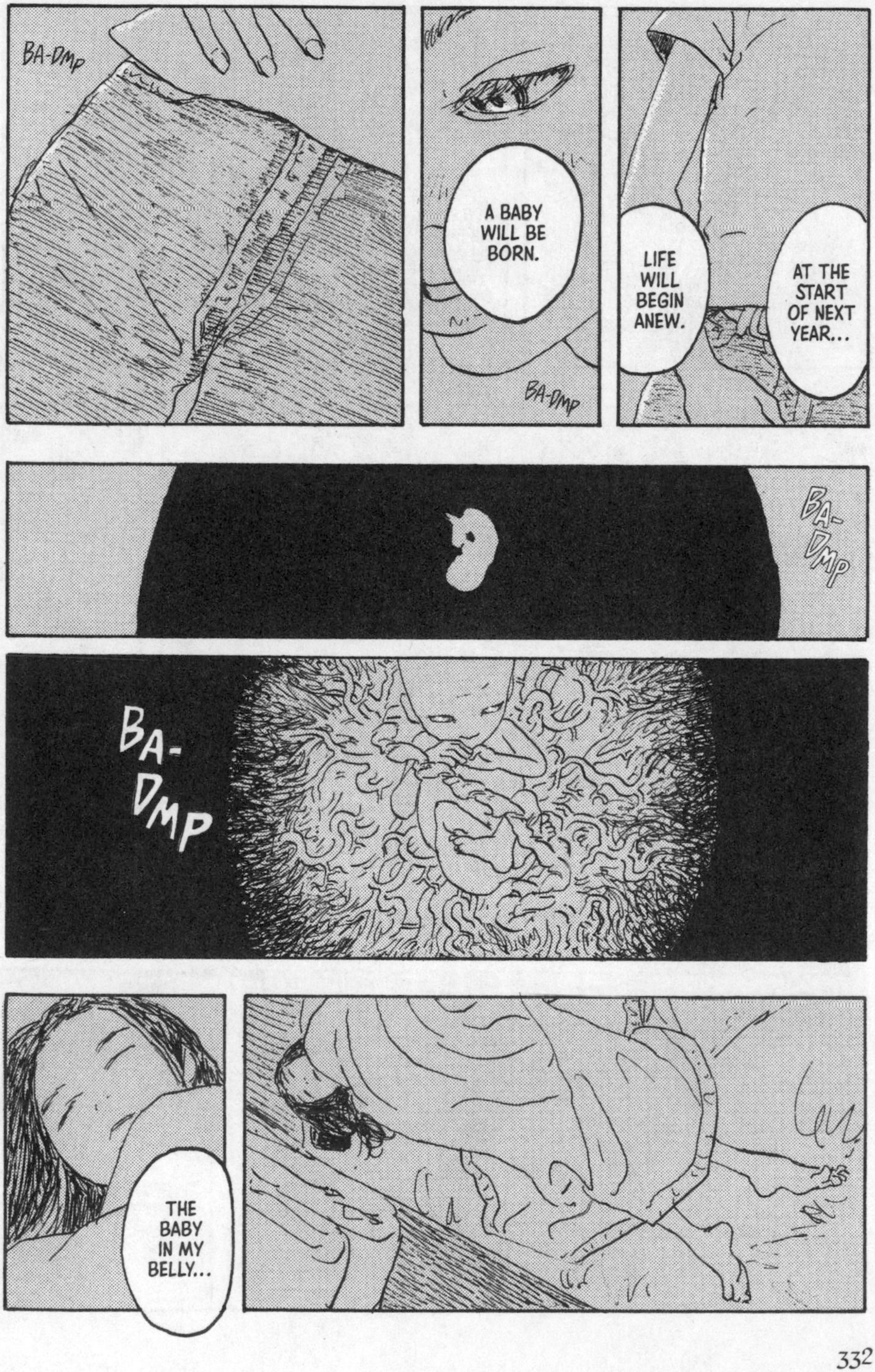
AT THE START OF NEXT YEAR...
LIFE WILL BEGIN ANEW.
A BABY WILL BE BORN.
BA-DMP
BA-DMP
BA-DMP
BA-DMP
THE BABY IN MY BELLY...

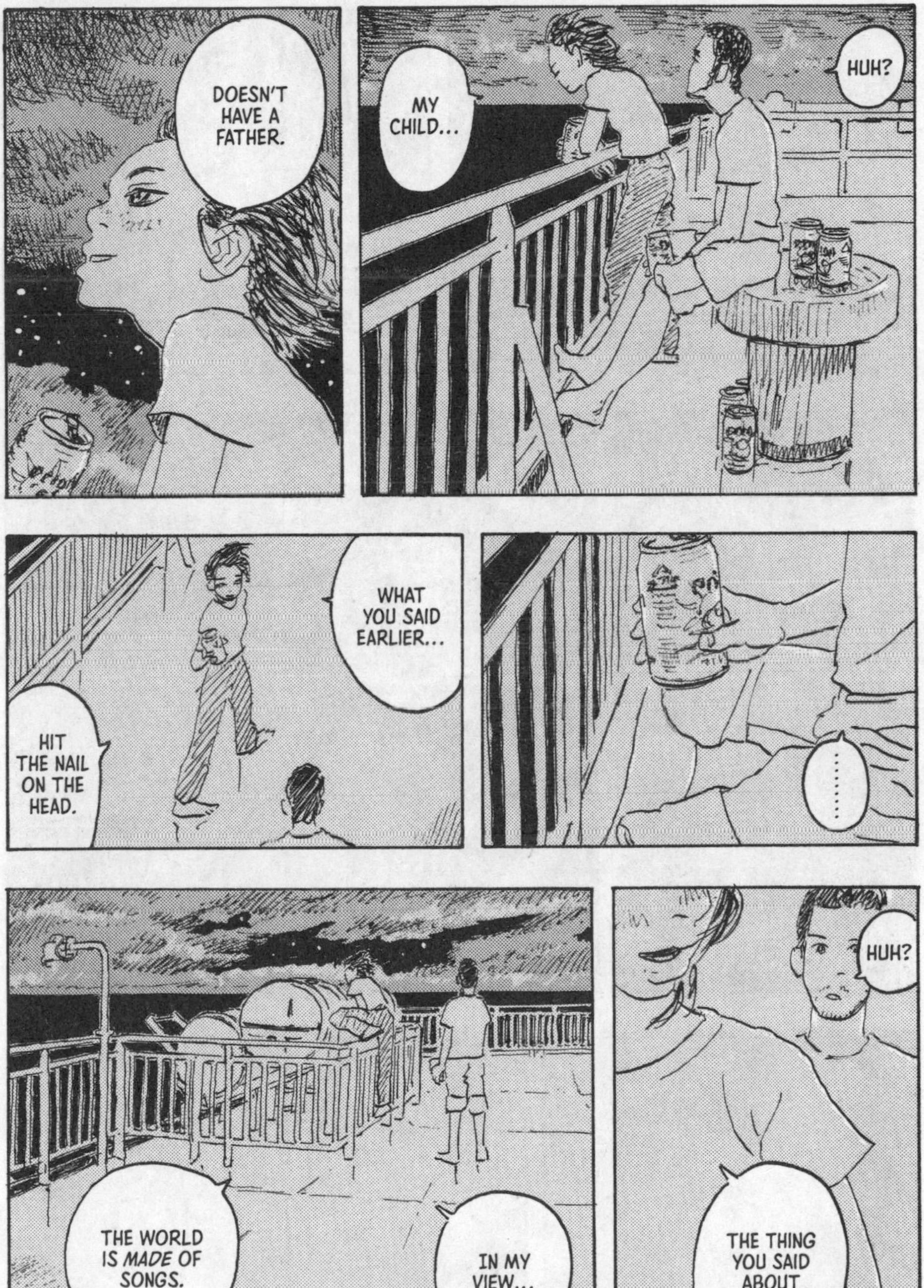
HUH?
MY CHILD...
DOESN'T HAVE A FATHER.
......
WHAT YOU SAID EARLIER...
HIT THE NAIL ON THE HEAD.
HUH?
THE THING YOU SAID ABOUT SONGS.
IN MY VIEW...
THE WORLD IS *MADE* OF SONGS.

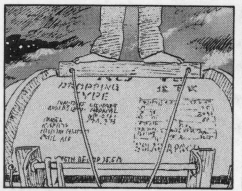

THE WORLD WAS *BORN* FROM SONG.

THIS FEELS GREAT!

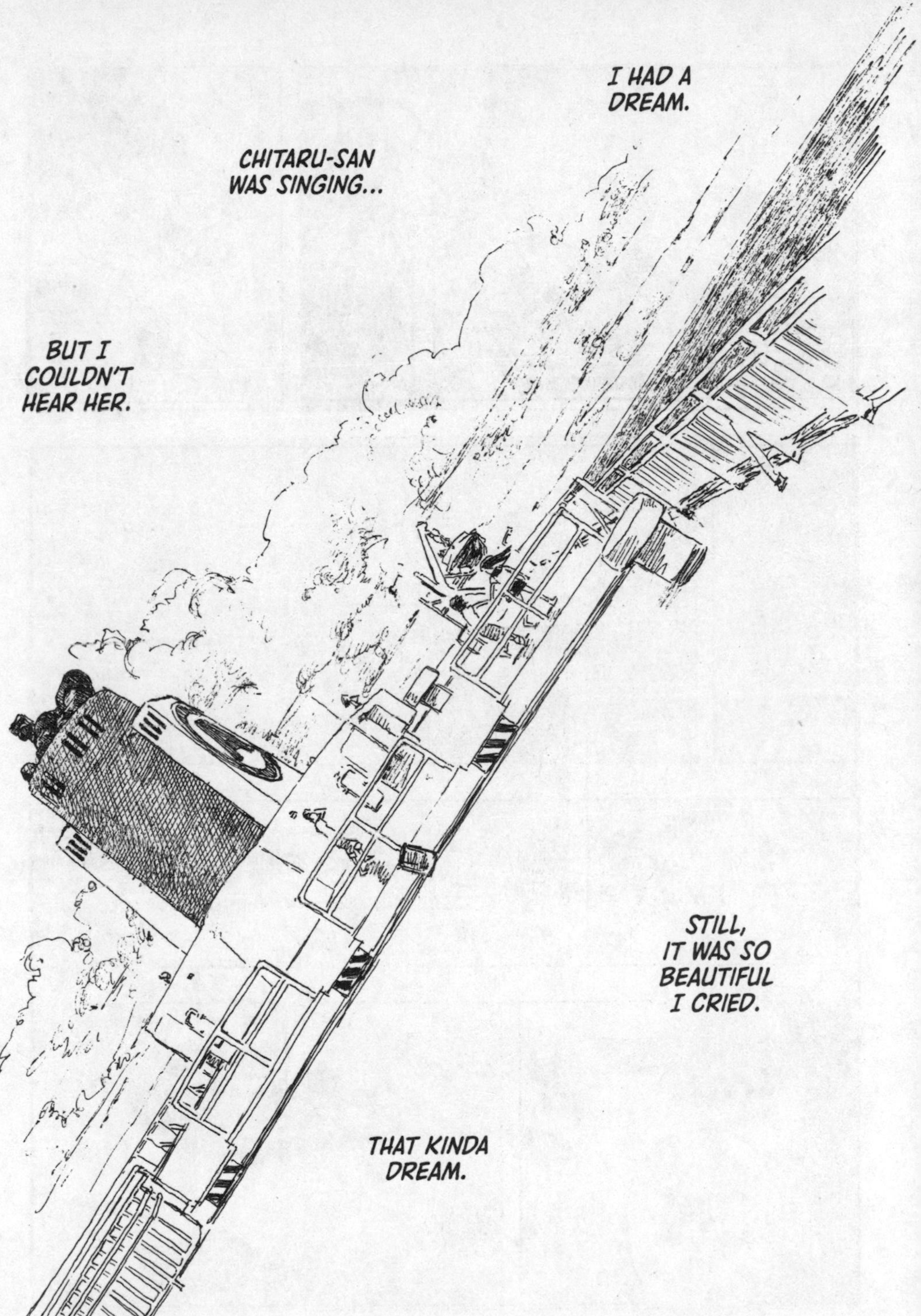
I HAD A DREAM.
CHITARU-SAN WAS SINGING...
BUT I COULDN'T HEAR HER.
STILL, IT WAS SO BEAUTIFUL I CRIED.
THAT KINDA DREAM.

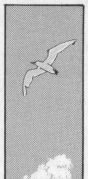

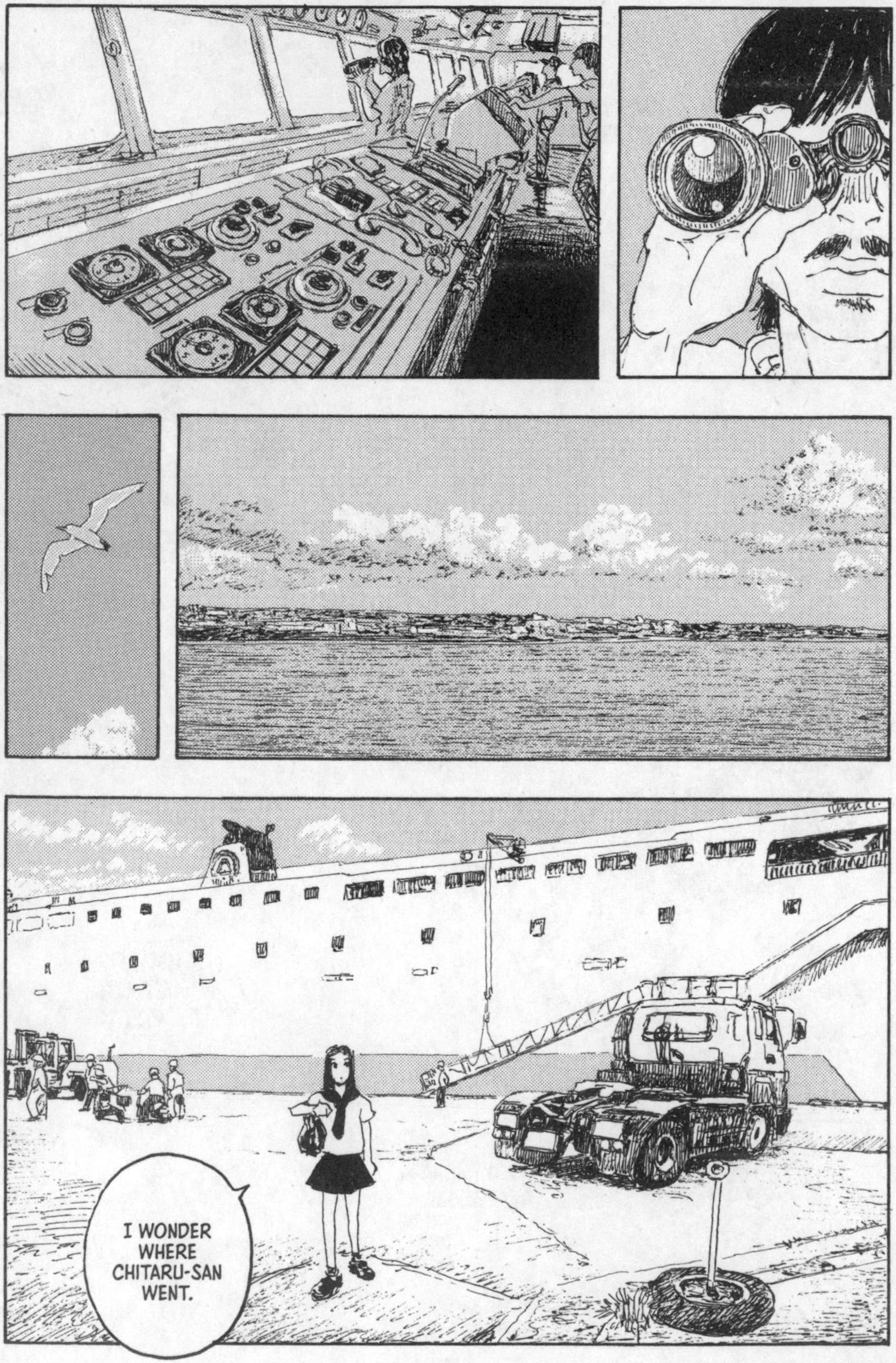
I WONDER WHERE CHITARU-SAN WENT.

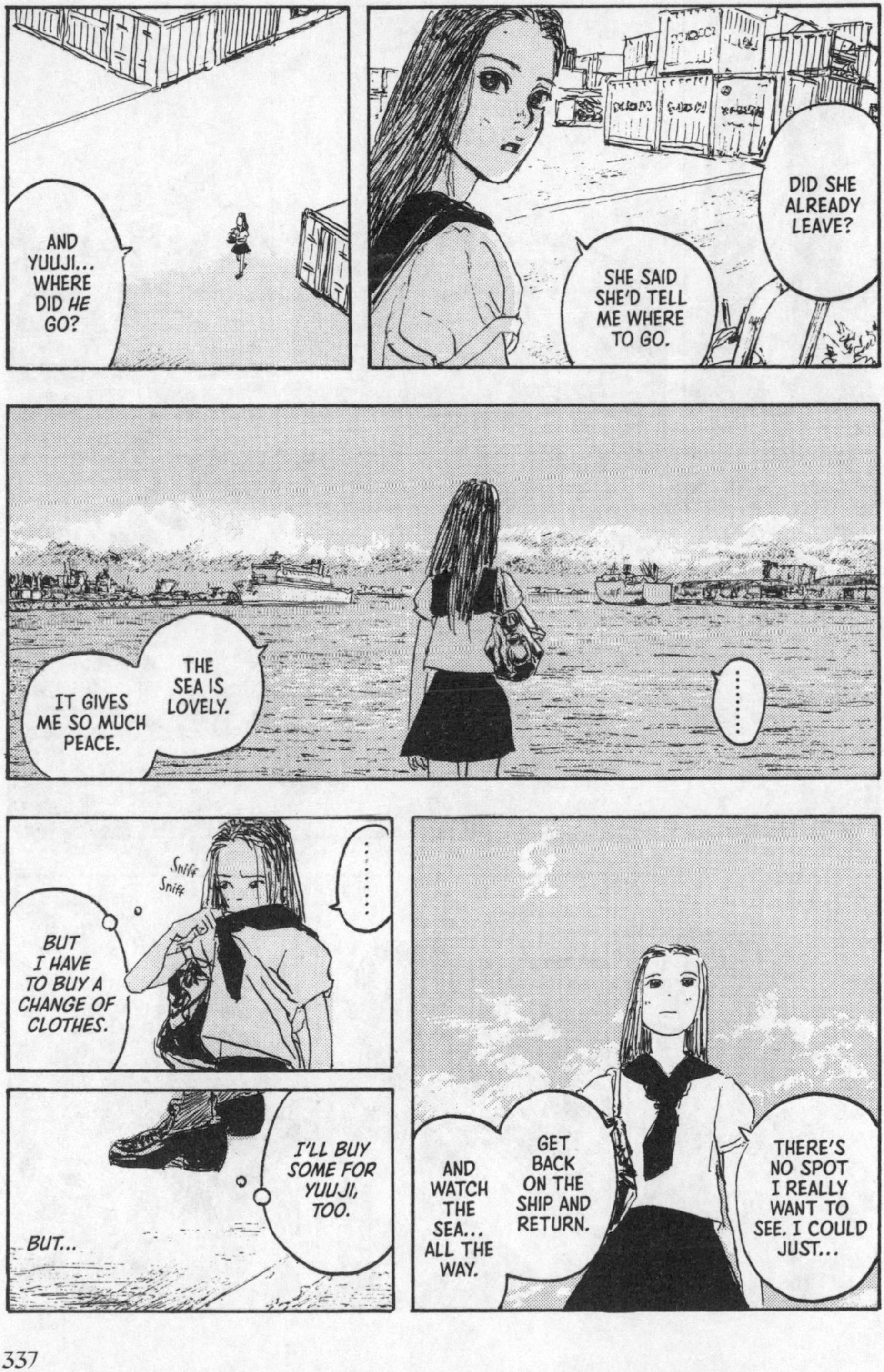
DID SHE ALREADY LEAVE?
SHE SAID SHE'D TELL ME WHERE TO GO.
AND YUUJI... WHERE DID *HE* GO?
......
THE SEA IS LOVELY.
IT GIVES ME SO MUCH PEACE.
THERE'S NO SPOT I REALLY WANT TO SEE. I COULD JUST...
GET BACK ON THE SHIP AND RETURN.
AND WATCH THE SEA... ALL THE WAY.
......
Sniff Sniff
BUT I HAVE TO BUY A CHANGE OF CLOTHES.
I'LL BUY SOME FOR YUUJI, TOO.
BUT...

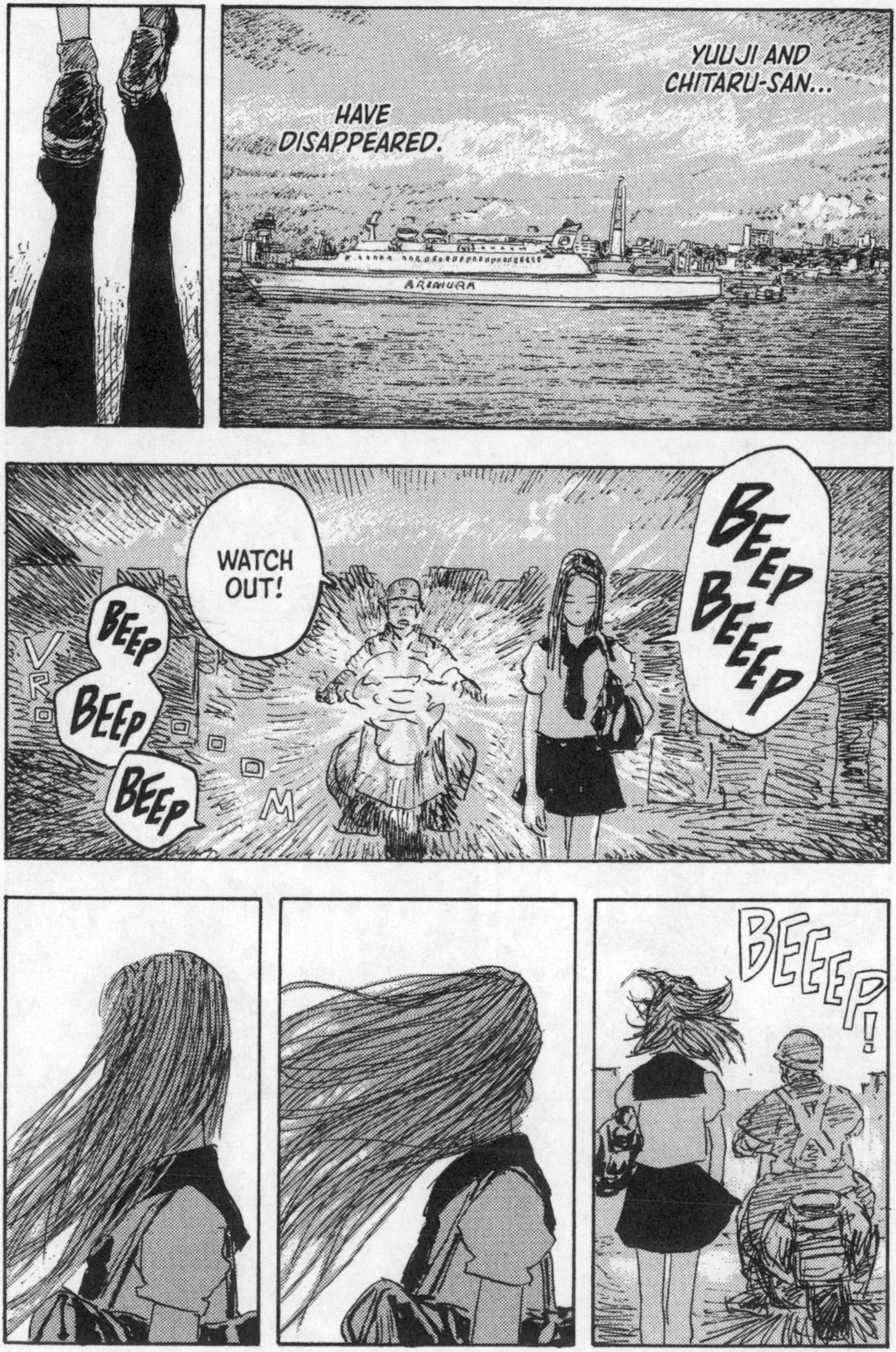
YUUJI AND CHITARU-SAN...
HAVE DISAPPEARED.
BEEP BEEEEP
WATCH OUT!
BEEP
BEEP
BEEP
VROOOOOM
BEEEEP!

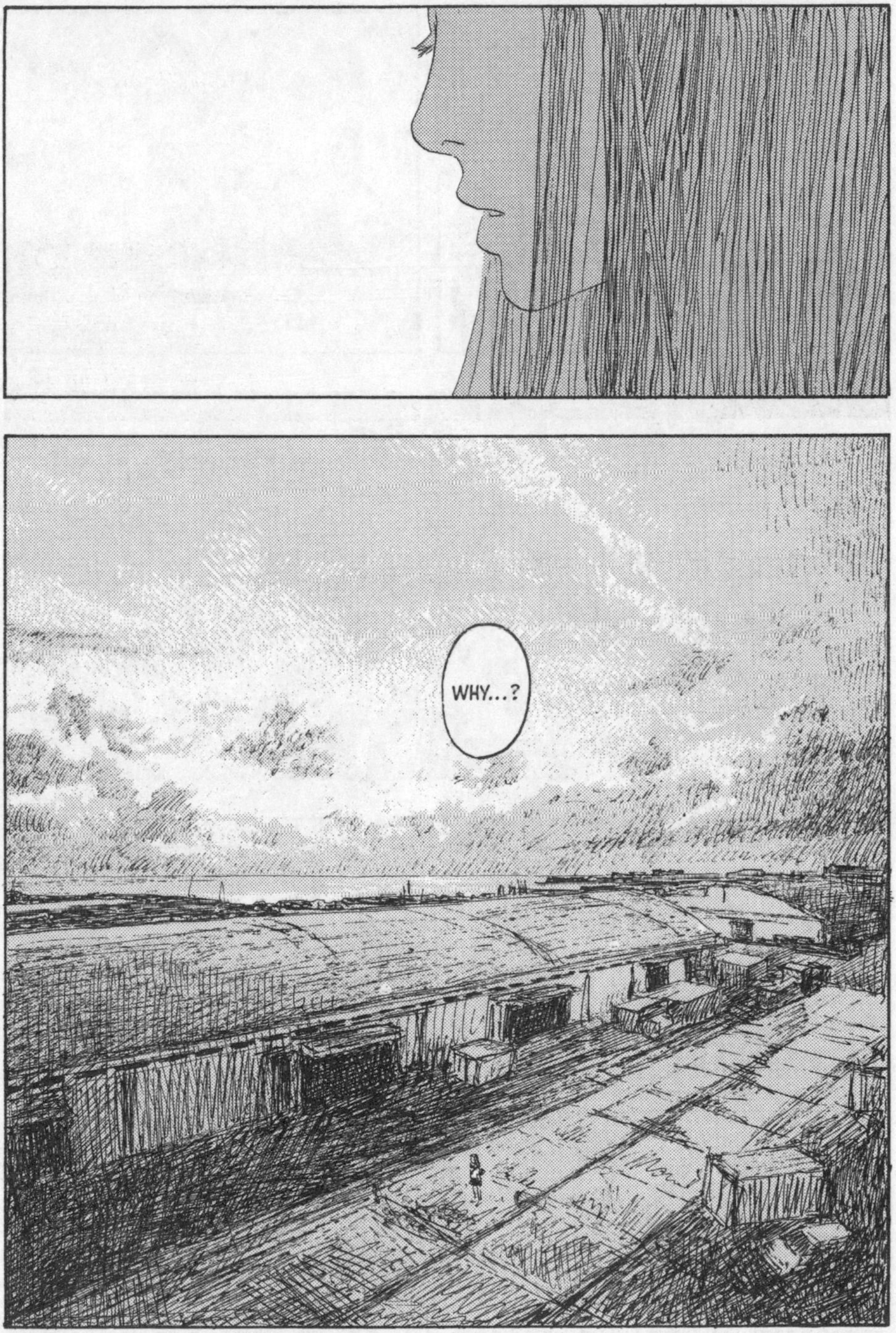
WHY...?

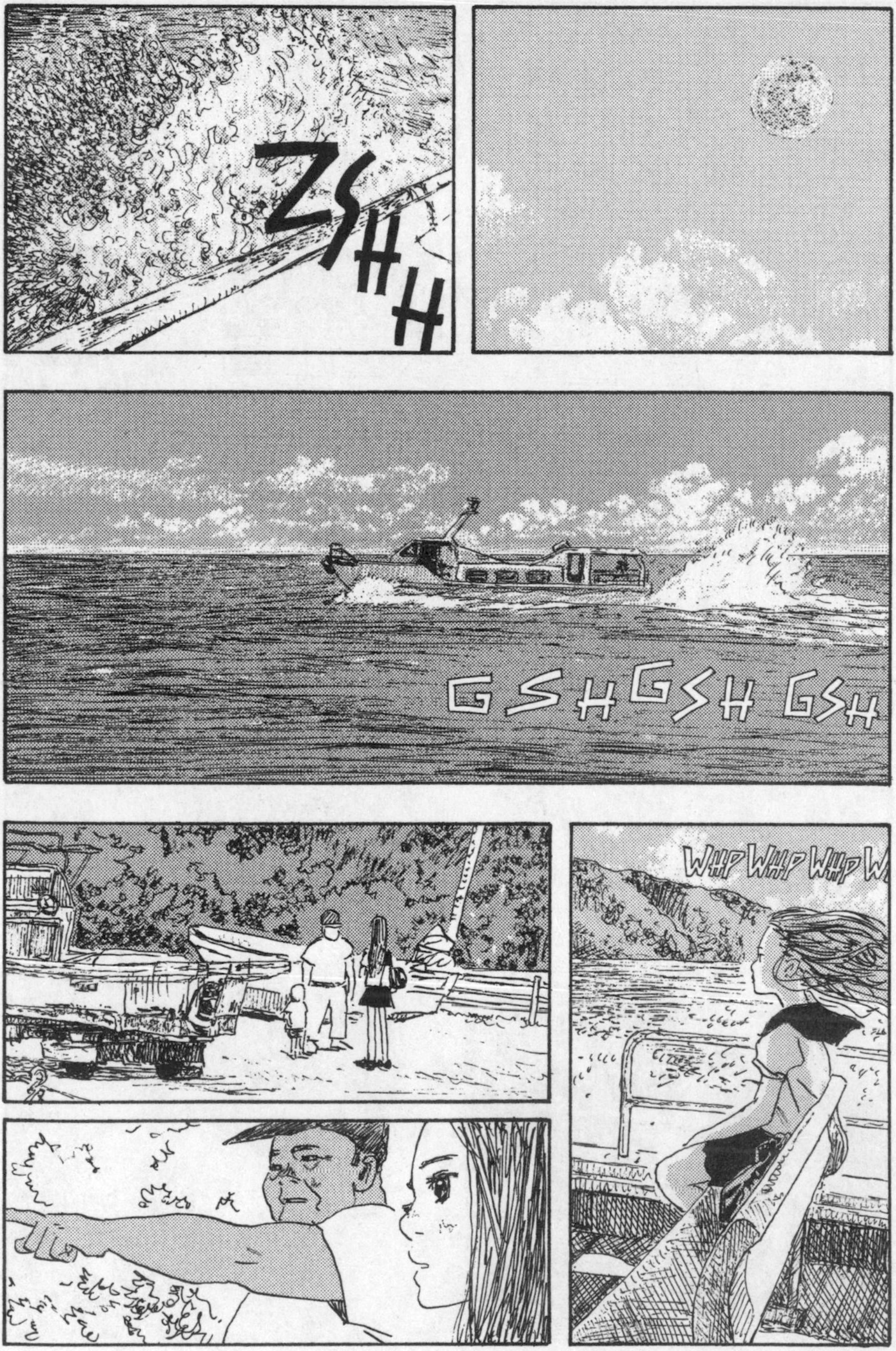
ZSHH
GSHGSH GSH
WHP WHP WHP

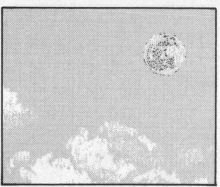

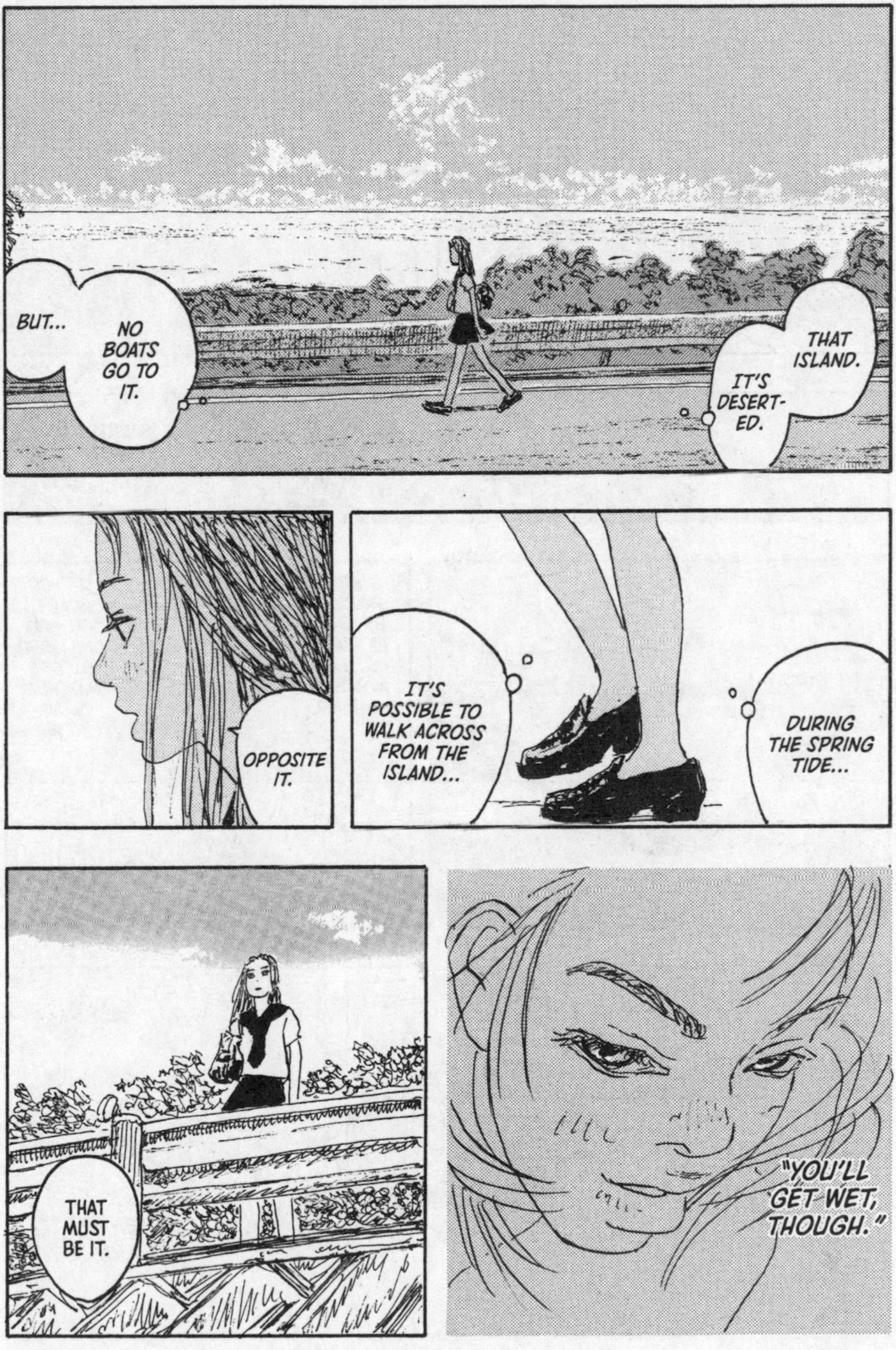
THAT ISLAND. IT'S DESERT-ED.
BUT... NO BOATS GO TO IT.
DURING THE SPRING TIDE...
IT'S POSSIBLE TO WALK ACROSS FROM THE ISLAND...
OPPOSITE IT.
"YOU'LL GET WET, THOUGH."
THAT MUST BE IT.

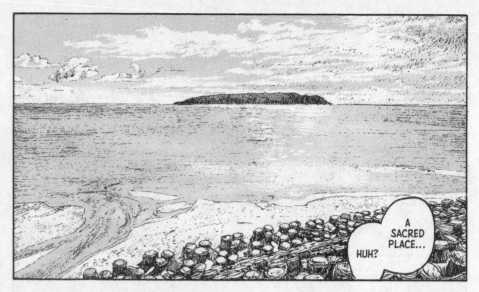

A SACRED PLACE...
HUH?
"IF YOU START WALKING ONE HOUR BEFORE MAXIMUM LOW TIDE...
TIDE CHART
High Tide
"YOU SHOULD BE ABLE TO REACH THE ISLAND WITHOUT SWIMMING."
WHY...
AM I LISTENING TO CHITARU-SAN?

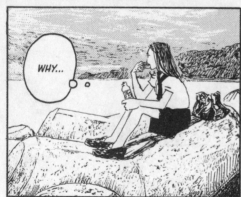

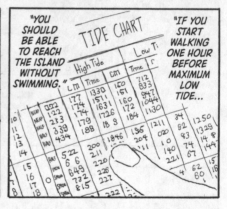

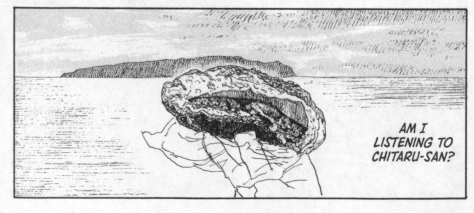

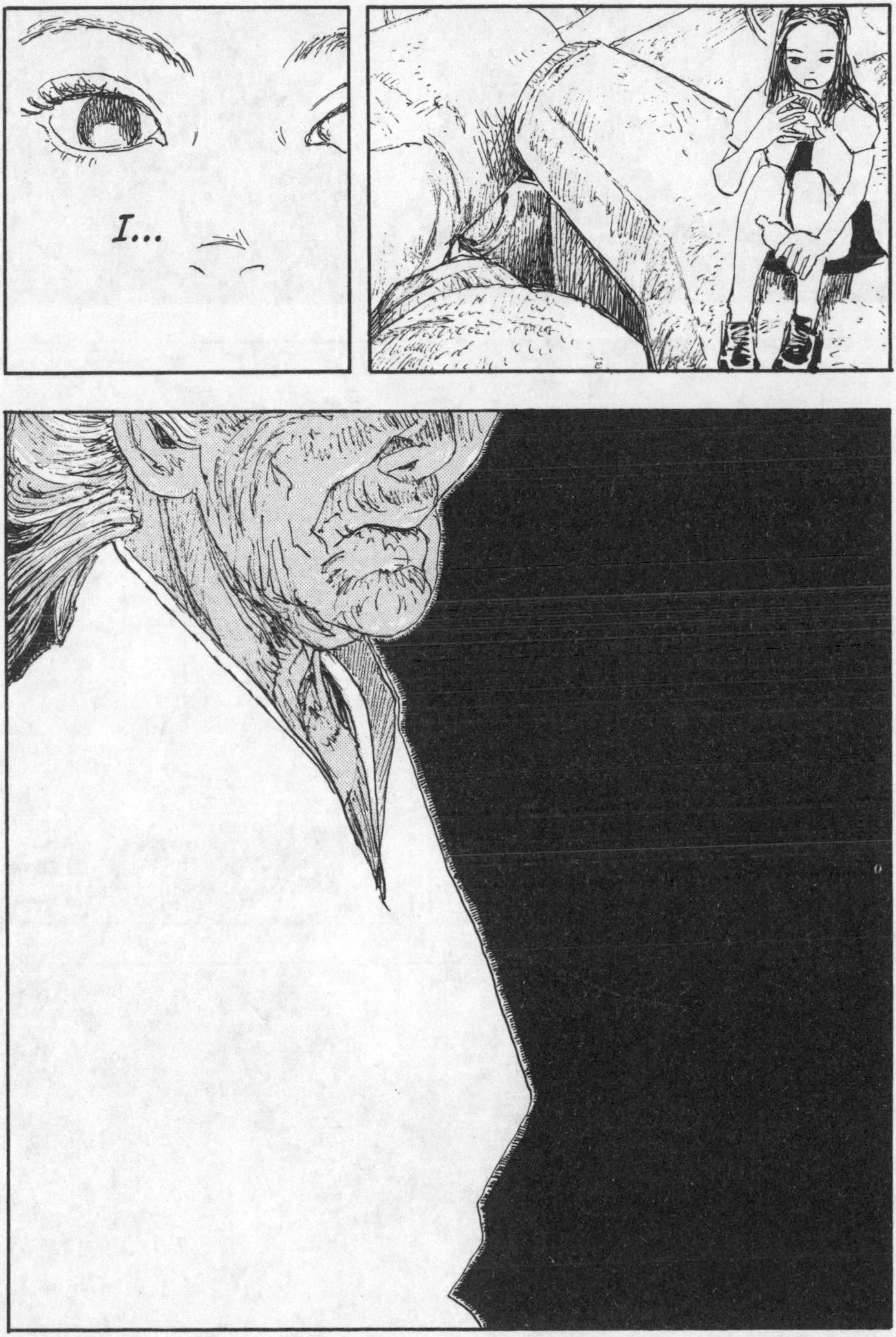
I...

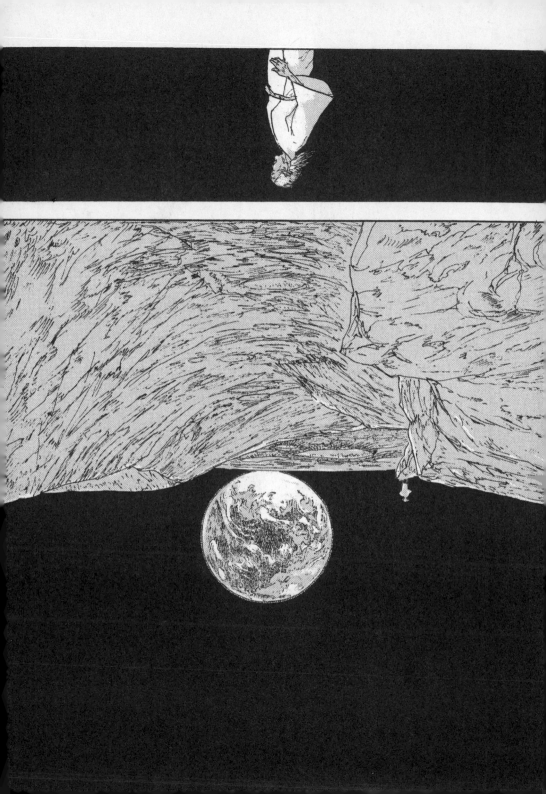

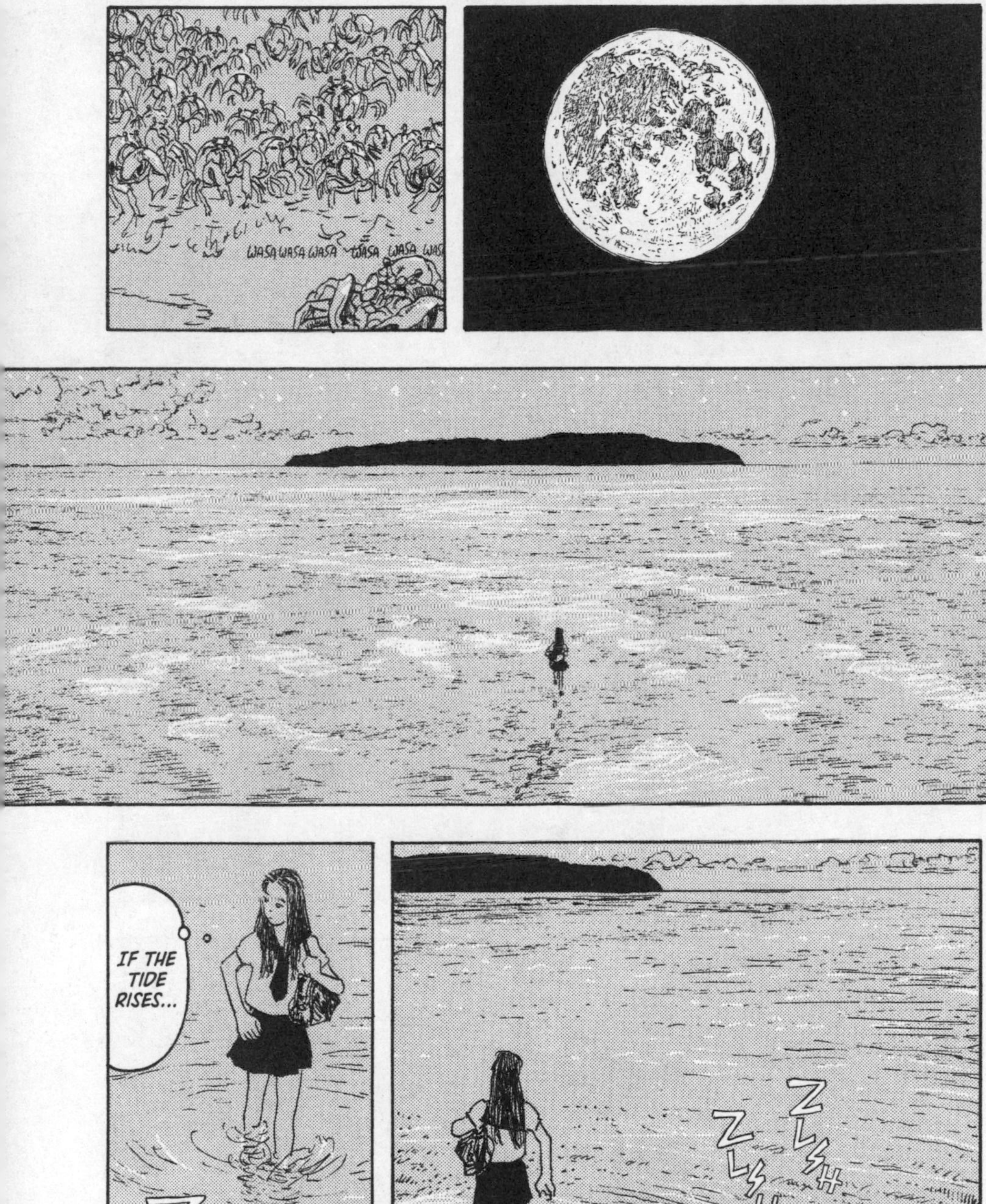
WASA WASA WASA WASA WASA WASA
ZLSH
ZLSH
IF THE TIDE RISES...
ZLSH

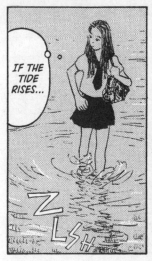

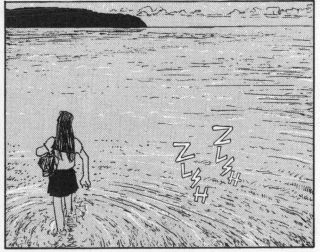

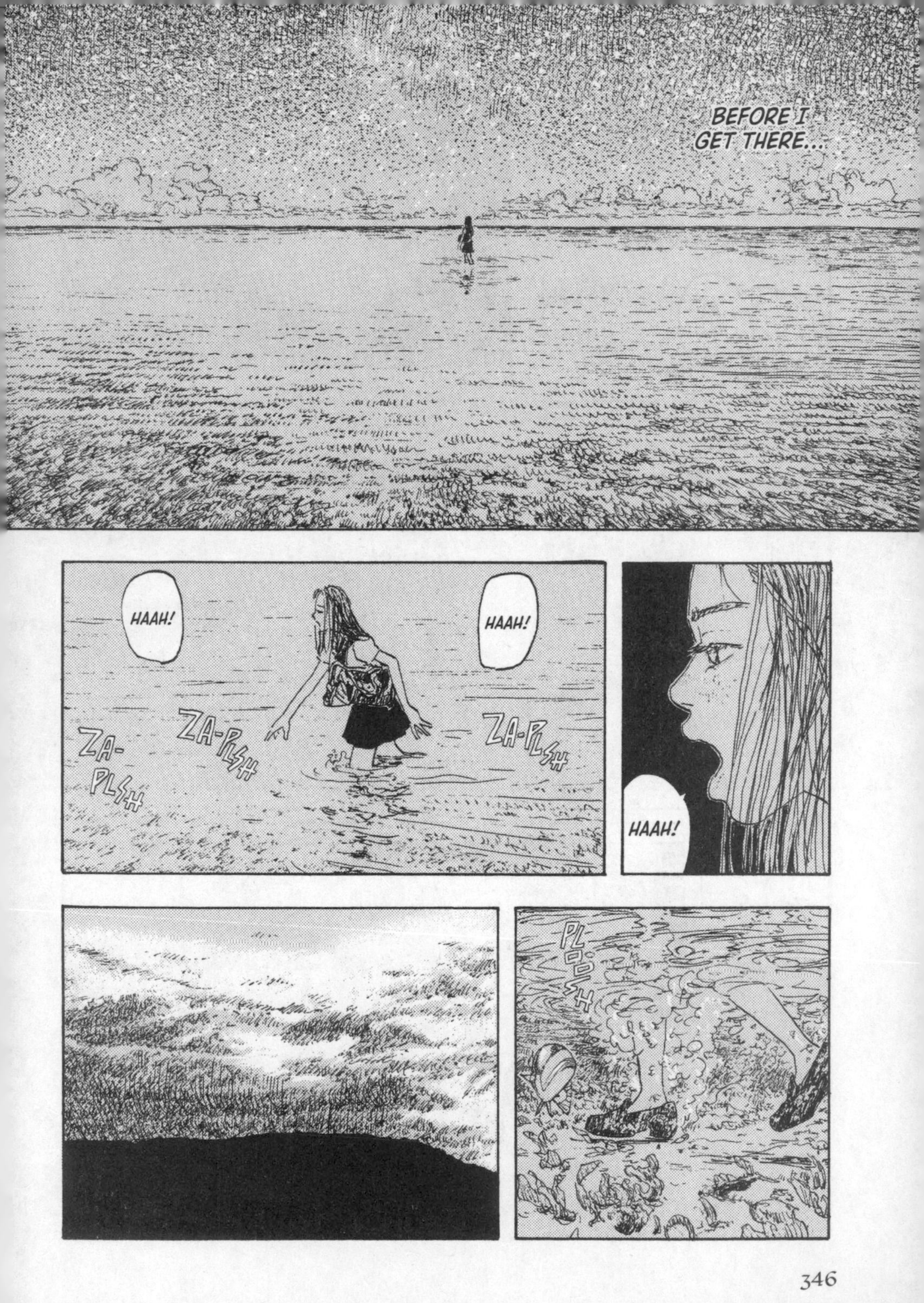
BEFORE I GET THERE...
HAAH!
HAAH!
ZA-PLSH
HAAH!
ZA-PLSH
ZA-PLSH
PLOOSH

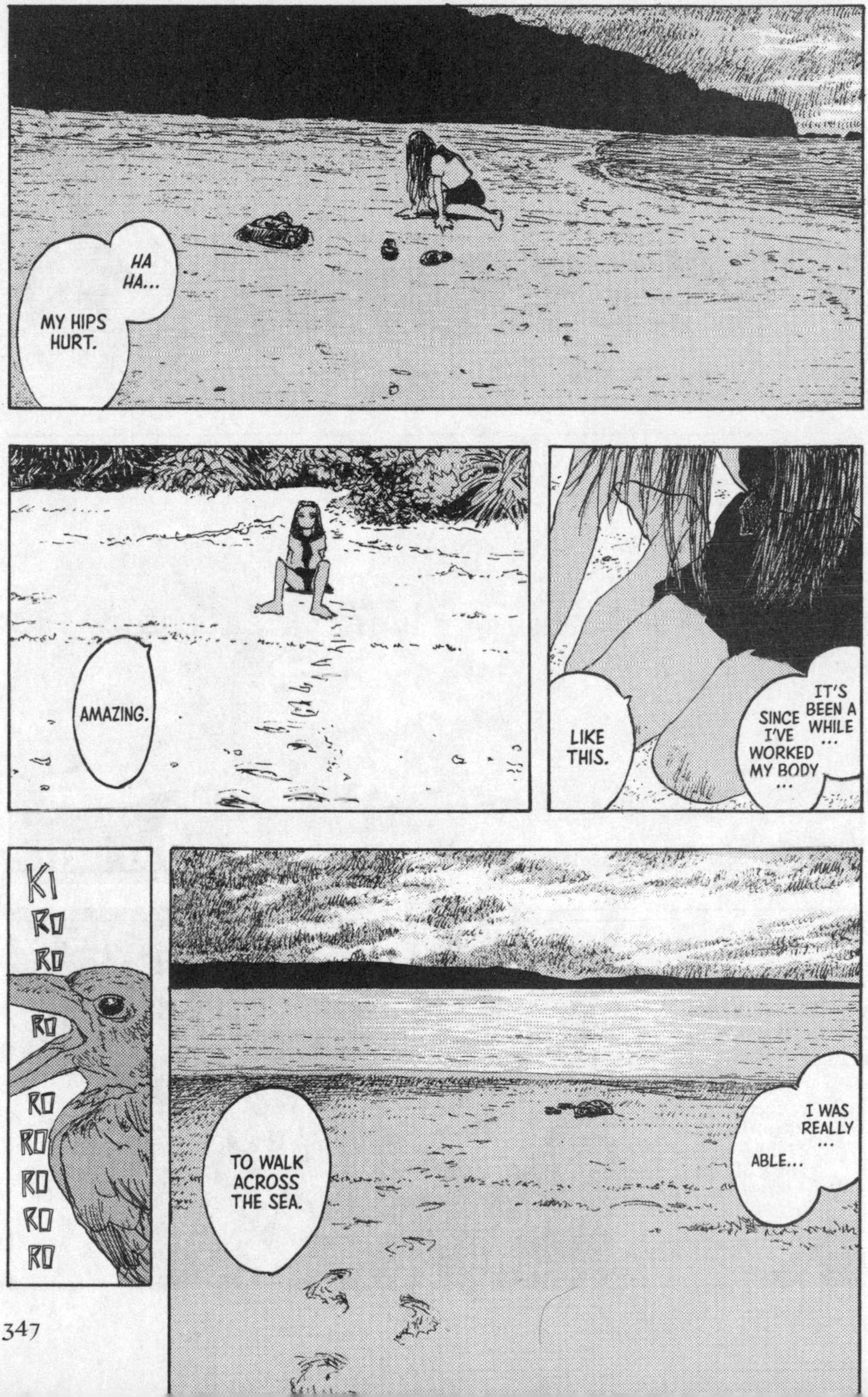
HA HA...
MY HIPS HURT.
IT'S BEEN A WHILE... SINCE I'VE WORKED MY BODY...
LIKE THIS.
AMAZING.
I WAS REALLY... ABLE...
TO WALK ACROSS THE SEA.
KI RO RO RO RO RO RO RO RO

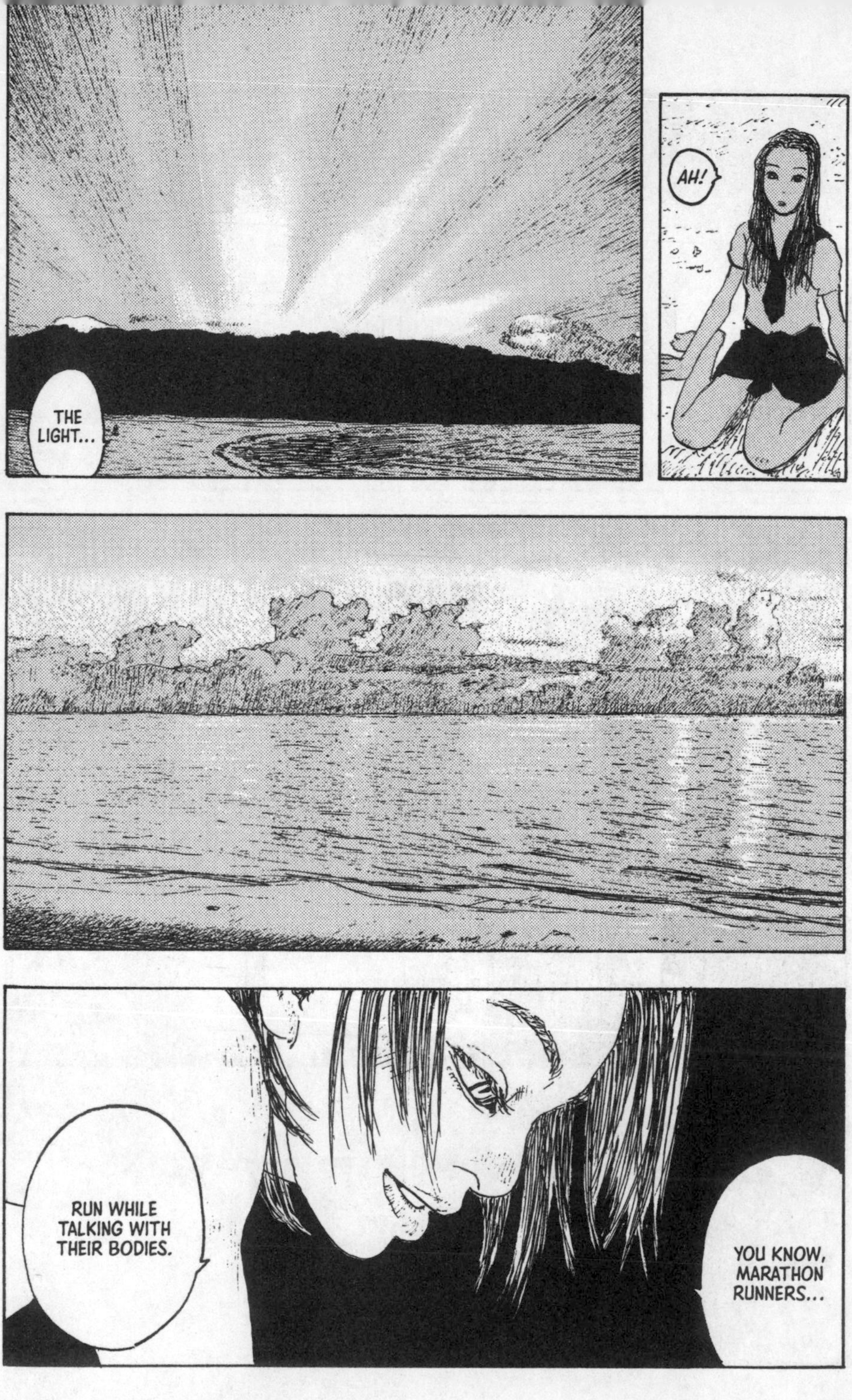
AH!
THE LIGHT...
YOU KNOW, MARATHON RUNNERS...
RUN WHILE TALKING WITH THEIR BODIES.

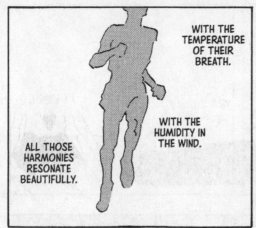

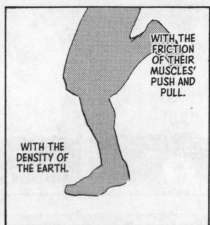

WITH THE FRICTION OF THEIR MUSCLES' PUSH AND PULL.
WITH THE DENSITY OF THE EARTH.
WITH THE TEMPERATURE OF THEIR BREATH.
WITH THE HUMIDITY IN THE WIND.
ALL THOSE HARMONIES RESONATE BEAUTIFULLY.
THEY RUN AS IF SINGING.
EVEN SWIMMERS...
EVEN THE PEOPLE WHO GROW BEAUTIFUL VEGETABLES IN THE FIELDS...
EVERYONE FEELS THE SONG OF THE WORLD.
I STRIVE TO ADD MY VOICE TO THE CHORUS, TOO.
TO BLEND IN...
WITH THE WORLD.
HINATA UNDER-STANDS.

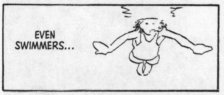

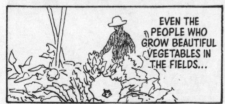

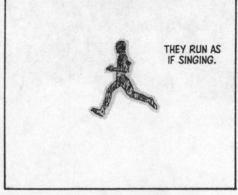

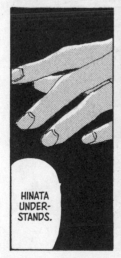

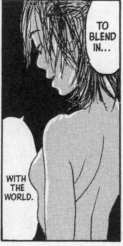

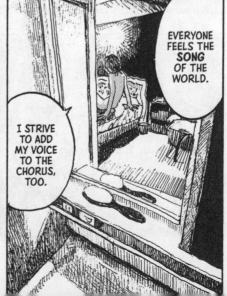

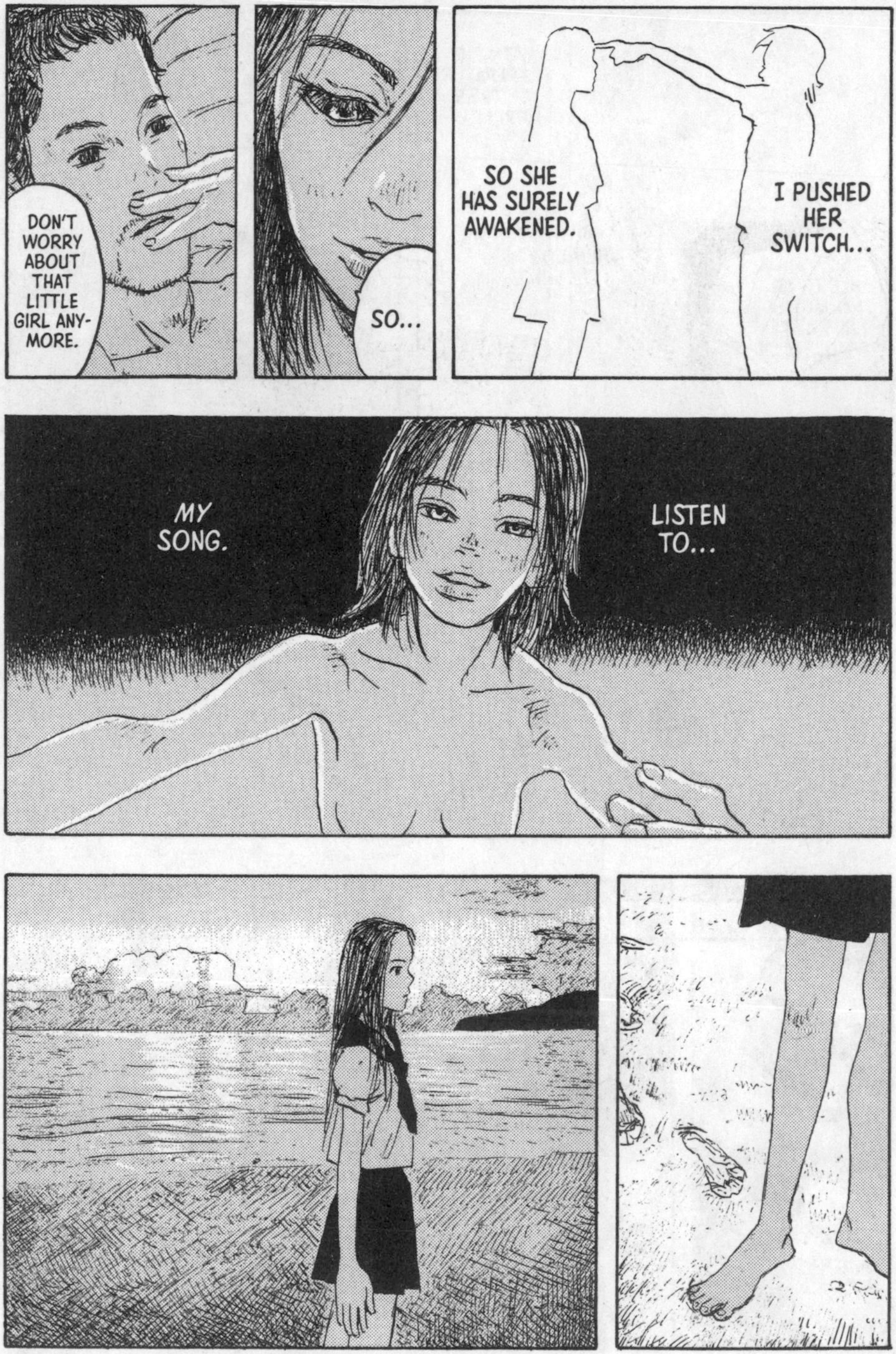
I PUSHED HER SWITCH...
SO SHE HAS SURELY AWAKENED.
SO...
DON'T WORRY ABOUT THAT LITTLE GIRL ANY-MORE.
LISTEN TO...
MY SONG.

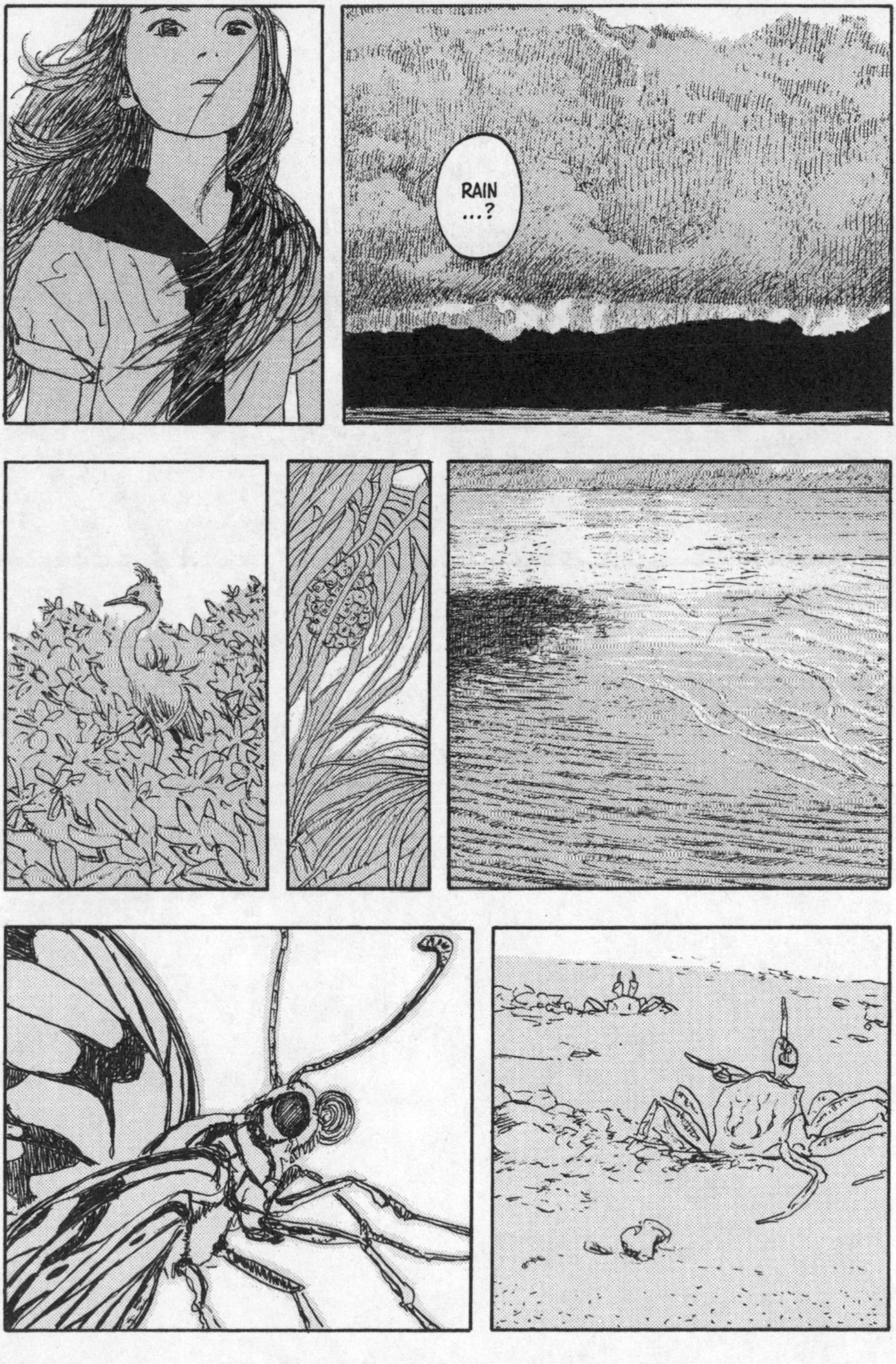
RAIN ...?

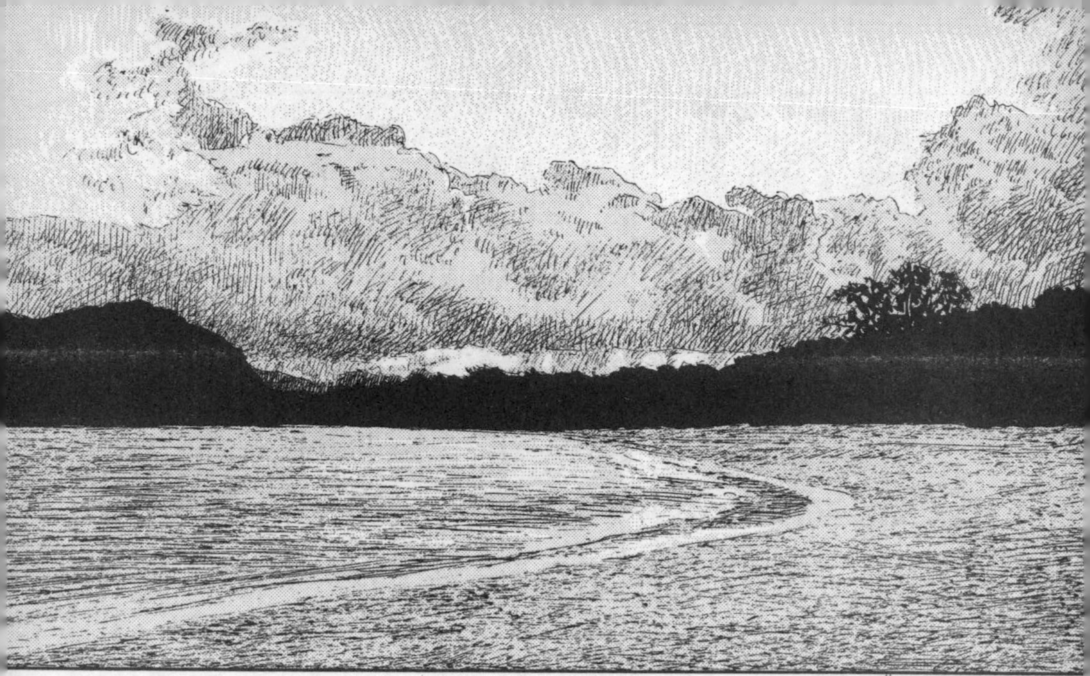

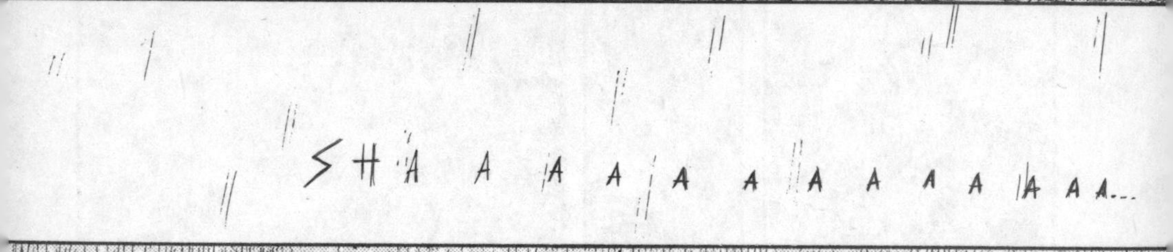
SHAAAAAAAAAAAA...

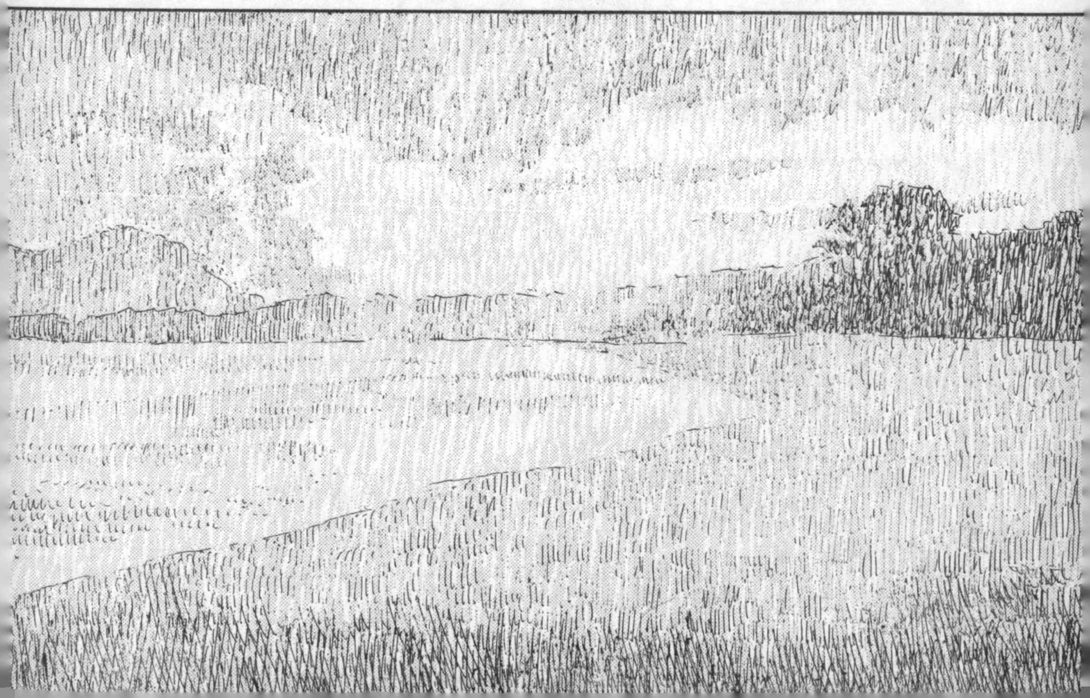

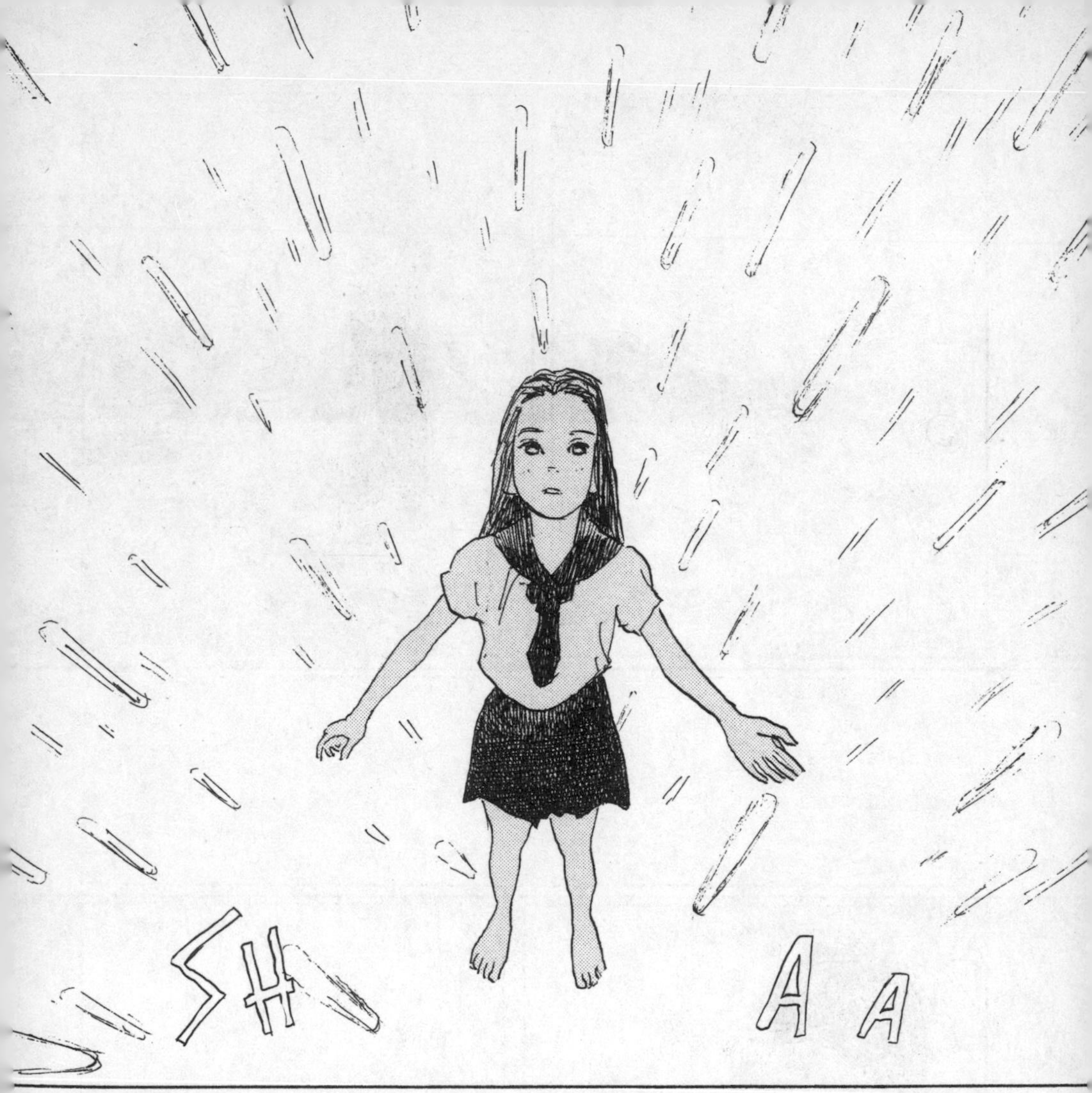
SHAA
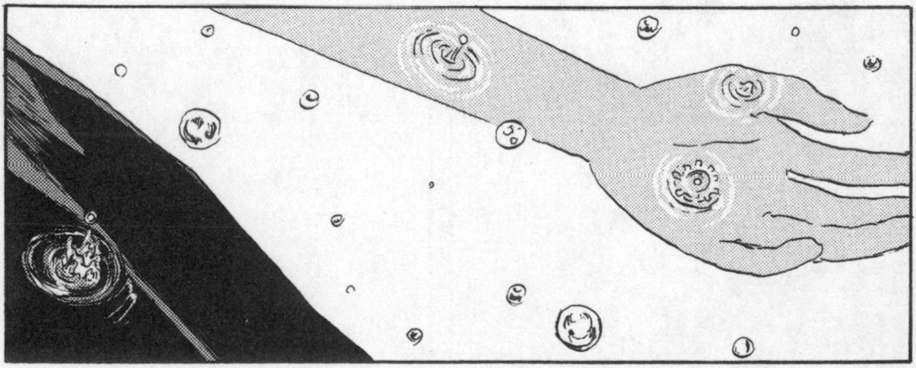

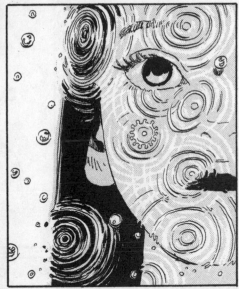

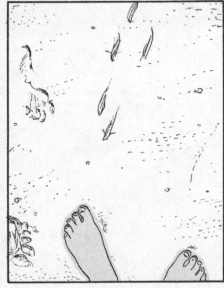

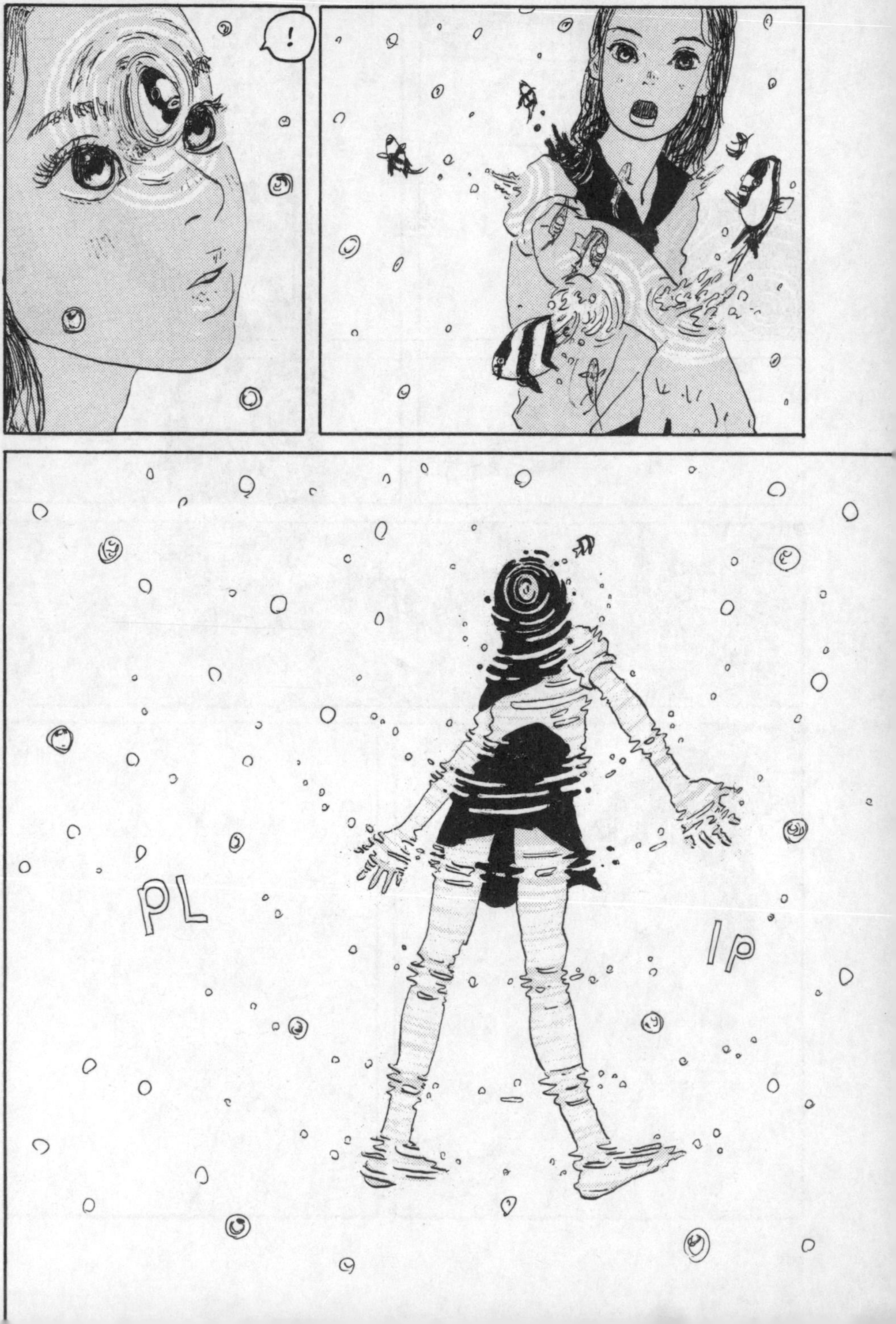
!
PL
lp

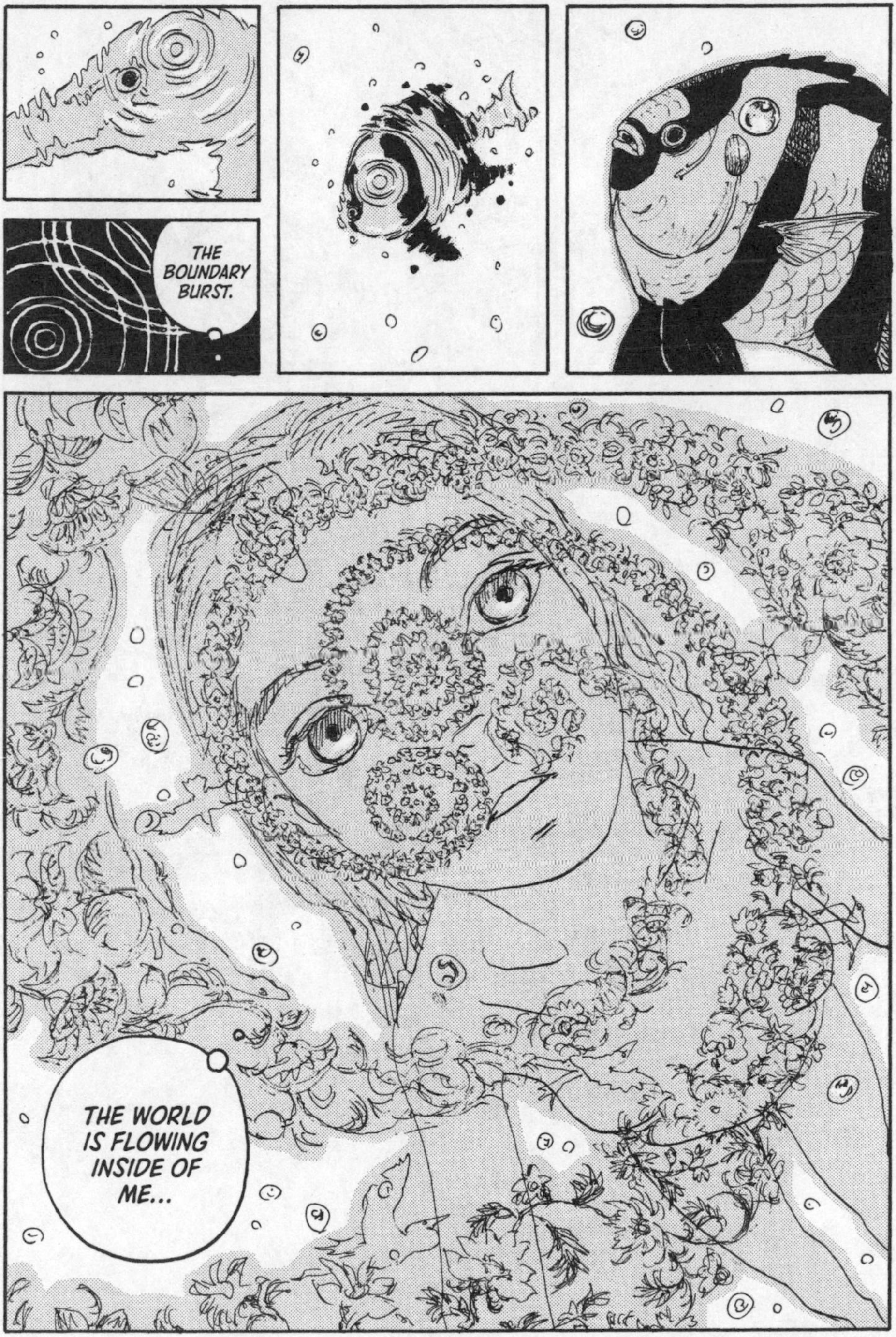
THE BOUNDARY BURST.
THE WORLD IS FLOWING INSIDE OF ME...

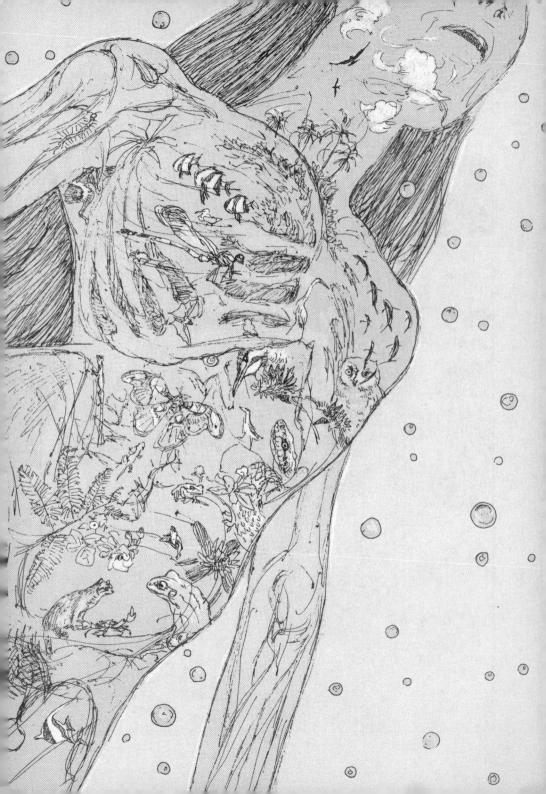

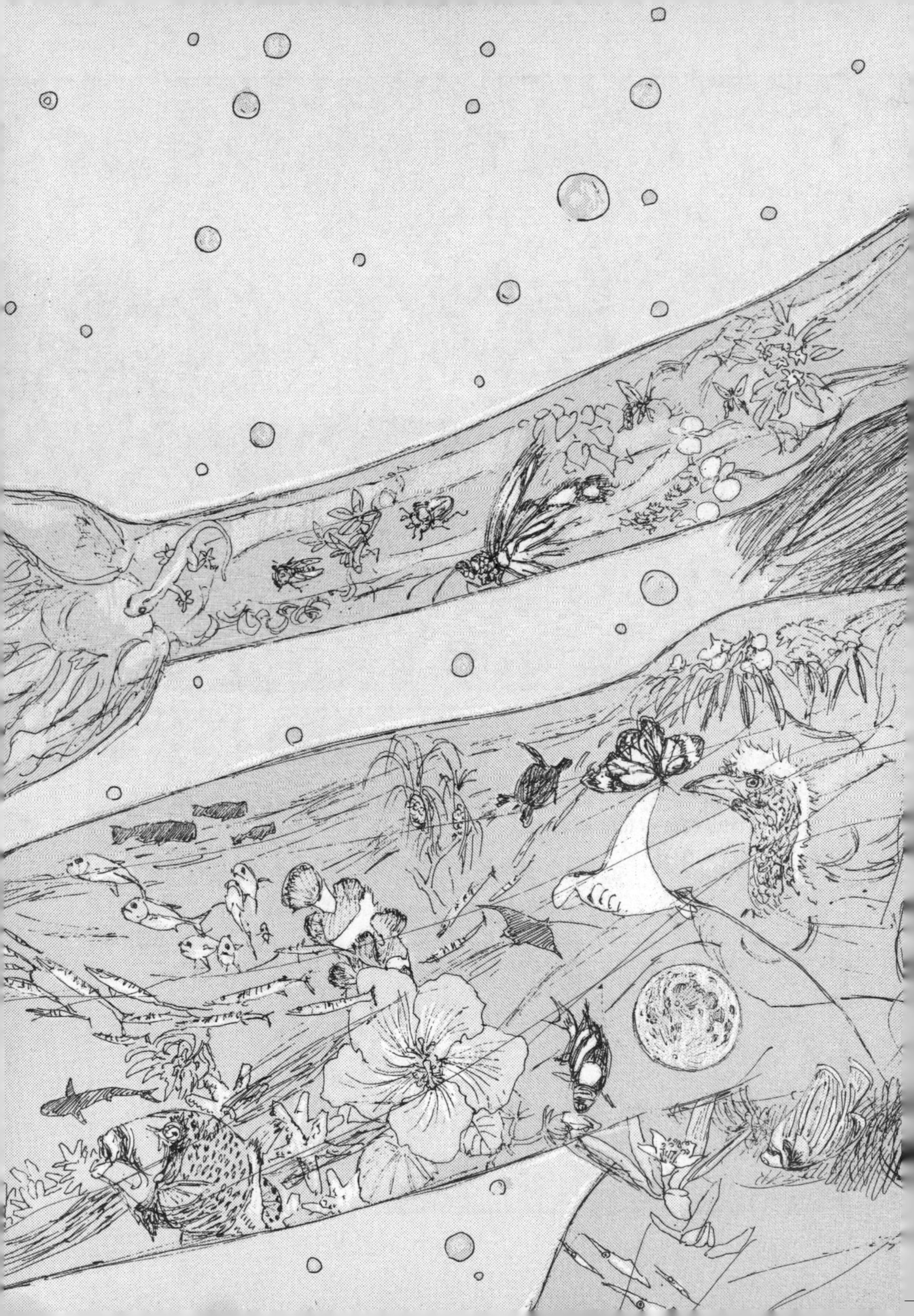

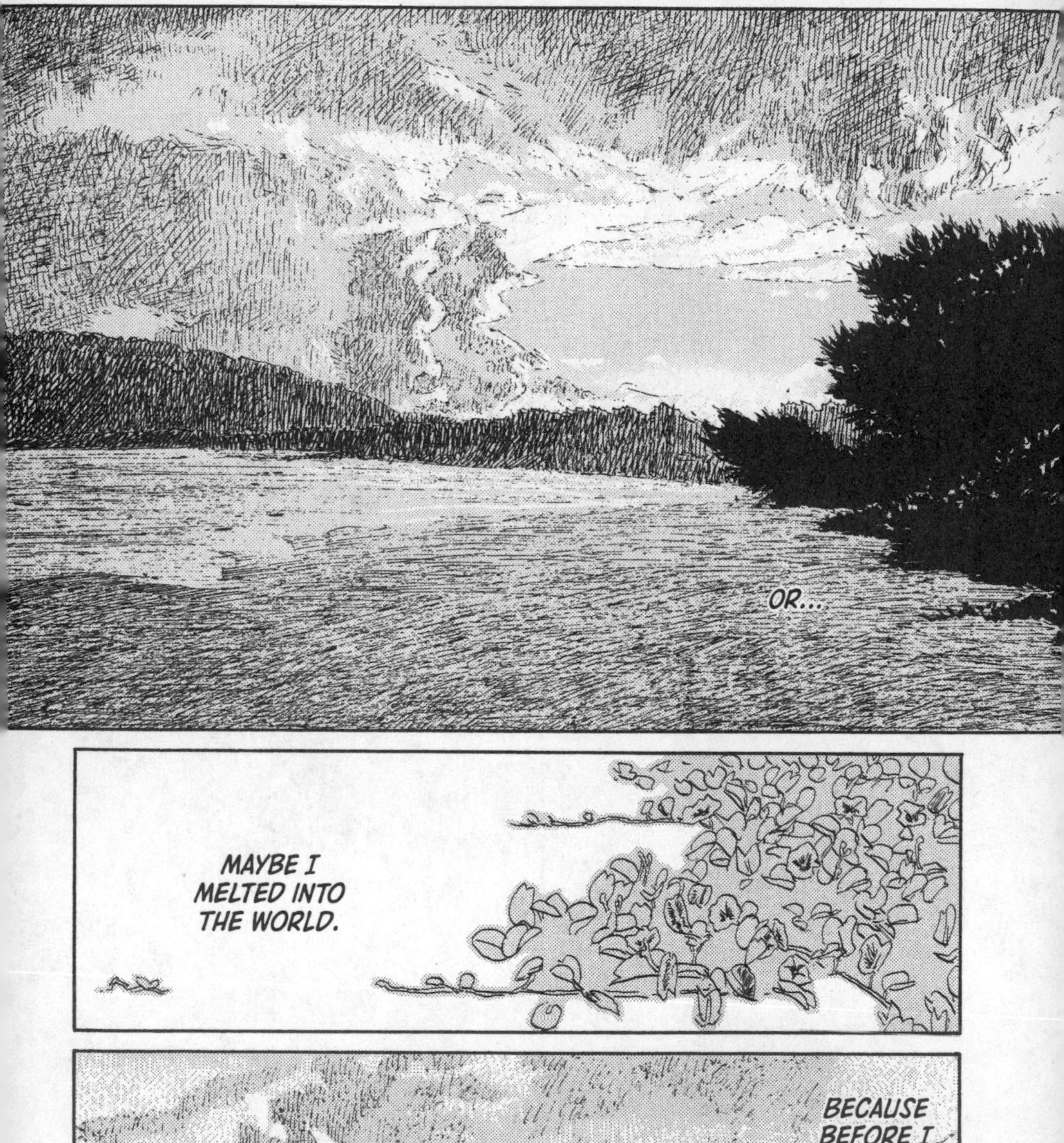
OR...
MAYBE I MELTED INTO THE WORLD.
BECAUSE BEFORE I KNEW IT...
I WAS SINGING IN A LOUD VOICE.

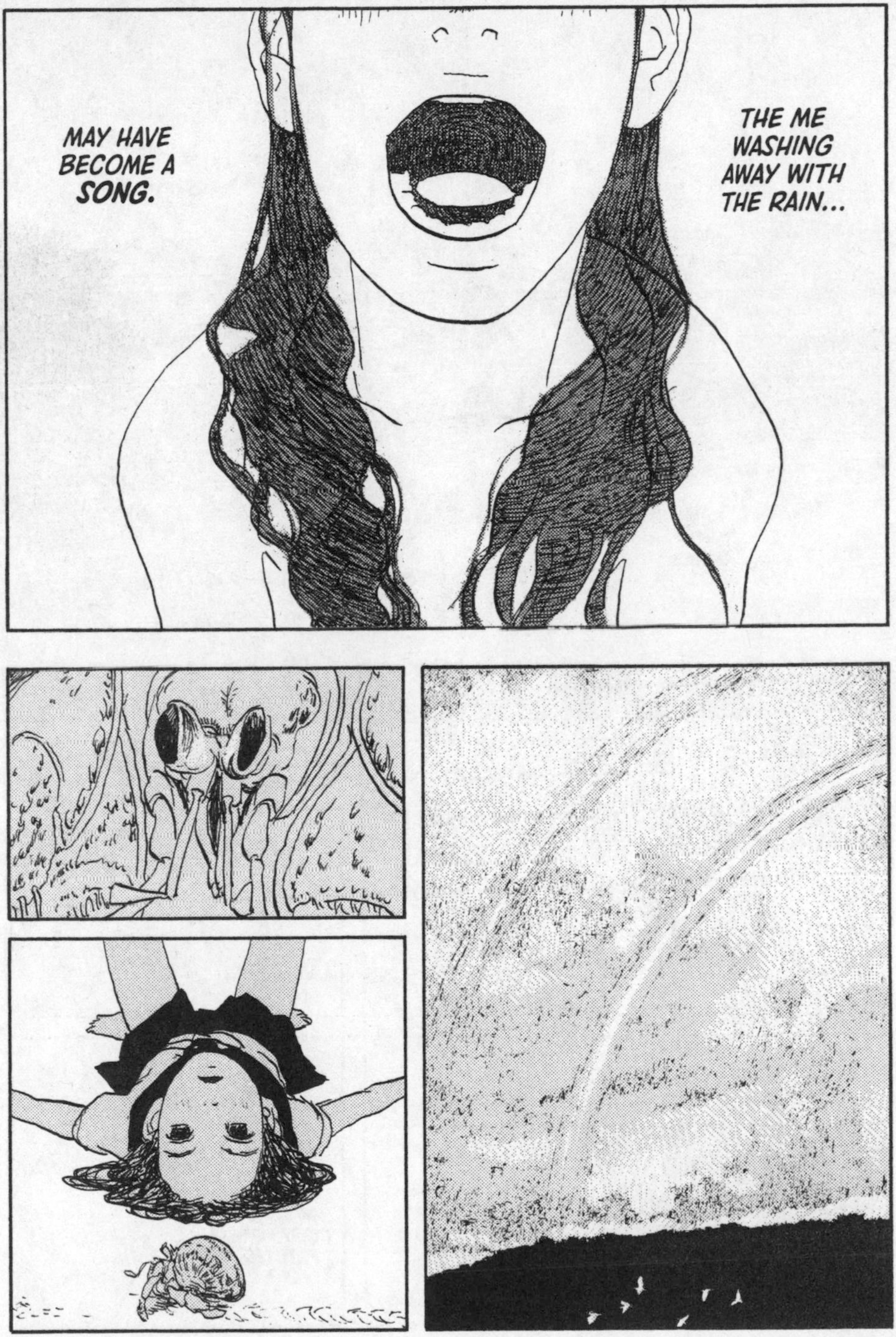
THE ME WASHING AWAY WITH THE RAIN...
MAY HAVE BECOME A SONG.

ZA-ZSHH...

TO THE
WORLD.

I AM
TUNED
...

IT'S LIKE
I BECAME
CLEAR...

AND THE
IMPURITIES
BUILT UP
WITHIN MY
BODY WERE
FILTERED
OUT.

ZSSHH

MAYBE...

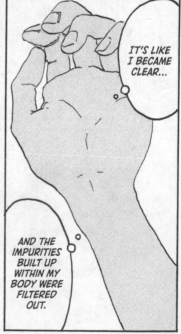

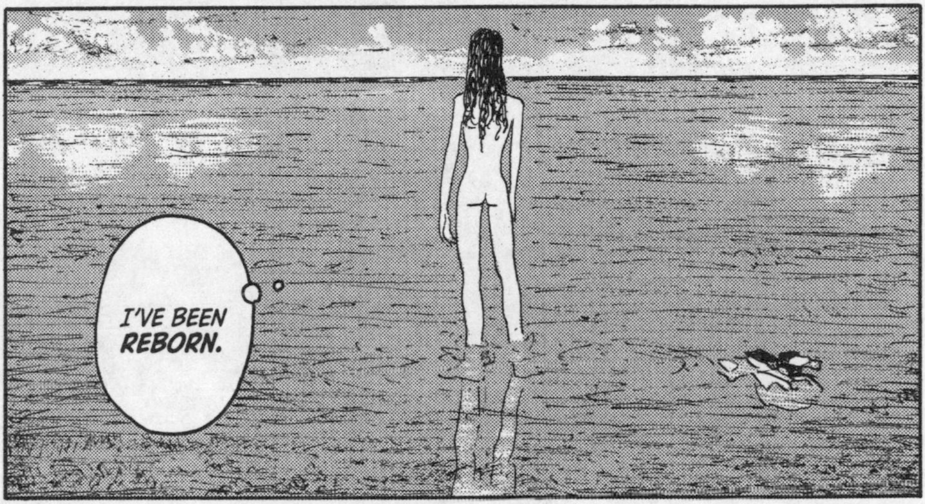
I'VE BEEN REBORN.

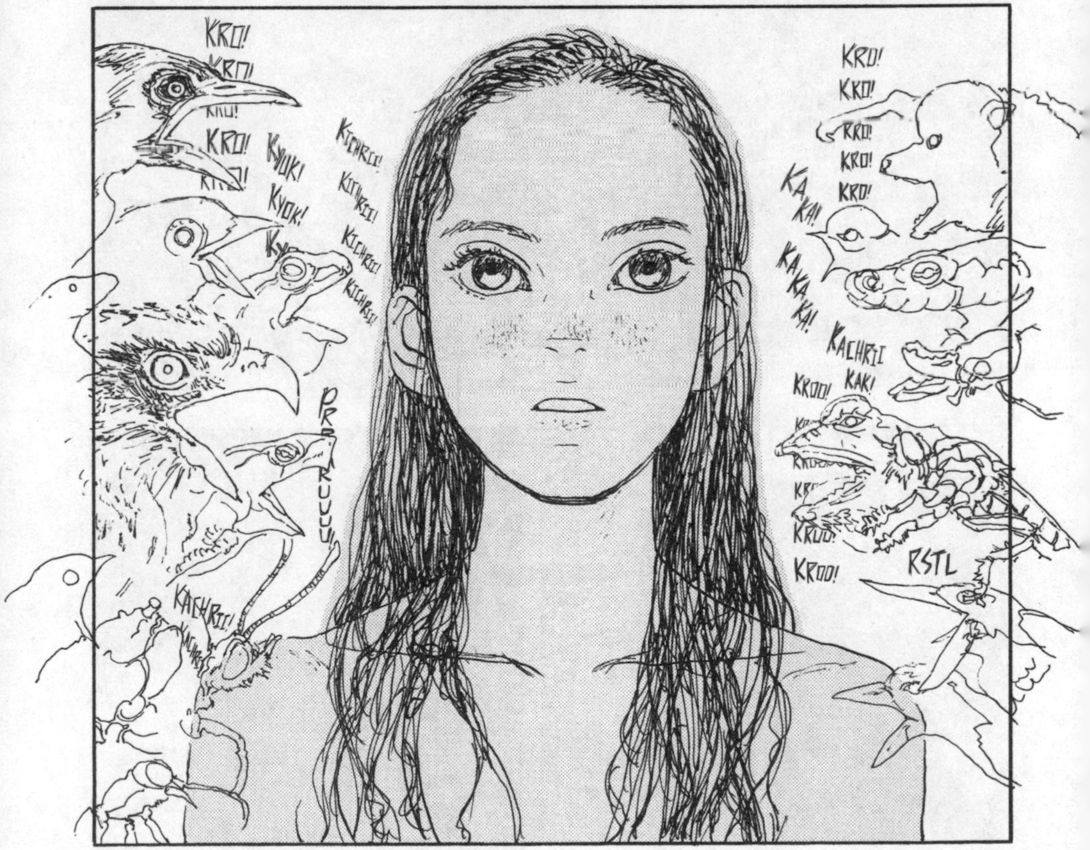
KRO!
KRO!
KRO!
KRO!
KRO!
KA KA!
KA KA KA KA!
KACHRII
KAKI
KROO!
KROO!
KROO!
RSTL
KRO!
KRO!
KRO!
KYOK!
KYOK!
KICHRII!
KICHRII!
KICHRII!
KICHRII!
PRRRUUU
KACHRII!

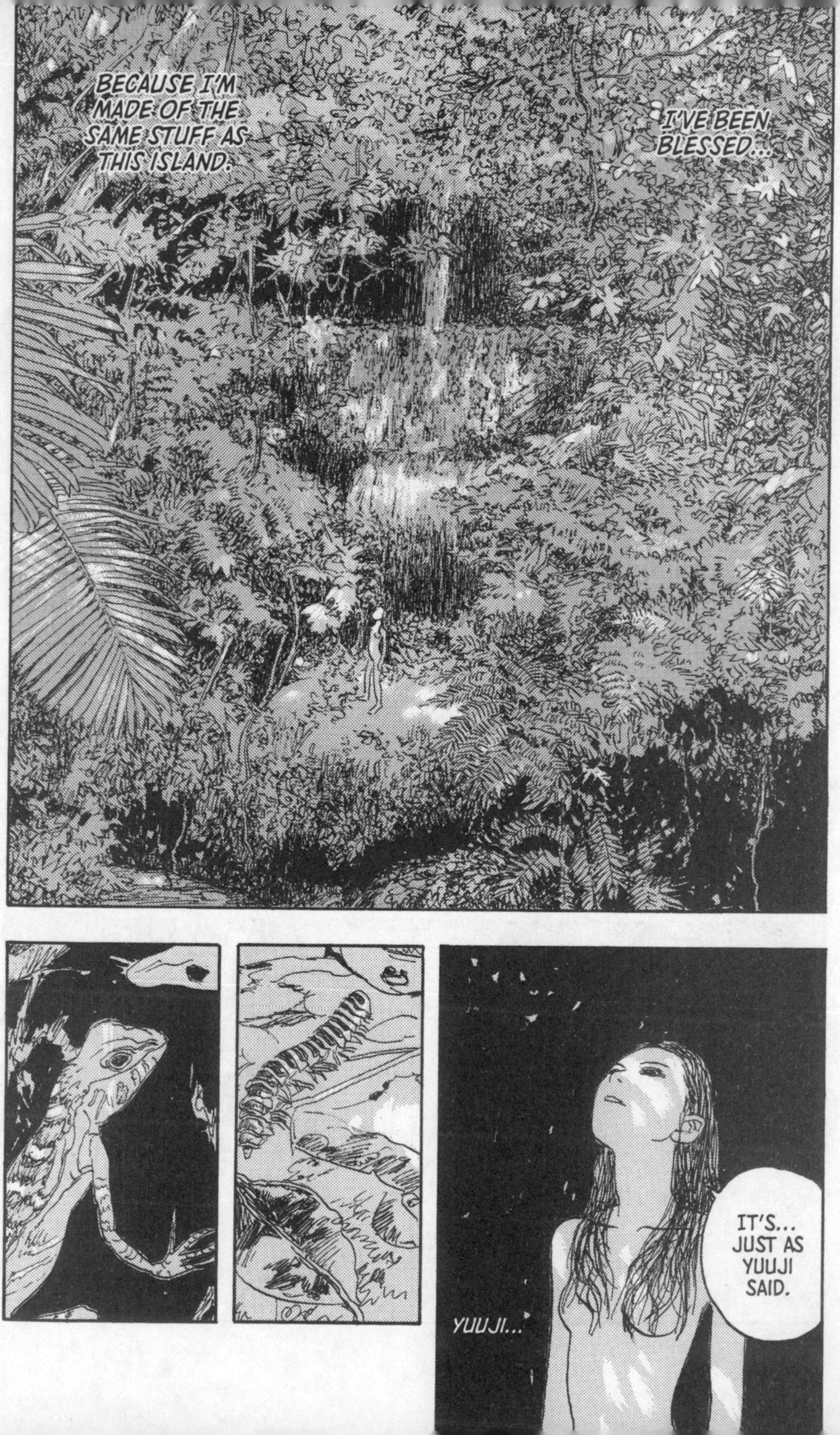
I'VE BEEN BLESSED...
BECAUSE I'M MADE OF THE SAME STUFF AS THIS ISLAND.
IT'S... JUST AS YUUJI SAID.
YUUJI...

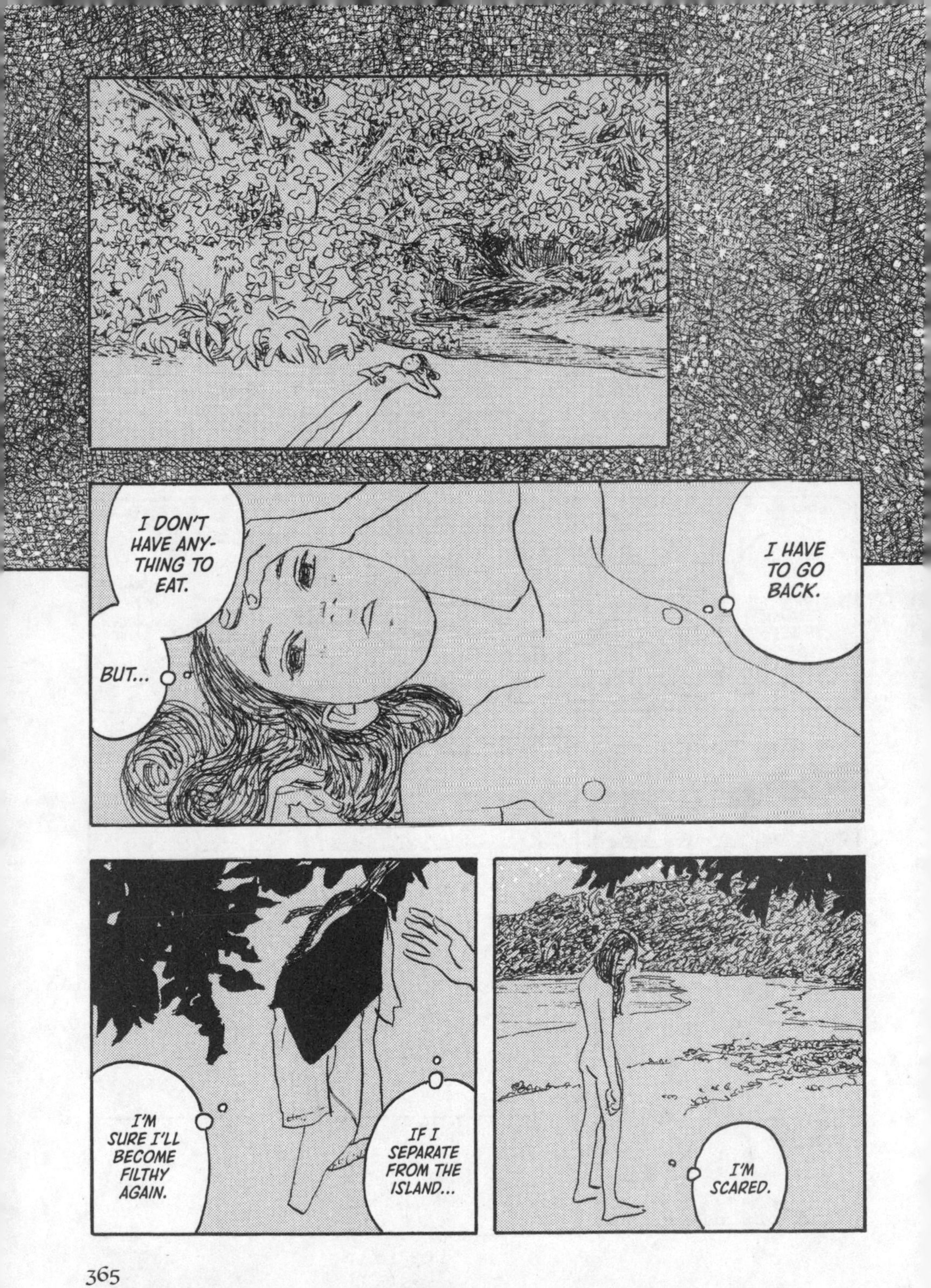
I HAVE TO GO BACK.
I DON'T HAVE ANY-THING TO EAT.
BUT...
I'M SCARED.
IF I SEPARATE FROM THE ISLAND...
I'M SURE I'LL BECOME FILTHY AGAIN.

I'LL RETURN TO MY GROSS OLD SELF...
FULL OF HATE, FEAR, AND DOUBT.
I CAN'T SING...
THE SONG ALONE.
AND WITH NO SONG...
I'LL GET MUDDIER AND MUDDIER...
AND BECOME OPAQUE SLUDGE.
I'LL SINK.
AS LONG AS I HAVE THAT SONG...
I CAN MAKE IT THROUGH.

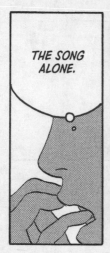

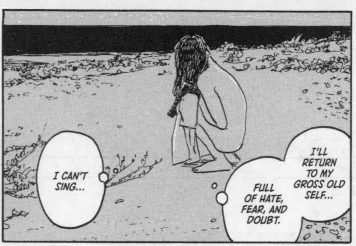

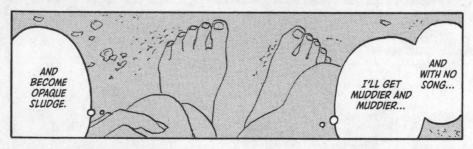

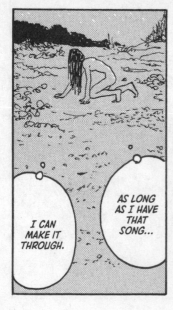

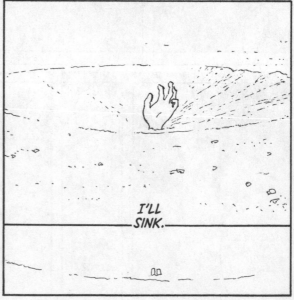

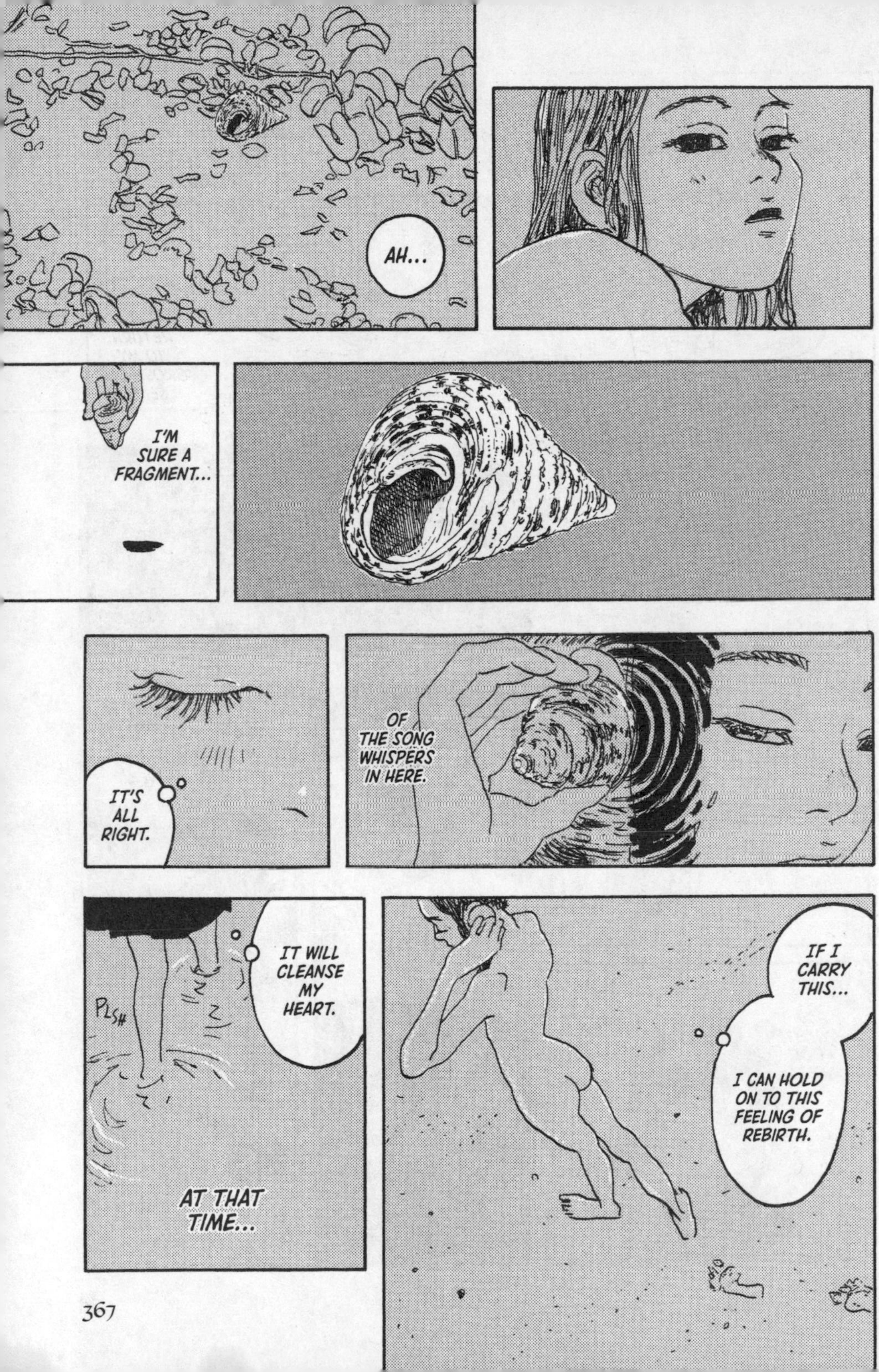
AH...
I'M SURE A FRAGMENT...
OF THE SONG WHISPERS IN HERE.
IT'S ALL RIGHT.
IF I CARRY THIS...
I CAN HOLD ON TO THIS FEELING OF REBIRTH.
IT WILL CLEANSE MY HEART.
PLSH
AT THAT TIME...

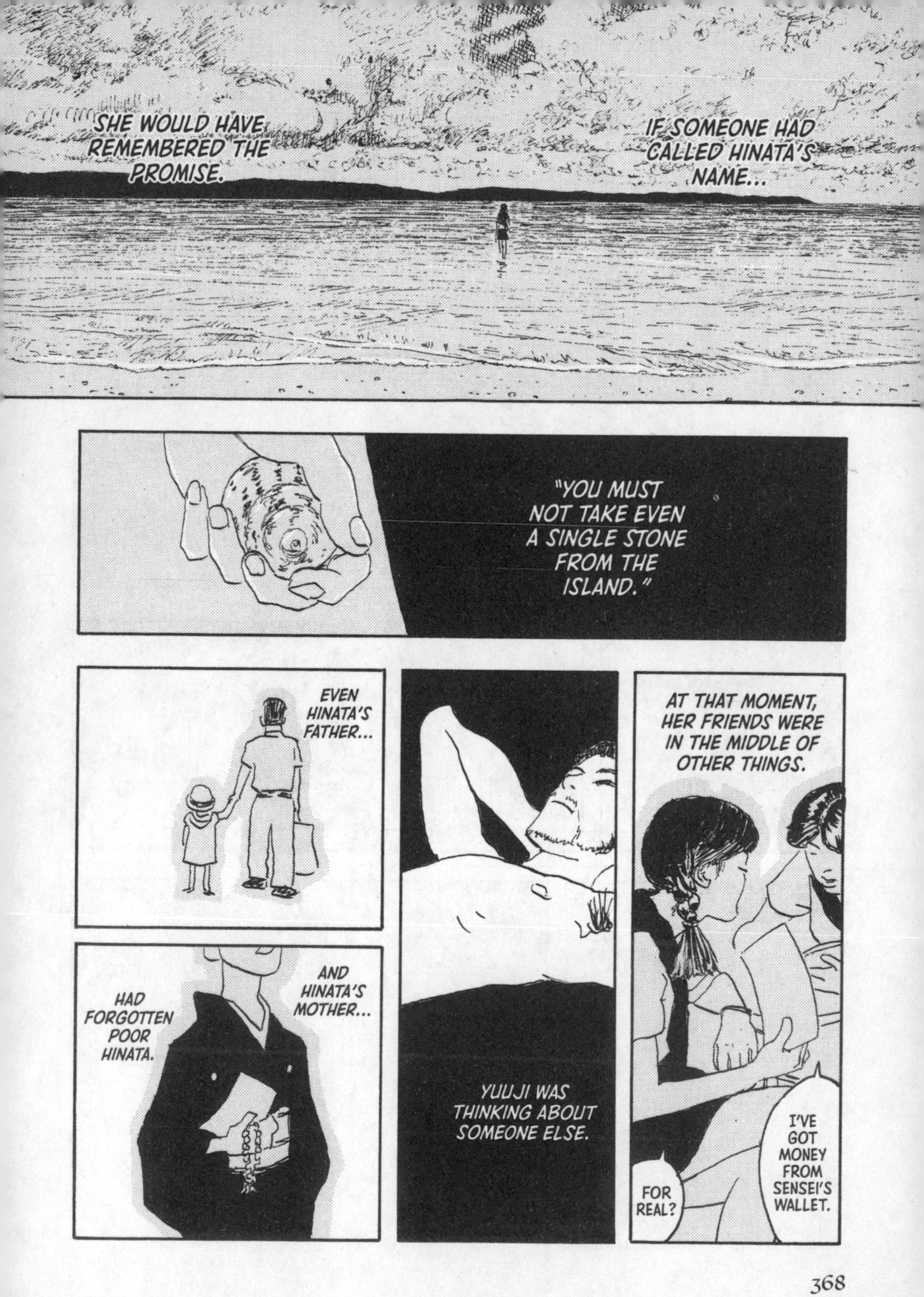
IF SOMEONE HAD CALLED HINATA'S NAME...
SHE WOULD HAVE REMEMBERED THE PROMISE.
"YOU MUST NOT TAKE EVEN A SINGLE STONE FROM THE ISLAND."
AT THAT MOMENT, HER FRIENDS WERE IN THE MIDDLE OF OTHER THINGS.
I'VE GOT MONEY FROM SENSEI'S WALLET.
FOR REAL?
YUUJI WAS THINKING ABOUT SOMEONE ELSE.
EVEN HINATA'S FATHER...
AND HINATA'S MOTHER...
HAD FORGOTTEN POOR HINATA.

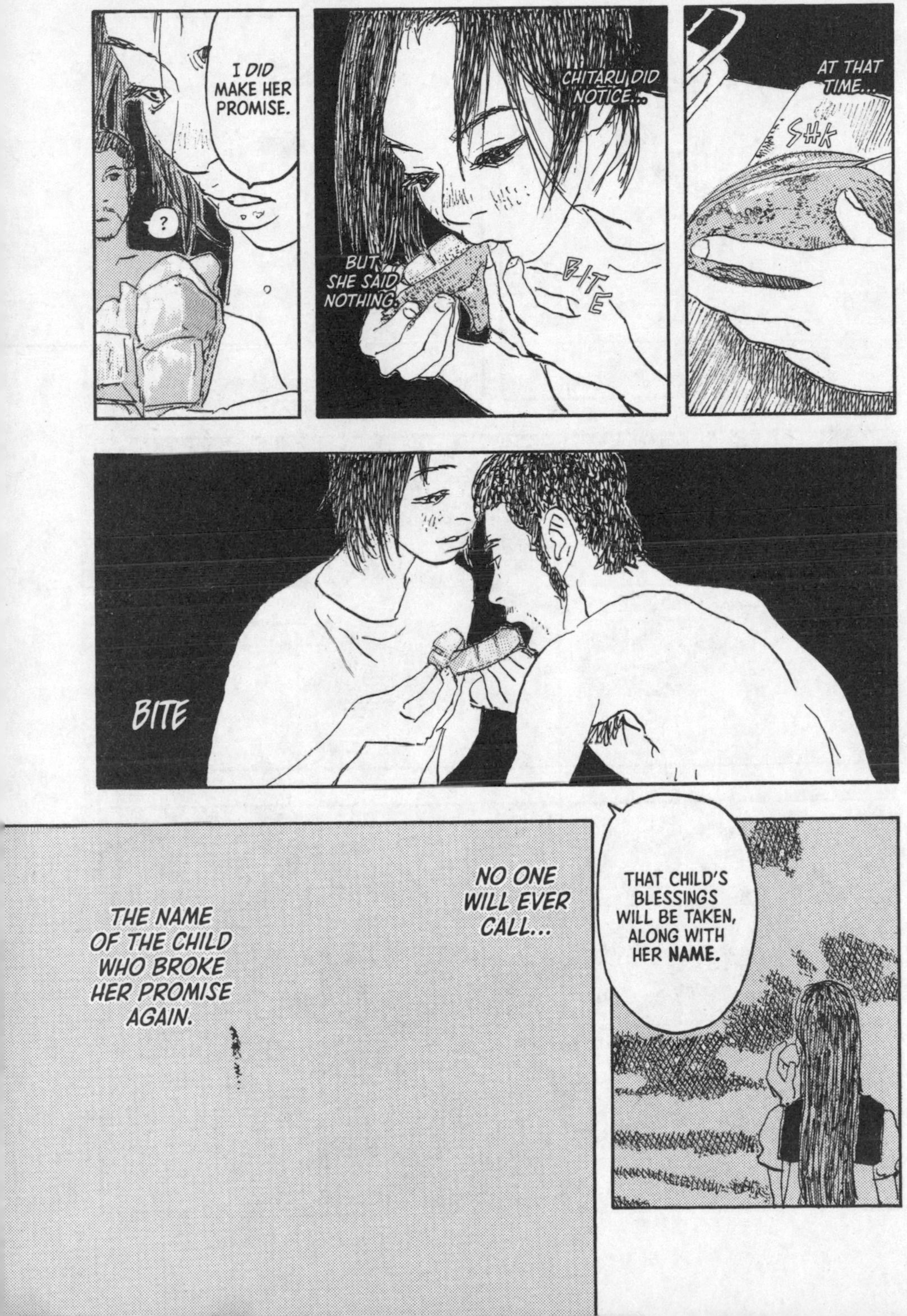
AT THAT TIME...
SHK
CHITARU DID NOTICE...
BUT SHE SAID NOTHING.
BITE
I DID MAKE HER PROMISE.
?
BITE
THAT CHILD'S BLESSINGS WILL BE TAKEN, ALONG WITH HER NAME.
NO ONE WILL EVER CALL...
THE NAME OF THE CHILD WHO BROKE HER PROMISE AGAIN.

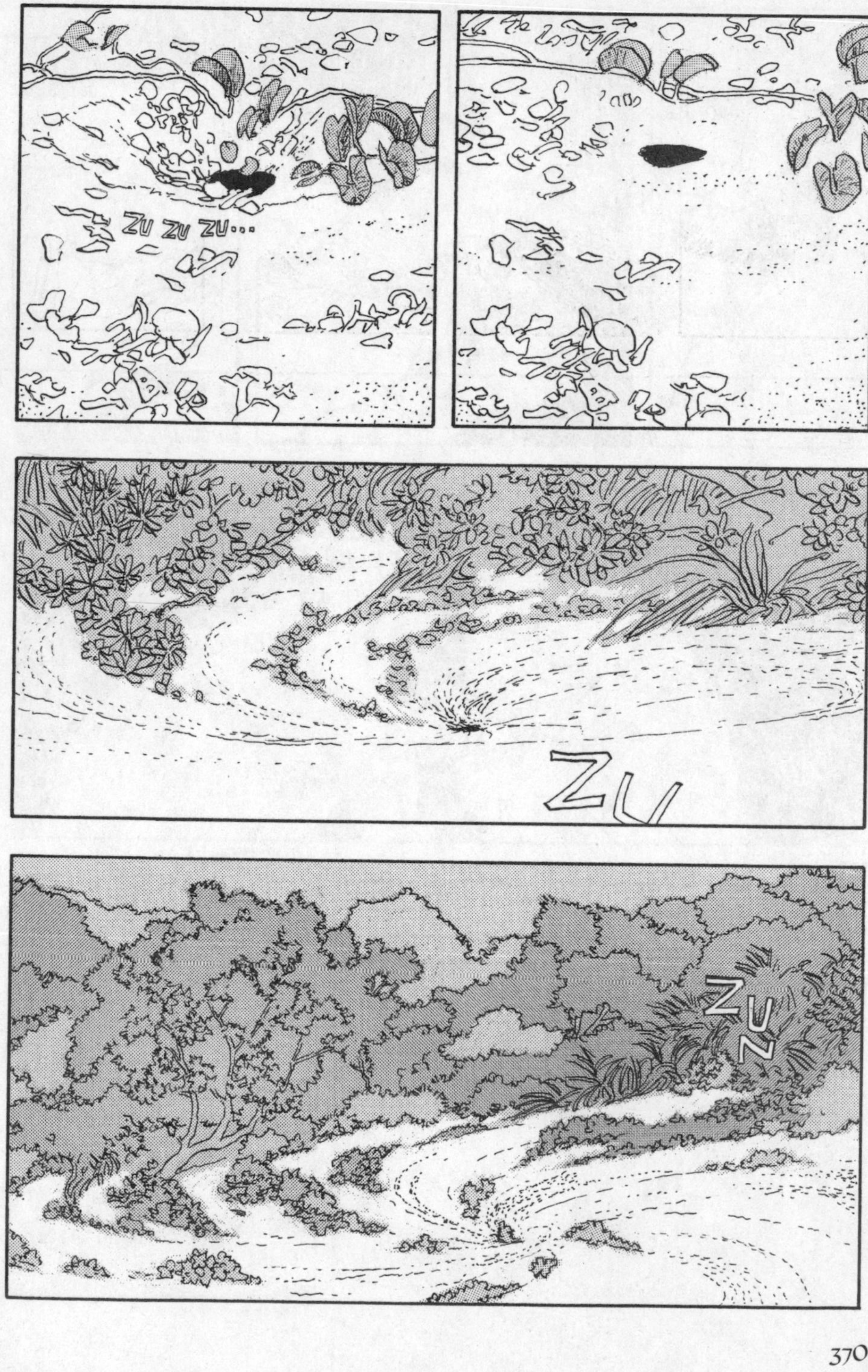
ZU ZU ZU...
ZU
ZU ZU

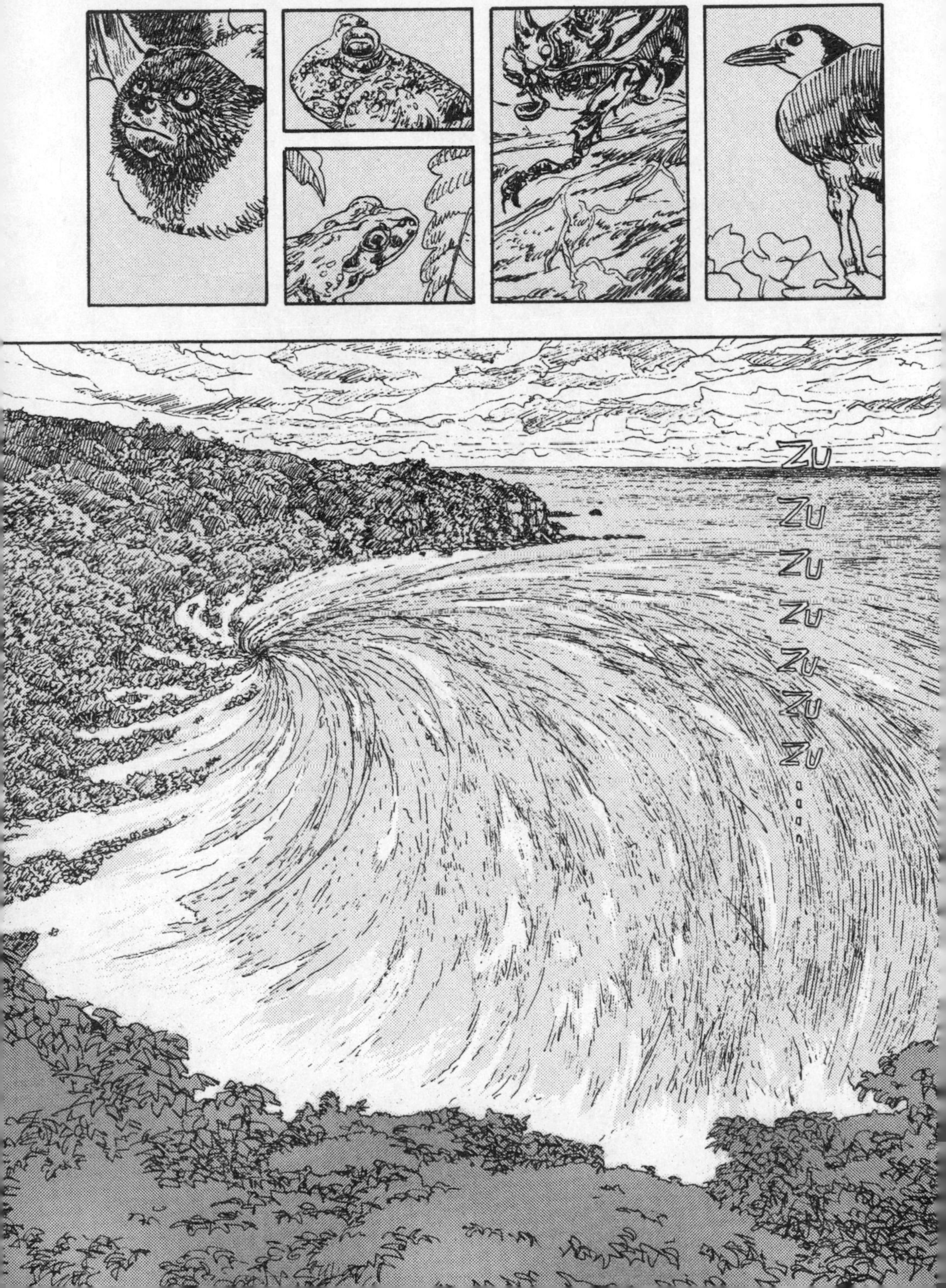
ZU
ZU
ZU
ZU
ZU
ZU
ZU.....

HARMONY
COLLAPSED.

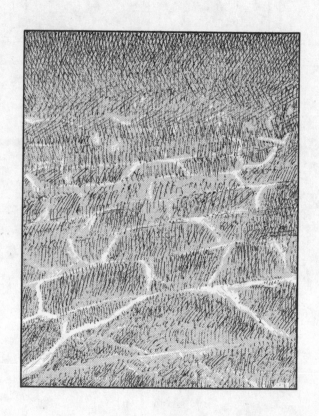

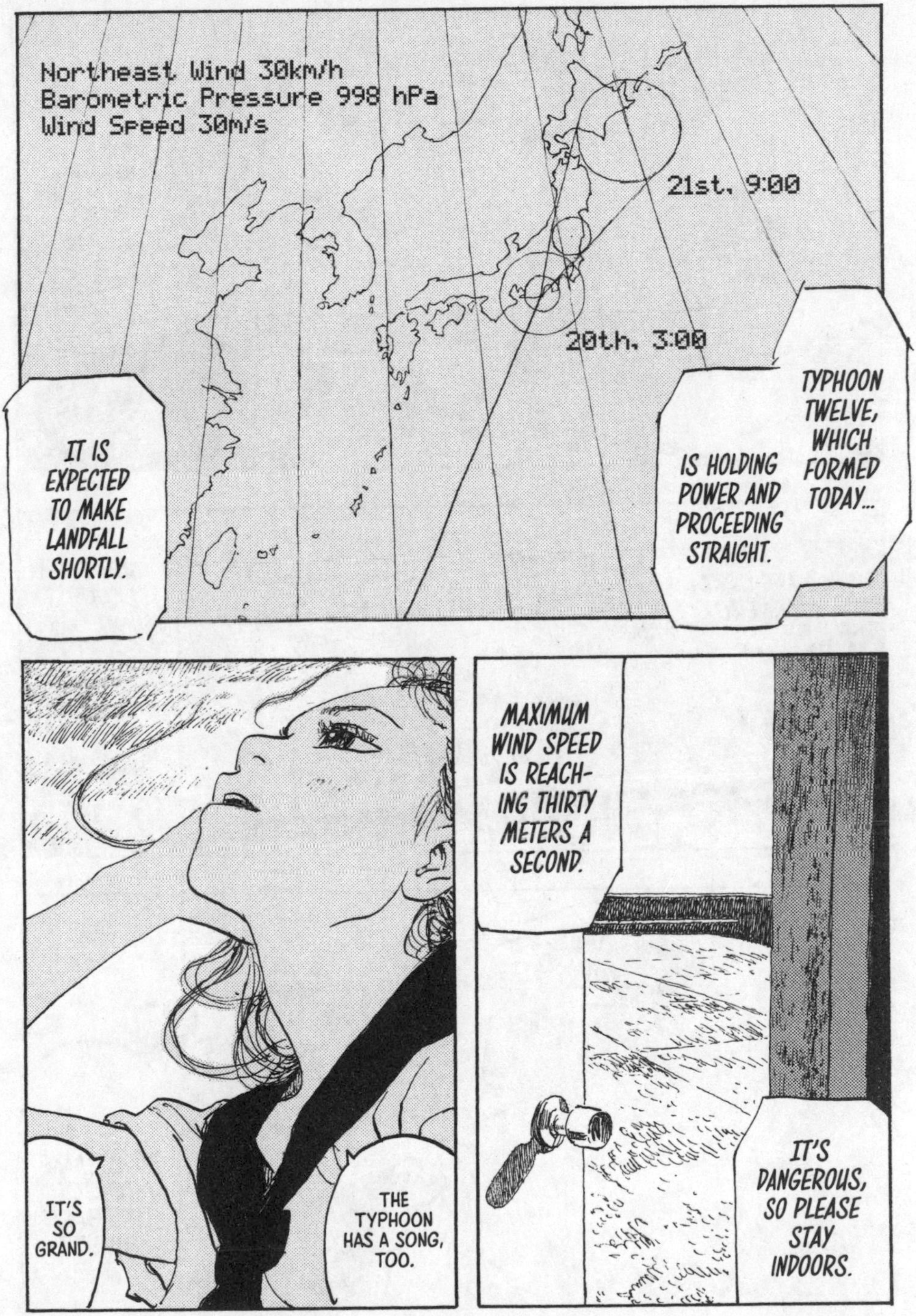
Northeast Wind 30km/h
Barometric Pressure 998 hPa
Wind Speed 30m/s
21st. 9:00
20th. 3:00
TYPHOON TWELVE, WHICH FORMED TODAY...
IS HOLDING POWER AND PROCEEDING STRAIGHT.
IT IS EXPECTED TO MAKE LANDFALL SHORTLY.
MAXIMUM WIND SPEED IS REACHING THIRTY METERS A SECOND.
IT'S DANGEROUS, SO PLEASE STAY INDOORS.
THE TYPHOON HAS A SONG, TOO.
IT'S SO GRAND.

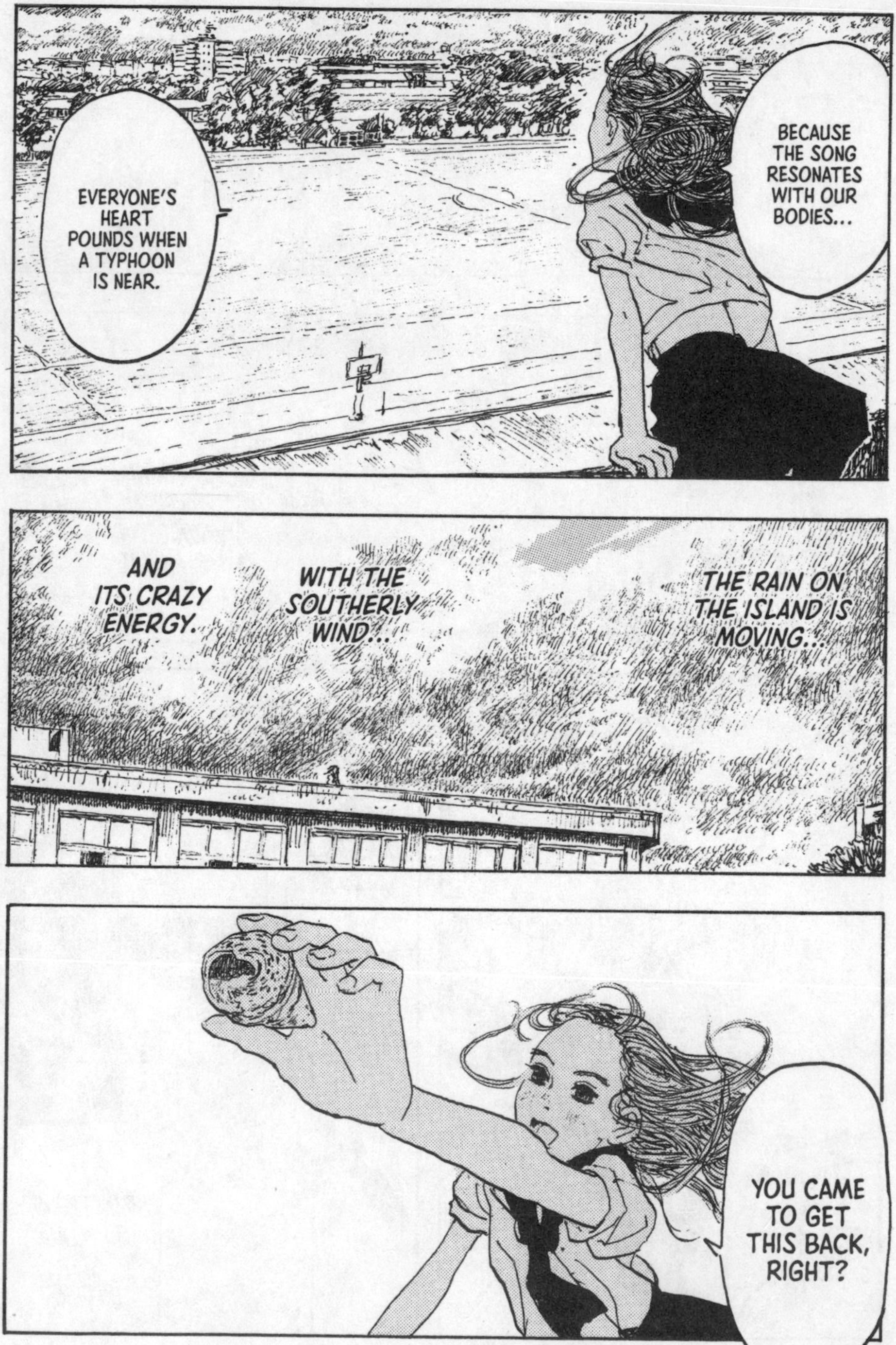
BECAUSE THE SONG RESONATES WITH OUR BODIES...
EVERYONE'S HEART POUNDS WHEN A TYPHOON IS NEAR.
THE RAIN ON THE ISLAND IS MOVING...
WITH THE SOUTHERLY WIND...
AND ITS CRAZY ENERGY.
YOU CAME TO GET THIS BACK, RIGHT?

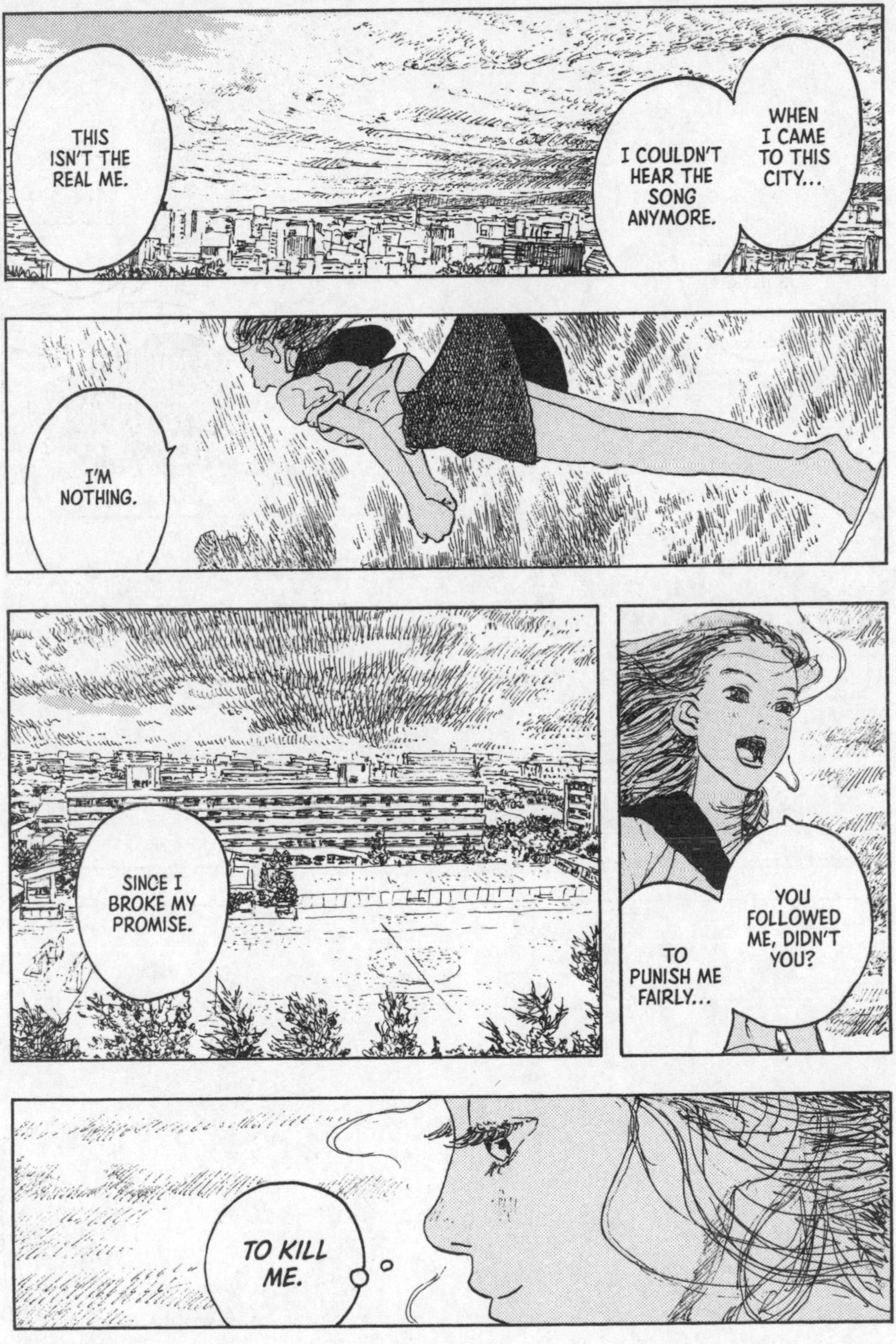
WHEN I CAME TO THIS CITY...
I COULDN'T HEAR THE SONG ANYMORE.
THIS ISN'T THE REAL ME.
I'M NOTHING.
YOU FOLLOWED ME, DIDN'T YOU?
TO PUNISH ME FAIRLY...
SINCE I BROKE MY PROMISE.
TO KILL ME.

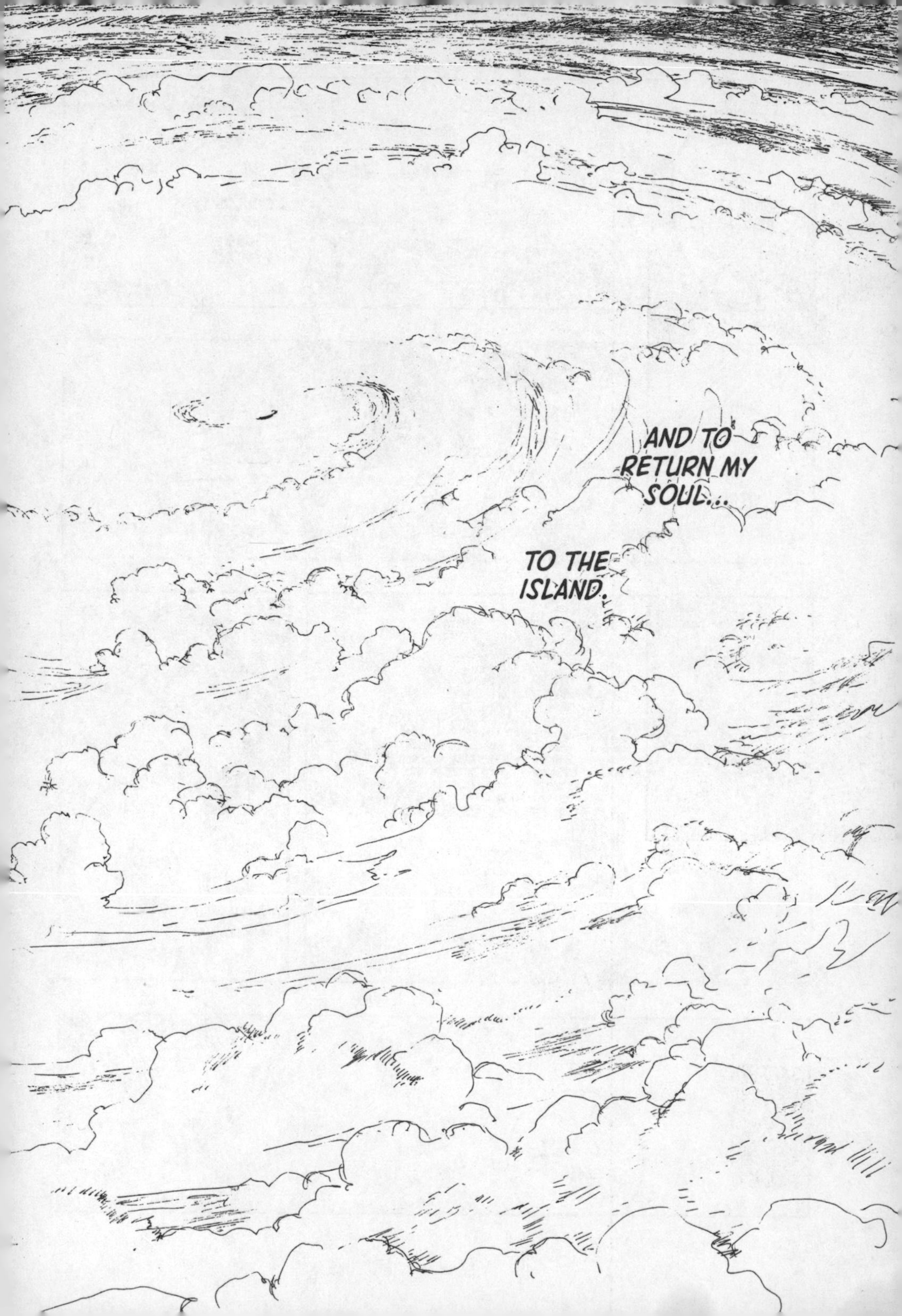
AND TO RETURN MY SOUL...
TO THE ISLAND.

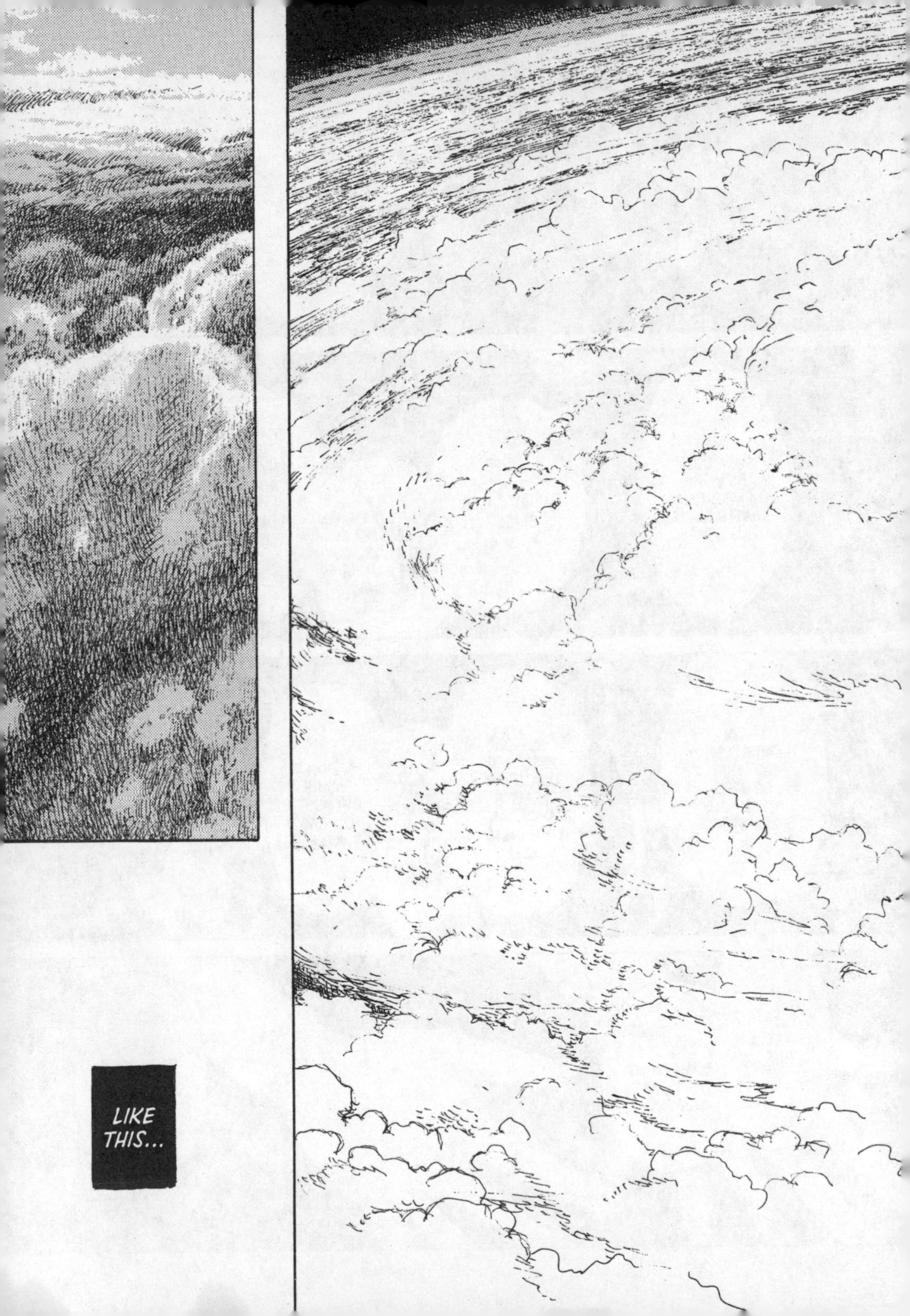
LIKE THIS...

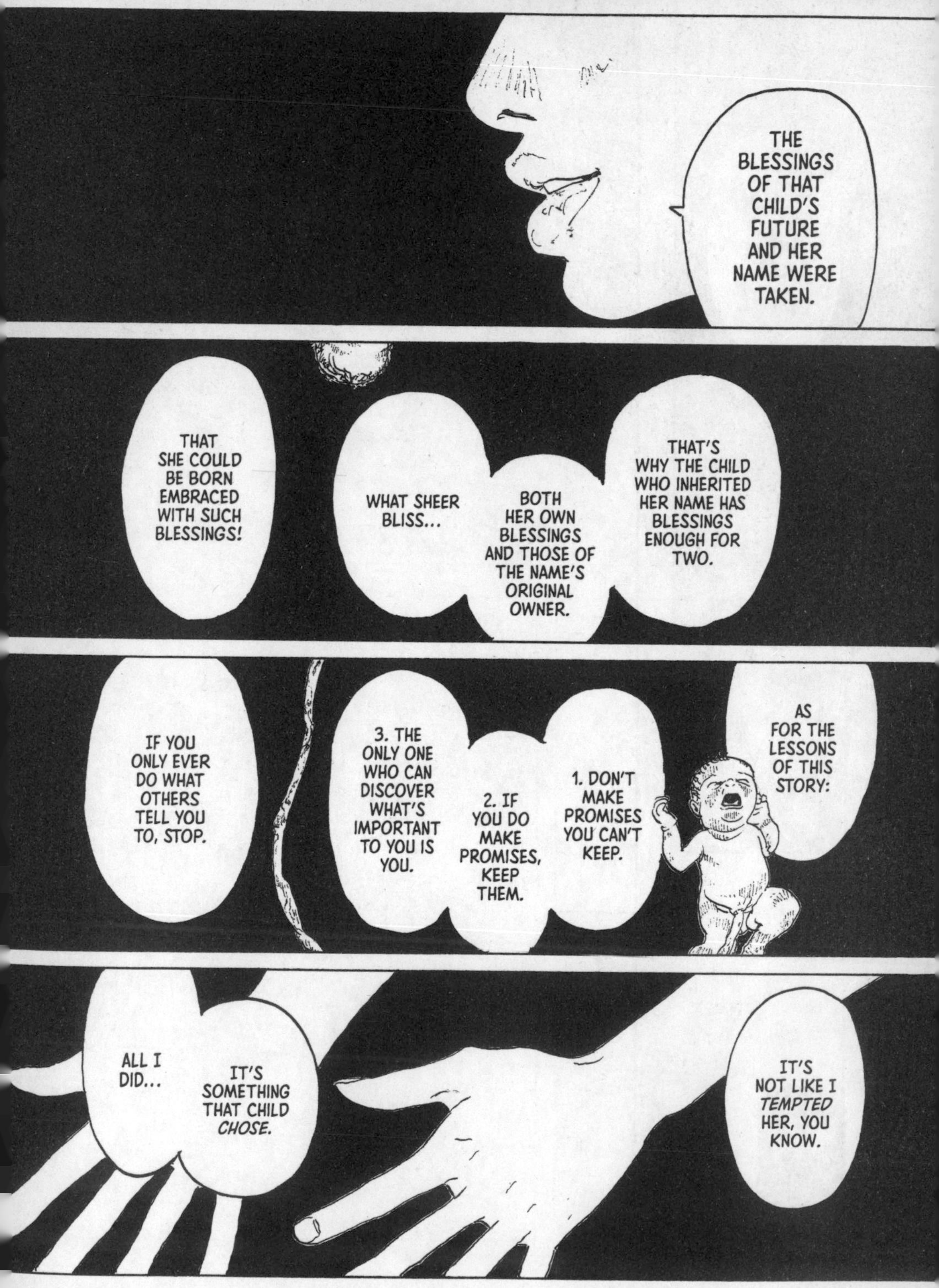
THE BLESSINGS OF THAT CHILD'S FUTURE AND HER NAME WERE TAKEN.
THAT'S WHY THE CHILD WHO INHERITED HER NAME HAS BLESSINGS ENOUGH FOR TWO.
BOTH HER OWN BLESSINGS AND THOSE OF THE NAME'S ORIGINAL OWNER.
WHAT SHEER BLISS...
THAT SHE COULD BE BORN EMBRACED WITH SUCH BLESSINGS!
AS FOR THE LESSONS OF THIS STORY:
1. DON'T MAKE PROMISES YOU CAN'T KEEP.
2. IF YOU DO MAKE PROMISES, KEEP THEM.
3. THE ONLY ONE WHO CAN DISCOVER WHAT'S IMPORTANT TO YOU IS YOU.
IF YOU ONLY EVER DO WHAT OTHERS TELL YOU TO, STOP.
IT'S NOT LIKE I *TEMPTED* HER, YOU KNOW.
IT'S SOMETHING THAT CHILD *CHOSE.*
ALL I DID...

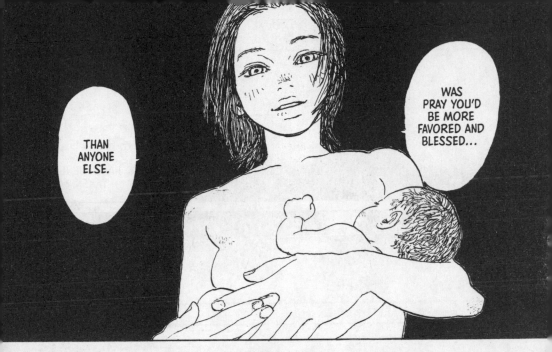

WAS PRAY YOU'D BE MORE FAVORED AND BLESSED...
THAN ANYONE ELSE.
MY WORD, SHE'S SO CUTE!
WHAT'S...
HER NAME?

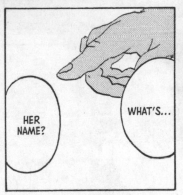

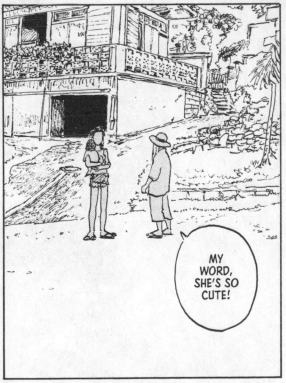

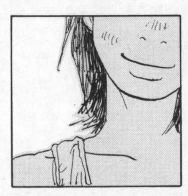

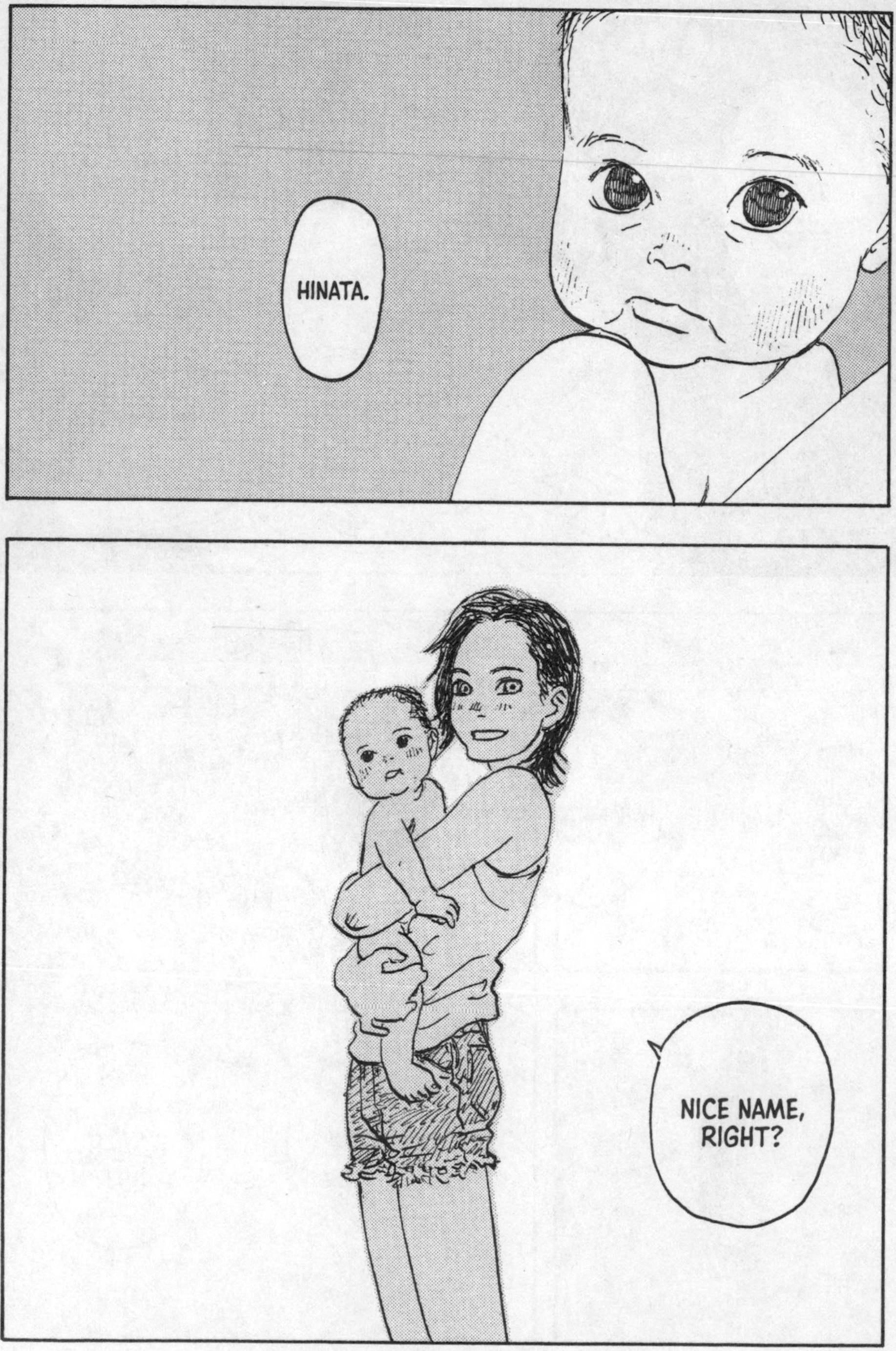
HINATA.
NICE NAME, RIGHT?

Thief of Songs ~ End

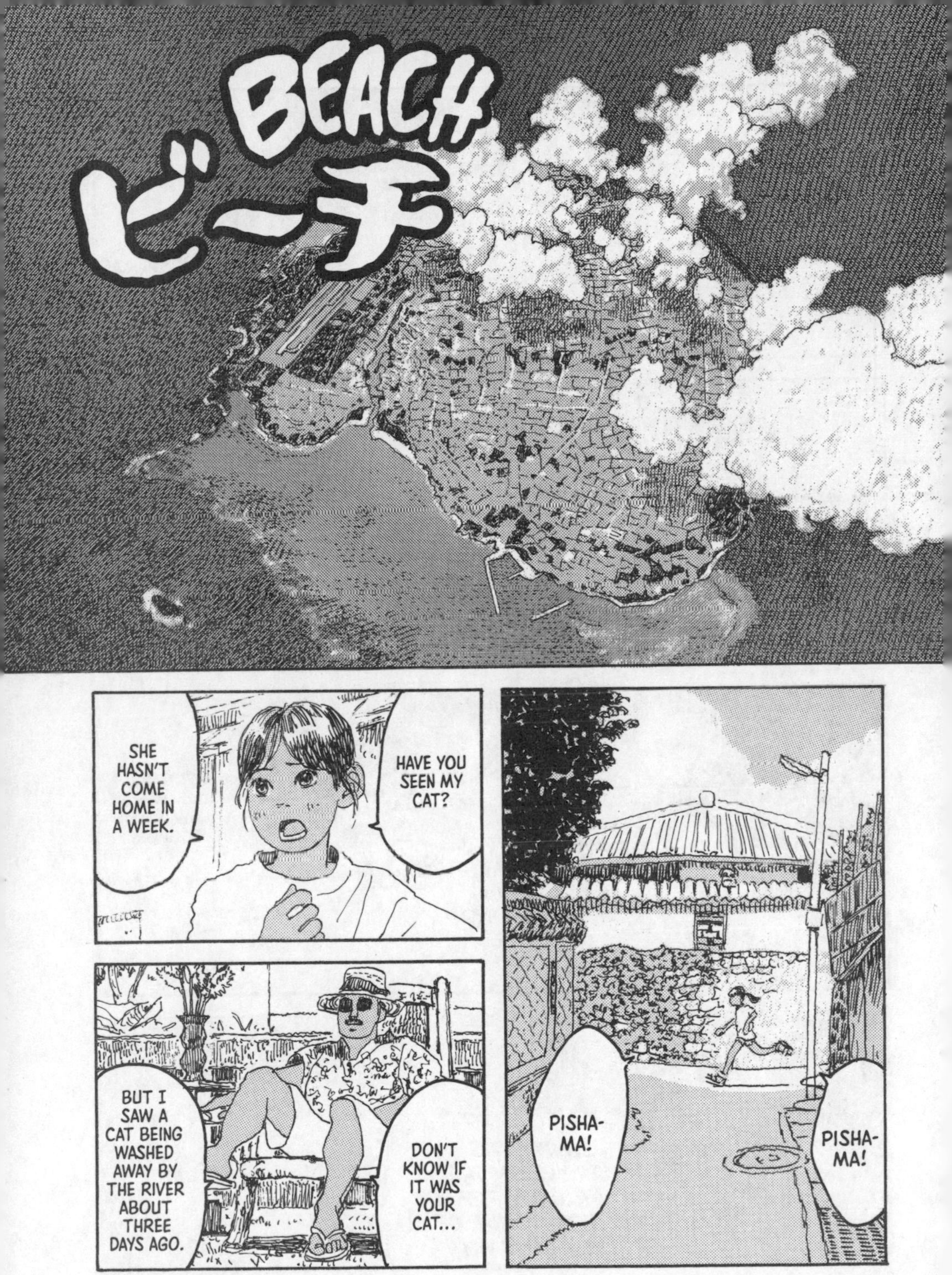
BEACH
ビーチ
PISHA-MA!
PISHA-MA!
HAVE YOU SEEN MY CAT?
SHE HASN'T COME HOME IN A WEEK.
DON'T KNOW IF IT WAS YOUR CAT...
BUT I SAW A CAT BEING WASHED AWAY BY THE RIVER ABOUT THREE DAYS AGO.

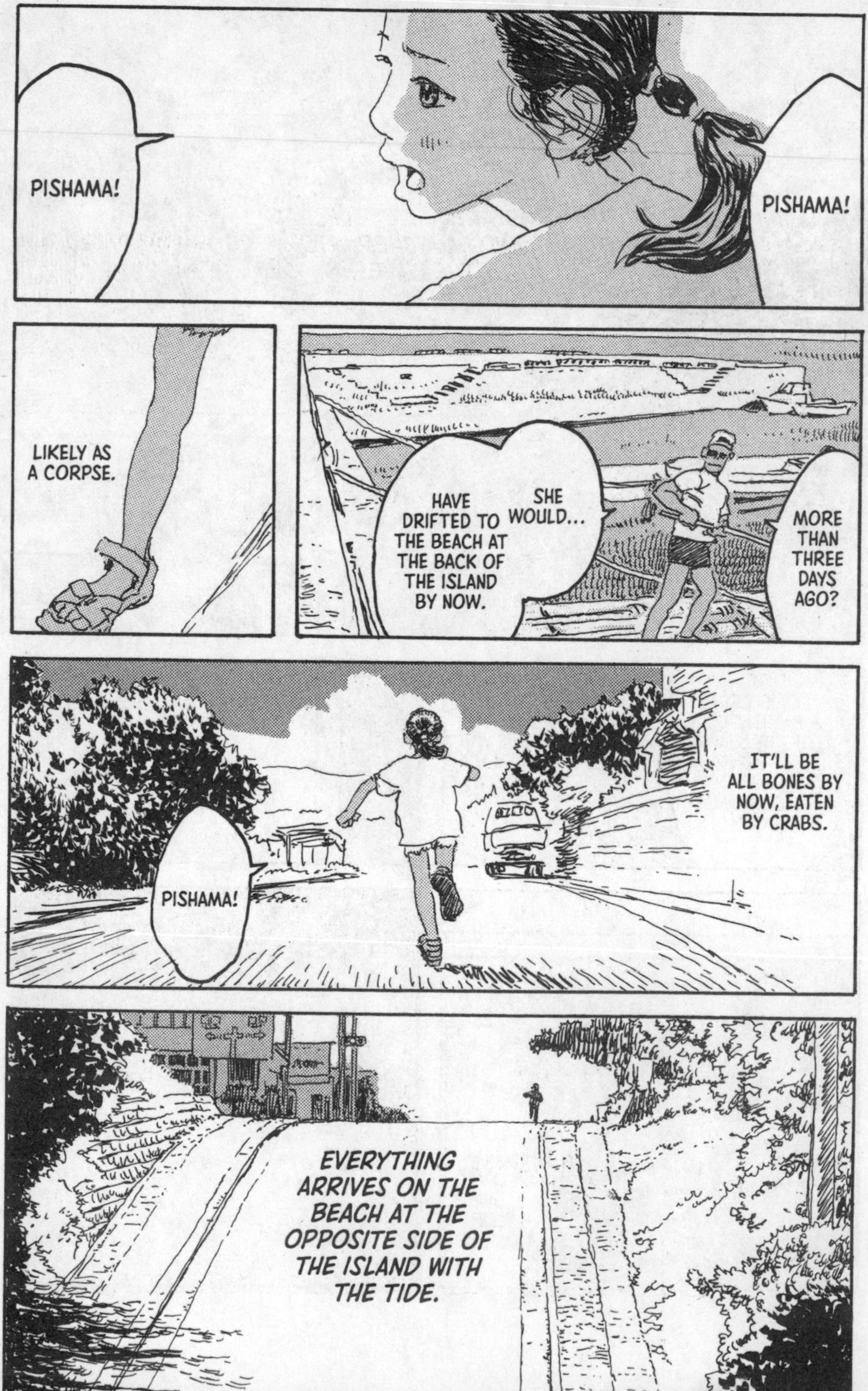
PISHAMA!
PISHAMA!
MORE THAN THREE DAYS AGO?
SHE WOULD... HAVE DRIFTED TO THE BEACH AT THE BACK OF THE ISLAND BY NOW.
LIKELY AS A CORPSE.
IT'LL BE ALL BONES BY NOW, EATEN BY CRABS.
PISHAMA!
EVERYTHING ARRIVES ON THE BEACH AT THE OPPOSITE SIDE OF THE ISLAND WITH THE TIDE.

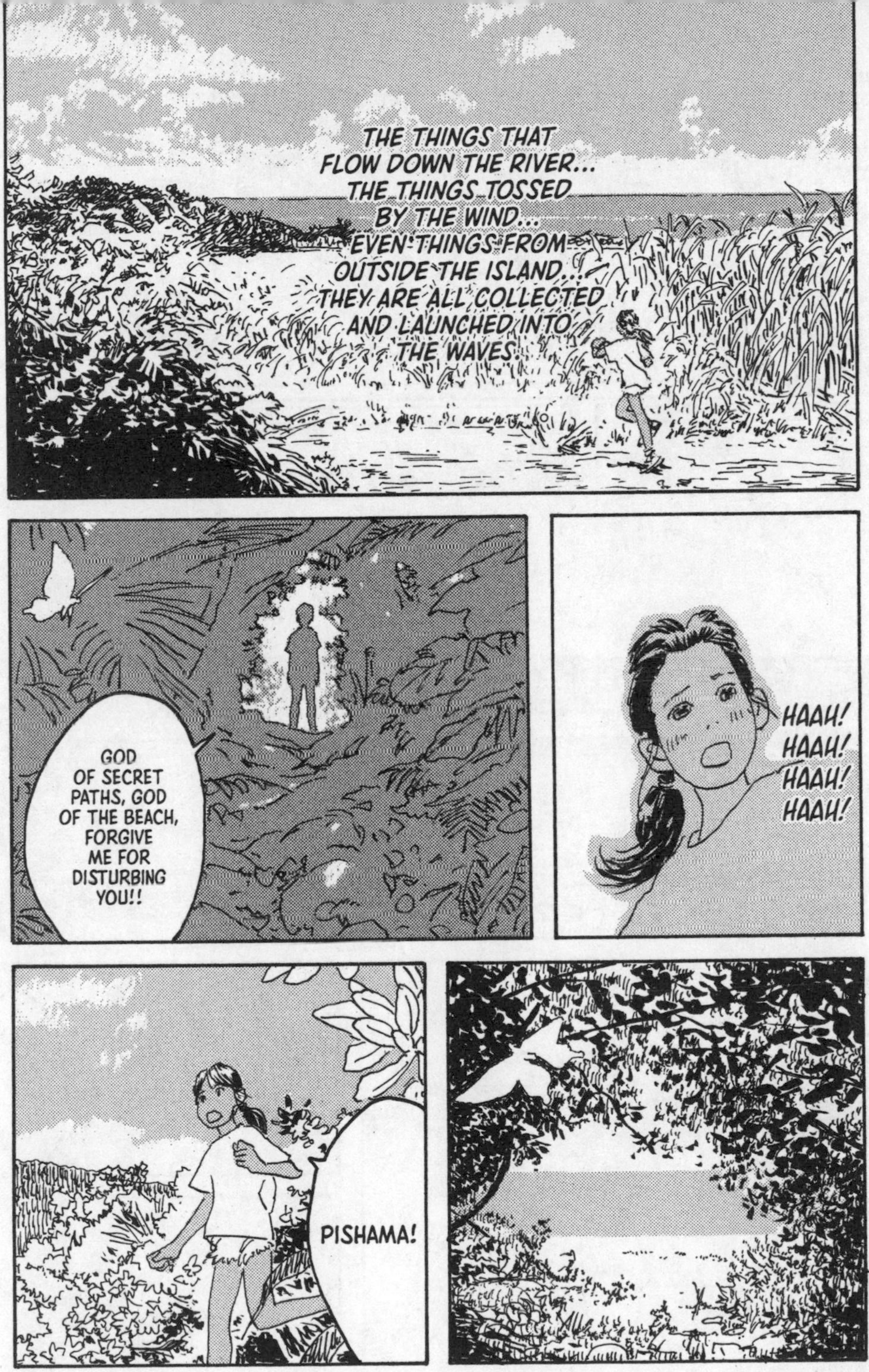
THE THINGS THAT FLOW DOWN THE RIVER... THE THINGS TOSSED BY THE WIND... EVEN THINGS FROM OUTSIDE THE ISLAND... THEY ARE ALL COLLECTED AND LAUNCHED INTO THE WAVES.
HAAH! HAAH! HAAH! HAAH!
GOD OF SECRET PATHS, GOD OF THE BEACH, FORGIVE ME FOR DISTURBING YOU!!
PISHAMA!

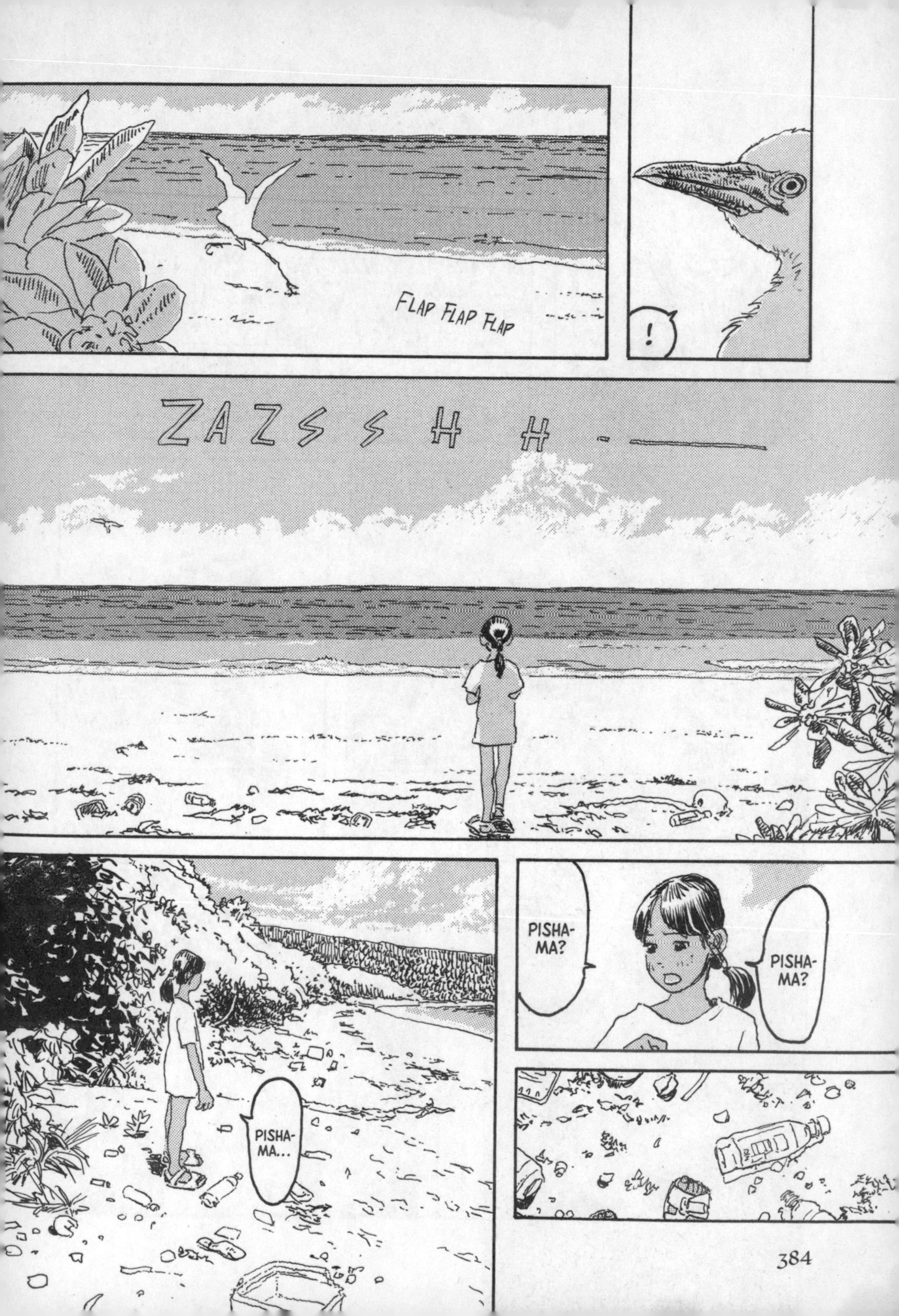
!
FLAP FLAP FLAP
ZAZSSHH—
PISHA-MA?
PISHA-MA?
PISHA-MA...

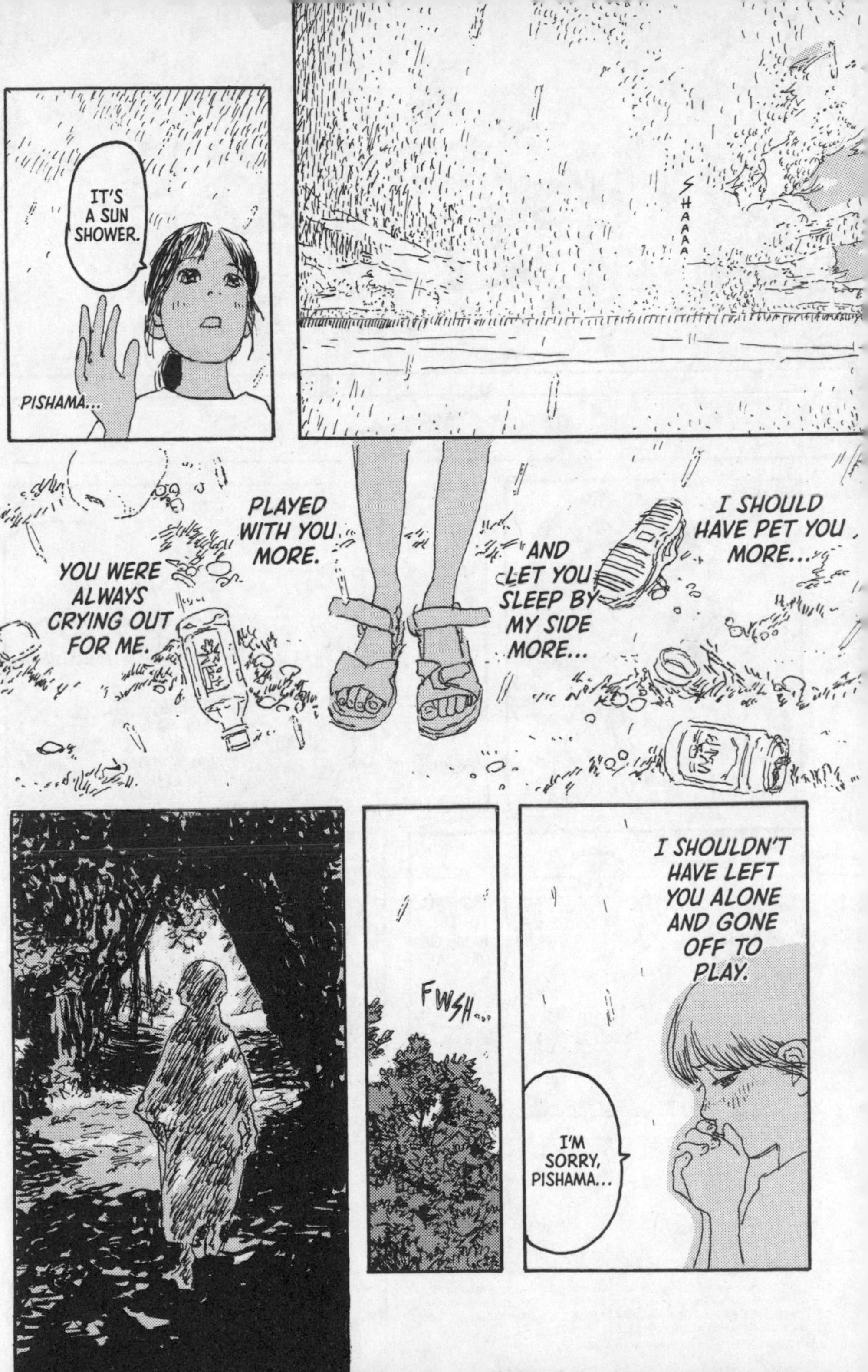
SHAAAA
IT'S A SUN SHOWER.
PISHAMA...
I SHOULD HAVE PET YOU MORE...
AND LET YOU SLEEP BY MY SIDE MORE...
PLAYED WITH YOU MORE.
YOU WERE ALWAYS CRYING OUT FOR ME.
I SHOULDN'T HAVE LEFT YOU ALONE AND GONE OFF TO PLAY.
I'M SORRY, PISHAMA...
FWSH...

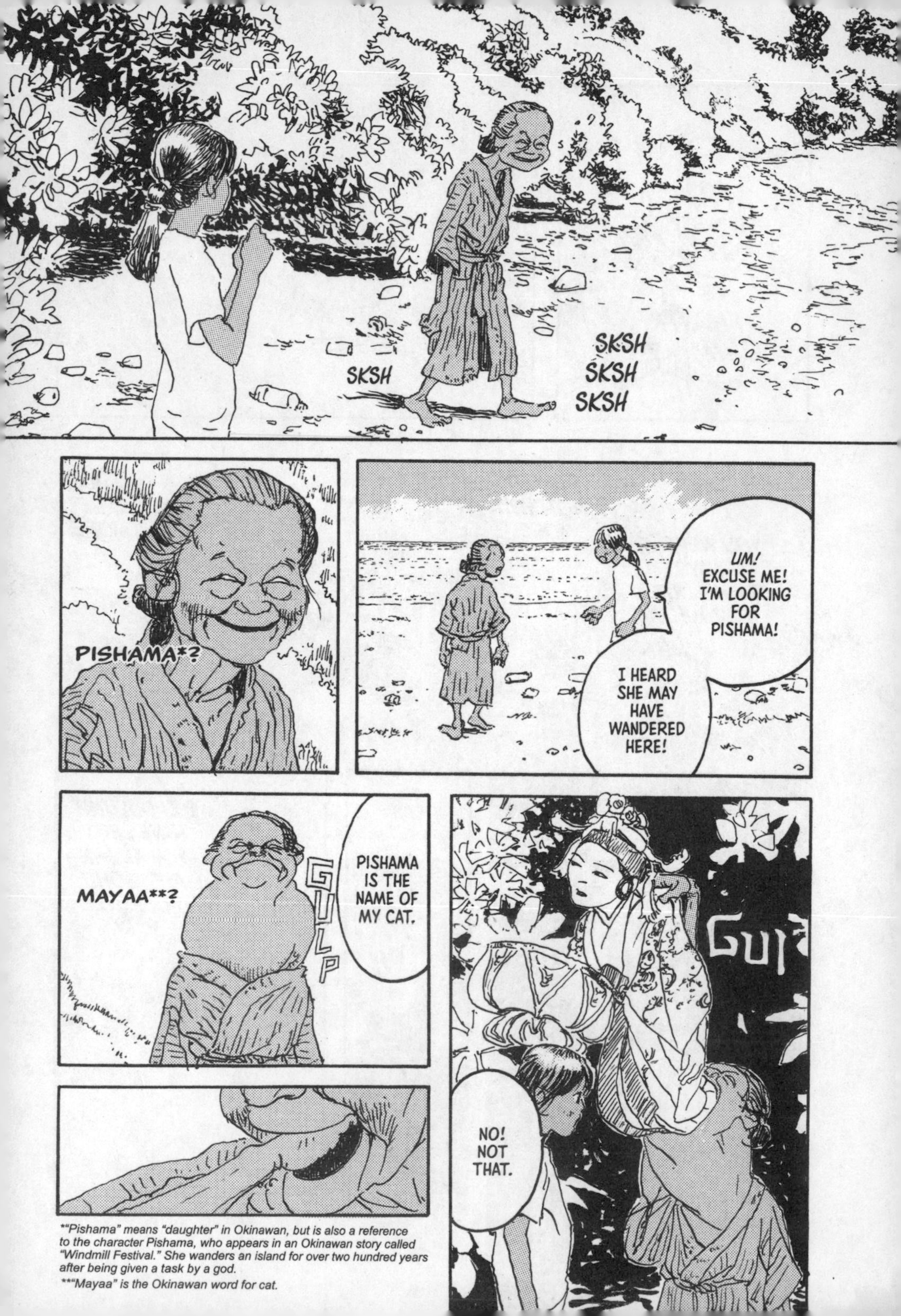
SKSH
SKSH
SKSH
SKSH
UM! EXCUSE ME! I'M LOOKING FOR PISHAMA!
I HEARD SHE MAY HAVE WANDERED HERE!
PISHAMA*?
GULP
NO! NOT THAT.
PISHAMA IS THE NAME OF MY CAT.
MAYAA**?
GULP

*“Pishama” means “daughter” in Okinawan, but is also a reference to the character Pishama, who appears in an Okinawan story called “Windmill Festival.” She wanders an island for over two hundred years after being given a task by a god.

**“Mayaa” is the Okinawan word for cat.

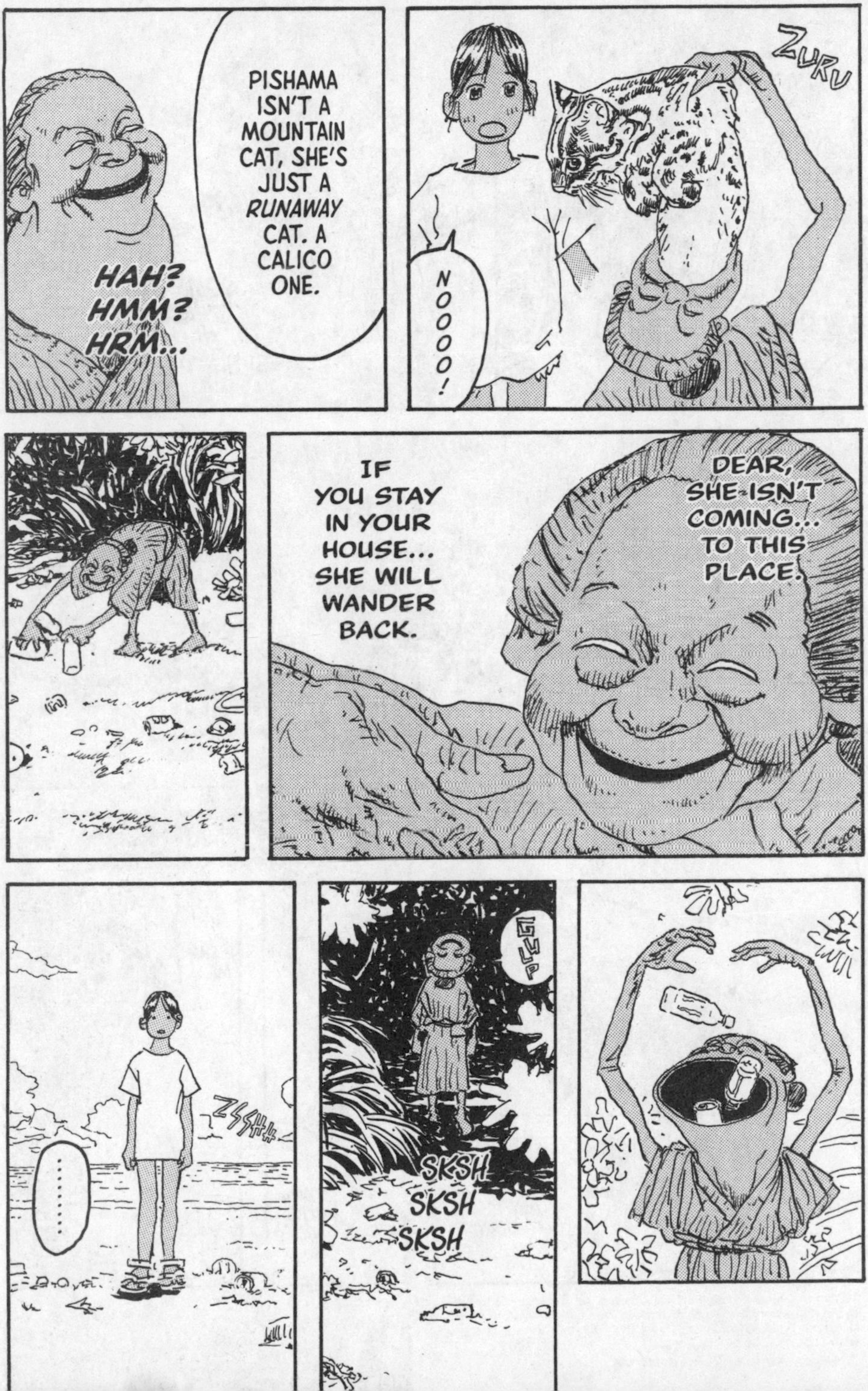
ZURU
NOOOOO!
PISHAMA ISN'T A MOUNTAIN CAT, SHE'S JUST A *RUNAWAY* CAT. A CALICO ONE.
HAH? HMM? HRM...
DEAR, SHE ISN'T COMING... TO THIS PLACE.
IF YOU STAY IN YOUR HOUSE... SHE WILL WANDER BACK.
GULP
SKSH SKSH SKSH
ZSSHH
......

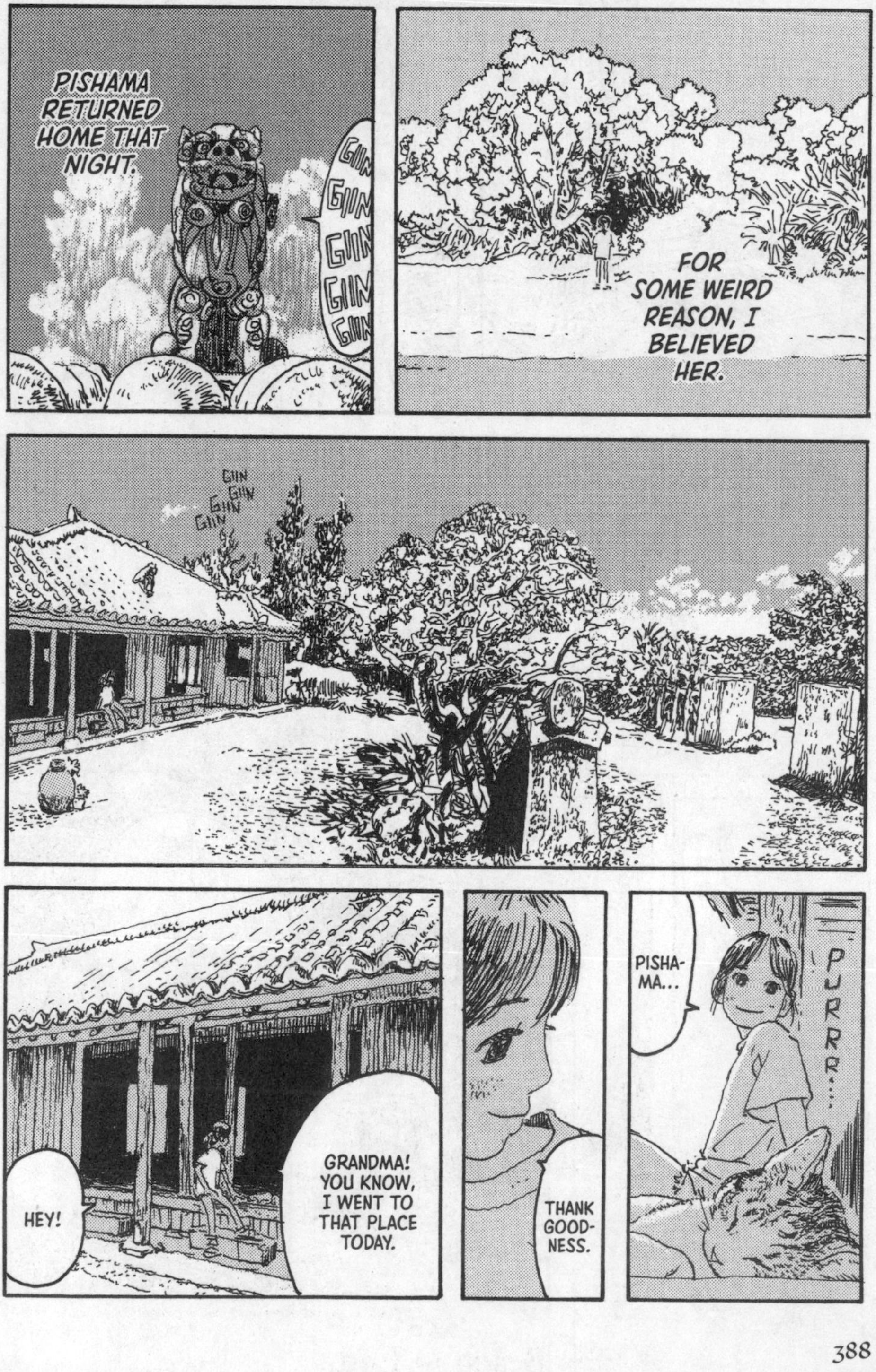
FOR SOME WEIRD REASON, I BELIEVED HER.
PISHAMA RETURNED HOME THAT NIGHT.
GIIN GIIN GIIN GIIN GIIN
GIIN GIIN GIIN GIIN
PISHAMA...
PURRR...
THANK GOODNESS.
GRANDMA! YOU KNOW, I WENT TO THAT PLACE TODAY.
HEY!

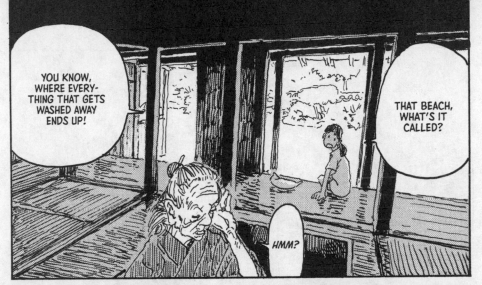

THAT BEACH, WHAT'S IT CALLED?
YOU KNOW, WHERE EVERY-THING THAT GETS WASHED AWAY ENDS UP!
HMM?
WASHED AWAY? ENDS UP?
GIN GIN GIN GIN
AAH... OH!
THAAAT PLACE.
IT'S CALLED GUSO*.
Jii Jii

*"Guso" is an Okinawan word meaning "afterlife" or "underworld."

Beach ~ End

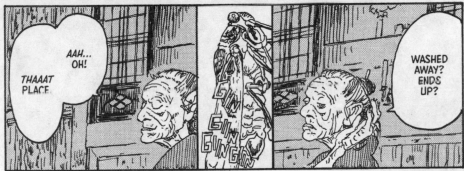

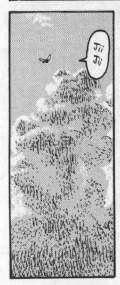

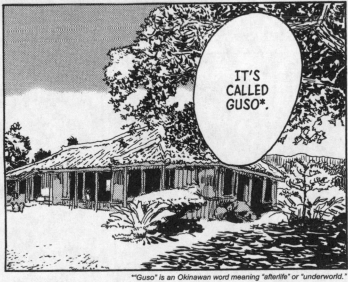

SEVEN SEAS ENTERTAINMENT PRESENTS

witches

story and art by Daisuke Igarashi   THE COMPLETE COLLECTION

TRANSLATION
Kathryn Henzler

ADAPTATION
Jamal Joseph Jr.

LETTERING
Aidan Clarke

ORIGINAL COVER DESIGN
Atsuhiro Yamamoto

COVER DESIGN
H. Qi

PROOFREADER
Leighanna DeRouen

COPY EDITOR
Dawn Davis

SENIOR EDITOR
Jenn Grunigen

PRODUCTION MANAGER
Lissa Pattillo

PREPRESS TECHNICIAN
Melanie Ujimori

PRINT MANAGER
Rhiannon Rasmussen-Silverstein

EDITOR-IN-CHIEF
Julie Davis

ASSOCIATE PUBLISHER
Adam Arnold

PUBLISHER
Jason DeAngelis

MAJO Vol.1,2
by Daisuke IGARASHI
© 2004 Daisuke IGARASHI
All rights reserved.
Original Japanese edition published by SHOGAKUKAN.
English translation rights in the United States of America, Canada, the United Kingdom, Ireland, Australia and New Zealand arranged with SHOGAKUKAN through Tuttle-Mori Agency, Inc.

Seven Seas press and purchase enquiries can be sent to Marketing Manager Lianne Sentar at press@gomanga.com. Information regarding the distribution and purchase of digital editions is available from Digital Manager CK Russell at digital@gomanga.com.

Seven Seas and the Seven Seas logo are trademarks of Seven Seas Entertainment. All rights reserved.

ISBN: 978-1-64827-839-6
Printed in Canada
First Printing: March 2022
10 9 8 7 6 5 4 3 2 1

//// READING DIRECTIONS ////

This book reads from *right to left*, Japanese style. If this is your first time reading manga, you start reading from the top right panel on each page and take it from there. If you get lost, just follow the numbered diagram here. It may seem backwards at first, but you'll get the hang of it! Have fun!!

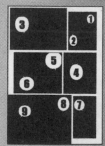

Follow us online: www.SevenSeasEntertainment.com